THE BLUE GUIDES

Countries	**Austria**
	Belgium and Luxembourg
	Channel Islands
	Corsica
	Crete
	Cyprus
	Egypt
	England
	France
	Germany
	Greece
	Holland
	Hungary
	Ireland
	Northern Italy
	Southern Italy
	Malta and Gozo
	Morocco
	Portugal
	Scotland
	Sicily
	Spain
	Switzerland
	Turkey: Bursa to Antakya
	Wales
	Yugoslavia
Cities	**Boston and Cambridge**
	Florence
	Istanbul
	Jerusalem
	London
	Moscow and Leningrad
	New York
	Oxford and Cambridge
	Paris and Versailles
	Rome and Environs
	Venice
Themes	**Churches and Chapels of Northern England**
	Churches and Chapels of Southern England
	Literary Britain and Ireland
	Museums and Galleries of London
	Victorian Architecture in Britain

*A 12C Norman tympanum preserved inside Holy
Sepulchre Church, Northampton, showing a man set
between a dragon and a small figure*

BLUE GUIDE

CHURCHES AND CHAPELS OF NORTHERN ENGLAND

Edited by Stephen C. Humphrey

A & C Black
London

W W Norton
New York

First edition 1991

Published by A & C Black (Publishers) Limited
35 Bedford Row, London, WC1R 4JH

© A & C Black (Publishers) Limited

Published in the United States of America by
WW Norton & Company, Incorporated
500 Fifth Avenue, New York, NY 10110

Published simultaneously in Canada by
Penguin Books Canada Limited
2801 John Street, Markham, Ontario LR3 1B4

ISBN   0–7136–3171–6

A CIP catalogue record for this book
is available from the British Library.

ISBN   0–393–30724–7 USA

Stephen Humphrey was trained as an historian. In 1979 he was
elected Hon. Secretary of the Ecclesiological Society, an old-
established body then in decline. He has invested considerable time
and effort to restore its reputation as a respected society, especially
as a publisher. Over the years he has written numerous pamphlets
and papers in journals on architecture and local history. He has often
lectured and guided parties on tours. He has lately embarked on the
publication of an annotated list of all churches and chapels which
have ever existed in England, the most comprehensive such list ever
to be attempted.

With 13 drawings by the **Reverend Brian Roy**

Typeset by CRB Typesetting Services, Ely, Cambs.
Printed and bound in Great Britain by
William Clowes Limited, Beccles and London

PREFACE

The pair of volumes, of which this is one, describes a selection from the many thousands of churches and chapels in England. To a large extent, the buildings chosen are those widely considered to be 'the best' in terms of their antiquity, their historical associations, and the magnificence of their architecture and fittings. The choice was influenced by a wish to represent all periods of architecture. There was in addition a need to give recognition in a touring guide to some much-visited churches which are not always 'the best' architecturally. An attempt has been made to draw attention to private chapels and to non-Anglican churches, for such buildings are omitted in traditional books on parish churches. Finally, there are a few special pleadings, such as any compiler would doubtless wish to make.

The volumes are arranged largely by the traditional counties of England. The popularity of these counties is obvious enough, but it should also be remembered that they usually correspond with the Church of England's diocesan boundaries, which are equally ancient. The county texts are the work of 17 writers; entries initialled 'S.C.H.' are the work of the editor.

ACKNOWLEDGEMENTS

A work of this sort requires the help of innumerable people. My thanks go first and foremost to Miss Freda Gould, who arranged in advance so many of my tours of the churches described, and who assisted too during some of the tours themselves. Miss Anna Zaharova fulfilled a similar role for my early tours. I gladly thank the staff of Top Grade Services of Barrett Street, London for typing much of the text so efficiently, and the staff of Mercury Secretarial Services Ltd of New Cavendish Street, London for endless copying (and especially to Mr Jack Coachworth for his unfailing pains to secure the best results). The staff of the Redundant Churches Fund kindly helped me to gain access to numerous churches in their care and commented on my text. I also gratefully acknowledge my debt to the National Monuments Record, whose staff have provided much help over illustrations. Gratitude is due too to Mr David Williams, formerly of the Council for the Care of Churches, to my mother (Mrs G.L. Humphrey) for reading and commenting on much of the text and for valuable further help, to Mr John Warbis for matters photographic and for driving me round Suffolk in 1987, to Miss Mary Boast and Miss Pauline Casey. I must also express my thanks in general to fellow-members of the Ecclesiological Society for information and advice over the years, with special mention of the late Gordon Barnes, sometime Chairman, who taught me so much about Worcestershire and Gloucestershire in many splendid tours, Mr T.F. Blood, also formerly Chairman, and the late Mr Maurice Henley, Vice-President, who helped with illustrations and other matters. The worthy contributors to the text all deserve my gratitude for what they have done *beyond* writing their counties. Hospitality, information and advice have been freely provided.

Incumbents, churchwardens and caretakers throughout England have been agreeably helpful. A number of particular debts need to be mentioned. I was specially fortunate in Yorkshire in the help I received. Canon C.J. Hawthorn of St. Martin's, Scarborough was very helpful over his distinguished Bodley church and on related Bodleian matters. The Reverend H.E. Hutchinson read my text for the East Riding and made useful comments. Canon Barry Keeton of Howden Minster corrected my information on statues and effigies in that church. Canon J.H. Armstrong of All Saints', Pavement, York has been very helpful on more than one occasion. Mr John Hutchinson suggested subjects for entries in the West Riding, and made comments on my choices for the East Riding. The Reverend R.M. Harvey opened Wadworth Church for me at no little inconvenience to himself, and gave me much information. Mr Leslie Hayes took great pains to show me round St. John's, Leeds and to discuss its history. In Rotherham, Mr Martyn Taylor specially opened the medieval bridge chapel and explained various features. Mr B. Heath was an exceptionally agreeable guide at St. Wilfrid's, Cantley. At Fulneck, Mr J. Ingham enabled me to see the Moravian Church and explained its history. My visit to the church at Adel near Leeds led me to meet Mr Brian Roy, who not only discussed that church in detail but went on to provide some admirable drawings for this work. Much useful information was provided by the Reverend S.M. Hind about Womersley Church and elsewhere.

In Lancashire, where so many churches are locked outside services, special access was gladly afforded at Mossley Hill; Warrington;

St. Agnes's at Sefton Park, Liverpool; at St. Helen's, Sefton (by Canon O.J. Yandell, who discussed the church in detail); St. John's at Lancaster; St. Walburge's at Preston (by Father Leo Caton, who gave me much of his time in explaining features in the church); and at the Friends' Meeting House in St. Helen's, where Ada Williamson, Clerk of the Meeting, was my guide. Miss Margaret Hodge, Domestic Bursar of Manchester Polytechnic, kindly allowed me to see the former Christian Science Church which is now in her care.

At Dukinfield, Mr Norman Stephens introduced me to the Unitarian Church at no more than a moment's notice. Much farther north, at Crosby Ravensworth, Westmorland, Canon R.H. Gurney welcomed me and discussed his church in the busy circumstances of a flower festival. In County Durham, the Reverend Michael Waters was exceptionally helpful at Ushaw College, again at just a moment's notice. In the same county, Canon A.H. Nugent of Brancepeth made detailed and valuable comments on the entry for his church. The Reverend T.J. Ganz gave much information about Tutbury Church, Staffordshire. I was guided and made very welcome at St. Chad's, Stafford (by Mrs Joan Eley) and St. Michael's, Lichfield (by the Reverend D.A. Smith). Mr Bruce Scott was notably helpful at St. Mary's, Clumber, Nottinghamshire, in the difficult circumstances of a major restoration. The late Mr Vivian Leleux was most helpful concerning Holy Sepulchre Church, Northampton. The Archdeacon of Northampton gave useful comments on St. Peter's in that town. In Huntingdonshire the Reverend P.J. Shepherd was informative and welcoming at Yaxley, as was Canon K.S.S. Jamal at Fletton.

For information on Essex I am indebted to Mr C.R. Starr. At Harlow I was enabled to see the Baptist Church, Potter Street by Mr Percy White. Mr R.J. Lloyd welcomed me at Radwinter Church on more than one occasion and gave me much information. At Blackmore, Mrs Skrimshare specially opened the church and discussed its history. In Suffolk I was helped at Blythburgh by Mr R.I. Collett, and at Bury St. Edmund's, admission to the Unitarian Chapel was made possible by Mr Ben Johnson (Chairman of the Trustees) and Mr Philip Orchard, who explained its history and the works proposed for it. I am grateful to the Reverend L.J.H. Hard for help with All Saints', Cambridge over many years. In Hertfordshire, Mr A.G. Trower was helpful and hospitable in respect of the old church at Stanstead Abbots. I acknowledge too the permision granted me to view the chapel of All Saints' Pastoral Centre, London Colney. On the churches of Bedfordshire, I have learned much from Mr C.J. Pickford, the County Archivist. At Edlesborough in Buckinghamshire I was enabled to view the church by Mrs J.C. Horne.

The late Mr John Pinder commented on my entry for St. George the Martyr, Southwark, and gave me other useful information. The Reverend Nicholas Richards commented in considerable detail on the entry for St. Mary's, Rotherhithe. My text for St. George's, Hanover Square was much improved by the advice of the Reverend W.M. Atkins. Mr Ian Anstruther and Mr Robert Elleray both read my text for Sussex and made valuable comments. At St. Nicholas's, Arundel Mr David Robinson opened the church specially and provided much information, and at St. Michael's, Brighton the Reverend D.G. Hewetson kindly unlocked the church when I visited in 1986 and explained various features. In the same year I went to All Saints', Selsley, Gloucestershire, where the Reverend I.E. Burbery was markedly helpful and most agreeable.

A NOTE ON BLUE GUIDES

The Blue Guide series began in 1918 when Muirhead Guide-Books Limited published 'Blue Guide London and its Environs'. Finlay and James Muirhead already had extensive experience of guide-book publishing: before the First World War they had been the editors of the English editions of the German Baedekers, and by 1915 they had acquired the copyright of most of the famous 'Red' Handbooks from John Murray.

An agreement made with the French publishing house Hachette et Cie in 1917 led to the translation of Muirhead's London Guide, which became the first 'Guide Bleu'—Hachette had previously published the blue-covered 'Guides Joanne'. Subsequently, Hachette's 'Guide Bleu Paris et ses Environs' was adapted and published in London by Muirhead. The collaboration between the two publishing houses continued until 1933.

In 1931 Ernest Benn Limited took over the Blue Guides, appointing Russell Muirhead, Finlay Muirhead's son, editor in 1934. The Muirheads' connection with Blue Guides ended in 1963 when Stuart Rossiter, who had been working on the Guides since 1954, became house editor, revising and compiling several of the books himself.

The Blue Guides are now published by A & C Black, who acquired Ernest Benn in 1984, so continuing the tradition of guide-book publishing which began in 1826 with 'Black's Economical Tourist of Scotland'. The Blue Guide series continues to grow: there are now more than 40 titles in print with revised editions appearing regularly and many new Blue Guides in preparation.

'Blue Guides' is a registered trade mark.

CONTENTS

HISTORICAL INTRODUCTION

Beginnings in the Roman Empire

On July 25th in the year 306 the Roman Emperor, Constantius Chlorus, died at *Eboracum*, the Roman city of York. On the same day and in the same city his son, Constantine, was proclaimed Emperor in his place. The proclamation probably took place at the main entrance of the Roman military headquarters, which directly underlies the S transept of York Minster. This was where a disastrous fire occurred in 1984. The equally dramatic proclamation of 306 was an event of marked significance in the earliest Christian record of this island. The accession of Constantine was one of the most momentous events in Christian history, for less than 20 years later he became the first Christian to be the sole ruler of the Roman world. Without Constantine, the future of Christianity might have been very different, as its story outside the Roman Empire suggests. Although Constantine's conversion is normally dated to 312, he might have become a Christian in some sense long before then. It is possible that he might have been drawn to Christianity in York itself, for just eight years after his proclamation a bishop from the city attended the Council of Arles. No doubt a Christian community was an obvious part of the York which Constantine knew.

These events of 306 took place in a city which was the military capital of a Roman province. *Londinium* was its commercial and administrative capital. At that time the English nation was still living in Angel and elsewhere across the North Sea. The Christian history of this country thus predates the change from Roman Britain to the English kingdoms. It goes back not merely beyond the Reformation, when the Church in western Europe was still united, but to that much remoter period when the Latin West was in full communion with the Greek East; in other words, when Christendom was one and when it acknowledged (with minor exceptions) the civil power of the Roman Emperor. The Christian world of Constantine's day was in fact centred much more in the Greek East than in the Latin West. The great Council of Nicaea in 325 was attended by only a handful of bishops from the Roman Empire's western provinces (and none from Roman Britain) in contrast to hundreds from the East. Egypt, Syria, Asia Minor: these were the Christian heartlands of the 4C, and they were also the richest parts of the Roman Empire. Constantine's church building schemes took place in Nicomedia, Antioch, Jerusalem and Constantinople as well as Rome; and even in Rome, where he built the two great basilicas of St. Peter on the Vatican Hill and St. Paul outside the walls, the East was recalled in their largely Egyptian endowments and in their further income from Antioch in the case of St. Peter's and Tarsus in that of St. Paul's, both sources being entirely appropriate in view of the connections of the two saints with those cities. In the course of time, all the major Christian cities of the East (Jerusalem, Antioch, Alexandria and Constantinople) fell under the power of Islam, leaving Rome in an unrivalled position. Rome, however, had another major advantage: it was acknowledged to be the burial place of St. Peter and St. Paul. This fact was to be of continuing importance long after the Roman Empire had faded.

A few traces of Christianity in Roman Britain are familiar as rather disconnected facts. The first English historian, St. Bede the Venerable, wrote in the 8C of 'an old church, built in honour of St. Martin during the Roman occupation of Britain', which stood in his day on the E side of Canterbury and which had been brought back into use in the late 6C. From an earlier period—the early 4C at the latest—may be recalled the martyrdom of St. Alban at *Verulamium*. The record of the Council of Arles in 314 shows that *Londinium* then had a bishop called Restitutus and that there were bishops in York and Lincoln too. Archaeological evidence which has received publicity includes the Water Newton hoard of Christian silver in Huntingdonshire; lead baptismal tanks, including the one found at Caversham, Berkshire, in 1988; the Christian mosaic from Hinton St. Mary in Dorset; the 'country house chapel' in the villa at Lullingstone in Kent; and, above all, the basilican church at Silchester in Hampshire. To these one can add the multitude of objects stamped with the *chi-rho* symbol ✗)— which the Emperor Constantine made a Christian symbol—or with an *alpha* and an *omega* (α, Ω). All these facts speak of a Christian Church in Roman Britain whose bishops were in full communion with those elsewhere in the Empire. It was of course a Church which moved from being persecuted into the toleration which Constantine's success bestowed; and, later in the 4C, a Church which became an integral part of the Roman establishment.

From the days of persecution there were martyrs to recall and honour. Over their graves in the cemeteries (which always stood outside Roman towns), shrines were built. In Continental cities a clear connection has been shown between such shrines in late Roman cemeteries and later churches (which are often cathedrals). Xanten, Cologne and Trier are principal examples. In England, one such early shrine is known: that of St. Alban, an inhabitant of the Roman town of *Verulamium* who was martyred there at an unknown date in the 3C or early 4C. His cult is the earliest of a local saint in this country for which there is evidence. In 429 St. Germanus of Auxerre visited St. Alban's shrine. We do not know whether the shrine was continuously maintained; a gap in the post-Roman period is possible. Knowledge of the site was clearly never lost.

It is wrong to assume that churches in the Roman Empire were necessarily poor, even in the days of persecution. 'Primitive poverty' or 'primitive simplicity' are erroneous labels. In the year 303, during Diocletian's persecution, a record was made of the belongings of a house-church at Cirta in N Africa. The clerk of the court listed two golden chalices, six silver chalices, a silver bowl, seven silver lamps, seven short bronze candlesticks with their lamps, two torches, eleven bronze lamps and chains, and innumerable items of clothing, apparently for use in baptism. The hoard of silver from Water Newton appears to have belonged to a comparable church. One major difference between the early Church and later times was that a bishop would have regular, direct dealings with *all* the worshippers of his diocese, before the pressure of numbers overwhelmed the Church's early practice. The word *parochia*, a parish, originally meant a diocese. Subsequently, when places of worship multiplied, there was still a sense of belonging to one, central congregation. One reflection of this is the Italian tradition of baptism not in a local church but in the central church or cathedral. Hence, for example, the very prominent baptistery next to the cathedral in Florence.

Baptism in general had a prominence in the early Church which it later lost. Many people, including the Emperor Constantine himself, were not baptised until the ends of their lives. Adults (not infants) would become full members of the Church in the presence of all its existing members.

The history of the Church in this country suffered much discontinuity as Roman Britain became England. The economy, population and towns of Roman Britain all decayed. A new pagan English population settled in large areas of the country. Surviving Christianity must have rubbed shoulders with paganism in many districts. Elmet, near Leeds, remained non-English territory, and probably Christian, until the 7C, by which time the conversion of the English was beginning. The SW (Devon and Cornwall), Wales and the NW remained non-English for centuries and therefore preserved Romano-British or Celtic Christianity alongside that of the new English Church. It has become academically normal in recent years to emphasise continuity between Roman Britain and the English kingdoms. Specific instances of sites in continuous occupation, however, are few, although archaeology will doubtless reveal more in the future. The church at Rivenhall in Essex is an unsuspected example yielded by excavations in recent years.

The Early English Church

The English Church began at the very end of the 6C. Pope Gregory I (reigned 590–604) had wanted to lead a mission to England in person, but in the event he sent a group of evangelists under a Roman monk called Augustine. The group had the good fortune to arrive in Kent when its ruler, King Aethelberht, was the most important ruler in England. In early English history, there were a number of distinct kingdoms in this island and at any given time one of them was usually recognised as suzerain of the rest. King Aethelberht happened to have a Frankish Christian wife, Bertha. According to Bede, she had worshipped since her arrival in Kent in a church which had been built in Roman times, that is, in a building which had presumably survived from the 4C. Posterity identified her church with that of St. Martin, which still stands on the E side of Canterbury and thus claims to be the oldest church in continuous use in England. Augustine and his missionaries made much headway in Kent; King Aethelberht's capital, Canterbury, became the centre of the new English Church, and Augustine himself became the first Archbishop of Canterbury in 601. The spread of Christianity throughout England was substantially a matter of politics. Kent directly influenced Essex (in which kingdom London lay) and Northumbria. In each case there was a setback after an initial success, and then renewed evangelisation produced a more permanent result.

Northumbria was arguably the key to the conversion of England in the mid-7C. Three successive Kings of Northumbria—Edwin, Oswald and Oswy—held suzerainty in most of England. Their power and their marriage alliances allowed them to influence religion in other kingdoms. Although both Edwin and Oswald were ultimately defeated in battle by the notorious pagan King of Mercia, Penda, Northumbria recovered on each occasion to ensure the survival of Christianity in the N and to oversee its introduction into Mercia itself.

A marriage alliance between Penda's son, Peada, and a daughter of King Oswy led to a mission by four priests in the E part of Mercia, around Peterborough, where Peada ruled in his father's lifetime. Penda himself died in battle in the year 654. The favourable background for Christianity under Peada and his queen continued under the next king, Wulfhere, another of Penda's sons. Wulfhere was King of Mercia from 657 to 674. He achieved dominance in England S of the Humber, and in his day, the great Mercian abbey of Peterborough began to set up daughter-houses in the Midlands and southern England. The evidence for these foundations constitutes an interesting account of evangelisation in the first century of English Christianity.

A 12C monk of Peterborough, Hugh Candidus or Hugh White, wrote a chronicle in which he stated that from Peterborough 'many other monasteries were founded and from that house monks and abbots were constituted at Ancarig, which is now called Thorney, at Brixworth, at Breedon-on-the-Hill, at Bermondsey, at Rippingale, at Woking and at many other places'. Bermondsey and Woking are both S of the Thames; their early connection with Peterborough speaks of King Wulfhere's control of southern England. Breedon-on-the-Hill in Leicestershire has a church of St. Mary and St. Hardulph which possesses significant pre-Conquest sculptures. Brixworth in Northamptonshire is even more notable, for its church of All Saints is a famous pre-Conquest building, which might date from the late 7C, or at least from the 8C, and excavations there have yielded evidence which must relate to the monastic foundation from Peterborough. The church is the principal survival of the story of Mercian evangelisation in the age of Bede and a reminder of the way in which the early English Church grew.

Dedications

Peterborough's name reminds us that in the 7C and 8C, St. Peter was by far the most frequent choice among known dedications of churches. Bede's 'Ecclesiastical History of the English Nation', which was completed in 731, mentions 25 dedications in total, of which eight are of St. Peter and three are of St. Peter and St. Paul together. An ancient dedication to St. Peter is one indication that a church might be of particularly early foundation. In Bede's time, St. Peter was held in great honour throughout the western Church. A famous manuscript of the Bible, the 'Codex Amiatinus', which is now in the Laurentian Library in Florence, was written in Bede's monastery of Jarrow in Northumbria and was taken to Rome by Abbot Coelfrid in 716. It was given to the Pope, but its dedication was strictly to the shrine, or indeed the relics, of St. Peter. Similarly, the pallium or scarf of office which Roman consuls had once worn and which, in due course, Popes sent to archbishops, was considered all the more important from the fact that before being granted by the Pope, it had been laid on St. Peter's tomb. The pallium still appears in the arms of the See of Canterbury.

The antiquity of other dedications is less consistent. There are some indications that All Hallows (or All Saints) and St. Martin might have had above-average early use. The Apostles and prominent Roman martyrs clearly formed the majority of early dedications.

Local saints in England were not commemorated until long after their deaths, in some cases centuries later. So, for example, a dedication to St. Augustine of Canterbury does not imply an early 7C foundation; more than likely it would be 10C, 11C or 12C. It is sometimes stated that churches dedicated to the Virgin Mary are of early foundation; this is not so. Comparatively few are recorded as bearing her name in the first couple of centuries of English Church history. Her over-whelming popularity over all other saints arose as late as the 12C. The original form of a dedication to her was 'Holy Mother of God', which reflects the title of *Theotokos* (literally 'God-bearer') which had been bestowed on her at the Council of Ephesus in 431.

The Danish Invasions

It is conventional to put together all churches from the time of St. Augustine to the Norman Conquest as pre-Conquest. Yet in many ways it is unsatisfactory to consider as one group buildings whose origin may be up to four and a half centuries apart. It would be ludicrous to put into one group churches built in the comparable span from Elizabethan times to the 20C. Although developments in pre-Conquest architecture, liturgy and Church government were relativ-ely very gradual, there were nevertheless clear differences between one century and another. The most obvious division in pre-Conquest Church history is before and after the Danish or Viking invasions of the 9C. Many monasteries, which had been founded in the 7C and 8C, did not survive the onslaught. The daughter-houses of Peter-borough which were discussed above, did not preserve their original status. Some, such as Brixworth, remained as parish churches with-out Peterborough connections. Others, such as Bermondsey, disap-peared entirely, to be re-founded under quite different patronage at a later date. Peterborough itself, which was attacked in 870, was not re-founded as a Benedictine monastery until 972. It was one part of the great Church renewal which took place in the reign of King Edgar (959–75) and under St. Dunstan, St. Ethelwold and St. Oswald.

Shrines and Relics

If the Danish invasions represent the great divide, what were the common factors from the 7C to the 11C? Above all, there was a common emphasis on shrines and relics, which continued until the Reformation. We are familiar with the subject of pilgrimage to a great shrine such as that of St. Thomas Becket at Canterbury, but much less so with the innumerable minor shrines throughout England and with the existence of quite small relics in parish churches. Churches were sometimes built to a plan which was chiefly geared to the circulation of pilgrims. The early crypts which survive at Hexham and Repton and under Ripon Cathedral were all designed to display relics and to ensure an orderly passage of pilgrims. St. Edmund's Abbey at Bury St. Edmund's was a typical example of the same thing on the most grandiose medieval style.

Relics divide into two groups: the bones of saints; and objects associated with them (or, in exceptional cases, objects reputedly associated with Christ). The first group would range from the entire remains to just one small fragment. All Saints' at Brixworth, for example, seems to have had a throat-bone of St. Boniface, which was as treasured in its reliquary as the entire mortal remains of an Apostolic martyr. It is true that pilgrims brought money to a church and especially to cathedrals and abbeys, and that there was some hankering for a local saint in places where no local martyr had existed, but it is very wrong to look upon the movement as mercenary. In the 10C, King Aethelstan—who had all the power and riches a king could have wanted—collected relics incessantly for what he clearly considered to be their spiritual worth. Rome achieved its pre-eminence in the western Church because it could claim the shrine of St. Peter, and it was the accepted site of his burial which led to the building of St. Peter's basilica halfway up the Vatican Hill. Such an awkward site was used for Constantine's great church, and for its successor, only because the principal Apostolic martyr was considered to be buried there. The word martyr comes from the Greek for a witness: a witness to belief in the Resurrection of Jesus. No more revered position in the early Church could exist than that of a martyr, whose death was recorded for posterity in a *passio*. The date of his martyrdom, known as his birthday in Heaven, was reverently recorded in liturgical calendars and marked more or less widely in Christendom. Not all saints, of course, were martyrs. Local English saints were often bishops, or founders or foundresses of churches and monasteries. But martyrdom was a special crown. So St. Thomas Becket was honoured more than St. Anselm, and St. Edmund more than St. Dunstan.

Pre-Conquest Buildings

Surviving pre-Conquest churches have been described in minute detail in many books and articles. Yet much that has been written has been oblivious or neglectful of the liturgy and customs of the early English Church. Buildings have been considered with little reference to their use. Shrines and relics, as discussed above, form just one subject which needs emphasis. Church organisation must also receive attention, for its history from St. Augustine's mission to the fully-established parochial system of the Middle Ages is a very long and complicated one. Monasteries loom large in much of the pre-Conquest period, especially for the influence they had on what survives of pre-Conquest art and architecture. Peterborough's scattered daughter-houses form just one small part of the story. In County Durham, it has been argued persuasively that almost all surviving pre-Conquest fabric and sculpture was monastic in origin, with a considerable number of monastic sites arranged in loose clusters. The word 'monastery' is used a little vaguely in relation to the early English Church. Monasteries existed in the absence of a modern parochial system; they were mission centres which were bound to remain prominent and influential long after a network of local churches had appeared.

Archaeology has added much to our knowledge of pre-Conquest churches in recent decades, even in cases where documents and standing fabric have been eloquent. Sometimes, standing fabric which was considered of much later date has been identified as pre-Conquest. The church at Rivenhall in Essex, now seen to be substantially pre-Conquest, was previously thought to be 19C. Archaeology has often revealed a succession of churches, beginning with a small pre-Conquest plan, which would typically be enlarged and rebuilt down to the 15C. Occasionally, there would be contraction—aisles would be demolished and arcades filled in—but medieval expansion was more usual.

Various pre-Conquest features are distinctive. They include 'long-and-short work', or quoins which were laid alternately vertical and horizontal; pilaster strips or lesenes; tall, narrow naves, and doorways of like proportions; central towers with re-entrant angles (that is, towers which are wider than their naves, chancels and transepts); very small windows, often with a single stone at the head; lateral chambers or *porticus*, sometimes placed side by side as if to form an aisle, but prevented from being one by transverse walls; doorways placed high up in towers, presumably affording access to W galleries; and triangular-headed windows and doorways. Some features are found equally in pre-Conquest and Norman churches, such as the reuse of Roman materials, the use of small, paired belfry windows, and E apses. In the case of apses, however, some very early pre-Conquest churches do have the distinctive feature of an arcade to separate the E end from the nave (examples are Reculver, Brixworth and St. Paul-in-the-Bail, Lincoln). A few pre-Conquest features seem very strange to us today. One is the turriform nave, whereby a tower's lowest stage formed a nave. This is strange because the proportions of such a church are very different from those which we consider normal. W galleries in churches seem normal enough, but pre-Conquest ones clearly emerged from towers and not at all in the manner familiar from the 18C and early 19C. Divisions in pre-Conquest churches seem odd, too: upper storeys apparently occurred quite frequently, and a ground-plan may be divided into distinct rooms as at St. Peter's, Barton-on-Humber, Lincolnshire. The influences which dictated these arrangements are not nearly so obvious as they are for the High Middle Ages; they were probably much more varied. If we knew as much about pre-Conquest Church life as we do, say, of the 15C, I suspect that the influence of the Greek East would be much more prominent than we have allowed.

The Norman Conquest

The Norman Conquest of 1066 and later was not an absolute divide in architecture or in Church life. Some 'Norman' churches had been built in England before the Conquest (such as the Westminster Abbey built by King Edward the Confessor), and some bishops in King Edward's reign were Normans. Conversely, some churches built after 1066 followed pre-Norman conventions—we label them 'Saxo-Norman'—and a few Englishmen remained as leaders of the Church amidst many newcomers. Some features shared by pre-Conquest and Norman churches were mentioned above. Nevertheless, there was a significant change in the scale of church building. Existing cathedrals and churches were rebuilt to dimensions which greatly exceeded those of their predecessors. Norman design has a regularity and a heaviness which we would not connect with earlier times. *'Ponderosum opus'* was the label given in the Middle Ages to the Norman Barnwell Priory Church in Cambridgeshire: heavy, ponderous work.

Norman churches often feature endless courses of small, squared ashlar, such as we see at St. Andrew's, Weaverthorpe, in Yorkshire. St. Andrew's is a most attractive example of the plainest Norman design, featuring little more than some small single-light windows, which are deeply-splayed within. Usually, there would be flat buttresses, possibly a stringcourse, a decorative corbel table just below the roof, shafting and mouldings round windows and doorways, and perhaps figurative carving in the capitals of the main doorway and in the tympanum above it. Within a Norman church, the piers of arcades were round and squat in the earliest buildings, supporting square abaci and round unmoulded arches. The abaci later became octagonal and eventually round; the piers became less heavy; capitals changed from the 'cushion' type to scallops and then to waterleaf; and, gradually in the 12C, zigzag and other mouldings appeared over arches, doorways and windows, becoming quite lavish by c 1175. A special type of Norman church was the 'round church', in which a round nave or rotunda derived from the Holy Sepulchre in Jerusalem. This type was prompted as much by pilgrimage to the Holy Land as by the Crusades.

The Foundation of Churches

The Norman period of the 11C and 12C is distinguished also by the number of new church foundations. Although we do not know when most ancient churches were first built, documents and archaeology tell us of enough to allow us to gauge the whole picture. More ancient churches—and this is particularly clear in towns—were founded in the 11C and 12C than at any other period. It may be said that the great majority of English churches were founded either in those centuries, or in the 19C and 20C. In towns, it was a combination of merchant wealth and a keenness to build churches which explains the great wave of Norman foundations. The number of monasteries founded in Norman England in contrast to other periods speaks very clearly of the vast scale of giving to churches at that time. The Church has been the recipient of money and land in every century, but it must not be forgotten that the scale of giving has fluctuated very markedly from one age to another. In England, the Norman period and the 19C have been the two great periods of giving.

The Parochial System

The practice of each church building serving a defined area called a parish has been part of the English scene for so many centuries that it is difficult to imagine earlier arrangements. Those arrangements centred on 'minster churches', which served wide areas, far larger than normal parishes. The word 'minster' comes from the Latin *monasterium*, which also gives us 'monastery'; but minsters were not often the same as monasteries. Minsters were gradually complemented by a spread of local churches, whose means of financial support were to cement the parochial system as we know it. Ancient parishes were more or less fixed permanently in the 12C, in the Norman period and just after. At the time of Domesday Book (1086), the older arrangements were still apparent; by 1200, the 'modern' system had effectively been reached. The parish of that time was not merely a geographical area, within which one priest had the 'cure of souls'. It was instead a grouping of legal and financial rights—the right to collect tithe, the right to bury (and to collect fees from burials) and the right to baptise. Churches had to be supported from their own income, and so it was important that their exclusive rights within their parishes were safeguarded. The result was that from c 1200 the parochial system was largely set fast. It became exceedingly difficult to create a new parish, for there were enough already, and all of them defended their rights. Even a chapel of ease which had long existed could not become a parish church without great difficulty. The great church of Holy Trinity at Kingston-upon-Hull, for example, was originally a chapel of ease to All Saints' at Hessle, further up the River Humber; Hessle was the more ancient place, and Hull was a medieval 'new town'. Consequently, Holy Trinity Church had no burial ground for many generations; burials took place at Hessle. Not until 1661 was Holy Trinity Church constituted a full parish church, by which time Hull was a major and prosperous port and was many times larger than Hessle. Market Harborough's main church lacked a burial ground for the same reason. In later centuries (from the 17C to the 19C), the division of an ancient parish was usually effected by Act of Parliament, because by then a parish had *civil* purposes as well as ecclesiastical ones. It was only in the 19C that the Church was enabled to create new parishes more easily, allowing the division of those inherited from the Middle Ages.

The Ownership of Churches

Although many major churches were founded and endowed by kings and given to bishops, the great majority of ancient churches were founded by layfolk for their own use. They were not given to bishops or to a diocese or any other ecclesiastical authority; they were private properties or 'proprietory churches'. Such churches could be bought and sold like a house or a farm, and it was possible for one to be owned by two or more people (or by two or more institutions). Divisions of ownership led to the use of technical terms such as 'mediety', 'moiety' and 'portioner', which lingered for centuries in some places. The proprietory church was normal in late pre-Conquest and Norman times, but was gradually brought within the Church's system of government. As the Middle Ages proceeded, the idea of the absolute lay ownership of a church faded, to be replaced by the lesser notion that an individual had the 'advowson', the right to present a priest. Ownership by institutions—by which is chiefly meant monasteries—was also modified so that resident priests had defined rights to complement those of the institutions.

The rights over a church largely concerned the entitlement to its income, which derived from tithes, surplice fees and its real estate (or 'glebe'). The issue at stake was always the division of that income between the owner and the resident priest. Certain parts of the income were always reserved to the priest, but the Church eventually legislated to ensure that parish priests received a fixed and adequate share. Bishops were said to 'ordain a vicarage' when they stipulated such fixed shares. The priest on the spot became a 'vicar', or substitute for the non-resident 'rector'. The owner, who came to be called the 'patron', still had some property rights (which depended on the local historical circumstances), but they were not exclusive as they had once been, and moreover he had certain duties, of which the upkeep of the chancel was the most common.

The proprietory church and the existence of innumerable small parishes (especially in towns) both resulted from lay initiatives. They produced a system which bishops had not planned and which was only gradually assimilated into Church government. A system planned by the Church itself would have been very different.

The position of the medieval clergy as literate men in a largely illiterate world led to their being recruited by kings for the purposes of civil government. Bishoprics were often filled by the equivalents of today's cabinet ministers. Numerous Bishops of Winchester, for example, held the office of Lord Chancellor, which was the nearest equivalent of the modern position of Prime Minister. Lesser officials received Church offices, too, to give them an ecclesiastical income to support their civil duties. Popes also had an administration to pay for, as large as any king's and of much longer standing; and so its officials were supported from the revenues of cathedrals and parishes throughout Europe. 'Papal provisions', or the appointment of (non-resident) papal officials to Church positions, were very numerous in the Middle Ages.

The Gothic Styles

From the late 12C until the 16C the Gothic styles of architecture were in use; and Gothic design continued, alongside Classical buildings, into the 18C in some places, by which time the Gothic Revival got under way, to ensure the use of Gothic styles into the 20C. So on any reckoning, Gothic forms are central to English church architecture; a Gothic church is the normal English idea of a church. By Gothic we mean one of the various styles which succeeded the Norman and preceded the revived Classicism of the 16C and later. In the early 19C, the architect Thomas Rickman labelled those styles 'Early English', 'Decorated' and 'Perpendicular', and English architectural writers have kept to those labels ever since. They are precise enough for most purposes, but it must always be remembered that architectural style is constantly changing, and that there are no firm boundaries by date. Between the heydays of any two styles there will always be a transitional style, or a series of them. 'Transitional' is in fact a formal label applied to late 12C buildings, which begin to show the supersession of Norman design by the Early English style. The crucial change was the arrival of the pointed arch in the last quarter of the 12C to replace the round arch of the Normans. All Gothic styles use the pointed arch, whether shallow or steep.

The Early English style is very roughly the style of the 13C. It is sometimes called the 'lancet style', because its chief characteristic is the tall, narrow, pointed window we call a lancet. Usually they are single-light, but at the E end of a parish church there may be a group of three (which are said to be 'graduated' if the middle one is taller); and very occasionally there will be more. The chancels of Eccleshall in Staffordshire and Haltwhistle in Northumberland are good examples of a simple lancet style. In the middle of the 13C, plate tracery came into use. Typically, two lancets would be placed side by side, with a quatrefoil added above them in the centre. All these elements would pierce the full thickness of the wall, rather than being divided by relatively thin mullions and transoms as in later centuries. Tracery formed by such internal divisions, or bar tracery, superseded plate tracery in the later 13C. By c 1300 three forms had developed. One was Geometrical tracery, in which foiled circles and triangles predominate. Elaboration quickly developed, as one may see in the windows of Howden Minster in Yorkshire. Another form was Y-tracery, in which a mullion divides into a Y-shape at the head of a two-light window. Thirdly, there is intersecting tracery, which is really Y-tracery repeated and overlapped so that a series of straight intersections are formed in the head.

Within an Early English church, it is normal to find round piers with round capitals and round abaci. The capitals developed out of the late Norman forms into what is called 'stiff-leaf' design. Arches, which had often acquired a shallow chamfer as well as a pointed shape in the late 12C, were normally given two full chamfers in the 13C, and sometimes they became very steeply pointed. For doorways, sedilia and blind arcading, the trefoil-headed arch was frequently used. Purbeck marble, which had appeared in some 12C Norman churches (e.g. Iffley, Oxfordshire), became very widely used in the 13C. The E parts of Beverley Minster in Yorkshire exemplify its lavish use. Finally, mention must be made of dogtooth moulding on nave arches, chancel arches and windows. Dogtooth is as characteristic of the 13C as zigzag is of the 12C and ballflower of the 14C. West Walton Church in Norfolk is a foremost example of the Early English style in all its elements.

In the 14C, the ogee curve appears, and this is the most characteristic element of the Decorated style. It is a double-curve, one part of which is convex and the other concave. Above the apex of an ogee arch, over doorways, belfry windows, etc., there will often be a crocketed upright. The ogee curve is the crucial element in 'flowing' or curvilinear tracery, in which all manner of patterns are created. A more regular pattern is found in Reticulated or net-like tracery, whereby cusped circles are pulled into ogee shapes on two sides to create the semblance of a net.

The Decorated period is known for some elaborate chancels, in which the regular features of sedilia, piscina and doorways are joined by an Easter sepulchre and a benefactor's tomb. A full set of these features in a lavish ogee style is found at Hawton in Nottinghamshire, Patrington in Yorkshire and Heckington in Lincolnshire. 14C naves will generally have octagonal piers and octagonal moulded capitals, with double-chamfered arches. Adornment might come in the form of ballflower moulding.

The Perpendicular style is the normal style of the later 14C and the 15C. Its name comes from the upright panel tracery which windows of that period reveal. Perpendicular windows were the largest of all medieval windows, regularly comprising several lights at the E end of a parish church or in other principal positions, and reaching as many as 15 lights in exceptional cases such as the W window of St.

George's Chapel, Windsor. With the use of buttresses, it became possible to create walls of glass, as in King's College Chapel at Cambridge or at Holy Trinity Church, Hull. The large medieval windows always have one or more transoms (which are sometimes battlemented) to divide the lights horizontally. The lights in Perpendicular windows are sometimes almost round-headed rather than pointed; and arches themselves are typically four-centred or shallow-pointed. The main windows of a church were often supplemented in the 15C by a substantial clerestory above the nave arcades (and very occasionally in the chancel too). Such a clerestory was typically part of a 15C remodelling of an earlier church, which would also include the replacement of some windows (especially the main E window), the rebuilding or heightening of the tower, and the addition of chancel chapels. The top of the tower would be given crocketed pinnacles, and they would appear also above buttresses to the nave and chancel.

Perpendicular arcades are formed most usually of piers of clustered shafts, perhaps with additional mouldings in the angles, and with capitals which are small and of limited detail. Sometimes there are no capitals at all, or they are just decorative bands (as in All Saints', Rotherham, Yorkshire). Octagonal piers of 14C type continued in use in the 15C in many places, and occasionally they will have concave faces (as at Northleach, Gloucestershire). 15C arcades are frequently very tall.

Spires

Medieval spires range from the 13C to the 16C. Norman churches had usually been given flat-topped towers or low, pyramidal caps. The earliest spires were of the broach type, whereby the transition from tower to spire—from a square to an octagon—is achieved by placing half-pyramids at the four corners, perhaps with gabled lucarnes in between. Later, it became normal for spires to be recessed behind ornamented parapets. Sometimes the two types are mixed; and in any case recessed spires began in the 13C, not so very long after the broach type. Pinnacles became more elaborate and more numerous as the Middle Ages advanced, and they are sometimes connected with the spire by flying buttresses.

Medieval Fittings

Most surviving medieval fittings tend to be 15C or 16C. Very few go back to the pre-Conquest and Norman periods. Fonts are exceptional. They were very often preserved when the church for which they were made was replaced in the later Middle Ages. Most fonts are of stone, but some attractive early ones are of lead. Norman fonts are particularly numerous, and they may display carvings which are as valuable as tympana and capitals. 15C fonts are also frequent, but decoration is generally limited to quatrefoils. 15C covers are often more notable, amounting to intricate, spire-like works in the best East Anglian examples such as that at Ufford, Suffolk. A 'Seven

Sacrament' font will bear carvings to represent the Sacraments recognised throughout the medieval Church. Fonts are often placed near the main door of a church, or at least at the W end, to symbolise the entry into the Christian family at baptism. The octagonal shape which they frequently possess is also symbolic—of regeneration—for the Resurrection was looked upon as having occurred on the 'eighth day'.

Most medieval woodwork tends to be 15C and 16C. Screens in particular date from the late Middle Ages because churches were more likely to be divided up by that period. It was the great age of the guild chapel and the chantry chapel, which were often divided by screens from the rest of the church. The principal screen would be the chancel screen, which could extend across the aisles where they continued alongside the chancel. The chancel screen was usually the Rood screen, for above the loft would be placed the Rood—a carving of the Crucifixion, flanked by the Virgin Mary and St. John and sometimes by further figures. The Rood loft would be reached by stairs at one end of the screen; the entrances to such stairways remain in many places where Rood and screen have long gone. Beneath the loft, chancel screens will usually comprise an enclosed base and openwork tracery above, arranged as in windows. The base was sometimes painted, typically with portraits of saints. They have rarely survived in great clarity, but enough generally remains to recognise St. Catherine from her wheel, St. Edmund from his crown and arrows, etc. All these saints were painted according to late medieval fashions and practice. Thus St. Edmund will look like a 15C king, not a 9C one, and St. Martin will be vested like a 15C bishop, not a humble 4C pastor; both are far from their historical realities. So numerous are these later medieval depictions, and so regularly were they copied in the 19C, that we take them as 'correct'. It must therefore be remembered that they are quite anachronistic. St. Martin would not have worn a mitre, St. Gregory would not have had a triple tiara, etc. Their times were worlds away from what the 15C knew.

Guilds were very numerous and important in late medieval times. They are usually thought of as *trade* guilds, but many of them were unconnected with trades. They offered their members spiritual benefits, especially the saying of Masses after their deaths. The belief in Purgatory, in which forgiveness is sought after death for unforgiven venial sins and temporal punishment is undergone until complete expiation is achieved, excited in the late Middle Ages a conspicuous level of allusion to death and to the need for expiatory prayer. Guilds in late medieval town churches often acquired their own chapels, which were sometimes new additions and sometimes adapted parts of the existing fabric. Rich individuals might found and endow a chantry, and this too might have its own chapel. The minimum endowment would be for a priest to say Mass regularly, especially on the 'obit' or anniversary of a person's death. A chantry would do for the individual what a guild would achieve collectively. The grandest chantry chapels were elaborate stone enclosures, comprising a tomb, an altar and an intricate vaulted canopy. Winchester Cathedral has an exceptional number of these.

Further categories of medieval woodwork which are also predominantly 15C and 16C are pulpits and seating. Pulpits survive from the 14C; but they were often introduced into a church for the first time in the late Middle Ages. Their panels may be painted in the manner of screen bases, or they may have niches for statues. Devon is the county for colourful pulpits, as it is for colourful screens. Seating for layfolk is chiefly of interest for the carved finials of benches (such as poppyheads), and the straight-topped, carved bench-ends which are so much a feature of West Country churches. The Instruments of the Passion are the favourite subjects of carvings on bench-ends. It should be noted that they very often date from the 16C, and sometimes from after the Reformation. Seating for the clergy may include medieval stalls, and stalls may incorporate misericords or small tip-up seats which often bear carvings. They tend to represent secular subjects, and, as with bench-ends, sometimes involve satire against abbots and bishops. Misericords were provided to relieve clergy who would otherwise have to stand through long choir offices.

Rarer items of woodwork which might be found in a chancel are sedilia, pyx-canopies, and aumbries or small cupboards. Sedilia are nearly always of stone and form part of a chancel's S wall, but very rarely they are wooden and detached. A fine four-seat example exists in Beverley Minster. Medieval pyx-canopies (to hold the Reserved Sacrament) are also very rare. Only one is in use today—at Dennington, Suffolk. The grandest is found at Milton Abbey in Dorset, a four-stage example with tracery and a spire which is now fixed to the chancel's N wall. Aumbries were used to store precious items and were normally placed on the N side of a chancel.

It should be noted that fittings which are normally wooden may sometimes be of stone. There are a few stone chancel screens (examples are Compton Bassett (Wiltshire) and Great Bardfield (Essex)), and pulpits are sometimes made of stone (including a canopied 15C case at Arundel in Sussex, and also some colourful Devon examples, as in St. Saviour's, Dartmouth). Early seating is also normally of stone, in the form of a continuous sill along the outer walls and occasionally around pier bases.

Medieval ironwork is usually a matter of decorative ironwork on door leaves. Hadstock in Essex has the only pre-Conquest example, but Norman cases are more numerous and later medieval work is fairly frequent. The earliest work comprised C-shaped hinges. Subsequently, the curls split and gradually became barbed straps and fleur-de-lis. The hinges themselves became scroll-shaped rather than C-shaped. Elaboration on later doors is marked. A few churches have medieval wrought-iron screens or grilles; there is a fine example at Arundel in Sussex. Also of wrought-iron are closing-rings on doors, and the occasional sanctuary ring. They typically show an animal head holding the ring in its mouth. Sanctuary in medieval churches did not give permanent freedom from arrest and punishment; it was a prelude to exile overseas as an *alternative* to trial and punishment in England.

The familiar eagle lecterns began in the 14C in wood, but many from the 15C onwards are of brass.

Wall paintings often formed an important feature of medieval interiors, sometimes covering the entire wall surfaces in one or more series. Most of them have a predominantly orange-red colour, but blues and greens may appear too. The Infancy and Passion of Christ, the life of the Virgin, and the lives (but particularly the martyrdoms) of saints formed the principal subjects. The saints appear in the dress and attributes of the time they were painted (as discussed under screens, above). Over the chancel arch there would normally appear the Last Judgement or 'doom painting', in which the Risen Christ presides over the judgement on the last day or 'doomsday'. To his left will be the 'goats'—the damned—and to his right (or place of honour) the 'sheep', or the blessed, all as in Chapter 25 of St. Matthew's Gospel. St. Michael will be weighing souls, and the Virgin Mary will be pleading for mercy on their behalf. The mouth of Hell and the New Jerusalem will receive those who have been judged, and all around will be the general resurrection, heralded by angels with trumpets. The power of that scene in the restricted world of a medieval village, where death was never far away, needs no emphasis. The 'doom' at Wenhaston in Suffolk is perhaps the most celebrated example. Another subject which tended to have a fixed place in a church was that of St. Christopher carrying the Christ Child, which was usually found on the wall opposite the south door. Most of the series or 'cycles' depicted in medieval wall paintings are ubiquitous, but some are rare. Battle in Sussex, for example, has an unusual series about St. Margaret of Antioch. Here we must remember that artists used both historical and legendary lives of the saints, and the apocryphal New Testament as well as canonical Scripture. The whole body of writings which was widely known in the Middle Ages must be familiar to the interpreter of medieval art.

Medieval stained glass is present in few parish churches in more than fragmentary form. Only a handful of churches in a county, on average, will have complete windows or a series of them. Even where there are such windows—most notably, in various York churches—the glass has often become jumbled through incorrect replacement in the past, or it is obscure for want of cleaning and restoration. Nevertheless, medieval stained glass is an important subject, for it was certainly central to the appearance which a late medieval church was intended to have. It performed the same didactic role as mural painting, but it also had a memorial and expiatory function too. A window's inscription will seek mercy for the soul of a donor, who will appear as a kneeling figure in the lower part of a light. Sometimes a window derived from collective giving. The delightful series of windows at St. Neot in Cornwall resulted from donations by different groups in that village. Depictions of Biblical scenes and of saints are most usual, with the larger schemes often presenting New Testament subjects alongside or opposite their Old Testament prefigurations. Some windows were purely decorative, with patterns of greyish glass known as *grisaille*. Tabernacle or canopy work became more prominent as the Middle Ages proceeded. In the very late medieval period, Flemish artists took the lead in stained glass design, most notably at King's College Chapel, Cambridge.

Medieval Monuments

Monuments are found in and around churches from the 7C to the present, but few survive from before the later Middle Ages. Pre-Conquest standing crosses are known to be memorials in many cases, and there is the very occasional named monument such as that to Herebericht the priest at Monkwearmouth in County Durham. Almost all early monuments, however, are anonymous. They comprise slabs with a raised cross or with incised decoration. Often they have been referred to in guides—wrongly—as 'coffin-lids'. Gradually, figures began to appear on slabs. The earliest are of abbots and bishops; most cathedrals have an example. The next stage, reached in the 13C, was to have the effigy raised on a tomb-chest, whose sides would be decorated with blank tracery, heraldry and small figures. These figures were usually 'weepers' or mourners. Occasionally there will be a 'bedesman', a figure praying for the deceased's soul. Medieval monuments were highly coloured, but little colour remains on most of them today. Even if effigies are never portraits, they are obviously valuable sources for medieval armour and civilian dress. The old story that a knight's crossed legs indicate a Crusader, incidentally, is fiction; it was merely a fashion of c 1300. Inscriptions are not widespread until the late Middle Ages, a fact which contributes to the anonymity of many monuments.

From the 13C another form of memorial existed: brasses. England is exceptional in Europe for the number of its brasses. They occur more in the E counties than elsewhere, nearer the Continental source of the latten from which they were made. Brasses are sometimes reused or engraved on the reverse; they are then known as 'palimpsests'. A brass will often be quite small and was clearly an inexpensive memorial in contrast to a stone tomb-chest with effigy.

In the late Middle Ages both stone and brass memorials sometimes show a skeleton or a decaying corpse. Such reminders of death accorded with the pessimistic mood of the late Middle Ages. A call to repentance in view of ever-imminent death was the intention of such memorials. Inscriptions often underlined the point.

Here and there a heart burial will be seen in the form of a small plaque, with a heart clasped by two hands.

The Reformation

The Reformation in the 16C divided the Church in western Europe permanently for the first time. It divided not only the Church in one country from that in another, but also produced in due course different Churches or *denominations* within each country. The Reformation in England was not eventually so drastic as that which occurred, say, in Switzerland or the Netherlands. King Henry VIII broke with the Pope but he did not repudiate the doctrines in which the Pope believed. So long as Henry lived, the Latin Mass continued, bishops remained as before, and even the chantry chapels survived. The king was responsible, however, for major acts of destruction in carrying out the Dissolution of the Monasteries and in stripping cathedrals and other churches of their shrines.

If we take together the century and a half after King Henry VIII's initial break with the Papacy, the continuities in the English Church are as obvious as the discontinuities. Above all, the Church retained its bishops, whereas in many reformed Churches elsewhere, the episcopate was abolished. With the bishops there survived in England the full panoply of medieval Church government, with the exception, of course, that appeals from Church courts no longer went to Rome. Nevertheless, the Reformation brought with it no little destruction to church fabric. Under King Henry VIII all the monasteries in England were dissolved; their lands and possessions were confiscated and passed permanently into lay ownership (which is why some country houses have names such as Woburn *Abbey* and Nostell *Priory*). In addition, the rich and magnificent shrines which existed in the country's major churches were plundered and dismantled. Pilgrims could no longer see the bejewelled and gilded monuments which stood over such tombs as those of St. Thomas Becket in Canterbury Cathedral or of St. Edmund at Bury St. Edmund's. In the reign of King Edward VI (1547–53), destruction went much further. All the chantries and colleges were dissolved. The fabric of many chantry chapels survived, but their entire reason for existence had gone. No longer were prayers and Masses said for the souls of the deceased. The Latin Mass itself was superseded by the English service in Archbishop Cranmer's new Prayer Book of 1549. Plate, vestments and 'images' of all sorts—especially Rood groups on screens—were destroyed, sold, melted down or otherwise reused. By and large, 16C destruction ended when King Edward VI died. The Elizabethan Church more or less kept what it had inherited. The lurch towards Continental Protestantism around 1550 was followed by a more stable period under Queen Elizabeth I, in which the mainstream Church saw itself as following a middle way between Puritans on the one hand and Catholics on the other.

Mention of Puritans introduces the struggles of the 17C, which were ultimately just as destructive as those of the mid-16C. The Puritans were those who tried, from the late 16C, to push the Church of England even farther away from the medieval Church towards the more extreme Continental models of the Reformation. Ultimately they failed, but during the 1640s and 1650s—when the Civil War occurred and when Oliver Cromwell was in power—they did achieve ascendancy in England. It was during these years that some particularly appalling destruction occurred. Stained glass and sculptures especially suffered. It was during the Civil War too that the one break in the episcopate occurred. The office of bishop was abolished and all the property of the country's bishoprics was forfeit to the state. The Anglican Church's privileged position was replaced by a Presbyterian ascendancy. Parish churches usually lost their Anglican incumbent; almost all lists of Rectors and Vicars which one may see displayed in churches will mention 'Commonwealth intruders'. In 1660, upon the Restoration of King Charles II, these Cromwellian changes were reversed. Bishops once again presided over the Church of England, which resumed its status as the Established Church. Property which had been confiscated under Cromwell was restored. In 1662, a new Act of Uniformity reaffirmed the beliefs and liturgy of the Anglican Church, automatically removing the 'Puritans' and like-minded men from the parish churches of the land. Nonconformity was thus distinguished from the New Anglican order and gradually crystallised into a number of formal denominations. Initially, these groups were persecuted, but in 1672 a measure of relief was allowed, and in 1689, after the 'Glorious Revolution', toleration of worship was generally permitted to Protestant Nonconformists, subject to their registering their chapels and meeting houses. Right down to the 19C, however, they were still excluded from public offices and from the ancient universities. None of this toleration in the late 17C was extended to those who maintained an allegiance to the Pope. It is true that judicial executions or martyrdoms ceased in 1681, but imprisonment remained normal until the late 18C, when Catholic Relief Acts gave Catholics the same rights which Protestant Nonconformists had enjoyed for a century.

Nonconformity

Nonconformity or Dissent—the 'Free Churches' of today—is generally considered to divide into two strands: the denominations surviving from the 17C ('Old Dissent') and those arising from the
evangelical awakening of the 18C ('New Dissent'). There were also
the Unitarians, whose emergence in the later 18C was a dynamic
element in the ranks of Old Dissent. The Unitarians became particularly important in Birmingham, where their members in the
Victorian age included many influential figures, above all Joseph
Chamberlain. Old Dissent proper comprised the Religious Society of
Friends (the Quakers), Independents (later Congregationalists), Baptists, and Presbyterians. The last of these declined in 18C England,
when many Presbyterians became Unitarians or Independents. The
Baptists were divided into Particular and General streams down to
1891. Both streams were chiefly found in southern England. The
Friends have always been a small but influential group, seen as one
of the more subversive parts of Nonconformity in the 17C, but
appearing to be the least evangelistic sect by 1800. The Independents shared with the Baptists a belief in autonomous churches (or
congregational government), but disagreed with them over baptism.
Baptists practise believer's or adult baptism, as opposed to infant
baptism. In theology the Independents were Calvinist, a position
they shared with the Presbyterians and Particular Baptists.

The evangelical awakening of the 18C led to the formation of the
various Methodist Churches by John Wesley (1703–91) and others in
the century or so after 1738. Wesley launched his life's work from
within the Church of England and he viewed his ministry as comple-
mentary to that of the Established Church. He wished to concentrate
on those areas where the Anglican presence was weak. Subsequent
to his death, the Methodists divided into a number of separate
groups. The mainstream Wesleyan Methodists remained the largest
group. Second to them were the Primitive Methodists, who
pioneered 'camp meetings' in the early 19C. Smaller Methodist
groups were the New Connexion, the Independent Methodists and
the Bible Christians. Each of these denominations, or 'connexions' as
they called themselves, consisted of societies or churches which were
grouped into circuits. The circuits were in turn grouped into
districts—roughly equivalent to dioceses—and were ultimately gov-
erned by an annual conference. Ministers were stationed in a circuit
for three or four years, and were thus expected to serve (or 'travel in')
a number of circuits during their active ministry. The Methodists
therefore put an emphasis on central government, quite unlike the
organisations of Baptists and Independents. In theology, they have
always been Arminian (like Anglicans and Catholics) and not
Calvinist.

The maximum division between Methodists was reached in 1849.
The groups began to reunite in 1857, when some of the smaller
groups joined to form the United Methodist Free Churches. The new
denomination merged in turn in 1907 with the Bible Christians and
the New Connexion to create the United Methodist Church. Finally,
in 1932 the Wesleyans, the Primitive Methodists and the United
Methodists came together in full Methodist reunion.

16C and 17C Churches

Very little church building took place in the century or so after the Reformation. There was some revival in the second quarter of the 17C, but not until the Restoration did church building occur on any significant scale. The style used until the mid-17C was almost always a late form of Perpendicular. Windows would usually be square-headed and they would have arched and uncusped lights. It was a matter of medieval forms without much of the detail which makes a genuinely medieval church interesting. Inside a late 16C or early 17C church, the story was normally as much Classical as Gothic. Such new fittings as there had been since c 1540 would display some Classical features. Early 17C pulpits form the most frequent category, following a canon or order to install pulpits in all churches. They invariably feature blank arches. Communion tables replaced medieval stone altars following the Reformation, and so they are frequently Elizabethan, with distinctive bulbous legs. Screens of the period are largely parclose screens, built to surround a private pew. Such pews—which could be substantial structures—were in a sense the successors of the old chantry chapels. Many communion rails remain from the 16C and 17C, for they were inserted to protect the altar either where screens had gone or where propriety considered the post-Reformation arrangement inadequate. In the N of England, a number of churches were given woodwork which is associated with Bishop Cosin of Durham. It was fitted from the 1620s until the later 17C. Brancepeth and Haughton-le-Skerne in County Durham and St. John's in the centre of Leeds are the best examples of the style. Cosin (1595–1672) was a younger contemporary of Archbishop Laud (Archbishop of Canterbury (1633–45) and previously Bishop of London), who attempted to embellish churches in the decade before the Civil War. He sought, in common with other influential Churchmen, an Anglican ideal in opposition to both Catholics and Puritans, but at that time the Puritans were strong, and Laud became their enemy, suffering execution in 1645. The 17C Anglican divines were to become important again in the 19C, when their example was attractive to the proponents of the Oxford Movement.

Stained glass was by no means absent in the 17C, but it was substantially heraldic. This did not offend the Puritan zeal against 'images', which reached such a destructive peak in the 1640s.

Post-Reformation monuments form an immense subject, involving foremost works of sculpture. The contribution of the Elizabethan and Stuart periods was to introduce the new Classical style and to develop a number of different forms of monument. Recumbent effigies on tomb-chests now mingled with reclining or semi-reclining effigies. The grandest monuments had large arched canopies on Classical columns, with long inscription plates and much heraldry. More modest and thus frequent types were of two kneeling figures facing one another, often across a prayer-desk, or of figures kneeling in a line, the standing figure in a niche, and the frontal bust or half-figure framed by Classical columns and a pediment. Shakespeare's monument at Stratford-on-Avon is the best-known example of this last type. It is also typical of its time in being the work of a Flemish sculptor, for in the late 16C and early 17C Flemish designers became markedly prominent in monumental sculpture, and many of them formed the 'Southwark School' (see the introduction to

London South of the Thames). Nicholas Stone was the one notable English exception to the Flemish rule.

Amidst the Perpendicular Survival of the early 17C, there was one undisputed Classicist: Inigo Jones. His Queen's Chapel in Marlborough Gate, London (built 1623–27) was the first completely Classical church in England, totally different from its contemporaries. Jones also designed St. Paul's, Covent Garden (1631–38). Not until Wren's time in the later 17C were there further Classical churches, and even then they had Gothic contemporaries (most notably in Oxford).

The Great Fire of London of 1666 provided the opportunity for Sir Christopher Wren to design a new St. Paul's Cathedral and no fewer than 51 parish churches. A summary of their features is found in the introduction to *The City of London*. A few churches with affinities to Wren's were built outside London, such as All Saints', Northampton. These late 17C Classical buildings are of particular note for their fine woodwork and for their plans. It is a commonplace that Wren's churches were 'fitted for auditories', meaning that the pulpit was as much a focus as the altar, and that the longitudinal plan of the Middle Ages was superseded. It would be wrong, however, to say that the altar was regarded as a minor fitting. Chancels may have been shallow—mere alcoves—or absent altogether, but almost always in the late 17C (and the 18C) a large and ornate reredos would be placed behind the altar, which would probably be all the more prominent for the absence of a deep chancel and a chancel screen.

By the late 17C the 'box-pew' was the normal new seating of a church: high, enclosed pews, set amidst panelled column bases, wainscoted walls, doorcases, pulpit and reredos, would create a sea of dark woodwork at ground level. Above would be round-headed windows with plain glass and cobweb ironwork, and walls with small memorial plaques. The ceiling might be embellished with plasterwork, and a little colour would be given by the prominent royal arms. In the larger cities (London, Norwich, Bristol) civic grandeur and merchant wealth would be represented by upright sword-rests and ornamented mayoral pews or seats. All this presented a very different scene from a pre-Reformation church, but it was still a seemly and sumptuous setting for worship.

The 18C

The 18C has usually been portrayed as a somnolent backwater in Church history, a static phase in the building and upkeep of churches, and in the wider life of the Church. Anglican churches have been considered neglected, 'Old Dissent' has been seen as declining and lacking fire, and Catholics viewed as dwindling in numbers. As with so many traditional accounts, all this is substantially inaccurate. Georgian churches were portrayed as neglected and inadequate partly because the Victorians wished to emphasise and justify their new ideas in architecture and in worship. It was part of their polemic to paint their predecessors as neglectful. They wished to stress that because their arrangements were 'proper', 'Christian' and worthy, those of previous generations were inadequate and unworthy. It is true that the scale of new church building in the 18C was only a fraction of the 19C's achievement, but England's 18C population rose very little, whereas in the 19C there was a colossal increase. In fact, new Anglican churches were built in all the major towns, and there were innumerable new non-Anglican buildings. 'Old Dissent' was less thrusting than it had been in the 17C, but it was certainly alive and building as much as the Church of England. 'New Dissent', by which is chiefly meant the Methodists, was immensely energetic and successful. These 18C churches and chapels were built in or near the centres of what were then much smaller towns; their surroundings have become depopulated over the last century and thus so many of these buildings have been demolished. Their absence today should not lead us to picture Georgian neglect of church building.

Nobody who has studied 18C vestry minutes and churchwardens' accounts from different parts of the country could conclude that neglect of church fabric was normal. Repairs and 'beautifications' were as numerous as at any other period. Sometimes, as at Beverley, buildings were saved from collapse. In most cases, work was relatively minor. Apart from the reinstatement of ancient fabric, refittings were common. The stereotype of an 18C interior is a familiar one: box-pews, a three-decker pulpit standing in the centre, benches for the poor also in the centre, a reredos at the E end with inscribed panels of the Creed, the Lord's Prayer and the Commandments, the royal arms prominently displayed, galleries to N and S for worshippers and at the W end for the organ and singers, and sometimes upper W galleries for the 'charity children'. Pulpits were not always in the centre, but often they were moved there to provide more space for pews at the sides. They were almost always very tall ('six feet above contradiction') so that the preacher could address the congregation in the galleries as well as those in the nave. Smaller churches in the country would often lack the N and S galleries but perhaps they would have an elaborate box-pew, reserved for the local landowner, complete with fireplace and wig-pegs. Examples of interiors of smaller 18C churches are Tong near Bradford and King's Norton in Leicestershire. The grander interiors were urban ones and trace their descent from Wren's designs for St. Andrew's, Holborn and St. James's, Piccadilly. Pews in all these churches were bought and sold as private possessions. This was regarded as normal, even if it was strictly contrary to Church law.

Of the buildings themselves, virtually all the early 18C ones were Classical, and so too were the majority of the later ones. At the beginning of the century the Gothic Survival was still more notable than the Gothic Revival. Nicholas Hawksmoor consciously revived Gothic for his towers at St. Michael's, Cornhill and at Westminster Abbey, but far more ubiquitous were the towers of rural churches which were rebuilt on late medieval lines, in a style which their builders had received as standard, not 'revived'. Very few parishes outside the major towns would think of employing a well-known architect or 'gentleman surveyor'; a local master mason would be employed instead. By the end of the 18C all Gothic work was revived. The revival, however, amounted to no more than a decorative use of medieval features on normal 18C shells. Pointed windows (often without tracery or cusping), ogee labels over windows and doorways, battlements and quatrefoils were all applied without much or any attention to medieval precedents. It is usual to label all this 'Gothick', reserving Gothic for later work. The plans of 18C churches, whether Classical or Gothic, generally followed the medieval precedent of an E–W rectangle. Only a few Classical works had centralising plans, such as Joseph Bonomi's St James's at Great Packington in Warwickshire and Nicholas Revett's church at Ayot St. Lawrence in Hertfordshire. 18C plans did not neglect chancels, as is traditionally claimed. In new churches, a chancel would perhaps be shallow in contrast to medieval examples, but it was not excluded. A Greek cross plan would automatically have a chancel in one of its arms. In existing churches, chancels were rebuilt or refitted in many cases, as at Bruton in Somerset, St. Clement's in Cambridge and St. Paul's Walden in Hertfordshire. It must be recalled that in the 18C the Sacrament was taken relatively infrequently. The chancel was not the permanent honoured focus of a church as it was for the Victorians. It was a part of the building which had a specific but intermittent use. It was not adorned in the 19C manner with coloured tiles, mural painting, gleaming brass and so forth; but in many cases it did have a reredos (or a religious painting) to give due honour to the communion table, and in a surprising number of 18C churches there was stained glass in the E window.

From the churches' financial viewpoint, the 18C was a different world to subsequent times. Royal briefs could be sought to collect money throughout England for rebuilding or repairs. Church rates could be levied on a regular basis, as normally as the poor rate or the highway rate. Pew-rents were regularly collected. Finally, in the cases of rebuildings, Acts of Parliament were often obtained, and by their authority loans could be raised on the security of parochial income, such as that from burial dues. By 1900 all these sources of income were either unknown or were highly unusual. In the case of London in the 18C, there was an exceptional source of income for church building, and one which resulted in some exceptional churches. An Act passed in 1711, known as the 'Fifty Churches Act', provided Government money for the building in London of some very grand parish churches in districts which had little or no church provision. Barely a quarter of the intended fifty churches were built, but most of them were of the first significance: Nicholas Hawksmoor's St. George's, Bloomsbury, St. George's-in-the-East, St. Anne's, Limehouse, and Christ Church, Spitalfields; Thomas Archer's St. Paul's, Deptford and St. John's, Westminster; and James Gibbs's St. Mary-le-Strand. Hawksmoor, Wren's chief successor, was a master of Baroque, as was Archer; Gibbs was closer to Wren himself, especially in his steeples.

18C monuments could claim a book by themselves. They tend to be the tallest and grandest of all church monuments. In the Gothic 19C they were looked upon as 'pagan' for their Classical obelisks and urns, and for their trumpeting of their subjects' worth in the place of the medievalising piety which the Victorians favoured. Standing figures, which had appeared in the 17C, became frequent in the 18C, and sometimes there are two or three in aedicules. A full architectural surround, sometimes from floor to ceiling, was normal. Of the sculptors, the three who are notable in the early 18C were all foreign: L.F. Roubiliac, Peter Scheemakers and J.M. Rysbrack. The last two were Flemish, like their Elizabethan predecessors in the Southwark School. Of English sculptors, Thomas Green and Edward Stanton must be mentioned. Peter Scheemakers's son, Thomas, and his pupil, Joseph Nollekens, were prominent later in the 18C. The late 18C and the early decades of the 19C may be taken together. They formed the age of the two John Bacons, father and son, Sir Francis Chantrey, John Flaxman, and the three generations of Richard

Westmacotts. Their works appear frequently in these volumes. Smaller monuments of note—in the form of busts or profiles in medallions—were more numerous by this time than the huge works of the earlier 18C.

Non-Anglican Churches

By the beginning of the 19C non-Anglican churches were both numerous and significant. Their earliest examples in the 17C were almost all domestic in character: see the Friends' Meeting Houses at Brigflatts (Yorkshire, West Riding) and Thakeham (Sussex), and the Unitarian Chapel at Ipswich (Suffolk). Their use for worship is shown only in the arrangement of windows. During the 18C a more ecclesiastical character appeared. The typical form was that of the Classical oblong, with two tiers of arched windows along the sides, and a W or entrance front with a pediment and perhaps an ornamented doorway. What would be missing in Anglican terms would be a tower. The non-Anglican interior, however, would differ very little from a contemporary Anglican one. Catholic churches of the late 18C and early 19C used the same general designs as those of the Protestant Nonconformists.

Two particular strands of non-Anglican design in the 18C need to be mentioned. Thomas Ivory's Octagon Chapel of 1756 in Norwich set off a fashion, mainly among the Methodists, of octagonal buildings. The other strand concerns the churches of the Countess of Huntingdon's Connexion. Selina, Countess of Huntingdon (1707–91) set up chapels, with chaplains to serve them, which were nominally still Anglican (like Wesley's arrangements), but which in time formed a separate denomination (of Calvinistic Methodists—Calvinist in theology but Methodist by government). Her chapels were stately affairs, grander than most non-Anglican buildings and evangelical Anglican in character.

Classicism stayed in the non-Anglican denominations long after the Established Church had abandoned it. The Gothic Revival was only beginning to enter the picture in the 1840s, in a manner which Anglican churches had known in the 18C. For long after the 1840s, however, the Baptists in particular continued to use the grandest Classical manner. Most denominations did turn to Gothic in time, and by the end of the 19C many of their churches were indistinguishable externally from Anglican ones. Internally, however, they differed. Free Church E ends were dominated by a platform for the preacher, behind which a large organ would be placed. A plain communion table would stand in front of, and below, the platform. In a separate category were the Catholics, who, despite Pugin, never adopted Gothic exclusively; some late 19C Catholic churches—above all, the London Oratory Church at Brompton—were entirely Classical. In the Victorian period, the main non-Anglican development was perhaps less the triumph of Gothic than the immense size and grandeur which some non-Anglican buildings reached. Sir Titus Salt's Congregational (now United Reformed) Church at Saltaire (Yorkshire, West Riding), the Unitarian Church at Todmorden (ditto) and the great Free Church buildings of Birmingham reflected their patrons' wealth and influence, which would have been unimaginable to their fellow-religionists of the 17C and 18C. This was especially true in the industrial cities. Rochdale had 15 mayors who belonged to the United Methodist Free Churches, a denomination which was markedly strong in that town. The national position of the Free Churches was transformed by the end of the 19C. After the General Election of 1906, there were no fewer than 157 Free Church MPs; in the 18C none of them would have been eligible in the first place.

The 19C

When the 19C opened, the Industrial Revolution was beginning to increase the national population. The growth in population in the 19C was unprecedented in English history. The first national census of 1801 recorded nearly nine million in England and Wales; by 1901 the total was 32½ million. So it is not surprising that church building was often undertaken to increase accommodation for worshippers; to provide more 'sittings', as it was put. But it was not merely a matter of more seats in more churches for more people. The 19C was a rare period in which gifts for church building sharply increased. It is a fact that although donations for church purposes are common to all periods, they rise and fall without proven reasons. The 11C and 12C constituted a peak; and so too did the 19C. Initially, generosity was the Government's also. Parliamentary grants were made in 1818 and 1824. But these were not repeated. Royal briefs were abolished in 1828. Church rates ceased to be compulsory in 1868. The great engine of 19C church building was personal giving.

It is the scale of church building in the 19C that needs to be stressed. A large town which had two or three Anglican churches by 1800 would have 30 or 40 by 1900, not to speak of up to double or treble that figure in Free Church buildings and mission halls. The ancient parish of St. Mary, Newington, in S London, for example, had just one Anglican church in 1800. Two more were built in the 1820s. By 1892 there were 15. In Bournemouth, Alexander Morden Bennett built eight churches as well as the main church of St. Peter. Schemes of Victorian church building spoke regularly in tens or dozens. Bishop Thorold launched a Ten Churches Fund in S London in 1882, and Bishop Blomfield's Metropolis Churches Fund built or helped 78 churches.

Free Church congregations either grew up in newly-populated areas, or they were formed from disputes in existing congregations. In most cases such disputes concerned the choice of a new pastor. A preacher would be invited to supply the pulpit for a few weeks, after which half the congregation would want him as their permanent pastor and half would not. The dispute would be resolved by a division into two congregations; one would keep the existing church building and the other would build a completely new one. In 1818, a new pastor was needed for the Camden Chapel at Camberwell, S London. Two candidates appeared: Joseph Irons and Edward Andrews. In the event, neither of them was appointed, with the result that their supporters formed two new congregations and built *two* new churches—the Grove Chapel for Irons and the Beresford Chapel for Andrews. Camden Chapel itself later became Anglican.

Church Building in the 19C

The early 19C was a period in which the Classical and Gothic styles co-existed more or less equally. Classicism went through a Greek phase in the 15 years after Waterloo and produced such notable churches as New St. Pancras' in London. Gothic became much more widespread than it had been in the late 18C. The main Greek Revival architects of the day were just as ready to turn their hand to Gothic. The churches built by the Commissioners under the parliamentary grants of 1818 and 1824 often used a simple Perpendicular style, with tall, thin windows, equally thin pinnacles and the use of crocketed hoodmoulds over doorways and windows. A few contemporary churches, such as St. Luke's, Chelsea, London (by James Savage, 1820–24) were of much better quality; the money needed for them was usually raised locally and not given by the Commissioners. Outside London, there were similar churches in scholarly Gothic, such as Pensax, Worcestershire. After c 1840 this scholarly Gothic became widespread and normal. Overlapping with its onset, there was a brief neo-Norman phase. Neo-Norman may be found from the 18C into the 20C, but only c 1840 did it become a normal style for a few years.

The Victorian Gothic Revival differed from its 18C and early 19C antecedents in both style and conviction. Earlier Gothic churches almost all used Gothic forms in ways which were not medieval. They were built without a belief in Gothic as the *only* appropriate Christian style. A.W.N. Pugin (1812–52) was the great proponent from the 1830s of the view that Gothic was synonymous with Christian, and that there must not be a random use of Gothic elements but a scholarly copying of medieval precedents. The Cambridge Camden Society of 1839, which became the Ecclesiological Society in 1845, similarly argued for faithfulness to medieval Gothic and for its exclusive worth, such that we speak of churches designed in Gothic before the 1840s as 'pre-Ecclesiological'. At the same time the Oxford Movement, a movement of theology and Church order which began in 1833, taught its hearers to claim a Catholic inheritance for the Church of England as well as one derived from the Reformation. These various lines of argument came together from c 1840 to prompt, in due course, profound changes in the Victorian Church.

Obviously, widespread change was not immediate. Just as, in one direction, scholarly Gothic had been used in some places well before 1840, so in the other it must be stressed that the impact of the Oxford and Ecclesiological Movements on the Church of England was by no means as immediate and strong as past comment has alleged. The new movements eventually secured widespread acceptance and influence, but for long after 1840 the number of Anglican churches which were built or reordered in precise accordance with their teachings did not comprise a very large proportion of the whole. A church which followed high fashion in its architectural style could still have a plan and fittings which owed as much to old ideas as to new. For example, Sir Gilbert Scott's St. Giles's, Camberwell, in S London, was a Gothic work of the new scholarly type when it was built in 1842–44, but inside it was given galleries and an altarpiece which included the usual inscribed panels of 18C convention. Architectural change preceded liturgical change as a general rule.

The Victorian Church Interior

The Victorian Gothic Revival was not merely one of architecture. It revived a wide range of medieval fittings and practices. Open benches replaced box-pews. Tiles were laid down, most frequently in the chancel and less often throughout a church. Mural paintings were reintroduced. Memorials once again took the forms of recumbent effigies on tomb-chests, and of brasses. Sedilia were duly placed on the S side of a chancel, and occasionally an Easter sepulchre would appear on the N. Side chapels, with their own furnishings, reappeared. Fonts, pulpits and reredoses were made by the thousand in wood, marble and alabaster, featuring in their carvings the standard iconography of the High Middle Ages. Chancel screens were revived, either in wood or in brass; but the Roods to go above them were only beginning to appear at the end of the 19C, and they tend to be 20C additions. Choirstalls in the chancel are characteristically Victorian, for choirs were no longer placed in the W gallery. A large new organ would typically be placed at the E end, too, in a N or S chapel or special chamber. In a similar position there would often be a new vestry. Above all in a Victorian church, there would be new stained glass. The art of making stained glass had never completely disappeared after the Reformation, but the quantity and quality of its production after c 1840 overwhelmed that of the previous three centuries. A small number of firms supplied the greater part of the market. William Warrington, Thomas Willement, Clayton & Bell, Morris & Co., John Hardman & Co., William Wailes, Heaton, Butler & Bayne, the Gibbs family, Ward & Hughes, James Powell & Sons, the O'Connor family, Lavers, Barraud & Westlake, Burlison & Grylls, and C.E. Kempe were the principal designers. Many of them also undertook mural painting, and sometimes woodwork and brasswork too. Very few churches in England do not possess some of their work.

Victorian Restorations

The installation of all the above fittings almost always accompanied a restoration. 'Restoration' was no neutral term in Victorian usage, but implied the *improvement* of a church and a revival of its presumed appearance in the High Middle Ages; or, if it were a later and Classical building, changes to mitigate a style and plan which were considered disagreeable. Victorian restoration was no once-for-all effort; a church could undergo a number of intermittent changes. 'Restoration' should imply conservative repair, but in Victorian days it involved much radical replacement. Decorated window tracery would replace Perpendicular work; porches, arcades, aisles and entire chancels were rebuilt; roofs were totally replaced; walls were 'scraped' of their plaster; and serviceable fittings—even medieval screens—were swept away for new ones. Towards the end of the century a more conservative view began to emerge. See how St. John's, Leeds, a 17C church, was drastically altered in the 1860s but carefully reinstated from the 1880s onwards. William Morris's Society for the Protection of Ancient Buildings (1877) was founded specifically to stop radical restorations.

Victorian Church Architects

A.W.N. Pugin. Although Pugin was the major early theorist of the scholarly Gothic Revival, he was not the most significant designer of its churches. For one thing, he was a Catholic who was almost never employed by Anglican parishes. Unfortunately too, his fellow-religionists rarely had the money to build according to his ideals, and often they did not share his passion for Gothic at all. Only the 16th Earl of Shrewsbury was a rich and wholehearted Catholic patron of Pugin, and together they built St. Giles's at Cheadle, Staffordshire, which, after cleaning and restoration in recent years, is a splendid example of what Pugin advocated. The style is Decorated; the fittings are designed and placed as they would appear in a lavish 14C church; and every surface is painted. St. Giles's is a magnificent work, but it was unique in Pugin's career.

Sir Gilbert Scott and his Contemporaries. Sir Gilbert Scott (1811–78) was the most prolific of all Victorian architects. He was regarded as the Wren of his day, and was consulted on the restoration of innumerable cathedrals and major churches. Countless parish churches were designed in his office, but his personal contribution to many of them is difficult to judge. He regarded All Souls', Haley Hill, Halifax as his best parish church, and it is certainly among the most magnificent 19C churches, lavish in its architecture and in its fittings. Scott's hallmark was the use of the late 13C Geometrical style.

Scott's chief contemporaries among church architects were William Butterfield (1814–1900), J.L. Pearson (1817–97), G.E. Street (1824–81), William Burges (1827–81) and G.F. Bodley (1827–1907). These architects were, with Pugin and with Scott himself, the leading figures in Victorian church building. Their combined church output was immense, for the great wave of 19C church building allowed architects to design churches almost exclusively. Butterfield was noted for his 'structural polychromy'—the use of bands of coloured brick or stone. His masterpieces were All Saints', Margaret Street, London, and the chapel of Keble College, Oxford. J.L. Pearson's churches show the influence of 13C French Gothic; they generally have apsidal E ends and, unusually for the Victorians, they are vaulted. The best examples of his work are St. Michael's, Croydon (Surrey); St. Stephen's, Bournemouth; St. Agnes's, Sefton Park, Liverpool; St. Augustine's, Kilburn; St. Peter's, Vauxhall, in S London; and, last but not least, Truro Cathedral.

G.E. Street wrote important books on Continental Gothic after much travelling in the 1850s and 1860s. His early use of medieval English precedents thus gave way to French and Italian models. He tended to favour an earlier Gothic style than his contemporaries; not for him the complexities of 14C 'flowing' tracery. Many of Street's churches are rather small—such as those he designed for the Sykes family in the East Riding of Yorkshire; larger and more significant ones are St. James's, Pimlico, London; St. Peter's, Bournemouth; and the church of St. Philip and St. James, Oxford. William Burges shared with Pearson a love of 13C French Gothic, but he often showed an extravagance of material and detail which distinguishes his work from Pearson's. His churches at Studley Royal and Skelton-on-Ure in Yorkshire (West Riding) are his best parish churches. G.F. Bodley practised for more than 50 years as a Gothic architect. He had been Scott's pupil, but reacted against Scott's Geometrical style. He shared in the use of French and Italian models in the 1850s and

1860s, but then moved to an English 14C and 15C style, to which he kept for the rest of his career. His early, 'Continental' works include All Saints', Selsley (Gloucestershire), St. Martin's, Scarborough, and St. Michael's, Brighton. All Saints', Cambridge (1863–64) was his first 'English' work. The masterpieces of his mature style were Holy Angels, Hoar Cross (Staffordshire), St. Augustine's, Pendlebury, Manchester, and St. Mary's, Clumber (Nottinghamshire. The Gothic Revival never reached so attractive a phase as it did in Bodley's hands.

Further Victorian Architects

So huge was the field of Victorian church building that there are countless architects of lesser standing to add to the seven already mentioned. R.C. Carpenter was a designer of some attractive Decorated churches c 1850. William White, another of Scott's pupils and close to the Ecclesiologists, designed a few important churches in London and elsewhere. S.S. Teulon, for long labelled a 'rogue architect' for his independent Gothic style, designed innumerable churches, of which St. Stephen's, Hampstead, London ranks as the most important. James Brooks designed notable churches in London, chiefly in Haggerston. Butterfield's pupil, Henry Woodyer, was responsible for Holy Innocents, Highnam (Gloucestershire). S.W. Dawkes was a notable architect in the same county, who also built St. Andrew's, Wells Street, London, now removed to Kingsbury, Middlesex. J.D. Sedding produced the two very different London churches of Holy Redeemer, Clerkenwell and Holy Trinity, Sloane Street—the one Italianate and having an early baldacchino, and the other an Arts and Crafts ensemble. Among Victorian provincial architects, the works of W.H. Bidlake in Birmingham demand attention, and in Lancashire the firm of Paley & Austin designed numerous churches of considerable merit.

After c 1875 a number of architects moved away from the mainstream Gothic of the previous and their own generation. G.G. Scott, Jr (1839–97) produced in St. Agnes's, Kennington and All Hallows', Southwark, both in S London, two churches which were notable for their use of Perpendicular, a medieval style which the High Victorians had tended to regard as 'debased'. Norman Shaw, better known for his secular works, designed St. Michael's, Bedford Park in a style which borrowed from Classicism. J.F. Bentley turned to Byzantine models for his Westminster Cathedral. For the Methodist Central Hall in London in the early 20C, Lanchester & Rickards used a French Classical style. Mainstream Gothic continued in this period in the hands of Sir Arthur Blomfield, Temple Moore, Charles Hodgson Fowler, F.A. Walters (for Catholic churches), Ninian Comper, and the heirs of Sir Gilbert Scott (his son, J.O. Scott and his grandson, Sir Giles Gilbert Scott). Comper lived until 1960 and, although he turned increasingly to Classicism in the 20C, represented the Gothic tradition well into the days of the Modern Movement.

The 20C

In the 20C, the great cities have lost much population from their centres. It has been a familiar pattern in all denominations for churches to be closed in city centres and in the inner suburbs. It would not be hard to show that for every 'inner-city report' of recent years, half a dozen inner-city churches have been closed. The more historic churches in the ancient city centres and in country villages have almost all been retained and cherished, at ever-increasing costs of maintenance. The Free Churches have contracted most markedly, but all denominations have lost clergy in large numbers. Long gone are the days when an Anglican parish might have had an incumbent and up to six curates, and not be unusual. Such a parish, with a church built in 1863 in a teeming district, may well have been suppressed in 1963 and be absent today as if it had never existed.

From the First World War onwards, churches drew away from the Victorian mould. Interwar Gothic became more and more diluted—as in the work of Sir Edward Maufe—although traditional plans tended to remain. After 1945 all 19C and early 20C models were widely abandoned. It was claimed in so many cases that a totally new plan had been devised, or that a building was a product only of the 20C and borrowed nothing from past ages. In reality, no plan is ever new; there is always a precedent. The real mark of a mid-20C church was a complete absence of decorative detail. It was surely this fact, in churches no less than in secular buildings, that has brought so much popular hostility to 20C design.

It would be wrong to underestimate the extent of new church building in the 20C, especially for new suburbs and to replace buildings bombed in the Second World War, but most church work of the last half-century has been a matter of repair and reordering. 'Reordering' is to recent decades what 'restoration' was to the 19C, a compelling fashion which has removed much of value in fabric and in fittings from the past. The crucial element in many reorderings has been to introduce a 'central' altar—at the E end of the nave, or under the crossing, and certainly well away from the traditional E end. Such a position was not unknown in past ages, but it has become normal in the later 20C. The drawback in so many reorderings has not been the new plan but the aesthetic nullity of so many new fittings. Often they are discordant in their settings, and remarkable for their starkness. The Second Vatican Council (1962–65) prompted in the Catholic Church the same changes which the Liturgical Movement had brought to the Church of England. If only that Council had occurred in 1865, or 1905, rather than 1965, its artistic results would not have been so dismal.

Much has been said about the 20C retreat from 19C teachings. It must be remembered, nevertheless, that Gothic and Classical churches continued to be built by some architects. Mention has been made of Sir Ninian Comper's work. His great churches of St. Cyprian, Clarence Gate, London and St. Mary, Wellingborough (Northamptonshire) in the early 1900s were followed between the wars by the chapel at All Saints' Convent, London Colney (Hertfordshire) and St. Philip's, Cosham (Hampshire). The Anglican cathedral at Liverpool, begun under Sir Giles Gilbert Scott in Edwardian days, was completed only in 1980 in a full Gothic style. Perhaps the foremost mid-20C Gothic architect has been S.E. Dykes Bower, designer of the E parts of St. Edmundsbury Cathedral (Suffolk) and the postwar additions to Lancing College Chapel in Sussex. H.S. Goodhart-Rendel designed a few notable churches in a style which sometimes veered to the Romanesque and included enough detail to be attractive in traditional terms.

Conclusion

All churches might be called ripples of the Resurrection. The faith which they express is reflected in the styles and customs of every age since Christianity began. The many and diverse subjects which the history of the Christian Church in England encompasses are linked together over the centuries by the basic tenets of Christian belief, shared by innumerable individuals whose craftsmanship, memorials and local connections we may see and appreciate today. In St. Ethelburga's, Bishopsgate, in the City of London, we see inscribed in the pavement the words *'Bonus intra, melior exi'* (enter a good person, leave a better one); who could fail to be moved in that way by the message we see of countless ages of faith in our churches?

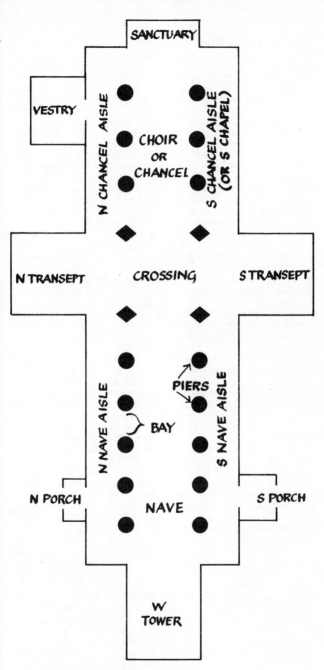

Standard ground plan of a church

GLOSSARY

ABACUS: The uppermost part of a column, above the capital: a thin, flat slab of various shapes and treatments.

ABBEY: A monastic house under an abbot, or a church which was once monastic but is now parochial (e.g. Tewkesbury Abbey) or a cathedral (e.g. St. Alban's Abbey) or a royal peculiar (e.g. Westminster Abbey). The name also applies to country houses in private ownership which occupy the sites of medieval monasteries (e.g. Woburn Abbey).

ACHIEVEMENT OF ARMS: A full work of heraldry, consisting of the shield or coat of arms, the supporters, crest and motto.

ADVOWSON: The right to nominate a priest for a benefice.

AGNUS DEI: Latin for the *Lamb of God*, a title which St. John the Baptist accords to Christ in the first chapter of St. John's Gospel. It is also used as the title of a prayer (based on St. John's Gospel) which is said (or sung) before the distribution of Holy Communion. In art, a lamb is often shown carrying a cross or a crossed flag.

AISLE: From the Latin *insula*, an island. A lateral and subsidiary part of a nave, a chancel or (more rarely) a transept, and running parallel to it. An arcade usually separates the two. The word is also used to mean a space between pews or benches, which is also called an *alley*.

ALTAR: A stone table, or a wooden one with a stone slab set into it, which is the focus of a Communion service. In the Middle Ages everywhere, and in the Catholic Church still, an altar will contain a relic of a saint. A 'high altar' is the main altar of a church.

AMBO: A reading-desk or pulpit.

AMBULATORY: A processional way round the E end of a larger church, comprising the choir or chancel aisles and the retrochoir E of the high altar.

ANGEL: From the Greek word for a messenger. An angel is an intermediary between God and Man. Medieval writers arranged them into nine orders, or three hierarchies of three choirs each: Seraphim, Cherubim and Thrones; Dominations, Virtues and Powers; and Principalities, Archangels and Angels. The Nine Orders of Angels sometimes form a subject in medieval Church art.

ANTECHAPEL: The W portion of a chapel, which is subsidiary to the rest and from which it may be divided by a screen (e.g. in King's College chapel, Cambridge) or by being the crossbar of a T-shaped building (e.g. in New College chapel, Oxford).

APSE: A rounded or polygonal termination to a church or chapel, most usually of the entire E end, less often of the transepts or subsidiary chapels. In early churches, apses were built at the W end too. The adjective is apsidal.

ARCADE: A line of arches. A *blind* arcade is fixed to a wall.

ASHLAR: Stone cut to squared shapes and smooth faces and laid in regular courses.

ASSUMPTION: The belief that the Virgin Mary was assumed into Heaven. The date of the feast is August 15th. In 1950 the belief was proclaimed to be a dogma of the Catholic Church, although it had been widespread since the early Middle Ages.

AUMBRY: A free-standing cupboard or a recess in a wall, used for storage, normally of sacred vessels or of books. Also known as an *armarium*.

BALDACCHINO: A canopy, usually supported on four or more pillars, which stands over an altar and occasionally over a font. In late 19C and 20C England, a number of architects favoured the baldacchino, above all Sir Ninian Comper. Also known as a *ciborium*.

BAPTISM: The initiatory Sacrament of the Christian Church. From the Greek word meaning a dipping. The form of baptism has varied in Christian history. It can be immersion (the submersion of the head), full submersion, affusion (a pouring) or aspersion (a sprinkling). A baptistery may be a detached building.

BARTIZAN: A projecting turret at the top of a tower.

BASILICA: A Roman public hall, aisled and with an E apse, which gave its name to churches which were built according to a similar plan. The word is loosely used for some early churches in England.

BATTLEMENT: A parapet which has a regular pattern of gaps between higher portions. The gaps are known as loops or crenellations, the flanking higher walls as merlons. Crenellated is a synonym for battlemented.

BAY: A division of an arcade, elevation or roof, which is marked out by piers, pilasters, buttresses, windows, ribs, etc.

BEAKHEAD: A moulding which resembles a succession of beaked heads.

BEDESMAN: One who prays for the soul of a deceased. The word is applied to small figures which may sometimes be found at the feet of recumbent effigies.

BELLCOTE: An open frame or turret, usually placed on the gable end of a church, to contain bells.

BILLET: A moulding consisting of short cylindrical or square blocks placed at intervals, sometimes in two parallel lines whereby the blocks of one line are positioned above the spaces of the other.

BOSS: A carved stone or piece of woodwork, placed at the junction of ribs in a vault or at the junction of members of an openwork wooden roof.

BOX-PEW: A bench in a church which is surrounded by high panelled sides and by a door; or a group of such benches.

BROACH SPIRE: An octagonal spire which sits on a tower without a parapet has angles which are covered by half-pyramids known as broaches. Broach spires generally date from the 13C and 14C.

BUTTRESS: An attachment to a wall which supports and strengthens it. A clerestory above an aisle roof sometimes needed a *flying buttress* to take the thrust of the upper wall over the aisle. Towers are more regularly buttressed. There are *angle buttresses*, in which the lines of the walls continue to create a 90° angle at each corner; *set-back buttresses*, also at 90° to each other, but placed away from the corner so that the angle of the buttressed fabric is visible; *clasping buttresses*, which encase the corners in a square of masonry; and *diagonal buttresses*, which extend from the corners at equal angles of 135° from each face.

CADAVER MONUMENT: A 15C practice, sometimes found at later dates too, to remind the living of the decay of the body and so to prompt them to seek salvation. Also known as a *memento mori*, a reminder of death.

CAPITAL: The upper part or capping of a column or pilaster, and usually its most decorative part.

CARTOUCHE: A mural monument with an elaborate curling frame.

CATHEDRA(L): A cathedral is a church in which is placed a bishop's chair or *cathedra*. A chair was the symbol of a teacher or philosopher in the

BROACH SPIRE · St MICHAEL AND
ALL ANGELS · HALLATON · Leics.

ancient world; a bishop has one
to symbolise his position as an
authoritative teacher of the
Christian Faith.

CATHOLIC: A Greek word
meaning 'universal'. Originally,
it implied orthodoxy or views
which were shared universally.
After the Reformation, it implied
traditional beliefs, which
Protestants questioned. It is used
as a title by those in communion
with Rome and also by members
of the Church of England and
the Eastern Orthodox Churches.

CHALICE: From the Latin *calix*, a
cup used for the Communion
wine. Usually made of precious
metal.

CHAMFER: An edge is
chamfered when the square
angle between two surfaces is
cut, usually at half a right angle
to each.

CHANCEL: The E part of a
church, often thought of as
being beyond the screen or
cancella.

CHANTRY: An endowment for
the saying or chanting of Masses

for the soul of a deceased. A chantry chapel, usually a small, enclosed chapel within a church, was sometimes specially built, and staffed by one or more chantry priests. All chantries were dissolved under King Edward VI, but many chantry chapels survive, for example the magnificent group in Winchester Cathedral.

CHAPEL: A small detached place of worship, especially one which is private rather than parochial or public, or a subsidiary part of a church. The word derives from the diminutive of the Latin word for a cloak: it was first used for the place where St. Martin's cloak was kept by *capellani* or cloak-keepers. In recent centuries in England, the word has been applied to buildings of the Free Churches in contrast to Anglican churches. 'Chapel' is sometimes used as a synonym for Nonconformity. A chapel of ease is a building which is dependent on a parish church.

CHAPTER (HOUSE): The governing body of a larger church, or a meeting of such a body. Originally, a chapter of the Rule (or statutes) would be read aloud at each meeting. A monastic chapter house will almost always be found to the S of the S transept.

CHEVRON: A zigzag decoration, especially in Norman architecture, or a V-shaped design in heraldry.

CHOIR: The body of singers in a church, or the part of the church in which they sing, usually towards the E end between the nave and the sanctuary.

CIBORIUM: Another word for a baldacchino, q.v.

CLERESTORY: An upper or 'clear' storey, designed to provide natural light in a church, most usually in the nave, but sometimes in the chancel as well. More often than not a clerestory will be a 15C addition to the fabric.

CLOISTERS: A covered walk around three or four sides of a quadrangle, with windowless outer walls and pierced (but often unglazed) inner walls, usually but not exclusively associated with cathedral and monastery churches. Each arm of the walk is known as an alley. The enclosed space within the quadrangle is the cloister garth and is sometimes known as a paradise.

COLLEGE: In its ecclesiastical sense, the word refers to a body of clergy living in an endowed community, but whose members are not monks or friars. Very often such a community was one of chantry priests. A collegiate church, however, is usually grander than this implies, being a larger church served by a body of canons or prebendaries.

COMMUNION TABLE: A wooden table for the celebration of the Eucharist or Holy Communion, which was originally distinguished from a stone altar. The terms are often used loosely today as if they were synonyms. A wooden table can have an inserted stone slab.

CONSECRATION: The word is used in speaking of the solemn hallowing or dedicating of a church. In the Church of England, this is usually the date of opening. In Catholic churches, it follows long after, sometimes a century or more later. The word is also used in the consecration of the water and wine in Holy Communion. Finally, it can refer to the consecration of a new bishop. In all these cases, the word means 'to make sacred or holy'.

CONVENT(UAL): Any monastic house, not merely of nuns, is a convent. Thus, it is proper to speak of the 'Prior and Convent of Christ Church, Canterbury' in the Middle Ages for the predecessors of the present Dean and Chapter. Conventual is an adjective which refers to a monastic house, particularly to its domestic buildings.

CORPORAL WORKS OF MERCY: In chapter 25 of St. Matthew's Gospel, these are given as feeding the hungry, giving drink to the thirsty, sheltering the homeless, visiting the sick, visiting prisoners and clothing the naked. The Church added a seventh, the burial of the dead.

CREDENCE: A small table or shelf near an altar, on which the bread and wine are placed before consecration.

CRENELLATED: *See* Battlement.

CROCKET: An embellishment in Gothic design which is applied to spires, gables and pinnacles. The shape is usually of a stylised leaf or a knob.

CROSSING: The junction between the E–W axis of a nave and chancel, and the N–S axis of N and S transepts. Often there is a crossing tower, which creates a quite distinct space beneath it.

CRYPT: A vaulted underground room in a church (or in a secular building), which usually underlies only a part of the superstructure. Crypts in early English churches were often used as shrines for relics. Later, they came to be used for burial, especially in the 17C, 18C and early 19C. Also called an undercroft.

CUPOLA: A small domed lantern, sometimes placed on a church tower in the absence of a steeple, and occasionally placed on the roof of the body of a church or chapel in the absence of a tower, e.g. over an almshouse chapel.

CUSP: The point formed where two foils meet in Gothic tracery.

DECALOGUE: The Ten Commandments. From the 17C to the 19C it was normal for an Anglican church to have the Commandments inscribed on a board at the E end, usually as part of the altarpiece.

DOOM PAINTING: *See* Last Judgement.

DOSSAL: A backcloth, normally behind an altar or on the N and S walls of a chancel.

EASTER SEPULCHRE: A specially-built recess, or a tomb used or adapted for the purpose, almost always on the N side of the chancel, which served to represent Christ's tomb during the celebration of Easter. Special recesses were most often built in the 14C. Today an altar of repose for the Reserved Sacrament fulfils the same function at Easter.

EMANCIPATION: The removal of restrictions on Catholics in 1829, but also used loosely of Catholic Relief Acts in the late 18C.

ENTABLATURE: The horizontal superstructure of a Classical design.

EUCHARIST: The Sacrament of the Lord's Supper or Holy Communion. From a Greek word which means 'to give thanks'.

FALDSTOOL: A small prayer desk, folding and portable.

FILLET: A raised band. The term is usually applied to those found on columns in a church.

FLEURON: A stylised flower carved in stone as an enrichment.

FLOWING TRACERY: 14C Decorated tracery, in which the ogee or curving element is dominant. Also called Curvilinear.

FLUSHWORK: A decorative chequerwork of black and white pebbles, often seen in East Anglian churches.

FOIL: A leaf, referring to the leaf-like shapes between the cusps of a Gothic window. Trefoil means with three foils, quatrefoil with four, cinquefoil with five, and sexfoil with six.

FRIARS: From the Latin *fratri*, meaning 'brothers'. The word was used from the 13C to distinguish groups of religious who worked amongst layfolk and without endowments from monks who lived in endowed

**14ᵀᴴ CENTURY EASTER SEPULCHRE
ALL SAINTS' ❖ HAWTON ❖ Notts ❖**

institutions quite detached from lay life. The principal Orders of friars were Franciscans (Greyfriars), Carmelites (Whitefriars), Dominicans (Blackfriars) and Augustinian or Austin Friars.

FRIEZE: A horizontal band of decorative carving.

GALILEE: A W porch or chapel. Famous examples exist at Durham and Ely Cathedrals.

GALLERY: The term refers either to a wooden gallery which is separate from the structure of a church (and whose purpose is to provide additional seating) or a stone gallery which is part of the structure. The latter type will rise above the aisles but be below the clerestory and will be open to the nave or chancel; it is also called a *triforium*. Wooden galleries are ubiquitous, especially in churches from the 17C to the early 19C, but a triforium will usually be found only in cathedrals and monastic churches, or in exceptionally substantial parish churches.

GARGOYLE: A grotesque waterspout, intended to throw water off a wall.

GEOMETRICAL TRACERY: Tracery of the late 13C which consists of circles and foils.

GREEK CROSS: A cross with arms of equal length.

GREEN MAN: *See* Wodewose.

GREYFRIARS: A name for the Franciscans, whose habit was grey (but is now usually brown).

GRISAILLE: Clear glass which is painted in geometric patterns and with leaf decoration within those patterns. It cuts out glare but admits more light than stained glass.

HALL CHURCH: A church in which the nave and aisles are of equal height.

HAMMERBEAM: A type of roof in which beams project from the side walls but do not cross the roof-space as tiebeams do. Instead, they carry posts or struts which support the rafters. There may be one or two tiers of hammerbeams.

HATCHMENT: A diamond-shaped board bearing a shield of arms, placed in a church after a funeral.

HIERATIC: Priestly.

ICONOSTASIS: An icon or image screen, normal in Eastern Orthodox churches.

INTERSECTING TRACERY: A form of tracery common in c 1300, in which mullions intersect as they curve in the window head.

JAMB: The side of a doorway, an archway or a window.

JESSE TREE: A genealogical tree of Christ's descent from Jesse via St. Joseph, often depicted in a Jesse window.

LADY CHAPEL: A chapel named in honour of the Blessed Virgin Mary, which was commonly added to medieval churches but which is not found in very early churches. In larger churches, a Lady chapel will often be found E of the high altar.

LANCET: A relatively thin, single-light window, characteristic of the Early English style.

LAST JUDGEMENT: The judgement of each individual at the end of time (at the Last Trump), as described in chapter 25 of St. Matthew's Gospel. Christ will divide the sheep from the goats, that is the righteous from the unrighteous, the former on his right, the latter on his left. A depiction, also known as a Doom Painting, was often placed above the chancel arch of a medieval church.

LATIN DOCTORS: St. Augustine of Hippo, Bishop of Hippo in N Africa, a foremost theologian of the early Church; St. Jerome, the translator of the Latin Vulgate, a standard 4C Latin text of the Bible; St. Gregory the Great, Pope from 590 to 604 and Apostle of England; and St. Ambrose, Bishop of Milan. A frequent group in medieval and Gothic Revival art, especially on chancel screens and pulpits. St. Jerome is always depicted as a cardinal and St. Gregory is shown wearing a triple tiara (both anachronistically).

LESENE: A pilaster strip (q.v.).

LIGHT: A vertical division of a window, divided from its neighbour by a mullion.

LINENFOLD: A wavy pattern, usually found in 16C and 17C woodwork, which resembles in a stylised way the folds in linen.

LONG-AND-SHORT-WORK: A feature of pre-Conquest churches in which quoins are alternately small and large, that is, laid horizontally and vertically.

LOUVRE: An arrangement of small horizontal boards which are placed in a sloping position one above the other. They take the place of glass in belfry windows to allow the sound of the bells to carry but to exclude rain.

LOW-SIDE WINDOW: A window found in chancels, usually on the S side at the W end, but sometimes on the N side. Its sill will be markedly low and its lower part will often be shuttered rather than glazed. No undisputed explanation has ever been given for this feature. Also called a lychnoscope.

LUCARNE: An opening in a spire.

LYCHGATE: A gate to a burial ground. From the Old English word *lych*, meaning a corpse or a dead body.

MARTYR: The Greek word for a witness; a person who had witnessed to the Christian Faith by suffering death in its name.

MEMENTO MORI: *See* Cadaver Monument.

MINSTER: A large church, originally one which had more than just a local or parochial responsibility. Minsters were normal from the 7C until the 11C and then ceased to have a formal status as the parochial system was completed. The word remains in use for certain large churches, such as the cathedrals at York, Lincoln and Ely, and collegiate churches such as Beverley and Southwell. Although minster derives from *monasterium*, a minster was not necessarily a monastery.

MISERICORD: The Latin word for mercy, which is applied to tip-up seats found in the choirs or chancels of churches. These seats were designed to provide relief during the long hours of standing during the daily offices of the medieval Church. They attract attention for their carvings, which usually reflect a mixture of piety and humour. Also known as a miserere.

MULLION: A vertical division of a window.

NAILHEAD: A moulding in which low miniature pyramids are repeated in a line, for example above an arch.

NARTHEX: A vestibule at the W end of a church.

NAVE: The main body of a church, which takes its name from the Latin *navis*, a ship, on account of a rectangular building with a pitched roof seeming like an upturned ship.

NICHE: An alcove or recess, usually intended for a statue.

OGEE: A double curve, one convex and the other concave, which was introduced in the early 14C as a characteristic part of Decorated design.

ORIENTATION: The siting of a church so that its altar is at the E end, facing the Orient.

PARCLOSE: A screen which separates the main part of a church from a subsidiary part, e.g. a chancel from its aisle.

PARISH: A defined district whose cure of souls is assigned to a particular priest.

PEDIMENT: A triangular or segmental gable over a portico, window, E end, W end, etc., of a Classical building. An open pediment is one in which the sloping sides do not meet at the apex. A broken pediment has the horizontal member interrupted in the centre.

PELICAN IN HER PIETY: A depiction of a pelican biting her breast, symbolic of self-sacrifice and thus of the Eucharist.

PERPENDICULAR TRACERY: Tracery from the later 14C onwards, in which upright panels are the main element. Also called Rectilinear.

PIER: A solid upright, often used loosely as a synonym for column.

PILASTER: A flat pillar placed against a wall, with a base and capital of a Classical order. A pilaster strip, found on the exteriors of pre-Conquest churches, has no base or capital.

PINNACLE: A decorative upright above a parapet, most usually on a tower but often on a nave or a chancel or their aisles. A pinnacle will frequently rise out of a buttress. It may itself be decorated with crockets.

PISCINA: A stoup with a drain, usually on the S side of a chancel, used for the ritual washing of chalices.

PLATE TRACERY: Tracery in the 13C which is pierced through the wall rather than forming parts of a continuous window.

POPPYHEAD: An ornamental finial on a bench-end.

PORCH: A roofed space immediately outside an exterior

PERPENDICULAR WINDOW · S. TRANSEPT
S.ᵗ PETER & S.ᵗ PAUL · LANGHAM · Leics.

doorway, usually single-storey but sometimes higher. The word is also used to translate *porticus*, which applies to chapels or chambers in pre-Conquest churches. Such *porticus* do not normally have exterior doorways.

PREDELLA: The term usually refers to a shelf at the base of an altarpiece.

PRESBYTERY: The word has three uses. Firstly, it refers to the entire E end of a church, more usually to a cathedral or monastery church. Secondly, it is used of a priest's house in the Catholic Church. Thirdly, it describes an essential part of the government of a Presbyterian Church, especially in Scotland.

PRIORY: A priory is a monastic house which is dependent on an abbey, either because it is a daughter-house of the abbey in question or because it is part of an order in which member houses are subordinate to the central one.

PULPITUM: A screen placed between a nave and a choir, with an opening in the centre, and usually with an organ in the gallery above. A feature of cathedrals and larger churches.

PYX: A receptacle for the Reserved Sacrament, especially when it is suspended over an altar.

QUOIN: A dressed stone at the exterior angle of a church.

RECTOR: The clergyman who had the right to receive the full endowments of a benefice. The title in use today no longer has implications of income. *See also* Vicar.

RELIQUARY: A container for relics, very often an oblong and gable-topped box, elaborately embellished.

REREDOS: A stone or wooden screen behind an altar, often arranged in arches or panels and adorned with painting or sculpture.

RETICULATED: Meaning 'net-like', this word refers to tracery of the early 14C in which circles are pulled at the ends into ogee shapes to create the appearance of a net.

RETROCHOIR: 'At the back of the choir', referring to the space at the E end of larger churches, behind the high altar. Such a place is usually reached by the choir aisles, which, together with the retrochoir, form an ambulatory (q.v.).

RIDDEL (POSTS): A riddel is a curtain at the sides or back of an altar. Up to four riddel posts are used as supports. An altar thus curtained is known as an English altar, for it was normal in late medieval England. In the late 19C and early 20C the arrangement was revived under the influence of Percy Dearmer and Sir Ninian Comper.

ROOD: A Crucifix. The Rood group, comprising the Crucified Saviour flanked by the Virgin Mary and St. John the Evangelist and sometimes by further figures, was placed above the Rood screen of a medieval church. A Rood loft was a small gallery above the screen. Revived in the 19C and 20C.

SACRAMENT: A rite in which God's grace is active. St. Augustine of Hippo wrote of a 'visible sign of an invisible reality'. The word is often used to refer solely to the Eucharist or Holy Communion. All Christians recognise the Eucharist and Baptism as Sacraments. Catholics and the Eastern Orthodox add another five: Holy Orders, Matrimony, Penance, Confirmation and Extreme Unction.

SACRING BELL: A bell rung at the consecration of the water and wine in Holy Communion. Also known as a saunce or a sanctus bell.

SALTIRE CROSS: A cross with diagonal arms, almost always used as a symbol of St. Andrew, who suffered crucifixion on such a cross.

SANCTUARY: The part of a church, usually its easternmost part, enclosed by the communion rails. In most churches it will be the E part of the chancel. The word also refers to the place of (temporary) refuge for criminals, which was recognised to exist in churches in the Middle Ages.

SEDILIA: Three seats (occasionally more) on the S side of the sanctuary, usually a prominent architectural feature of the S wall but sometimes a wooden structure placed against or near the S wall. The sedilia were intended for the use of the priest, deacon and sub-deacon during parts of the medieval Mass. Stepped sedilia are on different levels or steps. In some cases the sedilia are formed from the sill of a chancel S window.

SEE: A bishopric or diocese. From the Latin *sedes*, a seat or bishop's throne, which is a symbol of his right and duty to preach the Christian Faith authoritatively.

SEVEN DEADLY SINS: Pride, covetousness, lust, envy, gluttony, anger and sloth.

SHAFT: A small circular upright which is a subsidiary part of a larger feature such as a pier or a window. It can also refer to the upright portion of a standing cross (a cross-shaft). A shaft-ring is a decorative band which encircles a shaft.

SHRINE: A receptacle for sacred relics, normally a highly enriched tomb of a saint.

SPANDRELS: The wall space between two arches or between a single arch and a square-cut frame above it. The word usually applies in churches to the nave arcades.

SPLAY: A slanted side, especially to a window. Very early churches often had markedly narrow windows, which would light their interiors better by being splayed. Double-splayed means splayed inside and out.

SQUINCH: A supporting arch in an angle.

SQUINT: An opening in a wall, often at an oblique angle, which enabled a person to see the high altar from an aisle or from a room next to the church proper. Also known as a hagioscope.

STALL: A seat, especially in the choir or chancel of a church, usually with arms and often with misericords (q.v.).

STEEPLE: The word is normally used to refer to a Classical tower and its superstructure, or to the superstructure alone.

STIFF-LEAF: A term applied to carved decoration of capitals, which is particularly characteristic of the Early English period.

STOUP: A receptacle for holy water, usually near a door.

STRAPWORK: Characteristic 16C and 17C decoration which consists of curving and interlaced bands like straps.

STRINGCOURSE: A horizontal moulded course of stonework which is often to be seen on exterior walls and particularly on towers. Sometimes a stringcourse which was originally external will now be found within a church as a result of expansion.

TABERNACLE: The word has four uses. Firstly, it refers to a Sacrament house or receptacle for the Reserved Sacrament (especially in Catholic churches). Secondly, it was used in the 17C and 18C to mean a temporary church. Thirdly, it is used by Baptists as a title for some of their churches. Finally, it can mean any niche or canopied recess.

TERM: A support for a bust or similar carving, which tapers towards the base.

TESTER: A canopy over a pulpit, which is also called a Sounding Board.

TETRAGRAMMATON: Greek for 'four letters', applied to the Holy Name, especially as written in Hebrew as the central feature of a painting in a church.

THREE-DECKER PULPIT: A term used for a type of pulpit found in churches from the 17C to the 19C, which comprised three parts at different levels. The highest was the pulpit proper; below it was a reading-desk; and at the bottom came the clerk's pew.

TRANSENNA: A screen of lattice work.

TRANSEPT: If a church is built in the shape of a cross, its N and S arms are known as transepts. Sometimes only a N or only a S transept exists.

TRANSITIONAL: A halfway stage between one style and another, used most frequently to refer to the change between the Norman and Early English styles in the later 12C.

TRANSOM: A horizontal division of a window, found in late

Y-TRACERY – NOSELEY *[eic's.]*
EXTERIOR

Gothic designs. Transoms are sometimes embattled.

TRIFORIUM: *See* Gallery.

TYMPANUM: The space between the horizontal lower edge of a pediment and its sloping sides, or between the lintel of a door and an arch above it. A Norman doorway often has carving in its tympanum and this is perhaps the most frequent use of the word concerning churches.

UNDERCROFT: *See* Crypt.

VENETIAN WINDOW: A motif in Classical design by which an arched and taller middle light is flanked by two lower square-headed lights.

VESICA: The shape of an oval with pointed ends, which was occasionally used as a feature in wall paintings (to surround a figure of Christ or of the Virgin Mary) and more rarely for windows.

VICAR: From the Latin *vicarius*, a

deputy. A vicar was a deputy or substitute for a rector.

WEEPERS: Small figures in mourning on the sides of a tomb-chest.

WODEWOSE (or Woodwose or Woodhouse): A wild, hairy man, often carrying a club, who was the subject of many medieval carvings. He is very similar to the Green Man.

Y-TRACERY: Characteristic of 13C windows, in which a mullion divides into two in the window head.

CHESHIRE

Apart from the large urban areas around Birkenhead and Stockport, the county is characterised by the richly pastoral country of the Cheshire Plain, with its widely scattered villages and the picturesque cathedral city of Chester. Most churches (including those of the 19C) are built of red sandstone, which generally weathers badly, but some 17C and 18C buildings are of brick, and the timber-framed churches of Cheshire are the earliest of their kind in Europe. The county possesses one major Norman church, an excellent example of the Decorated style, a number of very fine Perpendicular churches, some splendid 17C monuments and woodwork, and four superb Victorian edifices.

The finest surviving pre-Conquest work is the pair of cross-shafts at Sandbach (probably early to mid-9C); they are decorated with carved figures, animals, heads, vine scrolls and interlace, and one has panels of biblical scenes. The only major Norman church is St. John's, Chester, where the early 12C crossing and parts of the nave and chancel survive; the arcades are Norman, whilst the triforium is Transitional and the clerestory (and the N porch) are Early English. The most important Decorated church is Nantwich. The tower and S porch at Astbury, the S porch and part of the tower at Bunbury, and the N transept at Great Budworth are also Decorated. Amongst the finest Perpendicular churches are Astbury, Bunbury, Great Budworth and Malpas. The earliest surviving longitudinal timber-framed churches in Europe are at Lower Peover and Marton, which may well be 13C and are certainly 14C at the latest. The W towers at Great Budworth, Lower Peover and Malpas have tall arches opening into the nave, whilst the W tower at Bunbury is embraced by the aisles; the tower at Astbury carries a spire (rare in this county), and Nantwich has an octagonal crossing tower. St. John's at Chester, Great Budworth and Nantwich have transepts; Astbury, Malpas and Nantwich have two-storey porches; and there are Perpendicular clerestories at Astbury (with particularly large windows), Great Budworth, Malpas and Nantwich (with two windows per bay). Chester Castle chapel has a late 12C or early 13C quadripartite vault, the chancel at Nantwich has an extremely rich Decorated lierne-vault, and there is a Perpendicular rib-vault in the tower at Malpas; also Perpendicular are the magnificent low-pitched camber-beam roofs at Astbury, Great Budworth and Malpas, whilst the late 15C chancel roof of Cholmondeley Castle chapel has arch-braces and hammerbeams.

The earliest example of pure Classical architecture is the N chapel at Over Peover (c 1648–50); it is of ashlar, one bay wide and three bays long, and the arcade to the nave has semicircular arches on piers, whilst the external walls have lunette windows between pilasters. Other 17C and 18C buildings are of red brick with stone dressings, such as the Unitarian Chapel at Wilmslow (1694), Cholmondeley Castle chapel (1717–18, probably by William Smith of Warwick), and Congleton (1740–42, by William Baker). One of the finest neo-Classical churches is St. Thomas's, Stockport (1822–25, by George Basevi), ashlar, with a grand Ionic portico. An early example of the Gothic Revival is the tower at Congleton (1760–86). St. Alban's, Macclesfield (1838–41, by A.W.N. Pugin) in the Perpendicular style introduces the more 'correct' Gothic of the Victorian period. High Victorian vigour is brilliantly exemplified by Hooton

(1858–62), by J.K. Colling, largely Italian Romanesque but with French Gothic and Byzantine elements, and by Eaton Hall chapel (1873–84, by Alfred Waterhouse), inspired by 12C and 13C France. Late Victorian refinement is magnificently represented by St. George's, Stockport (1893–97, by H.J. Austin), Perpendicular with traces of Art Nouveau, and the sublime Decorated Eccleston (1899, by G.F. Bodley). The swan-song of the Gothic Revival is the Lady Lever Memorial at Port Sunlight (1914, by W. & S. Owen).

The earliest church furnishing is the font at Chester Cathedral (possibly Venetian Early Christian, given in 1885); it is rectangular, the sides carved with the chi-rho and the alpha and omega between peacocks, winged lions, eagles, and interlace. From the 13C come a knight's effigy at St. John's, Chester, stalls at Great Budworth, and chests at Lower Peover and Malpas. Dating from the 14C are tomb effigies at Astbury, St. John's at Chester, Nantwich and Bunbury (with some original colour and its iron grille); stone piscinas and sedilia at Bunbury (also the remains of a stone reredos), Malpas and Nantwich (plus an aumbry); a wall painting at St. John's, Chester; and the magnificent oak choirstalls with misericords and canopies at Nantwich. The two finest screens (both c 1500) are at Astbury and Mobberley—the latter has eight bays with a richly traceried dado, elaborately ribbed coving on both sides, and corbels for the former loft parapet. Other Perpendicular woodwork includes the screen dado at Daresbury (with square panels of very flamboyant tracery), parclose screens and choirstalls at Astbury and Malpas, and bench-ends at Great Budworth. The most interesting brass is Roger Legh's (1506) at St. Michael's, Macclesfield, according to which the pardon for five Paternosters, five Aves and one Credo is 26,000 years and 26 days. There is a wall painting of c 1500 at Astbury, and Perpendicular stonework includes fonts at Great Budworth and Malpas, the screen and pulpit at Nantwich, and an incised tomb-slab and a superb monument with many figures at Malpas. The Perpendicular stone screen at Bunbury (1527) is painted with the earliest Renaissance motifs in Cheshire.

The only notable later 16C work is a damaged tomb effigy (1575) at Great Budworth. The most impressive Jacobean monument is Francis Fitton's (1608) at Gawsworth: a table-tomb on six Composite columns, the spandrels decorated with branches and shields in strapwork cartouches, the painted effigy in armour and his skeleton in a shroud beneath. Also particularly fine is the white, grey and black marble tomb (possibly by Edward Marshall) of Sir Richard Wilbraham (1643) and his wife at Acton; the vigorously modelled effigies rest on a boldly shaped sarcophagus, with rectangular panels on the sides and rich armorials against thick volutes at the ends. Other notable 17C monuments include those at Bunbury (1601), Malpas (1605), Astbury (1609), Nantwich (1614) and Chester (St. John's; 1693, by Edward Pearce). There is much splendid 17C woodwork; the rich 1650s fittings of Cholmondeley Castle chapel are the most complete. There is also particularly good work at Astbury (including a splendid font cover), Chester (St. John's) and Lower Peover. A rare survival is the painted plaster tympanum (1663) at Baddiley, which has the Lord's Prayer, Commandments, Creed and royal arms in panels beneath arches borne on columns.

Among 18C fittings, Congleton preserves its 1740s interior, with mural paintings by E. Penny, and there is a painting by Francis Hayman at Malpas. There are 18C altar rails at Bunbury and Great Budworth (with a contemporary altar), and a font at Cholmondeley

Castle chapel. There are handsome Georgian monuments at Malpas (one of 1815 by Sir Richard Westmacott), Lower Peover (1725), Chester (St. John's; 1729), and Astbury (1796, by Thomas King of Bath). Rich 19C ensembles are provided by the fittings of Eaton Hall chapel (by Waterhouse, with F.J. Shields's mosaics, a Century Guild crucifix and a tomb by Sir J.E. Boehm); St. George's, Stockport (by H.J. Austin); and Eccleston (by Bodley, with Farmer & Brindley's reredoses and a tomb). St. Alban's, Macclesfield has furnishings by A.W.N. Pugin, and Marple contains superb Arts and Crafts/Art Nouveau work by Henry Wilson (1895–1924). An outstanding example of High Victorian Gothic is the gilded metal hanging cross (c 1876) at Dunham-on-the-Hill (from Chester Cathedral), designed by Sir Gilbert Scott and made by Francis Skidmore of Coventry. Good 20C work includes the oak lectern by Bridgman's of Lichfield at Congleton, the wrought-iron gates and pulpit (1920) at Stockport (St. Thomas's), and the superb oak chancel screen by F.H. Crossley (1921) and the painted triptych by D. Brown (1967) at Bunbury. Amongst the notable monuments are those at Malpas (1904, by E. Hilton), Eccleston (1909), by Detmar Blow & F. Billerey; and 1953, by G. Ledward), Port Sunlight (1914, by Sir William Goscombe John), and Great Budworth (1925). A Modern work is the aluminium figure by M. Murray (1969) at St. John's, Chester.

There are fragments of early 14C stained glass at Nantwich, fragments of c 1500 at Astbury, 16C roundels at Bunbury, and Flemish glass at Cholmondeley Castle chapel and Malpas. The prettiest 17C glass (showing Dutch influence) is the small window at Farndon, depicting Royalist Cheshire gentry of the Civil War, with pikemen and musketeers, weapons and trophies. Congleton has one 18C window. St. Paul's, Boughton, Chester contains glass by Morris & Co.—the E window (1881) was designed by Sir Edward Burne-Jones, and the SE window (1887, depicting angels playing musical instruments) is probably by William Morris. There is also Morris glass at Low Marple. Eaton Hall chapel has a complete set of remarkable windows by F.J. Shields, and Eccleston was completely glazed by Burlison & Grylls. There is 19C glass by William Warrington at Malpas and Astbury; by William Wailes and John Hardman & Co. at Nantwich; by Clayton & Bell at St. John's, Chester and Nantwich; by the firm of O'Connor and Ward & Hughes at Astbury; C.E. Kempe at Nantwich, Great Budworth, Malpas and Bunbury; Edward Frampton at St. John's, Chester; and Christopher Whall at Marple. There are outstanding 20C windows by Shrigley & Hunt at St. John's, Chester, Irene Dunlop at Astbury, H. Clarke at Nantwich, and Christopher Webb at Bunbury. There is postwar glass by L.C. Evetts at Bunbury and by Pierre Fourmaintreaux at Great Budworth.

Barthomley has the only church in England dedicated to St. Bertoline, an 8C prince who became a hermit after the loss of his young and beautiful wife, and who lived a life of great piety on a small island on the river Sow in Staffordshire. In the 5C St. Patrick sailed up the Mersey and landed at Bromborough, baptising at the well which retains his name. Chadkirk Chapel near Romiley takes its name from St. Chad, who visited this district on a mission in the 7C. The 10C St. Plegmund gave his name to Plemstall (or Plemondstall), where he lived as a hermit before he became Archbishop of Canterbury. The relics of the Mercian princess St. Werburgh were brought to Chester soon after 907 and her shrine, in what is now the cathedral, dates from c 1310.

The writers of Cheshire include the 14C chronicler Ranulph

Higden, a monk of St. Werburgh's Abbey at Chester; the 16C historian and cartographer John Speed, born at Farndon; the hymn-writer Bishop Heber, baptised at Malpas in 1775; Lewis Carroll, baptised at Daresbury in 1832; Elizabeth Gaskell, buried at Knutsford Unitarian Chapel in 1865; and Charles Kingsley, who was a Canon of Chester Cathedral, 1870–73.

Astbury, *St. Mary.* One of the principal Perpendicular churches of Cheshire, with magnificent woodwork, St. Mary's is approached up the sloping village green and through an arched gateway of the 15C or 17C. The present church is largely a Perpendicular rebuilding of a 14C church of the same size, and was lightly restored by Sir Gilbert Scott in 1862.

The church is built of millstone grit. The Decorated tower, referred to in a will of 1366, stands N of the N aisle. It has a recessed spire, a rare motif in Cheshire, rebuilt in 1838. The W window of the N aisle has flowing tracery, but the N windows of the aisle are earlier 14C with Y-tracery and cusped lights, and those of the N chapel have plain Y-tracery of the late 13C. The S aisle windows match those of the N, and the two-storeyed S porch with its priest's room is also Decorated. The Perpendicular W end has a thin three-storeyed porch, with a worn statue of the Virgin and Child in a canopied niche, and is flanked by extremely tall two-transomed windows.

The nave and chancel are structurally one. The nave bays have a grid of mouldings, running vertically up the piers to the roof, and in two horizontal bands, one above the arches and the other below the clerestory. The large four-light Perpendicular clerestory windows, together with those at the W end, fill the interior with light. There is a narrow W gallery on four stone shafts. The nave and both aisles have magnificent low-pitched roofs with camber-beams and many bosses. The nave roof, completed in 1493, has very elaborate wall plates and two carved pendants, one over the chancel screen for the suspension of the Rood, and the other (carved with the five wounds of Christ) over the high altar for the suspension of a pyx. The S aisle roof is even more elaborate, having angels bearing shields with the Instruments of the Passion, and another pendant over the S chapel screen.

The church has 17C box-pews with strapwork panels. The W gallery has a pierced wooden balustrade, and above it hang the well-painted arms of King Charles II. The S door is 15C, and the S porch contains architectural fragments. At the W end of the N aisle is part of an 11C circular cross-shaft with interlace decoration. In the nave, beneath the N clerestory, is a wall painting of c 1500, depicting a coat of arms and the Virgin knighting St. George. The splendid font cover is early to mid-17C; the cover itself has four broken pediments surmounted by a pierced obelisk, and is wound up and down from a canopy with a broken pediment and Doric pilasters. The pulpit is Jacobean with two tiers of blank, round-headed arches. The wooden eagle lectern is probably 17C, with terrifying talons. The chancel screen of c 1500 is one of the two finest in the county; it is ten bays long and lierne-vaulted, with attractive openwork tracery filling the heads of the arches and the top of the dado. The coving was renewed in the 19C. The N and S chapels also have wooden screens. The chancel stalls and the parclose screen to the S are of c 1500. The very fine pierced altar rail is Jacobean or mid-17C. The stone reredos dates from 1866. On the N side of the chancel there is a recumbent effigy of Lady Egerton (1609). In the S chapel is an effigy of Ralph

Davenport (1387?), and a monument to Peter Shakerley by Thomas King of Bath (1796).

The stained glass in the N aisle W window is of c 1500 and comprises three figures and many fragments. The E window by William Warrington (c 1858) has scenes from the Infancy, the Passion and the Resurrection. The N aisle E window also by Warrington (c 1861) depicts the Expulsion of Adam and Eve from the Garden of Eden, the Annunciation, the holy women at the sepulchre, and St. Michael vanquishing the devil. The S aisle E window by Ward & Hughes (c 1872) depicts the Transfiguration, and that to the S shows the holy women at the sepulchre. The finest window is a gorgeous Annunciation by Irene Dunlop, with the Holy Spirit in the form of a dove encircled by cherubim, and Gabriel wearing a rich white dalmatic with a fiery halo and feet (c 1907). The other S aisle windows, reading from E to W, show the Virgin as Queen of Heaven with the Christ Child, and Christ the King with a young child (Irene Dunlop); Joshua and Aaron (c 1912); and two by the firm of O'Connor (1871). The W window depicts Christ the Consoler (c 1882).

Bunbury, *St. Boniface.* One of the major Perpendicular churches of Cheshire, St. Boniface's houses excellent 16C and 20C fittings. Architectural fragments of the Norman church are preserved and many Decorated features remain. The church was largely rebuilt after Sir Hugh Calveley founded a college in 1386, and the S chancel chapel (the Ridley chapel) was built by Sir Ralph Egerton of Ridley c 1527. The clerestory is of 1863–66 by Pennington & Bridgen and, following severe war damage, the nave and aisle roofs were rebuilt by Marshall Sisson in 1950.

The church is built of red sandstone. The massive W tower, embraced by the aisles, has a Decorated lower part and a three-light W window with curvilinear tracery, whilst the W door and upper parts are Perpendicular, with louvred bell openings (enlarged in 1675) and a crenellated parapet with crocketed pinnacles. The buttressed aisles have large four-light Perpendicular windows, differing between N and S. The N aisle's openwork parapet dates from 1840, and the Perpendicular N door is flush with the wall. The crenellated S aisle parapet was renewed in 1861, and the Decorated S porch has a statue of a bishop in a niche. The Ridley chapel has Perpendicular windows, whilst those in the chancel are curvilinear, with particularly flamboyant tracery of c 1343 in the five-light E window. There is a 14C treasury N of the chancel.

Inside the church, the base of the tower has arches on three sides, and corresponds to two bays of the eight-bay aisles. The slender Perpendicular piers of the six-bay nave have four shafts and four hollows. The spandrels of the N arcade have small animal and human figures. The stringcourse beneath the clerestory windows has stone angel corbels, from which rise the wall posts of the nave roof. This is low-pitched, of oak, panelled, with small painted bosses; the aisle roofs are plain. The nave and aisles are spacious and light, as is the Ridley chapel, but the three-bay chancel is comparatively dark.

The octagonal stone font of 1663 has a contemporary painted oak cover with scrolls. Near it is a deplorable stone statue of Mrs Jane Johnson (1741), and three early 18C charity boards. The former E window of the S aisle has an iron grille of c 1527. There are a number of 13C to 15C stone monuments at the W end of the N aisle. In the Lady chapel at the E end of the N aisle there are the remains of a 14C carved stone reredos. In front of this is a good painted triptych of

1967 by Denise Brown, depicting the Adoration of the Magi (in an English farmyard), flanked by the Annunciation to the Shepherds and the Flight into Egypt (with Bunbury in the background). A two-tier Baroque chandelier of 1756 hangs in the nave, and above the chancel arch are the painted arms of King George II. The Gothic carved oak pulpit on a stone base has an 18C stair rail.

The superb oak chancel screen of 1921 by Frederick H. Crossley has a linenfold panelled dado, Perpendicular tracery in the upper lights, and friezes of vines and animals above and below a 12-bay gallery, with different tracery and friezes on the E side. In the chancel are carved oak choirstalls with poppyheads and and a painted tablet to George Spurstow (probably by Randle Holme, 1669). In the middle of the chancel is the tomb of Sir Hugh Calveley (1394)—an alabaster effigy on a table-tomb with empty niches, preserving some of the original colouring and its simple iron grille with spikes. The altar rail has heavy turned oak balusters of 1717, the altar dates from 1659, and the reredos has linenfold panelling with a carved vine cornice. On the N of the sanctuary is the badly painted tomb of Sir George Beeston (1601), having a recumbent effigy beneath an arch flanked by columns, and a tablet above with a carved surround of military trophies. On the S of the sanctuary is a Decorated piscina and stepped sedilia beneath cusped ogee arches. The excellent painted stone screen of 1527 to the Ridley chapel is high, with 12 cusped ogee-headed lights, and is carved with the arms of Egerton and an inscription; the oak double doors have linenfold panelling, and in the upper parts carved wooden grilles. Inside the chapel, the dado of the screen is painted with the earliest Renaissance work in Cheshire, in grey on red and green panels simulating low relief carving. Inside the chapel is a reproduction of the small kneeling brass of Sir Ralph Egerton (1527).

The church possesses two superb postwar windows (E and W) by Christopher Webb which are notable for their fresh colouring, clear iconography and the use of the tracery in their composition. A window of the S aisle depicts Sir Hugh Calveley, St. George and St. Adrian, and Sir Ralph Egerton (c 1909). The N aisle E window shows the Annunciation (Webb, 1961). A window on the N of the chancel depicts Christ with St. Michael and St. Boniface (L.C. Evetts, 1952), and on the S three Old Testament figures (C.E. Kempe, 1905). There are 16C roundels in the Ridley chapel.

Chester, *St. John the Baptist.* St. John's is the only major Norman church in Cheshire. Originally founded long before the Conquest, and refounded as a collegiate church in 1057, the church became the cathedral of Bishop Peter of Lichfield in 1075. The See was transferred to Coventry in 1095, but St. John's remained a cathedral in name until the later Diocese of Chester was formed in 1541. In 1547 the college was dissolved and St. John's became a parish church.

The sandstone exterior is largely 19C. The upper part of the NW tower fell in 1881, and the ruins of its 12C base remain. The Early English N porch was destroyed when the tower fell, but was rebuilt with the old stones by John Douglas in 1882. Richard Charles Hussey restored the N side and built the NE bell tower in 1886–87. The E wall was built in 1581, and the ungainly neo-Norman window of the early 1860s is by Thomas Mainwaring Penson. To the E are the ruins of the Norman arch to the Lady chapel and the 14C choir chapels; a 13C oak coffin is set in one of the walls. At the SE is the so-called

Chapter House of c 1300. The S side and the W end, together with the interior, were restored by Hussey in 1859–66.

The interior is dominated by architecture of the early 12C. There is a four-bay Norman nave (originally three bays longer), a Norman crossing, and the first bay of the Norman chancel; both transepts have been shortened to one bay. The lowest storey of the nave and chancel is Norman, and has drum piers with scalloped capitals and double-stepped arches. The chancel has a Norman gallery, whilst the nave triforium is Transitional and has four pointed arches on ringed shafts in each bay. The nave clerestory is Early English, also with four arches per bay, the shafts with leaf capitals, and the windows alternating with blank arches.

In the N aisle there are three medieval stone effigies (not *in situ*): a knight of the Carrington family (c 1270–90) in chain-mail with crossed legs; an early 14C priest; and a half-figure of Agnes de Ridlegh (1347). On the NW pier of the crossing are the remains of a 14C wall painting of St. John the Baptist. The sandstone altar rail is neo-Norman. The reredos of 1876–77, designed by John Douglas, encloses a painting of the Last Supper by Heaton, Butler & Bayne. The pair of brass chandeliers in the sanctuary was given in 1722. The brass eagle lectern of 1887 is based on a 16C example at Wrexham. Next to the lectern is a small and very crude mid-17C font. The Lady chapel is entered through 17C oak gates with very rich wrought-iron railings and finials; similar ironwork separates the two sanctuaries. Dating from c 1925 are the early 17C-style screen dividing the S transept from the choirstalls and the early 18C-style altar rails. The oak reredos of the Lady chapel is formed from two panels of the former high altar reredos of 1692; it has Corinthian pilasters and swan-necked pediments, garishly painted, and carries a large face-less aluminium figure of the Virgin Mary, made by Michael Murray in 1969. To the S of the Lady altar is the splendid monument to Diana Warburton (by Edward Pearce, 1693)—an upright skeleton holding an inscribed shroud and flanked by Corinthian half-columns, with an urn and putti on a segmental pediment above and a tomb-chest beneath. In the S transept is the handsome marble wall monument to Cecil Warburton (1729), with a high-relief bust in a circular medallion within a rich architectural surround. In the S aisle is the fine Baroque cartouche of Mathew Anderton (1693), and several painted heraldic wall tablets by the Randle Holme family, dated variously between 1628 and 1682.

The W window depicts events in the history of the church and the city (by Edward Frampton, 1887–90). A window in the N aisle is the finest in the church, a memorial to the Chester architect Thomas Meakin Lockwood (by Shrigley & Hunt, 1901): referring to the building of Solomon's Temple, it depicts Hiram, 'architect and artificer' (1 Kings 7: 13–50). The E window depicts the Marriage at Cana, and commemorates the wedding of the future King Edward VII (by Clayton & Bell, 1863).

The organ was first used in Westminster Abbey for Queen Victoria's Coronation in 1838.

Chester Castle, *Chapel of St. Mary de Castro.* The chapel of St. Mary de Castro is on the first floor of the late 12C or early 13C sandstone Agricola Tower. The chapel has quadripartite vaulting, with slender keel-moulded ribs rising from slim round shafts with waterleaf capitals. There is a pointed altar recess, and fragments of 14C wall paintings.

Cholmondeley Castle, *Chapel of St. Nicholas.* Situated in the park of Cholmondeley Castle, the chapel contains the most complete mid-17C woodwork in Cheshire. Originally a timber-framed building of the late 15C, the chapel was restored in 1651–55 by Robert Cholmondeley, Earl of Leinster. In 1717–18, under the first Earl of Cholmondeley, the chancel was encased in brick and the rest of the chapel rebuilt, probably to the design of William Smith of Warwick. The transepts were added by the second Marquess of Cholmondeley in 1829.

The chapel is cruciform, with a three-bay chancel, three-bay transepts, two-bay nave, and a 19C vestry in the SE corner. It is built of red brick, with a moulded stone cornice and door surrounds, windows with keystones, and rusticated quoins. The steps to the W door have fine wrought-iron railings of c 1713–15, probably by the Davies Brothers of Wrexham. There are circular windows above the transept doors and on the S of the chancel, whilst the other windows are mostly round-headed.

The elaborate arch-braced and hammerbeam chancel roof is late 15C, and has pierced tracery and a frieze around the wall plate; it was altered c 1652, and the carved heads were probably added in the 1860s. The transepts are separated from the nave by an elegant arcade. The chapel has plastered walls and ceilings with a deep cornice, and is painted an attractive pale pink with the mouldings picked out in white.

At the W end, a staircase with turned balusters of 1719 leads to the State Gallery (family pew): this has oak panelled walls and strapwork flanking a coat of arms over the W door, and is furnished with Gothic side tables and chairs. The nave and transepts have simple box-pews of 1829. There are six hatchments of the Cholmondeley family, 1827–1968. There are also three oil paintings: 'The Holy Family with Saints' by the School of Palma Vecchio in the S transept; 'The Rest on the Flight into Egypt' by the School of Pietro da Cortona and 'The Adoration of the Shepherds' attributed to Bonifazio de' Pitati in the N transept. The Commandment boards of 1655 on either side of the chancel arch were originally behind the altar. Also of the 1650s are the carved oak Jacobean-style pulpit with an early 18C stair rail and the clerk's desk and lectern. The five-bay chancel screen of 1655 has Corinthian columns supporting an elaborate cornice of pierced strapwork, surmounted by the carved arms of the Earl of Leinster (facing E) and the Earls of Cholmondeley (facing W). The high oak panelling of 1651–55 in the chancel has tapering pilasters with Ionic capitals and a frieze with triglyphs and crude cherubim. The choirstalls are probably of 1829. The font on the N of the chancel, probably of 1718, is a fluted semicircle of grey fossil marble with an ogee oak cover. The 1650s oak altar rail has five openwork panels with horizontal ovals. The altar frontal was made from the crimson velvet robes worn by the second Marquess as Lord Great Chamberlain of England at the Coronation of King William IV in 1831. The E window contains Flemish roundels.

Congleton, *St. Peter.* Situated in a quiet backwater above the centre of the town, St. Peter's is a fine example of an 18C parish church, with a well-preserved interior. The present building was erected on the site of a chapel built in 1405 and subsequently altered, and incorporates the lower part of the medieval tower. The church was rebuilt by William Baker in 1740–42. The tower, raised in 1760 and completed in 1786, is of stone in the Gothick style. It rises from the main entrance, through the ringing chamber with an ogee-hooded window, through the clock chamber with three circular dials, to the belfry with four ogee-hooded, louvred windows, and is crowned with eight crocketed pinnacles. The church is of brick, six bays long, with two tiers of cast-iron framed windows, round-headed above and segment-headed below. The centre of the E end breaks forward with a Venetian window flanked by niches. The N porch, set at an odd angle, has two pairs of Roman Doric columns.

The interior is dominated by three galleries supported by square piers carrying Tuscan columns. The nave ceiling is coved, with a fine Rococo central ornament. The colour scheme of the interior—particularly the deep turquoise of the nave ceiling—is most regrettable. The marble font is 18C and has a baluster stem and a fluted bowl. The church is furnished throughout with oak box-pews, the mayor's pew having a mace holder in the form of a lion. The fine brass chandelier of 1748 has two tiers of eight arms, crowned with a dove bearing an olive twig in its beak. The components of the 18C oak three-decker pulpit have been set on either side of the sanctuary step with the reading desk centrally placed in front of the communion rail—the only surviving example of this arrangement in the county. The communion rail is three-sided, and also 18C, but the communion table is a late 19C reproduction of an 18C design. The fine oak reredos (1743) has two pairs of Corinthian columns, with painted panels of the Commandments, the Creed and the Lord's Prayer; its carving is in the style of Grinling Gibbons. Above it is a Pelican in her Piety within an open pediment. The E window is flanked by mural paintings (1748) by Edward Penny of Knutsford of St. Peter and St. Paul. In the S aisle is a 20C oak lectern, by Messrs Bridgman of Lichfield, with the Evangelists round an Ionic column. Also in the S aisle hang the crudely painted arms of King William III. The 18C glass in the semicircular head of the E window depicts the descent of the Holy Spirit in the form of a dove. The rest of the window dates from 1922. In the S aisle there is a memorial tablet to Sir Thomas Reade (died 1849), one of Napoleon's keepers at St. Helena and liberator of the slaves at Tunis; the tablet is by Thomas and Edward Gaffin and shows an African kneeling by a palm tree.

Dukinfield: see Lancashire

Eaton Hall, *Chapel.* The chapel at Eaton Hall is probably the most magnificent Victorian country house chapel in England. It was built in 1873–84 by Alfred Waterhouse for the first Duke of Westminster. Situated on one side of the forecourt, between the house and the stables, the chapel played a vital role in the picturesque composition of Eaton Hall, which, as remodelled by Waterhouse, became the largest Gothic Revival house in England. The house was demolished in 1961–62, except for the chapel and the stables, and a new house was built in 1971–73 by John Dennys.

The chapel is built of buff sandstone, with a grey slate roof. Gothic in style, it was inspired by 12C and 13C French examples, but has been handled with an originality that is purely High Victorian and typical of Waterhouse. The tower is 175ft high, and is joined to the (ritual) N side of the chancel by a two-storey structure with a bridge above. The tower has tall paired openings, four clock-faces of vitreous enamel with corner pinnacles corbelled out, and a short but very elaborate gabled octagonal spire. The tower contains a 28-bell carillon with a repertoire of 31 tunes. There is an octagonal stair turret with a spire at the NW corner of the nave. The walls of the nave and chancel have gabled buttresses between windows of two lights with a cinquefoil in a circle, above which rises a steep roof behind a corbelled parapet.

Inside, the pink sandstone walls are tall and narrow, with slender shafting. The five-bay nave has a narthex carrying a gallery at the W end. The chancel comprises three bays and ends in a three-sided apse. The chapel is rib-vaulted in pink and buff banded stone with gilded bosses—those in the nave are carved with the symbols of the Evangelists and the Apostles; those in the chancel show the Holy Spirit in the form of a dove, the Pelican in her Piety, the Lamb of God, the sacred monograms XPC and IHC, and the Instruments of the Passion. The narthex wall facing the nave is of carved stone with wrought-iron grilles, with a four-light window above the gallery. There are two-light windows on the N side of the nave and at the E end, while the bays on the S side of the chapel (which faces the stables) have blank arches with tracery and shafting similar to that of the windows.

The interior is richly furnished, with many items designed by Waterhouse. All the stained glass was made by Heaton, Butler & Bayne, and designed by the minor pre-Raphaelite artist, Frederic James Shields (1876). The W window depicts St. John the Baptist, St. Peter, St. James the Greater and St. John the Evangelist; the nave windows show New Testament figures; and the chancel windows illustrate the Te Deum. The blank arches of the S wall are filled with mosaics depicting Old Testament figures and were designed by Shields and executed by W.H. Burke in 1884. The nave walls below sill level have brass bracket candelabra and a blue and gold inscribed mosaic band above a panelled wood dado. The font of pink and cream alabaster has eight colonnettes around a central pillar. The pulpit and low chancel screen are of pink-veined alabaster with deeply pierced panels of foliage. On the S side of the screen is a brass lectern, with a book rest in the form of the portcullis of the Westminster arms, complete with hanging chains. The organ occupies the two bays of the chancel corresponding to the tower, and has elaborately stencilled pipes. In the sanctuary, the brass altar rail has wheat ears amid scroll-work between twisted colonnettes and the openwork alabaster reredos has gables and arcades. The altar crucifix (of silver, copper, enamel and mother-of-pearl) was commissioned in the mid-1880s from A.H. Mackmurdo and was made by Clement Heaton of the Century Guild. The low blank arcades on either side of the altar are filled with painted and gilded plaster panels, with the symbols of the Evangelists amid foliage and lilies. To the S is a monument to Constance (the first Duke's first wife; died 1880), with a white alabaster effigy by Sir Joseph Edgar Boehm resting upon a white and gold Renaissance chest carved with cherubim and foliage.

Eccleston, *St. Mary the Virgin.* Situated in the prettiest village of the Eaton Hall estate, St. Mary's is perhaps the most beautiful church in Cheshire. Built for the first Duke of Westminster in 1899 by G.F. Bodley, it replaced a church of 1809–13 by William Porden, of which a fragment remains in the churchyard. The churchyard is entered through fine wrought-iron gates of c 1722 by Robert and John Davies of Wrexham (from Emral Hall, Flintshire); also in the churchyard is the bronze tomb of Earl Grosvenor (1909), designed by Detmar Blow and Fernand Billerey and executed by E. Madeline, with statues of St. Edward the Confessor, St. George and St. Hugh.

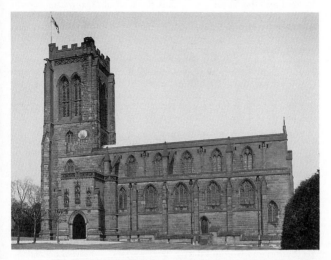

The S side of St. Mary's by G.F. Bodley, 1899, built for the first Duke of Westminster

The church is built of red sandstone in the Decorated style. This is one of Bodley's finest churches, exemplifying the refinement and sensitivity of his mature style. The buttressed W tower, its N and S walls in line with those of the clerestory, has tall paired openings pierced with quatrefoils, and a frieze below a crenellated parapet. The two-storeyed S porch has statues in canopied niches and a pierced parapet. The nave and chancel are continuous, with flat-roofed buttressed aisles, plain parapets, and flying buttresses to the clerestory in alternate bays. The windows are placed high in the walls and have Reticulated tracery, particularly complex in the E window. A three-bay vestry projects to the N.

The church is rib-vaulted throughout, with richly carved bosses. The baptistery in the tower opens into the six-bay church. The N and S aisle windows are different in size and internal treatment. Shafts rise from the piers to the vault, and a stringcourse runs between the tops of the arches and the recesses for the clerestory windows.

The church is completely furnished to Bodley's designs. The Thessaly marble font has a high oak cover carved with St. John the Baptist, St. Luke, St. Lawrence, St. John the Evangelist, St. Stephen, St. Mark, St. Matthew and St. George, and an angel finial. High over the tower arch is an elaborately gilded organ case with trumpeting angels at the corners. The pulpit and tester are of oak, carved with linenfold panelling, on a Thessaly marble base with wrought-iron rails to the steps. An oak screen with elaborate tracery extends the width of the church, and there are simpler screens on either side of the chancel. The carved, painted and gilded stone high altar reredos, executed by Farmer & Brindley, has two tiers of figures beneath rich canopies: in the centre is the crucified Christ with angels holding the crown of thorns beneath, and on either side are the Virgin Mary, St.

John, St. Peter and St. Paul, and angels bearing the sacred monogram and the Instruments of the Passion. Statues of the Archangel Gabriel and the Virgin Mary flank the E window, representing the Annunciation. On the S of the sanctuary is Bodley's monument to the first Duke of Westminster (1901; he died in 1899)—a white alabaster effigy carved by Leon Joseph Chavalliaud on a tomb-chest beneath a carved oak canopy. The (S) Grosvenor chapel has a Farmer & Brindley reredos with Christ flanked by St. Augustine and St. Paulinus. On the N wall is a monument to Hugh William Grosvenor (1914), a bronze relief in a Classical sandstone surround. To the S the second Duke of Westminster has a memorial of a bronze bust (1953) by Gilbert Ledward in an oval niche of green marble wreathed with oak leaves. All the stained glass is by Burlison & Grylls.

Great Budworth, St. Mary and All Saints. A largely Perpendicular church, begun in the 14C and completed by 1527, St. Mary and All Saints' is sited on a hilltop in a delightful village. It is built of red sandstone and comprises a W tower, nave with aisles and S porch, N and S transepts, and a chancel with N and S chapels. Nearly the whole church is crenellated, with diagonal corner buttresses and many gargoyles. All the window tracery was repaired in 1848–63. The long N transept is Decorated but the rest of the building is Perpendicular. The tower was probably built in 1500–20 by Thomas Hunter; it is in three stages, and over the door are the arms of Dutton, Warburton and Norton Priory.

Inside, the nave arcades are of six bays, the N side being older than the S, and the springers and capitals are carved with heads and other motifs. The clerestory has shafts between, and two bands beneath, the four-light windows; it originally had E windows (now blocked) too. Above the chancel arch can be seen the former entrance to the Rood loft. The two transepts open off the aisles, and are raised above burial vaults, the N being longer than the S. The chancel is of two bays, with a wagon roof, and the five-light E window has mixed curvilinear/panel tracery.

The 15C octagonal font has quatrefoils and heads on the bowl and a panelled stem with emblems of the Passion. At the W end of the S aisle there is a benefactions' board of 1703, with carved scrolls and painted cherubim. The S transept forms the Warburton chapel and contains 13C oak stalls, early 15C bench-ends with curious fleur-de-lis poppyheads, a damaged alabaster effigy of Sir John Warburton (1575), and a medieval stone altar slab. In the S chancel chapel, behind an iron screen of 1857, there is an early 18C communion rail with slender turned balusters, an altar of 1703 with cabriole legs and claw and ball feet, and a monument to Sir Peter Warburton (1813) with a woman kneeling beneath an urn. The sanctuary has a pair of wrought-iron standard candelabra, and a Victorian Gothic wooden screen to the N chancel chapel (now the vestry). Also on the N of the chancel is the organ in a good Gothic Revival case of 1839. The choir prayer desks (inspired by the S transept bench-ends) are by John Douglas, c 1883. On the floor of the nave is a very fine Gothic Revival brass to Joseph Leigh (1840). The N transept forms the Lady chapel and has a handsome stone screen by Anthony Salvin. In the N aisle there is an Arts and Crafts sandstone tablet to Lord Barrymore (1925). The stained glass in the three E windows is by C.E. Kempe: the S chancel chapel has six scenes from the life of St. Peter (1888); the chancel depicts the Passion (1883); and the N chancel chapel shows the Adoration of the Magi (1901). The Expressionist glass in the

Lady chapel was designed by Pierre Fourmaintreaux and was made by the Whitefriars Glass Studios in 1965.

Sir Peter Leycester, the great 17C historian of Cheshire, is buried in the Lady chapel.

Hooton, *St. Paul.* St. Paul's is largely Italian Romanesque in style, but with French Gothic and Byzantine elements. Designed by James K. Colling, it was built in 1858–62 at the expense of the Liverpool banker Richard Christopher Naylor of Hooton Hall (cf. Kelmarsh in Northamptonshire).

The church is of red and cream ashlar and red rock-faced stone, with grey slate roofs. The W end has a large rose window above an Italian Romanesque porch, with red granite columns supporting a gabled round arch enclosing a carved tympanum. The clerestory has round-arched windows, whilst the aisle windows have paired lancets beneath a round relieving arch. The transepts have similar plate tracery. The octagonal crossing lantern with its short spire, 95ft high, is set on a larger square tower base. The chancel aisles continue as an ambulatory around the semicircular E end. On the S of the chancel is the former private family entrance, a short cloister walk and porch, both originally open.

The interior is of cream ashlar with red ashlar banding, and has round arches throughout. The aisles and ambulatory have lean-to roofs, whilst the nave, transepts and chancel have impressive wagon roofs with semicircular ribs. The three-bay nave has arcades borne on Petershead granite columns with richly carved French Gothic capitals. Over the crossing is a dome supported on pendentives, which is a Byzantine motif; but the dome stops and opens into the octagonal lantern, which is wholly original. The chancel has two bays and then a five-bay semicircular apse. The ambulatory is a French motif. The arcade is borne on red granite columns, their capitals richly carved with foliage; the shafts in N–S pairs.

The font has a bowl of dark green serpentine, set on a five-column stem of dark red marble; it received a medal at the Great Exhibition in 1851. In the N transept is an Italianate painted Second World War memorial. The Caen stone pulpit has marble colonnettes at the corners and a taller one supporting the book rest. There is an Arts and Crafts brass processional cross, and a pair of Puginesque Gothic brass altar candlesticks. The W rose window contains stained glass of the 1860s. The rest of the glass is later. The aisle W windows are by Kempe & Co. and the E windows of the ambulatory are by Heaton, Butler & Bayne.

Low Marple, *St. Martin.* St. Martin's was built in 1869–70 by John Dando Sedding, who also designed the pulpit with bronze reliefs, the Rood screen, and the painted plaster relief of angels in the chancel. Sedding's pupil Henry Wilson, working in an Arts and Crafts/Art Nouveau manner, added the N chapel with its plaster vault of trees and birds in 1895–96, and the N aisle in c 1909; his furnishings include the inlaid communion rail and altar with a crucifix and four candlesticks in the N chapel, a large Michelangeloesque plaster relief of St. Christopher, a superb Art Nouveau font cover (c 1900), and a large War Memorial bronze relief of the Agony in the Garden (1924). The E window (1869–70) and the chancel S windows (1873) are by William Morris; the W window (1892), the nave S window

(1899), and the painting of the Annunciation in the N chapel reredos (1896), are by Christopher Whall.

Lower Peover, *St. Oswald*. The earliest surviving longitudinal timber-framed churches in Europe are at Lower Peover and Marton. The interior of St. Oswald's is outstanding as an (altered) example of this type of church, and also for its 17C furnishings. The present structure of the nave and chancel is probably late 14C and 15C; the W tower was probably built c 1500, and the aisles were altered and reroofed by Anthony Salvin in 1852–54.

The three-stage crenellated tower of Alderley sandstone has diagonal buttresses; above the W door is a Y-traceried W window, three-light mullioned windows for the bell ringers' chamber, lozenge clock-faces on three sides, and Y-traceried bell openings. On the S face is a sandstone war memorial crucifix of 1921. The oak-framed body of the church on a sandstone plinth is an exact rectangle, with only the tower and the S porch projecting. The church originally had a single roof, but Salvin gave the nave and aisles three separate roofs, with three lower roofs for the chancel and E chapels. The mullioned windows have arched lights of equal height. The heavily restored exterior has much lozenge and chevron bracing.

The four-bay nave arcades have octagonal posts of oak (possibly 13C), which carry big arched braces supporting cambered tiebeams. The aisles were originally lower and narrower, but are now plastered and have lighter roofs than the nave. The two-bay chancel has chamfered posts and arch-braced trusses. The Shakerley chapel (S) is of c 1610, and the Holford chapel (now organ chamber and vestry) (N) is of 1624.

The church is furnished with very simple 17C oak box-pews: some of them carry the Shakerley crest, and many of those in the aisles have half-doors, to retain rushes on the floor. The pews on either side of the door to the tower have overhanging canopies, probably 19C. The simple large round font was probably brought from Norton Priory in 1322, and its cover is Jacobean. By the font are two breadshelves of 1720 and 1739, to accommodate bread charities, with brass tablets recording these gifts—they were last used in 1966. The N chapel screen (1624) may contain parts of the medieval Rood screen. The lectern and the pulpit are from the 17C three-decker, which was rearranged by Salvin. The patron's pew, on the S side of the nave, has a wooden cresting around it. The low chancel screen is Jacobean. A black and gilt 19C Gothic Revival wrought-iron chandelier hangs in the choir. On the S side of the sanctuary are two brass tablets, of 1667 and 1696, to members of the Cholmondeley family.

The S chapel has a painted Gothic Revival triptych (originally from the high altar) by Alfred O. Hemming (active 1889–94) depicting the Crucifixion flanked by the Annunciation. Also in the S chapel are handsome monuments to Godfrey Shakerley (1696), with Ionic columns, and to Katherine Shakerley (1725), with twisted Composite columns and cherubim. The S chapel sanctuary screen has two tiers of balusters with three large spheres above. The stained glass all dates from the late 19C.

Macclesfield, *St. Alban*. Designed by A.W.N. Pugin in 1838 and opened in 1841, St. Alban's is a stone church of considerable size in the Perpendicular style. It has a large unfinished W tower, an aisled nave with slender soaring piers, a chancel with a seven-light E window, and a S chapel. There is an impressive Rood screen, and the chancel and chapel have richly stencilled wall decorations and carved stone reredoses.

Malpas, St. Oswald. St. Oswald's is one of the best examples of Perpendicular work in Cheshire, with a very fine nave roof and chantry chapels and an outstanding tomb. The structure is late 14C and was largely rebuilt above sill level in the late 15C. The churchyard is entered through two superb sets of early 18C wrought-iron gates from Oulton Hall, attributed to the Davies Brothers of Wrexham.

The church is built of red sandstone. The massive buttressed W tower has a round-arched 14C doorway, a Reticulated five-light window of 1864 by Henry Clutton, and simple two-light Reticulated bell openings. The E windows of the aisles are 14C, the other aisle windows are 15C, and the clerestory has four-light Tudor-arched windows. The two-storeyed S porch has a window of two trefoil-headed lights flanked by empty niches. The tower, nave, aisles and porch have crenellated parapets with crocketed pinnacles and gargoyles. The chancel has a five-light basket-arched E window, four-light N and S windows, and ornamented buttresses. N of the chancel is a Classical brick vestry of 1717 by Gardner and a 19C organ chamber.

Inside, the tower has a Perpendicular rib-vault. The six-bay Perpendicular nave arcades have slender lozenge-shaped piers with eight shafts and varied capitals. The nave and aisles have magnificent low-pitched, camber-beam, panelled roofs with painted and gilded bosses and angels (restored 1957–66). The chancel is of three bays, without aisles, and has Decorated sedilia and a piscina and a low Perpendicular camber-beam roof with bosses. Beneath the E end is a two-bay crypt.

The 15C octagonal font has quatrefoils, traceried stem panels and fleurons, and an oak cover of 1627. The handsome Gothic Revival pews with pierced ends date from the 1880s. Above the nave arcade hang three pairs of hatchments belonging, W–E, to the Dods of Edge Hall, the Tarletons of Bolesworth Castle, and the Cholmondeleys of Cholmondeley Castle. In the floor S of the pulpit is an incised white alabaster slab depicting Urian Davenport (1495), Rector of Malpas, in Eucharistic vestments. Above the chancel arch hangs a large oil painting of 'St. Peter's Denial of Christ' by Francis Hayman, given in 1778. In the S aisle there are a magnificent 13C oak chest covered with elaborate iron scrolls; six of the original box-pews of 1680; and tablets to John Stockton (1709), a cartouche with cherubim and a skull, and Mrs Bridget Kynaston (1644), a splendidly vigorous Baroque memorial with standing angels. The E bay of the S aisle is the Brereton chapel; its N counterpart is the Cholmondeley chapel. Both have high oak screens with inscribed head beams; the tracery differs, but in both cases some of the panels are cast-iron facsimiles of 1717(?). In the S chapel is the superb alabaster monument to Sir Randal Brereton and his wife Eleanor (1522), with naturalistic recumbent effigies on a tomb-chest with 20 statuettes beneath Gothic arches and pinnacles. An alabaster monument to Sir Hugh Cholmondeley and his second wife Mary (1605) stands in the N chapel, with stiff recumbent effigies on a tomb-chest which has strapwork corner pilasters, five kneeling children, a baby in swaddling clothes and the adult figures of Sir Hugh's heir and his wife. There is also a tablet to Lady Cholmondeley (1815) by Sir Richard Westmacott, with two angels. Against the S chancel wall are fine 15C stalls with nine misericords (six of them much restored); also a tablet to Charles Wolley Dod (1904) by Edward Hilton, with trees in bronze flanking the inscription.

The N aisle W window and the N window of the Cholmondeley chapel have Flemish roundels. The aisle E windows are by William Warrington (1845). The E window is a memorial to Bishop Heber, the lower part showing scenes from his life, with above them David composing the Psalms, the Magi, the descent of the Holy Spirit at Pentecost, Paul preaching to the Gentiles, and John on Patmos writing the Revelation. The S aisle windows include two by C.E. Kempe.

Reginald Heber, Bishop of Calcutta, was born in the Higher Rectory in 1775, and wrote many well-known hymns including 'God that madest earth and heaven', 'Brightest and best are the sons of the morning' and 'Holy, Holy, Holy'. 'Higher Rectory' recalls the fact that there were Rectors of the Higher and Lower Moieties until 1885, a long survival of a medieval division of the benefice (cf. Grantham in Lincolnshire).

Nantwich, *St. Mary.* Situated in the centre of the town, St. Mary's is the most important Decorated church in Cheshire, with an octagonal crossing tower and richly canopied stalls. The present church partially incorporates a 13C church and also has some fabric in the Perpendicular style. It was restored by Sir Gilbert Scott in 1854–61.

The church is built of red sandstone, with buttresses, battlements, gargoyles and pinnacles. At the W end, Sir Gilbert Scott installed a seven-light window with Geometrical tracery and a late 13C-style doorway (replacing genuine medieval work). The two-bay, two-storeyed Perpendicular S porch has a 19C lierne-vault. The windows of both aisles are Decorated, having ogee lights. The S transept has largely Perpendicular windows, including the large eight-light S window. The N transept has Decorated windows. The church is crowned with an octagonal crossing tower, which has Decorated ogee-headed bell openings and a stair turret 101ft high. The side walls of the chancel are Decorated, with windows beneath crocketed gables, and highly ornate pinnacled buttresses. The seven-light E window is Perpendicular, but it has a crocketed ogee gable which intersects the crenellated parapet. There is a two-storey Decorated treasury N of the chancel.

The four-bay nave has very tall Decorated arches. The clerestory was added in the late 15C or early 16C. The low-pitched roof (presumably by Scott) rests on large wooden angel corbels. The aisles have internal flying buttresses. The crossing tower is borne on four great piers with densely clustered shafts; the low wooden vault by Scott has painted and gilded ribs and bosses. Both transepts are of three bays: the N bay of the N transept was once the Lady chapel and has springers for a vault. The three-bay chancel has an extremely rich 14C stone lierne-vault with many carved bosses, the only medieval example in Cheshire.

The richly panelled octagonal font is Victorian. In the S aisle hangs a small watercolour of 'The Widow's Mite' by Jules Bouvier senior. The Victorian brass eagle lectern is flanked by fine standard candlesticks, and the wooden nave pulpit of 1601 by Thomas Finche has two tiers of blank arches. In the S transept (brought here from Wybunbury in 1982) is the alabaster monument to Sir Thomas Smith and his wife Ann (1614), having two recumbent effigies beneath a coffered arch flanked by pairs of Ionic columns, with much good strapwork. Also in the S transept is a battered alabaster effigy of Sir David Cradok (c 1380), and a small neo-Classical marble tablet to William Sprout (1807) with an angel holding a portrait relief. There are 20 late 14C carved oak choirstalls, with notable misericords and extremely complex triple-arched canopies. On the N of the sanctuary is an ogee-headed aumbry, and on the S are a piscina and sedilia beneath nodding ogee arches. The oak altar of 1638 has eight bulbous legs. The reredos of 1919 has a large statue of Christ Crucified flanked by the Virgin Mary and St. John the Evangelist and other saints, beneath rather dry Gothic canopies.

The stained glass in the W window illustrates Christ in the Temple (Clayton & Bell, 1875). The windows of the N aisle, reading W–E, depict Abel, Enoch, Job and Noah (Clayton & Bell, 1877); a colourful modern composition of animals, fishes, birds and planets (1985); and Christ the Good Shepherd with David and Miriam (Reuben Bennett of Manchester, 1901). In the S aisle is a gorgeously jewelled window of 1919 by Harry Clarke of the Virgin and Child with Saint Cecilia and a warrior saint. The S transept window depicts the Life of Christ from the Annunciation to the Baptism (William Wailes, 1858). In the N transept, the N window (incorporating some old glass) illustrates the Tree of Jesse (C.E. Kempe, 1876); and the E windows (John Hardman & Co.) depict the Transfiguration (1864) and the Archangels Raphael, Michael and Gabriel (1862). There are glowing fragments of early 14C glass in the SW chancel window. The E window depicts the Passion from the Agony in the Garden to the Resurrection (1876).

Port Sunlight, *Christ Church.* Built by William and Segar Owen in 1902–04, Christ Church is of red sandstone in a free Perpendicular style. The church is long and wide with aisles, transepts, tower and apse, and is richly furnished. Adjoining the W end is the Lady Lever Memorial of 1914, also by William and Segar Owen, a three-bay loggia richly decorated with buttresses, canopied niches, crocketed pinnacles and an embattled parapet; inside, beneath a tierceron-vault with many rich bosses, stands a green marble tomb-chest with bronze effigies of Lady Lever and William Hesketh Lever, first Viscount Leverhulme, by Sir William Goscombe John.

Stockport

St. George. St. George's is one of the most magnificent late Victorian churches in Cheshire. Designed by Hubert James Austin of Austin & Paley, it was built in 1893–97 at the expense of the brewer George Fearn. The schools and vicarage, also given by Fearn, form a group with the church.

It is built of red Runcorn sandstone, ashlar-faced inside and out. The style is Perpendicular, with traces of Art Nouveau (more pronounced in the furnishings, which also incorporate Jacobean elements). The church is large, cruciform and crenellated throughout, and comprises a nave with aisles and porches, a tower and spire, transepts, and a chancel flanked by a N chapel and a S vestry. The W window between octagonal turrets is flanked by the aisle windows and, beyond them, the two porches; the N porch carries a statue of St. Augustine of Canterbury. The high crossing tower, with panelled stonework and carved inscriptions, bears a spire (236ft high) between thin flying buttresses connecting it with four pinnacles. The E window between heavy buttresses is surmounted by a statue of St. George, while above the N chapel stands the Virgin and Child.

The seven-light W window has internal buttresses and a deeply pierced parapet below. The six-bay nave is high and wide. The stonework above the arcades is panelled, and each bay has a pair of square-headed two-light clerestory windows incorporating a triforium. The nave roof of oak, with both hammerbeams and tiebeams, has a band of pierced tracery panels. The N transept opens into the lower N chapel, which has a marble-paved three-sided apse. Above the panelled stonework of the crossing piers is inscribed the opening of the Te Deum and in the corners, above the heads of singing angels, are squinches which carry the triforium around the base of the tower. The panelled ceiling of the tower is stencilled in red and green on white with the sacred monogram and has rich gilded bosses. The two-bay chancel, paved with variegated marbles, has five-light side windows with a triforium, a seven-light E window with internal buttresses, and a good stone rib-vault with carved bosses.

The octagonal font of Derbyshire alabaster, with luxuriant swirling foliage on the bowl and pierced tracery around the stem, stands on a base of red Mansfield stone shaped like a Maltese cross. The aisles have wooden panelling and the pew-ends are carved with Gothic tracery. At the ends of the aisles there are oak screens, with a figure of St. Cecilia above that to the S transept. Between the N transept and the crossing there stands a very fine Gothic oak screen with fruit and flowers in the spandrels and a frieze of Art Nouveau angels' heads. The N chapel has an oak reredos with figures of St. John the Divine and St. John the Baptist beneath an Art Nouveau frieze of vines. Beneath the chancel arch there is a low stone screen with brass gates and a brass eagle lectern supported on four crouching lions; the chancel screen is continued to form the panelled base of the Runcorn stone pulpit, ornamented with statuettes of St. Paul, St. Matthew, St. Mark, St. Luke, St. John and St. Peter, beneath a circular oak tester. The handsome oak choirstalls beneath the tower are richly carved with many figures. The elaborate organ case, designed by Austin, has a Jacobean-style base with linenfold panelling, and a Gothic framework for the pipes with tiers of angels playing musical instruments. The communion rail is of oak, with tiny panels showing the Instruments of the Passion, and brass balusters. In the S sanctuary wall, carved in stone, are canopied sedilia and a piscina with a credence shelf. The Derbyshire alabaster reredos is carved with Christ Crucified flanked by the Virgin and St. John, with St. Columba, St. Aidan, St. Cuthbert, St. Oswald, St. Chad and St. Bede. The stained glass of the W window depicts figures symbolising the seven gifts and 12 fruits of the Spirit; the tiny window high above contains the arms of the See of Chester. The E window shows Christ in Majesty with angels and scenes from the life of St. George.

St. Thomas. Built by George Basevi in 1822–25, St. Thomas's is one of the finest neo-Classical churches in Cheshire. It has a tall W tower with a cupola, two tiers of side windows (reflecting internal galleries), and an E portico of six fluted Ionic columns. The interior has galleries with fluted Corinthian columns, and against the richly decorated E wall there is an Ionic tabernacle framing a painting of

Christ Transfigured (1855; by Zahner after Raphael). The chancel was sensitively remodelled by J. Medland Taylor in 1890, and the fine wrought-iron gates and pulpit were added in 1920.

Wilmslow, *Dean Row Chapel.* Dean Row is one of three almost identical Unitarian chapels in Cheshire, along with Macclesfield (1690) and Knutsford (1689). Originally Presbyterian, the congregation was founded in 1672 and the chapel built in c 1690. It had become Unitarian by the early 19C, and underwent major restorations in 1845 and 1971. The long rectangular chapel is built of red brick with sandstone dressings and a stone-flagged roof. The symmetrical eight-bay S front has two tiers of two-light, mullioned windows with brick hoodmoulds, and bronze war memorial plaques in the centre. The two projecting end bays contain small porches to the ground floor and galleries; the upper level is reached by two flights of external steps parallel with the front. Both gables have stone coping and ball finials, with a bellcote to the W. The interior retains the original W gallery, inscribed with the names of past ministers. In 1845 the S gallery was taken down, the 17C box-pews were rearranged and the pulpit, with three tiers of recessed moulded panels, was moved from the middle of the N side to the E. The communion table at the E end is enclosed by a rail, and through an opening above it may be seen the organ of 1894 in the E gallery.

CUMBERLAND

Cumberland comprises a vast and varied area: the mountain heart of the Lake District, the coastal region from the Solway in the N to Millom in the S, the Solway Plain, the city of Carlisle and its environs, the lower Eden valley, the North Pennines, and the N outposts of Bewcastle and Nicholforest. The slates and volcanic rocks of the central massif, the sandstone of the coastal areas and river valleys, the gritstone and limestone of the Pennines, and the washed cobbles from the becks have, for hundreds of years, provided the building materials.

It was not until after 1092, when William Rufus ousted the Scots from the N of the county and built a castle at Carlisle, that Norman churches and monastic establishments began to appear. These buildings, added to, altered, and restored over the centuries, provide the considerable corpus of Norman and Gothic architecture which remains today. A special feature is the church towers in the Border regions which were fortified against incursions by the Scots. Of later period is the fine church at Arthuret, built c 1609 in the Perpendicular style, and the noteworthy Georgian churches of St. Andrew, Penrith, St. Cuthbert, Carlisle, and St. Mary, Wigton, and the tiny Dales churches and chapels, low, whitewashed, with nave and chancel in one, which are sometimes crowned with a bellcote. Church building in the 19C and 20C added more than 100 places of worship to the number previously existing. Erected generally in neo-Norman and Gothic styles, the latter included the strict Gothic of A.W.N. Pugin at Our Lady and St. Wilfred, Warwick Bridge. Notable exceptions are the inventive styles of Philip Webb at the church of St. Martin, Brampton, and the completely idiosyncratic design, by Sarah Losh, of St. Mary's, Wreay.

Monuments of distinction are the group in white marble by Joseph Nollekens at Wetheral, the statue of the recumbent Robert Southey by J.G. Lough at Great Crosthwaite, the oval wall tablet by Musgrave Watson at Sebergham, and the Dacre and Howard tombs in the priory ruins at Lanercost. A fine baldacchino by Ninian Comper is at Workington St. John.

There is little medieval glass, although the E window at Greystoke has some 15C glass arranged with other fragments, and Edenhall has several 14C figures and some Flemish glass in its E window. Of 19C and 20C glass, in contrast, there is an enormous volume, contributed by more than a dozen studios, country-wide. One outstanding example is the set of 14 windows by Morris & Co. at Brampton, which includes the magnificent E window of five lights, all designed, except for the two erected after the 1914–18 War, by Sir Edward Burne-Jones.

At Keswick, a hub of present-day tourism, lie two writers: Robert Southey (1774–1843), poet-laureate and biographer, who is buried at nearby Great Crosthwaite; and Hugh Walpole (1884–1941), who was interred at St. John's Church in the town, where a Celtic-style cross marks his grave.

Arthuret, *St. Michael and All Angels.* Perhaps it is of no small significance that when King James VI gave permission for money to be collected throughout the country for the rebuilding of Arthuret Church, the patron of the living, Richard Graham, later created baronet, was His Majesty's Warden of the Border. This was in 1606.

Three years later, the building of the present substantial edifice was begun in replacement of the small 12C church on the site, which had been derelict since the Battle of Solway Moss in 1542.

The exterior of the red sandstone church is of a Perpendicular building of unbroken roofline with a sturdy W tower attached, a crocketed pinnacle at each of its corners and capped by a squat parapet spire. Aisles and clerestory are embattled, the walls are buttressed and the windows are all under square heads. The lights are four-centred. In the six-light, transomed E window, which has Y-tracery, it is interesting to note that whereas the original 17C top tracery light was typically oval in shape, the present one, in the restored window of 1868, is circular. In the churchyard are the remains of a wheel-head Maltese cross, considered to be Norman.

A chancel with two-bay side chapels, a shallow projecting sanctuary, a chancel arch and a nave divided from its N and S aisles by five-bay, double-chamfered arcades, comprise the rectangular interior. The W pier in each arcade is of a normal octagonal shaft and capital, but the remaining three, perhaps to accommodate some aspect of the earlier structure, are each fitted with a respond to both nave and aisle, the former rising with reduced thickness to roof level, the latter rising vertically to the clerestory.

Since the 16C the Grahams of Netherby have been intimately connected with the church and there are a number of wall tablets to the memory of individual members of the family. An early one, of 1657, is to Sir George Graham, while another commemorates Sir James Graham, Bt, a prominent politician who was MP for Carlisle in 1825 and for Cumberland in 1830. He died in 1861. During his career he held high offices, including those of Home Secretary and First Lord of the Admiralty. The pictorial E window (1868) is dedicated to him, and depicts the Apostles. A stained glass window inserted in 1970 at the E end of the S aisle wall is by Stanley Murray Scott and depicts, in the upper lights, St. Michael slaying the serpent in the company of rejoicing angels, and, in the lower lights, the carpenter, architect and stonemason at the building of the 17C church. A small brass engraved with a cross fleurette and a heart held between two hands is attached to a chancel pillar. It was found in the ruins of the old church and represents a heart burial, perhaps of a knight who did not return from the Crusades. The pulpit, carved with moulded panels and inlay, must be Jacobean.

In the churchyard is buried a notorious character in Archie Armstrong, born in Arthuret, who was a retainer and jester at the courts of King James VI and King Charles I. His too-caustic wit is said to have offended Archbishop Laud, and he was sent home in disgrace.

Aspatria, *St. Kentigern.* St. Kentigern's is a handsome red sandstone building of 1846–48 by Travis & Mangnall in the Early English style, with a high four-stage tower. The church is aisled and has six-bay arcades. The arch over the NW vestry door, supported on scalloped Norman capitals, is composed of zigzag and criss-cross work from the original Norman chancel arch, a relic which must have inspired the erection of the tower's archway to the nave, and its W portal. The height of the Early English chancel arch is striking and its proportions are superb. In the chapel at the E end of the S aisle are the brightly painted monuments of the Musgrave family of Hayton Castle, dating from 1500 to 1812. The font is of the early or mid-13C, its square bowl carved with coarse leaves with which a serpent is entwined. Among the fragments of stonework is part of an elaborately carved hogback coffin-lid believed to be 11C, and a 5ft length of a pre-Conquest cross-shaft. In the churchyard stands a replica of the Gosforth Cross (q.v.).

Bewcastle, *St. Cuthbert.* Of the present church only the E wall with its three stepped lancets and some of the masonry of the windowless N wall remain to indicate its 13C date. The W tower was added in 1792. The site lies within the perimeter of a Roman camp built as a N outpost of Hadrian's Wall. The church is famed far and wide for the cross-shaft, now headless, which stands in what is now the churchyard, a relic which ante-dates the church by some six centuries. According to the runic inscriptions on the shaft, the cross was erected to the memory of Alcfrith, King of Northumbria and son of Oswy, who himself succeeded Oswald, King and Saint, slain in battle in 642. 'Pray for his soul' demands the inscription. The shaft, 14ft in height, is historically and archaeologically a major artefact. On the W face, apart from the runes, there is carved the figure of Christ standing

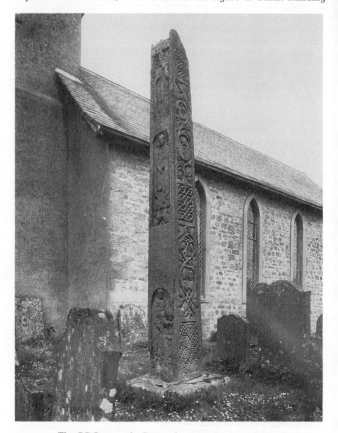

The 7C Bewcastle Cross, the most famous of standing pre-Conquest crosses in England

upon a lion and an adder; above is St. John the Baptist with the Agnus Dei, and below, St. John the Evangelist, with the Eagle. Carved on the other sides are knotwork, vine scrolls, chequer work, fruit and foliage, and birds and animals. The execution is masterful and sophisticated, and must have drawn its inspiration from far beyond Britain's shores, perhaps through the influence of such men as St. Benedict Biscop, who founded the monasteries of Monkwearmouth and Jarrow, and St. Theodore, a Syrian Greek from Tarsus in Asia Minor, appointed to the archbishopric of Canterbury in 668. Despite the passage of many centuries, the shaft is remarkably well-preserved.

Boltongate, *All Saints.* All Saints' is a small country church within sight of Skiddaw, built in the 15C by Ralph Neville, Earl of Westmorland. It replaced a 12C Norman church damaged or destroyed during a long period of Border warfare. The building's distinguishing feature is its stone roof.

Externally, the church is a Perpendicular building of sandstone rubble, with W porches N and S, a transept on both sides of the nave, and a vestry on the NE corner, all of these erections having lean-to roofs of stone slabs. A parapet runs round the W end from transept to transept, access to it being given by a stair turret capped by a low steeple, situated behind the N transept. A bellcote sits behind the W gable. The Perpendicular windows exhibit an interesting variety of tracery, and some have hoodmoulds with carved heads as label stops. The Decorated vestry window must be a reused piece. On the S side of the chancel a rectangular opening, now a window, is believed to have been originally for the issue of alms or for the confession of lepers.

The interior is an aisleless nave, with very small transepts, which in pre-Reformation days were chapels, and a long narrow chancel divided from the nave by a pointed arch. Over the nave is the church's unique feature: the tunnel-vault of stone, even more steeply pointed than the chancel arch, the inspiration for which must have come from Scotland. Built in the same fashion are the roofs of the transepts. The corbels issuing from the walls of the nave may have been used in the construction of the stone vault, but their function is debatable. Several of the corbels in the W wall are mounted with decorated capitals from the Norman church.

Among the stained glass windows is one of 1884 in the S wall by C.E. Kempe Studios, depicting St. Paul attended by four female Virtues. The lower W window of c 1855, with figures of Zacharias, Amos and Jeremiah in the main lights, angels in the tracery, and coats of arms in the predella, is attributed to Thomas Willement.

Brampton, *St. Martin.* When the Reverend Henry Whitehead came to St. Martin's in 1874 as Vicar, he found a Georgian building of 1789 in disrepair and a parish troubled by the problem of appropriated pews. He decided that a new church was needed and by the generosity of George Howard, ninth Earl of Carlisle, who had invited him to Brampton, and the Earl's family and friends, this was made possible. The architect chosen was Philip Webb, who had designed William Morris's Red House at Bexleyheath in Kent in a new style based on rural vernacular architecture, and whose commissions were, in the main, for country houses. Webb produced a design which incorporated some facets of his domestic architecture, treated period styles freely and held some surprises. The new church was consecrated in 1878, the tower, due to shortage of money, having to be roofed at its lowest stage, and not reaching completion until 1906. As a result of a decision at the outset that any commissions for stained glass windows should be given only to Morris & Co., the church has 14 fine windows by this firm, including the E window, ablaze with colour, dedicated to Charles Howard, the father of the ninth Earl, who had been Chairman of the Building Committee.

The E end of the red sandstone church closely overlooks dwellings and other property, the N side faces onto a busy street, there is rising ground to the S, and a steep fall to the W. The most comprehensive view is therefore from the NW. On the N side three two-light windows under embattled gables, separated by buttresses, lie between the high chimney of the vestry at the E end and the lofty tower with the porch at its foot on the W. On the S side four low, wide and gabled buttresses stand between small, segment-headed windows, while three embattled dormers pierce the roof. At the E end, the masonry of the high E window forms a recess between the low vestry and organ blocks. Many of these features seem to be reflections of Webb's domestic innovations. His treatment of the tracery of the windows is inventive and a free adaptation of period styles. In the battlemented tower, a pinnacle at each corner, there are surprises; the bell openings on the E and W sides differ from those on the N and S, while the gable ends to the ridge roof which supports the spire face E and W only.

The inner entrance porch leads up into the nave by two ogee-headed openings at the base of a high traceried arch which gives light to the nave from the W window. Four-bay arcades of 14C style, with octagonal piers and octagonal moulded capitals, divide the interior without the intervention of a chancel arch. Above the nave, ribbed vaulting of timber springs from stone pilasters on the inner side of the arcade above each pier and dies into the flat wooden roof above. Asymmetry is a surprising feature of the rectangular interior: the N aisle is wide, it has large two-light windows, three of its bays have wooden transverse tunnel-vaulting bracketed to the masonry, and the fourth, the easternmost, has a flat roof, and its arcade arch is boxed-in to form an extension into the church of the upper storey of the vestry, which has a window overlooking the chancel. In contrast the S aisle is narrower, it has single-light windows, and, running for its whole length, a lean-to roof in two stages, with supporting struts to the outer spandrels of the arcade at the level of the dormer windows. The organ and a three-light window occupy the easternmost bay.

The stained glass by Morris & Co. is an artistic feature of the first importance. Apart from the two windows in the War Memorial chapel, the glass spans a period of 20 years from 1878, and all within that period was designed by Sir Edward Burne-Jones. The E window Burne-Jones considered his finest work: it includes the Good Shepherd attended by nine angels, the Pelican in her Piety, the Virgin, St. Dorothy, St. Martin and St. George. In the N aisle are two windows of 1878 depicting Adam, Noah, Enoch and Abraham in the one, and Moses, David, Solomon and Elijah in the other, and one of 1880 figuring St. John the Evangelist, St. Luke, St. Peter and St. Paul. In the S aisle, easternmost, of 1886, is a three-light window of Hope, Charity and Faith, and W of it, three windows erected in 1888 to the memory of Bessie Howard, infant daughter of George and Rosalind Howard, depicting all the children of the Holy Family, and Jesus with other children. In the SW chapel is the children's window of 1896, in which Samuel presents himself to Eli with the words, on a scroll, in Latin, 'Here am I, you called me.' Also in this chapel, a circular window with two angels with trumpets and two with scrolls announcing the arrival of souls into Paradise, is a tribute to Henry Whitehead by his widow. He died in 1896. The two windows in the porch depicting Isaiah and Ezekiel, and Jeremiah and Daniel, are a tribute to Henry Whitehead from the parish. The panel bearing the Sacred Heart and the symbols of Bread and Wine which is incorporated in the reredos of the high altar, is also a piece of craftsmanship from the Morris workshops. In the War Memorial chapel the jewelled painting of Christ seated alone at a table prepared as for a feast, ignored by the busy world outside, is by Byam Shaw.

Bridekirk, St. Bride. The present neo-Norman church, 1868–70, by Cory & Ferguson, replaced an earlier building, the roofless chancel of which stands in the churchyard. The church is cruciform, with E apse and central tower. The SW doorway and its tympanum, the door to the S transept, and the arch to the organ recess are reused pieces from the Norman church of c 1130. The interior is of brickwork, and brickwork has also been used in the vaulted chancel roof and in the semicircular arches of the crossing, where brickwork provides even the semblance of dogtooth decoration. The church is noted for its especially fine 12C font, which, according to the runic inscription on the E face, is believed to have been carved by Richard of Durham. It is oblong, with deep tapering sides carved in two bands with mythical birds and animals, foliage, and scenes depicting the Baptism of Christ and the expulsion of Adam and Eve from the Garden of Eden. A number of medieval coffin-lids are arranged around the external wall of the apse.

Gosforth, St. Mary the Virgin. St. Mary's comprises a nave and chancel, a N nave aisle and two vestries on the N. There is no tower, but there is a W bellcote, whose three openings are arranged in triangular fashion. The chancel is 13C, but the rest was rebuilt in 1896–97. In the churchyard stands the famous Gosforth Cross, a relic from the late 10C or early 11C. At 14½ft in height it towers above all the other monuments in the churchyard. Slender, round below and square above, and still crowned by its cross-head, the cross displays in its carving an intense Scandinavian influence. The lower round portion represents the interlaced branches of the Sacred Tree of the Northmen, while the four upper faces bear representations of horsemen and other human figures, dragons, snakes and plaiting. Only on the E face is there any Christian work: a carving of Christ with outstretched arms, and below Him, two figures. One is a man with a spear, believed to be Longinus, and the other a woman, said to be Mary Magdalen. Other artefacts are two 10C carved hogback tombstones excavated from the foundations of the church in 1896, and now displayed at the E end of the N aisle.

Interesting survivals from the 12C Norman church are the capitals in the chancel arch, that on the S side carved with three faces framed in strapwork, the one on the N side decorated with the head of a 'green man', and a pair of detached arms. In the wall of the S porch are set carved grave-slabs of the 13C or 14C.

Irton, St. Paul. The church is a rebuilding of 1856–57 by Miles Thompson of Kendal, and comprises a nave, chancel and a W tower with a higher NE stair turret. The chancel was enlarged by William

White in 1872. The church is situated on an eminence in open country and commands fine views of the mountains towards Wasdale and Eskdale. In the churchyard S of the church stands the ancient cross, complete with head, for which Irton is justly famed. It is of red sandstone, 10ft in height, is carved on each face and dates from the 9C. According to authority it is Hiberno-Celtic. The decoration includes plaiting, incised saltires, vine scrolls and interlace, and on the W side, where now there is a completely eroded space, originally there was a dedicatory inscription in runes. The cross-head is the only Christian symbol.

The church possesses two stained glass windows by Morris & Co., both using figures designed by Sir Edward Burne-Jones. Situated at the E end of the N aisle, one (dated c 1906), depicts St. Paul at the Athenian altar of an unknown god in one light, and the Sibyl consulted by the Emperor Augustus at the birth of Christ in the other; the second, of c 1877, is of St. Agnes with a lamb, and St. Catherine of Alexandria, in separate lights.

Lanercost, *Priory Church of St. Mary Magdalene.* Lanercost Priory was founded by Sir Robert de Vaux in c 1166 for Augustinian canons. It was consecrated in 1169 when little more than the sanctuary is likely to have been built, and was completed in c 1220, except for the W front, which was only finished after the lapse of a further 50 years. The priory church was basically cruciform, with chapels on both sides of the choir, and a N aisle to the nave. S of the nave was the cloister, with the conventual buildings enclosing it on three sides. King Edward I and Queen Eleanor paid a visit in 1280, and the King was back again in 1300 and 1306 during his prosecution of the war against Scotland. In the ebb and flow of hostilities the priory suffered at the hands of the Scots, and on each occasion it had to be repaired or rebuilt. As a result the canons suffered an impoverishment which lasted up to the Dissolution in 1536. The priory was subsequently acquired by Sir Thomas Dacre, who converted part of the buildings into a dwelling, taking up residence in 1559. The N aisle was enclosed to serve as the parish church, while the remainder of the priory was left to decay. In the early 18C, on the demise of this branch of the Dacre family, the priory again came into the possession of the Crown. In 1740 it was decided to enlarge the parish church. The aisle was united with the nave, and the resultant space sealed off at the transepts by a wall with a window of three arched lights. The roof was restored, and the whole repaired and refurbished. From this new beginning has developed the handsome modern church. The priory ruins, bought by the Earl of Carlisle in 1869, are now in the custody of English Heritage. Much restoration work has been carried out in recent years.

The first impression of the exterior is of a W front with a fine portal, a frieze of blank arches, tall stepped lancets, and the beautifully carved 13C statue of St. Mary Magdalene in a niche in the gable. Behind is the nave made new in the 18C, and beyond the nave, the magnificent ruins of the 12C transepts, choir and sanctuary, and the remains of the Perpendicular tower, all roofless, lancets gaping, but much of it still standing up to the level of the eaves, and still remarkably well-preserved.

The W door gives access to the parish church, where a 13C four-bay arcade divides nave from N aisle. On the S side stands the wall which used to separate the nave of the priory from the cloisters, blank in its lower part, but pierced by four lancets above. Below the roof of the nave, on both N and S sides, its arches supported by clustered shafts with decorated capitals, runs the elegant clerestory and passage which terminates at the delicately shafted W window of three lancets. Stairs at the W end lead, through an anteroom, to the Dacre Hall, where an ancient kingpost roof of rough timber will be found.

Erected in a blocked NW doorway is part of the Lanercost Cross of 1214, the base of which stands in the meadow outside the church. In the vaulted cellarium S of the cloister are gathered many Roman and medieval artefacts. Among the stained glass windows in the N aisle are three by Morris & Co., all designed by Sir Edward Burne-Jones: one of c 1875 of St. Luke the Physician, another, the Annunciation to the Shepherds, of 1890, and a third of c 1895 depicting two Angels bearing away the body of Moses for burial in Moab. St. Cecilia is the subject of a window of c 1947 by the Irish artist and glazier, Evie Hone.

In the priory ruins are the tombs of the Dacres and more recent ones of the Howards. Among them is the tomb-chest, some 15ft in length and standing under a low Perpendicular arch, of Sir Thomas Dacre (died 1525), an outstanding example of the heraldic stone-mason's art, and in contrast, a charming recumbent effigy in ter-racotta of Bessie Howard, by Sir Edgar Boehm. She died in 1883 aged four months. Buried in the churchyard is Dr Thomas Addison, who was Physician at Guy's Hospital in London from 1824 until his death in 1860 and who diagnosed the medical condition known as Addison's Disease.

In 1982, the priory's cartulary, which was compiled between 1252 and 1364, was rediscovered after disappearing in 1826.

Penrith, St. Andrew. The present church was built in 1721–23, incorporating the tower of the earlier church, but adding a new W door to it. Since the rebuilding, a choir vestry has been built onto the S side of the chancel and considerable alterations have been made to the interior. Nevertheless, St. Andrew's remains a handsome, gal-leried Georgian church. It has an unusual style of roof, notable murals in the sanctuary and relics of early Christianity in the churchyard.

The church stands in cloistered quiet despite its situation in the town centre and only a matter of yards from the A6. It is of red sandstone. There are two tiers of round-headed windows with prominent keystones, separated by broad pilasters which run up through a moulded cornice to a solid balustrade with capstones. The nave is of eight bays, the chancel of two. The E window is of the Venetian type, its masonry forming a shallow projection from the E wall of the chancel. The W bay of the lower tier on both S and N sides is occupied by a door which leads into a cross-vestibule, the S door having above it a sundial of a type fashionable in the early 18C.

In the churchyard are relics 1000 years old; one the so-called Giant's Grave, on the N side of the church, the other the Giant's Thumb. The Giant's Grave is an arrangement of four sides of hogback coffins flanked by two Gosforth-type crosses, round in the lower half and square above. Interlace, a serpent and a small figure have been identified on the hogbacks. The crosses are nearly twice the height of a man, but are badly eroded. Interlace has been found on both, together with the figures of a man and a woman, a serpent and the Agnus Dei. The Giant's Thumb, to the NW, is a 10C cross of less height than the others, has a head of the wheel type, and bears scrollwork and interlace. An illustrated reconstruction of both the Giant's Grave and the Giant's Thumb will be found in the church vestibule or the tower upper landing.

Entry is by way of a Classical portal of Tuscan columns, frieze, and pediment in the W wall of the tower which, although Norman in its lower portion, is 15C above, as witness the straight-headed bell openings with two cusped lights. A two-arm staircase leads up under a massive double-chamfered, pointed arch still bearing socket holes from a previous structure, to a landing, thence into the gallery of the church, where there is a royal coat of arms of 1723, the date of the completion of the church. On either side of the tower staircase is an effigy in white softstone, of Anthony Hutton, Counsellor-at-law (died 1637), on the one hand, and of his wife on the other. On the landing stands an old muniment chest, and in the wall a stone recording the 2260 deaths from plague in 1597.

Entering the body of the church by the ground floor vestibule, the well-proportioned interior is revealed. A panelled gallery, supported by Tuscan columns, occupies three sides of the nave, while similar but more slender columns carry the roof. The chancel, raised in height in 1887 and slightly less wide than the nave, is flanked by the Lady chapel on the N side and by the magnificent sweep of the organ casing and the panelling of the clergy vestry below, on the S. Over the sanctuary a round-headed arch with keystone rustication springs from rectangular pilasters, the side walling of the E window curving up on both sides into the vault behind it. On the curved walling are paintings of 1845 by Jacob Thompson, a locally-born artist; 'The Agony in the Garden' on the S side, 'The Annunciation to the Shepherds' on the N. Of particular interest is the roof, erected in an unusual style of coffering, the present colour scheme for which, and for the supporting pillars, was designed in 1972 by Stephen Dykes Bower.

Fittings of interest are the two brass chandeliers in the nave, each of 24 candle sockets, which were purchased with the 50 guineas' reward given by the Duke of Portland to the citizens of Penrith for their harassing of the Scots during their incursion of 1745. The pulpit, decorated with carved panels, fluted colonnettes, etc., is believed to be the top section of the three-decker which, prior to c 1861, stood in the centre of the chancel. The font, of Caen stone and Shap granite pillars, is of 14C design, but made in 1864. On display in the S aisle is a Bible of 1613 used in the old church. An interesting 17C cartouche is set in the wall at the E end of the N aisle; it is surmounted by the head and bust, decolleté, of a female, with bucolic female cherubs as supporters and a cherub head at foot, all in white and red marble. In a window in the N aisle are fragments of 15C glass. In the S aisle is the Neville window, a modern window designed to display two fragments of old glass purporting to represent the heads of Cicely Neville and Richard Plantagent, and the 'Bear and Ragged Staff' emblem of Richard Neville, Earl of Warwick. Recent research suggests that the heads are those of Cicely Neville's parents, Ralf Neville and Joan Beaufort. The White Rose of the House of York features in the border. All the remaining stained glass, except for the easternmost window in the N aisle, erected 1913, is 19C. Most of the windows are unsigned. The E window, however, is by Hardman & Powell, of Birmingham, the St. Andrew window in the Lady chapel is evidently by Burlison & Grylls, and that in the N wall of the chapel is by G.J. Baguley, of Newcastle-on-Tyne.

St. Bees, *St. Mary and St. Bega.* St. Bees' Benedictine Priory was founded c 1120 by William de Meschines on the site of a 7C nunnery which was destroyed by the Danes in the 9C. Both Norman and Early English work survive in the church and priory, the building of which was completed in the early 13C. After the Dissolution in 1539 the lead was stripped from the roofs and the priory fell into decay, and not until the early 17C were repairs undertaken. At the same time the four bays of the monks' chancel and the W bay of the nave were walled off and excluded from what then became the parish church. In 1817, with the establishment at St. Bees of a theological college, the ancient monks' chancel was reconstructed to form a great hall, the walling at the W end of the nave was removed and the W door brought back into service, and the E end of the parish church was appropriately reordered. The style and condition of the church today are the result of an extensive restoration carried out by William Butterfield in 1855–68. One bay of the ancient chancel now forms the E end of the church, the three bays beyond the E wall serving as the Music Room of St. Bees School.

The exterior is of a cruciform building in rose-coloured sandstone comprising a four-bay E end, N and S transepts, nave and clerestory, side aisles, and a square central tower with a narrow stair turret in its NE corner. Apart from the Perpendicular clerestory the fabric is mainly Early English in style, although some Norman work survives. Of the Norman survivals the finest is the W doorway of c 1160, once richly decorated with chevron and beakhead ornament in the arches, and still impressive after more than 800 years. Opposite the W door is erected a Norman lintel, the dragon with plaited tail in its decoration showing Scandinavian influence. Of the priory's S chancel aisle built in the late 14C or early 15C, few traces remain, and three of the arches which gave access to it are now blocked up, and fitted with modern windows which light the S side of the Music Room.

Chancel, N and S transepts and the crossing, and a nave divided from the aisles by six-bay arcades, form the interior. The arcades are Early English, the piers alternately round and octagonal, the capitals decorated with simple nailhead. One pier in the N arcade, however, consists of composite keeled shafts. As part of Butterfield's restoration the aisles were walled off from the transepts, and each wall pierced by a large cinquefoil opening of sharp curves suggestive of the Decorated period. The piers and arches of the crossing divide the chancel from the nave, and here there is Early English work superimposed on the Norman. The chancel E wall is windowless except for a cinquefoil high up in the gable, but its blankness is relieved by the stone mouldings of Early English arches and tracery, and coloured tiling. The S transept houses the organ, which was built by Henry Willis in 1896–99.

A dominant feature of the interior is the fine cast- and wrought-iron screen, painted and gilded, which Butterfield designed in a late 13C style for the lofty arch between nave and crossing. Among the monuments is an ornate canopied Gothic tomb of Cotswold Stone in the chancel, a memorial to Maria Claudine Lumb, a child aged four who died in 1865, and whose sleeping effigy in Carrara marble lies in the recess. In the SW corner of the nave a tablet depicting a draped female bowed over a sarcophagus is by John Bingley. Exhibited at the E end of the S aisle are many artefacts from the priory, among them carved coffin-lids and grave-slabs of the 12C and 13C, recumbent effigies from the 14C and 15C, and part of a cross-shaft of the 10C or 11C. Erected in 1955 on the E wall of the St. Bega chapel in the N transept are modern representations of the Virgin and Child, and of St. Bega portrayed as a young girl.

Among the stained glass windows are two sets of note, one erected in the N aisle, the other in the S aisle, and both in the 1860s. Depicted in the N aisle are subjects from the Old Testament, and in the S aisle, stories out of the New Testament. The windows were manufactured by William Wailes of Newcastle-on-Tyne.

Warwick-on-Eden, St. Leonard. The date of foundation is uncertain, but it would appear to fall within the first quarter of the 12C on two points of evidence: the fact that the church was an endowment conferred on the nearby Wetheral Priory, founded c 1100 and its mention in a charter of King Henry I in 1131. The present church is noteworthy for its Norman apse of a form unusual in England, and for the massive Norman arch and responds at the W end of the nave. The apse has, on its external wall, 12 narrow pilasters with intervening round-headed recesses of similar width, examples of which are known from France, while the arch in the nave has scalloped capitals with some simple decoration, including the corn-cob motif. The Norman arch, believed to have been the original chancel arch, may have been removed to its present position in the early 16C by Prior Thornton, of Wetheral, whose rebus, a thorn tree growing out of a tun, or barrel, is carved on a buttress situated on the S side of the apse. A further feature of the building, extensively restored in 1869, is the splayed base of old masonry by which the walls of the present nave are supported. The stained glass window in the modern baptistery is of 1911–13 by Henry Holiday, and was executed by Powell's, of Whitefriars. It depicts the Apostle Paul preaching.

Wetheral, The Holy Trinity, St. Constantine and St. Mary. Of the Norman church dating from the time of the foundation of the nearby Wetheral Priory c 1100, nothing now remains. Rebuilding over the centuries has given the present edifice 13C arcades, a 16C exterior, and a tower of 1760 restored and redesigned in 1882. In 1791 a Gothic-style chapel was built over the mausoleum of the Howard family of Corby Castle on the N side of the chancel, to house one of the finest works of the sculptor Joseph Nollekens. The sculpture commemorates Maria Howard, wife of Henry Howard, who died in childbirth at the age of 22. Carved in white marble, the dying mother, her dead child in her lap, is supported by one arm of the draped figure of Faith, whose other hand points to the skies. Nollekens is said to have wept when he heard that his masterpiece was to be hidden away in a private chapel. Today the sculpture is available for public viewing.

Whitehaven, St. James, High Street. St. James's is a Georgian church built to the designs of Carlisle Spedding in 1752–53, the third church to be erected to serve the needs of Whitehaven, whose prosperity was increasing as a result of a flourishing coal trade. Viewed from the bottom of the long steep hill by which the church is approached, the W tower and its embracing side aisles present an imposing façade.

The church stands within a walled area of churchyard now cleared of gravestones. The four-stage tower, rusticated at the corners, crowned by pinnacles, with a pedimented portal, an upper pediment in the second stage, and clock and bell openings above, is a striking external feature. The dark red St. Bees sandstone chosen for the portal effects a pleasing contrast with the paler Whitehaven sandstone of the remainder of the tower. By comparison with the façade, the rendered side walls, pierced by two tiers of plain rectangular windows with stone surrounds, lack architectural interest. At the E end, blocked-up openings in the walls of the apse provide evidence of the former existence of three sets of Venetian-style windows.

The interior, painted in cream and pale pastel colours, comprises an apsidal sanctuary, nave and side aisles, aisle chapels, and W, N and S galleries. A segmental arch with keystone rustication divides the apse from the body of the church. Within the apse a straight-sided pediment supported by fluted Ionic pillars forms the centrepiece, behind which, around the curve of the apse, runs a cornice and an arcade of Ionic pilasters. The gallery is supported by Tuscan columns which continue to the ceiling unfluted but terminate in Ionic capitals. A coffered frieze decorates the gallery foot. The ceiling is of plaster, and is embellished with two roundels of 18C Italian stucco work, painted white on a blue background. They represent the Annunciation and the Ascension. Access to the gallery is by a two-arm staircase with close balusters in the vestibule at the W end. In 1979, under a reordering scheme, most of the gallery seating above the aisles was removed to provide space for parish activities. The side chapels are enclosed by screens which are supported by small, paired Ionic columns.

As one enters the eye is attracted by the centrepiece of the apse, a fine Transfiguration by the Milanese painter, Giulio Cesare Procaccini (1548–1628). The painting was presented to St. James's by William, third Earl of Lonsdale. The font, of Florentine marble and 17C workmanship, was a gift from George Augustus Frederick Cavendish-Bentinck, who was elected MP for Whitehaven in 1865. In the SE chapel a block of coal and a lighted miner's lamp form a simple memorial to the men who lost their lives in a Whitehaven pit disaster in 1947.

Much of the stained glass is the product of the workshops of two Lancaster firms, Shrigley & Hunt, and Abbott & Co. From the former are Our Lord, Mary and Martha of 1917, and the Good Samaritan of 1924, both in the S aisle, and a Good Shepherd window of 1924 in the N aisle. All four windows from Abbott & Co. are in the S aisle: a Virgin and Child of 1970, 'Well done, thou good and faithful servant' of c 1930, an Annunciation of c 1918, and one commemorating a life lost in the Great War, 1914–18. A window of 1976 by L.C. Evetts, typical of his style, is to be seen in the N aisle.

Wigton, *St. Cuthbert*. St. Cuthbert's, built in 1837, was designed by Ignatius Bonomi in the style of c 1300. The red sandstone building has a W façade with a gabled buttress at each side, three stepped lancets, which are recessed and shafted, a cinquefoil window in the gable, and a portal of two orders of round shafts and capitals and a pointed arch. The nave walls of five bays are buttressed and have two-light windows with Y-tracery. The E end was extended in 1857, after Bonomi's death. The E window is of five stepped lancets. There is no tower.

Wreay, *St. Mary*. St. Mary's, a rebuilding of 1840–42, can be described as the most idiosyncratic church building in the county. It was designed by Sarah Losh (1785–1853), one of the two daughters of John Losh, chemical manufacturer and ironmaster, who had settled at Woodside, a house N of the village. Sarah's beloved sister

Catherine had died prematurely in 1835, an event which determined Sarah to replace the dilapidated post-Reformation chapel
with a new building as a memorial. The two sisters had made a tour
of France, Italy and Germany two or three years after the Battle of
Waterloo, and Sarah would therefore have some knowledge of
Continental architecture. She was also artistic and well-read. In the
building of the church, of which she was her own architect, she
recruited the skills of local craftsmen and even sent one of the
stonemasons to Italy to study the architecture of Antiquity. The
result was a mixed French and Italian Romanesque style. Sarah
Losh's deep interest in nature is displayed in the wealth of carvings
of birds, animals, insects and plants and her contemplative spirit is
shown in the use in decoration of the arrow, a symbol of death, and
the pine cone, of eternity.

The external view is essentially one of a nave with bellcote,
surmounted by an eagle, on the W gable, and an E apse, the nave
lighted by a clerestory and a lower tier of windows. In the W wall the
18 dwarf, roofline, round-headed windows are an inspiration from
the Italian Romanesque, while in the wall of the apse the round-
headed blind arcade could be either French or Italian. The W door
and the main W windows are of three orders, the inner and outer
rusticated, the centre carved in flat, high relief with motifs of floret,
butterfly, corn sheaf, fossil shell and thistle. Gargoyles are usually
gross creatures, but here they are the alligator, crocodile, tortoise and
serpent. In the churchyard, steps leading underground are protected
by a railing composed of metal arrows. The mausoleum, where the
white marble effigy of Catherine Losh sits in contemplation of a pine
cone, is rectangular, flat-roofed, constructed of heavy slabs of yellow
sandstone, and purposely primitive. The effigy was the work of
David Dunbar, who had studied under Chantrey. In the grave
enclosure Sarah and her sister lie beneath a rough-hewn slab of rock,
as do many others, one of the slabs carved with a recumbent palm
tree, another acting as base for a large pine cone carved in stone. In
contrast is the elegant Bewcastle-style cross-shaft, rivalling the
original in height, which Sarah raised to her parents.

Entry is by way of a W door decorated with arrows, whence steps
lead down into the aisleless nave, a rectangular space with plain
walls lighted by a clerestory and a lower tier of windows. At its E end
the chancel arch, of lesser width than the nave and rusticated on the
soffit, rests uneasily on the carved Roman heads which serve as
imposts. In the chancel, following the curve of the apse, stands a
colonnade of round-headed arches supported by 14 sturdy round
shafts with carved capitals and square abaci, stone sedilia occupying
the intervening spaces. In the wall of the apse, behind the colonnade,
are seven lucarnes, gleaming gold, and above, in the gable of the
apse, a gallery of round-headed openings.

Carved wood and bog oak from Woodside are used for the pulpit,
the two lecterns—one an eagle, the other a pelican—the Archangels
Michael and Gabriel on the sides of the chancel arch, the company of
angels and palm trees above it and the several wall brackets. On the
inside of the W door is carved the gourd plant which sheltered Jonah
before Nineveh, being consumed by the grub which destroyed it. In
the chancel, 13 of the gable lights are filled with thin sheets of
alabaster etched with leaves and fossil forms through which the light
filters, while in the nave all the windows are of stained glass, most of
it small fragments cleverly arranged to form patterns. The font is of
alabaster, its panels carved by Sarah Losh herself. The cover is of

mirror glass decorated with lotus flowers carved by another hand. The portrait in oils of this remarkable woman hangs on the W wall accompanied by the family coat of arms.

DERBYSHIRE

Derbyshire is justly famous for the Peak District which takes up approximately the N half of the county. The eastern strip is largely industrialised and contains most of the large centres of population. The SW is rolling, pastoral countryside. Derby itself, the largest town, was made the seat of a bishopric as recently as 1927. As for building materials, Derbyshire has a variety of limestones and sandstones (including gritstone), with clays for brickmaking in the E. Brick was notably used at Repton Priory in the 15C. Chellaston was the site of one of the great alabaster quarries, which had a marked effect on the county's monuments. Lead was important too, especially around Wirksworth. Some carboniferous limestones when polished formed the 'Derbyshire marbles', of which the Ashford variety, a black material, was used for example in the altarpiece at Chatsworth. The mineral wealth of the county has meant that in prosperous times a number of fairly large-scale churches have been built. Wealth produced, too, Derbyshire's great mansions (Haddon Hall, Chatsworth, Calke, Kedleston, Hardwick, etc.), the chapels of some of which are as notable as the parish churches.

The pre-Conquest period may not be well-represented but what there is at Repton is of the highest importance. The vaulted crypt there was the burial-place of two Mercian kings, Ethelbald and Wiglaf, and also the shrine of their kinsman, St. Wystan. An apparent memorial to King Ethelbald is especially remarkable. For pre-Conquest carvings, Wirksworth and Eyam are the most important sites. Wirksworth has a panel of eight scenes arranged in two rows, carved in c 800. Eyam has a well-preserved churchyard cross, also of c 800. The shaft is truncated, but the cross-head remains. Bakewell has a similar example. Some 11C crosses also survive. The Norman period presents two important but utterly different buildings. Melbourne is built on a cathedral-like scale whilst Steetley at the opposite end of the county represents a perfect small building of nave, chancel and apse. Melbourne's scale derives from its use by the Bishops of Carlisle. Bakewell was originally intended to repeat Melbourne's two W towers. Sandiacre also has extensive Norman work, and significant Norman fabric may be seen at Crich and Brassington.

The Early English period of the 13C saw the building or rebuilding of a number of large-scale cruciform churches, most notably Ashbourne, Wirksworth, Chesterfield and Bakewell. All these except Wirksworth have transept E aisles, a mark of size. Ashbourne retains a brass dedication plate of 1241, and its S chancel doorway is a particularly grand example of 13C work. Doveridge has a 13C chancel of note, and Hartington has 13C work in its chancel, N transept and nave tower arch. The Decorated style is best represented in the chancels of Norbury, Sandiacre and Tideswell. St. Mary's, Chaddesden is substantially Decorated of the mid-14C. It is notable in Derbyshire that Reticulated and flowing tracery continued to be used later in the 14C than was usual elsewhere. The great church at Chesterfield is also largely Decorated, but with varying features. Many of the county's best towers and spires are 14C too: Repton's of c 1340; Ashbourne's (copied in the 19C by G.F. Bodley at All Saints', Cambridge); Ashover's; and Breadsall's. The spire at Chesterfield, 228ft tall, is famous for its freak twisting.

The Perpendicular style is somewhat scarce. The towers of

Tideswell and Youlgreave are among the better examples. Ashbourne's E window dates from c 1395. The other instances of 15C fabric are quite minor. Perpendicular, however, continued in use into the 17C, and there are noteworthy examples at Carsington (1648) and at Foremark (a chapel-like building) as late as 1662. The opposite end of the spectrum in 17C style is shown in the entirely Classical chapel of Chatsworth House, a magnificent example of late 17C decoration and workmanship. On a far more humble scale (but grand for its denomination in the 17C) is Elder Yard Unitarian Chapel, Chesterfield, built in 1694. Its principal façade is quite a substantial composition for a non-Anglican building of its day.

18C and early 19C Classical churches are not spectacular. Among them are Trusley, built of brick in 1713, the Moravian Settlement Chapel at Ockbrook, 1750, Mapleton (whose W tower has a dome and an oversize lantern), and the altogether grander but idiosyncratic Hassop, built in 1816 by Joseph Ireland, and St. John's, Buxton (1811). The grandest of all Derbyshire's Georgian churches, All Saints' in Derby (by James Gibbs, 1723–25), has been the cathedral since 1927 and is therefore outside the scope of this work.

The 19C produced much restoration but little of the quality of neighbouring Staffordshire in new buildings. St. Mary's, Derby by A.W.N. Pugin is one of the very few large-scale works by a major architect. Among other national figures, Sir Gilbert Scott largely rebuilt Edensor in 1867, Benjamin Ferrey designed Scropton (1855–56), and William Butterfield built Bamford (1856–60), giving it a tall, thin spire. Butterfield was perhaps more notable in the county as a restorer. A local architect, H.I. Stevens of Derby, designed many churches, but none of them are remarkable set-pieces. Alsop-in-the-Dale has a neo-Norman W tower from as late as 1882–83 (by F.J. Robinson), 40 years after it was the fashion, but complementing the church's genuine Norman work. In the early 20C, G.F. Bodley remodelled the chancel of Elvaston and added the grand N aisle of Kedleston Church. A little later, P.H. Currey and C.C. Thompson designed St. Mary's, Buxton (1914–15) in the Arts and Crafts manner, and restored St. Chad's, Wilne after a fire (1917–23). J. Harold Gibbons designed the brick-built St. Cyprian's, Frecheville (1953), with some attractive exterior detailing.

Turning to fittings, Derbyshire possesses a number of interesting decorated Norman fonts. Among the better examples are those at Ashover (made of lead and featuring the Apostles under arcading) and Youlgreave, which has a rare side stoup. There are some medieval screens such as the rare and unusual 14C Geometrical stone screen at Ilkeston and the late 15C and early 16C wooden screens at Chesterfield. An early 14C wooden screen stands under the tower at Kirk Langley. At Fenny Bentley and at Ashover screens of the early 16C use the 14C ogee style. A Rood loft (without a screen) survives in All Saints', Wingerworth. Morley has some 14C tiles in its N chapel. Of fonts later than Norman, Ashbourne has a good 13C example, decorated with trefoil arches, and Bakewell has a 14C octagonal font with figures under ogee arches. Medieval wall paintings are best represented by the large-scale 15C survivals in Haddon Hall's chapel, 14C remains at Melbourne and some late 13C work at All Saints', Dale Abbey. Medieval stained glass is best seen at Norbury where the chancel windows are filled with 14C glass. Haddon Hall has three windows with good figures and an inscription which dates them to 1427. Ashbourne has some heraldic glass of the 1390s in the tracery of its E window, and 13C and 15C fragments in its N transept windows. Dalbury has a St. Michael which could be 12C, and Cubley and Egginton have 14C glass, the latter including some figures.

As in Staffordshire it is with medieval alabaster monuments that Derbyshire comes alive. This is not surprising since the county possessed the most famous of the alabaster quarries at Chellaston. Bakewell has the earliest alabaster memorial (1385), to Sir Godfrey Foljambe and his wife. It is unusual for its date in comprising two frontal half-figures under a canopy, with shields above. The finest alabaster tombs are late 15C ones at Norbury (see entry). For collections of medieval and 16C alabaster and stone monuments, Ashbourne is difficult to surpass for a parish church. The monuments there are of the Cockaynes (14C–16C) and the Bradburnes (15C and 16C). Further good examples can be seen at Youlgreave (an alabaster effigy to another Cockayne, Thomas (died 1488) and an alabaster panel to Robert Gylbert (died 1492)); Ashover (alabaster effigies of Thomas Babington (died 1518) and his wife, with numerous weepers, etc. under ogee arches on the sides of the tomb-chest); Kedleston (15C and 16C Curzons); Tideswell (Vernon and Manners tombs, 15C and 16C); and Morley (14C and 15C Stathums, plus an effigy of Katherine Babington, died 1543). A monument at Fenny Bentley to Thomas and Agnes Beresford (died 1467 and 1473), in the form of two shrouded figures, is in fact Elizabethan; no fewer than 21 children on the sides of the chest are shown shrouded too. A shrouded figure appears as late as 1710 on a brass at Beeley. The best examples of medieval brasses can be seen at Hathersage (especially the one of Robert Eyre, died 1459), Ashover, Norbury, Tideswell (including Robert Pursglove, bishop and prior, died 1579) and Wirksworth.

Elizabethan and 17C monuments combined the medieval tradition of tomb-chests and recumbent effigies with Classical dress and also introduced new forms. At Wirksworth a fully Classical monument (to Anthony Lowe, died 1555) slightly predates Queen Elizabeth. The standard monument of figures facing each other across a prayer-desk may be represented by Francis Fitzherbert (died 1619) and his two wives at Tissington and by William Davenport (died 1640) and his wife at Doveridge. A group of monuments of the period at their best can be seen at Chesterfield (mainly to the Foljambe family), with a further good group at Bakewell.

A huge, magnificent Classical wall monument at Edensor commemorates the first Earl of Devonshire (died 1625) and his brother, Henry Cavendish (died 1616). At Elvaston there are Stanhope monuments from the 17C to the 19C. The one of the third Earl of Harrington (died 1829) is a rare work in England by Antonio Canova. Other Cavendish monuments exist at Bolsover (17C and 18C, including one of the second Duke of Newcastle designed by James Gibbs and sculpted by Francis Bird, 1727). The church at Kedleston has one of the richest collections of monuments with work by Robert Adam, Peter Scheemakers and J.M. Rysbrack, and continuing into the 20C with Sir Bertram Mackennal's memorial to the Marquess Curzon of Kedleston (died 1925). Ashbourne also possesses a group of 18C monuments and chief among these is the one to Penelope Boothby (died 1791) by Thomas Banks. Finally, it must be remembered that Derby Cathedral is very important for 18C memorials.

Turning to post-Reformation furnishings, Haddon Hall and Hardwick Hall have fittings from the early 17C. Chesterfield has a very good Jacobean pulpit. Good 17C fittings appear too in the

Willoughby chapel at Wilne (after 1622), at St. Edmund's, Castleton and in All Saints', Dale Abbey. The church at Foremark has furnishings of 1662, still in a Jacobean style. The late 17C decoration and fittings at Chatsworth House's chapel are of the highest standard and of national importance. The tiny church at Trusley has a complete set of 18C fittings, including a fine three-decker pulpit. At Hartington there are 18C painted panels of the Patriarchs of Israel. St. Mary's at Chesterfield has a fine 18C candelabrum and St. Werburgh's, Derby retains an early 18C reredos of note.

St. Mary's, Chesterfield has many 19C and 20C furnishings of merit, including reredoses by J. Harold Gibbons and work by Temple Moore. Norman Shaw designed various items for the church at Great Longstone. William Butterfield provided fittings for churches at Monyash, Hathersage and Ault Hucknall. Items designed by G.G. Scott, Jr may be seen at Bakewell. St. John's, Buxton has some opulent Victorian furnishings. An exceptional lectern of 1903 exists at All Saints', Mackworth. For collections of 19C and 20C stained glass, Ashbourne and Chesterfield are outstanding. The artists at Chesterfield include Heaton, Butler & Bayne, William Warrington and Sir Ninian Comper. At Ashbourne there is work by C.E. Kempe, Burlison & Grylls, Christopher Whall, Hardman & Co., William Warrington and the Bromsgrove Guild. Morris & Co. glass can be seen at Youlgreave, Wirksworth, Darley Dale (very early) and Ashford-in-the-Water. Melbourne Church has work by Clayton & Bell, Powell's and Henry Holiday. Tideswell has glass by Heaton, Butler & Bayne, and Hardman & Powell.

The historical associations of Derbyshire's churches must begin with Repton, as did the architectural account. St. Wystan's Church was a central place in the secular and religious history of Mercia from the 7C to the 9C. Its dedication, a very rare one, commemorates the Mercian prince whose death in c 850 was viewed as a martyrdom. St. Werburgh (Blackwell, Derby and Spondon), St. Alkmund (Derby and Duffield) and St. Chad (Longford and Wilne) are other Old English saints represented in Derbyshire. From more recent centuries, George Fox, founder of the Society of Friends, was tried at Derby in 1650. There too, in what is now the cathedral, 'Bess of Hardwick' (Elizabeth, Countess of Shrewsbury, died 1608) is buried and the Young Pretender of 1745 (Prince Charles Edward Stuart) is remembered, for his campaign from Scotland reached as far S as Derby. The great sculptor, Sir Francis Chantrey, was born at Norton on the Yorkshire border and was buried there in 1841; Thomas Hobbes (died 1679), the author of 'Leviathan', is buried at Ault Hucknall; Dr Samuel Johnson, the great 18C writer, was married in St. Werburgh's, Derby in 1735; the inventor of cotton-spinning machinery, Sir Richard Arkwright (died 1792) lies at St. Mary's, Cromford; and George Stephenson, famous railway pioneer, was buried at Holy Trinity, Chesterfield in 1848. Hathersage has links with Charlotte Brontë, who used the name of Eyre from the church's tombs for her novel. In the 20C, Kedleston was the seat of the Marquess Curzon, the greatest of the Viceroys of India and a leading member of numerous Governments down to his death in 1925.

Ashbourne, *St. Oswald.* St. Oswald's is a large and architecturally complex building of more than regional importance. It is cruciform and has aisled transepts and a fine series of monuments. George Eliot once described it as 'the finest mere parish church in the kingdom'. Archaeology has revealed traces of pre-Conquest and Norman churches on the site. The dominant feature of the church is the spire rising to a height of 212ft. It was added c 1330, damaged in a gale in 1698, partially demolished and rebuilt in 1783. It has numerous canopied windows to reduce weight and wind resistance. The oldest part of the church is the chancel built by 1241 in the Early English style. There are pairs of tall lancet windows to N and S, but the large E window is Perpendicular, c 1395, and the W bays have Decorated windows. The transepts, nave and S nave aisle also reveal work from all three Gothic periods. The main churchyard gate posts are unusual in that each pier is topped by four skulls surmounted by an obelisk. These date from c 1700.

The chancel was dedicated in 1241 by Hugh de Patishull, Bishop of Coventry. Its four bays are of greater length than the four-bay nave. Chancel and nave have a combined length of 176ft. The chancel roof was painted in 1963 to the designs of S.E. Dykes Bower. The nave is tall and spacious and is divided from the S aisle by four late 13C arches. There are seven triple-light Perpendicular clerestory windows on each side. There is no N aisle. The transepts date from c 1280 and both have E aisles. The N transept is also partitioned by a medieval wooden screen, the E section being filled with the tombs of the Cockayne, Bradburne and Boothby families. The S transept is divided by its arcade, the E section serving as a small Lady chapel, also containing the organ and vestry. The S wall of the transept is pierced by two large windows, that in the Lady chapel being Perpendicular and the other Decorated. The four massive tower piers were until comparatively recently hollow. In an attempt to strengthen the tower, three of the piers were filled with concrete in 1912–13 and the SE pier containing stairs was filled in during the restoration of 1931–32.

The nave capitals and vaulting shafts possess some fine late 13C stiff-leaf capitals and heads. The SE crossing pier capital depicts a 'Green Man' and a head of King Edward I. The middle capital in the S arcade depicts Blanche, wife of John of Gaunt. The font at the W end of the S aisle is early 13C and has decoration of trefoil arches interspersed with fleur-de-lis. The pulpit is made entirely of various Derbyshire stones with inlays of Blue John. In the SW tower pier the door is possibly a pre-Conquest survival; it has seven Norman metal serpent hinges, representing the seven deadly sins. On the S wall of the Lady chapel the oldest brass inscription in Britain records the dedication of the church on 24th April 1241. It translates: 'In the year one thousand two hundred and forty one from the Incarnation of Our Lord on the eighth (day) before the Kalends of May this church was dedicated and this Altar consecrated in honour of St. Oswald, King and Martyr, by the Venerable Father, the Lord Hugo de Patishull, Bishop of Coventry'. The organ was built in 1857 by Hill & Beard and contains some 2400 pipes. The low wooden chancel screen was designed by Sir Gilbert Scott in 1876 as a memorial to Canon Errington, Vicar 1850–72. On it there are four angels, carved by Bridgeman's of Lichfield, representing praise, prayer, baptism and holy communion. The brass chancel gates are testimony to one of Ashbourne's former industries, that of brassmithing. The tiled floor by Campbell of Stoke reproduces many of the patterns of the medieval tiles found in the church during the 19C. The reredos was designed in 1950 by Leslie Moore and the tempera panels were painted by Donald Towner. The landscape scenes are views of neighbouring Dovedale.

Amongst the many monuments in the chancel, two on the N wall are worthy of mention. The first is the tomb of Robert de Kniveton (died 1471) set under a large ogee arch. The other is a tablet by Sir Richard Westmacott to George Errington (died 1795). The N transept contains no fewer than 13 monuments from the 14C to the 19C and all but one of them are crowded into what was the Boothby chapel (the E aisle), which is closed off by two 16C parclose screens. The monument outside the Boothby chapel, set against the N wall of the transept, is to Sir Thomas Cockayne (died 1592) and his family. It depicts the life-size figures of Thomas and his wife Dorothy Ferrers, kneeling facing each other across a prayer-desk. Below them are their three sons and seven daughters. Sir Thomas was one of the founders of the Queen Elizabeth Grammar School in Ashbourne. Inside the Boothby chapel, the first tomb is that of Francis Cockayne (died 1538). It is a Purbeck marble altar tomb with a fine brass under a canopy. Next to this in the NE corner is the altar tomb of Sir Thomas Cockayne (died 1537) and his wife Barbara Fitzherbert, with their figures and an inscription incised into the alabaster slab. Around the base of the tomb are shields and coats of arms of various related families. Sir Thomas was present at the Field of the Cloth of Gold in 1520. Next to this is the alabaster tomb of Sir John Cockayne (died 1447) and his first wife, Joan Dabridgecourt. Their recumbent effigies, he in plate armour, she in her finest clothes, lay on top of a tomb-chest which has standing angels holding shields interspersed with panels of tracery. This monument has been ascribed to the Chellaston alabaster masters, Robert Sutton and Thomas Prentys. The final Cockayne tomb is that of Sir John Cockayne (died 1372) and his son Edmund, killed at the Battle of Shrewsbury in 1403. The effigies are of Caen stone and the tomb-chest has quatrefoil panels. The Cockayne monuments represent every generation from 1372 to 1592 with one exception.

To the right as you enter the Boothby chapel is the very large tomb to Sir Humphrey Bradburne (died 1581) and his wife Elizabeth Turville. Their recumbent effigies lay on top of a richly ornamented tomb-chest which still bears traces of colour. Their 15 children, nine sons and six daughters, are depicted around the base. The tomb was the work of Richard and Gabriel Royley of Burton-upon-Trent. Next to this is the tomb of John Bradburne (died 1548) and his wife Anne Vernon. This is again of alabaster with recumbent effigies. Finally come the Boothby tombs and most important of all is the Carrara marble monument of 1793 to Penelope Boothby (died 1791 aged almost six). This is of international renown and the masterpiece of Thomas Banks. Penelope Boothby was painted at the age of three by Sir Joshua Reynolds as 'Simplicity'. At the age of nearly six she could speak words in four languages, English, French, Latin and Italian, hence the inscription being in those four languages. Her recumbent figure is a virtuoso piece of carving; the various textures of flesh and different fabrics seem real. Near her monument in the SE corner of the chapel are crowded together five more Boothby monuments, 1662–1838, all of which pale in comparison with Penelope's monument. The N transept also contains various fragments of carving from pre-Conquest times, as well as medieval floor tiles and a painted medieval panel depicting on one side St. Michael and on the other the image of Pity.

The church's other great treasure is its stained glass, dating from the 14C to the 20C. Most of the medieval glass is in the N transept, in the northernmost lancets of the W wall. There are five medallions of c 1340, depicting Herod sending soldiers, the Boy Jesus in the Temple, the Adoration of the Magi, the Three Wise Men and the Angels appearing to the Shepherds. The Boothby chapel N window contains an image of the Crucifixion, Christ in Benediction and the heads of St. Christopher and St. Modwena, all c 1400. The other medieval glass comprises the 19 coats of arms of c 1395 in the chancel E window tracery. The rest of the window is by C.E. Kempe, 1896, depicting Christ as the King of Kings, surrounded by saints. Other windows by Kempe are the nave W window, 1902, depicting the Tree of Jesse and the nave NE window, 1902, which depicts St. Oswald and St. Andrew. The other nave window is by Percy Bacon, 1910, and shows St. Columba holding a model of Iona and St. Chad one of Lichfield Cathedral. The W window of the S aisle is by Burlison and Grylls, 1872, with images of Christ and the Disciples, John the Baptist and the Nativity. Another window in the S aisle has the most important 20C stained glass in the church. The Turnbull window was designed in 1904 by Christopher Whall and inserted in 1905. The window depicts St. Cecilia asleep at the organ, and on either side of her are St. Barbara with the face of Monica Turnbull and St. Dorothea with the face of Dorothea Turnbull. In the S transept there is glass by John Hardman Powell, 1874, in memory of Canon Errington. The window represents the Te Deum. Some of the patterned glass at the top is medieval. Other Hardman & Co. glass is in the N transept: the Hartshorne windows, 1877, depicting the Benedictus, an agricultural window and the Holland memorial window of 1860. The other two lancets in the W wall of the N transept are by William Warrington, 1857. The chancel lancets are also by Warrington and date from c 1861. They caused a famous outburst from John Ruskin when visiting the church in 1875. In a letter to the Vicar he said of them that they were 'the worst piece of base Birmingham manufacture'. He went further in referring to the Life of David windows in the S wall as something '...which would disgrace a penny child's book of Jack the Giant Killer'. Finally, in the clerestory of the W wall of the S transept is glass by the Bromsgrove Guild, 1933, depicting the Good Shepherd.

St. Oswald's has a number of historical associations. In 1288 King Edward I held an inquisition in the church, out of which came the laws for lead mining. King Charles I visited the church on the way from the Battle of Naseby (1645). Handel and Rousseau were visitors when staying at nearby Calwich Abbey. Samuel Johnson was regularly here. Bonnie Prince Charlie came on his way S to Derby during the rebellion of 1745. The church has a long tradition of music and choirs. There have been only four organists in 130 years and a long line of all-male choirs.

Chatsworth House, *Chapel.* The chapel is the westernmost room of the S block of Chatsworth House. It rises through two floors and represents a perfect example of the taste of the late 17C. It was built in 1688–99 and has remained unaltered since that time.

The room is lit by three windows on the S side. These, although internally appearing on the first floor, are externally part of the same raised ground-floor façade. The height of the chapel rising through two floors is explained by the slope of the ground and the use of a piano nobile. The S front was part of William Talman's work at Chatsworth. At the E end of the chapel there is a gallery supported on two marble columns with elaborate Ionic capitals. The panelling rises to a cornice at first-floor level and consists of cedar panels which give off a distinctive smell. Attached to these are limewood carvings of garlands of foliage and fruit, the work of the London carvers Thomas Young, Joel Lobb, William Davis and a young local assistant, Samuel Watson. The massive altarpiece in the apse at the W end was designed by C.G. Cibber. He also carved the figures of Faith and Justice on either side of the lower pediment. The rest of the altarpiece was executed by Samuel Watson. The two black Ionic pillars which support the pediment and the two pillars supporting the gallery were all carved from a single block of local Ashford marble. Above the lower pediment is a painting by Antonio Verrio of the Incredulity of St. Thomas, 1693. The painted walls above the cedar panels are by Louis Laguerre and represent Christ healing the sick. The ceiling oval depicts the Ascension and was painted by Laguerre and Ricard. The doorway in the gallery has a broken pediment with a centrally placed urn from which hang garlands of flowers, and on either side on the pediment there are putti, the left-hand one with a violin and the right-hand one singing. The two large brass candlesticks which flank the altar were bought in London in 1691 for £60. The 21 high-backed chairs are contemporary with the chapel. Hanging from the gallery is the Garter standard of the 10th Duke of Devonshire (died 1950), which was formerly in St. George's Chapel, Windsor.

Chesterfield, St. Mary and All Saints. The church is the largest parish church in the county, 173ft by 110ft, and is famous for its twisted spire. There is also a wealth of fittings, monuments and stained glass from the medieval period to the present. The exterior is dominated by the three-stage central tower, surmounted by the spire, which date from the middle of the 14C. The spire is 228ft high and leans 8ft 7⁵/₈ins S and 3ft 9³/₈ins to the W. Quite how the famous twist occurred is a matter of conjecture. It is widely believed that one of the main supports, made from comparatively green timber, split due to its being rapidly dried out by the sun, and thus caused the twisting. The twisted appearance of the spire is further emphasised by the fact that the lead plate casing has been laid in herringbone fashion.

The church reveals a basically Decorated appearance but with Perpendicular E windows and clerestory windows in the nave and S transept. The N transept was rebuilt in 1769 and restored with the addition of a vestry in 1963 after a fire in 1961. The E end is unusual in being as wide as the nave and aisles with the addition of a polygonal chapel, the Lesser Lady chapel. In 1509–49 the W front was rebuilt. The church was thoroughly restored in 1843 by Gilbert Scott. Internally the oldest features are the four massive Early English tower arches, which date from the dedication of 1234. The 14C nave and aisles are of six bays; the nave pillars are quatrefoil in shape, with fillets on the shafts and hollows in the diagonals. These support moulded capitals and arches.

The E end is two bays in length, with octagonal piers supporting moulded capitals and arches. The W end has a gallery erected in 1843 as part of Scott's restoration. In 1986 this was extended to fill the first bay, the screen being glazed and acting as an inner entrance porch. At the E end of the S aisle there is a large crocketed ogee recess beneath which rests the effigy of a priest from the early 14C. Adjacent to this is the altar of St. Peter's chapel, which partially blocks off the end of the S aisle. The ornate reredos was designed by J. Harold Gibbons as a memorial to two servers killed in the Second

World War. In the N aisle St. Oswald's chapel has an altar built in 1939 which has four riddel posts surmounted by angels.

Against the NW tower pier there is a very finely carved wooden Jacobean pulpit of c 1620. This has been attributed to the master woodcarvers then employed at nearby Haddon Hall. The Rood beam above was designed by Temple Moore in 1915 and the figures were carved by a Belgian refugee. The central nave altar in the tower space was installed in 1944 and around each side are curved altar rails. In the N transept which bore the brunt of the 1961 fire, the present organ (formerly in Glasgow) replaced the 1756 Snetzler organ which was totally destroyed. In the S transept there is the very worn pre-Conquest or early Norman circular font. The S transept also has a very fine medieval wooden screen dating from c 1500 which separates it from the Lesser Lady chapel and the Lady chapel. The polygonal Lesser Lady chapel has an Elizabethan altar and modern statues in the niches. Above it is a copy of the Madonna and Child by Bellini. The Lady chapel proper is two bays deep, as are the chancel and St. Katherine's chapel on the N. The width and size of the E end is unusual for a parish church. The Lady chapel altar made of alabaster was designed by J. Harold Gibbons in 1936.

The outstanding feature of the Lady chapel, however, is the magnificent collection of Foljambe family tombs behind the altar. The first on the left is of Henry Foljambe (died 1510) and his wife Benedicta. This tomb-chest with a marble top and inlaid brasses was made by Harpur & Moorecock at Burton-on-Trent for £10. Around the sides of the chest are figures under arches. On top of this chest there is an alabaster kneeling figure, assumed to be Sir Thomas Foljambe who died in 1604 at the age of 13. The outsize head is a later addition from elsewhere. On the floor to the right is the brass to Sir Godfrey Foljambe (died 1529) and his wife Katherine. In the centre is the tomb-chest of Sir Godfrey Foljambe (died 1585) and his wife Troth. There is a very worn incised alabaster floor slab to George Foljambe (died 1588). Against the S wall the elaborate tomb of Godfrey Foljambe (died 1594) and his wife bears the date 1592, which means that it was installed two years before his death. The effigies lie on top of a sarcophagus, above which is an elaborate pediment supported by Corinthian columns with two figures in niches. Against the E wall there are memorials to James Foljambe (died 1588) and another unnamed family member who died in 1559. The memorial depicts a body wrapped in a shroud, with symbols of death and childhood.

In front of the Lady chapel altar there is a brass to Geoffrey Hare Clayton, Vicar 1924–34. He became Bishop of Johannesburg and finally Archbishop of Capetown in 1948–57. Both the Lady chapel and St. Katherine's chapel have brass candelabra dating from 1760. The high altar with its four riddel posts surmounted by gilded angels has a reredos designed by Temple Moore in 1898. It was coloured by J. Harold Gibbons in 1936. The silver sanctuary lamp is Venetian and dates from c 1650. St. Katherine's chapel has a 14C wooden Rood screen. Next to this the small Holy Cross chapel has a carved reredos with the central panel of the Crucifixion coming from Oberammergau. The side panels and colouring were undertaken by Leslie Temple Moore in 1934. The church also possesses a late 15C or early 16C processional cross.

The stained glass is all 19C and 20C. The W window by Heaton, Butler & Bayne (1890) shows scenes from the life of Joshua. The second three-light window from the W end of the S aisle was inserted in 1985–86 to commemorate the 750th anniversary of the church in 1984. It is by Graham Pentelow and depicts scenes of life and industry in Chesterfield during the past. The window above St. Peter's altar is by Sir Ninian Comper (1943) and depicts Jesus, St. Paul and St. Andrew. Also by Comper is the Holy Cross chapel E window of the Virgin and Child (1941). The N aisle has one stained glass window above St. Oswald's chapel altar, by Christopher Webb (1960), which depicts St. Patrick, St. Columba, St. Aidan, St. Wilfrid, St. Oswald and St. Hilda. Also by Christopher Webb are the E window above the high altar depicting the Apostles' Creed, 1947, the Lady chapel E window of the Nativity, 1946, and St. Katherine's chapel N window, 1957, depicting the Virgin and Child with angels. The E window of St. Katherine's chapel is by William Warrington (1868). Warrington was also responsible for the Lady chapel S window (1844). In the S transept the S window based on Raphael's Transfiguration is by John Hardman & Co. (1875).

One historical event of note here was the attack by the Lancastrians in 1422 on the Yorkists attending Mass led by some members of the Foljambe family.

Derby

St. Mary, Bridge Gate. The large Perpendicular-style church with a tall W tower was designed by A.W.N. Pugin and consecrated in 1839. There is a five-bay nave and polygonal apse. On the N side there is a large Lady chapel added by Pugin's son, E.W. Pugin. Much of the stained glass is by John Hardman. The church finds itself cut off from the city centre by the inner ring road which is very close to the W front. The church is currently, 1987, undergoing extensive restoration.

St. Mary's Chapel, Bridge Gate. The small brick and stone bridge chapel was built in the 13C and enlarged c 1400. It was restored in 1930. It is now hemmed in by a graceful 18C bridge on the N side and the large modern inner ring road and bridge to the S. The chapel is used by a number of denominations; currently, June 1987, permission to alter the interior is being sought.

Foremark, St. Saviour. Set on a hill in a seemingly isolated position, St. Saviour's was the estate church for Foremark Hall (some distance down the hill and screened by trees). The church's interest lies in the fact that with the exception of the five-light stained glass E window the church is little altered from when it was built in 1662.

The exterior reveals a low, battlemented W tower and a battlemented nave, all constructed of ashlar in a Perpendicular style. The one jarring note is the redbrick vestry on the W side of the tower, totally out of sympathy with the rest of the building. The nave has two five-light Perpendicular windows equally spaced along each wall, separated by a centrally placed buttress. Entrance is gained through the W door in the tower. The aisleless nave is whitewashed and has a rough-hewn timber roof with seven large tiebeams. The side windows are clear, flooding the church with light. There is also a modern skylight in the first bay of the nave.

The nave has box-pews on each side, 14 on the N and 13 on the S. These are contemporary, as is the three-decker pulpit and tester.

The top stage of the pulpit is polygonal, with each panel featuring a pedimented arch, the same motif which appears on the Rood screen. The screen has a large glazed pediment centrally placed. The glazing depicts the Holy Dove with an angel on each side. Flanking the large gates there are two arches on each side, all partially glazed, above which there are panels with dragons' heads. On top of the screen there are obelisks. The 18C communion rail of iron is an early example of the work of Robert Bakewell of Derby, who was also responsible for the magnificent double wrought-iron gates, surmounted by the Burdett family crest, at the E end of the churchyard. The E window depicts Christ and the Evangelists and was installed in 1891. Flanking it are the usual inscribed wooden panels. At the W end on the S side is the simple font with wooden cover. On the walls there are the royal arms and four Burdett family hatchments. On the N wall of the sanctuary there is a fine coloured memorial tablet to Col. Sir Francis Burdett (died 1892). There are also Burdett family memorials in the floor of the nave. At the W end the brass candelabra came from Westminster Abbey.

Haddon Hall, *Chapel.* The battlemented chapel at Haddon Hall is situated on the S side of the courtyard and possesses a good series of wall paintings, medieval glass and other fittings. Entrance is gained through a covered way by the clock tower. The nave is of two bays with a very narrow N aisle and a wide S aisle. There are two deeply splayed late 12C lancet windows in the S wall and one in the aisle's E wall, all of which are clear-glazed. The chapel has simple raftered roofs which date from 1624. Running along the wall is a stone bench. The S arcade has a circular pier and double-chamfered arches. On the N side there is an octagonal pier. A small wooden stair leads to a wooden balcony. The chancel is lit by large three-light N and S windows and a five-light E window. The clerestory is 15C.

Against the S arcade there is a simple round Norman font with a Jacobean wooden cover. On the N side stands a three-decker pulpit of 1724. The screen of the same date has balusters on each side which form the top part of the family box-pew. The altar rails consist of similar balusters. The large Nottingham alabaster reredos with nine coloured panels representing the Easter story was installed in the 20C. In front of the screen against the S arcade is a white marble tomb with the recumbent effigy of a boy. It is to Robert Charles John Manners, Lord Haddon (died 1894) and was designed by his mother, Violet, Duchess of Rutland.

The chapel has much medieval wall painting which was restored earlier this century by Professor E.W. Tristram. On the S wall of the nave there is a large St. Christopher with the boy Christ on his shoulder, wading across a river stocked with fish. On the banks are smaller figures, plants and trees. On the W wall three skeletons are depicted, which would have formed part of a scene of the Quick and the Dead. In the chancel, the N wall has two scenes from the life of St. Nicholas and the S wall scenes from the life of St. Anne. The walls also bear patches of a floral pattern. The stained glass is all medieval. The E window is dated 1427 in an inscription in the glass. The three inner lights have Christ on the Cross, the Virgin Mary and St. John. In the tracery there are a number of figures and the Annunciation. The N window of the chancel has St. Michael, St. Anne and the Virgin Mary, and St. George. In the S window there are fragments of figures of the Apostles.

Hardwick Hall, *Chapel.* The chapel is on the first floor and, apart from the kitchens, is the last room seen on the tour of the house. It originally rose through two floors but was altered in the 18C. The present chapel is fairly small, with a dividing oak screen between the chapel and the landing. There are simple oak pews and a 17C pulpit. On the side walls there are painted hangings of the Acts of the Apostles and a Mortlake tapestry of the Supper at Emmaus.

Hassop, *All Saints.* The church is set on a slope opposite the entrance to Hassop Hall and was built in 1816–18. It was the work of Joseph Ireland and his assistant J.J. Scoles, at a cost of £2448 6s 7d. The plan is basically a rectangular box in the form of a temple. The W front is that of an Etruscan temple with four pillars supporting a simple entablature and a very deep plain pediment. The N and S sides are pierced by Grecian-style windows. The interior has a coved and coffered ceiling in blue and white, with pink and white walls. There is a gallery at the W end. At the E end the altar of inlaid marble came from Naples and the painting above, depicting the Crucifixion with the Virgin and St. John, is attributed to Lodovico Carracci.

Kedleston, *All Saints.* This cruciform church with its central tower has work from the Norman period onwards. It is chiefly 13C. The N aisle was added by G.F. Bodley in 1907–13. The fittings and monuments are particularly good.

The church sits partially hidden by trees and behind one of the flanking blocks of Kedleston Hall, a great Georgian mansion and the masterpiece of Robert Adam. The central tower has a Y-traceried louvred window in each face. The top stage is Perpendicular, battlemented and with pinnacles at the corners. On the S, E and N faces there are the original rooflines. The nave has a three-light W window with flowing tracery and a Norman S doorway with beakheads and zigzag decoration. The tympanum has a much-worn carving of a figure on a horse. The E end has 17C Classical urns and a sundial surmounted by a pediment which has a skull on top. The chancel S doorway and the main transept windows of three stepped lancets speak of the 13C church. The chancel has one original lancet in the S wall, all the other windows being later.

Within, there is no S aisle. Bodley's N aisle is separated from the nave by a three-bay arcade and by three wrought-iron screens by P. Krall. The soffits of the three arches have flower heads set in squares. Contemporary with the main fabric is the 13C piscina in the S wall of the chancel. At the W end of the nave there is an ornate font of c 1700 on a column with four leaves acting as a base. The circular tub has a wooden cover which is surmounted by an eagle on a ball. There are hatchments over the S door and above the nave tower arch. The floor is of highly polished marble in black and white squares. In the chancel, the altar has large silver candlesticks, a cross and hanging lamps. Nearby there are family pews dating from c 1700. The communion rails also date from this period.

The church is rich in monuments. In the N aisle stands the tomb of the Marquess Curzon of Kedleston (died 1925), Viceroy of India and Foreign Secretary, and his first wife (died 1906). The entire N aisle was built in her memory. The large white marble tomb-chest has Ionic capitals at the corners, recumbent effigies and, looking down on them from behind, two female figures. It was carved by Sir Bertram Mackennal. Various banners hang in this aisle. Against the W wall of the N transept is a large marble monument by Peter

Scheemakers, 1737, to Sir Nathaniel Curzon, Bt. (died 1718) and his wife Dame Sarah Curzon (died 1727). It consists of life-size male and female figures in Classical costume on either side of an urn. Behind them is a black marble obelisk surmounted by a crest. Against the E wall there is a large monument to Sir Nathaniel Curzon (died 1758), erected in 1765. It was designed by Robert Adam and executed by J.M. Rysbrack. It consists of a sarcophagus with an inscription flanked by shields. Above this are figures, one clasping a Bible, of Sir Nathaniel and his wife and two sons, all set against a pyramid-shaped tablet. In the S wall of the chancel in a recess is the effigy of Sir John Curzon (died 1406). On the N wall are a number of monuments, one of which, pedimented with Corinthian columns, obelisks and a crest above, is to the fourth Baron Scarsdale (died 1916). In the S transept is a large alabaster tomb-chest to Sir John Curzon (died c 1450) and his wife Joan. He is depicted in full armour, feet resting on a dog, his head resting on a helmet with an eagle on its top. On the N side of the chest are carvings of seven boys and ten girls. The S side has five figures under arches. Against the W wall is a foliate cross slab, possibly that of Thomas de Curzon (died 1245). It was found in the nave during alterations in 1884. The large monument to Sir John Curzon (died 1727) consists of two putti, one weeping and the other standing and playing a horn. There is a central pyramid-shaped tablet with a circular portrait medallion and a border of 18 putti. Against the E wall is a very large painted wall monument to Sir John Curzon (died 1686) and his wife Patience Crew (died 1642). At the bottom there is an inscription with a central garland of fruit and a skull and crossbones below. Two putti heads support a panel with portrait busts of four boys and three girls. These are beneath the main demi-figures of John and Patience, which are flanked by two angels with trumpets, holding back drapes. Three Corinthian columns support an entablature which carries a large central crest and two figures.

In the N aisle there are four windows by F.C. Eden. In the chancel the E window of three lights depicts the Crucifixion. The N and S windows are filled with heraldic glass.

Melbourne, *St. Michael with St. Mary.* Melbourne is the most important Norman church in Derbyshire as well as being one of the finest Norman churches in England. It has a number of exceptional features for a parish church. The reason for a church of this size and importance here was that the manor was granted by King Henry I to the Bishops of Carlisle on the founding of that See in 1133. Carlisle was increasingly unsafe due to repeated attacks by the Scots. The bishop therefore moved from Carlisle to Melbourne and set about building a church more worthy of a bishop. A further royal charter of 1229 from King Henry III endorsed the bishop's right to hold the duties of the cathedral at Melbourne. The church therefore would have been rebuilt between 1133 and 1229. There was a further large rebuilding of the E end in the late 16C and early 17C and a programme of restoration in 1862 by Sir Gilbert Scott.

The exterior is basically Norman, with some later alterations. The building is dominated by its tall central tower of two stages. The top stage with battlements and single louvred window in each face was added in 1602. Beneath this the Norman fabric shows the original rooflines and blocked clerestory and triforum windows. There are also the remains of blank arcading which ran round the double-height chancel. Originally, the E end had three apses. The footings and blocked arches in the walls of the transepts as well as the rebuilt E end with the inserted Perpendicular windows are evidence of this. The rebuilding took place during the 17C. At the W end of the nave there are two further rare features of note. There are twin low W towers, the plain parapets of which were added in 1954, replacing Scott's low pyramidal roofs. These towers internally form part of the one-bay-deep triple narthex. The twin towers and the narthex are very rare, at least for an English parish church. The W front has a doorway with five orders of decoration (much renewed), and a Perpendicular window above. The N transept has in its E wall two triple-light Perpendicular windows. The exterior as a whole is somewhat disfigured by the blue metal drainpipes.

Internally, the narthex has very coarse stone vaults. The five-bay nave consists of four pairs of large drum pillars some 4ft in diameter and 15ft tall, whose bases have four angled spur projections. Those of the most easterly N pillar are supposed to represent the symbolic crushing of the Devil. The nave arches have chevron patterns and are supported on elaborately carved capitals. The clerestory on the N side is the original design and unique for a parish church. It consists of triple-arched openings with a wall passage behind, each with two columns and a taller central arch, which corresponds with the round-headed window in the outer wall. The S side was rebuilt in the Early English style and has pairs of pointed arches with two pointed windows behind. The four tower arches are roll-moulded, with pairs of half-columns as responds. Above this on each side is a triple-arched opening and higher still two further tiers of triple arches. Originally those in the E face would have opened into the chancel. Within the tower space there is the metal cage which guides the bell ropes. The chancel tower arch has some finely carved capitals depicting animals and naturalistic details. There is a squint from the N transept to the altar. The transept, which now serves as the Lady chapel, has a triple-light Perpendicular window inserted in the Norman arch which once led into an apse. The chancel is of two bays and originally had an upper level with blind arcading running between the two levels of windows on the outside. The E end reveals evidence of the former apse, although it is now squared off and possesses a five-light Perpendicular window.

At the W end in front of the middle bay of the narthex there is the font dating from the late 12C or early 13C, a plain bowl on four columns. On the NW tower pier the remains of a 14C wall painting depict a large devil at the top and, beneath him, two women with a smaller devil on each of their backs. Opposite this, on the SW tower pier, traces were found of a Crucifixion. Against this pier used to stand the Victorian pulpit, c 1870, raised on four marble columns with heads of saints in roundels on each face. It was removed from the church in 1988. Opposite its former position is a brass eagle lectern given in 1891. The choirstalls and nave and aisle pews date from the Victorian restoration, as does the nave roof. The S transept is taken up by the organ and vestry. The organ was placed here in 1892 and rebuilt in 1957. The Rood in the central arch of the nave tower arch was inserted in 1937. The Lady chapel altar was installed in 1911 and the main altar in 1891. In the chancel there are two painted hatchments, to the first Viscount Melbourne (1748–1828) and the third Viscount (1782–1853).

In the vestry in the S wall there is the badly damaged recumbent effigy of a knight dating from the early 13C. At the W end of the same wall is an incised tomb-slab with a foliate cross, also ascribed to the

13C. There are a number of marble slabs in the vestry to the Hardie or Hardinge family. In the N transept there is a series of Gothick marble tablets to the Cantrell family, 1836–56. In the S aisle is placed a painted memorial to William Dawson (died 1603) and his wife (died 1602), the monument being put up in 1614. In the N aisle hang the flags of Australia and Melbourne, which were presented in 1948 by Archbishop Booth of Melbourne.

The church has some good 19C stained glass. The E window depicting the Crucifixion is by John Hardman & Co. (1867), as is the S chancel window which depicts the Risen Christ with sleeping soldiers. The window on the N side of the chancel shows the Triumphant Christ and is by Clayton and Bell (1869). In the N transept the N window is by James Powell & Sons (1865). The image of Moses and the tablets is by Henry Holiday. Above the altar the three-light window depicts Christ in Majesty and was installed as a memorial to Philip Robin (died 1918).

One historical footnote was that the Prime Minister of the time, Lord Palmerston, took part in the ceremony to mark the completion of Scott's restoration on the 28th September 1862.

Norbury, *St. Mary and St. Barlok.* Externally and internally, this is one of the most satisfying churches in Derbyshire. It is set on a ridge above the River Dove in idyllic surroundings and close to the late 17C manor house which has a wing dating back to the 12C. The church has a tower rising from the middle of the S side, the lower stage acting as a porch and main entrance to the church. The tower is low, and has set-back buttresses, battlements and corner pinnacles in the shape of elongated obelisks surmounted by spheres. The bell chamber has a louvred two-light window in each face. The tower, the nave and its aisles are all 15C, with aisle and clerestory windows of three cusped lights, four-centred in the aisles, square-headed in the clerestory. The S side has battlements. The chief feature externally, however, is the chancel, which is almost as big as the nave. It is of four bays and is lit by massive three-light N and S windows and a large five-light E window. The result is that the chancel appears spacious and light. The tracery is intersected, but very different from the usual plain variety. There are pointed trefoils and quatrefoils, and floral carving at the intersections. The date must be c 1300. The bays are divided by buttresses and the battlements are of a tooth-like design.

Internally, there is a small four-bay nave with octagonal piers with moulded capitals. There is no S aisle due to the position of the tower but the SW bay serves as a vestry and the SE bay as a chapel. There is no chancel arch, so adding to the spacious feeling of the chancel. The chancel walls are each four inches wider apart at the top. The nave and chancel have 15C wooden roofs.

At the W end of the nave there are two decorated shafts from pre-Conquest crosses. There is also a pre-Conquest or Norman carved stone reused as one of the spiral stairs in the tower. The SW bay has a large plain alabaster tomb-chest upon which is inlaid a brass with a Latin inscription. The tomb is that of John Fitzherbert (died 1531). On the wall of the vestry are some Victorian casts of the brasses in the church including the palimpsest of Sir Anthony Fitzherbert in the chancel. The lower of the two W windows contains some medieval stained glass fragments in the middle light. These represent the Holy Trinity. In the nave the Early English circular font is supported on clustered shafts. The SE chapel has a very well-preserved effigy of a cross-legged knight. This is the tomb of Sir Henry Fitzherbert (died 1315). The chapel has two windows filled with 15C glass, restored in 1962. The window over the altar depicts, in the central light, St. Anne teaching the Virgin Mary, to the left St. Winifrid and to the right St. Zita of Lucca. Beneath these figures are the arms of the Fitzherbert family and the images of Nicholas Fitzherbert, his first wife and their 13 children. The window in the S wall depicts in the centre light St. Barlok and on either side St. John the Baptist and St. Anthony. Beneath these figures are Nicholas Fitzherbert with his second wife Isabel and their three children. There is a traceried nine-arch screen to the chancel, which is raised on three steps. In the chancel the choirstalls date from c 1340 and have some fine carved bench-ends. Behind the stalls and running round the chancel is a continuous blind arcade. There is a double piscina in the S wall.

The chancel possesses a series of magnificent tombs and monuments. There are two exceptional alabaster tomb-chests. That on the left-hand side is to Sir Ralph Fitzherbert (died 1483) and his wife Elizabeth (died 1491). Their effigies lie on a chest whose sides are decorated with figures beneath nodding ogee arches. The other alabaster tomb-chest is that of Nicholas Fitzherbert (died 1473). His recumbent effigy in full armour has round his neck a collar with stars and roses, which denoted allegiance to King Edward IV. Around the sides of the chest are very finely carved figures, each under a separate arch, representing his 17 children. In between these two tombs and set in the floor there are the remains of a large brass to Sir Anthony Fitzherbert (died 1538) and his wife Dame Maud (died 1551). It is a palimpsest brass, for the figure of Sir Anthony in judge's robes is on the reverse side of a memorial to Matilda de Verdun (died c 1316), which more than likely came from the recently dissolved Croxden Abbey. Dame Maud is shown in her mourning clothes. The brass was moved here from the nave in 1842 when it was complete with an inscription. There are a number of incised alabaster slabs. Near the tomb of Nicholas Fitzherbert is an effigy of a shroud-wrapped body. This has been tentatively identified as being the memorial to Elizabeth, wife of Ralph Fitzherbert. Near this is an incised slab with a chalice, in memory of Henry Prince, Rector 1466–1500. On the N side there is a slab with the incised effigy of Alice (died 1460), first wife of Sir Nicholas Fitzherbert.

The windows of the chancel contain an unusually large amount of medieval glass. The E window has 15C glass which was restored in 1973–83. The glass came from all parts of the church in the restoration of 1842. The centre light depicts St. Edward the Confessor, St. Chad, St. Fabian, St. Margaret and Mary Magdalene. The two lights on either side are filled with the Apostles, each with a portion of the Apostles' Creed. The tracery above contains heraldic devices of the Fitzherbert and related families. The other chancel windows remain to be restored and show well the difference that restoration makes. Apart from the damage caused by a burglar in 1984, they are virtually complete and unaltered since the 14C. They represent a magnificent and rare example of glazing of the early 14C and contain many heraldic devices.

The church has close connections with George Eliot. Robert Evans, on whom Adam Bede was based, sang here. He reputedly made the N aisle altar. His parents George and Mary Evans, who were likewise used as the models for Adam Bede's parents, are buried in the churchyard.

St. Barlok is virtually unknown. He was possibly a pre-Conquest hermit, perhaps Irish.

Repton, *St. Wystan*. Repton has a fine 14C W tower and a graceful recessed spire rising some 212ft, but it is famous for its very early pre-Conquest crypt which was rediscovered in 1799 and for the other remains at its E end of a large pre-Conquest cruciform church. It is recorded that an abbey was founded as early as 660. It was here that St. Werburgh and Aelfthryth were abbesses. St. Guthlac was also a member of the community. The crypt was certainly standing when the Danes wintered at Repton in 874–75. As a result of excavations undertaken by Dr H.M. Taylor and Professor M. Biddle, it is now considered that the crypt could date back to at least 757 and the church itself from before 874. In the Old English Chronicle, the mausoleum at Repton is recorded as being the burial place of King Ethelbald (died 757), King Wiglaf (died 840) and St. Wystan (died

The E end of St. Wystan's, showing pre-Conquest pilaster strips; the church was the burial-place of early Mercian kings

850). The first two were Kings of Mercia; Wystan was Wiglaf's grandson, who was murdered by a kinsman. King Cnut moved the saint's relics to Evesham in the 11C. The crypt was built as Ethelbald's mausoleum, but became a shrine after 850, when it was remodelled.

The church reveals not only pre-Conquest work but fabric from all three Gothic styles. The exterior is dominated by the W tower and spire which were completed in 1340. The clerestory of the nave with its battlements is Perpendicular. The porch (with a parvise), N aisle and S chapel are 14C Decorated. On either side of the porch there is evidence of the Early English S aisle with lancet windows. The vestry on the N side of the tower was built in 1939. The unbuttressed chancel and E end of the N aisle are different from the rest of the church in their stonework, which is more irregular, and there are the very large stones at the corners and the pilaster strips, which all point to the pre-conquest origins of this part of the church. The chancel is built over the famous crypt; the ground at the E end has been dug away to reveal the extent of the pre-Conquest work, and in particular the stepped plinths.

The crypt itself is roughly square, three bays by three bays, making nine vaulted bays supported on four circular pillars and on wall pilasters. The pillars have a fillet running spirally around them, and plain square capitals. Access is gained by a steep stone staircase from the N transept, much of which is original. There are the remains of a similar staircase in the S transept. The E and S faces of the crypt have two rectangular 15C windows and the N face has a doorway which currently opens out onto the long-term excavations.

The porch contains a collection of pre-Conquest carved stones and most importantly, two columns and capitals which were removed from the E end of the nave during alterations in 1854. The nave is of six bays with hexagonal piers carrying double-chamfered arches, the W four being 14C and the last two dating from the 1854 alterations. The clerestory above has seven pairs of double-light Perpendicular windows. The wooden roof is also 15C. Above the chancel arch there is a doorway with an apparently original pre-Conquest step and lintel which would indicate the existence of an upper room. The chancel walls are pre-Conquest, with an inserted 13C lancet window in the N wall and a four-light Decorated E window. By the two flights of stairs down to the crypt there are the bases and lower portions of the pillars now in the porch.

At the E end of the N aisle, by the steps to the crypt, there is a large alabaster tomb-chest with the recumbent effigy of a knight (perhaps Sir Robert Frances of Foremark) dating from the end of the 14C. Above this on the E wall of the N aisle in what is now St. Catherine's chapel is a large monument to Francis Thacker (died 1710). It consists of a pediment supported by columns between which is his centrally placed bust. In the S transept, which is now used as the Lady chapel, the monument on the S wall is to George Waklin (died 1617) and his wife Ellen (died 1614). They are depicted kneeling and facing one another, with their son kneeling below them. In the next bay of the S aisle is the upright incised alabaster slab to Gilbert Thacker (died 1563). It also shows his wife and two children. He was responsible for the demolition of the priory church (which existed from 1172 to 1538 where Repton School now stands) and much of the monastery buildings.

With one exception, the stained glass is 19C and 20C. In the N wall at the E end there is a two-light window with a medieval fragment depicting a king. In the S wall of the S transept there is a four-light window with glass inserted c 1911 which depicts St. Diuma, St. Trystan, St. Guthlac and St. Chad. The S aisle W window by Dudley Forsyth of London depicts Aelfthryth, Abbess of Repton. Much of the stained glass is apparently by James Powell & Sons.

Sandiacre, St. Giles. The church is rich in Norman features and also has a particularly fine and little-altered Decorated chancel, which is almost as big as the nave.

The church sits on a ridge overlooking the Erewash valley. At the W end is a fairly low three-stage 13C tower of roughly dressed stone, topped by a spire, with a two-light louvred window in each face. The nave is built of the same coarsely dressed blocks, but the chancel is of more finely dressed stone. The chancel has buttresses rising to crocketed pinnacles and a band of quatrefoil decoration running above the windows. There are also a number of gargoyles. The inner doorway of the S porch is Norman and has roll-mouldings and three capitals of volutes and scallops. The aisleless nave has the remains of stone corbels which formerly supported a lower roof before the nave was heightened in the 15C and clerestory windows were inserted. In the S wall the four-light window is Decorated. There is also a large splayed Norman round-headed S window with attached shafts and decorated capitals, which is matched in the N wall. The Norman chancel arch is supported on numerous shafts and massive capitals with scallops and primitive carved figures. On the N side the decorative frieze continues along the E wall. The chancel was built by Bishop Roger de Norbury of Lichfield, who was prebend of Sandiacre in 1342–47. It is a wonderful example of Decorated Gothic, almost as large as the nave, with three-light windows on each side and a very large six-light E window, all with flowing tracery. Each window has a hoodmould which terminates in small carved heads. In the S wall there are very fine sedilia and a piscina under four gabled canopies, with ogee arches and five crocketed pinnacles. The gables have panels of flowing tracery.

At the W end of the nave a modern gallery houses an organ by Church & Co. of 1977. At the W end also is the 14C octagonal stone font which has the shape of a chalice. Each panel of the tub has foliate carving and the heads of demons and animals. The top has recessed battlements between each panel. Behind the altar the wooden painted reredos depicting the Crucifixion was dedicated in 1947. There are a small number of monuments. In the chancel on the S side there is a small tomb-slab with a foliate cross and two dragons on either side of the shaft. By the altar rail a brass plate with a crest to Howard Charlton (died 1638) was restored in 1855 by Thomas Broughton Charlton. On the N side of the nave there is a small metal plaque to Joseph Chadbourne (died 1722).

Stained Glass. In the S wall the four-light window has figures of St. Werburgh, St. Chad, St. Giles and St. Elizabeth. On the N side the large round-headed window depicts St. Michael above a view of Lincoln Cathedral. Below, an airman prays under a tree, with coats of arms on either side. The window is by M. Bell (1956). In the chancel there are a few medieval fragments in the N window. The E window depicts the Evangelists.

Steetley, All Saints. Set near some farm buildings in Whitwell parish in the far NE corner of Derbyshire, this apsidal chapel is justly famous as a classic example of Norman architecture of c 1150, which was sympathetically restored in 1876–80 by J.L. Pearson. In a neatly tended small graveyard amongst trees, the impression is of the smallness of the building, 56ft long by 15ft wide. The apse is lit by three small shafted windows. Beneath them runs a band of interlace carving, which wraps round the four semicircular buttresses of the apse. There is a corbel table below the steeply pitched roof. The only non-Norman feature is the three-light Decorated window in the S wall of the chancel. The nave is lit by four deeply-splayed round-headed windows, one each in the N and S walls and two in the W wall. The S door has five orders. The inner three consist of simple moulding, and then come interlaced foliage and carved medallions. In the course of restoration Pearson replaced two missing orders on each side. The arches have zigzag and beakhead decoration. The gable above, divided into smaller lozenge-shaped divisions, each containing a foliate cross, is the work of Pearson. At the E end of the nave roof there is a Victorian bellcote.

The chancel arch within has triple bands of decoration on the nave side, supported on four half-shafts with richly ornamented capitals. Working outwards the arches have zigzag, battlements and a curious ball shape set in a small semicircular recess. The capitals are richly decorated with foliate scrolls, scallops and depictions of a double-bodied lion, St. George and the Dragon and Adam and Eve. The E face of this arch is altogether plainer. The arch dividing chancel from apse is again a triple arch but plain, just the outer arch being decorated with a billet frieze. The four half-shafts have foliate scrollwork and scallop capitals. The apse has four shafts supporting a vault, the ribs decorated with a simplified beakhead pattern, meeting at a central decorated boss depicting the Lamb of God. At the W end there is a square stone font with a wooden cover dated 1975. Against the N wall is an incised tomb-slab with a foliate cross and the hand of God touching a chalice below. Next to it is a paten. Both of these rest on a three-legged altar table. The tomb-slab is believed to be that of Lawrence Le Leche who died of the plague in 1349. Also on the N wall of the nave there is a Victorian wooden panel with images of St. Gabriel, St. Mary, St. Jerome, St. Giles, St. Blasius, St. John the Baptist, the Suffering and the Glory.

Tideswell, *St. John the Baptist*. Known as 'The Cathedral of the Peak', this church of impressive proportions and appearance is helped by its unity of architectural style, being largely Decorated, with some Perpendicular additions, all built in c 1340–1400. The church was restored during the 1870s by John Dando Sedding.

The dominant exterior feature is the W tower which was the last part to be constructed, in c 1400, and is therefore Perpendicular. The W face has a very large five-light window above the W door. The belfry has pairs of louvred two-light openings and there are tall polygonal corner turrets which finish in equally tall crocketed pinnacles. These turrets and the top of the tower are battlemented. There is a stair turret in the SE angle of the lower stage. The aisles, nave, porch, transepts and chancel are all battlemented and a feature is made of the buttressing. The buttresses of the chancel each carry a pinnacle. The two corner buttresses of the S transept have niches and gargoyles. Above the chancel arch there is a small pinnacled and niched bellcote. The E window of five lights is a good example of flowing Decorated whereas the four three-light windows on each side of the chancel, which are tall, square-headed and with quatrefoil tracery, show the move towards Perpendicular.

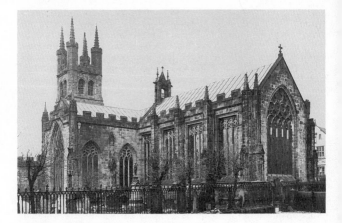

St. John's, 'the Cathedral of the Peak'

Internally, the five-bay nave has quatrefoil pillars carrying moulded capitals and arches. Above, there are two-light clerestory windows with a quatrefoil in the head. The tower arch is very tall. The easternmost arches of the nave are wider and open into the transepts. The chancel arch leads the eye into the light-filled chancel. The altar is in front of a stone reredos which is positioned away from the E wall, thus creating a vestry to which access is gained by a door on the N side. The reredos has two large niches filled with statues in 1950. The nave roof is medieval. The N aisle roof dates from 1632–35.

Both the N and S porches have internal wooden screens. The tower space also has a wooden screen, designed by John Oldrid Scott in 1904. In front of this is an octagonal font dating from the 15C, with badly worn shields and quatrefoils on each face. The nave and aisles have box-pews of 1824–27. In front of the chancel screen stands the hexagonal stone pulpit dated 1875. Beneath this the ornately carved priest's chair and stall are the work of Advent Hunstone of Tideswell. His also are the intricately carved N transept screen and organ case. The N side of the organ case has a series of canopies which terminate in three angels holding shields.

The N transept has always been used as the Lady chapel. It has ten medieval stalls with plain misericords which were originally in the chancel. In the E wall next to the altar and under the ornate wooden organ canopy there are two niches, one containing a 1952 Madonna and Child. Beneath these there are two female recumbent stone effigies, one of c 1300 and the other c 1375. The S transept serves in part as the Lytton chapel. The altar tomb dates from 1883. In front of the wooden screen is placed a 14C bell with a Latin inscription which translates, 'I have the name of Gabriel who was sent from Heaven.' On the E wall is fixed a good marble pedimented monument with Ionic capitals to the Statham family, put up in 1716. Above this is a painted hatchment. In the angle of the S and E walls there is a niche with a head support and a canopy. Hatchments flank the S window. The transept is dominated by a large alabaster tomb, restored in

1873. On the tomb-chest there are two recumbent figures of a knight and his wife, which have been incorrectly attributed as Sir Thurstan de Bower and his wife Lady Margaret. In the S aisle there is the brass of Sir Robert Lytton (died 1483) and his wife. The aisle also has painted inscriptions of the Creed and the Lord's Prayer, which are matched in the N aisle by painted panels of the Commandments.

In the centre of the chancel stands a large restored tomb-chest with traceried open sides, through which can be seen a stone corpse. It is the tomb of Sir Sampson Meverill (died 1462). The Purbeck marble top has a series of inlaid brasses depicting God under a canopy holding a crucifix, and a number of shields and inscriptions. On the N wall a large brass plate commemorates Canon Samuel Andrew (died 1900). In the N wall also there are two shallow ogee arches in front of which are two brasses. The first of these is to Bishop Pursglove (died 1579) and depicts a figure in full regalia. E of this is the brass to John Foljambe (died 1383), but the present brass was made in 1875. Above the E ogee arch a marble tablet with a broken pediment is in memory of Martha Eoly (died 1769). The stone reredos has two large niches surmounted by pinnacles. The niches contain statues carved in 1950 by Jethro Harris of Oxford, which represent Zacharias, the Archangel Gabriel, St. Peter and St. Mary Magdalene. The roof in the chancel has carvings of angels holding shields.

The stained glass in the church is mainly Victorian. The E window depicts the Tree of Jesse, and is by Heaton, Butler & Bayne, 1875. In the S transept the E window (1873) depicts the Risen Christ and the S window depicts Christ with the Evangelists. The large W tower window depicts Christ in Heaven with St. Chad and Lichfield Cathedral in the bottom left-hand corner and St. Cuthburga and Wimborne Minster in the bottom right-hand corner. This window dates from 1907 and is by Hardman & Powell.

Wirksworth, *St. Mary the Virgin.* A large and impressive cruciform church with a dominant central tower, its size is due to the wealth and importance in former times of Wirksworth as the centre of the lead industry. The church has a wealth of fittings and architectural details but pride of place must go to the pre-Conquest carvings.

The church is set in a close with houses backing on and is reached down a series of narrow lanes. The churchyard is largely turfed over. The dominant feature is the three-stage tower surmounted by a small recessed spire. On the W face of the tower are seen the original higher rooflines. The nave clerestory with its three pairs of double-light windows dates from the extensive restoration undertaken by Sir Gilbert Scott in 1870–74. The W front was restored in 1906–08.

Internally, there is a very wide nave of three bays with N and S aisles. The nave pillars are quatrefoil in shape and have fillets on the shafts. These support double-chamfered Decorated arches. Both the N and S transepts are divided by 14C stone arcades. Perhaps the most impressive internal architectural features are the four massive piers which carry the central tower and date from the late 13C. The chancel is separated from its aisles by arcades with octagonal piers. The sanctuary extends for two bays E of this.

Although the present church can be dated back only to 1272, there is a large number of stone fragments from earlier churches on the site. The most impressive of these is the justly famous Wirksworth stone dated to c 800, which is in the last bay of the N aisle. It was discovered during alterations in 1820. On it are the remains of eight superbly carved scenes, arranged in two rows. These have been interpreted as representing Christ washing the feet of the Disciples, the Crucifixion, the body of the Virgin Mary being taken for burial, the Presentation in the Temple, the Descent into Hell, the Ascension, the Annunciation, and St. Peter in a boat with the Virgin Mary and the baby Jesus in her arms. He has a scroll representing St. Peter being given the mission to spread the word. W of this in the N aisle is a further, very small pre-Conquest carving depicts Adam, the Serpent and the Tree of Life. At the W end of the N aisle is the war memorial with a painting in a blocked-up doorway of a calvary.

Hanging from the S side of the nave is the flag of the Wirksworth Volunteers dating from 1798. Against the tower piers are the wooden pulpit, designed by Sir Arthur Blomfield in 1895, and the brass eagle lectern. The N transept houses a large Norman font which has a circular tub on a cluster of columns. (A second font of 1662 stands in the S aisle.) Against the W wall of the transept there are an incised tomb-slab with a foliate cross, sword and sling, and another foliate cross slab. Built into the N wall are a large number of Norman carved stones which represent figures, a lamb around the shoulders of a man, beakheads, human heads and ornamental work. The E half of the transept is separated by a screen, surmounted by the carved arms of King William IV. Much of this half of the transept is taken up by the organ which was made by Brindley & Foster of Sheffield in 1899. In front of this is a glass case containing a 1602 'Breeches' Bible. The S transept is also divided in half, the E half serving as a vestry. Built into its walls are many carved fragments of pre-Conquest and Norman origin. One of note is near the N corner of the W wall; it depicts a lead miner with his tools. The S choir aisle, which is also the chapel of the Holy Rood, has an altar with two riddel posts surmounted by angels, designed by Temple Moore in 1897. The reredos (also by Moore) depicts the Crucifixion, St. Chad, St. Cecilia, St. Barnabas, St. Mary Magdalene, St. Stephen and St. Peter.

A fine collection of tombs and brasses is found at the E end of the N choir aisle. Against the N wall and in an upright position is the Blackwell brass. This consists of more than one original brass to the Blackwell family collected together. The main figures are those of Thomas Blackwell (died 1525) and his wife. Above this is a marble monument depicting a putto blowing a trumpet, to Sir Philip Gell (died 1688) and his wife Elizabeth (died 1719). On the E wall an alabaster memorial with a broken pediment and a centrally placed crest commemorates John Gell (died 1671). Two alabaster tomb-chests stand near the E wall. The first (N) has an incised lid with the figures of Ralph Gell (died 1564) and his wives Godith and Emma. Around the sides are the figures of his children (four sons and ten daughters) and shields. The second tomb-chest carries the recumbent effigy of Anthony Gell (died 1583). In the chancel on the N wall two monuments are placed above one another. At the top is a large columned and pedimented monument to Henry Wigley (died 1683), put up in 1714. Beneath this is the monument to John Lowe (died 1690), with cherub heads and a skull. Also in the chancel stands the finest monument, to Anthony Lowe (died 1555). It consists of a tomb-chest with a recumbent effigy whose feet rest on a skull. Around the sides of the chest are grieving children (W), two cherubs holding the family crest (N) and a Tudor rose (E). Above the chest Corinthian fluted pilasters rise to a cornice. Much of the tomb was painted in the recent past with bright modern paints, which are only slowly toning down.

The stained glass is predominantly 19C and 20C. In the S aisle two windows (1959) by Christopher Webb represent the seasons. In the N transept the N window (1909) depicts Gabriel, the Virgin Mary, Christ, St. Elizabeth, Raphael, Enoch, St. Stephen, St. John, St. Paul and Elijah. It was made by Morris & Co. after designs by Sir Edward Burne-Jones. All the windows in the chancel are by William Warrington (1855). The four lancets depict miracles and the E window parables.

One of the Vicars of Wirksworth, Richard Willey (1705–14), became Dean of Lincoln, and Bishop successively of Gloucester, Salisbury and finally Winchester. A curate of the parish, Abraham Bennet, FRS, wrote and experimented with electricity, publishing a paper in 1789.

COUNTY DURHAM

County Durham is a small and little-known but rather special county. Through the medieval period it was a County Palatine ruled over by the Prince-Bishop, who had viceregal powers. These powers were gradually removed from the 16C, but the Palatinate was not finally abolished until 1836. In the 19C coal mining was the major industry, and its workings dominated and disfigured the landscape in many parts of the county. Now, many mines have closed, and (except in the industrial conurbations of Tyneside and Teeside) County Durham has regained its rural image of rolling hills and unexpected valleys. Traditionally it was bounded on the N by the Tyne, and on the S by the Tees. Since 1974 it has lost, administratively, its NE corner to the new county of Tyne and Wear, and its SE corner to Cleveland, and in return it gained the bleak moorlands of NW Yorkshire and some villages S of the Tees. The most common building stone is sandstone, which can be rather dull but is sometimes enlivened with lovely 'watermark' patterns. In the SE some whitish limestone is occasionally used for churches; and in the W, the much-prized Frosterley marble—a carboniferous stone capable of taking a high polish—was quarried and used decoratively like Purbeck marble. It is no longer available. County Durham has some of the most important pre-Conquest churches in the country, and some grand Early English buildings; and in many churches the unique 17C furnishings, part Gothic and part Renaissance, introduced by Bishop John Cosin, can be found.

County Durham has some of the earliest pre-Conquest churches in the country. Several were founded in the remarkable flourishing of religious life in Northumbria in the 7C and 8C. St. Benedict Biscop introduced Continental religious life at Monkwearmouth in 674 and Jarrow in 681. He stocked their libraries with books, which stimulated the writings of Bede. Bede's contemporary and possible pupil, Archbishop Ecgberct of York, founded the 'School of York'; and this school produced Alcuin, the head of Charlemagne's palace school. Bede writes of the foundation of Jarrow and Monkwearmouth. Other pre-Conquest churches existed which he does not mention, such as Escomb. The most common pre-Conquest type of church is the single-cell or string of cells, found at Monkwearmouth, Jarrow, Escomb and Seaham. The proportions are tall and narrow. Later, naves became wider. The nave at Hart, though much altered, retains these proportions. A more complex arrangement, dating from the 10C or 11C, is the cruciform church with central tower, of which a good example survives at Norton. Monkwearmouth and Billingham have late pre-Conquest towers. The best fragments of sculpture of this period are the pieces of a late 8C or early 9C cross at South Church, St. Andrew Auckland, in a church otherwise almost entirely of the late 13C.

For the Norman period, the finest and grandest work is, of course, in Durham Cathedral. Nearby, on the other side of Palace Green, the castle has a Norman undercroft chapel, late 11C. Of roughly the same date is the upper part of the central tower of Jarrow, raised on a pre-Conquest base. Lanchester has a good Norman chancel arch on a renewed base. The most spectacular Norman survival is the N arcade of Pittington, built in the time of Bishop le Puiset, c 1160–70. Many churches in County Durham were rebuilt in Early English style in the 13C. Hartlepool, Darlington and Chester-le-Street are substantial buildings; but the largest is South Church, St. Andrew Auckland, rebuilt from 1292 by Bishop Bek as a collegiate foundation. The Bishop's chapel of Auckland Castle, built in c 1190 as the Great Hall, has noble Early English arcades, with shafts of Frosterley marble in the piers. Sedgefield, a church externally mostly Perpendicular, has arcades of this period with richly carved capitals. Amongst 13C church towers are Hartlepool and Darlington and also Sherburn Hospital chapel, with tiers of blank arcading. West Boldon has a notable 13C tower and stone spire (rare at this date); another spire, of lead-covered wood, is at Ryton. At Gateshead, St. Edmund's chapel, incorporated into Holy Trinity Church in 1892–93 (now a community centre), has a fine W front with a deep portal, tiers of blank arcading, and a seven-step lancet window. Stepped lancets at the E end are a feature of several churches: Dalton-le-Dale, Gainford, and elsewhere. In contrast, there is little Decorated work, the best being the E and W windows of Houghton-le-Spring. The W window has Reticulated, and the E window flowing tracery. From the Perpendicular period dates Houghton's two-storeyed Guild chapel of the Holy Trinity, built after 1480. It is on the S side of the church and was formerly detached. Sedgefield has been mentioned already; another church which is externally mostly Perpendicular is Egglescliffe. The chancel of Brancepeth was rebuilt in the 15C; and the octagonal stage and spire were added at Chester-le-Street.

There was little church building in the county in the 17C (but much internal refurnishing, as described below). In the 18C a few Classical churches were designed, of which James Paine's Gibside Chapel, 1760–69, was the most accomplished. Stockton dates from 1710–20: it is brick and rather staid. Less restrained is Holy Trinity, Sunderland, 1719, also of brick with stone dressings, which received a nearly circular apse in 1735. A Classical-style W tower was built at St. Mary's, Gateshead in 1740 (the belfry stage being added c 1773). The church at St. John's Chapel is a plain Classical building of 1752. St. Hilda's, South Shields has a W tower heightened and Classically-clad in c 1764, and the rest of the church was remodelled in 1810–12, with an apse. Castle Eden, 1764, is a delightful early Gothick work with an endearingly absurd pointed Venetian E window. Inside, Classicism persists in the Corinthian columns installed in 1800 when the aisles were added. More elaborately Gothick is the chapel of Croxdale Hall, 1807, but this is not shown to the public.

The 19C Gothic Revival in County Durham is dominated by local architects. Many of the 'national' architects built at least one church, but their works are mostly unmemorable. The exception is E.B. Lamb's Christ Church, West Hartlepool, 1854. As usual with Lamb, it is the eccentricity of the design, especially the tower and features of the interior, which is memorable. Of pre-Ecclesiological churches, Holy Trinity, Stockton, of 1834–38 by John and Benjamin Green, is perhaps the most impressive, even after the demolition of its octagonal stage and spire from the tower in 1957. Ignatius Bonomi's work at Pittington in 1846–47, with John Cory, is sensitive. In extending the exquisite Norman N arcade eastwards, no attempt was made to hide the junction or to improve upon the original design. Less sensitive was William Burn's recovery of Raby Castle chapel from dereliction in 1847. He blocked medieval windows, sedilia and an aumbry and obscured the vaulted ceiling with plaster. At Durham, J.P Pritchett rebuilt St. Nicholas's in 1857–58. Later in the 19C the partnership of Austin, Johnson & Hicks (afterwards Hicks & Charlewood) built grand and impressive town churches: St. Michael's,

South Shields, from 1881; St. Oswald's, Hartlepool, 1897–1904, in Perpendicular style; and St. Chad's, Gateshead (by Hicks alone) in 1904, Decorated, and with an unusual octagonal central tower. Many Catholic churches were built in the county in the 19C. At Esh Laude, the pre-Emancipation chapel and buildings of 1798–1800 were concealed as a farmyard; but St. Mary's, Sunderland, 1835, by Ignatius Bonomi, is grandly post-Emancipation yet clearly pre-Ecclesiological, its bold Early English façade being tacked on to a brick body. A.W.N. Pugin worked at Ushaw College chapel, but his work was re-done on a grander scale, incorporating elements of his design, by Dunn & Hansom in the 1880s. He also designed St. Mary's, Stockton, and published his grand design in his 'Present State of Architecture'; but only the W front was built and the rest was completed by others. His son, E.W. Pugin, built churches at Crook, at Brooms (Leadgate), Consett and at Castle Chare, Durham. The outstanding 20C church is E.S. Prior's St. Andrew's at Roker, Sunderland, 1906–07. W.D. Caroë took R.J. Johnson's chancel extension at Stockton, 1904–06, and gave it a thoroughly Baroque dressing in 1925. He also altered St. Michael's, High Street West, Sunderland, extensively in 1933–35 in a free Perpendicular style.

The work of John Cosin so dominates the history of church furnishings in the county that it is easy to overlook earlier work, although there is not much of outstanding significance. Frosterley marble is often found, usually in medieval fonts. Parts of a well-preserved Norman cross survive at Kelloe, showing richly sculpted scenes from the life of St. Helena. An early 13C sculpture, a panel of Christ seated in a mandorla, is at St. Mary-the-Less, Durham (formerly in St. Giles's). There is a 15C font at Hart, showing male heads and symbols of the Passion. Sets of 15C stalls remain in churches which were collegiate until the Reformation: at Lanchester; South Church, St. Andrew Auckland (1416–17); and Staindrop (c 1408), which also has the only medieval screen. Fine 16C stalls from Auckland Castle, made for Bishop Ruthall (1509–23) are in Durham Castle chapel. Jarrow has an early 16C set, and also 'Bede's chair', thought to be 14C. A further set is at Heighington, which also has an early 16C wooden pulpit with linenfold panels.

John Cosin (1595–1672) was Bishop of Durham from 1660. He arrived in the 1620s as chaplain to Bishop Neile, a Laudian sympathiser, and was soon a Prebendary of Durham Cathedral, Vicar of Elwick and Rector of Brancepeth. He was a fervent supporter of Archbishop Laud's policy of restoring and beautifying Anglican churches and worship, and it is clear that he was the driving force behind the numerous schemes of refurnishing in County Durham in the 1620s and 1630s. As Bishop he furnished a new chapel at Auckland Castle and at its consecration in 1665 urged clergy and laity to do likewise. His relations and friends were willing followers: his father-in-law, Marmaduke Blakiston, at Sedgefield in the 1630s; his son-in-law, Denis Granville, at Easington and Sedgefield in the 1660s; his brother-in-law, Ralph Blakiston, at Ryton from 1660; Eleazar Dunkon, Bishop Neile's chaplain, at Haughton-le-Skerne from the 1620s, and Isaac Basire at Egglescliffe from 1636. There were many other more tenuous connections with Cosin which led to a long list of churches which received 'Cosin' furnishings. A good deal disappeared in the 18C and 19C, but much remains. Cosin took a close interest in the work, and the persistent elements of the style suggest that the choice of the design was his. It is the combination of Gothic (and even Romanesque) with Jacobean and, later, Baroque which is characteristic and instantly recognisable. The earliest work seems to be at Billingham, the early 17C font cover and the screen, dated 1625. A similar font cover is at Darlington. Brancepeth has an almost complete set of furnishings, including a screen with typically exuberant canopy work, the inspiration for which may have been the (stone) Neville screen in Durham Cathedral. Haughton-le-Skerne has fittings similar in style and probably also of the 1630s, although the traditional date is 1662. Similar too is the chancel of Sedgefield, with a few pieces from the 1660s. Of the post-Restoration work the most complete example is Auckland Castle chapel; similar work is at Ryton, at Kirk Merrington (screen and stalls) and at Easington (the top part renewed in 1852–53). At Egglescliffe the style begins to become somewhat debased, and Redmarshall has pews very similar. The rest of the furnishings there have disappeared. The style was still being employed in the early 18C at St. Mary-le-Bow, Durham, with screen and stalls of 1707 and a reredos of 1731.

The best Georgian fittings are at Gibside Chapel, and date from c 1812. Holy Trinity, Sunderland is well furnished with early 18C fittings, including a baluster font of 1719 with an ornate Baroque openwork cover with fat cherubs and a dove hovering at the top. Seaham has a good set of 18C box-pews. The best range of 19C fittings is at Ushaw College. A surprising piece is Sir Ninian Comper's lavish choir screen of 1907, brightly painted and complete with Rood figures, in the tiny 19C church of Elton.

County Durham has very little medieval stained glass. Most notable are imported early 13C panels (probably French) at Lanchester, showing the Annunciation of the Shepherds, the Adoration of the Magi and the Flight into Egypt. There are a few 12C or 13C fragments, some possibly French, in Raby Castle chapel. Then there is scarcely anything until the mid-19C. At Ushaw College there is a fine array of glass by John Hardman, designed for Pugin's smaller chapel of the 1840s and filled out by Edward Frampton to fit the windows of Dunn & Hansom's enlarged chapel. There is good early Morris & Co. glass at Christ Church, Sunderland, of 1864, in the E window. At St. Oswald's, Durham, the W window of 1864–66 is by William Morris and Ford Madox Brown. Daniel Cottier's glass at Birtley (1872) and Felling (1874) is worth study. Hunstanworth has nave windows of 1879–81 by C.E. Kempe. The medieval monuments at Staindrop, and the 'fake medieval' Lumley tombs at Chester-le-Street, are described in the gazetteer. Norton has a well-preserved effigy of a knight, early 14C, originally a Fulthorpe, but his shield was altered in the 16C to carry the Blakiston coat of arms. The best brass is a large late 14C plate to a priest at South Church. Staindrop has a good range of 18C and 19C monuments. Joseph Nollekens's big monument of 1775 to Bishop Trevor of Durham is in the chapel of Auckland Castle.

There have been many distinguished Bishops of Durham. John Cosin has been mentioned already. Nathaniel, Lord Crewe (Bishop, 1674–1722) was a notable benefactor of the diocese and of the University of Oxford; William Van Mildert (1826–36) gave part of the endowment of the See towards the foundation of Durham University; John Lightfoot (1879–90) and Brooke Foss Westcott (1890–1901) were notable theologians. Henry Phillpotts, Bishop of Exeter (1831–69), was previously Rector of Stanhope, one of the richest livings in the country. He is supposed to have inspired Anthony Trollope's absentee clergyman Vesey Stanhope in 'Barchester Towers'. J. Meade Faulkner, writer and antiquary, was Librarian to the Dean and Chapter of Durham, and is commemorated in the cathedral cloister. Famous statesmen from the county include John Lambton, first Earl of Durham (1792–1840), Governor-General of Canada, and Sir Anthony Eden, first Earl of Avon (1897–1977), Prime Minister, whose family formerly owned Windlestone Hall near Rushyford.

Billingham, *St. Cuthbert.* One of the lesser-known pre-Conquest churches of the NE, Billingham stands on a low hill with its village clustering around, overlooking marshes to W and S, much as it must have done when founded (or refounded after Viking destruction) by Bishop Ecgred of Lindisfarne in the 9C. But now it is dominated by the vast industrial works of Teesside to S and E, and sprawling 20C housing to the N. The churchyard is of considerable size.

The tower and nave are pre-Conquest. The nave may in fact predate the 9C. The W tower was added to it in c 1000. It is tall and unbuttressed, crowned with a Perpendicular parapet, and is entered from the nave only. The second stage has typical pre-Conquest windows; the belfry stage has twin openings surrounded by raised bands. On the E side, the tower rests on the walls of the nave. In the 12C a N aisle was added and small clerestory windows were inserted. The S aisle followed in the early 13C. The clerestory windows on this side were altered in Perpendicular style. The chancel was rebuilt in 1847, and again, in grander style with aisles, in 1939 by G.E. Charlewood.

The tall, narrow proportions of the nave suggest an early, perhaps 7C or 8C foundation. The door to the tower may be of this date. The N wall was pierced, quite roughly, in the 12C to form an arcade of pointed arches. The fourth pier from the W is wider than the others, suggesting that perhaps a pre-Conquest side-chamber survived the alterations. Of the same 12C date is the chancel arch. The S arcade, early 13C, has more elaborate columns, each with four attached shafts.

Billingham preserves some 17C woodwork, earlier than the Cosin-style work seen elsewhere in the county. The screen, dated 1625, is now at the W end. It is quite simple, with arches and turned balusters. The font cover, a tall pyramidal piece, is also early 17C and is similar to the one at Darlington. Some early sculpted stones, including part of a cross-shaft, are built into the walls of the tower. On a S windowsill is part of a grave-cover; a finer piece, late 7C or early 8C, with a cross and alpha and omega, is in the British Museum. There is a brass, now lacking a head, to Robert Brerley, a priest in an almuce, 1480. The E window has glass of 1939 by Marion Grant.

Bishop Auckland, *Auckland Castle, Chapel.* The chapel of the palace of the Bishops of Durham is a building of the late 12C and early 13C, founded by Bishop le Puiset as a great hall, altered by Bishop Bek in the early 14C, and converted into a chapel by Bishop Cosin in 1661–65. Since the hall was a room with clerestoried nave and aisles, the transformation was quite easily effected. Cosin filled it with some of his most sumptuous and impressive furnishings, most of which survive.

The exterior was given its final form by Bishop Cosin and his mason, Robert Morley. The S side is the 'show' front. Cosin refaced it with ashlar, studded with a design of slightly projecting stones in a regular pattern. The windows were renewed. In the aisles the tracery is a fair approximation of the 14C Geometrical and Reticulated forms;

but the clerestory windows were enlarged under round heads and filled with tracery in patterns of foiled circles. The parapets are castellated and have crocketed pinnacles, and at the ends 17C-looking slim, domed turrets.

The 13C arcades are particularly stately and elegant, very tall and wide, with sharply-pointed, many-moulded arches of Frosterley marble. These are supported by slim quatrefoil piers: two shafts in each pier are of Frosterley marble, and two are of light sandstone. Most of the capitals are moulded but two have waterleaf. The roof is wooden, but slim vaulting shafts on stiff-leaf corbels were provided in the spandrels of the arches. They now bear late 19C angels, rather oversized and balancing, it seems, precariously on their tiny supports. The W end was the dais end of the medieval great hall, and there are remains of the blank arcading of pointed trefoil arches which marked out this end of the room.

The main door is decorated with fruit-laden swags, and the door to the W has Gothic openwork tracery. Halfway down the chapel, facing each other across the nave, are the pulpit and reading-desk, square, heavy and lacking the magnificent canopies of Brancepeth or Haughton-le-Skerne. They have poppyheads, Gothic tracery, and Classical garlands and terms. Three screens divide the chancel and aisles. They are mostly Baroque, with towering openwork of acanthus foliage above the main beams. Below are Gothic motifs: elaborate openwork tracery, moulded uprights, and blank cusped arches of the panels below. The chancel stalls are canopied above the principal seats, and the canopies are supported by shafts decorated with ornament inspired by the Norman piers of Durham Cathedral—an example of the remarkable eclecticism of Cosin's choice of motifs. The reredos is by C. Hodgson Fowler, 1884. Cosin had hung a tapestry of Solomon and the Queen of Sheba here. The organ is a Father Smith instrument of 1688. Stained glass of Cosin's period survives at the W end, decorated in blue and white with a pattern of diamonds—'Cosin's fret'. The rest of the glass is by Burlison & Grylls, of the 1880s, with one SW window of 1905 by James Powell & Sons. Cosin is buried in the middle of the chapel under a black marble slab. Joseph Nollekens executed the monument to Bishop Trevor (died 1771). His lively seated statue is set in a big Baroque canopy with a concave projecting cornice.

Brancepeth, *St. Brandon.* John Cosin, Rector of Brancepeth 1626–40, provided the church with a splendid set of fittings in c 1638. Virtually all that he provided has survived. The church itself is a medieval building, big and spreading, with a tall W tower. It stands in isolation in the grounds of the castle, which is a spectacular neighbour.

Brancepeth consists of tower, nave and aisles, transepts, and a long chancel and S chancel chapel. The unbuttressed tower has a Norman lower stage with tiny round-headed windows, then two stages with Early English openings, and a heavy battlemented parapet. The nave is Early English, the clerestory Perpendicular, with little pinnacles on the plain parapet. The aisles were widened in the late 13C or early 14C, and extended W to embrace the tower. Of the same period are the transepts. Many of the windows, though renewed in the 19C, have flowing tracery. The chancel and S chapel were rebuilt in the 15C and have large Perpendicular windows filling most of the wall surfaces. Only the N porch gives a hint of the interior style. It was built by Cosin in the 17C. The arches are still pointed; but the surface is decorated with Ionic pilasters, with strapwork and with diamonds at the bases. Cosin's arms are placed above the doorways in the frieze and small cherubs' heads surmount the pilasters. The pediment is rounded; at the side are castellations.

The interior is so dominated by Cosin's work that little more need be noted. The nave has Early English arcades of two bays, extended E by one bay at a later date. The nave roof, with interesting bosses, is 15C; and there is more 15C work in the arch between the chancel and S chapel. It is a wooden tunnel-vault, with an angel over the arch on the chancel side. The S chapel altar has, as a frontal, an elaborate 14C Flemish chest. It was assembled in the 20C by Robert Thompson of Kilburn. Over the chancel arch, on the W face, are two unusual sections of wooden panelling. One, painted white, is squared, with bosses: each of the 27 panels holds a different design of tracery. It may have come from Durham Cathedral in the mid-17C, where it had been part of the medieval Jesus altar. The other, upper, panel may be of Cosin's time. It is divided by ribs and has symbols of the Passion in the panels.

Much of the woodwork, and certainly the chancel ceiling, was installed c 1638. The craftsman was Robert Barker. Pews and benches, pulpit and desk, are shown on a seating plan of 1639. The Rood screen and choirstalls may be of the same date; but the font cover is probably later and is similar in design to the one of 1663 in Durham Cathedral. The pew-ends in the nave have Jacobean strapwork rising to poppyheads. In the transepts are pews with similar fronts, but with pierced friezes, and pediments, alternately round and triangular on the fronts and all triangular on the wall panelling. The pulpit is a bold piece, square and decorated with small attached balusters, arched panels and a back-plate with Cosin's usual diamond. Above rises the opulent tester, with triangular pediments and finials over, corner pinacles and a tall central openwork finial carried on scrolls. More sumptuous still is the screen. Here the motifs are entirely Gothic. The dados are copied from 15C panelling which now forms the reredos. The doors are pierced with tracery, but the flanking openings are blank. Above are three canopies, filling the arch, with crocketed pinnacles, recalling the Neville Screen and bishop's throne in Durham Cathedral. In the spacious chancel the choirstalls have strapwork and acanthus poppyheads at the ends, and tracery on the other surfaces. Over them is a canopy with an openwork parapet supported on balusters. The chancel is panelled in wood, with Gothic motifs and Classicising cherubs' heads. The ceiling over the altar is adorned and serves as a canopy of honour. The communion rail is Cosin's, as is the table (dated 1628, slightly earlier than the other furnishings). On the N wall of the chancel is a blank memorial tablet to Cosin. Its exact date is uncertain: it has terms exactly like those on the pre-1640 pulpit, but the swags are more typical of post-Restoration work.

Two monuments stand very proudly in the church. One, a knight in chain-mail and cross-legged, in the centre of the chancel, is of Robert Neville (died 1319); the other, of wood, is in the N transept and is of Ralph Neville, second Earl of Westmorland (died 1484) and his wife. He founded a Jesus chantry in the church. A third stands under the tower and is thought to commemorate the wife and child of the third Earl of Westmorland. There are two medieval brasses, to Thomas Claxton (died 1403), a knight in armour, in the N nave aisle; and to Richard Drax (died 1456), Rector, who was also Abbot of Jervaulx (Yorkshire, North Riding), a half-length, with symbols of the Evangelists at the corners (in the chancel, W of the cross-legged knight).

In a N aisle window are three roundels of Flemish stained glass. Much 19C and early 20C glass is to be seen in the transepts.

Chester-le-Street, *St. Mary and St. Cuthbert.* The church is now entirely Early English and later, but it has a long pre-Conquest history, partly as a cathedral. From 883, when monks brought the body of St. Cuthbert from Yorkshire, it was the seat of the Bishop of Lindisfarne until 995, when the See was removed to Durham. The famous Lindisfarne Gospels rested here in the days of the cathedral. Bishop Egelric rebuilt the church in c 1050, but there are no discernible remains of this rebuilding. Bishop Bek made the church collegiate in 1286. In the N aisle are the Lumley monuments, a series of 14 recumbent effigies assembled by John, Lord Lumley in the 1590s as a genealogy in stone, representing his forbears from the reign of King Edward the Confessor.

The W front is dominated by a splendid soaring spire of c 1409. The tower is squat and well-buttressed, with a large stair turret. In the W face is a large Perpendicular window, but earlier paired lancets survive higher up. Above is an octagonal stage with battlements and pinnacles. The S aisle engages the tower; on the N side is a well-preserved anchorage or anker house. There were anchorites from 1383 to the Reformation, and then four poor widows, for whom additional rooms were made on the N side. In the original upper cell is an unusual ancient window, partly mullioned and transomed, hewn out of a single block of stone. On the N side, further E, is a projecting chapel of 1829 by Ignatius Bonomi, with a Perpendicular-style window and an external stair. This is the Lambton pew, with a burial vault below which formerly held the remains of John Lambton, first Earl of Durham (died 1840). At the E end a blocked arch marks the entrance to a crypt, once the 'bone-house' and in the 17C and 18C the vault of the Hedworth family. Some of the buttresses on the S side of the church rest on medieval grave-covers. The S porch was rebuilt in 1742.

The nave, long and dark, is of five bays. It has no clerestory. The arcades have circular piers and moulded capitals. They are 13C, like the S door. Originally three bays, the arcades were extended westwards. In the S aisle, one original 14C window with Reticulated tracery survives at the W end. The N aisle windows are Decorated and Perpendicular. There was a N transept where the box-like gallery of the Lambton pew now stands. The chancel is 13C but the chancel arch is of 1862 and the E window is also a Victorian replacement. Two of the S windows (the E and the third from E) and the sedilia and piscina are 13C.

The chancel furniture, screen and choirstalls, were added at the millenary in 1883. The altar, resplendent in scarlet with vine-scrolls in gold, and the reredos are of 1927, by Sir Charles Nicholson. In the canopied niches are statues of the patron saints, St. Cuthbert bearing the head of St. Oswald. Nicholson's scheme continues on the N wall with three panels illustrating the history of the founding of the church, painted by A.K. Nicholson. A brass to Alice Lambton (died 1434), formerly in the S aisle, is now in the vestry. The font, at the W end of the S aisle, is 15C, octagonal, with shields of local families on the bowl. Near the font is an effigy of a priest (or bishop?), c 1300. In the N aisle are the Lumley effigies crammed closely together, the genealogical conceit of John, Lord Lumley (died 1609). The monuments do not mark the burial places of those whom they commemorate. Most are 16C inventions; but the third from the W is c 1260, representing Sir William Lumley, a knight in chain-mail, cross-legged, his feet on a wyvern and lion. For the ninth and tenth from the W, Lord Lumley appropriated late 13C monuments from Durham Cathedral graveyard. They are of local Frosterley marble, and purport to represent Ralph, Lord Lumley (died 1400) and Sir John Lumley (died 1421). Tablets over each monument give the details, with a long introductory effusion at the W end. Lord Lumley (buried at Cheam in Surrey) began another row for himself and Sir Thomas Lumley.

There is much 19C stained glass. The E window, 1877, commemorates St. Mary in the upper lights, and the early history of the church below (the arrival of the monks, 883; King Athelstan presents a copy of the Gospels, 934; King Edmund visits the shrine, 944; Bishop Ethelwold of Ely visits the church, 970). The two heads in the topmost lights are medieval. In the N aisle, windows show further scenes from the church's early history. Roman and pre-Conquest sculptural fragments are in the anchorage, now a museum. From an upper room a squint looks down on the S aisle altar. One of the fragments, part of a late 9C cross-shaft found in the walls during the 1862 restoration, shows a horseman with a shield, riding under a two-headed beast with EADMUND inscribed on it.

Darlington, St. Cuthbert. Darlington conjures up 19C images, especially of railways. It comes therefore as something of a surprise to discover the church, one of the grandest and most attractive Early English churches in the county, a cruciform building with a low central tower and a tall, elegant spire, built by Bishop le Puiset at the end of the 12C. Darlington was an important episcopal estate, and the church was collegiate, with a dean and four canons, throughout the medieval period. Sir Gilbert Scott took the view that the bishop had been influenced by the church of St. Cross at Winchester, Hampshire, built by the bishop's uncle.

Nave, chancel and transepts are of equal height, and have roofs of the original steep pitch. The W end is stately and attractive, with tiers of lancets, some windows and some blank, rising up into the gable, flanked by turrets decorated with more lancets. Below is a grand portal, the deep and much-moulded arch crowned with a tall gable. Lancets continue round the clerestory to the transepts and chancel; the E end, with its lancets in tiers and flanking turrets, was carefully rebuilt by J.P. Pritchett in 1864–65. The nave aisles, rebuilt in the 14C, enclose the gabled N and S portals. In the early 14C the tower was raised, and the band of trefoil-headed windows in the belfry stage is of this date. The spire originally had lucarnes, and was 8ft taller, but was slightly truncated in a rebuilding of 1752.

The church is most richly decorated in the chancel and transepts; after one bay of the nave, the style is simpler, and piers with clustered shafts are replaced by alternate round and octagonal piers. Perhaps this indicates financial stringency, or the parochial part as opposed to the collegiate. In the chancel, the lancet windows alternate with blank arcading. There are early 14C sedilia and a piscina with ogee arches. The S transept is more richly ornamented than the N transept, and has two piscinas with trefoil heads, indicating the positions of medieval altars.

The chancel is enclosed by a stone Rood screen or pulpitum of c 1400, installed presumably to support the tower arch when the spire was built. In the chancel is a fine set of 15C stalls (the three NW stalls were replaced in the 19C) with misericords. In the chancel also there is a Perpendicular Easter sepulchre with four-centred arch. The mosaic reredos of 1875, with wings of 1878, is by John Dobbin of Darlington, and was originally intended for Westminster Abbey. At the crossing is a marble pulpit of 1852, and a modern altar arrangement—altar, rails, and chairs in light wood, by George Pace. The S transept houses the font, with its splendid 17C Cosin-style cover, huge and many-tiered, with a slim crocketed spire at the top, all in Decorated style. In the transepts are fragments of medieval wall painting. There is a wealth of 19C stained glass by Clayton & Bell, Burlison & Grylls, John Hardman & Co. and William Wailes. There is a monument to General Sir Henry Havelock, the hero of Lucknow in the Indian Mutiny.

City of Durham

After the cathedral, the most rewarding ecclesiastical buildings of the city are the two chapels of **University College**, across the Palace Green in Durham Castle. This former residence of the Bishops of Durham was given to the newly-established university in 1833. The Norman chapel, a semi-basement building, is the oldest part of the castle, which was founded by William the Conqueror in 1072. It has a nave and aisles of six bays, and is covered with groined vaults. The piers are circular and not at all cyclopean, as those in the cathedral are. The sandstone has the lovely 'watermark' patterning often found in County Durham. The capitals are richly and vigorously carved with stars, leaves, faces and animals, and rudimentary volutes. The windows on the N side were enlarged in 1840.

The other chapel was built by Bishop Tunstall in the early 16C, and was enlarged in the late 17C by Bishops Cosin and Crewe. Its chief glory is the set of stalls, made for Bishop Ruthall (1509–23) and formerly at Auckland Castle. Some of the original misericords survive, including a man transporting his enraged wife in a wheelbarrow, and a muzzled bear. The bench-ends are very ornate, with poppyheads, coats of arms and tracery. Cosin replaced one in the late 17C: it has acanthus decoration. He provided a screen at the W end, with his usual blend of Gothic and Classical motifs. Some of the organ pipes and part of the case came from the Father Smith organ of 1683 in the cathedral. The reredos is by C. Hodgson Fowler, late 19C; the E window is by C.E. Kempe.

E of the cathedral is **St. Mary-le-Bow**, now a heritage centre. Its little tower is of 1702, incorporating parts of the medieval gate or bow which stood adjacent to it and which fell in 1635. The church is simple, nave and chancel only, and all the windows, in 14C and 15C styles, were inserted in 1843 by Bonomi & Cory. The church has important early 18C woodwork, continuing the Cosin style. The altar is of 1687, and the font and cover are 17C, but the main work was done from 1703. The Rood screen is of 1707, and has turned balusters, garlands, leaf decoration and an acanthus frieze. The chancel stalls are contemporary and have poppyheads and heavy garlands on the ends. The communion rail is of 1703. Nave and chancel are panelled. The panelling of the sanctuary, and the reredos, which has round-headed panels separated by Corinthian pilasters, and an IHS in a sunburst as a centrepiece, are as late as 1731. The W gallery was installed in 1741.

Down South Bailey is **St. Mary-the-Less**, now St. John's College chapel. It is neo-Norman of 1847 by George Pickering. He reused some original material, and preserved the plan of nave and chancel, but derived most of his decorative details from the gallery of the castle. The church houses an excellent early 13C sculpted relief which was brought from St. Giles's. It portrays Christ in a mandorla, with the emblems of the Evangelists around. The head of Christ is missing. In the chancel is Cosin-style panelling, with ogee-headed tracery, poppyheads, obelisks and cherubs' heads. There is a monument by John Cory to Joseph Boruwlaski (died 1837), the celebrated Polish 'Count' and dwarf who lived to a great age, was a well-known Durham personality and is buried in the cathedral.

Across the river, in Church Street, is **St. Oswald's**, much rebuilt in 1834 by Ignatius Bonomi after damage by subsidence, and again after a recent fire which damaged the chancel. The church has Norman arcades and chancel arch, and a Perpendicular W tower. The W window is an early work of Morris & Co., 1864–66. In Old Elvet is **St. Cuthbert's**, 1826–27, by Ignatius Bonomi, small and modest, in Perpendicular style. Bonomi's W gallery, on slim cast-iron piers, and his chancel screens, remain. The tower is of 1865. J.P. Pritchett's **St. Nicholas's**, 1857–58, stands proudly in the Market Place. It is in Decorated style, with a good tower and spire. The interior was reordered in 1979–80 by Ronald Sims. Over the river in Crossgate is the church of **St. Margaret of Antioch**. It was much restored by C. Hodgson Fowler in 1865–80, but preserves Norman arcades and chancel arch, and a 15C W tower. Close to the station is **Our Lady of Mercy and St. Godric**, Castle Chare. It is a tall church in a prominent position by E.W. Pugin, in Decorated style. The apse is multi-gabled. Pugin & Pugin added the Perpendicular-style W tower in 1909–10. **St. Giles's**, at the top of Gilesgate, on the edge of a steep hill overlooking the city, preserves original Norman features, especially the stark N wall of the nave, with three small windows set very high.

Escomb, *St. John the Evangelist.* This is a small, remarkably complete two-cell pre-Conquest church set unworthily amongst plain, modern houses. Bede does not mention it, but architectural and archaeological evidence point to the late 7C. It has nave, narrower chancel and S porch; slabs in the grass mark out the sites of a porticus on the N side of the chancel and an annexe on the W end of the nave (see its roofline on the W wall). The church was superseded in 1863 by a Victorian building up the hill, but this was demolished in 1970. The ancient church, having been repaired by R.J. Johnson in 1875–80, was fully restored and refurnished in 1965 to Sir Albert Richardson's designs.

Much of the masonry may have been brought from the Roman fort at nearby Binchester—many large blocks have typical Roman tooling. One stone has LEG VI (that is, the Sixth Legion from York) inscribed on it. The chancel arch (but not the jambs which are pre-Conquest in style) shows Roman influence in its radiating voussoirs and may have been completely reused. Five original small windows survive. All have monolithic lintels. The others are tall 13C lancets or 19C insertions. The N door, unusually, has stone jambs and lintels mortised like wood. The porch may be 12C, using stone from elsewhere in the church. The S door was probably enlarged then. On the S wall of the nave is a very early pre-Conquest sundial, apparently *in situ*, its dial marked with three lines and surmounted by a serpent.

St. John's, a two-cell stone church from the time of Bede

Inside, the original windows, deeply splayed, preserve grooves for shutters. The chancel arch is typically tall and narrow. Traces of wall painting survive: scroll work under the chancel arch 12C or 13C; and faint marks of various dates on the N wall of the nave. Many fragments of sculpture have been found, including an incised cross on the wall behind the pulpit. The stone cross behind the altar is 9C or 10C.

Gibside Chapel. This exquisite 18C chapel, built as a mausoleum for the Bowes family, was given to the National Trust by the 16th Earl of Strathmore in 1965. George Bowes inherited the estate in 1722 and in 1729 embarked on an ambitious scheme of landscape design. In c 1747 he laid out the avenue, at one end of which the chapel stands; the other end is terminated by a tall column crowned by a statue of British Liberty. Bowes died in 1760, leaving money for the building of the chapel. It was built to James Paine's design but was left internally incomplete in 1767, and was finished in 1812 by Bowes's grandson. The later architect is not known, but the furnishings somewhat resemble those in David Stephenson's All Saints', Newcastle.

The chapel faces NE along the avenue of Turkey oaks, more like a small villa than a church. Paine modelled it upon Palladio's Tempietto at Maser. In plan it is a Greek cross with the corners filled in, crowned with a drum and shallow dome. The façade facing the avenue has an imposing portico; the other façades are relatively plain, the ends of the cross having Diocletian windows (i.e. semicircular, with three vertical divisions). The portico is of six columns with Ionic capitals. The inner four columns break forward and are crowned with a pediment and plain parapet. The outer bays are closed with arches and balustrading; in front of them flights of steps rise to the projecting portico; the balustrade is repeated in the parapet above the entablature. Six urns decorate the parapet. The drum is embellished with swags.

The interior is cool, light and spacious, the wall surfaces painted a pale pink-brown, the architectural details picked out in white. The arms of the cross have become apses with groin-vaulted ceilings. The plasterwork above the rich entablature is by the early 19C architect; Paine planned sumptuously coffered vaults and dome, and large-scale paintings on the pendentives of the drum. He also wanted statues in the niches of the apses, which are all blank. The dome is supported by four engaged columns with Composite capitals. Similar columns are almost embedded in the corners of the apses. The arched spaces filling in the cross have pilasters with Ionic capitals.

The focal point should be the altar, almost centrally placed, and surrounded by a simple rail; but it is dominated by the splendid free-standing triple-decker pulpit to its W, partly under the crossing.

The stately three-decker pulpit of Gibside Chapel, a private chapel built by James Paine in 1760–69 in a Greek-cross plan

Stairs rise on either side of the desks to the oval pulpit, surmounted by an oval, inlaid tester. The pulpit is made of mahogany, the other furnishings of cherrywood. In the apses are curved seats for servants and visitors; in the corners, pews for family, agent and chaplain, all with uniformly panelled fronts. The furniture is all early 19C.

Hartlepool, *St. Hilda.* Hartlepool Church stands on the Headland, a little promontory close to the sea; a majestic, venerable building, with the old town clustering around it. The town now preserves few relics of its antiquity and its important medieval role as the chief port of Durham, and close to it has grown 19C West Hartlepool, with its docks and works and railways. Hartlepool was a pre-Conquest monastery, founded c 640 by St. Aidan of Lindisfarne. St. Hilda was head of the community c 649–57 before she became Abbess of Whitby. The church was built in sumptuous style by the Bruce family, Lords of the Manor, between 1200 and 1250 (Robert Bruce, King of Scotland, was a relative), perhaps as their burial place. The nave, with its fine Early English arcades, and the first bay of the chancel, survive. The aisles have Perpendicular windows. The rest of the chancel, which had been demolished, was rebuilt in 1924–27 by W.D. Caroë, in a style slightly later than the rest of the church. In c 1250 the W tower was built, large and quite finely detailed, with arcades of lancets, some blank. It gives an impression of strength and solidity, but either the foundations were inadequate or the construction was bad, for it began to subside soon after it was built, and had to be shored up with six massive and rather ungainly buttresses. Behind the high altar is a decayed male effigy on an altar-tomb of Frosterley marble, said to commemorate the founder, Robert Bruce. It had lain outside until the chancel was rebuilt.

Jarrow, *St. Paul.* The present building incorporates surviving parts of the famous pre-Conquest church, which is notable as the home of the Venerable Bede (died 735). St. Benedict Biscop founded Jarrow in 681, a few years after Monkwearmouth, the two coming under a federal abbot. Bede's remains lay here until 1020, when they were removed to Durham. The church originally comprised two churches linked by a chamber which is now the central tower. It preserves the oldest English dedication inscription, recording the date of 23rd April 685. The monastery was refounded as a Benedictine house c 1074 but the monks were moved to Durham in 1083, and Jarrow became a cell of Durham. The original W church survived, in a much patched and altered state, until 1782. The present nave and N aisle are by Sir Gilbert Scott, 1866.

The chancel, originally the E church, is late 7C. It may once have had a chancel further E, but a 19C vault has prevented excavation. On the S side, three tiny pre-Conquest windows remain, two with original stone *transennae* or roundels. The large window in this wall is early 14C, with Decorated tracery. The E window and the NE window have 13C intersecting tracery, and on the N side there is also a Perpendicular, square-headed window. Between the large windows is a pre-Conquest door, now blocked, with a single lancet above. The tower is late 7C at its base, late 11C above. On the first floor there is, on the N side, a window in late pre-Conquest style with carving over. The window on the S side has become a door to the first floor. Above are late pre-Conquest openings to N and S, double-headed with a baluster-shaft, and to the W a blocked triangular-headed window. The tower narrows considerably above the third stage, which is flat-topped and has Norman openings. W of the tower all is 19C, Scott's aisle being as big as his nave, and under a separate roof. Doorways under the tower confirm its early date. The S doorway is blocked, but the N leads to the vestry. On the first floor, a door in the E wall of the tower led to a gallery in the chancel. It can be seen, high up on the nave side.

The nave has been largely cleared of its furnishings. A new chancel arrangement has been made at the E end, incorporating an elaborate early 20C bishop's chair by W.H. Wood. Some of the early carved stones and stained glass are now in the Bede Monastery Museum at nearby Jarrow Hall. Others are displayed in the N aisle. The dedication stone, *ex situ*, is in the nave, above the chancel arch. The inscription is: DEDICATIO BASILICAE S(AN)C(T)I PAULI VIII K(A)L(ENDAS) MAI(I) ANNO XV ECFRIDI REG(IS) CEOLFRIDI ABB(ATIS) EIUSDEMQ(UE) ECCLES(IAE) D(E)O AUCTORE CONDITORIS ANNO IIII (The dedication of the church of St. Paul on 23rd April in the 15th year of King Ecgfrith and the fourth year of Ceolfrith, abbot, and with God's help the founder, of the church). A late 7C or early 8C stone (the upper part of which is in the Museum of Antiquities in New-castle) stands in the SE corner of the nave. It has an inscription which reads IN HOC SINGULARI SIGNO VITA REDDITUR MUNDO (by this sign alone life is given back to the world). In the chancel is 'Bede's Chair', probably 14C, with a high back of rough planks, covered with carved graffiti and equally rough, almost vertical, arms. At the entrance to the chancel is a large 20C wooden statue of Bede by Fenwick Lawson. Also by Lawson are figures of Christ ascending and St. Michael and the Devil. The central window on the S side of the chancel, a small, original *transenna*, contains pieces of the oldest stained glass in England, made in the monastery workshop in the late 7C and discovered during excavations in the 1970s. It was placed here in 1980. The E window, of three saints, is by L.C. Evetts, 1950. The lancet window on the N side has glass of 1985 by John Piper, a two-armed cross, with two Bs (for Benedict Biscop) below. A bust at the W end commemorates John Hodgson, incumbent 1808–23 and a well-known local historian and amateur archaeologist.

In the monastery in Ceolfrith's time was written a complete manuscript of the Bible, which was given to the Pope in 716. The manuscript survives today in the Laurentian Library in Florence and is known as the Codex Amiatinus. It is the finest of the earliest English manuscripts to survive.

Monkwearmouth, St. Peter with St. Cuthbert. St. Benedict Biscop founded a monastery here in 674. From this early date the W wall of the nave survives, as well as the lay-out of nave and chancel (originally separate churches of St. Peter and St. Mary). The masons and glaziers were sent from France by Abbot Torhthelm, one of the founder's many Continental associates (Biscop had been professed as a monk at Lérins and had seen 17 monasteries in all). Monkwear-mouth was twinned with Benedict Biscop's other foundation at Jarrow after 681. The church is presently being restored after a major fire in 1984. The setting is very much an industrial one, but open space surrounds the church itself.

The church has a tall, slender pre-Conquest tower which was built in stages. The lowest or porch storey was added soon after the church was built. A little later, another stage was added (originally with flanking N and W *porticus*, of which the gables are still visible). The quoins are of large stones laid side-alternate. There have been

openings in all four faces of the lowest stage, including an ornamented W doorway with banded balusters and animal carvings. The
stringcourse above is also carved with animals. Later, perhaps in the
10C, the tower was doubled in height; the belfry windows have twin
round-headed openings in a large blank arch. The rest of the church
was rebuilt in the 13C and 14C, and consists of four-bay nave,
chancel and a N aisle which continues N of the chancel. The aisle
was rebuilt and enlarged by Austin & Johnson of Newcastle in 1875–
76. The chancel's E window, of five lights, is 14C. At the SE corner is
an octagonal addition of 1973, an 'historical interpretation centre' but
officially called the Chapter House.

There is a collection of early sculptures, of which the finest is a
gravestone of c 700 inscribed HIC IN SEPULCRO REQUIESCIT CORPORE
... HEREBERICHT PRB (in this tomb lies the body of Herebericht the
priest). This was found in the ground floor of the tower in 1866,
covering, with other slabs, a 'relic chest' with the arranged bones of
12 people. At the E end there are bench-ends with carved lions,
probably original. There is a damaged effigy of a 13C or 14C priest in
vestments, called 'The Master of Wearmouth' (from the days when
Monkwearmouth was a dependency of Durham Cathedral Priory;
the Master represented Durham). A knight's effigy, much damaged,
thought to represent William Hilton (died 1435), lies in a recess much
renewed in 1872–75 (on the N side of the chancel).

There is 20C stained glass, by L.C. Evetts, the chancel's E window
being of 1969 (showing St. Aidan, St. Bede, St. Peter, St. Paulinus and
St. Cuthbert). Another window shows Coelfrith, Benedict Biscop's
successor.

Roker, *St. Andrew.* A magnificent early 20C church, of great energy
and inventiveness, by E.S. Prior, 1906–07, Roker stands proudly
amidst comfortable Edwardian suburbia. It is Gothic Revival in spirit
and arrangement, but all the motifs are treated in an original manner.
It has been called 'the cathedral of the Arts and Crafts movement',
and is furnished and decorated by such craftsmen as Ernest Gimson,
Eric Gill and Morris & Co.

Roker is a big, bold building in rough Marsden stone, seen perhaps
to best effect from the road running due E to the sea. The tower is at
the E end, with only a slight sanctuary projecting E of it. It bears
down crushingly on the church, like the keep of a fortress, with four
huge hexagonal corner turrets. Originally the turrets had pointed
caps. They are joined at the top under the parapet by a deep
segmental arch, with broad four-light belfry windows below. There
are transepts and a long nave. All the windows are shallow and
pointed, with stocky tracery of wide mullions and plain triangular
heads to most lights, except for the S transept E window, which is
round, with intersecting tracery forming a cross.

The massive arches of the nave seem to spring directly from the
floor, but are in fact supported by tiny paired piers with cushion
capitals. Behind the piers run narrow passages, vestigial aisles to
provide access to the pews. The arches span the nave elliptically. The
transept arches spring diagonally towards the narrower sanctuary.
The big E window fills the E wall, its tracery not appearing so harsh
within as it does without.

The ceiling of the sanctuary was painted in 1927 by Macdonald
Gill, and was restored in 1967 by Maurice Partland. The theme is
Creation. Texts from Genesis, the Benedicite and Psalm 104 divide
the blue walls, representing the sea, in which fish and a whale

disport themselves, from the land above, fruitful with trees and animals. Over this the heavens open out, with birds and stars and the moon, and in the centre a huge pink alabaster sun. The hand of God appears above the clouds, bestowing a blessing upon Adam and Eve. The reredos is a tapestry of the Adoration of the Magi by Morris & Co., from a design by Sir Edward Burne-Jones; the chancel carpet is a Morris design. Ernest Gimson designed the chancel furnishings—choirstalls, organ gallery, pulpit and tester, and the exquisite lectern, of ebony inlaid with ivory, mother-of-pearl and silver, with candle-brackets of polished wrought-iron. His also are the altar cross and candlesticks (of burnished wrought-iron, lacquered to prevent tarnish), the processional cross and the altar furnishings of the Lady chapel. The stone font, a plain shallow bowl on four carved supports, is by Randall Wells, with a cover by Robert Thompson of Kilburn. There are many examples of Eric Gill's skill in lettering. He designed the texts of the scrolls on the chancel walls, the dedication tablet inside the SW door, the table of Vicars, the tablet in memory of Jane Priestman (in whose memory the church was built) inside the NW door, and, on the Lady chapel wall outside, the foundation stone. The stained glass of the E window, showing the Ascension, is by H.A. Payne of Birmingham. Also by Payne is the S transept glass, depicting Christ's words 'Come unto me, all ye that labour and are heavy laden, and I will give you rest'. Angels swirl about the Cross, while Christ at the foot embraces a kneeling woman, and 'all sorts and conditions of men' worship. The round window in the E wall of the S transept has glass attributed to Burne-Jones, made by Thompson & Snee of Gateshead, and features emblems of the Evangelists. The other windows are plain, thick and translucent, set in small square panes, a novel process developed by Prior c 1890, allowing light in by day but twinkling and sparkling under artificial light at night. The war memorial at the W end has names by Macdonald Gill, with those for 1939–45 added by L.C. Evetts.

Staindrop, *St. Mary*. Staindrop has some pre-Conquest walling in the nave, but was extensively rebuilt in medieval times. From the early 15C to the Reformation it was collegiate, and has stalls and a screen (the only remaining pre-Reformation screen in the county) provided for the college of priests. The founder was Ralph Neville, first Earl of Westmorland. There are many monuments of the Neville family, and also of the Vanes, Earls of Darlington in the 18C and Dukes of Cleveland in the 19C, whose seat was Raby Castle.

In the 12C the nave was lengthened to the W, a tower was built, and aisles (which embrace the tower) were added. In the 13C a short belfry stage with corbelled top was built on the tower, and in the 15C a tall belfry stage was added. The chancel was rebuilt in the 13C, and transepts and a N vestry were added. The N transept preserves triple lancets with trefoiled arches. The vestry has an upper storey which may have been a priest's house. The aisles were widened in the 14C, when Ralph, second Lord Neville (died 1367) founded a chantry. The S aisle has windows under four-centred arches, with Reticulated tracery. At its SE corner is a small sacristy with a stone roof. The windows of the chancel have 15C Perpendicular panel tracery. In the 15C too the nave clerestory, with four square-headed windows on each side, was built.

The nave arcades show two phases of building. The three E bays were built first, c 1170. The piers are round, the arches are round and the capitals have some leaf decoration. The hoodmould over the arcade is enriched with nutmeg ornament. The W bays, somewhat later, preserve the round arches but have shafted piers and moulded capitals. One capital on the S side has been cut away: the tall pulpit stood against it until 1849. The tower arch and the chancel arch are 13C, pointed. From the upper chamber of the vestry a three-light window opens into the chancel. The fine sedilia are 13C. There are no internal shafts, but foliage and a head terminate the trefoil arches. These are deeply moulded.

A pre-Conquest sundial has been incorporated, upside down, over the chancel arch in the NE corner of the nave. The screen of c 1408 is plain, with ogee heads to the lights. The stalls—12 each side—have poppyhead bench-ends decorated, like the backs, with Perpendicular blank tracery, and misericords. The font, of local Teesdale marble, is 15C, octagonal, and decorated with plain shields. The communion table is 17C. There are fragments of medieval stained glass in the S aisle E window and in the vestry. There is much 19C stained glass, mainly by Clayton & Bell and by C.E. Kempe. Note the E window of the S aisle, in memory of the second Duke of Cleveland (died 1864), depicting Christ (as Salvator Mundi) and the Latin Doctors. The church was extensively restored and refurnished by John Cory in 1849–51.

In the S wall of the S aisle are two tomb-recesses. One, under a tall, richly decorated canopy, which has a finial termination supporting a plinth for a statue, is an effigy of Euphemia de Clavering, mid-14C. In the canopy the space is filled with trefoils and quatrefoils. In the other are 13C effigies of a lady and a boy, apparently placed there c 1850. In the SW corner is the monument to Ralph Neville, first Earl of Westmorland (died 1425) with his wives. The tomb is of alabaster, and a stove which formerly stood too close to it has calcined and damaged it somewhat; but the effigies are unharmed. Next to it is the oak monument to Henry Neville, fifth Earl of Westmorland (died 1560), with his second and third wives. Small thin pillars around the monument support depressed ogee arches, in which Neville's children kneel. Over the S door is the monument to John Lee (died 1793), Attorney General, the tablet topped by his bust and books, and with the usual eulogistic epitaph. The monument is by Joseph Nollekens, as is the monument to his wife, Mary Lee (died 1813). In the chancel are tablets to the Vane family: Henry, second Earl of Darlington (died 1792), reclining on a sarcophagus, with a relief of Raby Castle behind him; Margaret, Countess of Darlington (died 1800), 'Friend of Virtue Order and Religion', a fleshy female figure leaning on books on a podium in a Gothic ogee arch; and Katherine Margaret, Countess of Darlington (died 1807), whose 'pious and virtuous Conduct through Life' won her this obelisk on which she is shown being conducted from her death couch by an angel. All three monuments are by Robert Cooke of London. Sir Richard Westmacott designed the white marble tomb-chest of William, first Duke of Cleveland (died 1842). His recumbent effigy is clad in ducal robes and he wears his ducal coronet. Nearby is the monument of Sophia, Duchess of Cleveland (died 1859). She lies shrouded on a tomb-chest, while in a frieze above, her soul flies off to heaven with an angel.

In the churchyard is William Burn's Gothic mausoleum to the second Duke of Cleveland.

Ushaw, _St. Cuthbert's College, Chapels (closed to the public)._ Ushaw, a vast Catholic seminary, stands proudly on rising ground W of Durham. It is the successor of Cardinal Allen's English seminary at

Douai in Flanders, which supplied priests for England and Wales from 1568 until its dispersal at the French Revolution. The land at Ushaw was bought in 1799, and the main block was ready in 1808. The Classical, pedimented block is surrounded now by Gothic buildings mostly of the mid- and late 19C, a time of great expansion. To the left of the entrance front is the almost overwhelming chapel, with its many-gabled apse, of 1882–84 by Dunn & Hansom, replacing (and almost doubling in size) A.W.N. Pugin's chapel of 1844–48. Many features of Pugin's design, and fittings by him and John Hardman, were reused in the rebuilding.

The chapel is T-shaped, like Pugin's original and like many Oxford college chapels. Pugin's building had a square E end but Dunn & Hansom replaced it with the vigorous gabled and pinnacled apse. They reused many parts of Pugin's chapel. The tracery of the apse windows, 14C in style, is Pugin's. The five-light E window was Pugin's W window, and the seven-light W window was his E. In his gabled niche over the W window is a carving of the Coronation of the Virgin.

The main chapel (St. Cuthbert's) is long and spacious. Pugin's screen divides it from the antechapel. The windows are set in engaged arcades, with shafts rising to the richly decorated roof. Stalls run E–W in collegiate fashion. They were designed by Pugin, with misericords and poppyheads, and more were made to fill the enlarged chapel. Behind them rise wooden canopies decorated with a band of the text 'Magnificat', and (on the parapet) shields of the Bishops of Durham to the Reformation, then the Vicars Apostolic, and finally the Bishops of Hexham and Newcastle. High above the windows runs the prayer of St. Cuthbert. The sumptuous high altar and reredos, the tabernacle soaring up high, are of 1890–91 by P.P. Pugin. The panels were painted in 1908. John Hardman made the sanctuary lamp, and near the altar stands a statue of the Virgin by Karl Hoffmann. Pugin designed the magnificent brass eagle lectern, and Hardman made it. It is supported at its base by tiny lions, who seem remarkably serene and untroubled by the great weight of the ponderous brass bearing down on them. The Second Vatican Council (1962–65) necessitated some re-arrangement, on the whole carried out sympathetically and unobtrusively in 1982. The architect was Wilfrid Cantwell. A podium with slender brass railings abuts the lectern. Need it to have been quite so large? Further E is a freestanding altar, a slab of marble supported by similar delicate brasswork. E of it is a recent brass celebrant's chair. A wrought-iron screen encloses the sanctuary: ten delicate bays with Gothic motifs. All the metalwork was executed locally by Ron Field. The stained glass of the E window is by Hardman, and depicts the life of St. Cuthbert. The upper parts of the apse windows are also by Hardman, the lower panels being added by Edward Frampton in the 1880s.

The antechapel has a constellation of small chapels. Pugin's screen incorporates tiny chapels N and S of the central entrance. J.F. Bentley decorated the central bays by 1894. The sculpture was executed by Hoffmann. On the N side is Bede's chapel, with an altar by Bentley; to the S is the chapel of St. Gregory the Great, with paintings of c 1925, designed by S.P. Powell and executed by Elphege Pippet. In the antechapel stands Hardman's paschal candlestick, of brass, exhibited at the Great Exhibition of 1851. The great W window is by Hardman; it was Pugin's E window, and he thought it 'the finest work of modern times'. The subject is the Church Triumphant. Hoffman's statue of Our Lady of Help is in the antechapel; the Virgin's cloak carries the Star of David. In the SE corner of the antechapel is the Lady chapel, reconstructed, after Pugin's design, in the 1880s. The wall arcade, fleur-de-lis tiles, stone altar and sanctuary lamp, and Hardman's stained glass (all windows except the SE) come from Pugin's chapel. At the S end of the antechapel is the Sacred Heart chapel, with a screen of 1883 by Basil Champneys, and Pugin's original high altar and reredos. The W end of the antechapel was extended by S.P. Powell in 1925–28 to provide two fan-vaulted chapels, of St. Thomas and of the English Martyrs.

The cloister corridor leads to a succession of chapels. On the right the Oratory of the Holy Family, 1852–53, probably designed by Pugin, is octagonal and lit by clerestory windows. Opposite, and opening by a traceried arcade onto the cloister corridor, is E.W. Pugin's chapel of St. Carlo Borromeo, 1857–59. The capitals are richly carved with naturalistic foliage. The W window is by John Hardman. At the end of the corridor is St. Joseph's chapel, designed by Pugin in 1852 for domestic staff of the college, and completed by E.W. Pugin in 1854. E.W. Pugin designed the reredos (with a Hoffmann figure) and the roof, with its painted subject, the Descent of Joseph. This is now the chapel of the Salesian community at Ushaw. Running parallel with the main chapel, on the N side of the cloister, is St. Bede's chapel, formed in 1967 in part of E.W. Pugin's museum of 1856–58.

HEREFORDSHIRE

Remoter than well-heeled Worcestershire (to which it is now administratively joined), Herefordshire has kept its distinctive character.
This character—as far as it affects the churches and chapels of the
county—has three chief features. First, Herefordshire is border country, as its S and E boundaries clearly show: those villages within sight
of the Black Mountains often have strongly defensive church towers
and dedications to Welsh saints. Second, this is a sandstone area, and
the dark red soil of the land explains the pink-grey stone used
throughout the county. Third, Herefordshire is still very rural, and
has hardly a single major industry not associated with agriculture:
even Hereford itself retains the feel of a market town. It is thus a
county of working villages whose churches are still important focal
points, and the sense of continuity they represent is strong. By
contrast with East Anglia, however, Herefordshire was not a place
where huge fortunes from wool enabled rich burghers to build
extravagantly: most of the churches are relatively small-scale (the
largest being monastic rather than secular foundations) and the great
period of church building activity was well before 1350. Indeed, it
was from its earliest phase that Herefordshire contributed something
of national significance—its school of Norman sculpture which
enriched arches, tympana, fonts and corbels with artistry and craftsmanship of outstanding quality. Perhaps the most notable features
from later periods are the use of ballflower decoration (both inside
and outside buildings) in imitation of Hereford Cathedral, some eye-
catching spires and half-timbered upper storeys of towers. More than
one church in the county is located actually in a farmyard.

If Shobdon is the earliest place where the work of the Herefordshire School can be seen, it is at Kilpeck that its style can best be
appreciated *in situ*. Here it is apparent that the workshop created a
successful synthesis of Scandinavian, Anglo-Saxon and French
styles, and that their carving was highly skilled—there is nothing
provincial about the best of their work. Brinsop and Leominster
contain notable examples; so do Eardisley and Castle Frome (fonts)
as well as Fownhope, Rowlstone and Stretton Sugwas (tympana).
Other Norman churches that deserve attention include Moccas,
Peterchurch and lonely Garway, with its massive tower, and the
remains of a Templar round church. The building which best illustrates the advance from Norman to Early English Gothic is Abbey
Dore. None of the church W of the crossing has survived, but the
assurance with which the choir and retrochoir is handled proves that
the Gothic inspiration had reached Herefordshire by the end of the
12C. The outstanding churches of the next two centuries are probably Madley and Weobley (the latter most notable now for its tower
and resplendent spire of c 1340) but both had Norman origins.
Kingsland, however, is also worth mentioning as an impressive
church belonging entirely to one period (late 13C–early 14C), and
having an intact chantry chapel attached to the N porch. Geometrical
tracery and ballflower ornament can best be seen in the outer N
chapel of Ledbury and in the S aisle of Leominster Priory. There are
no purely Perpendicular churches but the chapel of Hampton Court
and the great W window of Leominster have distinguished tracery.
One keeps coming back to Leominster, for (despite being untypically
large) it best illustrates the history of church building in Herefordshire. It also shows most forcefully the impact of the Reformation

on a county that was otherwise relatively little affected: the Priory transepts, chancel and monastic buildings have entirely disappeared, and the present E end of the Priory is as unexciting as the W front is impressive.

With a few isolated exceptions, the story only revives in the later 18C. In 1679 Monnington-on-Wye was completely rebuilt apart from its Perpendicular tower while Tyberton Church (in the grounds of Tyberton Court) was remodelled in 1719–21. Stoke Edith (1740–42) makes an interesting comparison with Tyberton. Then comes Shobdon, mid-century and heavily influenced by Strawberry Hill; it is one of the most important Gothick churches in England. Hereford itself offers some instructive early Victorian contrasts: the church of St. Francis Xavier has a full-blooded stucco Doric portico (1838–39) while St. Nicholas' (1842) and St. Martin's (1845) stand midway between Commissioners' Gothic and A.W.N. Pugin. Elsewhere in and around the town F.R. Kempson and T. Nicholson provided competent but generally unexciting new churches and restorations to order. Sir Gilbert Scott built Eastnor (1852) and in 1866 G.E. Street restored Monkland. In the 1880s J.P. Seddon produced an exotic Italian church overlooking the Wye at Hoarwithy. But the only major architect to work regularly in Herefordshire during the second half of the 19C was G.F. Bodley. None of his work here is large-scale but all of it is interesting, especially his earliest church (Llangrove, 1854–56), the very late chapel at Hom Green (1905) and his decoration of Kinnersley, where he is buried. One other church must be mentioned: W.R. Lethaby's Arts and Crafts thatched church at Brockhampton by Ross (1901–02).

Relatively little medieval glass has survived, not even in the cathedral; some of the best has been resited. The E window at Ross-on-Wye, for example, contains four 15C figures originally from a window at Bishop's House, Stretton Sugwas. The best place to see early 14C glass is at Eaton Bishop which, from internal evidence, can be dated at c 1330. Brinsop also has 14C panels in its E window. The drama of Abbey Dore is heightened by the spectacular glass of its E windows, dated 1634. There is fine heraldic glass in the chapel of Coningsby Hospital, Hereford. Of 19C glass, C.E. Kempe's is the best represented, from as early as 1874 (Bridstow), with an impressive set of windows at Ledbury and others at Leominster, where the E window (by Kempe & Co.—i.e. post-1907) is especially effective. John Hardman & Co., whose N transept window of Hereford Cathedral is so memorable, made glass (to Street's design) at Monkland and also at Upton Bishop—where Clayton & Bell also contributed a window. There is good work by Comper at Brinsop (1920s) and by M.E. Aldrich Rope at All Saints', Hereford (1930s). There is no significant postwar glass.

Woodwork. There are plenty of examples of 17C woodwork—pulpits, communion tables and rails—but very little earlier work has survived. The glorious exceptions are the 15C choirstalls of All Saints', Hereford and the 16C Rood loft of St. Margaret's, which can be compared with Llangwm (Gwent) and Patrishow (Powys). The Laudian reordering of Abbey Dore includes a fine screen of 1633 in high Jacobean style, while at Shobdon the furnishings are, of course, an integral part of the Gothick effect. Of decorated woodwork it is sufficient to notice the Tudor painted roof of Almeley, and the chancel roofs at Kingsland and Kinnersley (both of these being examples of G.F. Bodley's celebrated sense of colour). The only criticism that may be offered of Kinnersley is that the decorative scheme Bodley introduced (embracing roofs, walls, chancel arch and organ case) overpowers the fine 1635 wall monument to the Smallman family. There are indeed many good **monuments** in Herefordshire, though few that are outstanding: at Bacton, Blanche Parry (Maid of Honour to Queen Elizabeth I) kneels before a rather uncomfortable-looking Virgin Queen; at Ross, Col. William Rudhall, dressed to kill in the high Roman fashion, looks suspiciously like King Charles I. Beneath the E window of Burrington Church are some 17C iron slabs which are impressively cast. Holme Lacy, Much Marcle and Hope under Dinmore have large-scale 18C monuments.

Herefordshire can be proud of its remaining collection of royal arms and hatchments spanning 300 years: Elizabeth I (Elton), Charles I (Abbey Dore), Charles II (Monnington), William III (How Caple and St. Peter's, Hereford), George I (Leominster and Tyberton), George III (Dilwyn) and Victoria (Aconbury). The county is also conspicuous for the number of its unusual dedications—again, a reflection of its proximity to the Celtic influence of the Welsh borders. St. Dubricius makes five appearances (Ballingham, Hamnish Clifford, Hentland, St. Devereux and Whitchurch). There are also St. Clodock (Clodock); St. Dinabo (Llandinabo—a unique dedication in Great Britain); St. Deinst (Llangarron—a dedication shared only with Itton in Gwent); St. Weonard (St. Weonard's—also unique) and St. Tysilio (Sellack—a dedication found elsewhere in Wales but not in England). Most unusual of all is SS. Cosmas and Damian (Stretford). This tiny church has a shrine and parallel naves and altars dedicated to these two 4C saints, who were venerated as patrons of physicians and surgeons. Only three similar dedications exist, in SE England.

There are no great, and few famous, men associated with Herefordshire's churches. David Garrick, the actor, was baptised in All Saints', Hereford. John Kyrle, Pope's 'Man of Ross', is naturally associated with Ross-on-Wye. Francis Kilvert is buried at Bredwardine, a few miles (but across the border) from Clyro where most of his diary was written. After the Reformation S Herefordshire was one of the strongest Recusant areas in the country, and for a century priests were able to serve the old Catholic families with relative freedom. This came to an end with the Popish Plot, when John Kemble, who had worked as a priest in the county for 54 years, was executed in 1679. He is buried at Welsh Newton, and was canonised in 1970 to join St. Ethelbert and St. Thomas of Hereford as the third recognised saint this small county has produced.

The Churches of G.F. Bodley. Herefordshire is closely associated with the architecture of George Frederick Bodley (1827–1907), the most influential ecclesiastical architect and designer of the later Victorian era. His work in the county spans 50 years and includes churches and church restorations, schools and parsonages. Although he never lived in the county, he married into a local family (the Reaveleys of Kinnersley Castle) and is buried in a Herefordshire churchyard.

In 1854 Bodley designed Christchurch, Llangrove (formerly Long Grove). This model village church (dedicated 1856) should be compared with his contemporary work in Gloucestershire at Bussage and France Lynch. Built of local red sandstone, its most striking feature is the W end with two prominent lancets and three flat buttresses. As at Bussage the porch forms a termination to the S aisle. The careful asymmetry of the S chancel windows is worth noting, as is their experimental tracery. The interior is unfussy, but there are some significant details: above the chancel arch a cross with equal arms (distinctive Bodley motif) is set into the wall; there is no screen, but a low wall (as at France Lynch) with inlaid marble designs. Most important of all, however, is the S arcade: chamfered rectangular pillars, without capitals, support arches that are radically free of mouldings. The confident clear-cut rhythm of this arcade would have seemed modern 50 years later.

Of the original church at Canon Frome only the brick tower remains. Bodley's rebuilding of c 1860 was an original response to a difficult site: the church stands within 20 yards of the imposing Canon Frome Hall. It has a steep roof with overhanging eaves, and a blind N wall. The tracery of the rose window is 13C French in character; the other windows look forward to English Gothic. Inside the church, the N aisle is lit chiefly by a cleverly hidden dormer, and the pulpit is an ingenious example of early Bodley design.

At Burrington, a remote hamlet near the Shropshire border, Bodley designed a church which was favourably noticed by 'The Ecclesiologist' in 1857. However, when the building was finally dedicated in 1864 only the chancel was Bodley's work: the patrons had insisted on using their own architect for the nave. The best features are in the sanctuary: a deeply recessed lancet window and a piscina with credence shelf above distinguish the S wall, and the steps to the altar are decorated with increasingly ornate encaustic tiles. (Bodley was to use these tiles again in other local work.) Across the road is the former parsonage, built by Bodley in 1862 and of considerable interest—the earliest signs of Bodley's move towards a vernacular style in domestic architecture.

Bodley's restorations had begun in 1857 with the tiny church of Brampton Abbotts near Ross, where he also built the adjacent school. He produced here, in the chancel, his earliest boarded wagon roof, opened up the 14C windows and added a half-timbered porch. His other work is in the NE of the county. At Almeley the pews and choirstalls are worth noting, and at Kingsland Bodley provided a beautiful painted chancel roof: the dominant colours are green, white and red, each bay celebrating one of the nine orders of angels. The sanctuary bay is richly coloured in Venetian red. Lyonshall (restored 1870–73) is one of Bodley's earliest collaborations with Thomas Garner. The S elevation (porch and windows) and, inside, the screen and pulpit show how sympathetic and skilful Bodley could be as a restorer. But the most important work is at Kinnersley where Bodley restored and enriched the church over a span of 30 years: walls, roofs, chancel arch and organ case are painted in characteristic style and colour (note especially the chancel roof). Reaveley family gravestones in the churchyard and the W window (Burlison & Grylls) were all designed by Bodley.

His last complete work in the county is at Hom Green, near Ross-on-Wye. Built in 1905, it is a miniature masterpiece in local sandstone with Cotswold stone dressings, dedicated to the Paraclete after a vanished medieval church. A narthex, spanning the W front, serves as a porch: shuttered grilles offer a view into the church even when locked, and the interior is astonishing, for a single arcade on octagonal pillars rises to the centre of a wagon roof, dividing the church lengthways. It is then bisected again by a screen separating the family choir from the nave. Sadly, the church is now abandoned, but a key is obtainable from the nearby cottage. In the same year that Bodley built Hom Green, he sailed to America to begin work on

Washington Cathedral. He was nearly 80 and the effort exhausted him. He died in 1907 and is buried at Kinnersley.

Abbey Dore, *St. Mary*. A 17C parish church fashioned out of a great Cistercian abbey, founded in 1147 by Robert of Ewyas and rebuilt in the 13C. After the Dissolution the buildings decayed and by 1630 it had become a cattle shed where 'Sir Gyles read prayers under a sheltering arch'. It then belonged to Sir John Scudamore and, influenced by Laud, he set about rescuing the crossing, the presbytery and the ambulatory. He built a tower over the S chapel, blocked the arcade leading to the ruined nave, and employed John Abel, the King's carpenter, to reroof and furnish it. This high and unusual building was reconsecrated on Palm Sunday, 1634, Sir John's birthday. At this time the pulpit, pews and music gallery were all W of the screen, leaving the presbytery (chancel) free for Communion services.

The walls are of local sandstone and the roof stone-tiled. Scudamore employed David Addams of Ross to build a tower for £90 and two buttresses for a further £13 6s 8d. The roof of the ambulatory was lowered and, as a result, the top of the stringcourse where it passes over the lancet windows has been lost. A 13C N door, with hinges bearing a wolf's head, has recently been replaced by a new one. The tower has battlements and there is a 17C timber-framed S porch.

The transepts are entered down steps and the length and height of the crossing can then be appreciated. The plastered walls have a large painting of the arms of Queen Anne, a skeleton, figures, and many texts, one near the door, signed 'William ... er of Hereford 1701'. The W wall of the crossing has a fine gallery, standing on columns similar to those of the screen which seals off the presbytery. It is a massive affair with the arms of Scudamore and Laud on either side of King Charles I's. Running the full length are words which can also be found in Monnington Court and on the market hall which Abel built at Leominster: *Vive Deo Gratus/Toti Mundo Tumulatus/Crimine Mundatus/Semper Transire Paratus*. 204 tons of timber, at 5s a ton, were provided for the roof and furnishing. The roof is flat, supported by braces and pillars of wood, resting on the broken columns of the abbey. The huge stone mensa is raised within four-sided Laudian communion rails, and has groups of medieval tiles on either side. The E end of the presbytery has an arcade of three bays above which are three lancet windows with good glass of 1634. The multiple shafts with stiff-leaf capitals at this end, and in the ambulatory, are amongst the best features of the church.

Apart from a lectern by R.W. Paul, the furniture was made by Abel; the pulpit with tester, stalls, panelling and prayer desk are all of a piece. There is a vandalised poor box of 1639 with the words, 'He that from ye Poor his eyes will turn away/The Lord will turn His eyes from him in ye later day'. In the ambulatory are some splendid bosses with scenes ranging from St. Katherine with her emblems to the Coronation of the Virgin. Near the sanctuary is a small memorial to John le Breton, a Bishop of Hereford whose heart was buried here in 1275; and in the ambulatory two mailed knights, one with an arm missing. John Aubrey claimed that it had been taken 'by a Mower to wett his scythe'. There are fragments of medieval glass in the ambulatory and three modern windows at the E end showing Richard Coeur de Lion, the Crucifixion, and Archbishop Laud respectively.

The S chapel has been screened off and is now the mausoleum of the Hoskyns family, a table-tomb of Sir John Hoskyns acting as communion table. He was a judge in the Marches and a friend of Sir Walter Raleigh. He was also the legendary director of a Morris dance performed before King James I. The dancers were ten Herefordshire ancients whose combined ages totalled 1000 years. There is fine calligraphy on many of the ledger stones which pave the church, and under a draped urn in the presbytery, a monument to a previous Rector, the Reverend John Duncombe, 'the Historian of the County'. On the N wall of the crossing is a humble slate memorial to the founder, 'the Good Lord Scudamore', scholar, diplomat, royalist, benefactor; the friend of Milton, Laud and Grotius; and the propagator of Herefordshire's most famous cider apple, the Red Streak, 'for which let the Minister and all ye people thankfully remember him and duely praise God'.

Brinsop, St. George. A small rectangular church, built between 1300 and 1350, with a Victorian bell turret, it is notable for the remains of a 12C building and the work of Sir Ninian Comper in the 20C. The nave and chancel are in one, and the N aisle and chapel are almost as large, all under one roof. The patron saint is much in evidence: on a tympanum of the Herefordshire School (c 1140) he is majestically slaying the dragon. The voussoirs of the arches are decorated with pleated figures, angels, doves, and Sagittarius in the style of similar work at Rowlstone. Beyond the screen Comper takes over with an alabaster reredos and altar, gilded angels, a shining celure, all adding golden opulence to the richness of the 12C carving. Comper's windows are good, but are eclipsed by a splendid 14C St. George with shield, spear and sword.

Brockhampton by Ross, All Saints. Nave, crossing tower, short transepts, chancel and high porch with a pyramidal roof. It replaced the medieval church of the Holy Trinity whose remains are in the grounds of the neighbouring hotel. All Saints' was built in 1901–02 by W.R. Lethaby to commemorate the parents of the donor, Alice Madeline Foster. It is a small country church with creepers on the walls and, except for the roof of the porch, it is thatched.

The sturdy central tower has a stair turret slightly protruding, and small square windows with inset tracery. The roof is steeply pitched, as are the arches of the porch. The nave windows are low and horizontal, while the large window in the S transept is a vertical oblong with thick diagonal stone bars, intersecting and dividing it into diamond lights. The S porch has a door into the nave with fine ironwork, and has five carved panels over, one with a cross and the others with flying birds.

Inside, Lethaby used concrete for the vaulting and gave character to the building by using, throughout its length, a succession of steep pointed arches, rising directly from the side walls. They lead the eye to an E window with three lights and a separate, small rose window above. The nave windows have cylindrical shafts, forward of the glass, standing on the wide sills. The glass is by Christopher Whall, brilliantly coloured, but sometimes sentimental. The E window has St. Margaret and St. Cecilia, with attendant cat, kittens and heavenly choir; while the large S window, dedicated to the donor's father, shows four angel musicians 'for music ever found an echo in his heart'. The architect used wild flowers as the unifying theme for the fittings, dividing the fronts of the choirstalls into 48 panels, each carved with a different species. These have been repeated on the embroidered hymn-book covers and on the altar cloth. The font is round and carved with interwoven tendrils of vine leaves and grapes. Two large tapestries near the altar are from the workshop of William Morris and were designed by Edward Burne-Jones for a window in Salisbury Cathedral. There is an alabaster figure of the Madonna on the altar, and the pulpit is carved with Christ preaching in the open air, while children play in the foreground. At the back is a carved wooden almsbox, paid for with money found in the pocket of one of the family, killed at Neuve Chapelle while serving in the Grenadier Guards in 1915.

Lethaby was one of William Morris's most able followers, Principal of the Central School of Arts and Crafts, and Professor of Design at the Royal College of Art. He was to become one of the founders of the Design and Industry Association and, in 1906, Surveyor of Westminster Abbey. He was a man of great integrity and, in his writings, made clear his uncompromising attitude to art and architecture: 'Art is not a special sauce applied to ordinary cooking ... It is the well-doing of what needs doing'.

Castle Frome, St. Michael. A small Norman church with nave, chancel and Victorian timber-framed bell turret and spire. The building is famous for its font, one of the later works of the Herefordshire School of craftsmen (c 1170). The bowl shows the baptism of Christ, a diminutive figure standing in a pool with fish and rippling water. John, much larger, with a maniple over his wrist, is touching Christ's head, as is a dove and the Hand of God. Around the rest of the bowl are the signs of the Evangelists and doves. Interlace is around the rim and the bottom, and the base rests on three menacing figures.

Eardisley, St. Mary Magdalene. A Norman church with a font to match that at Castle Frome. By the same school but earlier (c 1150). The figures are much more resilient than the sturdy John the Baptist at Castle Frome, and very similar to the warriors at Kilpeck. Again there is much interlace, the principal scene being the Harrowing of Hell, with Christ rescuing at speed a small man entangled in ropes. Other scenes include two men fighting with sword and spear, a cheerful lion with huge claws and tail rising from between its legs, and a puzzling half-length figure with halo and book.

Garway, St. Michael. A rectangular 13C church consisting of nave, chancel and S chapel, joined at a tangent by a 17C passage to a detached tower of great strength. The nave was imposed on a 12C round nave of the Knights Templar, its foundation uncovered on the N and its chancel arch incorporated in the existing building. There was also a 13C S chapel, rebuilt in the 16C. It stands above the Monnow, close to a massive dovecote with 19 rows of holes and the inscription that it was built in 1326 'per Ricardum'.

The church is of sandstone rubble with some tufa and has stone tiles. The tower is of two stages externally, but three inside, and has a pyramidal roof. There are large 17C buttresses on the S wall of the nave, while the N wall of the chancel, which is out of alignment, has a stringcourse of the 12C which has been cut by later lancet windows. The walls have masons' marks, a Maltese cross, a phoenix, and above the door, a hand raised in blessing.

The interior, except for the tower, is whitewashed and the chancel has a fine 14C roof of silvered oak. The round chancel arch is of three orders, the outer of varied chevrons and the inner composed of moulded voussoirs giving it a Moorish appearance. The inner order rests on plain shafts, the outer ones on detached columns with waterleaf capitals, except for one with a grotesque head with beaded foliage curling from the mouth, as at Kilpeck. The opening from the stairs to the Rood loft is exposed. The chancel windows are 13C reset and the stone altar has been built into the communion table. A two-bay arcade leads into the S chapel where there is a 13C piscina with trefoil head under which has been incised a chalice and wafer between a fish and a snake. The octagonal font also has a snake twined round a cross cut into one side. There is a dug-out chest and a 17C hutch, many coffin-lids reused in the floor, and sturdy benches, stalls and communion rails of the 17C. In the nave N wall is a gabled cross with the hand of God in the centre and heart-shaped openings on the arms.

The easily forded River Monnow, separating the Dioceses of Hereford and Llandaff, has always been a safe haven for those at odds with their bishop. And the fact that Garway was the chief Templar seat in the Marches had long brought down episcopal suspicion. So there has always been something faintly subversive about a parish which was placed under an interdict for barring its doors against the bishop in 1524; which gave sanctuary to a fugitive Prior of Monmouth in 1536; and which later gave harbour to recusants.

Hampton Court, *Chapel.* The chapel is an extension at the NE corner of the castle, dating from the mid-15C. According to Leland it was built by Sir Rowland Lenthall after taking many prisoners at Agincourt, 'by the which prey he beganne the new building and mansion place at Hampton'. He was given a licence to crenellate in 1434 and the castle and chapel date from then. The E window is of five lights and has remnants of 15C and 17C glass including several coats of arms. The best feature is the roof, mainly 15C but recently painted. It is divided into four bays by slightly cambered tiebeams which have tracery over. Each bay has 16 panels decorated with diagonal crosses, the panels having bosses of foliage, faces or negro heads at the intersections. The castle was restored by Sir Jeffry Wyatville in the 19C and the enriched parapet of the chapel may date from then.

Hereford

All Saints. Both because of its location at the busy junction of High Street and Broad Street, and because of its distinctive twisted spire, All Saints' dominates the centre of Hereford in a way the cathedral does not. An attractive, mainly late 13C church with some notable woodwork and a chained library, its peaceful interior contrasts with the bustling shopping area outside.

The church is built entirely of local sandstone. From the S one confronts an appealing clutter of aisles, buttresses, pinnacles and windows. A restored 14C porch (now disused) leads into the S chapel; entry into the church is down steps into the S aisle. From outside the tower's W door one looks up to see the terrific kink at the top of the octagonal 14C spire. The chief features of the N side are the great buttresses propping up the tower in the NW corner. There is no churchyard.

Inside, nave and chancel are flanked by aisles and chapels. First impression is of width not length, for the two bays W of the entrance are screened off to provide vestries, organ gallery and parish room. Of the two arcades, the earlier (13C) S arcade has a severely compressed first arch. There is a clerestory of four lights each side, and carved corbels support the roof of the N aisle. The baptistery is located in the S aisle. The chief architectural interest lies in the chancel and N chancel aisle (Lady chapel). There is no chancel arch but there was once a Rood screen; the staircase survives in the chancel S wall. With only single rows of stalls each side, and a minimum of other furniture, chancel and sanctuary are impressively uncluttered; their walls are limewashed. The sedilia are fragmented by the intrusion of a later doorway, evidence of the major 14C rebuilding; that this was undertaken piecemeal can be seen in the confusion of stonework and floor levels around the NW pier of the chancel. There is a piscina, and another rectangular opening in the E wall. Narrow doorways with chamfered ogee heads open into lockers either side of the high altar. To the S side of the five-light Perpendicular E window is a large wall painting of an indistinct female saint. The N chapel has a four-light E window and an attractive piscina with ballflower decoration and a quatrefoil basin. On the S wall are embedded some encaustic Malvern tiles, belonging to the 15C. Replicas of these were used in the Victorian restoration of chancel and chapels. In the S chapel can be seen the lower doorway of the Rood loft staircase. The original E window has been blocked and replaced by a small modern light just below the roof.

The most notable glass is in the two E windows. Each is by M.E. Aldrich Rope—bold 1930s attempts to create a fresh idiom for stained glass; the Lady chapel window has as its central subject the expulsion of Adam and Eve; the main E window displays the Holy City, the Ship of Faith and other themes from Revelation. The 15C choirstalls with vividly-carved misericords and elaborate canopies are the church's major feature. Free-standing, one range of five stalls each side, they can be seen to better advantage here than in most cathedrals. The pulpit, with characteristic Jacobean carving, is dated 1621. At the W end of the N aisle is a breadshelf, embellished with miniature obelisks, dated 1683, and an impressive chest, 14C in origin. The S chapel, reserved for use by Hereford's Russian Orthodox congregation, has an iconostasis. Here also is a chained library (originally 300 volumes; half are now in the British Museum) given to the church by Dr. William Brewster (died 1715).

David Garrick, the actor, was born in Hereford and a plaque commemorating his baptism in All Saints' is placed in the chancel.

St. Peter, St. Peter's Square. The oldest church in Hereford. The earliest visible parts are the chancel (late 12C) and the 13C tower. The S elevation dominates St. Peter's Square, but is rather diminished by having a bus shelter built against the church wall. There is no churchyard, only a sad little paved area at the foot of the E window.

Inside, there are pews everywhere. The N arcade is 13C with almost triangular arches (a Herefordshire characteristic); the S arcade was wholly rebuilt during the extensive restoration of 1884–86 by Thomas Nicholson. The S aisle ends abruptly in the blank wall of the tower, beyond which is the S chapel, notable for its sedilia and Jacobean communion table. The early 14C chancel arch was once spanned by a Rood loft (the staircase remains): the 19C screen, pulpit and lectern are well carved. Good woodwork too in the 17C panels of the organ case, and in the choirstalls with very late plain misericords—on several the carving was never completed. Carved arms of King William III are found in the N aisle. There is some striking stained glass, notably a late window depicting St. Peter by Kempe & Co. (1929).

St. Francis Xavier, Broad Street. Squeezed between shops and a Victorian post office, all that can be seen of St. Francis Xavier's (1838–39) is a tall, narrow stuccoed portico *in antis* with outsize Doric columns. Inside, the vestibule with stairs leading up each side to the gallery could belong to any Nonconformist chapel; but the suddenly wide rectangular hall of the church is wholly Catholic: there are no windows, all the light coming from the glazed sides of a dome which rises out of the coved ceiling. A balustraded wooden communion rail snakes its way across the whole width of the building; Ionic columns support the recess in the E wall in which stands a huge tabernacle, evidently modelled on St. Peter's, Rome. High Italianate wall paintings and statuary, and prominent stone Stations of the Cross adorn the church. A modern painting commemorates the local saint, John Kemble, martyred in Hereford in 1679 at the height of the Popish Plot.

Coningsby Hospital, Chapel of St. John, Widemarsh Street. When Sir Thomas Coningsby founded a hospital for old soldiers in 1614 he incorporated into the buildings a 13C chapel originally founded by the Order of St. John. Chapel and Hospital are both still in use. The chapel occupies the N side of the charming courtyard and is entered through what was once the Hall (now a museum).

There are plain sandstone walls and a trussed rafter roof: the chapel's character comes from its 17C furnishings—communion table and rails, pulpit and Commander's Pew—all of good quality. Excellent heraldic glass in a N window is dated 1614. The glass of the three-lancet E window was brought in 1984 from the disused chapel of Harewood Place (near Ross-on-Wye). It depicts the early history and insignia of the Knights of St. John of Jerusalem—high quality glass, possibly by John Hardman Powell (1864). In the adjoining museum is a 16C gold altar frontal from Spain, again with insignia of the Order.

St. Giles Hospital, St. Owen Street. St. Giles Hospital and chapel were established in 1682 on the site of a Templar round church. Of this only fragments survive (including a 12C tympanum) reset into the walls of the almshouses. The chapel (also 1682) was demolished in 1927 when the road was widened, but a replica was built nearby containing all the original furnishings, including neat pews and a substantial pulpit with a peg for the preacher's hat.

Hoarwithy, *St. Catherine.* An Italianate church with campanile and cloister walk and a Byzantine interior, built in 1880 by J.P. Seddon. A surprising addition to the Wye Valley, owing everything to the wealth and energy of the Reverend William Poole, a man described by the wife of one of his curates as 'So good, so grand, so autocratic and so often so difficult'. A great local eccentric, he ruled the village for 50 years, was chairman of the local bench, built a school, a vicarage and cottages, paid his curates and teachers himself, and fought tirelessly with bishops and bureaucrats. His memory still lingers. In 1944, one of his successors, visiting a dying man, found him shaking with terror. When he began to say that God was merciful, the old man started up, shouting, 'Its not God I'm afraid of, it's Mr. Poole'.

Mr. Poole became Vicar of Hentland, the mother church, in 1854 and found at Hoarwithy a building, 'as bare as the palm of the hand'. 30 years later he employed Seddon to incorporate it in the new church. It stands high and is approached by a flight of steps which pass the triple apse and the undercroft of the campanile to emerge onto the cloister walk which runs the length of the nave. The roof of this walk is supported by an arcade, the double pillars having leaf capitals, and the floor an interlace design in mosaic. The last arches form a porch protecting the door into the atrium. The doorway has a band of foliage with birds over the arch and lizard-like beasts on the capitals of the shafts. Beyond the atrium on the N side are well-designed outbuildings and vestry. The campanile has three stages and a tiled pyramidal roof.

The atrium, lit by three round-headed windows, has 'Keep thy feet when thou goest into the House of God' in the floor mosaic, and a tympanum of Christ, with the symbols of the Evangelists, over the door into the nave. On the inside there is another tympanum with three crosses. The aisle floor has a leaf-scroll mosaic, and the whole nave has kingposts, trusses, and tiebeams and was painted in terracotta, blue and green, by George Fox (of Eastnor?). The nave is divided from the chancel by three arches, the central one standing on two grey marble pillars with bases of red and green porphyry blocks. Two similar inner pillars support a cupola over the chancel. Each pillar has white capitals with Saints and Evangelists. The altar of marble, inlaid with lapis lazuli and crysalite, is raised on four steps. The ambulatory is lit by 11 windows and is surmounted by the golden vault of the apse, with the *pantokrator* the focus of the whole building. There are six canopied choirstalls and prayer desk on the S side, and an organ by Nicholson covering the mosaic of a peacock where Mr. Poole used to tell choirboys not to be too proud of their voices.

The furniture is of good quality and the stalls, made of oak from the Vicar's estates, were carved by Harry Hems from Seddon's designs. Over the canopies stand 13 named Welsh saints, of whom Dubricius and Weonard are the most local. Hems's name is on a cider barrel carved on the prayer desk in a scene in which Dubricius is conjuring drink in an emergency. The ambo, used as the pulpit, is marble with Cosmati work. The large brass lamps were copied from San Marco in Venice. The hexagonal font alone survives from the earlier church. The glass, designed by Seddon between 1890 and 1896, is remarkable for its restrained colouring. The 11 round-headed windows at the W end have named saints; two of the three on the N have more saints with swords; while five of the 11 in the apse commemorate Mr. Poole. They depict Christ as the light of the world, and the Evangelists. They were made by H.G. Murray of London. A large photograph of Poole still stands behind the altar.

Kilpeck, *St. Mary and St. David.* In the shadow of the castle ruins and surrounded by yews is one of the treasures of Norman Herefordshire: a small apsidal building superbly decorated by a company of craftsmen operating in the W between 1140 and 1180. Their exuberant talents enliven the portal, the W front, the corbel table, the chancel arch and the ribs of the apse.

The walls are of rubble with ashlar dressings of local sandstone and the external sculpture has been preserved by a porch (now removed) and the overhang of the roof above the corbel table. It is the door in the S wall which makes the immediate impact. The

The famous 12C carved S doorway of St. Mary and St. David's, a masterpiece of the Herefordshire School of sculptors

tympanum has a simple beaded Tree of Life, with the arch decorated in two orders. The outer one has medallions containing dragons, birds, snakes and fish, linked by ropework emerging from the mouths of a succession of intervening heads. The inner order has beakheads, snakes, beasts and an unexpected angel. The shafts are decorated on the left with two warriors with Phrygian caps, ribbed surcoats and trousers, enmeshed in belts and ropework. On the right there are two birds and a swirl of foliar trails and palmettes. The abacus above is decorated with a typical glaring head with beaded foliage coming from the mouth; on the left are two opposing beasts. The jambs are carved with snake-like dragons devouring one another. The W front has Viking-style dragon-head projections, a window with interlaced beaded bands, and two foliated heads like the one on the portal. The corbels which surround the building have birds, beasts, fertility emblems, musicians, a dog and rabbit, the Lamb and Cross, and two people embracing. The ferocity of many of these heads echoes the ferocity of the times. It is almost as if they were defending, from the battlement of the corbel table, the beauty of holiness inside.

Indeed, the interior is very different in both style and character. This is especially true of the chancel arch, decorated by three figures on each shaft. They have none of the lithe alertness of the men on the doorway; they stand, placidly devout, one above the other, nimbed, a book in one hand and a key, cross or scourge in the other. The way in which each succeeding reduced arch of chancel, apse and E window gives an illusion of space, is due entirely to the artistry of the builders. The apse is divided into three bays with recessed single-light windows, surmounted by zigzag decorated arches and rib-vaults, joining at the apex in four fearsome heads. The walls are plastered, and there are traces of a pre-Conquest building in the NE corner of the nave. The gallery is Jacobean with stepped seating; the huge font of breccia stands on five legs, and like the one at Bredwardine, is completely plain, though a carefully carved stopper has survived. There is a curious stoup with two hands clasped round the rim of its stomach and four snake-like creatures emerging from the base. With the four heads on the apse, it is quite alien to this beautiful interior.

Kilpeck is the least restored of all the churches built or enriched by these talented craftsmen. They were operating when the country was enduring the anarchy of King Stephen's reign and when the Welsh March was in turmoil. Kilpeck is a monument to their triumph over such difficulties and gives a curiously appropriate impression of inner peace amidst outward menace. So it is perhaps not altogether surprising that the Bishop of Hereford, visiting the church in 1397, should be told that the chaplain was not 'firm in the faith, because on many occasions he has celebrated rites at night with fantastic spirits'. In 1840 G.R. Lewis made the church famous by publishing, with his 'Essay on Ecclesiastical Design', a set of splendid lithographs of all the sculptural details. Amongst the many subscribers were Gladstone, Pugin, Cottingham, Thomas Wyatt, Newman and the Cambridge Camden Society.

Ledbury, St. Michael and All Angels. The church commands the town with its splendid detached tower and spire. Alongside is a large late 12C nave and chancel, to which have been added N and S aisles and chapels, and in the early 14C an outer N chapel, known as St. Katherine's. The walls are of a reddish local sandstone and the building lies in a beautifully kept churchyard, the tombstones still in their proper places, but mostly on the N or Devil's side.

The tower, the finest of the seven detached ones in the county, is of four stages, the first three dating from c 1230 and the fourth probably from the rebuilding of the spire by Nathaniel Wilkinson in c 1730. The spire is octagonal and with the tower is 202ft high. The W façade has a mid-12C recessed portal with chevron arch and faces biting from the capitals into the shafts. The window above is of three lights and is flanked by square turrets with pinnacles. The W window of the N aisle has good Geometrical tracery, that of the S aisle a closely matching restoration. The S wall is buttressed and the windows are of the typical Herefordshire Y-tracery. The finest work is in the outer N chapel where the four-light windows are enriched with ballflower ornament as are the jambs of the doors. The masonry throughout this chapel seems to have been the work of masons from Leominster.

Inside, the drastic scraping detracts from the effect achieved by the exterior, in spite of the great width of the building. The arches of nave and chancel stand on octagonal piers, while the clerestory windows from the earlier church are round. Also from that earlier building are the corbel tables exposed in the side aisles. The chancel arch is of three orders with the lower voussoirs in alternate grey and reddish stones; the shafts have scalloped capitals. The E responds of the nave have two corbels, one showing a fight between a lion and a dragon, the other a foliate head.

The chancel stalls (early 16C) have moulded misericords; of the same period is a chair carved with panels showing the Entry into Jerusalem and the Adoration of the Magi. The reredos, a 19C copy of Leonardo's Last Supper, has been up-staged by the Crystal Cross suspended over the altar in 1967. Of more importance are the monuments. In St. Katherine's chapel, now separated from the N aisle by glass doors, is the relief of a priest in Mass vestments, hands clasped in deep prayer, under a trefoil canopy, early 13C. From the next century, and now hidden behind the curtains of a vestry, is the effigy of a lady, her long dress overflowing the tomb on which she lies. In the sanctuary, under a canopy supported by three marble pillars, are Edward Skynner (died 1631) and his wife, Elizabeth, in a remarkable high-crowned hat, ruff and flowing dress. They kneel face to face, their dead child between them, and below are their ten other children, the five boys all bearded like their father, the girls all looking very like their mother. Other Skynners buried here include Captain Samuel Skynner by Thomas White. He is surrounded by naval trophies, being 'no mean proficient in maritime affairs'. There are also monuments by Westmacott, Flaxman and Charles Regnart; while a sleeping child, guarded by angels, and carved by Thomas and Mary Thornycroft, was exhibited at the 1851 Exhibition. In the chancel is a brass to William Calwe (died 1409), a chantry priest, with one of the earliest epitaphs in English, rather than Latin: 'Sey pat nost for sere Willia Calwe/That loved wel god and alle hallwe'. There is an assembly of good medieval glass in one window in St. Katherine's chapel, including Becket and King Canute. Many of the other windows, especially in the S aisle, are by C.E. Kempe, and very good.

Few national figures are here; it is very much a parish church. Elizabeth Barrett Browning's parents are commemorated and John Masefield remembered in his childhood how, 'Life's other glory topp'd the Church's spire,/A golden vane surveying half the shire'. It is the parishioners who figure most clearly here, in the wonderful selection of slate ledger stones, beautifully carved and lettered, covering the church's floors.

Leominster, *St. Peter and St. Paul*. Leominster claims to be one of the great parish churches of England. Certainly, together with Abbey Dore and Ledbury, it is one of the three great churches of Herefordshire. It stands a little apart from the Georgian town, in a spacious open churchyard of the original priory (dedicated to St. Peter and dating from c 1130), only the nave and W door of which remain; the parish church (dedicated to St. Paul) replaced the S aisle of the priory in 1239 and now forms the S nave. Exactly 300 years later the priory was dissolved. Destruction of the central tower, transepts and apsidal E end followed soon after. In 1699 a great fire badly damaged the remaining parts; some stonework still reveals the scars. Victorian restoration from 1866 onwards was largely the work of Sir Gilbert Scott.

The present churchyard gives direct access only to the W and S elevations. The W front (local sandstone rubble and ashlar) is a samplebook of styles: the Early English triple-lancet window of the N aisle; the splendid Norman doorway and window under the tower, whose higher stages are restored 14C; the great W window (Perpendicular with two slender buttresses rising up the centre) and finally the W window of the S aisle—late Geometrical tracery studded all over with ballflower decoration. Ballflower also covers the windows of the S elevation. The porch in the SW corner has good stiff-leaf carving. But it is the Norman doorway under the tower that is celebrated: it has three orders with carved capitals, clearly of the Hereford School, depicting birds, men (dressed in the same quilted trousers as seen at Kilpeck etc.), snakes, corn, lions and foliage.

Inside, the Norman N nave has a character quite different from the adjacent 13C S nave. Its arcades have mainly plain arches resting on great drum-like pillars with scalloped capitals. Triforium and clerestory emphasise height and create a powerful rhythm that halts abruptly at the E wall, a blank curtain put up after the Dissolution and pierced only by a modern round-headed window. The narrow N aisle has a doorway that originally led to the cloisters, and four crude gable-shaped windows with transoms. The S nave is effectively the centre of the present church. Lit from the W by the great 15C window of eight transomed and cinquefoiled lights, it is spacious if undramatic: there is no screen or chancel arch, and even the sanctuary is hardly raised above the level of the nave. In the sanctuary N wall can be seen a Norman door, archway and steps that led originally to the priory's Rood loft. The S aisle, containing the Lady chapel, is separated from the S nave by an arcade of six bays with slender pillars which were remodelled after the fire. The five windows of the S wall each have four lights and Geometrical tracery. In the sanctuary wall is a 13C piscina with a bishop's head set above, and stepped sedilia with trefoil heads, triangular hoods and ballflower decoration.

In the N nave there are faint traces of 12C decoration in the triforium, and masons' marks can be seen on the pillars. In the choir vestry (W end of N aisle) a 13C 'Wheel of Life' wall painting has all but disappeared. Arms of King George I can be seen at the E end of the aisle. The communion table in the N nave is Elizabethan. The handsome organ case is part 1739 and part modern. On display in the S aisle is a pre-Reformation chalice of distinction. There is much

good glass, notably the E window above the high altar: the Crucifixion (Kempe & Co., 1922) with the figures surrounded not by canopy
work but by antique white glass. In the S aisle there are (from the E)
two Kempe windows of 1897 (the Annunciation and the Shepherds at
the Manger), a German window depicting the Adoration of the Magi,
and then a Freemasons' window (the Presentation in The Temple),
by Geoffrey Webb 1938. There are two fonts: the earlier is 13C,
square with chamfered edges; the later, an octagonal design of 1842.
Leominster's Ducking Stool, still in use in the 19C, is proudly
preserved in the N aisle.

Madley, *The Nativity of the Blessed Virgin Mary.* An impressive
church, dominating the village with its splendid tower, nave, apsidal
chancel with crypt under, and S chapel. The N porch is based on the
N transept of a 12C building which was incorporated in the present
one when rebuilding began with the tower and nave in the early
13C. Between 1310 and 1320 a new chancel was extended into an
apsidal E end and a considerable drop in the ground gave room for a
crypt underneath. In c 1330 the S chapel was built and the S porch
demolished. The battlements of the tower are Victorian, while the
stair turret is carried above the parapet, a feature of many churches
in neighbouring Monmouthshire.

It is built of sandstone, ashlar and rubble and the roof is leaded and
stone-tiled. The tower is in three stages with clasping buttresses. The
W door has moulded orders under a window with three lancets. The
ringing chamber has two pointed lights and the belfry three. The
buttresses of the apse have ballflower decoration and pinnacles with
finials overtopping the eaves. The crypt is vaulted from a central
octagonal pier and can be reached from the aisles above. The S
chapel has large three-light windows to the S and a five-light one to
the E with ogee trefoils.

The Early English arcade of six bays has moulded capitals and the
clerestory has single lancets. The S chapel is separated by an arcade
of five bays. The high chancel arch has a door above and traces of
wall painting. The polygonal apse has a fine Reticulated E window
between two Geometrical ones. The sedilia, under three bays with
trefoil heads, has ballflower ornament. The piscina is of the same
date (c 1320). The font is huge and rough, and has been restored after
being reputedly vandalised by the Scottish army in 1645.

The furniture is not as outstanding as this glorious church
deserves. In the N aisle parts of a 15C screen have been cobbled
together with some 17C panelling to make a family pew or close.
With cushioned seats around the inside, it successfully protects the
occupants from anything that might be happening in the church. The
glass in the E window has the arms of England, Bohun and Warenne
in the top quatrefoils and below six roundels, two to each light. These
roundels have blue backgrounds and are set in ruby rings. Four of
them have scenes from the life of the Virgin, and two concern St.
John, though others think he is St. George. Below again are many
fragments of an early 14C Jesse window. Amongst them is the head
of Ezekiel, his splendid beard stained yellow with sulphide of silver.
The glass is only surpassed by that at Eaton Bishop, the adjoining
parish. It is likely that the same man worked on the shields in both
churches. The stalls in the chancel have undecorated misericords;
there are two chests, one medieval; and a badly damaged tomb-chest
of 1575 with the effigies of Richard and Anne Willison, signed 'This
Towm John Gildo made'.

As the only coloured glass is at the E end, the church is marvellously light, while the absence of tombs increases the sense of space. That spaciousness was enhanced until recently by the use of chairs. Unfortunately some run-of-the-mill pews have appeared. But it is still a marvellous setting for its annual musical festival. What is curious is the lack of evidence as to its benefactors. Where did the money come from? There is little information except for a reference in the cathedral archives to an agreement between the parishioners and the Dean and Chapter in 1318 that all offerings made before the statue of the Virgin would be spent on the new chancel.

Monnington, St. Mary. An early 15C tower guards a nave, chancel, porch and lychgate built between 1679 and 1680. It stands amongst apple orchards, looking across the water-meadows to the Wye beyond. Over the wall is Monnington Court where the benefactors, Uvedall and Mary Tomkins, lived. It seems likely that they employed Francis Jones of Hasfield, Gloucestershire to carry out the reconstruction. He had rebuilt Newent in 1675 with very similar windows and finials.

The tower is of three stages with embattled parapet complete with arrow slits. The stone is local sandstone and the roofs are of stone tile. The porch has an elliptical arch with, over it, the arms of Tomkins impaling Capel in a scrolled surround with 1679 and V & M T. The door into the nave is of this date with moulded panels and ornamental hinges. The lychgate is half-timbered and is approached from the village by a green lane with a brook in which Kilvert, whose sister was married to the Vicar, admired the marsh marigolds.

The interior is ceiled and whitewashed; the windows, round-headed, with mullions and transoms, have plain glass except for the Tomkins achievement; the whole marvellously light. Characteristic of the building is the use of twisted columns. They appear on screens, pulpit, communion table, rails, and royal arms. It has a unifying effect, and the high chancel arch, doing little to impede the transition from the nave, adds to that unity. It is still lit by oil lamps.

The furniture is almost all late 17C. The octagonal font, engraved 'V & MT 1680', has a cover with an acorn finial; the twisted legs of the communion table have at the top the same initials and '1679'. The screen has eight bays of twisted columns. The pulpit, stalls and reading desk have the same. Only the upright, open-backed Nonconformist settles have none. The arms of King Charles II, the finest in the county, are of oak, painted with twisted side columns supported by outer twisted iron shafts. It has been moved from the screen to the S wall of the nave.

There are Tomkins ledger stones in the chancel and on the N wall of the nave a memorial to Robert Perrot (died 1667), who distinguished himself fighting for Venice against the Turks, his bust looking as if he had come straight from the galleys. In the churchyard is the legendary grave of Owen Glendower. Kilvert firmly believed the legend and often grew lyrical about it. One of his favourite walks from Bredwardine was around Brobury Scar and through Monnington Walk, the avenue of trees planted in 1660. He especially enjoyed Sunday at Monnington: 'It is so calm and so serene. There is no hurry, no crowd, no confusion, no noise'. This is still true.

Much Marcle, St. Bartholomew. A 13C chancel and aisled nave, with a central 15C tower, and 14C N chapel. A large church notable for its monuments: **1.** A 14C oak effigy of a civilian in buttoned jerkin with sword, belt and wallet, his feet crossed on a dog. **2.** Altar-tomb with canopy over Blanche Mortimer, Lady Grandison, in wimple, with her tightly buttoned dress overhanging the dog at her feet. Her eyes are closed, a veil is falling over her shoulders, and her fine hands hold a rosary; probably the most serenely beautiful effigy in the county (1347). **3.** Alabaster and black marble altar-tomb to Sir John Kyrle and his wife. Sir John, with long hair, is in armour, his feet on a hedgehog (Kyrle); his wife has a ruff, slashed sleeves and dress open to reveal an underskirt, her feet on a paw (Mynors). Both have hands clasped in prayer (1650). **4.** Tomb-chest with effigies of a knight and lady (c 1400). He is in bascinet and full armour, gloved hands clasped and feet on a lion; she has a long pleated dress with a high scalloped collar, angels at her head and two dogs tugging her dress at her feet. There is important early Kempe glass in the chancel, including the first use of the individual wheatsheaf motif.

St. Margaret's, *St. Margaret.* High and remote above the Golden Valley, this is an undistinguished little church with a wooden turret. It consists of a nave and chancel separated by the finest screen in Herefordshire. It is of the Welsh type in silvered oak, undamaged and unpainted. A loft rests on two richly carved pillars with niches and delicate capitals. It is divided into panels and has a frieze of vine leaves, with cresting on the parapet and the same reversed at the base. The soffit is divided by ribs meeting in bosses, all different, carved with foliage, lions, faces and knots. The Rood stairs lead to it. The walls are painted with bordered texts and, in an old frame, 'The Duties of Churchwardens' printed in parallel columns in English and Welsh.

Shobdon, *St. John the Evangelist.* A 13C W tower to which were added in the 18C a nave, transepts and chancel, with battlements and ogee-headed windows. By 1756 the Hon. Richard Bateman of the adjoining Shobdon Court, a friend of Horace Walpole, had built one of the most surprising churches in the county, 'Rococo Gothick' at its most fantastic. There has been some argument as to which architect Bateman employed, and Richard Bentley, Sanderson Miller and William Kent have all been suggested.

The exterior gives little indication of what is stored inside. The embattled two-staged tower has a W door with an ogee arch and trefoiled window above. It opens into a narthex with access to the nave and gallery stairs. The Batemans had their own door into the family pew in the S transept, and their servants another into the servants' pew in the N transept.

On entering one is surprised by the beautifully restrained colouring, white and bluish grey, of this Rococo fantasy. It is a church with only one liturgical centre, the communion table behind white railings. The sumptuous family pew is also railed off and has a large marble fireplace and comfortable seating. The less luxurious servants' pews are also railed. There is a gallery, painted white, at the W end, built in 1810 and extended in 1829. The ceilings are coved and the chancel and transepts are separated from the nave by triple pendant ogee arches. The white pews have dome-shaped ends with quatrefoil openings and blue surrounds. There are two fonts, one from the Norman church and the other 18C.

The most elaborate object is the pulpit, a three-decker, with a sounding-board like a wedding cake. It has crockets and finials and bright red hangings. There are two magnificent Gothick chairs in the

*The pulpit at St. John the Evangelist's, a principal feature
of an ornate 18C Gothick interior*

sanctuary. The uniform colour scheme and the clear glass of the
windows with small lozenges enclosing quatrefoils of blue, red and
yellow make the church bright and cheerful. Only the 1892 lectern
and the 1907 glass in the E window jar. The window is particularly
unfortunate as it replaced the 1753 glass, some of which has been
arranged on screens in the N transept. It would be an act of mercy to
return it, even incomplete, to where it came from. There is a
monument by Joseph Nollekens to the second Viscount Bateman in
the nave.

As one emerges from the churchyard, a newly planted avenue
leads the eye to what the Viscount saved from the Norman church he
destroyed. He put together chancel arch, two doorways, and their
tympana on linking walls. He added a gable, pinnacles and battlements to dominate his park. Time has weathered the sandstone and
eroded the craftsmanship with which the team of men, who were to

move on to Kilpeck and Rowlstone, endowed it. One of the tympana has a Majesty, within a mandorla held by heavily-booted, diving angels. The other tympanum has the Harrowing of Hell, as on the font at Eardisley. Many of the features which recur elsewhere can be traced to Shobdon: the warriors in ribbed garments interlaced with ropes, the mythical beasts, the beakheads and writhing dragons.

The Norman church took the place of a timbered chapel dedicated to St. Julian, in c 1143, when Oliver de Merlimond, Hugh Mortimer's steward, founded a short-lived priory here. De Merlimond had been on pilgrimage to Santiago de Compostela, and the churches on the route may have influenced his choice of workmen. But this small team of craftsmen, assimilating Spanish, French and Viking elements, fashioned a style of their own which is as instantly recognisable as the Rococo Gothick inside the church. Set in a private, wooded parkland, they make a unique pair, and remain a tribute to the patronage of two men of taste, one from the 12C and the other from the 18C.

Stretton Sugwas, *St. Mary Magdalene.* A church with timber-framed W tower, nave and chancel, built out of the materials of the Norman church demolished in 1879. It contains two fine memorials of that earlier building, a tympanum and an incised slab. The tympanum of c 1150 has Samson in pleated garments, astride the lion, forcing its jaws apart with his bare hands. It is an almost exact replica, reversed, of a much smaller carving on the impost of the W doorway at Leominster. The incised slab commemorates Richard Greneway and his wife, Maud Harper. Their heads, under a canopy, rest on cushions and his feet on a dog. They wear long pleated gowns and she has an almost abstract starched head-dress. Their long hands are clasped in prayer. It is one of the most dignified memorials in the county, comparable with the effigy of Blanche Mortimer at Much Marcle. Maud Harper died on March 27th, 1473 and her husband some years later.

HUNTINGDONSHIRE

This little county, although now absorbed into Cambridgeshire for administrative purposes, has very much an identity of its own and churches with a character of their own. It is bisected by the A1 which runs through it from N to S. To the E of this trunk road, much of the countryside is flat and some is Fenland. To the W, Huntingdonshire is beautifully undulating, with pleasant hills and streams and stone-built villages. There are 86 medieval churches, also four which have been rebuilt but incorporate medieval parts, and five 19C churches. The main building material is limestone, although some churches to the S and E are faced with cobblestones, similar to many Cambridgeshire churches.

Work of all periods is well represented. Pre-Conquest work occurs at Great Paxton, Fletton and Woodston. There is Norman evidence in almost half the churches, but especially at Ramsey, in the arcades at Hartford, Eynesbury and Stibbington, chancel arches at Bury, Folksworth, Morborne, Haddon, Southoe and Warboys, and several good doorways, including a superb one at Southoe. There are also several fonts from the Norman period. The transition from Norman to Early English occurs at Farcet, Glatton and Alwalton. Pure Early English is seen at Chesterton, Holywell, Somersham and Leighton Bromswold. Decorated architecture includes Fenstanton's glorious chancel, the rare polygonal apse at Bluntisham and Tilbrook Church. Most stages in the evolution of Decorated architecture are represented here, including plate tracery, Y-tracery and the later Geometrical, flowing and Reticulated tracery. Perpendicular work is best seen in the larger churches, like St. Neots, St. Ives, Conington, Buckden and All Saints', Huntingdon. Of the post-medieval work, the 17C refurbishing of Leighton Bromswold is of supreme interest, also the tiny church at Little Gidding, the 18C chancel at Chesterton and the rebuilt tower and spire at Godmanchester.

A feature of Huntingdonshire exteriors is seen in its fine towers and graceful stone spires. The earliest of these are 13C (Chesterton, Water Newton, Alconbury and Buckworth) and they continued to be built throughout the 14C and 15C, ending up with the handsome spires recessed behind parapets seen at Buckden, St. Ives and Yaxley. There are 32 stone spires in all and some of the finest may be seen to the W of Huntingdon: Ellington, Easton, Spaldwick, Catworth and Keyston. Others occur along the Ouse valley to the E of Huntingdon. At Grafham, Houghton and Old Weston, the spires spring from octagonal belfry stages. Fine spireless towers occur at Brampton, Conington, Eaton Socon, Elton, Great Staughton, Huntingdon St. Mary, St. Neots and Stow Longa.

Church interiors contain much of interest. Several have ancient woodwork in their roofs—St. Neots, Somersham, Ellington and Great Gransden being fine examples. Over 20 churches have remains of medieval screenwork; the 14C screen at Offord Darcy, and the 15C screens at St. Neots and Tilbrook are of exceptional interest. Catworth has a 15C pulpit and Orton Waterville has a fine 16C one. Of the 17C pulpits Eynesbury's is particularly beautiful. Eynesbury also has a series of medieval benches, as does Glatton, whilst Brampton and Godmanchester possess stalls with misericords. Piscinas feature well including superb double piscinas at St. Ives and Leighton Bromswold, and several other examples of this unusual format which date from the reign of King Edward I, when there was one drain for the water from the cleansing of the chalice and another for that from the washing of the priest's hands. Other treasures include medieval lecterns at Ramsey and Bury, wall paintings at Molesworth and Broughton, a selection of ancient doors with fine ironwork, and box-pews at Old Weston and Farcet. Conington and Great Staughton possess some of the county's finest monuments; there is a heart shrine at Yaxley and the famous Capability Brown is commemorated at Fenstanton. Fine brasses may be seen at Sawtry and Diddington.

Buckden, *St. Mary.* This handsome church has a superb setting, backed by the Tudor brick Great Tower and gatehouse of Buckden Palace, with which it forms a pleasing contrast. The palace was the residence of the Bishops of Lincoln. The church is predominantly 15C and is a noble Perpendicular building. The aisles are lit by three-light windows, the N aisle being a little later and less ornate than the S. The chancel is 13C—it has an original doorway, but 15C windows. Of the 15C also is the beautifully proportioned tower and spire. The tower has set-back buttresses and pairs of double belfry windows and the spire is beautified by three tiers of lucarne windows. The entrance to the two-storeyed S porch is framed by a crocketed hoodmould. The parapet has corner pinnacles and creatures crawling round the stringcourse at its base. Inside, the porch has a vaulted ceiling with a central boss showing the Assumption of the Virgin Mary. The S doorway is 13C, with stiff-leaf capitals and its doors, which were once traceried, are 15C.

The interior is remarkably bright because the only stained glass comprises 15C fragments in two S aisle windows. Fine corbels may be seen on the tall and elegant 15C arcades, and supporting the roofs, which are 15C too. The nave roof was repaired in 1649 and the S aisle roof has an orchestra of angels with musical instruments. More angels appear on the cambered tiebeam roof of the chancel.

The font is 15C, the pulpit early 17C and in the clergy stalls are 16C Flemish woodcarvings of scenes from Our Lord's Passion. The sanctuary piscina is 13C, as are the three arched sedilia beside it. On the N sanctuary wall is a marble monument to Bishop Barlow, who died in 1691. He spent so much time living in ease at Buckden that people nicknamed him the Bishop of Buckden. Bishop Sanderson, who wrote the Preface to the 1662 Prayer Book, is buried in front of the altar here and Bishop George Pelham (died 1827) has a memorial by E.H. Baily in the N aisle. Also in this aisle is the large Gothic memorial to Robert Whitworth (died 1831), by Thomas Rickman.

Fletton, *St. Margaret.* Situated in the suburbs to the S of Peterborough, this unprepossessing church contains pre-Conquest carvings which are of national importance. The 13C W tower, with angle buttresses and Y-traceried windows, is crowned by a broach spire with two tiers of lucarne windows. Beside its W wall is part of a pre-Conquest cross, which bears the later inscription, *Radulf filius Wilielmi.* Many of the windows in the aisles and clerestory are rectangular and without tracery; these are probably of 17C date. The chancel is Norman and has a blocked S window of this period, its other windows being in the 14C Decorated style.

The homely interior has N nave and chancel arcades of c 1160 and an early 14C S arcade with octagonal piers. The Norman chancel arch has been given a later pointed head. The font is probably of the Tudor period. The main interest lies in the chancel where, in the E wall, just above the altar, have been set pre-Conquest carvings which were probably fashioned in the 9C. They were moved to their present position during recent years, having been set in an external buttress for many years. Here we see mythical creatures, angels, and Our Lord central, flanked by two figures—possibly His Mother and St. John. They compare with carvings at Breedon-on-the-Hill in Leicestershire and with the so-called Hedda Stone in Peterborough Cathedral. In the S chancel wall are two more figures, thought to be later than the others, representing St. Matthew and St. Michael.

In 1983, this much-loved and cared-for church was badly damaged by fire which was deliberately caused in the hope of destroying it. In 1984, however, it was reopened for worship, having been thoroughly and beautifully restored.

Godmanchester, St. Mary. Godmanchester is a small town of Roman origin, which is divided from the town of Huntingdon by the River Ouse. Its church is a large and dignified building, where we may enjoy fine craftsmanship from the 13C to the 17C and later. The earliest part is the chancel, which has shallow Early English buttresses and a renewed triple-lancet E window. Carved into the stone of one of the S buttresses is a beautiful circular design, rather like a rose window pattern, which may have served as an elaborate Mass dial. The chancel was given new windows in the 15C and the large windows lighting the aisles also date from this time. The Rood loft staircase vice may be seen where the S aisle and chancel join. Whilst the body of the church is mostly faced with brown cobblestones, the stately W tower is ashlar-faced. Above its deep W doorway is a pair of two-light windows. There are also pairs of large two-light windows in the belfry stage. The recessed spire which crowns the tower is beautified by three tiers of lucarne windows. The tower and spire are particularly interesting because they were built in 1623 and are fine examples of this period. The lofty S porch is probably 14C. It has large figures crowning the corners, handsome image niches and a sundial at the top. The inner entrance is also flanked by canopied niches and its 14C arch contains a pair of medieval doors.

The interior is spacious and remarkably wide. There are tall 15C arcades and both nave and aisles are spanned by arch-braced cambered tiebeam roofs. Above the chancel arch are two 13C lancet windows which retain traces of medieval painting in their splays. These may well have lit the E wall of a former central tower. The present W tower arch is also 13C, with stiff-leaf capitals.

The octagonal font is very worn and betrays its great age. Over the S doorway is a set of Hanoverian royal arms made in cast iron by Joseph Wallis of Colchester. The N chapel has a late 16C communion table with bulbous legs, and on the wall nearby is the brass of an unknown civilian, of c 1520. The S chapel is tastefully furnished and modern work of great taste and quality may be seen in the nave altar arrangement. The chancel screen and the reredos are the work of G.F. Bodley and were erected in 1901. In the chancel are some 15C stalls which have fascinating woodcarving on their armrests and the underside of their misericord seats. Amongst the armrest carvings may be seen a jester with his cap and bells, a king, a cat with dragon's wings and an angel on clouds. Beneath the seats are a fox and goose, a wyvern, a rabbit, a monkey, a horse and other creatures. Note also the traceried fronts and poppyhead ends. E of the main stalls are further sets of three and the ends of these terminate in fascinating designs, including poppyheads made up of four birds and of four hairy faces! This church has six stained glass windows by C.E. Kempe and a window by Morris & Co.

Great Gransden, *St. Bartholomew.* A beautifully situated church with a stately 15C exterior, which has large Perpendicular windows, an embattled Rood loft staircase turret, two fine porches and a handsome tower with pairs of two-light belfry windows and a lead-covered 'spike'.

Inside, the 15C work includes the four-bay arcades, the fine nave roof with original angels, the well-restored aisle roofs and many of the benches. These have straight-topped and buttressed ends and some have traceried backs and fronts. The ancient screen has traces of painting. The S chapel was tastefully furnished as a war memorial in 1948 to the designs of William Lea of Huntingdon. It contains a fine canopied niche, also modern glass in the SE window by Francis Spear. In the N chapel is a 17C communion table and a set of paintings given to the church in 1966. Another recent gift is a set of cast-iron royal arms near the N door. There are carved bosses in the chancel roof and some medieval glass remains in its SW window. In the sanctuary is a handsome 15C piscina recess.

A burial slab, with Lombardic lettering, commemorates the Reverend Thomas de Neusum, who died c 1330. Great Gransden's best-known incumbent was the Reverend Barnabas Oley (Vicar, 1633–86). He was President of Clare College, Cambridge (most of whose 17C Old Court he was responsible for building), Archdeacon of Ely and literary executor for George Herbert. He founded a school and almshouses in the village and in 1683 he gave a carillon mechanism for the church clock. He also donated the fine 17C pulpit which we see in the church today.

Great Paxton, *Holy Trinity.* As we approach the exterior of this pleasantly situated church, overlooking the valley of the River Ouse, we see little to indicate its importance as a pre-Conquest minster which was a nucleus for pastoral and missionary work in the surrounding villages. Only the two tall 11C clerestory windows each side of the nave (and the blocked half of a third) survive externally from the pre-Conquest building, which was a cruciform aisled church, its nave stretching a further one and a half bays W of the present nave. In the late 13C the chancel was rebuilt; one window of this date, with intersecting tracery, survives on the N side. About a century later the tower and S porch were added. The aisles were rebuilt in the 15C, when the Perpendicular windows were also placed in the chancel.

We enter beneath a 15C S doorway, by means of a fine old door, the ironwork of which may well be 13C. Inside we see something of the glory of the pre-Conquest building, which was erected c 1020. The nave is lofty and its arcades rest upon bold 11C piers, which have four attached columns with fillets between them, supporting large bulbous capitals and square imposts, from which spring the semicircular arches. E of the two and a half remaining bays of this arcade are the massive compound columns which supported the crossing arches, of which the N arch (c 28ft high) remains. 15C craftsmanship remains in the cambered tiebeam nave roof (restored in 1637), the benches (which have flat-topped and buttressed ends), the tower screen, which once formed part of the Rood screen, the parish chest, and probably the plain octagonal font. The N chapel has two carved image brackets which are studded with fleurons and foliage. Nearby may be seen what remains of the Rood loft staircase. Some fragments of 15C glass are preserved in the NW chancel window. The piscina in the S wall of the sanctuary is simple, but the sedilia beside it have superb 14C arches, framed by a hoodmould resting upon three carved heads. The elaborate reredos, by Percy Bacon & Brothers, was given in 1899. There is a ring of five bells in the tower.

Hemingford Abbots, *St. Margaret of Antioch.* A church set in a quiet and pretty corner, and built of brown cobblestones, apart from the chancel which was rebuilt in local gault brick early in the 19C. The windows in the aisles and clerestory are mostly 15C Perpendicular, although some aisle windows date back to c 1300. The tower and its recessed spire are remarkably elegant and well-proportioned, with clasping buttresses (note the beasts on the W buttresses), fine gargoyles and pinnacles. The spire has two tiers of lucarne windows, also two bands in the stonework. The porch shelters an Early English entrance arch to the church.

The arcades have 3½ bays and date from c 1300. This church at one time had a central tower. The octagonal font bowl may well be 13C. The nave and aisle roofs are 15C; the nave roof has 22 angels and a painted E bay. The royal arms beside the entrance are of c 1801–16. In the N aisle are the remains of a medieval wall painting of St. Christopher and a fine modern St. Christopher painting by Brian Thomas, 1978. Fine craftsmanship may also be seen in the glass tower screen engraved by David Peace in 1974 and in the high altar, which was designed by Peter Foster and is set beneath an E window with glass by Powell's of Whitefriars, showing the Crucifixion, St. Mary, St. John and ten other saints. A window in the N aisle contains glass by Kempe & Co., made in 1928.

Hemingford Grey, *St. James.* This church has an idyllic setting, right beside the River Ouse. Its distinctive tower (built c 1390) is capped by the stump of its stone spire, which was blown down by a hurricane in 1741. The ball finials on the spire and tower corners were added at this time. The S aisle is 14C, the N aisle and S porch were rebuilt in 1859 and the core of the chancel is 13C. Two original lancet windows remain in the N wall.

The interior has been made attractive, homely and comfortable by the installation of new floors and seating in 1977. The arcades are an unusual mixture of 12C, 13C and 14C work and the nave roof is 15C. On the N side of the chancel is a double aumbry, and on the S side is a beautiful late 13C double piscina, with intersecting arches supported by shafts of Purbeck marble. The E window of the S aisle has glass by Ward & Hughes, made in 1892, and the Resurrection window near the S door (placed here in 1906) is by C.E. Kempe.

Huntingdon

All Saints. Huntingdon's mother church faces the market place. To the E of it is the old Grammar School, which Oliver Cromwell attended and which was part of the 12C Hospital of St. John. All Saints' is not a large church (it is just over 80ft long), but there is great beauty in the stonework of its all-embattled exterior. The 15C S aisle has large four-light windows with fine corbels as label-stops to their hoodmoulds, also gabled buttresses, with carved creatures and niches. The S porch, with its niche and stoup, is also 15C. More carved creatures appear on the clerestory and the N aisle, the windows of the latter having 14C tracery and crocketed hoodmoulds. The NW tower was much restored with brick after the Civil War in the 17C. The elaborate organ chamber N of the chancel was added by Sir Gilbert Scott in 1859.

Inside are graceful 15C arcades, but one 13C arch remains at the W end of the N arcade. The 13C font is thought to have come from the church of St. John, and would therefore be the font at which Oliver Cromwell was baptised. The stone panelling beneath the S aisle E window forms a reredos for the Corpus Christi chapel, which was furnished by Sir Ninian Comper in 1931. What was the 19C chancel screen is now the Lady chapel reredos. The chancel has a fine 15C roof with good bosses. The clerestory windows contain glass by Clayton & Bell, who also designed the S aisle W window. The W window of the nave is by C.E. Kempe (1900) and the E window of the chancel is by his successors in Kempe & Co. (c 1920). Over the S door is the wall monument to Alice Weaver, who died in 1636.

St. Mary. This church lies to the S of the town centre. Its major external feature is the unusual and ornate W tower which, although not lofty, is a magnificent piece of 15C craftsmanship. It has large and unusual clasping buttresses, which are enriched with niches, traceried panelling, gables and carved creatures. The fine W doorway has an ogee hoodmould and is flanked by large canopied niches. Above the three-light W window and clock is a frieze of quatrefoils and pairs of two-light belfry windows. There is an embattled, stone-panelled parapet, and crocketed pinnacles at the corners. The E face of the tower was rebuilt after this part collapsed in 1607.

There are flat Norman buttresses at the SE corner of the nave and the SW corner of the S aisle, indicating that there must have been a large 12C church here. The chancel has an Early English priest's doorway with waterleaf capitals and dogtooth moulding, also a 13C lancet window on the N side and another reset in the vestry. Most of the windows in the church are 15C and the E wall of the chancel was rebuilt in 1876.

The arcades are basically 13C and have a variety of piers and capitals. Some were rebuilt following the collapse of part of the tower in 1607. St. Mary's contains a set of four 15C woodcarvings of Apostles with their emblems, a small stone near the chancel arch, inscribed 'R. Cromwell, I. Turpin, Bailiffs, 1609', and altar rails by Sir Ninian Comper, incorporating angels brought from Austria. There are several attractive wall tablets. One to members of the Carcassonnett family, made in 1749, is believed to be the work of Peter Scheemakers.

Leighton Bromswold, *St. Mary.* A memorable church in a beautiful hilltop village to the N of the A604. A tree-lined avenue leads to the lychgate, near which is a great stone, thought to have been a 'seat of judgement', where taxes were collected and criminals judged. Leighton's fine 13C Early English church, with its later (c 1330) Reticulated and 15C Perpendicular windows, had become dilapidated and roofless by 1606. Twenty years later the Reverend George Herbert, the celebrated writer, poet and Anglican Divine, became the parish priest here and set about restoring the church and making it beautiful, mostly with his own money. The building that we see today is much as he left it.

The Duke of Lennox paid for the bold, ashlar-faced W tower, with its large Classical windows and obelisk pinnacles. This is dated 1634. The church behind it is largely medieval, with nave, chancel and transepts. Notice, however, the stand-pipes on the chancel, which are dated 1632, also the small blocked low-side window in the S chancel wall. The chancel windows have intersecting tracery except for the three-light Perpendicular W window in each wall. The 13C aisles have been demolished, but their doorways have been inserted into the nave walls. The S doorway is splendid Early English work and its arch is embellished with dogtooth ornament.

The spacious interior has much which remains from George Herbert's 1630s refurbishing. Work of this period includes the tiebeam roofs, the circular font (said to have been formed from two 13C capitals), the benches with their characteristic armrests, the chancel stalls, the handsome twin pulpit and reading desk, both with back and sounding boards, also the lectern, the tower screen and the low chancel screen. The transepts have handsome four-light windows, with Reticulated tracery of c 1330. In the N transept are two alabaster effigies, portraying Sir Robert Tyrwhitt and his wife Elizabeth (died 1572 and 1578), and their daughter Katherine, Lady Darcy, who died in 1567. The lofty chancel has a large Perpendicular E window. In the S wall is a spectacular double piscina, with interlaced arches of early 13C date, and designed so that the mouldings as well as the arches are interwoven. In the N sanctuary wall is a double aumbry.

Little Gidding, *St. John the Evangelist*. This tiny fairy-tale church is set in the heart of the country, at the end of a cul-de-sac lane which leads from the Hamerton to Great Gidding road. All churches are pilgrimage churches, but this one is especially so, not only for its beauty and interest, but also because of its associations and the prayer and devotion which have been offered within its walls. It was here in this beautiful spot that Nicholas Ferrar (scholar, mystic and Anglican deacon, 1593–1647) formed a religious community, having bought the manor house at Little Gidding. By 1626 the community had c 40 members, including Ferrar's own family, his brother and sister and their families. These people lived under a simple Rule but no vows were taken. King Charles I visited Little Gidding; so did the Puritans in 1646, when they attacked and ransacked it. Nicholas Ferrar's manor house has long gone, but Manor Farm, beside the church, is the centre for the modern Little Gidding Community which now thrives here.

The little church is built of brick and is only 60ft long. Nicholas Ferrar greatly restored the medieval church in 1625 and in 1714 John Ferrar reduced its size and gave it the present remarkable stone W front, with its large doorway, side pinnacles and unusual bellcote and spirelet. To the W of the entrance is Nicholas Ferrar's table-tomb. Above the door as we enter, we are reminded that 'This is none other than the House of God, and this is the Gate of Heaven'. Few indeed could fail to sense that this is Holy Ground!

The colourful and cared-for interior is small and tunnel-like, with beautiful 17C and 18C furnishings. The seating is arranged in collegiate fashion, facing N and S, with panelling on the wall each side and texts in gold above. The church underwent a very sympathetic restoration in 1853, to the designs of Henry Clutton, and the 17C, 18C and 19C work blends so well that it is difficult to tell which is which. The chandeliers were placed here in 1853, but the candle sconces on the walls were made in 1920 by W.A. Lee. There are simple wagon roofs and the floors of black and white marble slabs enhance the Classical atmosphere here.

The eagle lectern is the one placed here by Nicholas Ferrar in 1625, although it may well originally date from the late 15C. Nearby is an hourglass stand. The remarkable font is of brass and has a cover shaped like a crown; it dates from the 17C. A wainscoted arch leads to the panelled chancel, at the E end of which is the reredos of 1714 which incorporates brass panels with the Lord's Prayer, Creed and Commandments, dating from 1625. The colourful windows arrived during Clutton's 1853 restoration and the glass is superb of its period. The E window shows the Crucifixion, but the nave windows are filled with armorial glass, with the arms of King Charles I, Nicholas Ferrar, and others. The brass memorial plates now on the wall near the chancel arch came from graves in the churchyard; these commemorate 17C and 18C relations of Nicholas Ferrar.

St. Ives

All Saints. This church occupies a quiet and picturesque position near the River Ouse, a sedate distance to the W of the town. The present church is largely a rebuilding of c 1470, with windows in the Perpendicular style of architecture. The large five-light E window of the S aisle, however, has intersecting tracery, with a large quatrefoil at the top, and dates from c 1300. The S porch entrance is flanked by canopied and vaulted niches and the S doorway has medieval doors. The N porch shelters a 13C doorway. We can see that there was a medieval sacristy to the N of the chancel. The crowning glory of the exterior is the graceful and elegantly proportioned 15C tower and spire. Its total height is 151ft, but its design and proportions make it appear deceptively taller. The tower has slender pinnacles and the spire is punctuated by two tiers of small lucarne windows. The pairs of double belfry windows are tall and elegant and beneath the four-light W window is a fine doorway with traceried spandrels, and two niches, containing later statues.

The interior is lofty, dignified and colourful. The long-established Anglo-Catholic tradition here has embellished this church with beautiful adornments and has saturated it with an atmosphere of devotion. The aisles embrace the tower, which is supported upon three sturdy arches and has a tierceron star vaulted ceiling. It contains a ring of eight bells. The octagonal font, with interlacing arches, dates from the late 12C or early 13C. Nearby is a chest dated 1783.

The nave has a 20C cambered tiebeam roof. There are medieval timbers in the roofs which span the wide aisles. The tall, thin four-bay arcades are remarkable because each pier has two large statues of saints. The statues are the work of Sir Ninian Comper (1897) but the brackets upon which they stand date from c 1470 and have fascinating carvings, including a dog biting its tail and another dog baiting a bull. Comper also designed the noble chancel screen and loft (1893), which contains the organ case, incorporating the Rood group. The organ is a three-manual instrument by S.J. Binns, with 22 speaking stops. The pulpit is a fine example of late 16C or early 17C craftsmanship in oak. The S chapel has an 'English' altar, designed by Sebastian Comper and a remarkable double piscina, with two arches, resting upon circular shafts and a rounded outer arch, bordered with dogtooth ornament. This is very early 13C work. To the E of it is an aumbry and flanking the E window are two image niches.

The chancel is lofty and its tiebeam roof is almost flat. It has figures standing on the wall posts and its E bay forms a panelled canopy of honour, with angel bosses, to the high altar. The grand reredos shows Our Lord with four English saints. The Brittin window on the S side of the chancel is by C.E. Kempe, and two windows (one in memory of the Watts family in the N aisle and the other in memory of Dr Grove in the S aisle) are by Comper. The five-light E window of the S aisle has stained glass ('Render unto Caesar...') which seems to be by William Wailes. The same attribution applies to the four-light W window.

Sacred Heart, Needingworth Road. This short and simple redbrick building in the Early English style was designed by A.W.N. Pugin and was first erected in 1843 in Union Street, Cambridge. It was taken down and rebuilt here in 1908. It is a simple building, with an aisled nave, porch, and stone-faced bellcote. A modern extension has been built onto the N side. The windows are small lancets and the four-bay arcades inside have circular and octagonal piers. The sanctuary has a piscina and aumbry and the W (but liturgically E) window is a triple lancet. This is a short church, so its interior appears rather lofty. It is homely and devotional and has been tastefully converted for liturgical requirements after the Second Vatican Council.

Bridge Chapel of St. Lawrence. St. Ives has a fine bridge over the River Ouse, built c 1415, upon which is the tiny bridge chapel of St. Lawrence, consecrated in 1426 and having an E apse.

The chapel of St. Lawrence standing on the 15C bridge over the River Ouse at St. Ives, Huntingdonshire, one of the five surviving medieval bridge chapels in England

St. Neots, *St. Mary.* This is a large and stately town-centre church, which was almost totally rebuilt in the 15C. Only one 13C lancet window remains in the N chancel wall. Wills refer to rebuilding from 1485 onwards, although it is possible that the scheme began in the late 14C. The 128ft high tower, which dominates the exterior and the town, was completed c 1535. It is faced with Weldon stone and is graced by panelled buttresses, punctuated by horizontal quatrefoil friezes and is crowned by an embattled stone parapet, with large pinnacles at the corners and smaller pinnacles at the centre of each face. The buttresses are gabled and terminate in pinnacles, after the fashion of the great towers of Somerset. The lower stage has blank tracery on the N and S sides and the tall pairs of double belfry windows give great dignity to the tower.

The embattled church has large four-light windows in the aisles and three-light clerestory windows. The NE Rood loft staircase turret rises above the nave parapet. The aisle buttresses are gabled and display a variety of carved figures. The N porch was rebuilt in the 19C; the S porch is larger and is two-storeyed. The exterior in general presents a uniform and handsomely proportioned appearance.

Inside, we are aware of the vast size of this ambitious building, which measures 158ft from E to W. The tower arch is remarkably lofty and the five-bay arcades are tall and elegant. The font, although rather plain, is believed to be 12C and may have come from the nearby priory. Near the N door is a fine canopied niche which is 14C. The 15C roofs are superb and are embellished with angels bearing shields and a host of animals and creatures. The nave roof has carved spandrels and richly decorated cornices. The parclose screens between the chancel and the two E chapels are 15C and the screen to the Jesus chapel (N) shows Renaissance influence. The chancel roof was restored in 1901 and its wall posts rest upon figures of the Apostles. In the Lady chapel (S of the chancel) is a late Elizabethan communion table, which was originally the high altar.

There is much 19C glass in the windows, nearly all of it showing scenes from the life of Christ. Clayton & Bell glass is well represented here, particularly in the W window of the tower, showing English saints and the four Latin Doctors. The Woman of Samaria window in the S aisle is by John Hardman & Co. The finest monument is the ornate memorial to the Rowley family on the S side of the chancel, erected in 1893 to the designs of Frederick A. Walters. Behind a grille lies the effigy of Mrs. Rowley, who died in 1886, carved by Thomas Earp. Above this rises a tall and extravagant canopy. The three-manual organ was built by G.M. Holdich in 1855 and has been restored by Bishop & Son, but it has been kept much as Holdich first built it. The tower contains a fine ring of eight bells; the tenor bell weighs 29 cwt.

Waresley, *St. James.* This small village in undulating countryside SE of St. Neots possesses a Gothic Revival church of great character, built between 1855–57 to the designs of William Butterfield. It is built in the style of the late 13C. Its roofs are steeply pitched and the building comprises nave and chancel, S vestry, transept and short aisle, and the Duncombe mausoleum on the N side. The S porch tower is slender, tall and has two very short and small S buttresses. The two-light belfry windows are set very high and the tower is crowned by a tall shingled and chamfered spire. Beside the pavement to the E of the church is a pump, set beneath a stone gabled well-house, also by Butterfield.

The interior contains most of its original Butterfield furnishings, including the font and its wooden cover, the benches, pulpit, stalls and altar rails. The arcade has circular piers and a smaller W bay. The chancel walls are embellished with tiled patterns in red and green, and texts in quatrefoils. There is grisaille glass in the N nave windows and a variety of very worthy pictorial glass. A window in the N transept is of 1865 by Heaton, Butler & Bayne. A three-light unglazed window gives a view into the Duncombe mausoleum, which has its own entrance from outside. On the N wall of the nave is a fine memorial to Lady E. Caroline Duncombe, who died in 1911, with an angel drawing aside a curtain to reveal a head and shoulders portrait of the old lady.

Water Newton. Christianity is known to have existed at Water Newton long before the present, largely 13C church of St. Remigius was built, because within the parish was the Roman town of Durobrivae, which grew up around a 1C fort built to defend a bridge across the River Nene. By the 4C it had grown to a sizeable Roman settlement. In 1975, 27 silver objects were unearthed in a field on the site of this town and much of this Water Newton Treasure (now in the British Museum) was clearly used by a Christian community. It dates mostly from the 3C and 4C and many items bear the Christian chi-rho (✸) emblem. Some are votive plaques; others are vessels which may have been used in connection with the Eucharist. The votive plaques are the only ones known to be Christian rather than pagan. This constitutes the earliest known collection of Christian silver anywhere in the Roman Empire and, if the attribution of use is correct, the earliest Christian church plate in this country.

(K.S. Painter, 'The Water Newton Early Christian Silver' (1977).)

Yaxley, *St. Peter.* Its noble tower and spire are a landmark across the flat countryside S of Peterborough. They draw us to one of Huntingdonshire's largest and most ambitious churches, where we may enjoy the craftsmanship of most periods of medieval architecture.

The tower was built in c 1485–1540. It is strengthened by clasping buttresses and has an embattled parapet, beneath which are gargoyles and carved figures. The four slender pinnacles are linked to the crocketed spire by elegant flying buttresses which are pierced by quatrefoils. There are three-light, transomed belfry windows. The wide aisles are mainly 13C and the fine S doorway is also of this date. E of the aisles are 13C N and S transepts, but the S transept was given its beautiful five-light window with Reticulated tracery c 1330. The chancel chapels are late 13C and the large E window, with its five lights and flowing tracery, dates from c 1320. Of the 15C are the S porch, the clerestory and several of the windows.

There is much of interest inside St. Peter's. The four-bay nave arcades are 15C but the arches to the chancel and E chapels are two centuries earlier, of which date is also the octagonal bowl of the font. There are faint 14C wall paintings of Our Lord's Resurrection appearances in the N chapel, an early 16C Doom painting above the chancel arch, and on the W wall of the nave there are later 16C texts and curious pictures of a gravedigger, a skeleton and other figures, and a set of 17C royal arms over the S door. The pulpit was made in 1631, but stands upon an earlier base. The fine screen was fashioned c 1500 and has traces of paintings of the Instruments of the Passion. The organ case and gallery above it were designed by Temple Moore, who restored the church in 1904–10. The organ was built by

William Hill in 1910. There are some medieval benches in the N transept, and a piscina and aumbry. Here may also be seen beneath an arch a carving of two hands holding a heart. This is a heart shrine and it marks the place where the heart of William de Yaxley (Abbot of Thorney, who died in 1293) is buried. The N chapel has 13C sedilia and a piscina, and some beautifully carved stone faces set high on each side. The 19C pulpit now in this chapel replaced for a while the 17C one. In the S chapel are more carved faces. There are two piscinas here, showing that the altar was moved further E c 1320. The chancel contains a set of stalls restored by Temple Moore, but with 15C traceried fronts and poppyhead ends. The fine painted reredos with nine figures against gilded backgrounds and four angels on posts, by Sir Ninian Comper, and the glass in the E window (Christ in Glory, St. Peter and St. Paul, and Gospel scenes below), by Geoffrey Webb, were installed in the 1940s.

LANCASHIRE

Lancashire is a very varied county in its geography, geology, and building materials. Perched on the W side of the Pennines, its landmass is bounded by the estuary of the River Mersey to the S, and subdivided by the Rivers Ribble and Lune, and the incursions of Morecambe Bay in the N. The S portion of the traditional county, which includes Greater Manchester and Merseyside, is low-lying, a N projection of the flat plain of Shropshire and Cheshire, and thus it continues, as we travel N, through the arable country surrounding Ormskirk, and on, beyond the Ribble to the Fylde peninsula. On the N side of Morecambe Bay—the Furness and Cartmel peninsulas—Lancashire enters the Lake District; and on the E side, the county ascends the Pennines, with outlying areas of higher land including the forests of Bowland, Pendle and Rossendale.

In the SW Nature provided the Triassic or New Red sandstones of the Liverpool area—sometimes these are of the poor quality associated with this stone, sometimes not. In the SE, there is carboniferous sandstone, and millstone grit. N of the Ribble, there is more millstone grit, and this and other carboniferous limestones became predominant in the N portions of the county. Lakeland Lancashire has Ordovician and Silurian stones, including the grey-green slate associated with Westmorland. In the medieval period, the county was extensively wooded, and timber-framing, for domestic building, large and small, was normal. Brick was introduced at the end of this period, and now many of the county's buildings employ the bright red bricks associated with Accrington. The New Red sandstones were quarried at Woolton and Rainhill (Liverpool), and nearby Runcorn, Cheshire. The first two of these quarries provided the hard dull-pink stone of Liverpool's Anglican cathedral. The carboniferous sandstones, in the N, are mainly grey or dull yellow, and tend to produce a very dour effect, but have the great advantage—as some of the New Red sandstones do not—of being resistant to the action of smoke, soot and rain. These stones were also traditionally split to form roofing slates. The millstone grit is used for building in the area around Lancaster, and the carboniferous limestones include that from Stainton, near Ulverston, which is grey-green, and can be polished, and is thus one of the so-called English 'marbles'. The slate of the Lakeland area is used for roofing, and increasingly, today, for cladding buildings of concrete.

In former centuries Lancashire was very sparsely populated, but the mechanisation of the cotton industry and the exploitation of coal caused the population to expand so considerably and rapidly that it became one of the most densely populated counties of England. This growth was concentrated in the SW, SE and mid-E regions. This late development, in historical terms, means that by far the largest number of churches dates from the 18C, 19C and 20C. Pre-Conquest remains include a few fragments, eg of crosses (Halton, Heysham, Winwick), and of the Norman period, only the odd tympanum (eg Altham) and doorway (eg Aughton, Bispham, Middleton, Whalley) can be seen. From the Transitional and Early English Gothic periods come the abbeys of Furness and Cartmel, and parts of the churches of Rochdale, Maghull, Wigan, Whalley and Ribchester. Decorated Gothic work includes that at Deane, Hale, Radcliffe and Whalley Abbey. The Perpendicular period produced the important town church of St. Mary, Lancaster (late 14C), the church that became

Manchester Cathedral (refounded as a collegiate church 1421), and St. John's, Tunstall (rebuilt c 1415), and additions at Deane, Middleton, Radcliffe, etc. In N Lancashire, the Gothic style continued to be used in the 16C, after the Reformation, when it was little used in the rest of England; this may be called Tudor Gothic, Late Perpendicular, or even Gothic Survival: St. Wilfrid's, Standish (16C) is the most important example. The 17C is normally known for its church monuments rather than buildings, though Prescot's nave may date from this century, and there are also the N chapel of All Saints', Wigan (c 1620), and W towers at Didsbury, Ringley and Bradshaw.

In the 18C, church building began again. Often, at this time, towns were provided with a second parish, eg St. Ann's, Manchester (1709–12). Other churches in the first part of the century include those at Burtonwood (1716), Ellenbrook (1725), Lowton (1732), St. Mary's, Rochdale (1740) and Hale (1754). Forms of worship other than that of the Church of England began to produce religious buildings in the 17C. Protestant Dissent created the 'meeting house'. The first were conversions of existing buildings, and then they were purpose-built. Lancashire's early meeting houses include the 'Ancient Chapel' of Toxteth, Liverpool (1618, rebuilt 1773). After the 1689 Toleration Act, registered meeting houses had legal status, and buildings from this time include Wrightington (Tunley Presbyterian, 1691), Yealand Conyers (Quaker, 1692) and Rivington (Unitarian, 1703). The evangelism of John Wesley, George Whitefield and their followers (from the 1740s) created the New Dissent, and the N of England was a focus of this. Wesley himself opened the chapel at Davyhulme, Manchester (1779), and Padiham's second chapel, opened in the same year, was designed by the local superintendent minister. Manchester's Oldham Street Chapel (1781) was in the heavy, battlemented Methodist Gothick style. Later Methodist churches include the large Cheetham Hill, Manchester (1837) and Baillie Street, Rochdale (1837, 1912). One rare and fascinating product of Nonconformity is the Moravian Settlement. The Moravian Brethren, who came originally from Germany, lived in self-contained communities which included chapel, work-places, residences, etc. Fairfield, to the E of Manchester, was the largest of the six or so established in Britain. Dating from 1785, its buildings were planned by Benjamin Latrobe senior, whose son was one of the architects of the Capitol, Washington DC.

Another important aspect of religion and religious architecture in Lancashire is Recusancy, or Roman Catholicism from the Reformation to the later 18C. Lancashire was the leading county of Recusancy, being the place where Catholic worship survived more strongly than anywhere else. At first, Masses were held in domestic premises, in secret. Later, Catholic chapels, like Dissenting meeting houses, were legal if registered, yet Catholics still feared an antagonistic populace. At Netherton, Liverpool, we see how a chapel (1793) would be discreetly hidden at the back of a modest house, and invisible from the road. Some of the first Catholic churches tended to take the exact form of Methodist chapels, and while this was largely due to the status of Catholicism, and the building industry which was available to Catholic builders, these churches also avoided drawing attention to their religion and faith: St. Patrick's, Park Place, Liverpool (1821–27) is a slightly grander, and later, version of the Methodist style.

It was in the 19C that Lancashire's population expanded at a terrific rate, and likewise the building of churches. In the Anglican Church, building was promoted by the Church Building Commission. Eighteen Commissioners' Churches were produced following the grant of money of 1818, and 63 following that of 1824. All were in a Gothic style, except St. Philip's, Salford. The first grant produced few in the N, less populous, part of the county, the second, rather more. Architects such as Sir Robert Smirke, Francis Goodwin and Philip Hardwick were involved, and Thomas Rickman's churches include the cast-iron building, St. George's, Everton, Liverpool (1812–14). The 1830s taste for Italianate, Romanesque and round-arched styles contributed St. Anne's, Aigburth, Liverpool (1836–37) and the tower of St. Thomas's, Ardwick, Manchester (1836). The mature Gothic Revival produced very many buildings, and for all denominations. Despite Lancashire's traditional Catholic strength, the county could be said to lack a Gothic Catholic church of the importance of A.W.N. Pugin's at Cheadle, Staffordshire, but he did build St. Wilfrid's, Hulme, Manchester (1842), and his son built St. Francis's, Gorton, Manchester (1866–72). Irish immigration increased the Catholic population, particularly around Liverpool, and other Catholic architects of note include J.J. Scoles and J.A. Hansom. Likewise, Lancashire acquired no major production of the new Gothic movement in Anglicanism, comparable with Margaret Street, London, or Leeds Parish Church; but William Butterfield built Holy Cross, Clayton, Manchester (1862–66), and Sir Gilbert Scott produced Christ Church, Denton (1848–53), etc. Local Gothicist J.S. Crowther restored Manchester Cathedral, and built St. Alban's, Cheetham, Manchester (1873–76). In the later Gothic Revival, however, Lancashire contributed buildings of national, and even international, importance: G.F. Bodley's St. Augustine's, Pendlebury (1871–74), J.L. Pearson's St. Agnes's, Sefton Park, Liverpool (1883–85), Leonard Stokes's St. Clare's, also Sefton Park (1888–90), and the works of Edgar Wood (First Church of Christ Scientist, Victoria Park, Manchester (1903), Methodist Church, Middleton (1897, 1899–1901), and others). The long-lived practice of Paley & Austin of Lancaster filled the county with many Gothic churches (some of the very highest quality), and also built them outside Lancashire; Aldridge & Deacon did similar work in Liverpool. In 1883, Manchester's Oldham Street Methodist Church was demolished to make way for a 'Central Hall'. These were the Methodist missions of the turn-of-the-century in the inner cities, and employed very advanced ideas. Neither chapel nor church, these halls were built in towns and cities up and down the land; Liverpool's (Renshaw Street, 1904–05) is in a muscular Art Nouveau style.

Much fine 20C church building has been done in Lancashire. In Liverpool, the city in which Giles Gilbert Scott created his vast Anglican cathedral (1904–80), he also built St. Paul's, Derby Lane, Stoneycroft (1916), with its very original plan. The interwar years saw the 'Art Deco' modernistic work of F.X. Verlarde, most of which was for the Catholic Church (eg St. Monica's, Bootle 1936), and that of Bernard Miller, for the Anglican Church. St. Christopher's, Norris Green, Liverpool (1932) shows Miller using the popular device of concrete parabolic arches within a calm, traditional brick box. Sts. Matthew and Aidan, Roundhorn, Oldham, however, is a piece of severe Classicism, recalling Lancashire's industrial past, and even the architecture of Nonconformism (Taylor & Young, 1933). St. Nicholas's, Burnage, Manchester (Welch, Cachemaille-Day & Lander, 1931–32) is thoroughly Odeon cinema-like. The same

architects' St. Michael's, Wythenshawe, Manchester (1937) antici-
pated the central-planned form of Liturgical Movement churches
(from the 1960s). Postwar churches include Catholic buildings by
Weightman & Bullen, eg St. Ambrose's, Speke, Liverpool, 1959–61;
their St. Mary's, Leyland (1959–64) was one of the first circular
Catholic churches, a form popularised by Liverpool's Metropolitan
Cathedral (Frederick Gibberd, 1959–67), and the new liturgy. In
1969—when ecumenism in worship had become desirable—
Lancaster University's chaplaincy centre was opened. Its plan was a
three-leaved clover, involving two chapels (Catholic, Anglican/Free
Church), and these could be opened out and linked across a central
concourse, uniting the worship areas. St. Helens' United Reformed
Church (Peter Bridges & Martin Purdy, complete 1977) is an uncompromising essay in modern church building design and theory.
Almost the entire volume is a gigantic lead-covered Mansard roof,
which houses internal terrace, theatre and 'free association' area.

The furnishings, decorations and contents of Lancashire's churches
are, like the buildings themselves, very varied. The Norman font at
Kirkby depicts Adam and Eve and the serpent—a coiled motif
repeated in the thick cabled base. Walton's Norman font bowl
depicts the Flight into Egypt, etc., and is supported on three squat
columns. Early tombs include those of Sir John Harrington at Cartmel
(1305, restored 1618–20), the traceried tomb-recess at Halsall (14C;
present effigy added 1563), and the alabaster effigies in the Derby
Chapel, Ormskirk, which may have come from Burscough Priory.
Alabaster fragments (late 15C) are now in the church of Our Lady,
Lydiate. Brasses include those found in Ormskirk, Manchester
Cathedral, Winwick and Eccleston (15C); Whalley, Childwall, Sefton
and Flixton (16C); and Manchester Cathedral, Preston and Lancaster
(17C). Lancaster has Decorated canopied stalls of c 1340 (which may
have come from Cockersand Abbey). Other canopied stalls are in
Manchester Cathedral and Whalley; these have misericords, as does
St. Helen's, Garstang and St. Mary's, Blackburn. Lancashire is not
well endowed with medieval glass, but there are fragments at Halsall
(14C), Upholland, and Billington. Cartmel Priory has mid-15C figures, and Cartmel Fell has 15C glass, which was originally in
Cartmel Priory. Ashton-under-Lyne has a cycle of 19 panels of the
life of St. Helen (late 15C–early 16C). Renaissance furnishings
include the amazing canopied stalls and choir screen of c 1630 at
Cartmel, and the cage-like screened pew at Whalley (1534, 1610,
1697). Woodcarving in the style of Grinling Gibbons is found in the
altar rail at North Meols (transported, early 20C, from St. Peter's,
Liverpool); Whalley's organ case (1729) likewise came from
Lancaster in 1813. Monuments of this period include those to Richard
Bold (died 1635) at Farnworth, Widnes (in alabaster); Edward
Chisnet (died 1653) at Standish; Richard and Elizabeth Legh at
Winwick (1687–90); and the Baroque monument to Katherine
Lowther at Cartmel (1700). Georgian interiors, undisturbed in the
19C, are rare and fascinating: Lancashire has the church at Tarleton
(1719), and the Old Church at Pilling, near Fleetwood, both of which
preserve original fittings, pews, woodwork, etc. Among later Geor-
gian monuments there are those to Sir William Lowther (died 1756) at
Cartmel, Joseph Nollekens's monument to Roger Hesketh at North
Meols (1791), and the monument to Mary, Princess Sapieha (died
1824) in the Bold chapel at Farnworth, by Pietro Tenerani.

With fittings and glass, as with buildings, Lancashire is richly
endowed with products of the last two centuries. Victorian glass

includes an Ascension at St. Michael's, Flixton (R.B. Edmundson, 1858) and an Annunciation at All Saints', Higher Walton (N. Westlake, 1864). From 1868 comes the Morris & Co. glass at St. John's, Tue Brook, Liverpool, with its outstanding wall and ceiling paintings (by C.E. Kempe). Pendlebury has glass by Burlison & Grylls (1871–74), and All Hallows', Allerton, Liverpool, has more glass by Morris & Co. (of which a detail appears on the cover of this book), as does St. Stephen's, Gateacre (1883). Late Morris glass—and rarely, set in a Nonconformist church—is that at Ashton-under-Lyne's Albion Congregational Church (1893–96). Ninian Comper inserted glass in St. Mary's, Rochdale, on which he had worked, in 1923 and 1926. St. Michael's, Wythenshawe, Manchester (1937) has glass by Geoffrey Webb, and St. Mary's, Rufford has a striking Christ in the Temple by Kaye & Pemberton (1953).

Ashton-under-Lyne, *St. Michael and All Angels.* St. Michael's is a large medieval town church, and yet its ecclesiastical independence from Manchester took till the later 13C to establish, its parish church status being normally dated from 1281. As a building, it has everything, and more, that civic status can give: important monuments, constable's pew, military flags, a large ring of bells (13), and an Earl's coronet displayed on the Lord of the Manor's pew. Outside, the stonework has that smooth, unblemished regularity that makes 'Perpendicular' unbelievable, rather as at Manchester Cathedral. Inside, the effect is all lateral, one-directional: a great long, seemingly thin, volume, filled up in every place with lavish decoration. This is a large ancient town church that has been much re-created, and endlessly ornamented in recent centuries; and somehow such churches give the appearance of having lost their way, despite (or because of?) all the effort expended. Several, and even surprising, are the compensations.

The present church was begun in the early 15C by Sir John de Assheton and completed in the early 16C, the tower being one of the later works. However, in the 18C, much decorative plasterwork was applied within the building (the medieval ceiling being covered in 1792), and in 1821, the N side of the building was reconstructed. In 1840–44, much of the rest of the stonework was replaced. In 1886–88 the tower was rebuilt, by J.S. Crowther, the architect who did extensive work at Manchester Cathedral. The N porch was a First World War memorial. However, within this curious sandwich of re-creation, medieval work still stands. Outside, there are some splendid 15C corbels, and if they seem to grimace at times, it is probably the result of having had to struggle through a thick layer of 19C masonry to catch sight of the world again.

The nave has five bays, and then a wide arch, with panelling and a royal coat of arms, marks the beginning of the chancel (two bays), but its presence is only noticed high above the springing, and in no way does it cut up this long unified space. The sanctuary has a wooden roof and a stone reredos. A seven-light window terminates the building. St. Michael's wooden—almost flat—roofs, with their beams and bosses and painted panels, look down on a similarly intricate mass of woodwork below: the 19C pews (whose bench-ends rise up to large poppyheads). Half-way down the nave, on the N side against a column, is the pulpit. Again, it is Gothic and decorated in carving. Amazingly, it is a three-decker pulpit but to any Georgian country church carpenter it would have been a nightmare. Dating from

1844, it is claimed to be among the last of such pulpits ever to be built. So a medieval church, re-created in the appropriate (Gothic) style in the 19C, used a device from the Georgian Protestant preaching house, but translated into a style alien to the form. The history of Ashton's fonts is also complex: the present marble font is early 20C, but there is also one of 1662. In 1980, an object believed to be the medieval font was found in a local garden.

But it is the medieval stained glass that is Ashton's glory. It is the most comprehensive collection in the county. It is said to date from c 1460–1517. It has had a chequered history of re-locations and restorations, and the present siting, raised away from the present windows proper, took place in 1974. It was probably made in York, where the glassmakers' guild church was dedicated to St. Helen, and it is St. Helen with whom most of the glass is concerned. Helen was a historical person, the mother of Constantine, the first Christian Roman emperor. She is said to have discovered the True Cross, and the sites of Jesus's life and death. Many legends and myths were woven around these facts, and these are depicted in 18 panels of the stained glass. In addition to this, a group of panels commemorate the lives of the donors, the Assheton family.

Cartmel, *Priory Church of St. Mary.* Cartmel Priory was founded as a house of Augustinian Canons in c 1190. A condition of its foundation was the provision of a priest and altar for the local laity; so from the first, part of the building functioned as a parish church.

The church's great size is related to its principal, monastic, function. The first parts of the building to be completed were the chancel, transepts, and the N wall of the nave, and this is of the Transitional period, and Norman in character; however, later work is found in all these portions, including windows, which were inserted in both the Decorated and Perpendicular periods. The N doorway is Early English, the S doorway—with its shafts and decorated round arch—is part of the earlier work, and led, once, to the cloisters. The nave, though begun earlier, is essentially of Perpendicular work, as is the tower.

In 1537, King Henry VIII's commissioners removed the canons from the priory and took much of the church's valuables, including its roof lead. However, the parishioners claimed their ancient rights to use their portion of the church—the S chancel aisle, known as the 'Town Choir'—and so the building escaped complete destruction. The non-parochial portions continued to rot and crumble until c 1620. A few years earlier, George Preston had begun the work of repairing and restoring the whole church. He it was who added the oak choir screen and canopies, which we see today. In 1820, however, the building was ruinous once again, and work paid for by the seventh Duke of Devonshire (1859) was carried out, the building being re-roofed and re-seated by 1870.

The nave is comparatively short (three bays) and of cruder work than the earlier building's. It has an arcade of sets of two octagonal columns. The S aisle contains the sculpture 'They fled by night' (1966) by Josephine de Vasconcellos. The N nave aisle contains a recumbent effigy of Frederick Cavendish. The aisle's W windows represent the Magnificat (S) and Te Deum (N). At the E end of the nave are four crossing piers, which support the tower, and the transepts are set beside this under-tower space, to N and S. On the nave aisle side of the NE pier is a pauper's bread shelf. In the chancel it is perhaps the 17C screen and canopy, and 15C misericords, that first hold our attention. The misericords have such subjects as the Trinity, a pelican, a mermaid, and an elephant-and-castle; but perhaps the later woodwork is actually more rare and curious than these. The actual structure is very Classical, indeed Renaissance, in its use of columns, pilasters, vestigial Corinthian capitals, and entablature: but in the panels, the carving is thoroughly Late Gothic in its tessellated forms (recalling the panels of Lancaster Priory's stalls and tracery). The work is Flemish, and carved in c 1620. To the N is the N choir aisle, or Piper Choir, said to be the oldest extant part of the fabric, with its Norman-style carving, and vaulting. The S choir aisle, or 'Town Choir', is where we see most work from the Decorated period, notably the E window (which has two of its outer lights blocked) and the Harrington tomb, which is set between this aisle and the sanctuary. Set in an arch, the monument has tracery rising above effigies, believed to be of the first Lord Harrington (died 1347), and his wife. It is suggested that the tomb was originally built elsewhere, and has been fitted in at a later date. There are crouching figures of mourners, placed on the other plinth of the tomb. In the sanctuary, there are sedilia (S), the tomb of the first prior (N), and above the altar, a large nine-light window, inserted in the Perpendicular period; it fills the E wall, almost too much, since outside it makes the masonry, arching over it, seem thin and weak. This window once had 80 panels of glass of the York School; the three central lights are remnants of this (restored in 1964). The 'Town Choir' aisle has part of a 'Jesse Window' (14C); there is much fine modern glass in the building, some the work of Shrigley & Hunt.

Outside, we see that the basic impression of the building—somehow not dispelled by the vast windows—is one of massive bulk, which is perhaps a legacy of its Norman/Transitional origins. The ends of the transepts—whose walls rise up to a flat battlemented parapet—enhance this, as does the double tower. The upper stage is daringly set at a 45° angle to the lower stage, the corners coming down on corbels over arches (and, as a result, the walls are of half the size of the lower stage's walls). This is an odd, perhaps unique, idea, but the diagonal setting of squares within squares, like this, is known to be something that Late Gothic masons found geometrically fascinating.

Dukinfield, *Old Chapel, Old Road, The Crescent.* Dukinfield is a place in historic Cheshire, not Lancashire, but its Unitarian chapel derives from a congregation formed at Denton across the border and is therefore included here. This Unitarian 'cathedral' stands at the highest point of the land, its gabled façade, with Decorated window and corner turrets, looking down on the town below. The name refers to a 1707 church, destroyed in 1839. The present Gothic building was opened in 1840. Despite its specifically churchlike appearance, the plan and arrangement is distinctively Nonconformist. The transepts at the centre of the nave, with the gallery all around (even over the door vestibule) shows the move towards the Nonconformist Gothic auditoria of the end of the century, with their wide, often centrally-planned space. The clustered columns are iron and narrow, thus not hiding the all-important pulpit, which is also raised on columns, and beneath which is the railed communion table. Above and behind the pulpit is the organ, somewhat grand for the date, if it is so. Behind the organ is the minister's small vestry, and being a Nonconformist building, a staircase from the vestry gives the preacher access directly to the pulpit in the church next door.

Farnworth, near Widnes, *St. Luke.* The fabric of this church goes back to the 12C. The nave has five bays, and its octagonal columns (mostly with moulded capitals) are of the 14C. Above these are dormer clerestories. At the W, but off-centre with the nave and W wall, is the 14C tower. There are N and S nave porches. The nave and chancel have wooden roofs, the former pitched, the latter panelled (15C) and nearly flat. At the E of the S nave aisle is a transept. The N nave aisle was rebuilt in 1855 as the Bold chapel. This contains most of the church's monuments, including a Chantrey of 1822, an effigy of a knight (c 1500 or 17C fake?) and a pair of alabaster effigies. There is also the monument, made in Rome, to Princess Sapieha (died 1824), by Pietro Tenerani, a pupil of Bertel Thorwaldsen. A curious feature of the chapel is a hinging door covered in book spines, said to come from Bold Hall, St. Helens. Also in the N nave aisle is a window, somewhat faded, by William Morris. An arch leads to the chancel, with its wide E window. Paley, Austin & Paley worked on this part of the church, and that was in the major restoration of 1894–95. Beside the transept, S, there is a pauper's bread shelf.

St. Luke's has a pleasant setting in a churchyard with fine trees. Externally, we see the very attractive qualities of local sandstone, well-weathered. From outside, the Bold chapel projects—even obtrudes—in a way that was less obvious within.

Lancaster Priory, *St. Mary.* Lancaster Priory, the ancient parish church of the county town, was built at the top of the hill which dominates the area all around. Nearby is the castle, and both stand 110ft above the River Lune. On this site there was once a Roman fort, and then a pre-Conquest church. The first Lancaster Castle was built after the Conquest by a relative of King William. The same man, Roger de Poitevin, gave land to the Benedictine monks of Séez, in Normandy, and they established a monastery on the site. In 1414, Henry V suppressed foreign monastic houses, and the priory was eventually given over to the Brigittine nuns of Isleworth, Middlesex. However, as part of this change, the priory became, as well as a monastic church, Lancaster's parish church, the people sharing the building with the nuns. The arrangement took effect after 1430, and one result was the building of the church which we see today.

In gritstone, and in the Perpendicular style, the church is a rectangle 145ft by 58ft. The nave has four bays, with a colonnade of three octagonal piers, with octagonal capitals; above is the clerestory, and at the W, a gallery. The S nave aisle has three three-light Perpendicular windows, and a porch at the W. A transverse arch gives directly to the chancel, which is also of four bays; similar arches terminate the nave aisles. There are several steps at this point, but no screens, such as we find at other major medieval churches in the county. But what we do find is a fine set of canopied stalls, and ten misericords. These fill one-and-a-half bays, and are set back between the columns, in no way interrupting the view of E from W, or closing in on the choir, as they often appear to do. The stalls can be described only as late Gothic, since they could have been made at any time from the late 14C to the late 15C. They are normally thought of as having been brought from the Premonstratensian abbey of Cockermouth, but they may have come from that at Furness. Unlike many such late medieval choirstall canopies, these do not break forward, and are straight, rather than curved or canted in plan. But fascinating and remarkable is the wealth of pierced tracery in the ogival tympana—note the variations, and the characteristic late Gothic flame and dagger motifs—and the tall pinnacles that subdivide the bays. The rears of each stall are ornamented with embroideries designed by Guy Barton, and worked between 1962 and 1975. Beneath the chancel, remnants of Roman and late 12C work have been found. Towards the E termination of the second chancel bay is the communion rail of ironwork and brass (1870), and beyond, the high altar. The reredos, consisting of four painted panels, depicts the Last Supper and dates from 1919. There is a passage behind the altar, above which is a five-light Perpendicular window, with glass dating from 1847. There are chapels N and S of the choir, each occupying two bays: St. Nicholas (N), St. Thomas Becket (S). Both have three-light windows filled with modern glass.

Of course, the building history of St. Mary's did not end with the late medieval period. In 1539, the priory was suppressed along with its mother house in Syon, but the Catholic faith lingered long in Lancaster, it being a centre for the resistance to the Reformation known as the 'Pilgrimage of Grace'. In 1540, the church was made part of the new Diocese of Chester (it had been in York), which was originally very large. In the 17C, the town was a centre of Quaker activities: the ornate pyramidal font cover dates from this time, being installed in 1631. The matching pulpit, though not now in its original form, was made in 1619. In the 18C, the state of the tower and bells caused much concern, and after various unsuccessful attempts to rebuild the tower, and even fear of total collapse, a new tower was eventually completed in 1775. Its Gothic style is typical of the time, its openings having superimposed sets of Y-tracery. The major modern Gothic works include the S porch, by which the building is normally entered, and the large N outer aisle. These date from 1903, and are the work of Paley & Austin, the Lancaster firm whose work is seen all over the county, and beyond. The N outer aisle is a memorial to members of the King's Own Royal Lancaster Regiment who fell in the Boer War. It is of four bays, and has an apsidal E end, with altar. The chapel has fine early 20C glass: its W window, slightly later, is a memorial to the dead of the First World War. Being a large civic church, Lancaster Priory is filled with fine monuments, furnishings, candelabra and objects of all kinds. These include a Crusader's casket, a monument by L.F. Roubiliac (mid-18C) and, perhaps most unusual of all, a set of four brass Coptic crosses, brought back in the 1860s. They are said to date from the 4C or 5C, and thus form a link with the early history of the Christian faith.

Lancaster, St. John the Evangelist. In the mid-18C, Lancaster, situated on the River Lune, became a prosperous port. St. Mary's Priory Church was inadequate for the number of inhabitants, and as a result, St. John's was built as its chapel of ease, and sited down in the busy town. Constructed in 1754–55, a W tower was added in 1784 by Thomas Harrison, an architect known for his work in Chester. The parish was only created in 1842. In the 1860s, the church was used for civic services by the Corporation, which was at that time in dispute with the churchwardens of the priory. These years saw the enlargement of the organ.

St. John's is a typical 18C Anglican building. Its nave has four bays, galleries over aisles, N and S, an organ at the W, and a short chancel with semicircular apse. It is pewed throughout (original pews remain in place) and the central aisle widens at the E, showing where the now-vanished three-decker pulpit stood. The semicircular-headed nave windows (four each side, one at the W end of the aisles) rise unbroken, despite the galleries. The slender columns above the galleries support a dentilled entablature, which sub-divides the roof areas (the central area is coved) and continues around the inside of the apse. Unusually, the apse is lit by two windows set either side of a central strip of blank wall. In the 1920s a chapel was added to the N of the chancel, and a vestry to the S. The tower has louvred bell openings beneath pediments, and above this is a rotunda with Tuscan columns and entablature. Finally, there is a short, slender spire.

In 1988 St. John's was vested in the Redundant Churches Fund.

Liverpool

Bootle, *St. Monica, Fernhill Road.* This Catholic church is one of that handful of pre-war British buildings which were inspired by the latest developments on the Continent, and particularly German churches of the 1920s. It is the work of F.X. Verlarde.

From the main road, we see a towering façade of display and effect: it is the W end, and has three two-light windows, on which large concrete angels stand, all producing a powerful vertical thrust. Over the door, there is a relief depicting St. Monica. On the N side (also on a road) we see thick, squat flying buttresses that rise up over high, narrow aisle roofs. Inside, the narthex is separated from the nave by a wide brick arch. The nave (six bays) is very wide with a flat, uniform ceiling. High up are small clerestory windows, in pairs. To N and S of the nave, transverse barrel arches of brick define the bays of the aisles, and the walls from which they rise are pierced with arch openings; these produce the aisles-passages, but the S aisle is much wider, a true aisle, and hence the buttresses we saw from outside. In the aisle walls there are long, thin, two-light round-headed windows. The E wall is un-pierced and plain; it is a great reredos, with ascending wooden-gilt figures with suspended baldacchino over the altar, with tabernacle. The 1930s fittings include a jazzy iron and curved chrome communion rail, which contrasts with the excellent low-relief stone-carved Stations of the Cross. On the S extremity of the narthex there is a chapel to St. Monica. The sculpture, inside and out, is unmistakably of its era, particularly the latter. Thirties sculpture could be crude and thickly-detailed: but this means it remains visible, when set high up on buildings, in all its details.

The high altar was reconstructed in the 1960s, and recently there has been a thorough reordering and refurbishing by Richard O'Mahony & Partners, producing a forward dais with free-standing altar and font, etc., on it.

Everton, *St. George, Heyworth Street.* This church by Thomas Rickman is very important for its early cast-iron interior (built in 1812–14). A local ironmaster, John Cragg, suggested this use of iron. In form and arrangement, it is a typical Commissioners' church, being an open rectangular box, with small sanctuary, pulpit set at the end of the wide nave, and lateral galleries the length of the building, set up against the internal colonnade. Here, however, the columns are tall slender iron ones, and the large Gothic braces to the nave ceiling and aisle ceilings are of the same material. Hence the upper parts of the building are a forest of thin tendrils of the new-found material, rather than heavy trusses of oak or stone tracery. But the style is Perpendicular and the iron goes a long way to ape the style, with none of the modern scruples of truth-to-materials. In fact, the structure is not so far removed from that of Coalbrookdale's iron bridge. However, what tends to be forgotten by those who have learned of the church from photographs and descriptions of the interior is that the outer structure is entirely conventional stonework—a thick envelope of local hard pink stone, and these two kinds of structure are married together. The W end of St. George's looks down over docks, to the Mersey.

Mossley Hill, *St. Matthew and St. James, Rose Lane.* This very fine, large church by Paley & Austin was built at the top of the hill in a pleasant suburb. It was built in 1870–75, but suffered extensive war damage, and needed major rebuilding (new roof, reproduction organ case, etc., by A.E. Shennan). The war took away large amounts of glass by Morris & Co. and Henry Holiday; some was replaced with stained glass (eg the nave's W window, by Carl Edwards), but much else was left clear, with the result that the church is very light. The nave has six bays, with alternating octagonal and shafted columns. The nave's aisles are terminated at the E, and linked to the crossing arch by internal flying buttress-type arches. The nave is filled with good oak pews (postwar). The pulpit is wooden also, but raised on stone. But then we come to the first of the spaces that have attracted us from our initial entry into the nave: the choir under the tower. This, and the sanctuary beyond, are vast soaring spaces, and rise much higher than the nave. Two powerful sets of arches (transverse and lateral) support the tower above, and produce this large choir. The choir beneath a tower, subdividing nave from sanctuary or chancel, is a familiar Paley & Austin plan. Powerful arches descend onto single piers: but each has a series of moulded arches, cut back and deeply chamfered, such that the lower parts of these piers have a series of eight strips set in a diagonal straight line. Inside the tower, above the arches, there is a grid of tracery, and there are windows, N, S and W. The tower's ceiling is of wood, and panelled. Beyond the under-tower is the sanctuary, with E window (the work, also, of Carl Edwards). To the S, at the E corner, a passage leads to an octagonal vestry (in it is a Boer War memorial of pleasant Art Nouveau copperwork). The vestry was built in 1873, having a splendid fan-like roof structure.

On the outside of the E wall, below the window, we see the architects mix their familiar warm stonework with curious fretted flushwork. At the W, there is a NW porch; at the SW there is a church hall (of brick, this time), about 12 years old. Two Morris & Co. windows (wartime survivors?) are reset in it.

Sefton Park, *St. Agnes and St. Pancras, Ullet Road.* (Known as St. Agnes's, Sefton Park or St. Agnes's, Toxteth Park.) This fine church of 1883–85 is the work of J.L. Pearson. Like many of this architect's works, this has a strong French influence.

The very red Ruabon brick, which covers the exterior, hardly prepares us for the cream-coloured Runcorn stone within, the whole of the interior being built of this. It is vaulted throughout. The style is that of the 13C, and the building's plan is characterised by a noble polygonal apse (which Pearson often employed) and a set of transepts at the W end of the nave (in addition to those at the crossing). This W transept is the most unusual feature of the plan, and suggests the transept on which large W towers are sometimes raised in very large churches. To the W, at the entrance, there is a narthex and gallery above, with triple W window above that. The nave has four bays, with cylindrical columns, and aisles. At the crossing, transepts open to N and S, and these have aisles at the W. The N transept houses the organ, the gallery of which is held on a large polygonal structure supported on 11 slender columns. The S transept has a wooden gallery set along its S wall. To the E of this transept, there is a projecting Lady chapel, rectangular in plan, and this also has aisles, with dark Purbeck shafts in the columns. This chapel is to the S of the chancel, which is one bay deep, and then the five-part apse extends from this. It has a narrow ambulatory passage. The chancel/apse is very beautifully proportioned, but its decoration and carved statuary and sculpture is the most impressive feature. This work is set in three tiers: in the main arcade spandrels (angels), within the arcade, and then suspended figures of saints above (the work of Nathaniel Hitch, 1893–95). At the centre of the apse is a large marble reredos, with sedilia beside it. Before it hang seven sanctuary lamps. At the entrance to the chancel there is no screen, and now a nave altar is sited before the chancel's entrance. The carved adornment seen in the apse is reflected around the building, a stringcourse holding various curious beasts and other objects (eg in the W transepts). A small access gallery runs around the church's upper walls. The Lady chapel's screen and reredos are by G.F. Bodley (1903–04). St. Agnes's Vicarage is the work of R. Norman Shaw (1887).

Sefton Park, *St. Clare, Arundel Avenue.* St. Clare's, built in 1888–90, is one of the most original and striking Catholic churches in the city, and one of the first works of a particularly brilliant *fin de siècle* architect, Leonard Stokes. Here we see many of the hallmarks of the most advanced Arts and Crafts Gothic. Basically, it is one volume, which rises sheer: it has a nave and aisles, but the aisles are simply circulation passages, tunnels cut through wide transverse buttresses which are within the building, and sub-divide the internal spaces. The deep arches over these aisles are circular, and above is a small triforium-passage. The deep arches that rise above this, and frame the principal windows, are pointed. The interior, one is surprised to find, is not of ashlar, but plaster, and this was an economy measure taken against the architect's wishes. Externally, the church is brick with stone dressings. There is no tower, but a small octagonal turret, set between the nave and N transept, in the re-entrant angle. The E window—set high up, and broad—is typical of the Gothic of the period. The presbytery is small and simple, and pleasantly sited together with the church.

Tue Brook, *St. John the Baptist, West Derby Road.* St. John's was built in the years 1868–70 by G.F. Bodley. It was commissioned by a Mrs Reade, whose husband was the first incumbent. It cost £25,000; Bodley also designed the Vicarage, in Green Lane. St. John's is a relatively simple church in a Decorated style, and a conscious evocation of an ancient English church. The tower and spire project at the W end of the building, beside which is a small NW porch, which forms the normal entrance. The nave is of five bays, with a clerestory whose windows are set over the spandrels between the nave's arches. The bay divisions of the outer aisle walls are set slightly off those of the arcade, producing six bays. On the aisle walls are Stations of the Cross and large paintings, with doors, depicting New Testament scenes. Above the chancel arch is a large painting involving the Crucifixion, and many other Christian themes and symbols. Beneath this arch, we enter the choir, which is closed off by an elaborate Rood screen and loft, in five sections. To the N, arches divide the N and S nave aisles from the Lady chapel (N) and organ space (S). In front of the organ is the altar of St. John, or Requiem altar. This was made as recently as 1950, and employed parts of discarded choirstalls. Beside it is the pulpit, and on the wall opposite, on the N, the statue of Our Lady, designed by Sir Ninian Comper (1919); Comper also designed the statue of St. John the Baptist which is raised on the final column of the nave, S side.

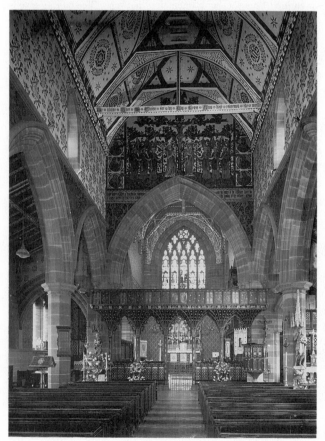

The interior of St. John the Baptist's by G.F. Bodley, 1868–70, whose lavish decorations were restored by S.E. Dykes Bower in 1968–71

Inside the choir, we see the choirstalls and organ case, all of oak, stained black, and painted and gilded. Set in the floor is a large brass memorial to Ralph Brockman (parish priest 1896–1925). Beyond is the sanctuary and high altar. The reredos is divided into seven painted panels, with Christ's baptism depicted in the centre. The E window is of five lights, and some of its subjects have faded somewhat. It is the work of Bodley, Ford Madox Brown, and C.E. Kempe. The sanctuary's S window, above the sedilia, depicts the angelic choir, and was designed by Sir Edward Burne-Jones. To the N of the choir is the Lady chapel, which has a floor of black and white marble and a wooden reredos depicting the Nativity. One of the last parts of the church to be finished was the space under the tower: this is now the chapel of the Holy Rood, and was consecrated in 1978. It is furnished with an altar and reredos, designed by Bodley in 1890 for Dunstable Priory, which were given to St. John's in 1966.

Perhaps the most striking and rare feature of this church, however, is the internal decoration: throughout the building, the walls and ceilings and all surfaces, whatever their material, are covered in stencilled decoration and painting and gilding that is very bright and rich. High up inside the nave's walls there are additional paintings by Kempe. Often, a church's sanctuary is decorated like this, but rarely the whole building. This work has required various restorations, the latest having been carried out recently—though there is clearly still repair and refurbishment to be put in hand. Externally the church is not quite as striking as some of Bodley's, but interesting is the effect produced by the blend of colours in the stone, which perhaps half-prepares us for the polychromy within. A pleasant composition is produced by the arrangement of the vestries around a little courtyard.

St. John's is one of Liverpool's principal Anglican churches of the Anglo-Catholic or Tractarian tradition. It has to be remembered that much of the city's religion is characterised by a tradition of very forceful Protestantism, and that the Anglican diocese (founded 1880) was from the first among the 'lowest' in the Church of England. Thus, from the founding of St. John's, its religion and its priests met with opposition from such as the Orange Order and National Union of Protestants, and then from its diocesan bishops. It is hard for us today to imagine priests being sent to prison, only a century ago, for using incense and wearing priestly vestments—but to understand St. John's, we have to see it against this historical background.

Manchester

Chorlton-on-Medlock, *The Holy Name of Jesus, Oxford Road.* This is one of the largest and best of the churches of J.A. Hansom (built 1869–71). It is administered by the Society of Jesus. Set in Manchester's university quarter, its W entrance opens onto a main road. It is in a Gothic style which is French in character, as seen in the apse and chancel. We enter through a vaulted narthex (with organ above), a space screened by columns and a Rood-screen-like structure. The wide nave has four bays, its vault suspended on slender columns. Left and right are the side aisles, and beyond are outer aisles consisting of confessionals (N) and side chapels (S). Of these chapels, the largest is the Lady chapel, a pleasant space, having circular top-lights and a painted and gilt reredos with triptych. The organ gallery, at the W, continues out over the aisles. W of the Lady chapel-outer-aisle there is an octagonal baptistery that projects externally, forming the building's corner. The Lady chapel is screened from the S aisle by beautiful tracery, set double-thick (ie one superimposed upon another, without them touching), all in a Perpendicular style; this feature is rarely found in such large measure, or used so skilfully. The confessional outer aisle (N) has somewhat inferior Decorated tracery. Beyond the nave are the transepts. They each have two chapels at the E, in separate bays. The southernmost chapel of the S transept has good post-First World War stained glass. Diagonal arches, at the E end of the nave, bring the width of the nave in, and make the transition to the narrower chancel, which has an ambulatory and polygonal apse, with altar in it. The reredos is a great pile of ascending Gothic canopies, with central and outer aedicules (by J.S. Hansom, 1890). In addition to this apsidal E altar, there is a modern free-standing one, set in the crossing space. Outside, the fine ambulatory rises, with N and S towers, flying buttresses and soaring gables—what a pity it is hemmed-in by ancillary buildings. Above the W entrance, Hansom planned a 240ft steeple; instead, there is a tower by Adrian Gilbert Scott. Completed in 1928, it is like a miniature version of that which his brother Giles built at Liverpool Cathedral (completed in the 1940s).

Fallowfield, *First Church of Christ Scientist, Daisy Bank Road.* Edgar Wood was Manchester's important Art Nouveau architect, and this 1903 church—though a church no more but the theatre of Manchester Polytechnic—is probably his best work. Perhaps Wood lacked the intense genius of C.R. Mackintosh, but here we see his skill and verve falling only slightly below that of the Glaswegian master. To be honest, the qualities of this building are largely those of domestic architecture but it was a religious building in the 'meeting house' tradition.

The building is very well-known from photographs in books—but how much bigger and imposing the reality is! The Y-shape of the plan is related to that of the turn-of-the-century 'butterfly' house of E.S. Prior and others, and its two small wings, at the front, contained a reading room (left) and hall (right). Between these rises the tall gabled entrance, with its tall, rough, vertical keystone device, and cruciform window (a kind of Venetian window gone mad), and lower down is the deeply-set door, beneath recessed brick arches. To the right is a stair tower that seems borrowed from Burges's Castell Coch, and right of that, a chimney with oversailing arches set on eight corbels. Here, all roofs are pitched (the main roof very steeply), and they generally fall away from the walls to a point near the ground. And everywhere there are the lovely features of *fin de siècle* domestic design: small battered buttresses, tiny leaded panes, tumbled-in brickwork, iron brackets connecting walls and gutter, white rendering, changing roof pitches, etc. The influences and echoes are too numerous to list, but if we look at the strong *porte cochère*, on the 'S' side of the hall, the spirit of W.R. Lethaby seems there to hover: the dome set on square, with brick and stone chequered parapet, clearly being composed of those archetypal forms described in 'Architecture, Mysticism and Myth' (1891). Beneath, *God is Love* is just legible in relief, on a rapidly-crumbling lintel stone. Strangely, at the back of the main building, a low range of meeting and committee rooms have flat roofs (did they ever leak?).

Through the arch (in which is set a 1903 foundation stone, granite, from Concord, New Hampshire) we cross a corridor, and enter another door. The main hall's roof has timber trusses, set on corbels, and has dormer clerestory-like windows. Low arches connect with small aisle passages through transverse arches. At the 'high' end, opposite the door, there is a marble mosaic 'reredos' behind what would have been a platform; some pieces of carved furniture from this part of the building are preserved at Manchester City Art Galleries. There are shallow transept-like spaces at this end of the hall, beneath low semicircular arches. Looking back towards the entrance end, we see the organ loft, with its curious wooden framed screen, and below, either side of the door, odd green tiled spaces disappear down behind a screen of stout metal balusters. The thin green tiles, similar to these, are vertically fixed. But the wing to the left of the main building (entered from the main hall by turning right) is the most beautiful part of the whole complex of rooms: architects at this time seemed to be able to endow small domestic spaces with a magical quality, at once light and spacious, and also intimate and cosy. The effect is presumably created by the tall oriels (rising externally above the roof), the small windows with deep embrasures, and the inglenook. Manchester City Council deserve much credit for the restoration (1974–76) of this memorable building.

Middleton, *Methodist Church and Schools, Long Street.* This church, built by Edgar Wood in 1899–1901, shows a very different side to the architect's work from that seen in his Manchester Christian Science Church. Here we have Art Nouveau Gothic, an original and brilliant style that marks the continuing evolution and growth of Gothic in modern times. The composition of the church and schools is very compact and intimate; it is urban in character, since the whole fits into a small rectangle set on a busy street, the church anchoring one lateral boundary, the school buildings and gateway enclosing the rest. The lower portions of the church are in warm pink stone, and above, and elsewhere, there are stock bricks—almost all laid as headers (ie. the smaller face showing). A stone archway, with balustered ironwork, leads to the schools' quadrangle; the buildings have canted oriels, high-pitched roofs, rendering, etc. The church has a strong 'W' window, with prominent verticals, overlooking the road; steps beside it lead to the entrance. Beneath the window, a curious set of eight monograms is raised up from the wall, by intaglio: presumably they are the initials of ministers and officials from the time when the building was erected. Some small windows in this façade are headed with strange thin vertical slits. On the church's 'N' side, there is a clerestory; the roof is steeply pitched. The interior is furnished with much woodwork in simple Arts & Crafts style, employing the low segmental-arch curve of C.F.A. Voysey and others. Also Voysey (or Baillie Scott)-like is the ceremonial chair, of oak, inlaid with sycamore and ivory; its armrests are curved. In stone, however, are the church's pulpit and attached low screen. The former has attached Romanesque columns and carved frieze. The church's stone columns are octagonal. The exterior has recently been cleaned, and the condition of this important church is very good: this is much to the credit of whoever organised and paid for the cleaning work.

Pendlebury, *St. Augustine.* This church is considered by many to be the best work of G.F. Bodley, and one of the finest English churches of modern times. His work includes the gatehouse and school, the latter now given over to other educational uses. The church dates from 1870–74, and was paid for by a Manchester banker, who donated £50,000. A drawing showing a tower, standing freely on the S side of the church, was exhibited at the Royal Academy in 1875; it was never built. The church is a very large brick structure, of basically one long, high volume; other than a porch at the SW and a vestry at the NE, it has no projections nor any buttresses extending beyond the walls (for reasons which will be explained). This great mass (a prism, rectangular with a sharp point at the top) reminds us of St. Bartholomew's, Brighton; it looks, as David Verey wrote, 'like the hulk of an enormous ship washed up on a forlorn beach'. And very grim the scene is today, the industrial housing that was once all around long gone (and little having replaced it), the area between the buildings, and the churchyard, in disarray, and the heavy steel gates fitted over all the original doors look hard and forbidding; the glories of Bodley's art are now a kind of paradise-closed-up.

Reviewing the work in 1877, 'The Builder's' critic drew attention to the 'somewhat unusual' plan and structural system for which the church is so famous: that of pierced internal buttresses, or buttresses brought into the building, and cut through with small aisle passages. This is why the building is able to have a very high roof, and not require wide transverse buttresses projecting outwards from the building. So inside, either side of the principal space (a long, wide hall—nave and chancel in one, unbroken) we see a series of transverse walls projecting out from the nave piers, which are vaulted together with transverse ribbed, pointed, barrel-vaults, this vault taking its form from the nave arches which it abuts. The building's side walls then abut these buttresses/vaults, and their windows descend only two-thirds or so down the wall's height to a stringcourse, outside (which is the level of the two-storey NE vestry's eaves). Outside, these internal buttresses poke out above the principal parapet, and on the outer walls emerge as a thin pilaster strip. The windows have a low arch, like a relieving arch, set over them, the windows, and the wall area around them, being recessed. The nave is of six bays. In the seventh, there is a Rood screen (but no chancel arch), and the organ is on the N side, in the 'buttress' space (its presence accounts for the blind N bay, at this point). Canon Frederick Sutton, who collaborated with Bodley on matters relating to organs, is said to have designed this organ case. The pulpit is on the N pier at the W side of the seventh bay, just before the screen. The altar is raised very high, on eight steps. The final (tenth) bay cants inwards—beside the sanctuary—and the aisle passages cease. The great reredos, with its tiers of painted figures, rises to about half the height of the E wall, and hence the wide E window only pierces the upper half of the wall. The window is divided by two vertical buttresses which flow through the window, and join a grid of tracery on the outside. The window thus has two outer panels (each with two lights) and one central panel (three lights), and there is much flowing curvilinear tracery at the top, raised higher in the central panel. The glass is all the work of Burlison & Grylls, a firm which Bodley helped found in 1870. Bodley worked with the glass-makers, devising schemes in which each window had a principal colour, an idea Bodley considered new, at least in modern times.

Whether or not St. Augustine's was the first English church to have internally-pierced buttresses, the idea was to have much influence in later English church building. The idea came originally from the great medieval cathedral of Albi, in the S of France, a building which has had a massive influence on British architects from Bodley to Basil Spence, and not only was Coventry Cathedral influenced by it, but those at Guildford and Liverpool (Anglican).

Preston, *St. Walburge, Weston Street.* It is surely due to the traditional strength of Lancastrian Catholicism that it was able, within just a few years of full emancipation (1829), to erect this vast and

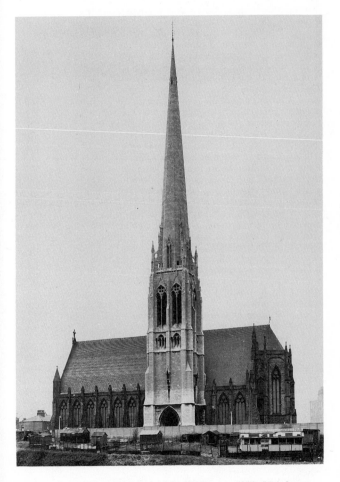

J.A. Hansom's church of St. Walburge, 1850–54, whose spire is 315ft high

breathtaking church (1850–54). Joseph Aloysius Hansom, inventor of the Hansom cab and founder of the influential journal 'The Builder', was an important Catholic architect in the period c 1840–70. Here he was able to create a work of powerful drama which dominates its surroundings.

Outside, it is the tower and slender spire—315ft high in total—which holds our attention, and when we approach the W façade, it is the large rose window; but once inside, it is the gigantic hammer-beam roof, covering a vast unified space, that holds us in awe. The interior has no divisions of screens or columns or walls; nowhere are there aisles or separated chapels. The roof is very steep and high, and descends down onto outer walls which are very low by comparison (only at the E does the wall of the apse rise up, and considerably so, with the result that E windows fill the large space formed by the high roof against the E wall—the rose does the same at the W). The church is of 13 bays, and there are 13 wooden trusses, each bearing two large carved saints. This is the architecture of repetition: the viewer standing at either end sees a forest of timber beams, truss after truss after truss. Beneath is the seating: fixed pews, with a central and two outer corridors. At least 1100 can be seated. There is an organ loft raised on iron columns, which fills the two W bays. A lower stage of the tower (flanking the building on its S side) opens into the church, forming a raised choir loft; a baptistery is set beside the tower's base. On the N side, in the ninth bay from the W, a pulpit is built out from the wall, the staircase to it seemingly set into the wall's width. The semi-octagonal apse has tall stained glass windows, and all together has just a hint of Italian Gothic E ends. Either side of the apse are two other windows, smaller because of the fall of the roof, and they look like aisle windows, though there are no aisles. They rise behind two chapels which flank the original chancel: Our Lady (N) and St. Joseph (S); the large marble E altar has a gold tabernacle surmounted by a tower-like structure with a crucifix. In recent years, a forward free-standing altar has been created by bringing part of the chancel platform forward a further bay (the fourth from the E), and the new work has been very carefully designed to blend with the old, using appropriate materials. On the S side, there is a war memorial which takes the form of a large triptych with hinged panels. It must be said that in this church, as with so much Catholic building of the 19C, the detailing and decoration are sometimes poor, but St. Walburge's reminds us that architecture consists of space, and the enclosing of space with structure; who can carp about crude carving or garish glass, when experiencing such space, and such structure, as this?

Rochdale

St. Chad. St. Chad was the great 7C Apostle of the Midlands, who sited the vast Diocese of Mercia at Lichfield. Much of S Lancashire was once part of that diocese, and churches dedicated to him are far-flung. While his remains were moved into Lichfield Cathedral in 1148, a document suggests that this Lancashire church also had relics.

It is situated on a steep hill overlooking the town, and it is first known from the later 12C. St. Chad's is another large civic medieval church which is now essentially one of 19C structure—particularly in its external stonework. The nave, of six bays, has alternating round and octagonal columns with capitals decorated with stiff-leaf. This is largely of the 13C, with a high arch to the tower of the 14C. The under-tower is screened, and its W window has William Morris glass, of 1872–74. To the tower was added a bell stage in the 1870s. The clerestory is of five windows, N and S (16C). The N aisle was rebuilt in 1854–55 and the S in 1873–75. In the former is the medieval font, unearthed in 1893. The latter has a S door, of 1907. An arch leads into the chancel (oak pulpit, of 1907, at its S). Original Perpendicular work survives in the choirstalls and screens—and this means it survived the years when St. Chad's was a Protestant preaching church, with fixed box-pews, galleries and plastered ceiling, which was the case until the mid-19C. The chancel, like the nave, has six bays and a hammerbeam roof adorned with two tiers of carved angels. The sixth bay is the sanctuary, with E window of six lights. This chancel was rebuilt and lengthened by J.S. Crowther in 1883–85. N of the chancel is the St. Katherine chapel. Its 1965 altar rail, complete with mouse, is the work of Robert Thompson of Kilburn. Also N of the chancel is a large parish chest. To the S is the present Holy Trinity chapel. This (like St. Katherine's) was a 15C chapel, but was acquired, in 1823, by the new Lords of the Manor, the Dearden family. James Dearden seems to have wished to create a bogus ancestry for his family, fitted to his new position, and so he filled the chapel with brass monuments, set in the floor, in the medieval manner. The problem is that they are forgeries, and date from the mid-19C. However, the monument to Jacob Dearden (died 1825) is genuine: a young woman leaning over a pedestal, etc., by R.W. Sievier—and there are others. From the church, a long steep series of steps leads down to Rochdale's excellent Gothic town hall, and Lutyens's war memorial beyond.

St. Mary, Toad Lane. St. Mary's was built and consecrated in the 1740s. It was a chapel of ease, a brick preaching church, with aisle galleries set on fat Tuscan columns, and a short chancel with apsidal sanctuary. This building was in use until February 1909. The new church was dedicated in February 1911, and was the work of Ninian Comper. Comper seems to have used some of the old building, but reconstructed those parts he used, and added new work. What was reused was the old church's N aisle, with a new arcade and altered windows. The original nave served Comper as an inner nave aisle, and Comper's own nave is now on the S side of this, there being two N aisles, and no S aisle at all. Inside, as a consequence of this and other design decisions, are two arcades, of very different heights.

The outer nave aisle has slender Tuscan columns with semicircular arches on them; the arches' soffits have an interlaced, diagonal moulding. This outer aisle has a chapel, screened, at the W. The central aisle houses the organ, at the E, which is raised above an open space, screened from the aisle. Above the organ is a wide, round arch. The screen, and its passageway above, is continuous with the Rood screen and loft of the nave. The nave has five tall columns, three circular and two octagonal (their sides gently concave), separating it from the aisle. Opposite the columns are seven wide, open Perpendicular windows (three-light) that look to the S. The nave's seating originally extended almost right up to the screen, but has now been moved back to make way for choir seating and a free-standing altar. On the S side of the nave, just in front of the screen, is the pulpit, part of which is the 18C original. The nave's portion of the screen has five parts, with Rood above, and two of the angels found in Ezekiel's vision. High above these is a Rood-beam-like tie, carrying a Christ-in-Judgement with two angels, in mandorlas. Inside the choir proper are rows of stalls, two each side. A squint is provided, giving sight of the sanctuary from the N nave aisle. There is an open communion rail and an 'English altar' with riddel posts surmounted by angels bearing candles. Two clear windows are set to the S of the chancel, and one to the N. The E window is six-light; stained glass depictions include a fine set of scenes from the early life of Christ (lower portion). Higher up, there are two depictions of Christ in mandorlas, and in the familiar Comper fashion where the portrait resembles a Roman youth. The building employs pink stone from Alderley, near Manchester, and brick outside. On the roof is a small cupola.

St. Mary's, with its existing Georgian building, was perhaps ideal material for Comper's singular genius to work on. This church is perhaps individual among its creator's works because of its scarcity of the familiar gilding and whitewashing, and more of the warm stonework and elaborate woodwork (appearing just as wood). But not untypically, we find that the whole was built up more gradually than may first appear: the W window (St. George and the Dragon, etc.) was completed in 1923, the Rood screen—perhaps the finest part of the whole building—in 1924, and the central volume's E windows in 1926.

St. Helens, *Hardshaw Friends' Meeting House, Church Street.* This is a typical Friends' meeting house, and is set back from the road, at the outer end of the street, near a traffic island. In the 1650s, Quaker missionaries passed through St. Helens on their way S, from the N part of Lancashire, where their movement arose (see Swarthmoor Meeting House under Ulvertson). The St. Helens Meeting was a product of this evangelisation: in 1679, the meeting house building, and much other property, was bequeathed to the local Quakers by George Shaw. In these early years, the Quakers were fined for their unlawful worship (here, in 1684); in 1689 the building became a registered meeting house. The 1679–92 building was reconstructed in 1763. It is the oldest building, still in use, in the town.

The building follows the common Quaker pattern of large meeting room (four roof trusses) with benches and table, set to the left of a central dividing passage, having a smaller room to the right. Unfortunately, most of the fittings and furnishings are recent: the screen, which traditionally divides spaces in a Quaker building, is here a structure of tall panels that move on a rail, and looks early 20C. However, this in itself is interesting, since in the first 30 years or so of this century, Nonconformists began sub-dividing many rooms and spaces within their buildings, for all kinds of extra-liturgical activities. The St. Helens screen surely replaces simple wooden panels that hinged or slid or folded, and Quakers used screens for similar purposes (as well as a measure of sexual separation). So here, old and recent Nonconformist use of screens is strangely linked.

Early this century, the meeting house was used by Presbyterians, and they are said to have erected the present rostrum or elder's seat, against the far wall: behind it, originally, there was a wide fireplace, as found in 1906. The windows preserve much original glass in diamond panes. Above the entrance door is a sundial, and at the rear of the house is a late 1960s service wing, tastefully matching in the colour and quality of its stonework.

Sefton, St. Helen. Sefton Church provides one of the most coherent pre-Reformation buildings in Lancashire. It has had modern work—which medieval church has not?—but it does not, like so many others in the county, emerge as a somewhat disconcerting co-existence of old with a lot of new. The thing that unifies it, and gives the whole its special character and feeling, is the woodwork, particularly the abundance of screens, and while the county is not poor in this feature, Sefton must surely stand supreme.

The chapel N of the chancel has Decorated windows, and a double piscina with fine Decorated details in the arch surmounting it; this is the oldest part of the fabric. The rest dates from the late 15C to c 1540, though the chancel's E window is late 19C. However, the curious pinnacles around the spire—like stone umbrellas that will not fully close—are of uncertain date, and dates suggested include the 17C and early 19C. The nave has four bays, but five clerestory windows (three-light, and round-topped, which are so common in Lancashire). The roof looks so authentically 15C that we would not know it to be the turn-of-the-century work of W.D. Caroë—Sefton has always been lucky in its woodwork: well, almost; at the NW of the nave there is a clutch of crude pine pews. These were the 'official' pews of the 'Mock Corporation' of Sefton, a Georgian dining club that decamped from church into the adjacent hostelry, and there held bogus civic proceedings, while tippling. But the nave's pews return us to the Sefton standard, with their fine, but odd, carved alphabet, the letters of which are set along the outside of the early 16C bench-ends. The S nave aisle has three windows (and S porch, with room over); the N nave aisle just has two windows. To the W of the nave is the tower, the W wall of which bears a mark revealing an earlier roof. At the E end of the nave, the screens begin. In the centre is the high, coved Rood screen, with its Renaissance putti-decorated frieze. In front, on the N side, is the pulpit, also of oak, which comes down to a sharp point—an inverted octagonal pyramid: this is the result of some reduction devised by Caroë. The sounding board is also octagonal. To right and left of the central screen are other screens, which divide the nave aisles from the chancel aisles; these are less high and simpler, particularly that to the N. The N chancel aisle houses the Blundell pew, which has stalls turned around three sides of a square. Beyond this is the Lady chapel, at the E of which is a modern altar, with the beautiful piscina adjacent, on its S side. An early 14C tomb-recess, in this chapel, has the effigy of a knight (13C), and there is another, bearded, of the 14C. Beyond this chapel is a vestry which extends around the E side of the building. Inside the choir (first and second chancel bays) are stalls, which are returned around beside the Rood screen, and there is also a lower, forward, row of stalls, also returned. The choir is screened from the chancel aisles, with late Gothic tracery panels. The second chancel bay of the choir, proceeding E, has the organ on its S side, and the third chancel bay is the sanctuary. On the N side is an aumbry. The reredos here is wooden, and Classical in style—a bit out of harmony with the rest, stylistically—but it is generally dated mid-18C. S of the choir is the Sefton chapel, which has many monuments of the Molyneux family, including brasses (16C) set in the floor of the chapel, and that of the Sefton pew, in the chapel, another abundance of carved screenwork, set on the S side. Sefton Church is filled with interesting objects and furnishings: there are hatchments to be seen, brass chandeliers, a late 16C chained Bible, candlesticks of rhinoceros horn and a vast oak chest. Sefton's furniture includes some work by Robert Thompson, the 'mouseman' of Kilburn, Yorkshire, including one of his very, very thick tables, finished with the adze so that its surface is covered in ripples. Opposite the Blundell pew is a cupboard by Thompson. Somehow this late Arts & Crafts work—since this is presumably the tradition from which it comes—can lose all sense of style and form in its absorption with quality of construction and materials. But perhaps Sefton Church is an appropriate setting for it, since all around it is a celebration of the glories of English oak, and English woodcarving.

Standish, *St. Wilfrid.* This church presents many difficulties to its historian, since it seems to be a fascinating mixture of different builds and styles. Discounting the (later) tower, gatehouse and vestries, here is a building that appears to be largely Perpendicular in style and period; and so it probably was, once. In the 1540s, however, it is known to have been in a ruinous condition, and building work was done soon afterwards, in the 1550s. In 1582, however, a contract was made for major rebuilding, and this was effected in a few years. The exterior work must thus be considered to be 16C Gothic; but inside, the internal columns (nave and chancel) are Tuscan, and have wide, thin abaci (the arches above them are Gothic, however), and of a Classicism that one expects to find in the following century. So, much of the work is typical of years earlier, and some, very avant-garde. The Rood loft stairs are more likely to be remnants from the pre-1540 building, than part of the 1580s work. The nave and chancel arches could conceivably be much older, also, having been reused. The nave has five bays, with clerestory of four-light windows, and the aisle windows are also four-light. The nave has various hatchments hanging in it. The roofs are all flat (or almost flat), of timber, with diagonal bracing. The pulpit, octagonal, of oak, dates from 1616. The chancel has two bays, and also the sanctuary. N and S of the chancel are tombs with recumbent effigies. The reredos is of stone, having seven panels. The E window has five lights. S of the chancel is the Standish chapel. A new liturgical area has been created in recent times, by bringing the communion rail forward to form a trapezoidal platform. The modern furniture it has suggests the hand of George Pace, who did much reordering work of this kind. The W tower with its upper octagonal stage dates from 1867. It is perhaps a little thin and weak for such a church. The E vestry (1913–14) and the gatehouse (1926) are the work of Austin & Paley, the latter being a pleasant little addition to this very architecturally unusual church.

Stonyhurst, *St. Peter.* Stonyhurst was a large house, dating from the 14C, 15C and 16C, which in 1794 was given to the Society of Jesus. They used it to house their English College, which was then evacuated from the Low Countries, where Catholic institutions were being suppressed, just as they had in England in the 16C; as a consequence, Stonyhurst became one of the great Catholic schools, with building work going on through most of the 19C. The W façade of the school has a gatehouse (c 1592–95) set at the end of a water-flanked avenue, and to the right of the school buildings, but separate, is the Stonyhurst parish church, which was built in 1832–35, just after the Catholic Emancipation Act of 1829. The work of J.J. Scoles, it has seven bays, and aisles with low-pitched roofs, each bay set between pilasters bearing large crocketed finials. The windows' tracery (particularly in the aisles, to the N) is very authentic, considering the date. There are small transepts to N and S. The corners of the building are in the manner of King's College Chapel, Cambridge, and their use reflects that found in the Commissioners' Gothic of about this time; but also, it reveals a certain confidence and show, which English Catholicism had perhaps longed to display, in the long years before Emancipation. The church also shows the competence Catholic Gothic had acquired before the coming of A.W.N. Pugin.

Ulverston, *Swarthmoor Meeting House.* Swarthmoor is an important early meeting house, of great simplicity and charm; its interiors and fittings are sufficiently undisturbed as to convey the atmosphere of the early Friends. While the Friends' leader, George Fox, came from Leicestershire, it has been said that the movement he founded really originated in the NW of England. In 1652 he visited Swarthmoor Hall, home of the Puritan Judge Thomas Fell, and his wife Margaret. As a result of this visit, Friends met in the Great Hall at Swarthmoor for 38 years. In 1687, Fox bought, for £72, an estate called Petty's, near the Hall, and gave it to the local Friends to convert into a meeting house.

Approaching the meeting house from the road, we see the traditional Friends' arrangement of hall to the left (rising to the building's full height), entrance-passage just off-centre, and two-storey space to the right. In front of the passage is a small porch, a stone above which records Fox's gift of the building in 1688. The meeting hall proper has three full-height windows (probably later replacements), and four beams above, the ceiling being flat. The rectangle of simple benches around a table is the normal interior form. The raised Elders' Bench is at the far end wall, opposite the passage. The two-storeyed portion, on the other side of the passage, comprises a gallery (raked) with small room below, and all these rooms and spaces can be connected up, since the passage's walls mostly consist of wooden screens that can be hinged up, and fixed on hooks set in the ceiling. The gallery, also, can be screened-off, or opened onto the main meeting hall. Movable screens are an interesting feature of early Friends' buildings. The leaded windows of the gallery, and room below, are probably contemporary with the original conversion. In the passage there are some plain wooden hat-pegs. The floors are of slate (and this, of course, is slate country).

Warrington, *St. Elphin.* Warrington's major church is dedicated to someone concerning whom nothing seems to be known, though the designer of an early-20C window in the S nave aisle has depicted him in a monkish habit, bearing a crozier. Today the church that bears his name is like many another large town church, with its gradual transformation from early medieval to largely 19C: but St. Elphin's also has a powerful 281ft tower and spire, which makes its presence known far and wide. A church stood on the site in the late 12C. Various parts of the present structure date from the 14C (the crypt beneath the E end, the E and N walls of the N transept, and large parts of the chancel). Much of the remainder is the work of F. & H. Francis, and dates from 1859–67. There was, in addition, some work done in the 17C (remnants are in the tower) and the early 19C (S aisle windows). The nave has four bays, with columns of eight slender shafts rising to a hammerbeam roof; there is no clerestory. The aisles date from 1833 (S) and 1859–67 (N); they retain their galleries. There is a large elaborate organ case (of 1909) at the W end. The pulpit and lectern, of 1878, are of sumptuous brasswork. Strong, deeply moulded crossing arches (on 13C-style piers) lead to the transepts, and, at the E, the chancel, of three bays (the crossing is ceiled with a flat timber roof). The chancel was made higher, in the mid-19C restoration. At the E is an 'English altar', with sedilia beside it (a reproduction in wood and plaster of 14C stone sedilia). The chancel has a wooden wagon roof. The E crypt has a ribbed vault (rebuilt in the 19C) set on six corbels, which are carved with floral patterns and faces (original). The central W corbel bears the face of Christ. St. Elphin's contains many monuments of interest. In the N transept, the former Boteler chapel, there are alabaster effigies of Sir John Boteler and his wife (late 15C). The S transept now houses monuments to the Patten family (1772, 1892, etc.), which were originally in a separate Patten chapel, sited to the W of the transept.

Whalley, St. Mary. Whalley owes its development to the Cistercian abbey founded there in the later 13C. NW of the abbey, the parish church was built. The fabric includes much work of the Early English period, with a S doorway with Norman capitals, and there are late Perpendicular aisle and clerestory windows and a Perpendicular E window and tower (at the W). The nave has four bays, with round columns and capitals. The four high clerestory windows are not aligned with the arches below. The steeply-pitched wooden roof has four trusses set over the columns. The first bay of the nave is largely filled with a big organ and organ loft. The N aisle has two projecting dormers and two flat-topped windows below. There is a N porch, at the W. At the E end of this aisle, there is a war memorial chapel, and there is another chapel at the E end of the S nave aisle. The chancel consists of five bays, the choir comprising three, the sanctuary two.

Whalley's church has one strong feature, not as yet referred to: a surfeit of glorious woodwork, in the form of benches, pews, screens, stalls and misericords. These begin in the nave, with its oak benches, those on the S side clearly being old, the others modern. The chancel, and N and S aisle chapels, are all separated by Perpendicular screens. But then there are the box-pews. The most elaborate of them, on the S side, is that known as 'St. Anton's Cage'. It bears the dates 1534, 1610 and 1830, and the last date is the least relevant to its history: it is the upper parts which are 17C, altered in the 19C. Beyond this, to the N, is a further carved pew of 1702, and there are others. The organ case, W, was made for Lancaster Priory in 1729. Beyond the Rood screen (three panels, either side of the central opening) are the choirstalls. These come from Whalley Abbey, and can be dated to the years 1418–34. Notable is the very intricate tracery of the canopies, and the way their rear panelling is occasionally cut away to reveal a window. There are 12 stalls on each side (two on the S side give access to doors). Beneath the canopies are seats with misericords, one of Lancashire's notable sets. Subjects on the N side include St. George and the Dragon, eagles, a rose, a pig, and a wife beating a man with a frying pan; on the S side, a dragon, a green man, an angel, a pelican, a lion, and a dragon. Set within these stalls are additional benches.

The sanctuary has a modern communion rail, altar with reredos, and stone sedilia with four attached columns and triple hoodmoulded arches. The E window has heraldic shields (25, and others in the S sanctuary windows). On the N side of the sanctuary, at the bottom of the wall, is the monument to Dr Thomas Dunham Whittaker (1822); it is a semi-reclining figure. Other monuments in the church include that to Elizabeth Whalley (1785), and Sir Richard Westmacott's monument to Sir James Whalley Smythe Gardener, of 1805.

Winwick, *St. Oswald.* St. Oswald was the Christian King of Northumbria who died in battle against King Penda of Mercia, in the 7C; it is thought that the battle, and Oswald's death, took place near Winwick. St. Oswald's Church is medieval, much transformed with rebuilding, and having a chancel by A.W.N. Pugin.

The W tower is of early 14C date. The nave has six bays, clerestory, and a fairly flat timber roof. The S arcade was rebuilt in 1836 in an early 14C style, and presumably approximates to what was there before (the S aisle was rebuilt at this time also). The dating of the N arcade is less certain. The arches appear to be of the 14C, but the columns have been held to be early 17C work. On the W wall of the nave, an inscription commemorates King Oswald's death. The clerestory is late Perpendicular, and marks on the tower's inside wall suggest that it had an earlier, lower, roof. At the E of the N aisle (this aisle was itself rebuilt in 1580) there is found the Gerard chapel. This has a damaged brass memorial to Sir Piers Gerard (died 1495), remains of an early cross, a damaged 14C font, and an inlaid communion table dated 1725 (once the principal communion table of the church). On the equivalent part of the S aisle is the Legh chapel. Despite the presence of the organ, we are able to see various monuments of the Legh family of Cheshire, including that made in Rome by R.J. Wyatt (for Ellen Benet Legh), the 1527 brass showing Sir Peter Legh and his wife, and several others.

Pugin rebuilt the chancel in 1847–48. We enter it through Pugin's Decorated screen of three bays. The painted wagon ceiling has a very high-pitched roof above it; the chancel thus rises above the nave. The side windows are three-light, and the E window is four-light. There are triple sedilia, carved panels around the altar, and encaustic tiles. The chancel's glass was designed by Pugin and made by John Hardman. At the E end of its roof, Pugin placed a small bellcote.

On the outside of the church's W wall, we can see a carving of a pig. This is the 'Winwick Pig', concerning which there are various stories and legends. It seems that the present carving is a replacement of a medieval one destroyed in the 17C (the fragments in the Gerard chapel may have been damaged in the Puritan years also). The original carving was set beside another depicting St. Anthony of Egypt, known as the founder of Christian monasticism. St. Anthony's mascot was a pig, and hence the carving's original presence. St. Oswald's is pleasantly set in an undisturbed churchyard. Built on a high point, its steeple is visible far around.

LEICESTERSHIRE

The Soar valley—or less romantically, the A6—roughly divides Leicestershire into two distinct areas. To the E is the higher, very picturesque part, to the W flatter ground which runs out into the West Midland plain. This distinction is reflected in the county's churches and their building materials. Moving E the geology becomes younger whereas—and this is an oversimplification—the earlier phases of surviving churches tend to be older. The characteristic W Leicestershire church is built of greyish Triassic sandstone and will tend to date mainly, or in some cases wholly, from the early 14C. In the E limestone or ironstone are the building materials from the Jurassic series that sweeps up through the E margin of the county. Typically the oldest parts of these churches are to be found inside, perhaps a Norman arcade, though more usually dating from the 13C, with various later additions. The typical E Leicestershire church has lean-to aisles, sometimes a chancel chapel, usually a W tower and invariably a S porch. In the W a characteristic feature is the provision of big aisles under their own gabled roofs. Sometimes there is one but they can be so large that they give the churches a two-naved appearance, e.g. at Broughton Astley and Thurlaston. This type may derive its popularity from the vast S aisle at St. Mary de Castro, Leicester. The finest example is to be found at Stoke Golding. Particularly in the S there is a large tract between the sandstone-using and ironstone-using parts that is overlaid by thick deposits of boulder clay and is devoid of decent building materials. Here whole churches—and the big building at Lutterworth is one of them—are constructed out of stones collected from the fields. Such walls present a browner version of the flint walls of Norfolk. In addition there is a variety of materials from the craggy outcrops of Charnwood—pink Mountsorrel granite and metamorphic rocks of various subtle hues. Swithland slates, arranged in courses of diminishing width, provide roof coverings of the highest quality and visual interest. In the E Collyweston slates, consisting of platy limestone, have been brought in from just across the border in Northamptonshire. Brick appears very early in the chapel at Bradgate Park, where the mansion was begun in c 1490. Otherwise it starts being used in the W from the early 18C (c 1726 at Sibson).

The great period of Leicestershire church building was some 30 or 40 years either side of 1300 and it is unusual to find a church that does not contain work of this period. Of earlier centuries, there is little pre-Conquest and Norman work but a substantial quantity, if not quality, from the 13C. Leicester was the site of a bishopric from the early 8C until shortly after 872 but pre-Conquest architecture is almost wholly absent apart from the late nave at St. Nicholas', Leicester. There is the usual scatter of sculpture including a complete cross at Sproxton and part of one at Rothley. But the key items and ones of international significance are the early 9C sculptures at Breedon-on-the-Hill. Leicestershire is not a great county for Norman work. The most impressive architecture comprises the decorated towers at St. Nicholas' (including reused Roman bricks) and Higham-on-the-Hill. The tower at Tugby is a very interesting one showing early features. The mighty crossing piers at Thurnby survive, though rebuilt, and the tower at Breedon, too, is Norman. The finest piece of all is the sedilia at St. Mary de Castro with their exquisitely carved capitals and a riot of zigzag in the arches.

Otherwise there are various arcades (e.g. Allexton, Lubenham and Theddingworth), doorways (e.g. Belgrave in Leicester (especially good), Great Glen and Horninghold), a stately tympanum at Hallaton, one with mysterious symbolism at Stoney Stanton, a pillar piscina at Broughton Astley, and some two dozen fonts.

13ᵗʰ CENTURY PIERS AND ARCHES ⋄⋄
STᵉEGELWYN ᵗʰᵉ MARTYR ⋄ SCALFORD ⋄ Leics ⋄

A good deal more survives from the 13C. It is rare to find a complete 13C building in this area, but the plain cruciform church at Mowsley is an example. The most common survival of 13C work is in arcades. Many were added to previously unaisled structures to create space for side chapels. The local evidence suggests that it was most popular to add a N aisle before a S one. Long chancels (e.g. at Illston-on-the-Hill and Great Bowden) were added in place of their short Norman predecessors. E Leicestershire is a rewarding place to notice the transition between Norman and 13C architecture. The magnificent capital at Twyford is from the same school as those at

Oakham Castle. Round arches have remarkable staying power into the early 13C in this area. It is to the 13C that the earliest spires belong. That at Hallaton is particularly pleasing. Other examples are at Horninghold and Shepshed. These are all of the broach type. Later came the parapet spire and a whole vocabulary of ribs, pinnacles, crockets, bands, spire-light crosses and different treatments to the parapets to provide variety and visual interest. There are several places where the serene beauty of the 13C may be enjoyed at its best: the beautiful foliage capitals at Somerby, the beautiful and unusually traceried windows at Stoughton, the crossing tower at Melton Mowbray and the college chapel at Noseley.

This last example carries us well into the golden age of c 1300. Apart from the 1860s and 1870s, there must have been more activity in Leicestershire's churches then than at any other time. Probably the most beautiful church of the time is Stoke Golding after the addition of the S aisle and chapel in c 1280–90. The rich tracery and openwork parapet are far more than the average village church could run to. The more typical activity was the rebuilding or adding of aisles, the standard pattern for the arcades being double-chamfered pointed arches on octagonal piers with moulded capitals. Tracery was often intersected, or some variant upon it, or Geometrical. The term 'Decorated' seems inappropriate to most work of the time in Leicestershire. But at Gaddesby, in the S aisle, the remodelling work provided an astonishingly ornate example. Other good work of the time is to be seen at Market Harborough, Claybrooke and several W Leicestershire churches. Kibworth Beauchamp is a wholly early 14C church and includes a local motif, also met with in N Northamptonshire—arcades without capitals.

Leicestershire's economic fortunes declined after the first quarter of the 14C and it is no doubt for this reason that Perpendicular work is relatively limited. Even churches which look like larger Perpendicular town churches are in fact 15C recastings of earlier ones. St. Margaret's, Leicester, Market Harborough and Melton Mowbray all fall into that category. At Market Harborough in c 1480, for example, the work involved refenestration, the addition of embattled parapets and the rebuilding of the nave arcades. The piers are tall, fairly slender and with the local device of no capitals in the E–W directions. At a great many places clerestories were added, sometimes (e.g. at Melton Mowbray) towers were heightened and new windows were put in. The 15C builders provided some fine steeples, especially a number with broach spires which still have Geometrical tracery (e.g. South Kilworth and Theddingworth). Croxton Kerrial in the far NE is a rare example of a wholly Perpendicular church. The greatest gem, perhaps, is the tiny chapel at Withcote, all of the 16C and retaining much of its glass of c 1530–40.

Leicestershire has a number of churches from the 17C and 18C that are of above-average importance. Staunton Harold is a rare example of a church erected during the Commonwealth—by a staunch Royalist, Sir Robert Shirley. It is still cast in the Gothic mould, though its furnishings are in the 17C tradition. The next key church is Gaulby, remodelled in 1741 and incorporating extraordinary chinoiserie in the form of pagoda-like pinnacles on top of a hybrid tower. Only half a mile away is one of the great 18C churches, King's Norton, a beautiful airy rectangle which has its furnishings more or less intact. Saxby (1789) and Stapleford (1783) are other good examples of late 18C church building.

The early 19C is represented by the fine tower at Kibworth

Beauchamp (1832–36), by a splendid furnishing and plaster-vaulting scheme at Appleby Magna (c 1830) and by St. George's, Leicester, a costly Commissioners' church of 1823–27. There is an important restoration by A.W.N. Pugin at Wymeswold (1844–46). Pugin was very active around Charnwood, which was a major centre for the Catholic revival. Ambrose Lisle March Phillipps de Lisle was the inspirational force and brought missionaries from Italy. For them, William Flint's Greek Revival church of St. Mary, Loughborough was built in 1833–34. Phillipps founded Mount St. Bernard Abbey in 1835 and Pugin was his architect for five years from 1839. He built a small church (now a workshop and house) at Shepshed in 1842, extended the chapel at Phillipps's house at Grace Dieu in 1841 and started the work, including a chapel, at Ratcliffe College in 1843.

Of the High Victorian period, Raphael Brandon's Little Dalby of 1851–52 is an excellent example of assured remodelling and improvement on an existing building. In 1860–62, Sir Gilbert Scott built a most uncharacteristic church in Leicester (St. Andrew's), which is in the blunt brick idiom more characteristic of William Butterfield. In 1865–66 Goddard & Son's Tur Langton takes up the brick theme again but in less stern a manner: it is a fascinating essay in polychrome and spiky decoration so beloved in the 1860s. Leicester is fortunate to possess Ewan Christian's masterpiece, St. Mark's (1870–72), impressively apsed and faced with Charnwood slate from the donor's own quarries. The magnificent church of St. John the Baptist in Leicester is by Goddard & Paget in 1884–85 and is as good an example of late 19C church building as can be found in most towns. Goddard & Co.'s church of St. James the Greater, Leicester (1899–1901, completed 1914) has a splendid Early Christian revival interior.

Of the Free Church buildings, the most imposing are Goddard & Paget's Melbourne Hall, Leicester, of 1880–81; William Flint's Congregational Church of 1844 in Market Harborough; Joseph Hansom's 'pork pie chapel' for the Baptists in 1845 (so-called because of its round appearance to the street); and the Wigston Magna Congregational Church of 1841–42. Some of the other buildings are moderately distinguished and many are unpretentiously charming, e.g. the little Gothick rectangle of 1837–38 in Evington for the Baptists, the Rearsby Wesleyan Chapel of 1849 and the delightful Hepzibah Chapel of 1807 for the Congregationalists in Newton Burgoland. Leading Nonconformists with whom the county is associated are George Fox (1624–91), who was born at Fenny Drayton and who became the founder of the Society of Friends; Philip Doddridge (1702–51), the great Nonconformist divine and hymn-writer who became minister at Kibworth Harcourt in 1723 and Market Harborough in 1725; and Selina, Countess of Huntingdon (1709–91), born at Staunton Harold and founder of the Countess of Huntingdon's Connexion, who is buried in Ashby-de-la-Zouch Parish Church.

As for the contents of churches, there is a scattering of screens (e.g. Burton Overy and Long Whatton) and the strange device at Eastwell which amounts to a plaster (?) infill between nave and chancel, pierced by a couple of windows and a small doorway. A complete set of benches survives at Croxton Kerrial and some fine ones, too, at Noseley. Wall paintings are few in number but those at Great Bowden and Lutterworth are worthy of note. Stained glass is better represented, pride of place going to a collection of important 13C pieces brought to Twycross in the last century. Other notable work is at Launde, Stockerston and, as mentioned above, Withcote. The post-Reformation furnishing schemes noted earlier at Staunton Harold and King's Norton are of the very highest order. The most spectacular post-Reformation item is the vast example of the arms of Queen Anne (1704) over the chancel arch at Long Whatton. Monuments, however, are very well represented in Leicestershire. Pride of place must go to Bottesford where the chancel is filled with fine monuments to the Earls of Rutland. Ashby-de-la-Zouch, Noseley and Stapleford are all worth visiting for their monuments. Other churches with monuments above the ordinary include Belton (Roesia de Verdun, 13C), Tilton-on-the-Hill, Edmondthorpe, Launde, Tugby, Lutterworth and Welham (vast monument of 1728 to Francis Edwards, now in its own special transept). At Wanlip is the earliest brass anywhere (date of death 1393) to have an inscription in English.

ELIZABETHAN MONUMENT to RICHARD NEEL.
S? THOMAS A BECKET · TUGBY · LEICS · ‌

Appleby Magna, St. Michael and All Angels. This church is distinguished on two counts. It is a good example of a typical, spacious W Leicestershire type—almost wholly early 14C and with aisles under separate gables. Secondly, a major restoration in 1829–32 produced a most unusual interior.

The Decorated work is clearest in the large Reticulated windows, though the vertical elements in the upper parts of the tracery hint at a transition to Perpendicular. The E window was new in 1879. The tower with its Perpendicular windows and detailing would post-date the aisles even though the S aisle butts on to it with a straight joint; it would seem the tower was shoved partly into the nave because of the lack of space to the W. The N and S doorways were removed c 1830 and the taking down of the S porch and the insertion of a new window was accomplished so skilfully that one would not suspect the work is not medieval. It is obvious in most places that the walls have been raised and the reason why is apparent inside.

The four-bay arcades are of the early 14C with quatrefoil piers and capitals but with fillets on the shafts and in the angles (slight differences between N and S). The arcade to the N chapel has plainer quatrefoil piers. The most immediately striking feature, however, is the plaster ceilings, the height of which required the walls to be raised. They were put in during what was the most expensive restoration, at £2970, in the county during the first four decades of the 19C. The Gothic ceilings are far removed from medieval workmanship both in technique and spirit (see the awkward rib sections to get a level ridge in the aisles). The furniture is of the highest quality as can be seen in the workmanship of the gallery and the box-pews. Some of the latter have been removed but on those that remain are the original pew numbers in brass figures. On these furnishings and also on the font and the vestry appears a unifying decorative motif of plain Y-tracery. The wide central alley in the nave was originally occupied by open forms for the poor. Stained glass is rare at this date but here 15 tracery heads have examples by William Collins of London and displaying a variety of motifs. Glass contemporary with the original aisles is to be found in the N window heads. The glass in the E window is by Lavers, Barraud & Westlake, 1879.

Belvoir Castle, Chapel. This is a fine example of a private chapel in a major country seat, in this case the seat of the Dukes of Rutland. The castle was founded in the late 11C but went through many vicissitudes. The buildings were totally remodelled in an imposing early 19C version of castle architecture and it is to this phase that the chapel belongs. Work began under James Wyatt in 1801 and continued under the Reverend (Sir) John Thornton after Wyatt's death in 1813.

The chapel is a tall structure in the S range, at the end of the Regent's Gallery. Its ecclesiastical character is unmistakable from the outside due to the tall, transomed Perpendicular windows in three bays and the flanking octagonal turrets. Their Gothic is a marked contrast to the surrounding architecture. It rises higher than the level of the Regent's Gallery from which it is approached down a spiral staircase on the visitor's tour. Before it is a small antechapel.

Inside, the shortness and height make for an impressive space. The ceiling is a plaster lierne-vault which is in keeping with the abundance of typical early 19C small-scale, light Gothic decoration. On the inner wall there are blank arches corresponding to the windows on the outside. There are galleries for the family at both ends. In the one at the E end is a painting of the Last Supper by Gaspard Poussin and over the altar, below a rich canopy, a reredos consisting of a painting of the Holy Family by Murillo.

On the walls are Mortlake tapestries of the Acts of the Apostles. The communion rail is a rich wrought-iron one of c 1700. The antechapel contains the coffin of Robert de Todeni, the 11C founder of Belvoir; it was discovered on the site of Belvoir Priory and bears his name in Lombardic lettering. There are also other coffins, including one with a 13C effigy of an abbot.

Bottesford, *St. Mary the Virgin.* The spire, rising some 210ft above the Vale of Belvoir, makes this church a landmark for many miles around. The great interest here, however, concerns the monuments to the de Roos family and their successors at Belvoir from the late 15C, the Manners family, who became Earls and later Dukes of Rutland. Their monuments practically fill the chancel and are as fine a collection over a period of four centuries as in almost any parish church. They include the only monument that records a death by witchcraft and successive monuments to eight earls. The building history of the church can be traced back to the 13C, with an addition in the 14C, major remodelling in the 15C and the early 16C, plus a large-scale restoration by Sir Gilbert Scott in 1847. Limestone is the building material, but with ironstone in the N transept and chancel.

Outwardly, this is a large Perpendicular church with aisles, transepts, S porch (formerly two-storeyed), and proud W steeple. But, starting on the S side of the chancel, 13C traces can be seen, a little dogtooth and traces of arches to a S chapel. This had gone by the Reformation, for early in the 16C simple, square-headed windows were placed in the chancel, including a row of six three-light clerestory openings. On the N a corresponding chapel was replaced by a vestry. At about the same time the roof pitch was lowered, even to below the top of the chancel arch. The N transept (see the gable-headed buttresses) and S aisle (with flowing windows) appear to date from the early 14C. The N aisle is 15C and butts up to the earlier transept, while the S transept butts on to the aisle and hence is later. Its S window is flanked by two niches, on the E of which the de Roos arms could formerly be detected, i.e. not after 1487. The de Roos family was also responsible for the tower. Their crest appears in the S spandrel over the W door; on the N, the shield bears the Instruments of the Passion. Apart from its height there is nothing special to commend the tower: it is not well proportioned and its small belfry windows are quite inadequate. The spire, equipped with crockets and three tiers of lucarnes, is altogether better. In the nave clerestory there are two windows per bay and a great quantity of panelling in the parapets, with pinnacles and large head stops. The N aisle is much restored but its W window has inventive tracery with both Decorated and Perpendicular elements.

Architecturally there is little to say about the interior and its sterility may be due to Scott's restoration. The arcades are of five bays with slender piers which have concave sides. This concave motif is also continued in the arches. The prominent filling at the top of the chancel arch carries the arms of Queen Victoria. Nearby, N of the pulpit, are three niches that would have stood above a medieval altar. In the chancel the 13C evidence reappears—on the S, a strip of dogtooth and a poor foliage capital above. Above the chancel arch are the almost indecipherable remnants of a Doom painting. The pulpit is a fine piece of 1631 covered in low-relief designs: its door was vandalously used to make up two bench-ends in 1971. The font is a 16C piece, apparently with legs resembling those on the first monument in the centre of the chancel (date of death 1563).

Belvoir Castle, on the escarpment overlooking the Vale and Bottesford Church, was founded shortly after the Conquest by Robert de Todeni. It passed by marriage to Robert de Roos of Yorkshire in the 13C, and by marriage again to the Manners family of Northumberland in the 15C. Sir Robert Manners's wife, Eleanor de Roos, died in 1487 and the family of Manners has held it ever since. Sir Thomas Manners was created first Earl of Rutland in 1526, and the ninth Earl became the first Duke of Rutland in 1703. The monuments are mentioned here in date order. A small figure of a knight with the lower part now missing and only about 1ft 6ins high (NE corner) represents Robert de Roos (died 1285). He is dressed in chain mail. This effigy was brought from Croxton Abbey, where Robert's heart was buried. His body was buried at Kirkham in Yorkshire, as is noted on an inscription just W of the N door. W of the S door is an unidentified, wimpled lady of c 1310–20. She may be Matilda de Vaux, wife of William de Roos. The 5ft canopied brass to Henry de Codyngtoun, a 14C Rector, is very good and includes eight small saints on the orphreys of his cope. John Freeman, Rector in the early 15C, has a smaller brass. Sir William de Roos (died 1414) and John, Lord Roos (died 1421) lie S and N of the altar respectively. Both wear armour and the SS collar.

The Rutland monuments begin with Thomas Manners, first Earl (died 1543) and Eleanor his wife (W of the altar rails). It was the work of Richard Parker of Burton-on-Trent at a cost of £20 and is carved from alabaster, like all six of the earliest Rutland monuments. The couple lie on a tomb-chest with weepers round the base and with early Renaissance detailing. The monument to Henry, the second Earl (died 1563) and Margaret his wife (W of the first Earl) is remarkable. It takes the form of an Elizabethan communion table, arranged lengthwise in the centre of the chancel with the couple beneath. The table has bulgy legs (cf. the font) and three small kneeling figures and an upright slab on top. Edward, third Earl (died 1587) and Isabel his wife (SW corner) lie on a monument by Gerard Johnson of Southwark. It is the first of the four elaborate canopied monuments. Then comes John, fourth Earl (died 1588) and his wife Elizabeth (NE), also by Johnson, and very similar in design. At ground level there are six kneeling figures. Both the Johnson tombs were set up in 1591 at a cost of £200, plus a further £20 paid to John Matthewe of Nottingham for painting them. Roger, fifth Earl (died 1612) and Elizabeth his wife (N) lie on a monument by Nicholas Johnson which cost £150. He was Ambassador to Denmark from 1603. He is placed at a higher level than his wife and they lie beneath a coffered arch. The vast monument on the S is to Francis, sixth Earl (died 1632) and his two wives, Frances and Cecilia. It is so large that the chancel roof had to be raised above it. He lies between the two women and, again, there is a coffered arch over them. It is this monument that is known as 'the witchcraft tomb', because in the inscription it is noted that he married Cecilia in 1608 and 'by whom he had two sons, both of whom died in their infancy by wicked practice and sorcerye'. This claim was founded on the belief that the Earl and Countess had been made ill and their two sons mysteriously stricken and killed by the evil spells of Joan Flower and her two daughters Margaret and Phillipa, following a dispute with the family.

Lady Katherine Manners also 'was set upon by their dangerous and devilish practices but recovered'. The three witches were arrested together with three others. Joan Flower died during her trial and her daughters confessed to their crimes and were hanged at Lincoln in 1618. The monument to George, seventh Earl (died 1641) which is W of the 'witchcraft tomb', is of marble and is by Grinling Gibbons. It was erected in 1686 at the same time as the monument to the eighth Earl and the two together cost £100. The seventh Earl stands portentously in Roman attire. Similarly the eighth Earl (died 1679) and Frances his wife (by the N door) stand in Roman dress either side of an urn. Their third son became the first Duke of Rutland in 1703. The first four Dukes were buried at Bottesford but they and most of the 18C burials were reinterred in the mausoleum at Belvoir in 1828.

Breedon-on-the-Hill, *St. Mary and St. Hardulph.* Breedon's claim to national, and even international, importance, rests on a major collection of pre-Conquest sculptures which are detailed below. The church itself occupies a dramatic location on top of a hill, a situation made even more striking by the quarrying away of the E side for agricultural lime and roadstone. At the end of the 7C, probably shortly after 675 but before 691, a monastery was founded here from Medeshamstede (Peterborough). King Aethelraed of Mercia confirmed the grant to Medeshamstede by one of his *principes*, Friduric, of land at Breedon. A monk at Medeshamstede called Hedda was to become Abbot of Breedon. The monastery may have disappeared during the Danish invasions of the late 9C but there is no clear evidence for this. The next definite date is the establishment of an Augustinian priory between 1109 and 1122 after Robert de Ferrers gave the church to Nostell Priory in Yorkshire. What we see today is but a part of the medieval building—its central tower and aisled chancel. Something of the structural change at the church can be read in the W wall. There is a low, blocked Norman arch from the old nave and above this a window with zigzag and angle shafts. Above is the old roofline. Later the W or parochial part was enlarged as the Perpendicular responds to the arcades show. This work was displaced S from the old axis of the church and, indeed, the NE respond sits right in the middle of the old Norman tower arch. Presumably all this was to respect the monastic quarters on the N and there was little communication between the parochial and monastic parts. On the N of the tower is a Norman doorway with more zigzag and angle shafts. Above the windows are now 13C lancets but their heads reuse 12C zigzag. The top of the tower is Perpendicular. The four-bay chancel and its aisles are 13C, to which campaign the NW lancet (note the unusual 14C transom in it) and E window of triple lancets belong. The present side windows are from a 14C remodelling—Reticulated windows to the N, and intersected and ogee intersected windows to the S.

Inside, the immediate impression is of a brightly lit, unrestored building. The box-pews, pulpit and W gallery of c 1793 survive. The arcades are tall with piers of different sections. They may have been altered in the 18C but with a general faithfulness to the 13C originals: a little 13C foliage survives in the NE respond. The N aisle is vaulted. So was the S one but the vaulting was probably removed in the 1790s. A good 13C doorway from the S aisle to the former S transept also remains. The pew of the Shirley family in the N aisle is dated 1627; it is an enormous, very private affair with lots of contemporary decoration.

The sculpture at Breedon falls into four groups. There are two types of frieze, a series of figure sculptures in a different style, and lastly a group of late pre-Conquest cross-shafts. The date of the friezes is now thought to be very early in the 9C and the figure sculptures perhaps of the period 820–50, though much later dates have also been suggested for the latter. Work from the same school as the friezes and figures at the E end of the S aisle is to be found at Fletton near Peterborough, thus pointing to Medeshamstede having a key role in the story. Otherwise there is nothing like the frieze sculptures anywhere in Great Britain or Continental Europe. They are certainly very different from Northumbrian sculptures and have an unexpected light-heartedness. The carving is highly accomplished and shows a delicate technique involving chisels and drills to give a small-scale, deeply-cut effect. The stones are both limestone and greyish sandstone (perhaps from Mansfield).

A good starting point is beneath the gallery. On the S wall the two types of frieze may be seen. The first is narrower, almost 6–8 inches in height and has two vine trails intertwined to form mandorla shapes. The second is broader, 8–10 inches and includes figures and maze-like slanted key-fret ornament. The figures are quadrupeds with their heads turned back to bite bunches of grapes. On the N wall is a frieze with a geometrical pattern of circles and lozenges superimposed. Moving to the E end, a long stretch of the first frieze appears behind the altar, with whorled vine scroll, the central spirals of which have three-lobed leaves, grapes and a single hollowed cup-like leaf (the latter device also being found on the figured frieze as a termination to animal tails and the wands held by two standing men). The best place to view the sculptures is in the S aisle. Here the frieze repeats some of the ornament seen at the W end. There are strange creatures that could have stepped out of an ancient nightmare, a long panel with birds in various attitudes, some strutting, some with wings outspread and at the ends of this frieze carved heads, the E pair of which have been suggested as secondary. At the E end is a large panel with a figure (the Virgin?) holding a book and giving a blessing in the Byzantine style; she is placed beneath an arch resting on piers with bulbous capitals. Also at the E end are three panels with eight standing figures, no doubt Apostles, each in an arched compartment. Parallels occur on the Hedda stone at Peterborough and at Fletton. A little further W are two fine bare-legged figures squeezed together in a rectangular panel, clearly in the same style as the friezes. Note the terminations of the wands they hold. Then there is a large panel of a regal, leonine creature with his head set in a similar way to some of the frieze beasts but the carving is not on the miniature scale. Beyond the long frieze is a mousey creature in the bottom corner of an otherwise defaced panel. Nearby is a fragment with two storage jars and part of a muscular leg: this may be from a scene of the Marriage at Cana. Finally, there is a bearded saint with a book. A short stretch of frieze occurs in the E wall of the N aisle and in the spandrels of the nave arcades. The designs are varied, including pelta ornament (over the NE pier), a warrior with a spear, a horseman with a spear and more birds and ornament. The largest sculpture is in the ringing chamber (viewing by appointment) and is a lovely 3ft high figure of an angel in an arched surround. The 'Breedon Angel' is probably Gabriel, who gives a Byzantine-style blessing, perhaps as part of a lost Annunciation scene. The early 9C is the most usually suggested date though David Parsons has pointed to the parallels with the Winchester School (e.g. the way the figure overlaps the frame) and this could mean a date as late as the end of the 10C. Certainly of late date (late 9C or 10C) are the various pre-Conquest cross-shaft fragments in the N aisle, which are unrelated to the style of the friezes and figure panels. Apart from interlace and degenerate vine scroll, one fragment has an interesting juxtaposition of Christian (Adam and Eve and the Serpent in the Tree of Knowledge) and pagan (a warrior being offered a drinking horn) themes. The piece to the E has beasts, including one in the Jellinge style from Denmark.

The monuments in the Shirley aisle should be noticed. Francis Shirley purchased the aisle in the 16C and the monuments are set behind a forbidding iron grille. Francis himself (died 1571) lies with his wife on a table-tomb with the mourners bearing shields in the base. John Shirley and his wife (monument of c 1585) occupy another table-tomb decorated with shields and pilasters. It was, like the first monument, made by Richard and Gabriel Royley of Burton-on-Trent. But the biggest monument is to George Shirley (died 1622) and his wife Francisca, who had died in 1595 in childbirth aged 31 (as the Latin inscription makes clear). It is a two-storey structure with a grisly cadaver below. In the upper part the couple kneel under coffered arches with their children—George occupies the E arch, his wife the W one. The monument is prominently dated 1598, after the death of Francisca.

The dedication at Breedon is unique. Hardulph is a shadowy figure mentioned in a 16C text which says he occupied a small cell in a cliff overlooking the Trent and that he brought books on the lives of the saints to the holy St. Modwen of the Burton-on-Trent area. The most illustrious name associated with the Breedon monastery is Tatwine, who had been a priest there and who became Archbishop of Canterbury in 731. He died in 734, the year before the Venerable Bede, who mentions him in his history. Tatwine was also known as a composer of riddles.

In the churchyard are many fine 18C slate headstones, including a large number signed by Thomas Allt of Breedon.

Gaddesby, *St. Luke.* There are three reasons why Gaddesby Church is of exceptional interest—it has the most spectacular Decorated work in the county; it has a marvellously unrestored interior; and its S side has puzzles to perplex the most experienced church enthusiast. Its structural history can be traced dimly back to the 12C. It enters the historical record in the mid-13C, when it came into the possession of the Knights Templar of Rothley; indeed it was not separated from Rothley until 1874. It is known that Robert de Gaddesby founded two chantries in the church in 1323 and 1333 and that Robert de Overton founded another, also in 1323. One of these must have been associated with the astonishing display in the W part of the S aisle but, unfortunately, there is no positive evidence. In fact there was extensive work going on throughout the church in the 14C, including the addition, at what was quite an early date, of a clerestory. However, different people or bodies were responsible for different parts, which accounts for the lack of unity of design. Gaddesby is a very good place to study the subdivision that so characterised churches by the 14C. Apart from work on the chancel in the 15C, the church was complete by 1350. There have been no major changes in post-medieval times apart from re-roofing (probably in the 18C) and the chancel restoration of 1859.

To understand and appreciate Gaddesby, it is best to begin inside. Low down to the right of the W door in the S aisle is the sole

14ᵀᴴ CENTURY DECORATION ⁖ S. AISLE ⁖ Sᵗ LUKE ⁖ GADDESBY ⁖ *Leicestershire.*

ornamented fragment (zigzag) from a Norman building (not *in situ*).
The W quoins of the nave seem to represent the W end of an early
phase before the erection of the 13C tower. In the spandrels of the
arcades, seen best from the N aisle, are the traces of walling through
which the arcades were broken and which are no doubt associated
with the W quoins. This seems to indicate a very long pre-13C
church. In the 13C the tower was started and was evidently not
meant to be flanked by the aisles (see the treatment of its base)—the
arches to the N and S are later additions between the buttresses,
presumably to integrate the tower into the overall space and provide
visual unity with the aisle arcades. To the 13C also belong the wide
chancel arch, the five-light E window with its grouped lights, and the
arcades. These are of five bays and have octagonal piers and
capitals. They are paired, though the details do differ slightly from N
to S. The earliest two bays seem to be at the SW on the evidence of
the shallow water-holding bases. On the E face of the tower the line

of the nave roof at this time can clearly be detected. Next, the beauties and complexities of the S aisle need to be considered. Inside, just E of the doorway, there is a jagged line sloping downwards towards the W, clearly showing two different fabrics. The direction of the line suggests that the one to the W is later. A rebuilding is not necessarily implicit: it could well be that those who paid for the westerly work were willing to spend more on higher quality masonry. This is certainly true of their successors who lavished a rare magnificence on the embellishment of an earlier structure.

The story can now be taken up on the outside where the abrupt junction between the ironstone of the E parts and the limestone ashlar facing of the W ones is immediately obvious. There is no reason at all to suppose that it was intended to continue the riches into the E area. The eaves course there, with its ballflower decoration, shows that it was put in at much the same time as the remodelling of the W parts: also the treatment of the E merlon of the parapet with its fleuron decoration seems to suggest some sort of full stop. Equally, inside, the eaves courses with their delightful carvings stop at that point. It seems there are at least three phases to be discerned in the aisle and it is not at all easy to distinguish which is which. The S doorway with its deep moulding and, on the right, shaft with elementary leaves, is of an early stage. At this time the aisle probably did not extend W beyond the line of the nave. Later, the westward extension embraced the tower and it is probably from that time that the large windows with their expansive Geometrical tracery of thin members date. They have been patched but their design is the same as in the late 13C. Of the same date is the W doorway. Then comes the grandiose work which surely cannot be before 1323, and more likely, is after 1333. That it is a remodelling of the earlier fabric is most clearly seen in the W wall. Here an unusual triangular window with curved sides and containing three quatrefoils with curved sides has been inserted, somewhat clumsily. It rises out of a new head provided to the W doorway. Above comes a riot of gables, pinnacles and three niches with bowed ogee canopies. The low gable comprises a trail, a fleuron frieze and, on top, an awkwardly treated parapet with stepped merlons leaning precariously at 90° to the angle of the gable. On the S the trail (note the mermaid in the W bay), fleuron frieze and stepped merlons continue. The buttresses are adorned on top with bowed ogees over canopies and are encrusted with crockets, gables and so on. Part of the wall is built out to accommodate a tomb-recess inside. It is worth noticing the stringcourse. This is exactly the same in both the W and E parts of the aisle and was an insertion during the 14C works. It starts S of the W doorway: N of this doorway the form is different and earlier, a further suggestion that the lavish work is a remodelling of an older aisle. So it would seem that work was in progress on both parts more or less simultaneously, but that the resources for the E area were much less. Finally, on this S side is the most tantalising puzzle at Gaddesby. Clearly there have been three porches. The present one is a humble 18C affair on the same axis as the preceding one. But before that, and planned during the 14C works, there was another. Its axis lay further E and this has awkward implications about the S doorway. This doorway now leads one straight into a pier (most unusual, and not so on the N). Although there is really no evidence in the wall fabric, one is forced to the uncomfortable conclusion that in the mid-14C the doorway lay further E and was later—and for what reasons one cannot imagine—moved W (hence the crude botching at the apex). This unlikely hypothesis is supported inside by the remains of a piscina largely destroyed by the move, a stringcourse beneath it which has been interrupted, and scars on the pier opposite the doorway (at bottom and top) made by a former screen that would have formed the E wall of the chapel, roughly in line with the eaves courses above.

Of the rest of the building there is less to say. The tower and broach spire are very fine but are overwhelmed by the sumptuousness of the S aisle. There is a W lancet, and belfry windows with Geometrical tracery. The three tiers of lucarnes also have Geometrical designs. The N aisle was evidently built at much the same time as the 14C work on the S. The buttresses share the attractive cusped gabled design low down and the stepped merlon motif is also repeated. The windows have various very pleasing Decorated designs, including rich flowing tracery. The clerestory is also early 14C. At one stage it had a high-pitched roof which disfigured the E face of the tower. The priest's door (N) was put in in 1859. The chancel was probably almost entirely rebuilt in the 15C: it is simple and clearly the Hospitallers (successors to the Templars as Rectors) did not wish to spend much money on it and reused some 13C windows. Before re-entering the church the Perpendicular window in the E wall of the S aisle should be noted. Its insertion into the 13C fabric is even more obvious than the 14C insertion at the W end.

The most striking feature about the interior is that it retains many pre-Victorian features, notably the cobble (N aisle) and brick floors and old seating. That in the nave is medieval and has been variously ascribed to the 14C or 15C. It is certainly crude and has remarkably high sills to step over: these would presumably have kept carpeting of rushes in place. Round the two pier bases on the S are circular seats which predated the advent of fixed wooden seating. The stone walling between the piers on both the N and S does not seem to be a survival of the aisleless nave but was put in at some stage after the building of the arcades, for it lies on top of the pier bases. It serves as a partition between aisles and nave and would have reduced draughts in the seats and supported a timber screen. In a clerestory N window the medieval glass from the church has been assembled. Mortice holes in the chancel arch indicate a former wooden filling in the head of the arch. Similar holes in the tower arch are the evidence for a gallery at the W end, as are the recessed padstones in front of it. It clearly was never needed for congregational space and must have been used by the musicians and/or singers. The font is 13C with cusped arches and basic foliage in the spandrels. Gaddesby has three worthwhile monuments. In the N aisle are the alabaster incised slab to William Darby (died 1498) and his wife, and a sandstone figure in armour with a Lancastrian SS collar on a table-tomb of c 1500. In the chancel is a splendid marble monument to Col Edward H. Cheney of the Scots Greys, whose distinction it was to have had four horses killed beneath him as he fought at Waterloo. The sculptor, Joseph Gott, with great virtuosity, has the redoubtable colonel step off one of the fallen horses. Below is an idealised battle scene. The monument was brought from Gaddesby Hall. Less satisfactory is the reredos of 1892 by John Ely. In front of the W doorway outside are what are probably the remnants of a medieval altar slab.

Hallaton, *St. Michael and All Angels.* The church is usually approached from the E through this delightful village of brick and stone. It is more spacious than many in this area and gives a first, though rather misleading, impression of Decorated richness. The 13C W tower has a good broach spire which is a fairly early example of the type.

The Decorated contribution comes from the aisles. The N one, particularly, commands attention with its flowing tracery windows and big polygonal buttress at the NE corner ornamented with five niches and the shields of the Bardolf and Engaine families who held two manors in Hallaton in the 14C. Above is a parapet enriched with quatrefoils. The S aisle is rather plainer but the windows are good. On the S they have flowing tracery but the E one is rather unusual. It is of three lights and in the head is a circle cut up into quarters like slices of a cake. Closer inspection reveals an earlier history. The chancel reached its present length in the late 13C. On either side are two two-light Geometrical windows, though the E window is a replacement of 1897 of a Perpendicular one. On the N wall, obscuring a former doorway, is a handsome monument of the Reverend G. Fenwicke, Rector for 38 years. The tower was started rather earlier and its spire was complete in the late 13C. This composition is rightly famous. The belfry lights have twinned pairs of lancets, shafted jambs and deeply moulded heads. The spire is of the broach type. It rises above a corbel course and has pinnacles at the bases of the low broaches. The lower tier of lucarnes projects rather more than one might wish and certainly more than would be expected in later developments. These lucarnes have surrounds of dogtooth ornament. Before entering the church the weather strip at the W end of the N aisle should be noted. It may indicate a narrow, low aisle before the present 14C one or perhaps a chamber in the angle between tower and aisle (a similar feature on the S side in a corresponding position can be seen from within the SW vestry of 1923). Within the N porch (W wall) is a precious survival from the early Norman church— a tympanum showing St. Michael kneeling triumphantly on the dragon and piercing its head with a spear. On the right expectant souls await deliverance. The roof of the porch is original 15C work.

Inside the N aisle is the oldest evidence of all, a pre-Conquest coped grave cover with interlace work. To understand the interior it is best to work forward in time. The three W bays of the four-bay N arcade are late Norman and have waterleaf capitals and a scalloped W respond. Only the two middle bays have round arches (with one step only). The W arch is a later, pointed replacement. The E respond of the S arcade is a very late Norman piece but has almost certainly been reset. It seems likely that the late Norman nave was of three bays and was extended E by a bay in the 13C as part of the campaign to lengthen the church. The S arcade is 13C too, as are the piscina and triple graduated sedilia (with dogtooth in the heads) in the chancel. Shafting enriches the chancel windows. It is noticeable from the level of the sedilia that the floor of the chancel was below that of the nave in medieval times. The 14C work seen outside is echoed internally in the piscina and sedilia of the S aisle and the arch from the chancel to the E part of the N aisle. Beneath this area lies a crypt which can be entered by steps from outside the E wall of the aisle. The Perpendicular contribution at Hallaton is slight: the key feature was the addition of the clerestory (partly blocked on the N). There is no proper chancel arch, only a plaster one, probably of the 18C. There was a general restoration in 1889–91 under Charles Kirk of Sleaford from which time most of the furnishings and fittings date.

The most mysterious feature can be seen both inside and outside the E wall of the chancel. Inside can be seen the first two steps of a spiral staircase leading upwards and outwards. A scar in the outside wall is obviously related. It has been suggested that the stair was to lead to either an outside pulpit or to an upper chamber. The complication is that above the outside scar can be traced the sill of a medieval window which would have interfered with the stair. Was the stair project ever completed?

The font is an unusual 13C piece, circular, slightly tapering and with four shafts on the bowl, each topped with a head. The pulpit is 18C and has linenfold, a late use of this motif. The excellent E window of 1899 is by C.E. Kempe and depicts the Nativity. Kempe, much earlier in his career, also provided the chancel S window with six angels and the S aisle E window with three archangels (1882). Monuments, apart from the pre-Conquest grave cover and several 13C and 14C ones, are confined to mural tablets, including two attractive ones of 1774 and 1789 in the spandrels of the N arcade.

King's Norton, *St. John the Baptist.* This remarkable Gothic church dominates the tiny village of King's Norton and was built at the expense of the Lord of the Manor, William Fortrey, using John Wing the Younger as his architect. The Wing family had already been associated with Fortrey. In 1741 the elder John Wing had remodelled Galby Church, only half a mile away, for Fortrey, involving an extraordinary tower with pagoda-like pinnacles and a mixture of Gothic and Classical forms.

The rebuilding of King's Norton was an altogether more ambitious project. The work began in 1757 and was finished in 1761 except for a crocketed spire completed in 1775. The church is approached through a fine iron gate (formerly at the hall) and a flight of steps. It is faced with Ketton stone but this conceals brick walling. To Addleshaw and Etchells, writing in 1948, it is a 'perfect expression of eighteenth-century Anglicanism, its lucidity, its classical view of life, its freedom from cant and humbug'. The plain, tall rectangle of the combined nave and chancel is a supreme example of rational, late 18C planning. This had seven bays and to its W is a noble W tower which doubles as a porch. But even if the planning is simple and logical, the architecture aspires to grandeur. Fortrey spared no expense and his architect gave him a Gothic building with a seriousness hardly matched anywhere at that time. A few details like the hoods over the windows and the use of three windows in the E wall do not have a medieval ring but most other features are direct descendants of 14C and 15C Gothic. The tower lost its spire after a lightning strike in 1850, but it still remains a coherent composition.

The interior is a precious survival because the original fittings remain exactly as they were in the late 18C. The only exceptions are the Victorian font of 1850 and, presumably, the loss of open forms to seat the poor in the wide alley in the middle of the nave. The most immediately striking feature is the three-decker pulpit standing on the centre line of the nave and in front of the chancel area. No other such arrangement survives in Leicestershire. The box-pews, W gallery and altarpiece are all original and have restrained Classical detailing. A trace of Gothic emerges in the gates to the chancel space on either side of the pulpit, and in the communion rails. Within the chancel area the seats face N and S and were probably for the families of the Lord of the Manor and the Rector.

Apart from the consequences of the fall of the spire the church was spared any changes in the 19C. This means the windows retain their clear glass, and the absence of stained glass, in addition to the whitened walls and the complete lack of monuments inside, creates a dignified interior devoid of all traces of fuss. E of the chancel William Fortrey built a tall monument with an obelisk to his father (died 1722) and mother (died 1733). On the N of the church is a good Rococo monument to John Smalley (died 1763).

Leicester

For a place of its size—280,000 people in 1981—Leicester has a particularly good collection of churches and also has a venerable ecclesiastical history. It had its own bishop, certainly from 737 until soon after 872, when the effects of the Danish settlement were felt. In 877 the town became one of the five main boroughs of the Danelaw. Where the cathedral was is not certain and most of the five surviving medieval churches of the old town have put forward claims. The present cathedral was elevated to that status in 1927, having formerly been the civic church of the town. In fact it is neither the grandest nor archaeologically most interesting. For the latter, one must go to St. Mary de Castro; for the former, probably to St. Margaret's. For the greatest antiquity one goes to St. Nicholas' with its late pre-Conquest nave.

There are several Anglican churches of the 19C which are worth visiting. The earliest is St. George's, a big Commissioners' church of 1823–27 by the local architect William Parsons (now a Serbian Orthodox church). Sir Gilbert Scott's first Leicester church, St. John the Divine (1853–54), is now converted into flats but is Leicester's first Ecclesiologically 'correct' church. His second, St. Andrew's (1860–62), is an extraordinary design, with the stark brickwork typical of William Butterfield and paralleled in Scott's output only by Crewe Green in Cheshire and Yiewsley in Middlesex. Two churches of the early 1870s are of considerable interest. St. Mark's (1870–72) is Ewan Christian's finest building and stands proudly as a focal point in Belgrave Gate. It has a richly treated spire, whose whiteness contrasts completely with the black slate, a tall, continuous nave and chancel and a bold apsidal end. St. Paul's, the foundation stone of which was laid on the same day as St. Mark's, has highly unusual detailing. Its simplicity pre-echoes some of the trends in church architecture of 20 or so years later. The architects were F.W. Ordish and J.C. Traylen, both local men. The two finest 19C interiors are to be found at St. John the Baptist (1884–85) and St. James the Greater (1899–1901, W end 1914). Both have fairly ordinary exteriors but, as usual in the late 19C, the real attention is lavished inside.

Non-Anglican Churches. Nonconformity was very strong in the town and produced many distinguished figures. The Unitarians who met at the Great Meeting House were among the intellectual leaders of Leicester. They started a Domestic Mission led by Joseph Dare whose reports brought the conditions of the poor before the public conscience. The Great Meeting House in Great Bond Street (E of the centre) was erected in 1708. It is of brick, square, with a hipped roof and has rendered pilasters at the corners. The porches and the loggia at the front that give it some distinction were added in 1866. Architecturally the most spectacular building is the Melbourne Hall,

Melbourne Road (S of the centre) of 1880–81 for an Evangelical Free Church. It is a vast, ambitious redbrick octagon with a row of top lighting and simple Gothic detail. The architects were Goddard & Paget of Leicester. The most unusual chapel is the 'pork pie chapel' in Belvoir Street, now an Adult Education Centre but formerly Baptist. It was designed by the Catholic Joseph Hansom, was opened in 1845 and derives its name from the semicircular shape of the body of the building facing the street. It is flanked by two smaller semicircular entrance structures. The style is a sort of simplified Greek Revival. Nearby, the Methodist chapel in Bishop Street has a large, spreading façade of 1815. It was designed by the Reverend William Jenkins.

The best church in the whole county from the 20C is the Catholic St. Joseph's on Uppingham Road and Goodwood Road. It is by T.E. Wilson and dates from 1967–68. It is built on a circular plan in buff brick and has a tall, thin tower linked to the main structure by a glass narthex which sweeps down under copper roofs on either side of the tower. The space for worship is oval, has a W gallery and an altar raised high on several steps. The lighting is subtle, coming through the narthex, through narrow slits in the walls and from a ring of top lights. The dome is supported on eight thin concrete piers. A very beautiful interior.

St. Margaret, St. Margaret's Way. Of all the churches in Leicester, St. Margaret's is the grandest. It lies a little way from the centre, but it is easily located by its proud 15C tower. This was being built in c 1444 but was probably not complete till the early 16C. Its top stage is panelled and the twinned belfry windows are contained by an ogee arch which rises up into a pinnacle. Much of the exterior is 19C renewal, but the overall impression is of a large Perpendicular town church. However, only the vaulted porch and the large four-bay chancel, with its big, transomed windows, were wholly built in the 15C. The clerestory was added to the nave at that time.

There was an important church here in Norman times but the only parts that could date from then are the vestiges of the transept arches, with characteristic upright leaves in the responds from the late 12C. At this time the church was probably aisleless. The S transept arch was heightened in an odd way in the 13C and a large S aisle thrown out. To this scheme the fine and richly moulded S doorway belongs. The N arcade was built rather later than the S one. The aisles flank the W tower. For such a large church it is not rich in furnishings or fittings. The sedilia in the chancel form the sill of the SE window. On the inside of the N door is particularly fine ironwork from the 13C. In the chancel is an alabaster effigy of John Penny (died 1520), Abbot of Leicester and later Bishop of Bangor and then of Carlisle.

St. Mary de Castro, Castle Street. The tower and crocketed spire of St. Mary's are a landmark over a wide area. Visually, they are the best part of this most interesting church, of which, unlike the cathedral or St. Margaret's, it is difficult to obtain a good general view. The structure has a fascinating development, the product of successive medieval building schemes plus a major contribution from the 19C. The complexity is such that it is by no means easy to gain a clear understanding about the early development. There may have been a pre-Conquest church on the site but the present building claims its origins from c 1107 when Robert de Beaumont, Count of Meulan and first Earl of Leicester, founded a college for a dean and 12 secular canons.

The church has a long, narrow nave and a chancel as wide as the nave and three-quarters of its length. On the N is a narrow aisle and a small transept, but to the S there stands an aisle of enormous dimensions which encloses the tower. To trace the building's history it is best to start inside at the W end. In the ground stage is simple blind arcading which could belong to the time of the foundation of the college. Higher up and seen best from just inside the S aisle is a row of blind arches pierced by two clerestory windows (the traces over the N arcade are rebuilt). At the E end there is again much Norman evidence but the lack of work connecting the two ends means that statements about the appearance of the 12C church are speculative. Suggestions that the church had transepts and a crossing tower have no supporting evidence and there is no reason to suppose it was anything other than a long, aisleless structure. The E parts are in two phases, both of which are later than the work at the W end. The earlier is marked by ornamental triangles between windows, the later (and more easterly) by quite elaborate windows and, outside, by twinned, semicircular buttresses. All this work has been much restored and the two E windows replaced a large pointed window with intersected tracery and date, rather surprisingly, from before 1840. A door in the N wall of the chancel shows that there was a sacristy and this would have been sited below the weather strip seen outside (the present vestry is based on designs by the noted ecclesiological writer, M.H. Bloxam of Rugby). There seems to have been no proper chancel arch: the present one is of 1844 and replaces a cheap elliptical affair. The last Norman works that have to be mentioned are the resited N and W doorways on the N aisle, with an abundance of zigzag, and the splendid sedilia in the chancel. The latter has deep arch heads full of flat zigzag and the capitals to the shafts have fine foliage carving. It is possible they were brought here from Leicester Abbey at some stage. The waterleaf capital in the W is

NORMAN SEDILIA
St MARY de CASTRO • City of Leicester.

perhaps a replacement of c 1180 but otherwise a date some 20 years earlier seems preferable.

In the 13C the history becomes clearer. Early on, single, round arches were built on either side of the W end of the chancel, but whether they were connected to transepts by this time, as might be expected, is not clear. The capitals have stiff-leaf foliage. A narrow S aisle was also built, the outer wall of which was 12ft 6ins S of the arcade, as discovered last century. The W part of this arcade survives and is low and has quatrefoil piers. The triple sedilia, now in the much larger S aisle, may have been sited in this early aisle. The 13C also added the N aisle (a clear straight joint can be seen at the W end) with its arcade with piers of complex section. The clerestory was also put on in the 13C and gave the nave walls their present height. The N arcade and the clerestory above were rebuilt by Sir Gilbert Scott in 1859–60.

Late in the 13C came the vast S aisle, which cleared away all earlier evidence on the site. It is likely that this aisle was associated with some institutional change at the church and was always linked to the parish rather than the college. The E end is dominated by an enormous window put in in 1846 and said to be modelled on the E window at Ripon Minster: it contains stained glass of 1847 by Forrest & Bromley of Liverpool. The side, lower windows are 1844 replacements for intersected ones. The Rood loft stairs in this aisle are astonishingly far W, for what reason and of what date is not clear. Also odd is the siting of the tower which was built rather later and, due to the lack of consecrated ground to the W, was placed within the body of the aisle. It must have been started c 1300, with the spire being finished perhaps a century later (the spire was rebuilt in 1785).

The Perpendicular contribution was slight. Battlements were placed on the nave and three bays of the N clerestory (all removed by Sir Gilbert Scott). The extant arch-braced roof in the chancel and the clerestory on the S aisle were also of this time. The medieval history concludes in 1547 with the suppression of the college under the Chantry Act; it never seems to have been particularly thriving. A notable date in the life of the church was 1426, when the young King Henry VI was knighted here.

Many of the Victorian changes have already been mentioned. There was a succession of architects starting with the local man, William Flint, in 1844, followed by Joseph Mitchell of Sheffield in 1846, and, finally, Sir Gilbert Scott in 1852. Scott's main early work was reseating and the insertion of the three big Early English arches on the S side of the nave. These replaced a huge semicircular affair of 1800 which had been put in so people could see and hear the popular Vicar, the Reverend Thomas Robinson. There is plenty of stained glass by William Wailes and a fine reredos of 1899 by G.F. Bodley. This is one of his typical tall pieces, richly treated with statuary and niches. The big fibreglass mural of Mary at Pentecost in the NW corner of the chancel is by Noel Black; will it stand the test of time? The chancel screen incorporates some pleasing Jacobean shafts of various designs. N of the font are a number of patterned medieval floor tiles.

St. Nicholas, St. Nicholas Circle. St. Nicholas' is the only church in Leicester, and one of the few in the county, to have any visible pre-Conquest work. It was built within the *palaestra* (exercise yard) associated with the Roman remains immediately to the W. The history of the church may be very old indeed and its proximity and relationship to the upstanding Jewry Wall must be more than a coincidence. Excavations have suggested that this Roman wall itself and two foundations running obliquely to the W end of the present church may have served as part of a narthex for an earlier church. It has been suggested that a church on this site may have been the 8C cathedral in Leicester. The existing church has a late pre-Conquest nave, rugged Norman additions plus various other alterations down to the 19C.

The W wall of the nave is almost certainly pre-Conquest but there is no distinctive work to confirm this (the large blocked doorway is Norman). In a county not famous for its Norman work, St. Nicholas' has a notable tower. It was started in the 11C and the lowest parts visible from outside include the reuse of Roman bricks in her-ringbone patterns. The rest, much restored in 1904–05, is a heighten-ing by two tiers and has blank, intersecting ornamental arches and twinned belfry windows (there was a late 13C or 14C spire until its removal c 1805). Other Norman work is to be found in the chancel (stringcourse on the N) and the S doorway, which has a little zigzag. The S aisle was remodelled c 1300 and the clerestory was added in Perpendicular times. The next change was the removal of the N aisle in 1697. This was rebuilt in 1875–76 and the dull Norman-style N transept was added in 1889. The Norman church had been cruciform so this change, in part, restored the old arrangements.

The pre-Conquest work is best seen from inside. Much of the nave survives intact though the insertion of the vast brick arch on the S side in c 1829 destroyed much there. On the N wall are two tiny double-splayed windows with double tiers of reused Roman tiles arranged in crude radial patterns in their heads. Similar windows on the S would have been destroyed c 1829. The plain gaunt arches of the N arcade and the tower are characteristic of the austere work of the early decades after the Conquest. In the arcade there is no stepping or chamfering on the arches and the earlier masonry of the nave wall serves as a simple pier. The tower arches have a single, blunt step. A little relief is afforded in the tier of blank arches around the inside of the tower. Chapels were added to the chancel in the early 13C though that on the N has disappeared. On the S (also traces on the N) there is unusual treatment of the pier and responds. The latter have, above the shaft-ring, a thick shaft instead of the thinner work below. The Perpendicular font was brought from St. Michael's, Stamford.

Lutterworth, St. Mary. Lutterworth Church is most famous for its association with John Wycliffe, who was Rector from 1374 to 1384 but is, in itself, a large and distinguished building of the 13C and 14C with important wall paintings and a strange and prominent top to its tower.

In 1703 the spire was blown down but the present top to the tower was not put on until 1761 in a rather heavyweight Gothick (date on SE pinnacle). It has enormous pinnacles, Y-tracery windows and flat strips at the angles with tall, recessed panels. Sir Gilbert Scott, who restored the building in 1867–69 at a cost of £7156, planned to put back the spire and also add an outer N aisle (as a model of 1866 inside shows). The tower was begun in the 13C and is marred by an extraordinarily massive NW stair turret. At the E end the church was complete to its present length. There are the two lancet windows at the W end and in the chancel, and the 19C restoration revealed that prior to the 14C there were two lancets in the E wall too. The remainder of the windows are late 13C and 14C insertions including some in the chancel which mark the transition from Decorated to Perpendicular. The clerestory is, as usual, a 15C addition. The fabric is of local cobble stones. The porch of 1881 is a posthumous work by Scott.

The interior has four-bay arcades of c 1300 with octagonal piers and double-chamfered arches. The tower arch is rather earlier. On the other hand, the chancel arch is later (Perpendicular) and has a panelled soffit. Above the nave is an excellent embattled tiebeam roof with arch-braces and tracery in the spandrels. The main timbers of the aisle roofs are also medieval. But the items of greatest interest are the 14C murals, one over the chancel arch and the other over the N doorway. Both suffered from over-zealous restoration and repainting by Burlison & Grylls in the 1860s but were returned to something like their original appearance in 1983 and 1984. Over the chancel arch, Christ is seated in majesty on a rainbow surrounded by angels at the Last Trump. This is not a conventional Doom for there is no New Jerusalem nor a gaping Hell's mouth and this 15C representation seems more accurately described as a Resurrection of the Dead. More problematic is the N aisle painting which dates from the early 14C. The work of 1983–84 uncovered traces of paintings of three skeletons a little further E which indicate the story of the Three Living and the Three Dead. The Three Living are well-attired and the two outer figures are evidently kings, both with falcons, one with a sceptre. The middle figure must surely be a queen and, it seems, the three figures have been repainted at some stage, apparently to represent King Richard II, Anne of Bohemia and John of Gaunt. It is not known whether this was in the 1860s or earlier. The lower parts of the figures are entirely 19C as is the bright border which follows medieval precedent at the top left-hand corner. In 1983–84 part of another, later painting with smaller figures of a priest and a cardinal was found and is to be seen against the lower part of the right-hand king's body. This could date from Wycliffe's time but whether it relates in any way to his views is not known.

The fine Perpendicular pulpit has six carved panels, but, contrary to popular supposition, it is almost certainly too late to have been the one from which Wycliffe preached. A rarity is the fragment of a medieval cope at the W end. Much-restored parts of a Perpendicular screen remain between the chancel and the N chapel. In the N aisle there is a good Elizabethan communion table resting upon lions. Several major Victorian stained glass painters are represented, including Clayton & Bell in the E window of 1884 (though date of death is 1869) and Warrington & Co. in the SW chancel window (1889). The best monument is a tomb-chest in the N aisle with a pair of figures. It lies under an arch at the top of which there is an angel bearing a soul in a cloth. Otherwise there are two 15C brasses, one in the N aisle to John Fielding (died 1403) and his wife Joanna (died 1418), and the other of c 1470 in the nave.

John Wycliffe's turbulent career ended with his ten years at Lutterworth, when he made some of his severest attacks upon abuses in the Church. He challenged many medieval superstitions, was a serious scholar and had his ideas taken up by other important groups, notably the Lollards and John Huss and his followers. The translation of the Bible into English during Wycliffe's time may have stemmed directly from his influence, though there is no evidence that Wycliffe himself made the translation. Wycliffe was condemned both in his lifetime and afterwards. This culminated with an order at the Council of Constance in 1415 that his remains be dug up and destroyed. This was eventually carried out in 1428. A marble monument was at last erected to Wycliffe in 1837 and is now at the E end of the S aisle. It is by Richard Westmacott, Jr in a very advanced style for its time.

Melton Mowbray, *St. Mary.* This is undoubtedly the grandest church in Leicestershire. It is cruciform, has a crossing tower and, most unusually for a parish church, two aisles to each transept. The superficial impression is of a major Perpendicular town church and this derives chiefly from the upper stage of the tower and the spectacular clerestory which rings the church with a glass wall of 48 windows. Below this much of the building dates from between c 1280 and 1320. But the real origins of the present structure can be traced to Norman times for, inside the ringing chamber (not open to the public), can be found the traces of Norman arches. Also, built into the N wall of the chancel low down (visible inside the vestry) is a zigzag fragment. St. Mary's was a major church throughout the Middle Ages and served as the mother church for a large area (probably the survival of the early minster arrangements), and even down to the 20C five chapelries were served from it.

The detail of much of the exterior is unexceptional and the effect of the church stems from its scale and proportions. The windows of c 1300 are mostly quite plain Geometrical and intersecting ones and the mighty clerestory achieves its strength from continual repetition of plain, broad windows of the late Perpendicular period. Without doubt the finest part is the crossing tower. The elegant lower stage, supported on the Norman masonry, is of the 13C. Each face comprises a group of three two-light windows, complete with shafts, transoms, dogtooth and different tracery patterns. Above comes the late Perpendicular belfry stage with four two-light divisions in each face, the outer ones being blind. Then there is a richly treated parapet, crowned by eight tall pinnacles. The beauty of the tower is sadly marred by the rather frivolous spirelet and the bulging stair turret on the NE angle. N of the chancel is a vestry dated 1532. The chancel and body of the church were almost entirely rebuilt in c 1300 and to the nave was added a Galilee porch with all the exuberance of the Decorated style around 1330. Ballflower is encrusted round its windows and doorway, and trails creep round the head of the latter. There are also several niches. This porch served as a chapel, as a piscina indicates.

The church is entered through a rich inner W doorway with the 13C motifs of rich moulding, stiff-leaf and dogtooth. The immediate impression is of the spacious six-bay nave with its quatrefoil piers. Then come the vistas of the aisled transepts in which the numerous piscinas indicate the positions of former altars. It is noticeable that the E arcades have a different pier shape (quatrefoil with fillets) from the simpler W ones (octagonal). In the N transept can be seen the way the roof has been heightened to its present level. Beyond the crossing with its 13C detail comes the chancel which is relatively small in comparison with the nave. This arises, presumably, from the fact that Lewes Priory, to which the church belonged from the 13C, was less inclined to spend considerable sums on their chancel than were the citizens of Melton on the rest. There has been much restoration—by R.W. Johnson of Melton in 1854–56 and Sir Gilbert Scott in 1865–69. Scott designed the E window in 1856.

Melton is not particularly rich in fittings but the following are worthy of note, starting in the chancel. This is provided with richly carved woodwork of 1890–93. In the chancel arch stands a lavish screen of 1906. In the vestry in the E aisle of the N transept is a table upon which, until 1925, bread for the poor was placed every Sunday. In the S transept is an alabaster monument with a particularly lovely figure of a late 14C lady, and also a monument to Sir John Burnett (died 1738) and his wife Mary; his bust is in a medallion held by two putti. The monument was executed by Thomas Naylor of Nottingham. The brass chandeliers in the transepts date from 1746 and hang from masses of scrolly ironwork. At the E end of the S aisle is the damaged effigy of a cross-legged knight, perhaps Hamo Belers who died in 1303. Over the chancel arch can be seen royal arms dated 1682. At the W end of the aisle, enclosed in a cupboard, is a most unusual thing for a church—a water pump. Above, in the SW window, is collected the ancient glass from the church dating from the 14C onwards. Elsewhere there are many 19C windows, mostly by William Wailes of Newcastle.

William de Melton, who was Vicar c 1285–1319 and may have played a major part in the rebuilding, later became Archbishop of York.

Noseley, *St. Mary.* Founded as a private chapel for the Lord of the Manor, Anketin de Martival, St. Mary's became collegiate c 1270 and was completed some 30 years later. It came to replace a church disused and demolished in the 16C which stood in the deserted village to the W. It stands proudly in the grounds of Noseley Hall and consists of a long, eight-bay rectangle with buttresses dividing each bay but with no division between nave and chancel. Its Y-windows are consistent with a late 13C date, though the embattled parapets, and wide E and W windows are from a late 15C remodelling. A tower stood in the somewhat unusual position on the N side of the chancel in the second bay from the E and was demolished at some unknown time after 1793. The chapel is extraparochial.

The interior is a most impressive space, though the stripping of the wall plaster in Charles Kirk's restoration of 1894 has made the appearance more austere. Piscinas in the N and S walls show where a screen would have divided the nave from the chancel. Another sedilia and double piscina (with dogtooth) stand in the chancel. The magnificent stall-ends are among the best medieval woodwork in the county. They may date from c 1473, the date of the death of William Hesilrig. Apart from the fine tracery, the ends depict a vase of flowers and a funeral. The numerous cocks are from the arms of Elizabeth Staunton, whom William married in 1458. The roof, of the slightly cambered, tiebeam variety and with tracery in the spandrels, is contemporary with the late 15C remodelling. Below the springing of the arch-braces are angels holding Instruments of the Passion and the Martival arms. The early 14C font is a good example of a popular Leicestershire type with different tracery on each face. The five-light E window has late medieval stained glass, including figures of St. John the Baptist, St. Thomas, and angels.

There is an extensive collection of monuments to the Hesilrig (Hazlerigg) family. Sir Thomas (died 1629) lies on a tomb-chest with shields below divided by pilasters and columns. Behind is the inscription and his numerous, kneeling progeny. Then comes Sir Arthur, a staunch Parliamentarian who died in the Tower in 1660 after the Restoration. He was one of the five MPs whom King

Charles I tried to arrest in 1642. He lies with his wife above their 12 children and behind is a big oval inscription between Ionic columns. Elizabeth (died 1673), wife of Sir Thomas (who does not have an inscription), is described as 'a Phoenix of her sex'—an allusion to her family name Fenwick and the phoenix appearing in the Fenwick crest.

Staunton Harold, *Holy Trinity.* The idyllic setting for the church, between the hall and the lake, says nothing of the tense circumstances under which it was erected. It was commenced in 1653 by Sir Robert Shirley. He was only 23 years old but was a fervent Royalist and a supporter of Laudian principles; to him there was a clear link between the two. In November 1656 he died in the Tower, suffering from smallpox. It is often said he was imprisoned for his church building activities but the issues really had more to do with his active support for the Royalist cause. He left money for completing and furnishing the building and it now stands as a monument to the dedication of its founder and as a major example of the survival of medieval architecture into the 17C. It is one of only a handful of churches erected during the Commonwealth, though it was not completed until c 1665.

Seen from the approach roads it looks like a normal later medieval building except that the E–W dimension is somewhat compressed. It has the usual W tower, nave, aisles and chancel. However, there are no side entrances, a sure sign of post-medieval work in the Midlands. There is a profusion of battlements (some pierced) and pinnacles (the intermediate ones are shaped like fleur-de-lis). The windows vary from square-headed Perpendicular ones in the clerestory to others of rather earlier design—cusped intersected (e.g. the E window) and Y-tracery. Work of very different character and dating from the last phase is the priest's doorway and the W entrance and plaque above. The latter bears the famous tribute to the ill-fated Robert Shirley: 'In the year 1653 when all thinges Sacred were throughout ye nation Either demolisht or profaned Sir Robert Shirley, Barronet, Founded this church; Whose singular praise it is, to have done the best things in ye worst times, and hoped them in the most callamitous. The righteous shall be had in everlasting remembrance'.

The interior is approached through a screen, which, like the rest of the woodwork, is by the joiner, William Smith. The screen, which supports the organ loft, is Jacobean in detail and this highlights the contrast between the architecture and the furnishings. The architecture is Gothic, very true to the medieval spirit though the spreading chancel arch is of rather unexpected proportions. The arcades are of three bays with octagonal piers and double-chamfered arches. Perhaps the most surprising feature is the strange painting on the wooden ceiling of the nave. It represents the Creation and is dated 1655 and is signed by Zachary and Samuel Kyrk. The ceilings of the chancel and aisles seem to have been painted in 1662 by a Mr. Lovett, who was paid £26 for 'clowding the iles' and £25 for 'clouding the Chancell' with its choir of cherubim.

William Smith's woodwork survives complete, notably in the pews and the panelling round the walls and up the piers. Even the candle holders on the pews remain. The font is very plain and has a fairly simple cover. However, the wrought-iron screen between the nave and the chancel, which was ordered from the master iron-worker, Robert Bakewell of Derby in 1711, is anything but ordinary. Above its delicate designs are the arms of the Shirleys. Hatchments to the family hang in the aisles, and over the chancel arch hang funerary banners and an achievement of arms. Other funerary banners and armour hang in the chancel. On the S of the chancel is the marble monument to Robert Shirley, Lord Tamworth (died 1714, aged 22) in a semi-reclining position. The organ is important for its early date; it appears to predate the Commonwealth and may have been made for the house and later moved to the church. Its case, however, is dated 1686. At Staunton Harold the old practice of separating the sexes during services is still observed (in this case men on the S, women on the N). Before the altar in a vault lies the body of Sir Robert Shirley.

The church was given to the National Trust in 1954 by the 12th Earl Ferrers, whose private property it had been.

Adjacent to the church is the Hall which now serves as a Sue Ryder Home. Most of it is work of the 17C and 18C. The small private chapel, later known as the Justice Room, was used by the recusant Sir Henry Shirley in the 17C and is lined with panelling from that period. High up on two sides are 11 contemporary half-length paintings on wood of various saints. (The chapel is not normally open to visitors though application may be made to the Administrator, Staunton Harold Hall, near Ashby-de-la-Zouch, Leicestershire, LE6 5RT.)

Stoke Golding, *St. Margaret.* This is undoubtedly the finest church in W Leicestershire. This is the result of a major remodelling around 1300 which provided the noble S aisle and later the rich S arcade and the windows on the N side. Apart from the rebuilt chancel it is practically untouched by Victorian restoration. The plan with nave/chancel and aisle/chapel being of almost equal size and importance, may have provided the inspiration for several 14C examples in the area (e.g. Broughton Astley, Thurlaston).

Between c 1290 and 1300 the S aisle was planned and built as an entity, and very nearly the same width as the nave. It has seven bays with a grand window arrangement—alternating three-light cusped intersected and three-light with quatrefoils in the head. The E window is of five lights with encircled trefoils in the head. The aisle is unusual for the pierced parapet. The tower was probably started in the very early years of the 14C and, with its spire, completed c 1350. The simple quatrefoil openings on the spire tell of economy not found in the earlier work. The N side of the church was refenestrated in the early 14C, starting at the W end. The most advanced and ambitious work is in the windows in the E part where there is lovely flowing tracery which differs from window to window. The early 14C E window is a generous one of five lights complementing the one in the S aisle; it has three circles in the head and the middle light stretches up to divide the two lower circles. In 1882 the chancel was rebuilt by W. Bassett-Smith but with the unfortunate idea of making the chancel roofline stick up above the others.

The interior is distinguished by its sense of length and the beautiful S arcade. This seems rather later than the aisle and, indeed, the bays do not correspond exactly with the windows. The arcade is of four bays with very delicate moulding in the arches. The effect is enhanced by the fillets on both the pier and arch members. The capitals abound with foliage of different kinds. One of them is populated with a series of heads below the foliage. On the N wall of the nave is a Latin inscription which may give the clue to the start of the great campaign. It is perhaps a 16C or 17C copy of an earlier original but it notes that in the reign of King Edward I (1272–1307) Robert de Campania and his wife '*fundaveru(n)t hanc ecclesia(m)*'.

INTERSECTING TRACERY
St MARGARET • STOKE GOLDING • LEICS.

They cannot truly have 'founded this church' since there is clear evidence of one already existing, so their generosity was no doubt more to do with remodelling or re-endowing it. That there was a church here in the 13C is demonstrated by the single lancet window in the S wall of the chancel (internal since the building of the aisle). The fabric of the nave N wall is almost certainly 13C too and therefore it is likely that the earlier church was a very long rectangle, on similar lines to the chapel at Noseley. No Perpendicular clerestory was added but the roof pitches were flattened; the old roofs to the nave and aisle remain. The steep pitch of the aisle roof can be detected in the masonry. Apart from the roughness of the walls, the unrestored nature of Stoke Golding is shown by the seating. This is of 1844 and the box-pews are rather old-fashioned for such a date.

The font is Decorated and has a series of figures round the bowl, including the patron saint (plus a kneeling donor) and St. Catherine. At the E end of the aisle is a double piscina; it is early 14C and, as such, a late example of the type. In the S aisle is the massive oak 'stocke chest 1636'.

Tur Langton, *St. Andrew.* This is an excellent and bold High Victorian design and was the work of the 26-year-old Joseph Goddard of H. Goddard & Son of Leicester. It was built in 1865–66 to replace a small medieval building at the W end of the village. Typically for its time it is built of polychromatic brick—even the spire is brick—with stone dressings, in a loose Early English style. It has much strong detail such as the large W window and those on the S side, though the N side which fronts on to the main street has much smaller-scale treatment. The interior has a warm, vibrant quality due to the lively detail and the light streaming through yellow-tinted glass. Note especially the notched brickwork, again typical of the 1850s and 1860s, and polychrome brickwork over the arches, and the busy wood and stone carvings. The chancel, lit by a ring of Heaton, Butler & Bayne glass, is more sombre. It is fortunate that the florid High Victorian churchyard railings survived the Second World War.

Withcote Chapel. This small rectangular chapel stands in a delightful situation beside the 18C hall. It is a rare example of early 16C architecture in this area and was started by the Lord of the Manor, William Smith (died 1506), as his private chapel and was continued by his successor Roger Ratcliffe (died c 1537). It has square-headed windows, battlements and angle pinnacles. There is no division between nave and chancel. The interior was remodelled in the 18C (probably 1744) and added the panelling, the partition at the W end and the fine reredos. Two fluted Ionic columns frame a painting in the centre, and there are pedimented wings, against which are placed 18C marble monuments. The seats and most inappropriate font are of 1864. The 16C glass is an important survival and the similarities with the figures at King's College Chapel, Cambridge, suggest that the same craftsmen may have worked at Withcote (perhaps including King Henry VIII's glazier, Galyon Hone). There are eight Apostles and ten Prophets, with their inscriptions partly discernible. The glass has lately been repaired by Keith Barley of York.

The chapel is in the care of the Redundant Churches Fund.

Wymeswold, *St. Mary.* Wymeswold is a place of pilgrimage for the restoration which A.W.N. Pugin carried out for his High Church patron, the Reverend Henry Alford (Vicar, 1835–53). The work of 1844–46 has been claimed as the best surviving example of a Pugin restoration. Pugin found a very dilapidated church, the earliest parts of which date back to the early 14C (the five-bay arcades). The big W tower with its twinned belfry windows is Perpendicular.

Pugin's work started with the rebuilding of the S aisle, which was in a particularly bad state, followed by the removal of the gallery and the brick wall blocking the tower arch. The style of the new work was Decorated and the aisle windows were copied from the finest Lincolnshire churches. The lavish two-storeyed N porch is rather more fanciful. Attention then turned to the chancel which had been built in Perpendicular times. Pugin was careful to put in a new E window in keeping with the style already in existence. The Perpendicular clerestory was retained.

Inside, practically all the furnishings and fittings are by Pugin, even down to the candle sconces. He removed the fragments of the Rood screen as they were extremely decayed but they can still be seen preserved in the S aisle. The chancel screen placed in the new chancel arch is Pugin's. The finishing touches were the fine painting on the chancel roof (a green ground with gold stars and quatrefoils with the IHC monogram) and texts which are always suited to their position (e.g. on the lectern, 'Thy Word is a Lamp unto my Feet...'). The glass in the E window was designed by Pugin and made by William Wailes of Newcastle; it depicts ten saints and cost £200. The chancel NE and SE windows are by Powell's and much of the other emblematic glass is by John Hardman & Co. There is much to admire but ultimately one is left with the impression of rather dull precision and it is hard to remember the revolution that Pugin's medieval accuracy introduced.

Henry Alford moved to London in 1853 and became Dean of Canterbury from 1857 until his death in 1871. The S aisle E window is a memorial to him. He was a man of many varied talents including hymn-writing. He is best remembered for 'Come ye thankful people come...'.

LINCOLNSHIRE

Despite the growth of tourism and personal transport, Lincolnshire still remains the largely unknown county that the 'Murray Guide' noted in 1898. The historical county occupies that great tract of E England between the Great North Road, the North Sea, the Wash and the Humber. The scenery varies from clay vales and fen to chalk uplands and limestone scarps, and despite the introduction of intensive farming and the resultant 'agri-prairies', there is much of interest. The churches, also being dependent upon the underlying geology for their materials, vary equally in type and style. Geologically the county is divided N–S into a number of sweeping belts. In the extreme W, the clay Vale of Trent of neighbouring Nottinghamshire strays into the county and comes to an abrupt halt at the foot of the scarp slope of the Lincolnshire Limestone, the Lincoln Cliff. In the S this latter becomes the fine building stone of the Stamford area. E of the Lincoln Cliff another band of clay stretches to the chalk uplands of the Wolds and these in turn give way to the Marshlands and the coast. In the SE corner are the Fens which lay undrained until the early 19C when the modest but distinctive churches of that area were built.

The marvellous buildings in the SW, at Stamford and also that wonderful group of 14C Decorated churches in the Heckington area emanating from the Ancaster quarry, are built from the fine oolitic freestones of the Lincolnshire Limestone. These stones could be transported by water to the accessible rich areas of the Marshlands and the S edge of the Wash bordering Norfolk. Up on the Wolds very little good building stone was available, though there was a little chalk in the Louth area, and Greenstone, a green sandstone which normally weathers brown, from the Spilsby area. Numerous churches in E Lincolnshire were built of this. In the poor stone areas brick became an important material, being used in quantity from the late 14C onwards. There are many medieval churches with substantial parts in brick: Lutton, Bardney (chancel), Freiston (N aisle), Tydd St. Mary and Sutton St. James (towers). There are a number of 18C brick Lincolnshire churches: the untouched Langton-by-Partney, Wyberton chancel and the tower at Bratoft. Bratoft is perhaps an exemplar for a modest non-limestone belt Lincolnshire church: its medieval body is of Greenstone with freestone dressings and the 18C tower is of brick. Timber church building is rare in Lincolnshire, but the 13C lead-covered timber spire at Long Sutton is remarkable.

What are the special attractions of Lincolnshire's churches? As far as buildings are concerned these are: the pre-Conquest churches where there are two outstanding ones and approaching 50 other examples; the 14C Decorated churches of the Heckington and Sleaford area; and the sumptuous churches of the Marshlands and the Fenland. The fittings that make Lincolnshire worth visiting are the chancel furnishings, the Easter sepulchres, sedilias, etc. associated with the 14C Decorated work, and perhaps the screen-work. Monuments, pre- and post-Reformation, stained glass and wall paintings are also present, in quality as well as quantity.

Pre-Conquest churches are well represented in Lincolnshire, though virtually nothing dates from before the Anglo-Danish period. Most of the surviving churches are later, some possibly as late as c 1100 ('the Saxo-Norman overlap'), but at Edenham the late 8C *in situ* sculpture is evidence of an important early church. There is no doubt that Stow and St. Peter's, Barton-on-Humber are the two best pre-Conquest churches in the county; the former because of its grandeur and its historical associations, and the latter for its role in the study of pre-Conquest churches. Much of the pre-Conquest contribution is in the form of towers and the majority of these make up an identifiable group: Alkborough, Bracebridge, Branston, Clee, Corringham, Glentworth, Hale, Harmston, Heapham, St. Mary-le-Wigford and St. Peter at Gowts at Lincoln, Marton, Rothwell, Scartho and Winterton. These towers from the 11C are characterised by being unbuttressed, tall and gaunt with no decoration. They are usually of two stages, the lower one taking up most of the height, with twin round-headed belfry lights divided by mid-wall shafts in the upper stage. The pre-Conquest style of church building carried on in Lincolnshire after 1066. Mid-wall shafts in the belfry lights in the otherwise very Norman tower of Boothby Pagnell form one example. Even so, the true Norman style came early. Before the Conquest the Romanesque feature of the tall, wide, equal-height crossing arches were built at Stow, and Bishop Remigius's 11C cathedral and its later 12C remodelling by Bishop Alexander were there for the whole county to see and emulate. Fine Norman parish churches include Long Sutton, which has a complete seven-bay 12C arcade, as has Whaplode, and Bicker has two surviving nave arcades of high quality. Of the equally common cruciform Norman church, Horbling retains the chancel, lower part of the central tower, W end and possibly parts of the S transept. Sometimes, as at Kirton-in-Holland or Aswarby, a Norman or 13C Early English S door remains from an earlier church in a later wide S aisle. For Norman sculpture, there are at least a dozen carved tympana surviving, none of them really outstanding. The font at Thornton Curtis is one of only ten black Tournai marble fonts in the country (one of the others being in Lincoln Cathedral), while the lead font from Barnetby-le-Wold has been described authoritatively as 'the finest of the surviving English lead fonts decorated with foliage motifs'.

Eight years before the end of the 12C St. Hugh, Bishop of Lincoln, began a complete rebuilding of his cathedral which eventually left only the W front surviving from the earlier work. Starting from the E, work progressed westwards in an idiosyncratic but pure Early English style, and when the W end was reached the builders immediately returned to the E end. By this time, 1256, the apsidal end of St. Hugh's Choir had become very outmoded, so it was knocked down and the Angel Choir built to the E in the fresh and more sumptuous Geometrical style. The result was one of the greatest 13C buildings in England and one that had a tremendous impact upon the buildings of the county. This impact was felt in the copying of details, such as columns from the St. Hugh Choir at St. Mary-le-Wigford, Lincoln, and Ruskington, or the influence of the Angel Choir on Crowland and Grantham. The great 13C parish church of Lincolnshire is Great Grimsby, St. James, a large cruciform building of the first half of the century. Only the nave and N transept survive intact. Deeping St. James and Moulton at the other end of the county are two 13C examples of exceptional quality. Also worthy of note are the church of St. Leonard, at Kirkstead Abbey near Wood-hall Spa, and the naves at Weston and All Saints', Stamford; in the case of the last also the blank arcading round the S walls. The 13C tower of Stamford, St. Mary has four stages of blank arcading and tall lancet belfry lights, shafted and heavily dogtoothed. Of equal quality is the tower at Gedney, though this has a Perpendicular top stage. In the S of the county a number of early spires begin to appear, all of the broach variety. At the very end of the century the magnificent tower and spire at Grantham were built in work much influenced by the Angel Choir. At 281ft the spire was the tallest in the country until overtaken in the 14C by St. Mary Redcliffe in Bristol (292ft) and Salisbury Cathedral (404ft).

The local influence exerted by the cathedral cannot be overestimated and it continued well into the next century. The form of Heckington with its ornamented parapets with projecting figure corbels, and large traceried windows separated by buttresses bearing crocketed and gabled statue niches, is no different from that of the Angel Choir built over 50 years previously. True, the detail is very different, but even here the cathedral had its contribution to make, via the commemorative tomb to Remigius and its associated Easter sepulchre, of the 1290s. During the second and third decades of the 14C there suddenly appeared in Kesteven a number of very grand set-pieces: Heckington, Navenby and the Sleaford nave. The patrons of these grand churches obviously vied with each other and there is evidence to suggest that certain wealthy chancery clerks of King Edward II who were Lincolnshire Rectors were the core of this competition. The chancel fittings follow a set pattern: a founder's tomb, sacristy doorway, Easter sepulchre, piscina and sedilia. All are highly decorated but the Easter sepulchres are by far the grandest. It has long been wondered why these wealthy patrons should be so interested in the Easter ceremonies as to build these great permanent stone monuments, particularly when during their extremely limited use during the year they would be veiled off. However, recent examination of the contemporary rise in popularity of the feast of Corpus Christi, plus reference to close Continental parallels, has led to the very reasonable suggestion that these structures were in fact Tombs of Christ and Sacrament Shrines. Lincolnshire took the Flowing Decorated style to its bosom. Large churches like Boston, Holbeach and Gedney were rebuilt at this time, and significant additions, like the S chancel aisle at Grantham, were made to many large churches, and countless smaller churches bear signs of the style coming through to them. Window tracery patterns ran riot as their asymmetrical sinuous curves gave an infinite amount of scope for invention. Towers and spires were also a feature of the Decorated period and these are also one of the glories of S Lincolnshire. The Heckington tower inspired those at Anwick, Donington, Ewerby and Silk Willoughby. This was the time of transition between the broach spire and the newer parapeted spire. The spire at Grantham of c 1300 is parapeted though, like Heckington, it retains small broaches, while the later spire at St. Mary's, Stamford is a pure broach, but highly ornamented with lucarnes, niches and statuary. Quite amazing is the series of spires at the foot of Lincoln Cliff, for example, Welbourn and Caythorpe, which have such pronounced entasis that they look almost like space rockets awaiting blast off. Even their flying buttresses look like fins and the crockets do not detract from the image.

The great Perpendicular churches tend to be in areas of prosperity: ports—the Stump at Boston; trading centres—the Stamford churches; areas with great economic activity—the string of Marshland churches; or they are the products of wealthy patrons as at Tattershall. The two grandest Perpendicular churches are Louth and Tattershall. Tattershall is a huge gaunt cruciform building devoid of ornamentation, while Louth with its battlements and pinnacles and steeple rising to 295ft is at the opposite end of the spectrum. The Marshland churches have a feel all of their own, not merely because many of them are built of the distinctive Greenstone, but also because of the way they fit into the countryside; proud buildings standing up in the flat and exposed landscape. The best is perhaps Theddlethorpe, All Saints, but Burgh-le-Marsh, Friskney, Croft and Addlethorpe all have much to offer, not least in the quality of their fittings. Perpendicular additions to existing churches include towers and clerestories. Boston Stump at 272ft high is the obvious example for a tower. Edenham represents a type of tower in the S with high parapets, crocketed finials and bell openings of four lights with the centre mullion rising right to the apex of the arch. All the 15C towers in Stamford are of this type. A variation on this is where the bell openings are set under an ogee hoodmould, the apex of which breaks through the top of the tower as a centre face pinnacle. This can be seen at Beckingham and on the 15C top stage at Long Bennington. There are some fine 15C clerestories. Many of them are in the Fenland area and representative examples may be seen at Gedney, Kirton-in-Holland, Pinchbeck and Algarkirk.

It is only recently that 16C and 17C building work has come to be recognised for what it is and distinguished as 'Gothic Survival' rather than genuine work of the Middle Ages. A few things can be identified: possible tracery in the E window at Friskney (1570), Tuscan columns in the nave at Metheringham erected c 1601, the rebuilding of the towers at Ruskington in 1620 and Barholm in 1648, the latter complete with inscription: 'Was ever such a thing since the creation A new steeple built in the time of vexation'. Also, almost certainly dating from the 17C was the remodelling of the tower at St. George's, Stamford.

Coming into the 18C we still have the odd tower, for example, Deeping St. James (1717), but now we also have complete churches. Unless it was casing a medieval church, as at Mablethorpe (1714) and Baumber (1758), Lincolnshire Georgian tends to be the typical Classical auditory church. Consequently there is not much 18C Gothick though the chancel at Baumber is in that style and the rebuilding at Doddington (1771–75) is Gothic. Langton-by-Partney (1720–30) is a Classical gem and untouched, and its partner at Well (1733) is almost as good. There is the grand town church at Gainsborough, possibly by Francis Smith of Warwick (1736–44), and there are also dignified churches at Cherry Willingham, by Thomas Becke of Lincoln (1753), and Saxby (c 1756). Moulton Chapel is something special: a tiny brick octagon of 1722 by William Sands senior of Spalding. Equally modest but of great charm because of its furnishings is Hannah-cum-Hagnaby, a tiny Greenstone church built in 1753. The Fens have a story all to themselves. Between 1816 and 1828 five modest but charming little brick preaching boxes were built in the Georgian tradition, possibly by Jeptha Pacey. They are: Carrington (1816), Frithville (1821), Langrick (1828), Midville (1819) and Wildmore (Thornton-le-Fen) (1816).

The county was strong in Dissent from the early part of the 17C and while much of this survived the Restoration it tended then to be concentrated in the Fenland and Marshland areas. There were also strong pockets of Quakerism in the N. Virtually nothing survives from this phase apart from the Friends' Meeting Houses in Lincoln (1689), Brant Broughton (1701) and Gainsborough (1704), and the Baptist chapels at Monksthorpe, near Great Steeping (early 18C) and possibly Maltby-le-Marsh, which though altered could date from

1690. A great loss as far as Nonconformist furnishings are concerned was the restoration of what is now St. Leonard's Church, Kirkstead Abbey, which from the 17C until at least the late 18C was a Presbyterian chapel supported by a prominent local family. These survived until the end of the 19C. In the second half of the 18C Methodism began to gain a foothold. A remarkable survival from this period is the Methodist chapel in the stable block of Raithby Hall at Raithby-by-Spilsby, the conversion dating from 1779. There are few later chapels of note in Lincolnshire. The façade of the Centenary Methodist Chapel at Louth (1835) is a confident expression typical of its age, while the carvings on the front of the former Methodist Chapel (1800) in Barn Hill, Stamford, are delightful. In the case of Roman Catholic churches, almost all the buildings date from after 1800. The exception is the chapel built in 1793 by the Young family of Kingerby in the upper storey of the wing of a farmhouse at Kirkby-cum-Osgodby.

A number of interesting churches were built during the very first years of Queen Victoria's reign. At the N end of the county is Haugham by W.A. Nicholson of 1840 (now in the hands of the Redundant Churches Fund), a delightful Gothic fancy built as a miniature imitation of St. James's, Louth in brick and stucco. All the furnishings are contemporary. At Stamford, John Brown of Norwich built the church of St. Michael in the High Street (1836). Although still a preaching box with galleries (sadly all gone after conversion to shops in 1982), the exterior shows the beginnings of the true Gothic Revival. There are many later Victorian churches but not much of outstanding quality. Gilbert Scott's Nocton (1862), G.F. Bodley's sensitive and sympathetic chancel at Brant Broughton (1876) and his later Bishop's Palace chapel at Lincoln (1898), and J.D. Sedding's chancel restoration at Stamford, St. Mary (1890) must be excepted from this, and J.L. Pearson's chancel restoration at Stow (1853–14), Scott's St. Paul's, Fulney, Spalding (1878–80), together with St. Nicholas's, Newport in Lincoln (1838), and J.S. Crowther's St. John's, Scunthorpe are also worthy of note. For the 'rogue architects', the Lincolnshire honours must go to J. Croft of Islington for Cold Hanworth Church (now unfortunately converted into a house). Local architects were strong on the ground, the most prolific being the Diocesan Architect, James Fowler of Louth. Probably his best churches are Binbrook and St. Swithin's, Lincoln, but unfortunately some of his restorations were a touch insensitve. Charles Kirk of Sleaford also did much, and one of his most charming works is the polygonal chancel at Quarrington (1862) with its touching inscription to his mother round the frieze. Edward Browning of Stamford worked in the S and his restoration of Uffington is distinctive, even if ruthless. G.G. Place of Nottingham also worked extensively in Lincolnshire; Manthorpe near Grantham being one of his new churches and Boston one of his major restorations. Coming to the turn of the century, the renowned Arts and Crafts designer, Henry Wilson, built and supplied the furnishings for a chapel at Walmsgate Hall (1901). The latter were incorporated into the new church at Langworth (1960) after the demolition of the chapel. The charming timber-framed church by Bucknall & Comper (1902–04) at Gosberton Clough must be mentioned. Lincolnshire's 20C churches are few and do not represent the best of contemporary church design. All that needs noting is St. Hugh's, Old Brumby, Scunthorpe (1939), by Lawrence Bond of Grantham. It is brick over a concrete frame with pantiles on a Mansard roof. Like many plain churches of the 1930s, much thought and energy has been put into the design of the font and cover, which forms the W focus of the church.

To consider the treasures of Lincolnshire's churches, it is perhaps best to start with the sculpture, as this covers not only one of Lincolnshire's highlights, the 14C, but the wide range of monuments from the 13C to the 19C, and sculpture from the earliest age. Brasses and incised slabs will also be included here. The earliest sculpture needs a good visual imagination to put it into its original context. Into this category come the very early pieces, probably 7C or 8C, from a screen in an earlier pre-Conquest monastic church at South Kyme, the late 8C roundels at Edenham, and the 10C carved head of Christ above what was originally the chancel arch, the W face of the E tower arch, at Barton-upon-Humber, St. Peter. It is in the 13C that funerary sculpture begins to appear, and at Kirkstead Abbey there is a fine mid-13C military effigy, with its legs missing, and two more effigies at Rippingale, one ecclesiastical and the other military. The 14C in Lincolnshire is rich in sculpture. There are the statues on the exterior at Boston (N and S clerestories and N aisle parapet), a single exterior standing figure in a tower niche at Heckington, a wealth of projecting sculpture from the buttresses, etc. and the richly carved Easter sepulchre, sedilia and piscina in its chancel. The lifesize female figure of c 1320 at Stamford, St. Mary is also worthy of close inspection. From the very end of the century comes the headless female saint at Pickworth which is remarkable for the survival of its medieval colour. Lincolnshire also possesses a number of interesting early brasses, two military brasses being among the earliest in the country. That at Croft is c 1300 and the half-figure at Buslingthorpe is only a few years later. The earliest figure brass of a lady seems to be that at Barton-upon-Humber, St. Mary (c 1380), again a half-figure, though that at Gedney is within 20 years of it. There is a good priestly brass at Boston of c 1400, and representative merchants at Boston (1398), Linwood (1419) and Stamford, All Saints' (1442, 1475, 1489). The best military brasses tended to appear at the end of the 14C: Broughton, Gunby, Laughton and Irnham. There are approaching 100 incised slabs with figures and many more without. By far the most impressive is the Flemish one to Wissel Smalenburg (1340) in black Tournai marble at Boston, but there are important ones also at Redbourne, a military figure, Sir Gerard Sothill (1410), and at Crowland to a master mason, William de Wermington (early 14C). The monuments in the NE chapel at Spilsby to the Willoughby and Bertie families range from the first half of the 14C to the early 17C, being concentrated from c 1348(?) to 1410 and 1580 to 1610.

For the 16C and early 17C, there are three superb monuments at Snarford to the St. Pol family and Robert, Earl of Warwick, and the tombs to the Heneage family at Hainton, also roughly of this period. The Exeter tombs at Stamford, St. Martin to the first Lord Burghley (1598) and to the fifth Earl and his wife (1704) are both of the very highest quality. The best collections for the 18C are the Ancaster monuments at Edenham, those to the Newton family at Heydour, and the collection at Belton to the Brownlow family which range from the 17C to the 19C.

Lincolnshire screenwork is significant and has a character of its own. In general, it is slightly heavier in appearance than that of Norfolk and not quite so soaring in its verticals. The heads of its arched openings also contain intricate tracery compared with the much plainer openings in Norfolk. The earliest surviving screen is that at St. Leonard's, Kirkstead Abbey which dates from the 13C.

This shows no trace of the county characteristics, but they are there by the early 14C in the screen at Ewerby. The best churches to visit for screens are Addlethorpe, where the parcloses also survive; Theddlethorpe All Saints', which also has parcloses, with early 16C Renaissance decoration; Stamford, St. John and the chapel at Browne's Hospital which have superb screens of c 1451 and c 1475 respectively. For the most complete screens, with coving and Rood lofts, Sleaford (restored by Ninian Comper, 1918) and Coates-by-Stow (restored by J.L. Pearson, 1883) are the best. For other medieval wooden furnishings there are the fine stalls and misericords of c 1390 at Boston, a few bench-ends, the odd pulpit or two (Claypole, Coates-by-Stow and Fishtoft—all Perpendicular) and a couple of ornate tall font covers (Frieston and Fosdyke). Coming to the end of the 16C and beginning of the 17C, the county is much better off. There are a number of pulpits—Navenby, Skirbeck and Wrangle are thought to be later Elizabethan, while there are dated examples at Boston (1612), Croft (1615) Burgh-le-Marsh (1623) and Skidbrook (1628). For the 18C the untouched furnishings at Langton-by-Partney and Well stand out for their completeness. Even the good Victorian churches tend to lack outstanding contemporary wooden furnishings and all that needs special mention are the choirstalls and screens at Stamford, St. Mary which are some of J.D. Sedding's best.

Lincolnshire is not a county where ancient stained glass survives in quantity, but glass of quality does exist. There is very little from the 13C apart from the cathedral; just a few fragments at Stragglethorpe. The 14C is better represented with the two N aisle windows at Heydour being among the best. Also worthy of note are the remains at Gedney (a Tree of Jesse), Carlton Scroop and Wrangle. The best of the 15C can be found in the chapel of Browne's Hospital, Stamford (1475). St. Martin's, Stamford has five windows of good 15C glass, the majority of it improperly removed from Tattershall church in the middle of the 18C, and Tattershall itself retains glass of interest, now all collected in the lower half of the E window. The glass at Messingham ranges from the 14C to the 16C. One of the few works of the 18C is the W window of the S aisle at Burton-on-Stather (1777). This depicts Christ the King holding an orb and is by James Pearson. The enamel style of glass painting continued into the 19C until superseded by the Gothic Revival and the attempts to rediscover medieval techniques. The outstanding example of this is the E window at Redbourne of c 1837 painted by William Collins using a design of John Martin, 'The Opening of the Sixth Seal'. It is a scene full of horror contrasting strongly with the pretty canopies and niches painted above and below. Most of the Victorian stained glass painters are represented and perhaps the most interesting are the windows by Henry Holiday at Hackthorn (1861), the Morris & Co. window at Ruskington (c 1874) and the Christopher Whall windows at Stamford, St. Mary (1890, 1891). Of equal interest is the work of Canon F.H. Sutton, Rector of Brant Broughton, who designed and actually made glass for his own chancel, rebuilt by Bodley in 1876, and the cathedral. It is so good that it has been mistaken for the work of C.E. Kempe. Boston and Grantham contain works of William Wailes, Kempe, Clayton & Bell, Michael O'Connor, John Hardman and James Powell. The 20C is not particularly well represented by stained glass, but Grantham has a number of large windows with postwar glass with the work of Harry Harvey, L.C. Evetts and John Hayward. One of John Hayward's most recent works (1980) can be seen at Billingborough and Francis Skeat's American commemorative glass was in 1985 inserted into a chancel window at Willoughby.

Medieval paintings also are not common in Lincolnshire, but the 14C and 15C wall paintings at Corby Glen are fine by any standard. High on the nave wall are Nativity processions with the shepherds on one side and the Magi on the other. At the E end is a Virgin and Child and opposite them, King Herod. In the N aisle are several scenes including a Weighing of Souls, St. Anne teaching the Virgin, St. Christopher and a Warning to Swearers. Pickworth also has extensive wall paintings. There is a part of a Doom over the chancel arch at Carlby, and at Goxhill there is a 15C Crucifixion in the S porch: a most unusual position. The panel paintings that usually go hand in hand with the survival of medieval screenwork hardly survive in Lincolnshire, but of great curiosity value is the 16C painting on wood under the tower of Bratoft Church depicting the defeat of the Spanish Armada. It is crude but dramatic and the painter, Robert Stephenson, went to great pains to sign his name in large letters.

Finally, a word on people. There are a number of saints who have special connections with Lincolnshire. Guthlac (c 673–714) was the founder of Crowland Abbey. About the year 701 he went to live there as a hermit. The subsequent abbey church was built on the site of his cell and his cult flourished particularly in the 12C. Scenes from his life can still be seen on the 13C tympanum of the W doorway of the abbey. St. Hugh (1140–1200), Bishop of Lincoln from 1186 until his death, was a Carthusian monk. Hugh was deeply loved in the diocese and his shrine in the cathedral was much visited before destruction at the Reformation. This regard has continued until the present day and representations of him with his symbol the swan abound in modern stained glass and statuary. St. Gilbert of Sempringham (1083–89) is famed as the only Englishman to found a monastic order, the Gilbertines. By the time of his death he had built 13 monasteries. St. Botolph (died 680), who gave his name to the town of Boston and whose townsmen were known throughout the Middle Ages as 'Botolph's men', was for long thought to have been personally connected with the town, but modern scholars feel that the monastery he founded in 654 was more likely to have been at Iken in Suffolk. Less well-known is St. Hybald, an obscure 7C monk who has four churches dedicated to him, all of them in Lincolnshire. He is thought to have been based in the village that now bears his name, Hibaldstow.

The diocese has been blessed with a number of notable bishops: Robert Grosseteste (bishop 1235–53) philosopher and scientist; John Williams (bishop 1621–41), the foremost of the moderate reformers in the pre-Civil War period; Christopher Wordsworth (bishop 1869–85), a renowned scholar; and Edward King (1885–1910), his much-loved successor, who was of Catholic persuasion and became a *cause célèbre* when prosecuted for Ritualistic practices in 1890. Like St. Hugh he is commemorated in stained glass and statuary all over the county, and his photograph can still be found hanging in many a Lincolnshire vestry. The most famous latter-day churchman born in the county was John Wesley (1703–91), the founder of Methodism, son of Samuel Wesley, Rector of Epworth, and almost equally famed is his brother Charles, the hymn writer, who was born at the Rectory four years later. King Henry IV was born in 1367 at Bolingbroke Castle, part of his father's estate. John of Gaunt is credited with the building of the grand and wide S aisle, now the nave, of Old Bolingbroke

Church. Lord Burghley (died 1598), Queen Elizabeth I's chief minister, was born at Bourne, educated at the King's School, Grantham, and though he built Burghley House just outside the county, his tomb and those of his family are in the nearby St. Martin's, Stamford. The Reverend Francis Willis MD (died 1807) was physician to King George III and his treatment of the king's madness is recorded on his monument (by Joseph Nollekens) in Greatford Church. Captain John Smith (1580–1631), one of the founders of Virginia, was born and baptised at Willoughby, and there is a modern commemorative window in the baptistery by Francis Skeat. Matthew Flinders (1774–1814) of Donington was a noted explorer of Australasia and is commemorated in the church by a contemporary monument and a modern stained glass window. Other famous Lincolnshire men are Sir Isaac Newton, who was born at Woolsthorpe Manor on Christmas Day 1642 and was baptised soon after in nearby Colsterworth Church, and William Stukeley (1687–1765), often called the 'father of British archaeology' who was born at Holbeach and after a late ordination became Vicar of All Saints', Stamford, from 1729 until 1747. It is to Stukeley that we owe much of our knowledge of the state of Stamford churches in the 18C. Lastly, mention must be made of Queen Victoria's Poet Laureate from 1850, Alfred Tennyson. Born of an old Lincolnshire family at Somersby Rectory in 1809, he was the son of the Reverend Dr George Clayton Tennyson. The church at Somersby contains a bust of Tennyson and a few souvenirs.

Barton-on-Humber, *St. Peter.* St. Peter's is one of the most famed pre-Conquest churches in England and holds an important place in the history of the study of early churches. It was the first church to be clearly recognised as pre-Conquest during the furious debate in the early 19C over whether any such architecture survived in England. Thomas Rickman pointed out that while there might be some legitimate dispute over a pre-Conquest date for the top stage of the tower, this was so clearly predated by the lower stages in a totally different style, that they must be pre-Conquest. His argument was largely accepted.

Today Barton has continued this tradition of being at the forefront in academic studies. After closure and redundancy in 1972, the church was vested in the Department of the Environment, which sponsored a total archaeological investigation. This has yielded a complete architectural history of the church. It has long been known that the present appearance of a W tower and annexe, attached to a much larger medieval church, gives a totally wrong impression for the earlier church. The excavation proved beyond doubt that the tower and W annexe are respectively the nave and baptistery of the first church on this site, built in the late 10C on a pre-existing cemetery. The baptistery was matched on the E side of the tower by a similarly sized chancel. The excavation also yielded some extremely interesting information on internal arrangements and use. The position of the font was identified in the baptistery, as was the position of the altar in the chancel—W of a central N–S screen or rail, and it was shown that there were doorcases on both arches to the chancel and baptistery. The investigation revealed evidence of former architectural features and constructional techniques. Surviving and sawn-off joists in the baptistery show it, and presumably the chancel, to have had upper floors entered from the surviving doorways in the tower nave. We are left with the strange vision of a church being divided into three rooms by doors and having upper floors. Radiocarbon dating of surviving wood gave a date of c 990. The presence of sockets for tiers of massive beams at the top of the 10C tower suggests a support to a very weighty roof and it is concluded this could only have been a spire-like structure. Constructional techniques were revealed by traces of wood left in the original putlog holes, showing how the scaffolding was erected.

The tower stands some 60ft high and is divided into three stages. The two late 10C stages rise to a height of about 47ft and have long-and-short quoins at the corner, which are matched by similar work at the corners of the baptistery. The lower stage of the tower has two tiers of decorative stripwork arcading on the N and S faces; the lower round-headed and the upper triangular-headed. The setting out was rather offhand and the arcades are wobbly and of unequal width, particularly where they contain doorways. In the upper tier are pairs of small round-headed windows with turned baluster columns. The second stage is completely plain apart from the belfry openings, consisting of triangular-headed windows on all four faces sitting on the dividing stringcourse. These also have turned baluster shafts, supporting through wall stones. Inside the tower, the space is dominated by the arches to the baptistery and former chancel. The chancel arch approaches 13ft in height and is 5ft 5ins wide with a stepped impost and integral outer pilaster strip; the baptistery arch is a little smaller and simpler. Immediately above the chancel arch (the tower side of the E arch) is a stone with an important incised head near its top carved in a 10C Anglo-Scandinavian style. It is thought to be the remains of a Christ in Majesty, where the rest of the composition was painted and has since disappeared. The baptistery, offset to the N by four degrees but in line with many of the pre-church graves on the site, is by comparison a much plainer building. It has small round-headed, double-splayed windows in its N and S walls and two circular windows in the W wall, the higher one to light the upper floor. All the stripwork, quoins and arches in the 10C work are of Yorkshire gritstone, reused from Roman buildings, while the rest of the fabric is of limestone rubble.

The original church was enlarged in the mid-11C. No trace of this second phase remains apart from the line of its roof on the E wall of the tower. As it cuts through the earlier twin belfry lights this was probably the reason for heightening the tower with a third stage. It is in the typical late 11C Lincolnshire Saxo-Norman style with tall pairs of belfry lights and mid-wall shafts. In the 12C the church was again enlarged and started the addition of a whole succession of aisles. The late 13C added a two-storey porch. In the mid-14C both arcades were totally dismantled and reconstructed to a new spacing. Also in the 14C a new W belfry window was added to the tower, and later in the century a timber-framed spire, but the latter had disappeared before the end of the 18C. The 15C saw the addition of a new chancel and a nine-bay clerestory. The only addition after the medieval period was the organ chamber on the N side of the chancel in 1897.

What can the visitor see surviving from these later alterations? The earliest after the Norman period is the 13C S aisle with its fine three-light Geometrical windows, although the two-storey porch has lost its upper chamber. Similarly, the N aisle also remains with Reticulated windows, unusually set alternately with pointed arches and square heads. The E window here, which like the W one has fine flowing tracery, is particularly interesting, incorporating as it does a Crucifixion scene with Christ, the Virgin and St. John carved into the mullions. It is now an internal window looking into the organ chamber. The mixture of 13C and 14C work in the arcades can be roughly distinguished: the dogtooth ornament indicates the reused 13C capitals and the foliage decoration, seen particularly on the responds, is 14C. The 14C upper two-light belfry window on the W side of the tower also survives. The 15C chancel and clerestory are also important elements of the building today and it can be seen that when building the chancel, the E wall of the S aisle was also rebuilt (slightly to the W of its former position), most likely to restrain the thrusts from the new chancel arch. The W window of the S aisle is also of this period. Much of the 15C work was carried out in brick.

St. Peter's has a relatively small number of outstanding fittings today. Among these must be mentioned the two 14C panels of stained glass in the E window containing two figures, the original N door with its accompanying ironwork and the restored 15C Perpendicular screen with a Rood loft of 1898. There are also a number of pieces of 17C funerary armour.

Boston, St. Botolph. The first view of Boston Stump rising majestically out of the fen is a dramatic and unforgettable experience, particularly if approached from the NE in the late afternoon with the tower silhouetted against the dying sun. Closer to, the church is equally impressive, dominating the market place with its sheer size: the tower rises to 272ft and the church encloses over 20,000 sq ft. Grand the interior certainly is, but this is possibly at the expense of proportion, especially across the extremely wide aisles. The magnificence of the church matches Boston's importance in the Middle Ages. During the 13C it was second only to London as a port but by the end of the Middle Ages silting of the Witham, shifting sands in the Wash, and a turning towards the Atlantic led to its decline. In the 17C Boston was a hotbed of Puritanism and Boston, Massachussetts, founded in 1630, was so named because of the large number of Bostonians in the emigrants.

The church is clearly seen to be a predominantly 14C building in the Flowing Decorated style with some major 15C Perpendicular additions. The seven-bay nave, with 14 clerestory windows, is Decorated, as are the W three bays of the chancel. The other two bays are Perpendicular. The present E window is a total replacement of 1851–53 by G.G. Place of Nottingham. Apart from the E and W windows of the aisles, the only other major Perpendicular addition is the Stump itself. Although an early record claims a starting date of 1309, the tower dates mainly from the 15C. The building took place in several stages. The first two stages of the tower to the top of the paired windows with the ogee canopies are obviously part of a single building campaign. The large proud lower windows, that on the W face having eight lights, and the paired lights above, are drawn together by the unifying stone panelling behind, while the parapet just above suggests the top of what already appears a very substantial tower. This was indeed the case, and it appears all that was originally intended after this was a spire. The reason for the change of mind is not known, but it was decided to continue upwards as a tower. The next stage was built as an open lantern, with an extremely large four-light window on each face, and is very crude compared with the rest of the building. Perhaps to compensate, the final stage, a delicate transparent octagon full of ornate detailing and supported by flying buttresses, was added a little later, probably early in the 16C. By this time all thought of a spire had been abandoned but it leaves the query of how the name 'the Stump' originated. The name is ancient and possibly derives from a period between building the different stages of the tower. On the other hand, it may merely be a description of the truncated appearance of the tower seen standing up starkly from the fen.

It is worth walking round the church before entering. The only remaining external chapel is the one tucked into the SW corner W of the porch, used variously over the last few hundred years as a school, fire engine house and vestry. It is a part of the 14C fabric separated from the church by a two-bay arcade. It was renamed the Cotton chapel in 1853 after a famous 17C Puritan Vicar, John Cotton, who fled with many of his congregation to Boston, Massachussetts in 1633. E of the porch on the aisle wall can be seen the traces of another chapel, thought to be that of the medieval Corpus Christi Guild. Between the clerestory windows are image brackets and canopies which formerly held statuary. Some of this survives: one figure on the S side and four on the N. The latter includes a Virgin and Child. There is also other medieval statuary at the E end of the N aisle; on the N and E faces of the NE pinnacle and along the adjacent E parapet.

The 14C S porch is large and ornate, remodelled in the 15C when an upper floor was added. This now houses a parish library, founded in the 17C. The door to the church, though restored, is the original and has complex flowing tracery patterns on its upper parts. On entering, the scale of the interior impresses, but the plan is very conventional. It is inside that the 14C reigns supreme and little can be seen of 15C additions. The exception is the tower, but this can only be seen in full glory from its base: a light airy space rising a full 137ft to the level of the vaulting, itself a Victorian completion of a medieval scheme, but inserted against the advice of Sir Gilbert Scott. His fears over the extra weight were well-founded and the tower had to be strengthened by Sir Charles Nicholson in 1929–33. Nicholson also had to provide new nave and aisle roofs. In the middle of the second bay from the E is a boss with the date 'AD 1929' and above it a motor bus to commemorate the donation towards the restoration by the local bus company. Other donors are also commemorated, the most amusing being the carving of a white elephant in the W bay of the S aisle to indicate the money raised by the churchladies' white elephant stalls. The chancel roof of 1781 was merely repainted by Nicholson as it had been fully repaired in 1909. The S aisle at first sight appears a total mystery with a multiplicity of tomb-recesses, blocked doorways, and sedilia and piscina, but if viewed as a medieval layout, it becomes much clearer. The two E bays were screened off to form a chapel and the blocked doorways one above the other indicate the loft stairways. Similarly, the W blocked doorway and recess indicate the former Corpus Christi chapel already noted on the outside. A major visual impact on the interior is the reordering carried out in 1985 by Ronald Sims of York. A new altar has been carried forward into the E bay of the nave and the predominant texture of the area is light limed oak. Incorporated into the reordering are the surviving parts of the 19C Rood screen and its six medieval return stalls. These are now set facing N–S. Successful in achieving what it sets out to do, the reordering has not solved the visual problem of the large unused void of the chancel stretching away behind the altar.

The contents of St. Botolph's are numerous and wide-ranging. The earliest item is a bronze 13C lion's head door knocker with two lizards composing the ring, to be found on the tower S door. The stalls in the chancel date from c 1390, but the canopies are the result of a sympathetic restoration of 1853–60. The stalls are noted for their carvings which include the elbow-rests, poppyheads, but most importantly the misericords. There are 62 in all. A complete and inexpensive listing of the misericords and stall carvings is available in the church. Also in the chancel are two major medieval brasses: on the N side of the altar is one to Walter Pescod (died 1398) and his wife under triple canopies, and on the S, that to a priest of c 1400, perhaps to John Strensall (died 1408). There are also a large number of empty stone indents whose brasses have long since disappeared, and 25 incised slabs, the majority from the 14C. By far the best of these is the black Tournai marble slab at the W end of the N aisle, a memorial to Wissel Smalenburg, a merchant of Munster who died in 1340. The figure is set within very ornate buttressing and a canopy. The other medieval monuments are to be found in the S aisle. Two recesses in the S wall contain 15C effigies of a lady in a horned head-dress and a knight wearing a Maltese cross of the Order of St. John of Jerusalem. To the E of these is a tall 14C tomb-recess, its canopy being cut by an 18C tablet. By the S door is a plain but unusual memorial to Richard Smith (died 1626), consisting merely of a plank inscribed with a rhyming verse. Near the font is a small inset brass in a large slab to John Tooly, 1686, with good lettering and escutcheon. On the N aisle wall there is a plain brass memorial to Abdias Howe, Vicar of Boston 1660–82. Howe, an avowed Puritan, entertained Cromwell and his troops the night before the Battle of Winceby in October, 1643. The N aisle also contains memorials to the Fydell family, the best of which is that to Richard Fydell of 1780 by James Wallis of Newark: a red and blue marble obelisk bearing a medallion portrait, all under a pediment. The pulpit is an extremely fine Jacobean work of 1612 with fine Ionic columns. The tester above is much restored and the steps are an 18C addition. The font, a very imposing and ornate structure mounted on four steps, was designed by A.W.N. Pugin and installed in 1853. The church also contains some fine 18C ironwork: the communion rail of 1754, and the large screen across the tower arch. The Corporation mace holder of 1727—front pew, N side—is worthy of note. Behind the high altar is a large reredos designed by W.S. Weatherby in 1891 and filled with its statuary in 1914. Weatherby also designed the altar triptych in the Cotton chapel. The former reredos, a copy of Rubens's 'Descent from the Cross', removed in 1845, now hangs on the N aisle wall. The stained glass is entirely 19C and 20C. The best is the E window by Michael O'Connor of 1853 and the E window of the S aisle by C.E. Kempe (1889).

Grantham, *St. Wulfram*. St. Wulfram's is a large stately church justly famed as one of Lincolnshire's best, set back in its own miniature close, originally a market place, off Swinegate. Pleasant houses line the close at the W end, and to the N is the attractive 18C Rectory next to the ancient King's School, where Lord Burghley and Isaac Newton were educated in the 16C and 17C. From the outside the church is a simple but large rectangle with N and S aisles to both the nave and chancel. The only projections are N and S porches and the 15C Hall chapel jutting out from the N chancel aisle.

Grantham is one of those few churches where it is better to start from the inside to understand it. A casual glance shows that the church with its six-bay nave and four-bay chancel has distinct differences in style. There are some remains of herringbone masonry in the chancel, which suggests an early date, and the nave appears to

St. Wulfram's: the early 14C W front includes the famous spire rising to 282ft

be 12C. But there are oddities that need explaining. The nave aisles and W end seem to date from towards the end of the 13C, but even here the N side is different from the S. The S chancel aisle, which has a crypt beneath, appears Decorated, while its N counterpart is Perpendicular. The nave is in two parts: the four E bays and the two W ones, the junction between them being marked by the two responds back to back, separated by a short piece of wall. The E bays, but not the W, have blocked clerestory windows above three of the arches, and the present arches cut right into them. It is clear the present arches cannot be original and they must have formerly been lower, presumably round-headed, to allow room for the clerestory. Round-headed arches to the main bays and clerestory fit the Norman character of the supporting columns, which look c 1180. The absence of the clerestory in the two W bays suggests the earlier church terminated before them and they were a W extension (in the late 13C). The whole was unified by constructing tall pointed arches on the older columns to match the two new bays. The work of extending W was part of a complete recasing of the W end. The W 13C work is most exciting and important and has led to many architectural historians trying to trace its origins. The N aisle is of the highest quality and shows affinities with the Angel Choir at Lincoln Cathedral, building in 1256–80. The large six-light W window derives from the E wall of the Angel Choir, but being of six lights instead of eight, has used pairs of three-light windows there to complete the design. The slightly taller centre light in the sets of three is an Angel Choir motif. Part of the work on the N aisle was the provision of a sumptuous N portal with niches each side set under triple canopies, sadly mutilated when the N porch was added. The doorway itself has an exquisite complex moulded arch with shafts and stiff-leaf capitals of the highest order. The S aisle is later and the windows with their plain intersecting tracery must be approaching 1300. The W window here cannot be trusted for dating, as its tracery was inserted by Anthony Salvin in 1854 to replace that of the 17C or 18C; and the S doorway and entrance to the S porch are earlier 13C pieces retained presumably from the previous aisle.

Ballflower appears prolifically at the lowest levels of the tower, suggesting that building must also have started about the turn of the 14C. But it is most probable that the tower was envisaged from the very beginning of the project and perhaps was its *raison d'etre*. It is clear from the size of the supporting piers that a large tower was intended, and almost certainly as a rival to the great tower of St. Mary Magdalen's, Newark, started some years before. The result is spectacular and soaring. Starting at the bottom, there are series of statue niches flanking the doorway and W window, though none of the existing statues are ancient, and above are two tiers of very steeply pointed blind arcading. The final two stages, which account for half the tower's height, leap clear of the body of the church and consist of tall window openings. The lower set have two distinct pairs of lights sitting on a deep band of quatrefoil decoration, and the upper two pairs are set under a single arch with a vertical central mullion that runs up to the apex. Inside, there is a high vault with 12 radiating ribs. From behind a small parapet, known locally as 'the Olliers', which has large corner pinnacles surmounted by original statues, springs the spire. It rises from small broaches through three sets of lucarnes that are most unusual. The upper two sets look like coronets in that they are to be found on all six faces of the spire, though they only pierce it on alternate faces. When built, the tower and spire (now a little lower at 272ft) were the tallest in the country, and the large-scale work—the N aisle is wider than the nave—was conceived, if not totally executed, as a single project. This gives a co-ordinated feel to the W front and the tower, which does not change styles (or centuries) halfway up as at Newark. Engaging the tower within the aisles was also part of the design, and not an afterthought like Newark, to create the screenlike appearance of the W front so beloved of the 13C.

The S chancel aisle, probably the chantry chapel of St. Mary founded by William Gunthorpe, was built next. In the full Lincolnshire Decorated style, with large five-light windows on the side and a six-light E window, all the tracery is sinuous, flowing and different. The exterior is curious and terminates at the E end with tall, round, military-looking corner turrets. The date of the chapel is c 1330–50, but the presence of large amounts of ballflower decoration on the frieze and on the gables of the buttresses suggests the earlier end of this range. Under the chapel is a contemporary crypt originally entered from external doors, but now via a 15C door from the S chancel arcade. The N porch dates from about the same time and is a most interesting structure. Its upper parts have been rebuilt, but it is clear it was a two-storeyed building with a stone vault between the floors. The doorways in the E and W walls suggest a processional way, and the presence of twin stairways to allow circulation of pilgrims led to the very interesting suggestion by Professor Hamilton Thompson that the upper room was used to house the relics of St. Wulfram. The presence of relics of St. Wulfram was recorded in 1565 when it was noted his shrine had been sold. The only other major additions to the church in the Middle Ages are the balancing Perpendicular N chancel chapel and the Hall chapel (now a vestry) projecting from the N side of the church. The E bay of the nave is wider than the rest, probably to accommodate a large stone pulpitum, the stone foundations of which were discovered during the 19C excavations. It appears the alterations to the bay were carried out during the mid- to late 14C.

Work on the tower and spire has been frequent. On a number of occasions the upper parts have had to be dismantled and rebuilt. The latest repairs were carried out in c 1985, when the statue of St. Wulfram on top of one of the tower pinnacles was conserved. The great 19C restoration was by Sir Gilbert Scott in 1866–68, when over £20,000 was spent. The most immediately apparent of Scott's works are the three parallel wagon roofs he inserted over nave and both aisles and his Rood screen. The roofs certainly complete the unity intended by the medieval masons, but they are somewhat forbidding. Also, to achieve this unity Scott removed a small clerestory to the chancel added in the 17C. Other restorations of the 19C were the N porch, 1877; the S porch, 1890, when contemporary directories state it was 'completely rebuilt'; and the Hall chapel, restored by Sir Walter Tapper in 1909.

Grantham today has few ancient furnishings. A little medieval work remains, such as the Saltby tomb-recess in the S aisle immediately E of the porch, which is supposed to date from 1369, and the similar Harrington tomb-recess a little to the E. Here the cusps of the arch are decorated with angels and the Instruments of the Passion. Dating from the 15C is the font: octagonal, with scenes, including an Annunciation, Nativity and Baptism of Christ, on the sides of the bowl, and small figures round the stem. Above it is a tall ornate cover of 1899 by Sir Walter Tapper. From the 16C, Grantham boasts the extremely interesting and famous chained library, founded by Francis Trigg, Vicar of Welbourn, in 1598. It is housed in a room, complete with its own fireplace, over the S porch. The best monuments date from the 18C. There are two by Henry Cheere, one in the N aisle of 1756 to the Lord Chief Justice, Sir Dudley Ryder, and the other in the S aisle to Captain William Cust. Also of note in the N aisle are monuments to Mrs. Middlemore (1701) and Sir Thomas Bury (1722), and in the S aisle, Edmund Turnor (1769) by Edward Bingham, and William Thorold (1808). In the S chancel chapel there is an 18C wrought-iron mace stand of c 1766.

Grantham is a church with much stained glass: so much that it darkens the church on dull days. As so much of the glass is worthy of note all the windows will be mentioned, starting with the W (tower) window, proceeding clockwise. (1) By William Wailes, 1856. (2) Adoration of the Magi by Wailes, 1853; rearranged after gale damage in 1979 so that the stained glass has clear glass surrounds. The lighting of the aisle is improved, but at the expense of the integrity of the glass. (3) Good window by Clayton & Bell, c 1865. (4) Clear-glazed. (5) Christ and Peter walking on the water, by John Hayward, 1980. (6 and 7) Both by C.E. Kempe, 1896 and 1898. (8) Weighing of Souls by St. Michael, by Harry Harvey, 1962. (9–11) Clear-glazed. (12) The E window. Large window of 1883 obscured by the enlargement of the reredos in 1901. (13) By Kempe & Co., 1920. (14) By Kempe & Co., 1927. (15) By Clayton & Bell, 1875. (16) Virgin and Child with Symbols of the Passion by L.C. Evetts, 1969. (17) A memorial commemorating an event in 1833, but the window itself is c 40 years later. (18) The Seven Sacraments by John Hayward, 1974. (19) Clear-glazed. (20) By Clayton & Bell, 1875. (21) W window of the S aisle was by Wailes, 1855, but only the tracery lights and inscription remain, the rest being reglazed in clear glass. There are other noteworthy Victorian furnishings. Sir Arthur Blomfield designed the reredos behind the high altar in 1883, which has painted figures of Prophets, kings and Apostles, and John Oldrid Scott installed the fine chancel parcloses (1886) and the W timber lobby (1888). Sir Walter Tapper enlarged and heightened the reredos in 1901, restored the reredos in the crypt and designed the present organ case in 1905–06. The external statues in the tower niches date from 1922 and 1956.

There are a number of interesting peculiarities in the history of Grantham Church. First, it was a prebendal church of Salisbury Cathedral, and from the very early 12C the town was divided into medieties with two Rectors, that is, the cathedral prebendaries. Two Vicars, of N and S Grantham, were first appointed in the early 13C, and though in the post-Reformation period the care of the parishes was frequently left to only one of them, it was not until 1713 that the offices were formally combined. During the early 17C one of these Vicars, that of the S mediety, brought Grantham to the forefront of the furious national debate between the reformers and the Puritans over the position of the altar. In 1627 Peter Titley, a reformer of Laudian persuasion, moved the altar, until then set E–W at the W end of the chancel, to the E wall where he set it N–S. The Mayor, a Puritan, tried to move it back and a free fight broke out in the church. The subsequent appeal by both sides to Bishop John Williams resulted in his famous 'Letter to the Vicar of Grantham'. This, because of its moderation and compromise (accepted by Titley) led to an attack on it by the more extreme Laudians, and resulted in a pamphlet war of great significance to the Church in the period leading to the Civil War.

Great Grimsby, *St. James, St. James's Square.* Grimsby is by far the largest town in the historic county of Lincolnshire. It is a medieval town, but the great expansion took place between 1850 and 1860 with the coming of the railway and the building of the fish dock. Consequently, with the notable exception of the parish church, the only buildings of architectural merit in the town date from after 1850.

St. James's is a large cruciform church set today in its own modern precinct, bounded by an inner ring road and by buildings of the

1960s and 1970s. The exterior looks mostly renewed and, apart from its size, does not evoke immediate interest. However, among the newer work are enough clues—clerestory lancets, W and S doorways, transept pinnacles—to show that the core of the church is 13C. The tower, however, is Perpendicular and has the uncommon feature of two-light belfry windows set within wide recessed blank arches, two on each face.

Entering the church, one is struck by the magnificence of the 13C nave arcade: six bays with columns of eight filleted shafts under octagonal abaci and roll-moulded arches; but it is the unusual arrangement above that commands attention. Instead of the normal pattern in large churches of arch, triforium and clerestory, the arches here have an arcaded wall passage sitting immediately on them, with taller bays jumping up at irregular intervals to encompass the clerestory. The transepts had E aisles and in the N transept the arrangement continues. For the later work, the Perpendicular tower fits into the crossing raised on flat piers with blank panel decoration. A fire destroyed the earlier one and a contemporary inscription on the NE pier commemorates its rebuilding by John Ingson in 1365. During the 16C Grimsby was in decline and the church building in poor condition. The 17C saw the collapse of the E end and in 1718 the nave was sealed off during patching repairs.

The dramatic change in Grimsby's fortunes in the 1850s naturally led to attention being turned to the church. The S transept was rebuilt in 1858–59 by Charles Ainslie, a kinsman of the Vicar, and the nave was restored and reroofed to its original pitch by R.J. Withers in 1874–77. The ruined chancel was rebult in 1882–84, but shorter than originally, and the tower strengthened. G.F. Bodley built the Lady chapel on the E side of the N transept in 1906, in a pleasant but modest Decorated style, and the Classical windows of the aisles, presumably of 1718, were replaced in c 1911 in a more flowing Decorated style. Sir Charles Nicholson built the chapel of the Resurrection on the E side of the S transept in 1920 and added the vestries. This chapel, with its side passage and fittings, is all of a piece and attractive. Bombing on 25th August 1943 caused great damage. Much of the N wall of the N transept was blown out, and almost all the stained glass badly damaged. Contemporary watercolours in the N transept by A.E. Wade show the extent of the havoc. The latest disaster was a serious fire in 1979, fortunately confined to the tower.

The only medieval contents are the 13C font at the W end of the N aisle, and the military effigy of Sir Thomas Haslerton of c 1400 in the N transept. There are no great later monuments, but one of 1808 in the N transept to the infant George Rye has the most moving inscription: 'Dear lovely babe early thy course was run,/Scarce morning dawn'd ere set your evening sun./Yet still sweet innocence thou'rt doubly blest,/Escap'd from wordly cares thy soul's at rest./When your fond parents drop the cumbrous clay,/May'st thou a cherub wing them on their way'. All the early 20C windows in the nave aisles were restored between 1947 and 1952, and the opportunity was also taken to commission new work. The best of this is the glass of 1954 in the transepts by Hugh Easton: four archangels in the N and the *Benedicite* in the S; and the glass of 1956 by L.C. Evetts in the Lady chapel illustrating the *Magnificat*. A large organ gallery of 1953, with internal porch below, dominates the W end. In 1972 the large carved altar reredos by Frank Roper of Penarth depicting the Virgin and St. James in a modern style was installed. Unfortunate visually was the introduction in 1984 of the suspended radiant electric heaters: they upset the rhythm of the medieval architecture.

Perhaps the most famous early son of Grimsby was John Whitgift (c 1530–1604), who became Vicar of nearby Laceby and in 1583, Archbishop of Canterbury.

Heckington, *St. Andrew.* Lincolnshire is a county famed for the quality of its 14C Decorated architecture: Heckington Church is the county exemplar, built in a consistent style during the first part of the 14C and featuring all the hallmarks of that style. Internally, there is a full set of chancel fittings: Easter sepulchre, founder's tomb, sedilia and piscina, all carved and of the very highest quality. The chancel was built by Richard de Potesgrave, a wealthy Chancery Clerk under King Edward II who became Rector in 1309, and the nave was almost certainly built by the Lord of the Manor, Henry de Beaumont, Earl of Buchan and cousin of King Edward II. The royal arms above the S porch are in their pre-1340 form which suggests the building was complete, or virtually complete, before then.

The best overall view is gained from the SE corner of the churchyard where the four elements of the church can be taken in: the ornate chancel, defined by the flowing tracery of the windows, particularly that of the seven-light E window (and also the S transept window), the buttresses with their crocketed canopies, image niches and prominent projecting sculpture and the roof with the large pinnacles and pierced wavy parapet; the simpler nave; the S porch matching the chancel in its elegance and style; and the relatively severe tall tower topped by the more ornate spire, transitional in form, having both broaches and large corner pinnacles, the whole set behind a parapet. The tower was obviously one of the last parts to be constructed. The exterior also gives the clue to the building sequence. On the N side it can be clearly seen that the N aisle and transept are slightly earlier and different in style from the chancel: the junction between the E side of the transept and the main body of the church shows a discontinuity in building. The window tracery also does not flow as it does further E, though the N window of the transept is a replacement of 1867 by Charles Kirk, so it may not be an accurate copy.

The S doorway appears at first sight slightly earlier than the main fabric, but is in fact contemporary with it. On entering one is struck by the starkness of the interior, for with the exception of the chancel fittings, it is extremely plain and bare. This impression is heightened, particularly in the chancel, by the gloom and green cast imparted by the glass. The overall impression is of a very tall and wide nave and chancel linked by a very open chancel arch. The nave is of five bays, the E one being wider than the others to accommodate the transept openings, and beyond them is a short unaisled nave bay built at the same time as the chancel.

At the E ends of the nave aisles short projections from the main arcade with a single blank arch indicate the beginnings of the transepts. The roofs, though built to their correct medieval pitches, are in fact Victorian reconstructions—that of the nave by Charles Kirk, 1867, and the chancel by James Fowler of Louth, 1888. These replace the low-pitched 15C roofs seen in early Victorian prints, which cut across the chancel arch. Fortunately the late medieval masons left the original gables standing to their full height.

The chancel fittings are magnificent and are the focus of the interior. They consist of the standard set for churches of this type.

Starting on the N, the founder's tomb-recess contains the effigy of the Rector, Richard de Potesgrave, in Mass vestments under a pointed segmental arch with ogee cusping. The figure has been raised about six inches at some time, and behind it is Potesgrave's chalice excavated from the tomb in 1800. Though in a glass case it is in very poor condition, as is the effigy which is green with algae. The priest's door to the right leads to a two-storey sacristy and beyond it is the Easter sepulchre (see p 221). This is one of the most famed pieces of 14C carving in England. It consists of a central triangular-headed opening flanked by two niches containing the three Maries and two angels. Beneath are four sleeping soldiers and above is the Risen

The Easter sepulchre in St. Andrew's, a sumptuous Decorated fitting in a remarkable 14C chancel

Christ censed by attendant angels. His fine crocketed canopy is supported left and right by curious flying buttresses with pierced parapets, and above the pinnacles are set against a background of typical seaweed-type foliage. The whole is topped by a cornice carved with small monsters, including a mermaid. On the S side the sedilia are set within a rectangular frame which is equally ornate: ogee recesses set under crocketed canopies with saints and angels above; left to right—St. Margaret, censing angel, the Virgin, Christ, censing angel, St. Katherine. The saints and Christ are being crowned by small angels and the censing angels are being replenished by angels holding incense boats. The stops to the canopies have a series of most interesting carvings all connected with food, and as some of them seem to involve the feeding of animals with grapes, they may be a parody on the Holy Sacrament. The double piscina to the E of the sedilia cuts through the windowsill leaving the ogee arch and large pinnacle freestanding.

There are a number of other medieval monuments, perhaps the most interesting being the 14C slab in the S transept. It is entirely plain apart from a quatrefoil towards one end in which is carved the sunken relief of the bust of a male figure. There are also three incised slabs: one in the S transept and two in the E bay of the nave. One of the two is to Margaret Allesdon, 1509, and bears the faint impression of a lady under a canopy, and the other, largely illegible, bears a Tau cross, c 1500.

There is much 19C and early 20C stained glass. The best glass, by T.F. Curtis of Ward & Hughes, 1897, is in the E window and illustrates the Te Deum in the main lights and the Benedicite in the tracery. The large Ward & Hughes S window of the S transept of c 1922 is not as good. It depicts Richard de Potesgrave showing a plan of Heckington Church to Henry de Beaumont, but the large pictorial scene spreading across all five lights is disruptive to the rhythms of the medieval window and tracery.

Lincoln

Lincoln feels like two towns: an upper historic one at the top of Steep Hill surrounding the cathedral and based on the old Roman *colonia* of Lindum, and a lower one to the S looking like a typical product of the Industrial Revolution and slightly shabby compared with its more elegant neighbour. Appearances are, however, misleading and the S suburb is almost equally ancient. The extremely long southern High Street was a very early piece of ribbon development and in the Middle Ages had along it 12 of Lincoln's 46 churches. The first church recorded in the city was one built of stone by St. Paulinus in c 628. A tradition dating back to the 12C has long identified this with St. Paul-in-the-Bail, formerly situated at the junction of Bailgate with Westgate. Though modern scholars do not think this link can be fully substantiated, the truth is even more interesting. The medieval St. Paul's was replaced by a Georgian building in 1786, which in turn was replaced by a Gothic building by Sir Arthur Blomfield in 1878. This was demolished in 1971. The site was then excavated and revealed a long sequence of churches and burials back to the late Roman period. The earliest church had been built on the courtyard of the forum of the Roman town, probably in the 4C, and the plan of this is marked out in the garden now on the site. A 7C bronze hanging bowl, discovered during the excavation and probably associated with the second church on the site, is now on display in the cathedral treasury.

It is thought that most of Lincoln's churches were in existence by the 11C. The churches of St. Benedict, St. Mary-le-Wigford and St. Peter-at-Gowts are the only ones remaining. Like St. Paul-in-the-Bail, all the others have been demolished or enlarged out of existence. There has been a long debate over the precise dating of St. Mary's and St. Peter's towers. Today it is felt that these towers are post-Conquest, built towards the end of the 11C. Study of the capitals and other decorative features on the belfry lights of the two towers has led to the conclusion that they ultimately derive from the work of Remigius at the cathedral.

With the destruction of so many of the medieval churches one would hope Lincoln to be rich in Georgian architecture, but there is less than one would expect. St. Botolph's has a tower of 1721 but it is not the most exciting, and Lincoln's best Georgian church, St. Peter-at-Arches (1724) by William Smith, was demolished in 1932. Much of it was incorporated into the new church of St. Giles, Lamb Gardens (between the Wragby and Nettleham Roads), by W.G. Watkins in 1936. The Victorian period is not represented by any important churches. Sir Gilbert Scott's St. Nicholas's in Newport, c 1838, is unremarkable and Scott afterwards repented of it. Perhaps the most interesting 19C ecclesiastical building in Lincoln is the former prison Chapel at the castle built in 1847. It is a unique survival of a total separation of prisoners system and is a horrific reminder of a short-lived prison philosophy. The local architect, James Fowler of Louth, is best represented in the city by St. Swithin's (1869, steeple 1888), now under threat of redundancy. Charles Hodgson Fowler is represented by All Saints', Monks Road; St. Faith's, Charles Street West; and restorations at St. Peter-at-Gowts and St. Helen's, Boultham. G.F. Bodley rebuilt St. Mary Magdalene's in Bailgate close to the cathedral in 1882; and in 1889 he made a fine reinstatement of the chapel at the Bishop's Palace, just S of the cathedral, from a ruined 13C shell.

St. Mary-le-Wigford, High Street. A church 'to awaken the curiosity of the stranger and to interest the enquiry of the acute antiquary'; so states a guide to Lincoln published in 1810. This is certainly just as true today, but the setting has changed dramatically in the intervening years. The church is now bounded on two sides by busy streets pounding with traffic and on a third by a railway. Though not large, the church is of the highest quality. Not only is the 11C tower of great architectural interest, but most unusually, its original dedication stone survives. The body of the medieval church is early 13C, very beautiful and much influenced by the contemporary work of St. Hugh's Choir at the cathedral. It consists of a three-bay nave with N aisle, and a two-bay chancel with N chapel. Post-medieval additions are the 19C S nave arcade and organ chamber, and work of the 1960s and 1970s, comprising a parish room to the SE, internal offices in the church and a small N porch.

The tower is typical of the tall slim Lincolnshire 11C towers; of two stages, the lower very plain, rising for most of the height of the tower, and the upper containing pairs of bell lights on each face, each of them divided by a central shaft set halfway back in the wall. The belfry lights repay attention. The W one is unique in that it has decorative detail on the twin arches, in the form of shallow Vs carved on the voussoirs to give a zigzag ornament. The mid-wall shaft of this opening has a pre-Conquest feel to it, though with volutes on the capital, while that on the E approaches the Norman with a cushion capital. The W doorway, with a later twin-light, square-headed window inserted above it, is most impressive, its height emphasised by its extreme narrowness. However, it has suffered from restoration. The doorway now acts as a window to an inserted office. Just to the right of the doorway and probably *in situ* is the original dedication stone. The inscription is in Old English and almost illegible, but transcriptions tend to agree on: MARIE/OFE 7 SCE/N CRISTE TO L/ AN 7 FIOS GODIA/EIRTIG ME LET WIRCE. This produces 'Eirtig had me built and endowed to the glory of Christ and St. Mary'. The tower is not bonded into the nave, which projects about two feet each side of it, suggesting the W wall of the nave is earlier.

The N and E elevations reveal 13C work with two lancets in the E chancel wall separated by a central buttress, and a single 13C window of three uncusped lights on the N nave wall. The rest of the fenestration here has been so altered that it is confusing, but all is made clear inside. The church is entered from this N side through a small wood, glass and leaded porch of 1974. The medieval interior is a delight. The tower arch is very powerful, being 20ft high and over ten feet wide, and above it is a round-headed doorway. The Early English work impresses with its beauty and delicacy rather than power. Stiff-leaf capitals, detached shafts with rings and moulded arches abound. The three-bay N nave arcade has octagonal columns with detached shafts, good stiff-leaf and plain chamfered arches. The chancel arch is similar but has keeled responds. The two-bay chancel arcade to the N chapel has a column of the St. Hugh Choir type: an octagonal shaft with hollow sides and four detached shafts, again with very good stiff-leaf. The two lancets of the chancel E wall are unified by a central narrower blind bay plainly plastered, with an elongated quatrefoil opening above. The N wall windows now make sense. The three-light second window from the W is shown to be original and its rear-arch has keeled shafts, good stiff-leaf capitals and a deeply moulded arch. Its pair to the W is seen to be similar and the later square-headed window has been cut into it. The later medieval work is fairly small-scale: Reticulated E and W windows of the 14C inserted in the N aisle and the square-headed windows in the N wall. All the additions on the S side are 19C. However, the S doorway is 13C and was incorporated into the new aisle. All the ceilings are modern. Making a large visual impact is the work carried out in 1974 by Bridges & Purdy of Birmingham, which won a European Architectural Heritage Year award in 1975. This comprises a two-storey insertion into the tower space, the lower of which is an office, two offices in the Victorian S aisle, a room connecting the church with the SE parish hall erected in 1964, and the small N porch. All the internal work was non-destructive and reversible, but the S aisle offices are unfortunate and visually disruptive.

Notable fittings include a piece of pre-Conquest interlace built into the lower part of the S jamb of the tower arch, and another smaller piece above the S door outside; and three monuments in the N aisles: (from the E) part of a 14C female figure in the N chapel; an alabaster tomb-chest with reclining effigies to Sir Thomas Grantham and his wife (1618); and a mutilated male effigy of the 14C in the NW corner. At the W end are two small inscription brasses: one on the N jamb of the tower arch to William Horn, a former Mayor of Lincoln (died 1459) and the other on the W respond of the S nave arcade to John Jobson (died 1525) depicting his tools, an axe and a knife, as a fishmonger. In the chancel is a brass chandelier of 1720, the gift of the City of Lincoln. Upon demolition of the Victorian church of St. Mark in 1972, a number of items were transferred to St. Mary's. These include the large incised slab with kneeling figure, to Leonard Laycock (died 1594) in the NW corner; the fragment of the 13C coffin lid set into the S aisle office wall; the made-up arch and pieces of zigzag, all 12C, built into the external W wall of the 1974 S extension; and the three stained glass panels signed 'I.M. 1873' in the N aisle, depicting Christ with the children.

St. Benedict, St. Benedict's Square, High Street. A fragment of a medieval church, consisting of a chancel, N chapel and repositioned W tower. The chancel is noted for its 13C work and the tower for the confusion it has caused architectural historians and archaeologists. The survival of St. Benedict's is remarkable. The nave and original tower were destroyed or severely damaged during the Civil War and for a large part of the 19C the church was disused and neglected. Demolition for a street 'improvement' was proposed in 1928, but public protest was so strong that it was reprieved and restored in 1932. In 1969 it became the Diocesan Centre for the Mothers' Union and the internal reordering dates from that time.

St. Benedict's is a typical modest town church. The first incongruity one notices is the tower. It is butted against the W wall of the church, overlapping both the chancel arch and the N aisle, blocking an earlier W continuation. The tower was re-erected in its present position c 1670. It has the general form of the Lincolnshire 11C towers, but closer inspection shows it to be much too squat and the twin belfry lights with their mid-wall shafts have some rather strange stones in them. A recent archaeological examination has revealed that there are no original 'Saxon' parts present, and so it is the form alone that was copied. The remaining part of the church is seen to consist of 13C, 14C and 15C work from the outside. The Early English period is represented by the beautiful but incomplete lancet at the E end of the S wall and the corbel table above. During the first half of the 14C three flowing Decorated windows were inserted, and the window set high in the W wall of the N aisle is contemporary. The E window probably also dates from this time, unless the strange vertical elements in its tracery means more replacement of c 1670. The rest of the windows—those in the N aisle—are fairly late Perpendicular work with flat four-centred arches. Blocking and large-scale repair in brick here meant that a full complement does not survive.

Inside, the picture is expanded. The outstanding feature is the 13C two-bay arcade on the N side with its octagonal column, detached shafts, stiff-leaf capitals and finely moulded arches (chancel side only). The present N aisle must be an enlargement of an earlier one as the N lancet was clearly on an external wall. This enlargement seems to have taken place in the 14C, if the corbels supporting the roof are to be trusted. They seem more trustworthy than the W wall with its high window which shows signs of disturbance. The N aisle roof seems to be later than its corbels and possibly dates from the time of the insertion of the Perpendicular windows. On the other side of the arcade the roof in the chancel is post-medieval and again could date from the 17C rebuilding. Inspecting the chancel arch with its 17C blocking, enough of the original is visible to show it is 13C, and on the other side of the blocking, under the tower, the 13C E respond of the nave also survives. Dividing the W bays from the rest of the church is a pale buff brick screen dating from the reordering of 1969 by Antony Parker & Partners. It is about eight feet high and encloses offices. Detailing includes small brick buttresses and heavy concrete lintels having the appearance of lead. The wall is staggered, and a domestic-type window and serving hatch look into the chancel and the N chapel respectively. The chancel may be divided from the N chapel by means of a curtain at abacus level. The work today looks dated, but the insertion was not destructive and is completely reversible.

Notable fittings include the 14C sedilia with a depressed ogee arch and drop tracery, a 13C double piscina a little to the E, and, set into the N wall opposite, a small attractive 13C head, probably of an angel. On an adjacent bracket is a small statue of Mary Magdalen holding a jar of ointment. This is a 1932 import into the church, is Flemish and dates from the first part of the 16C. Just round the corner on the other side of the arch is an attractive sconce in iron. The pulpit in the N chapel is 17C and stands on a plinth of Perpendicular stonework. Above it is a repainted royal arms of King George II, 1734. The font beneath the sedilia is 18C and has a circular bowl with swags, set on a tapering square column. Its cover is contemporary.

Louth, St. James. Louth is a small intact town set in the Lincolnshire Wolds. Being in an area not rich in indigenous building stone, it is a town of red brick, much of it Georgian, punctuated by a few splashes of ostentation, mostly Victorian, where stone has been proudly imported. The parish church of St. James dominates the town with its tower and spire. Like Boston and Grantham, it is the grand-scale town parish church with the conventional plan stretched to its limits. It has a magnificent W tower, but the soaring delicate spire here is one of the highest in the country and beats Grantham by a few feet. The plan is that of a nave, six bays long with aisles, and a chancel of four bays, also with aisles. As the tower and spire are engaged by the aisles, the resulting plan is a plain rectangle broken only by the N and S porches and the NE vestry. One of the disadvantages of stretching a parish church to such a size is that the interior has to be of outstanding merit to retain its architectural integrity, or the contents have to be of such a quality to disguise the problem. Louth does not quite make it on either count, but it is a tribute to the rest of the church that despite this, St. James's is still one of the great Lincolnshire churches.

The impression created by the tower and spire, whether from a distance or close up, is one of delicacy. The slimness of the tower and equally slim crocketed spire emphasise this, but the dominant source is the transition between the tower and the spire. Tall pinnacles receive the thrusts of transparent traceried flying buttresses set against a background of finely decorated battlements. In detail, the tower consists of three stages, with a huge W window with typical Perpendicular panel tracery set above an ogee canopied doorway. The second and third stages have pairs of two-light windows, the upper being taller and set under high ogee crocketed canopies. Crockets appear everywhere: on 24 buttress gables, and on the main and battlement pinnacles. The spire, which rises to a height of 295ft, also has crockets up each edge, but is otherwise plain with only one set of lucarnes set very low down. The tower was built in the 15C, but there are more precise details about the spire. Accounts show that it was started in 1501 and took 14 years to build. A tall full-length clerestory of ten bays rises above equal-length aisles, all fully pinnacled and battlemented. The E end has a pierced gabled parapet over a large seven-light, transomed Perpendicular window. The nave clerestory windows show perhaps lingering remains of the Decorated style. The body of the church was erected during the first half of the 15C and the chancel a little later, perhaps intermediate in date between the nave and tower.

On entering, the impression is of a large, over-restored and yet empty space, devoid of decoration. The nave arcades and chancel arch, being extremely plain, reinforce this feeling: the nave bays have plain octagonal columns, with sides alternately flat and hollow, and simple chamfered arches above, while the chancel arch is totally unadorned, not even having capitals or label stops! The aisles look very much restored. The puzzle of the nave is the W bay. It is separated from the rest by a short piece of walling and it may represent the result of joining the new tower with the already existing nave. Beyond the lofty tower arch is the immense volume of the tower space rising 86ft to the top of the second stage. Here it is crowned by a lierne-vault of great power made up of superimposed patterns of lozenges and squares, and lit on all four sides by the windows below. The chancel, which does not benefit from the greenish cast of the clerestory windows, has its four bays made up by quatrefoil pillars and moulded arches of two orders under plain ogee hoodmoulds. The latter continue upwards as shafts to the string-course and contribute to the overall panelled effect of the chancel. The three-light clerestory windows have conventional Perpendicular tracery.

The restorations which have left such a heavy mark on St. James's include the nave and aisle roofs of 1825. With its traceried boards and lightweight pierced arches above the ties, both typical of the date, the nave roof looks insubstantial for such a large building. Its carved angels are very much worth inspection though. The spire was restored in 1844 under L.N. Cottingham. The main 19C restorations were carried out in 1860–69 by James Fowler, who lived in the town. The work included the clearing of 18C galleries and seating, the present tiled paving, the chancel reredos, the restoration of the S chapel sedilia and the recreation of N and S chapels by introducing screening—the S chapel screen (very highly restored) came from a previous chantry in the N aisle and the N screen was a gift of Fowler himself. Fowler also totally rebuilt the S porch. Some time before 1882 the present chancel roof with its fine projecting angels (now gilded) was inserted. The main 20C restoration has been the consolidation of the NE bays of the nave arcade, c 1950, under Godfrey Allen. Sir Charles Nicholson refurbished the S chancel chapel as a war memorial. More recently, George Pace restored the N chapel, incorporating six late medieval stalls and displaying on the E wall two 15C angels holding Instruments of the Passion, from a former roof.

The few medieval furnishings are those that were largely collected into the N chapel. The present font is by Fowler, but at the W end of the N aisle is a late Perpendicular one found in a local garden and restored to the church. One of the church's treasures is a 'buffet', known locally as the 'Sudbury Hutch' because thought to have been given by a former Vicar, Thomas Sudbury (died 1504). Buffets were portable cupboards used for the display and storage of plate. This example bears portraits of King Henry VII and Elizabeth of York. Unfortunately, Dr. Eames, the noted furniture historian, has declared that it 'cannot be accepted as medieval'. On the E wall of the chancel are two good wall monuments. The earlier on the S side is to Thomas

Orme (died 1814) and has above the inscription a sarcophagus in relief upon an obelisk. The other by John Earle of Hull on the N side, to John Emeris (died 1819) has a relief of Faith. The most ambitious monument is in the N aisle, to William Allison (died 1844), 'a banker of this town'. It is of three bays, canted, with arches supporting a projecting ogee canopy. It is highly crocketed and pinnacled, and every square inch of the Caen stonework bears carved decoration. Its ironwork railing is equally pretty. There are interesting paintings at the W end of the nave: on the N side on a tower buttress (but possibly due to be moved to the S aisle) is a late 16C Madonna and Child adored by the Evangelist. When bought from a church in Rome in 1848 it was attributed to Tintoretto. It was presented early this century. On the S side of the nave, also on a tower buttress, is the Descent from the Cross by William Williams, purchased in 1775. The figures of Moses and Aaron come from an 18C reredos. Also in the church are two chests: one near the S door and the other, a domestic chest dated 1686, in the N aisle. The stained glass makes a marked contribution to the feel of the interior. The E window, which was badly fired and has lost paint, is by Clayton & Bell, as are the two W windows of the aisles. A prominent citizen, Cornelius Parker, paid for the glass in the W window, illustrating the Te Deum, and two windows in the S aisle illustrating Old Testament stories: they are all by John Hardman & Co. Two windows in the N aisle depicting Christ walking on the water and the Entry into Jerusalem are by Heaton, Butler & Bayne. The brass lectern of 1865 designed by R.J. Withers is a fine piece.

Stamford

Stamford is a beautiful unspoilt town in the SW corner of the county with a history going back more than a thousand years. The churches are built almost entirely of the local Lincolnshire Limestone, with Barnack stone predominating. Stamford does not have one medieval church dominating the town. It has instead five, the substantial remains of a sixth, now a school chapel, and an early Victorian church built on the site of a medieval predecessor. These seven remain from the 14 existing in the Middle Ages. Stamford was not dominated by a single lord of the manor and it was possible for wealthy individuals or syndicates to establish churches themselves. The major building periods in Stamford are the 13C and the 15C. It seems that like many of the other wool areas in the 15C, general economic decline was offset by the personal wealth of individuals who spent much of it in building and good works.

All Saints, All Saints Place (NW corner of Red Lion Square). A very early church, mentioned in Domesday, situated at the W edge of the pre-Conquest town. Today it dominates Red Lion Square, apparently a late Perpendicular building with a bold tall tower topped by a graceful crocketed spire. However, a closer inspection reveals that the external blank arcading wrapping itself completely round the S aisle is Early English and dates from the 13C. Entering by the 15C S porch, which has a fine ogee canopy and panel-vaulted interior, it is also seen that the core of the church is 13C: the ornate S arcade with its detached shafted columns and stiff-leaf capitals, the simpler N arcade, and the S chancel arcade with its interesting capitals. The rest is the result of a comprehensive rebuilding in the late 15C by the Browne family, wealthy wool merchants in the town. Their merchant's mark can be seen in a panel on the N face of the tower. The rebuilding included all the windows, the roofs with the grotesque corbel supports in the nave, and the vaulting of the tower, with its strange little men apparently supporting it. The panelled roof in the S chapel is particularly fine. Structural features of note are the unusual water disposal arrangements on the N aisle—channels cut for pipes on the buttresses with gargoyles halfway down them—the castellated N tower porch complete with mock arrow loops, and the original stone clock-dial on the E face of the tower. All these date from the rebuilding.

By far the most interesting of the original fittings are the brasses to the Browne family. The best is the double brass ascribed to William and Margaret Browne, 1489, in the S chapel immediately under the fine 13C double piscina. Among the others, on the E wall of the N aisle, are those to John Browne, died 1442, on twin wool sacks, with his wife Margery; and John Browne, died 1475, with his wife Agnes, over a Latin verse. Both men have fine examples of contemporary iron-framed purses hanging from their belts. Other contents of note are the warning to bellringers in a painted aedicule, dated 1694, beneath the vaulting of the tower at the level of an earlier bell ringing chamber, and the 17C hourglass stand to the side of the pulpit.

The church was repewed in 1857 by Edward Browning who earned the scorn of contemporary ecclesiologists by inserting box-pews. Major works were undertaken between 1871 and 1874 by Thomas Graham Jackson. He stabilised the whole S wall of the church. The reredos by J. Treadway Hanson and the low chancel screen were installed in 1878 and the N chancel vestry built, 1886. There is much Victorian glass: the W window dates from 1888, the gift of an American descendant of the Browne family. That just to its S is by C.E. Kempe and depicts Lincoln diocese and its neighbours. To the N are two windows by Sir Archibald Nicholson. The glass over the S porch and immediately to the E is by Heaton, Butler & Bayne, 1900.

St. George, St. George's Square. Originally this was a modest town church consisting of nave, chancel, aisles and tower, but it was enlarged in 1888 by J.C. Traylen. The medieval church has idiosyncratic nave arcades and a 13C tower arch which was lifted bodily to first-floor level in the 17C. The church is known chiefly for its chancel which has close connections with the Order of the Garter. It was built at the bequest of William de Bruges, first Garter King of Arms, who died 1449/50. The windows originally had kneeling figures of Knights of the Garter. A single head and a number of quarries bearing the insignia of the Garter survive, collected in the N chancel window. The roof is also original with demi-angels at the bases of the intermediate rafters, though the painting is 19C. As well as the Garter quarries, there is other medieval glass: 15C figures of St. Catherine and St. Anne teaching the Virgin survive in the S chancel window. Below these are the head of a Garter knight and the head of a bishop of c 1500. The E window, the Ascension, is by William Wailes and Clayton & Bell (1869) and the W window of the S aisle is a memorial to Traylen (died 1907), by Hugh Arnold. There is a fine monument to Sir Richard Cust and his wife, Anne, in the chancel with the mourning wife leaning on a pillar bearing the arms and portrait bust of her husband: signed by John Bacon the Elder, 1797. Other interesting memorials are the 14C incised slab to Blanche Wake, died 1380, daughter of Henry, Earl of Lancaster, from the Stamford Greyfriars; and a curious bellmetal plaque, 1626, in bellfounder's letters to Tobie Norris, bellfounder. The clock on the tower has an 18C dial and the mechanism, with a birdcage frame and anchor escapement, is signed Thomas Rayment, Stamford, 1792.

St. John the Baptist, St. John's Street (SE corner of Red Lion Square). St. John's is a delight: a small town church built all of a piece, and complete by 1451, if the record of stained glass inscriptions made by a local antiquary, Francis Peck, in 1718 is to be believed. Its character is typical of a mid-15C church and the nave arcades have arches where only the inner demi-shafts have capitals, and the outer orders run continuously from apex to base without interruption. The roofs are also original and have carved angels: those in the chancel are almost upright three-quarter-length figures, while those in the nave are almost horizontal. Their colour schemes date from 1856 and are not original. The church is noted for its original screenwork and stained glass. The screens are typically Lincolnshire in style—tall vertical bays with tracery in the window heads—and the glass as noted above dates from 1451. The screens had their Rood lofts removed in 1564, a doorway to the pulpit was cut through the N section sometime in the 18C, and in 1856 the main chancel screen was removed to give a better view of the newly installed E window! This is now set within the S arcade of the chancel and the rebates for its doors can still be seen. Much of the glass survived until the 18C. What survived into the 20C was last restored in 1974 by the York Glaziers' Trust, when the jumble in the S chancel window was redistributed in the E window of the S aisle and some of the aisle tracery lights. The former includes the upper part of a bishop from one of the main lights. Of particular note in the N aisle tracery lights is the depiction, in the window immediately E of the N door, of the Virgin giving protection to departed souls in the folds of her cloak while interceding on their behalf with God the Father, who is weighing them in a blanket. This is a unique depiction in English stained glass. Also of interest in this wool town is St. Blaise, patron saint of woolcombers, with his woolcomb, in the third tracery light of the next window E. Of the later glass, the E and W windows are by Oliphant and date from the 1856 restoration. In the S aisle, numbered from the E, windows two (1897) and four (1904) are by Heaton Butler & Bayne, and three (1897) and five (1913) are by Clayton & Bell. A small wall tablet with a mourning female figure in the S aisle is stamped 'Coade, London, 1800'.

The church has associations with Sir Malcolm Sargent the conductor, who was a native of Stamford and is buried in the town cemetery. He was in the St. John's choir during the early years of this century and learnt to play the organ here under his father, who was church organist.

St. Martin, High Street St. Martin's. The entry to Stamford from the S is unique and one of the most impressive in the country. The transition from country to town is sudden and total, and the tall tower of St. Martin's Church, tightly set, dramatically contrasts with the 18C domestic architecture. The church is a total rebuilding of the late 15C. The tower was built first, as this can be the only explanation of the earlier surviving roofline on the E wall of the tower. Internally it is the most spacious of the Stamford churches and though relatively bare, is the one that approaches most closely the grand town church. The chancel was described as ruinous in 1473, but the angels above the nave arcades hold shields bearing the arms of men who were bishops in the 1480s, suggesting a rebuilding during that decade. The W shield on the N side is of Bishop Russell of Lincoln (1480–94)— two chevronells between three roses—who was almost certainly a patron of the rebuilding.

Passing the mutilated water stoup beside the outer doorway, one enters the church through the S porch, a fine structure with a vaulted roof—the angel boss bears the arms of the See of Lincoln—and a room above. On entering one immediately notices the open arches of the tower encompassed by the aisles and the spacious nave of five bays. The chancel beyond the wide and tall chancel arch has a plain 18C plaster ceiling which amazingly survived the 19C restorations. N and S are chapels, the N one being the Burghley chapel containing notable tombs to the Cecil family, Earls and Marquesses of Exeter. The doubling in width of this chapel in 1865 is the only structural addition since the Middle Ages.

The Burghley monuments and the medieval stained glass are the most notable fittings and of national importance. The tomb to Lord Burghley, died 1598, is one of the grand tombs of the period. In a Renaissance style, it has the armoured effigy of the first Elizabeth's Lord High Treasurer under twin arched canopies supported by Corinthian columns. On top are much strapwork and obelisks. A little behind it in the Burghley chapel is the other great monument: that to John Cecil, fifth Earl of Exeter, dated 1704. Here the Earl and his wife in semi-reclining attitudes are portrayed as a Classical Roman nobleman and lady. They are flanked by standing figures of Victory and Arts. The figures were carved by Pierre Monnot, but it seems the backgrounds were carved and the whole erected by an English mason, William Palmer. Other monuments include one in the Burghley chapel to Richard and Jane Cecil, died 1552 and 1587, and a wall tablet in the N aisle to the Dutch painter, William Wissing, who died at the nearby Burghley House in 1687. Of curiosity value is the ceramic memorial to Thomas Goodrich of 1885, described as 'a rare cricketer and a good man'! In the detached churchyard to the E is a fine slate gravestone to Daniel Lambert, the famous fat man who weighed 52 stones 11 pounds and who died in the town in 1809.

The medieval glass dating from the 15C is placed in the E window and four adjacent S windows. Some of it is original to the church, but most of it came from Tattershall. It was removed in the mid-18C and installed in St. Martin's by William Peckitt. This explains the cavalier attitude to the restoration and why medieval glass was ruthlessly chopped up merely to make geometrical patterns. The most interesting glass is in the E window with 15C saints and angels, together with 16C shields; and in the window immediately W of the organ, which shows, left, Moses striking the rock and the soldier piercing Christ's side; centre, Samson carrying off the gates of Gaza and the three Maries at the tomb, and right, David and Goliath and the Resurrection. The scenes come directly from the *Biblia Pauperum*.

The font is an interesting survival from the earlier church, the bowl dating from the early 14C. The box-pews, like those in All Saints', are an interesting late example dating from 1844. Together with the woodwork in the Burghley chapel, they are by Edward Browning. Unfortunately, one must travel to London and the Victoria and Albert Museum to see another of St. Martin's notable fittings: a fine brass chandelier of 1732 sold for scrap by a former Vicar in 1892 for 4d. per pound!

St. Mary, St. Mary's Street. St. Mary's has long been considered the mother church of Stamford, but the historical evidence does not support this. The status was probably accorded to it because of its intimate connection with the town's administration; through its Corpus Christi Guild which later evolved into the borough corporation. The church occupied the whole of its existing site by the early 13C with the E wall extending to the site boundary, and this accounts for the stubby appearance of the church compared with the height of the present tower and spire. The tower was begun in the early 13C and an aisled nave and chancel built contemporaneously or added shortly afterwards. Still in the same century the two W arches were cut through the chancel behind the present choirstalls and transepts were built to the width of the N chapel—see the blocked lancet window in the W wall of the chapel. Probably at the same time a more easterly N extension was added to the chancel and the traces of this can be seen externally on the E wall. In the 14C a beautiful and late flowering of the broach spire was added to the already superb tower, and the N transept was extended into a large chapel with a second arch into the chancel and a tall open roof. It is called the Corpus Christi chapel and interestingly the first record of the Guild of Corpus Christi dates from c 1350.

For a number of years during the next century St. Mary's must have looked a strange sight as the whole church between the tower and the chancel arch was virtually demolished and a new Perpendicular building inserted in the space. The only traces of the earlier nave that remained were the responds of the arcades at both ends and the two steeply pitched rooflines on the tower wall. The SW respond (but not the renewed E one), with its detached shafts and stiff-leaf capital, shows that the original arcade was of very high quality as the similar one at All Saints'. The nave roof also dates from this Perpendicular rebuilding, but much more spectacular was the ceiling of the Corpus Christi chapel roof, the bequest of Alderman Hikham who died in the 1480s. This gilded and painted panelled wagon roof is one of the glories of the church and gives the alternative name to the whole chapel, the 'Golden Choir'. Its bosses deserve close inspection, as does the painted inscription to Alderman Hikham and his wife Alice along its cornice. The ceiling was last conserved in 1953 by E. Clive Rouse.

Much of the present internal appearance of St. Mary's is dominated by works of the 19C and the greatest impact was made by the work of John Dando Sedding in the chancel in 1890. He gathered about him a superb team of Arts and Crafts workers—Christopher Whall and the sculptor Stirling Lee among them and they were responsible for the screen, the choirstalls, the altar and its surrounding paving and the painted chancel ceiling. Christopher Whall designed both the windows in the Corpus Christi chapel, the windows in the chancel already being filled with Wailes glass of 1859 and 1860. The fine eagle lectern is by Watts & Co. There is other late glass of lesser quality: the W windows of 1880 and 1889 are by W.G. Taylor and the debased Arts and Crafts-style single light in the S aisle is by Edward Payne of Stroud, 1976. There are other notable contents in the church. The lifesize early 14C statue of a female saint on the E wall of the Corpus Christi chapel is virtually complete and of high quality. Below is a truncated late 14C military effigy under an ornate architectural canopy containing the only original 14C window in the chapel. Between the chapel and the chancel is the 1506 tomb to Sir David Phillips under a large canopy and with an integral W doorway. There is also a parish library started by the eye surgeon Richard Banister (c 1570–1626) and later supplemented. The earliest books are early 16C with fine stamped bindings.

St. Mary's is the Stamford church that today represents the Catholic tradition within the Church of England and its interior and fittings all suggest this. Catholicism was introduced in 1890 by an aristocratic young incumbent of the Mildmay family and it was he who commissioned and largely paid for Sedding to carry out his restoration.

Chapel of Browne's Hospital, Broad Street. The chapel attached to the almshouse founded by William Browne in 1483 has some first-class contents, despite the severe restoration of the hospital by James Fowler of Louth in 1870. The glass, which can be dated to 1475, is of the very highest quality, and garment borders and haloes have holes drilled in them for the insertion of deep coloured glass to give the impression of jewels. The woodwork, the screen and the stalls, is also original and of good quality. The screen is typically Lincolnshire and the stalls have misericords.

Stow, St. Mary. One of the great pre-Conquest churches in England, it is a large unaisled cruciform building of the 11C and 12C. Apart from the Victorian stair turret and small vestry on the N side, and the lengthening of the latter in c 1984, the structure has remained virtually unchanged for 800 years.

The first impression is of a Norman church and the large chancel and nave have the typical flat buttresses, round-headed windows and doorways of the period. There are some incongruities, however: the tower is wider than the chancel, nave or transepts and this is a most un-Norman characteristic. The nave and chancel are not bonded into the crossing, also suggesting the latter is earlier. The other obvious feature is that the transepts were not built in a single phase. On the S side, for example, a slight change in colour and material (about halfway up the 13C window) and the eroded lower quoins with some signs of fire damage, show a change in building programme. The tall narrow window is a part of the later phase and the similarity between the palmette decoration of its hood and that above the W crossing arch suggests they are contemporary.

Inside, the church appears severe, a feeling emphasised by the lack of aisles and the light they bring, and the height of the nave. This increases the impact of the crossing which dominates the interior. A tall round arch, 35ft high and 14ft wide, faces into the nave and is matched by three identical ones facing into the transepts and chancel. This purity of form is tempered by the presence of massive polygonal piers and their four pointed arches above. These were inserted in the 15C to support the present Perpendicular tower but left the earlier work undisturbed. The arches themselves are supported by jambs that are no more than pieces of walling with dressed stone on the soffits. They display an inner half-round column and an outer flat pilaster strip on each face. The pilasters do not reach the ground but spring from projecting corbels at the top of the plinth. Above they are stopped by chamfered imposts. The arches are round-headed, roughly square in section, but with a series of more sophisticated roll-mouldings. These contrast with the rubble infilling of the soffits. The W arch on the nave side has a hoodmould of palmette decoration similar in style to that on the small window in the S transept. The developed style of the arches, and the slight difference in scale, has led to the conclusion that they are later than the more primitive jambs, and for the reason given above the arches have been associated with the upper part of the transept. Correspondingly, the lower part is thought contemporary with the jambs of the crossing. The signs of fire damage on the lower parts provide the clue for the cause of remodelling.

There has been a long-running debate over the date of the crossing and transepts, the consensus until recently being that both were pre-Conquest. The difficulty has been associating the few known dated events with the structure. In 1965 Dr and Mrs H.M. Taylor concluded the lower parts of the transepts and crossing to be 10C and the upper, the work of Bishop Eadnoth I (1004–16). The nave, they felt, was the work of Remigius, c 1090, and the chancel 12C. The most recent work on Stow by Dr Richard Gem has revised this scheme. On architectural grounds he sees the crossing arches as Romanesque and not before the last quarter of the 11C. He describes the crossing below the arches as proto-Romanesque, seeing some influence there in the use of half-round columns alongside the more traditional rectangular pilaster. An equal height, equal width crossing was also an important feature of a large Romanesque church with transepts. Equally, though, the Stow crossing is still very pre-Conquest. It suggests the fairly late date of c 1050 and fits neatly with the period of a known endowment by Earl Leofric of Mercia. If Leofric did build the transepts and crossing, it is almost certain he was fitting them into a pre-existing building. Traces of an earlier nave and chancel were discovered during the 19C restoration and an archaeological excavation in 1984 revealed traces of perhaps more than one earlier building phase on the exterior of the present N wall. The presence of an original *in situ* doorway in the W wall of the N transept had previously hinted at such a possibility.

The revised dating scheme places both the present nave and chancel in the 12C. The nave is very plain with flat buttresses, small round-headed windows set at a high level and three doorways, two (W and S) ornate with multiple orders but restored, and the N more simple. Its interior if anything is even more simple and austere. The chancel is divided externally into three bays by flat buttresses and only a hint of what is inside is given by the two levels of windows: the lower with decoration and colonnettes, the upper smaller and plain. The interior is divided into the same three bays, but here they are separated by composite wall shafts supporting a vault. The elevation of each bay is tripartite with blank arcading below, and the upper parts occupied by the two levels of windows. The chancel owes much of its present appearance to a thorough restoration in 1850–52 by J.L. Pearson. The E wall is totally his, where he replaced a large late 13C E window with his own 'Norman' work. Similarly, the vault is completely 19C, but the Rector, George Atkinson, an antiquary and moving force behind the restoration, showed convincingly that the chancel was originally vaulted. Pearson's work of 1864 in the nave and transepts was more conservative, with the exception of the removal of the large Perpendicular W window. As with the chancel, it included raising roof pitches. One bonus was the removal of an inserted stone belfry stair which obscured the whole of the N side of the nave crossing; another was leaving the remainder of the post-Norman windows untouched.

Some contents of the church are worthy of note. Recently an important graffito of an early Scandinavian longship was recognised on the N face of the SE crossing pier, that is, the earliest part of the church. It is badly worn. Two slabs with late pre-Conquest interlace carving, long thought lost, were rediscovered in 1979 on the Rood stair. Other medieval contents include the 13C font with small carvings on the bowl and base, the remains of a late 12C or early 13C wall painting of St. Thomas Becket in a recess in the E wall of the N transept, and two 13C memorial slabs to females in the chancel with recessed heads in roundels. There are also 15C brackets on the E walls of the N and S transepts with carved figures, which are, respectively, musicians playing a double auloc and a crumhorn, and three heads. Woodwork includes parts of the medieval screen dado incorporated into the chancel stalls, late medieval benches in the nave and a 17C pulpit. Above the altar there is a recent head of Christ by Andrzej Kuhn of Freiston Shore.

NORTHAMPTONSHIRE

Northamptonshire is one of the great counties for churches. It lies within the Diocese of Peterborough but its churches in the extreme SW tip are nearer eight other cathedrals than their own. Scenically it has little to offer, but in building materials it is richly endowed. There is fine limestone from the Lincolnshire series, which was quarried at a number of famous medieval sites, including Weldon, King's Cliffe and Barnack. Also, from the NE come Collyweston slates, not slates in the true sense of the word but platy calcareous sandstone or sandy limestone, which splits to provide a most lovely roofing material. After the limestone the dominant building stone is Northampton Sand, an iron-bearing rock varying from a pale, honey colour to dark brown. There are fine churches everywhere but the greatest concentration is on either side of the River Nene as it glides gently NE from the county town.

This is a very important county for pre-Conquest churches. There are two particularly famous monuments, Brixworth and Earls Barton, both a short distance from Northampton and fully described in the gazetteer. Brigstock is the third important pre-Conquest building. The work is of two phases, the earlier being the lower part of the W tower and the nave. Later the tower was heightened and the semicircular stair turret added (just as at Brixworth). At Brigstock characteristic massive pre-Conquest dressings can be seen to advantage. Nearby at Geddington (famous for its beautiful and well-preserved Eleanor cross) is work of very different character—the survival of parts of the nave and the attractive decoration on its former external N wall of blind triangular-headed arcading, formed out of undressed stones.

Northamptonshire is not a county for major Norman work. The exceptions are both in Northampton itself—the churches of St. Peter and Holy Sepulchre. The latter is the earlier and is the best preserved of the English round churches. Its impressive rotunda with eight huge circular piers and surrounding aisle form the core of the early 12C building. St. Peter's is a long, aisled structure of the mid-12C which preserves its clerestory and internal carving of exceptional quality. Good 12C work survives at Earls Barton, notably a S doorway with beakhead decoration. Other work of interest occurs at Rothwell (q.v.), King's Sutton (q.v.), Spratton (late 12C tower), Duddington (arcades), Pitsford (tympanum) and Grendon (arcades).

The 13C is something of a golden age in Northamptonshire. The crowning achievement is the W portal at Higham Ferrers, which has a pair of doorways divided by a trumeau and, around them, carving of the greatest richness. There is much other 13C work at this church too. This was a period when many churches were enlarged and/or lengthened. Raunds is a particularly good example of 13C development with its W end defined by an early tower with extraordinarily ornate decoration and, at the E end, a beautifully serene six-light Geometrical window. Polebrook is a good place to see a variety of 13C architecture and also shows interesting structural development. Nearby Warmington was wholly built between the late 12C and late 13C and, apart from its overall beauty, has one feature of particular fame—the original wooden vault over the nave. At Hannington there is a rare feature—a 13C two-naved plan with a three-bay arcade on the axis of the chancel arch. Cottingham has unusual capitals in the N arcade, decorated with whole figures arranged horizontally. St. Peter's, Brackley has a good W tower and S arcade and there is 13C evidence too at St. James's Church, also at Brackley. This was built as the chapel of the Hospital of St. James and St. John which was founded in the mid-12C.

It was in the 13C that the building began of some of the steeples for which this county is justly famous—a county of squires and spires as it is so often called. The squires still inhabit a great many of the numerous country houses. Near these there is usually a church and nearly half of these had or have a spire. Those started in the 13C are invariably of the broach type such as King's Cliffe or Raunds. They vary greatly in height and the treatment of their details. At Deene the late 13C spire is one of the earliest to experiment with a parapet. The 14C saw the refinement of the parapet spire. A particularly graceful idea was to throw flying buttresses from pinnacles at the corners of the tower to the spire (e.g. Higham Ferrers and Rushden). Further elaboration was obtained by adding ribs and crockets to the angles of the spire, a device that successfully enlivens the outlines of the very tallest needle-like spires such as Higham Ferrers, Kettering or Oundle. But the supreme Northamptonshire spire is the late 14C example at King's Sutton, where all the possible devices are brought together in a delicate, harmonious whole. In the 15C an interesting and very beautiful method was adopted at Lowick and Fotheringhay to finish off a tower, namely the addition of an octagon, a considerable improvement on the strange, idiosyncratic double octagon of c 1380 at Irthlingborough.

There is good early 14C work in Northamptonshire. From that time there are some dated examples. At Harlestone Richard de Het rebuilt the chancel in 1320 and the rest was rebuilt in 1325. In the chancel at Geddington a rare inscription in Lombardic lettering tells of the paving of the chancel by William Glover, who died in 1369, and the building of the S chapel by Robert Launcelyn. At Higham Ferrers there are ambitious windows with that most characteristic feature of the early 14C—Reticulated tracery. For freer Decorated turn to Oundle or the chancel at Cotterstock which was built for a college of a provost and 12 chaplains established in 1337 to pray for the soul of Queen Isabella. A curious local feature, also found across the border in SW Leicestershire, is the use of double-chamfered arches without capitals (e.g. Stanford-on-Avon). The most striking feature from the late 14C is the use of strainer arches across the naves at Finedon and Rushden, and between the N aisle and chapel at Easton Maudit. The transition between Decorated and Perpendicular can be studied in the tower at Oundle, where ogees occur in the windows but the whole has strong vertical accents. There was generally less activity in the second half of the 14C than in the 13C and early 14C, a story that is repeated over most of the Midlands. There were, of course, many schemes which altered the faces of Northamptonshire's churches, notably the addition of clerestories and battlements. The finest tower in the county and beyond is Perpendicular and is found at Titchmarsh, a beautifully proportioned structure in four stages and with careful detailing. Several family chapels were added late in the period, such as the Griffin chapel at Braybrooke in the early 16C, the Chambre chapel at Spratton of 1505 and the Spencer chapel at Great Brington before 1522. The three major Perpendicular buildings are Fotheringhay, Lowick and Whiston, built shortly before 1534.

Northamptonshire has some interesting examples of church building in the 17C and 18C. The chapel at Steane (built in 1620 by Sir Thomas Crewe) has a full set of 18C woodwork in the nave and a mausoleum that contains the fine Crewe monuments. The chapel on the S side of the chancel at Apethorpe is a year later and is in a simplified Perpendicular style and houses the enormous and extra- ordinary monument to Sir Anthony Mildmay (died 1617). The chapel on the N side of Kelmarsh has interesting work of 1638–39, including a strange E window with circles and lozenges and swirly Carolean decoration in the parapet. The 17C story is more or less completed by Lamport with its plaster ceilings and Isham monuments, and by the expensive remodelling of All Saints', Northampton. Built 1723–25 is the almost factory-looking Aynho and 30 years later the proud civic church in Daventry. East Carlton is a lovely and careful example of Gothic Revival from 1788.

Although the towns of Northamptonshire grew in the 19C there was no major need for new Anglican churches except in North- ampton itself. Here the best new church is St. Matthew's of 1891–93 by the local architect, M.H. Holding. Further N at Kelmarsh is the most lavish High Victorian scheme of all, by J.K. Colling in 1874. Sir Gilbert Scott's remodelling of Ashley in the 1860s and the decoration of the chancel by Clayton & Bell are more subdued but still of interest. Middleton Cheney is to be visited for its Morris & Co. glass. But the real masterpiece of both the 19C and 20C is Sir Ninian Comper's glorious St. Mary's, Wellingborough.

Nonconformity was strong in the 18C and many chapels survive from that time. The earliest surviving building is the former Friends' Meeting House at Finedon of 1690 (now a funeral parlour). Only fractionally later, in 1695, is the core of the Congregational Castle Hill Meeting House in Northampton where Philip Doddridge, the important Nonconformist divine and hymn-writer, was pastor from 1730 till his death in 1751. There are early Baptist chapels at Irthlingborough (c 1723), Roade (1736–37) and Burton Latimer (1744). Architecturally, the United Reformed Church of 1874–75 in High Street, Wellingborough is highly notable, being planned as an ovoid shape with the pulpit at the narrow end.

Among church furnishings and fittings several interesting Norman fonts have survived. West Haddon and Braybrooke have figure sculpture (the latter including a mermaid, the former Biblical scenes). The font at Crick stands on three kneeling figures but the most interesting of all is at Little Billing, an early font with an unfinished Latin inscription. Stained glass is best seen at Stanford-on-Avon and figures from a 14C Jesse tree occur at Lowick. Wall paintings at Ashby St. Ledgers and Croughton are of interest. Brixworth houses a rare object, a medieval stone reliquary. Northamptonshire has two of the eight vamping horns said to exist in England. These 18C or early 19C horns were used, it seems, to amplify the voice of one of the singers and set the tune for hymns in the days of the old choir bands. One is at Harrington; the other, from Braybrooke, is in Market Harborough Museum (Leics.) . Two 20C masterpieces are housed at St. Matthew's, Northampton: Henry Moore's Madonna of 1944 and Graham Sutherland's Crucifixion, unveiled two years later.

Northamptonshire is particularly rich in monuments as might be expected in a county with so many prosperous country houses. At several churches one can see a sequence of monuments to a family spanning 300 or 400 years. Examples in the gazetteer entries are Great Brington and Stanford-on-Avon. Other churches in the gazetteer which are noteworthy for their monuments are Higham Ferrers, Cottesbrooke, and Lowick. In addition, notable series of monuments can be seen at Fawsley to the Knightley family,

Charwelton with three brasses and monuments to the Andrewes family, Dodford with its N aisle full of monuments and brasses chiefly to the Cressys and de Keyneses, Deene where the Brudenells are commemorated, Castle Ashby with Compton monuments, and Easton Neston where it is the Fermor family. At Warkton the chancel was specifically built shortly after 1749 to house monuments to the Montagus. These include two magnificent ones by L.F. Roubiliac to John, Duke of Montagu (died 1752) and Mary, Duchess of Montagu (died 1753). Also here is Mary, Duchess of Montagu (died 1775), designed by Robert Adam and sculpted by P.M. van Gelder. Nearby is Weekley, which houses monuments to Montagus of the 15C and 16C. Another monument of the highest quality is to Sir Edward Ward (died 1714) by J.M. Rysbrack at Stoke Doyle.

Ashby St. Ledgers, *The Blessed Virgin and St. Leodegarius.* Apart from its dedication, the church is important for its mural paintings, old furnishings and unrestored interior. The lack of Victorian restoration may have saved the murals, which were not discovered till 1927. Unfortunately, they are very worn but much can still be discerned of the 18 panels depicting the Passion, from the Entry into Jerusalem to the Resurrection, over and adjacent to the chancel arch. On the S wall of the S aisle, hard to see and tucked behind the organ, is the earliest painting (c 1320) depicting the scourging of St. Margaret. On the N wall of the N aisle is a large St. Christopher and to the left of the tower arch the grim figure of Death. The Rood screen is a rich, vaulted one and retains its medieval doors. Many Perpendicular traceried benches survive, as do two large Jacobean pews in front of the screen. On the N side of the nave is a three-decker Jacobean pulpit with tester. 18C box-pews in the aisles and a musicians' pew at the W end of the S aisle remain. The communion rails are 17C. There is a good series of monuments including a particularly fine brass set in the sanctuary to William Catesby. He was a favourite of King Richard III, was captured at the Battle of Bosworth (1485) and executed. He was mentioned by Shakespeare and is recalled as the first character in the doggerel: 'The Cat, the Rat, and Lovel our dog/ Rule all England under a hog'. His wife Margaret (died 1494), their three sons and two daughters, and shields are also represented. In the chancel a brass set in an enormous block of stone is to Sir William Catesby (died 1471) and his two wives; only the upper part of Sir William's shrouded figure remains. In the S aisle is a brass to Thomas Stokes (died 1416) and his wife Elena; below them are their four sons and 12 daughters. The fine wall monuments in the chancel are to the l'Ansons (who came to Ashby in 1612) and the Ashleys (who came in 1703).

St. Leodegarius (or St. Ledger) became Bishop of Autun in France in 663. He was martyred in 679. Another famous member of the Catesby family was Robert, who was one of the leaders of the Gunpowder Plot.

Ashley, *St. Mary.* In the 1860s Sir Gilbert Scott virtually rebuilt this church for the Reverend R.T. Pulteney and provided it with a richness of painted decoration by Clayton & Bell. The church is broadly faithful to its medieval predecessor. The medieval fragments, such as the windows on the N, indicate that the medieval building dated largely from c 1300.

The aisled nave is fairly routine but the polished granite shafts of the chancel arch prepare one for the glittering chancel interior, an interior that was the aim of so many mid-19C restorers but one which so often eluded them due to cost. The floor sparkles with tiles and stones and the walls are covered with paintings by Clayton & Bell— Apostles and St. Paul on the N, Old Testament figures on the S. Over the E window Christ sits in majesty surrounded by adoring angels. The paintings were restored in 1973 by Peter Larkworthy (great-grandson of Alfred Bell). The chancel windows are also the work of Clayton & Bell. Perhaps the most distinguished single item is the font with a bowl of a single piece of variegated pink marble. Its predecessor, an 18C baluster, stands in the chancel, its Classical simplicity ill at ease among such Victorian riches.

Aynho, *St. Michael*. Were it not for the 14C tower, this extraordinary building could be mistaken as an annexe to the adjacent house. It was rebuilt in 1723–25 by Edward Wing, carpenter and master builder of Aynho, in a style more associated with secular buildings of the time. The sides have virtually identical symmetrical façades of seven bays. In the centre is a doorway and, above, a large round-headed window breaking into a pediment. The windows are plain round-headed ones on the ground floor and segment-headed above. The tower is a bold Decorated piece. The interior is both a surprise and a disappointment. A surprise because the two storeys of windows outside lead one to expect galleries round three sides but there is only one at the W end (it was always so). A disappointment because the interior is so Spartan. The Victorian glass (E window by Thomas Willement, 1857) is out of keeping too. Furthermore, necessary work on the roof and ceiling in the 1960s by G. Forsyth Lawson & Partners, presumably on a tight budget, has left a ceiling which would be more at home in a domestic kitchen. Fortunately, the box-pews and wooden W gallery remain. At the W end is an early 17C wooden carving of the Crucifixion: it was originally given by King Louis XIII of France to the Sisters of the Hospital of St. Louis for their chapel and was presented to Aynho Church in memory of the last squire in the middle of this century.

Brixworth, *All Saints*. The age, the size and the grandeur of All Saints' distinguish it as one of the most important churches in the country. It is the largest pre-Conquest building still standing and was relatively little altered by later medieval changes. The original church had a W narthex, a nave entered from the W with lateral *porticus*, a choir and a sanctuary. At the E end there is the remarkable feature of a ring-crypt in the shape of a stilted semicircle, which may be an original feature. By the 12C the *porticus* seem to have gone, and a tower and stair turret had been raised in place of the narthex and the sanctuary was now polygonal. In c 1300 a S chapel was added and early in the 14C a new belfry was built and a spire was added. In the 19C the church was the object of much investigation by C.F. Watkins, Vicar from 1832 to 1873. He was responsible for a major restoration in 1864–66 under the architects William Slater and William Smith, when the main task was the dismantling of a later medieval sanctuary and its replacement by a polygonal one on the lines suggested by the two surviving bays on the NW side. The reason behind the initial establishment of such a major church was monastic; in fact, it was probably a royal foundation. The idea has been put forward that Brixworth was the site of *Clofesho*, a royal monastery where ecclesiastical councils were held in the 8C and 9C. The documentary evidence is limited but it seems that Brixworth was one of several monasteries founded from the abbey of Medeshamstede (Peterborough) some time after 675. The site seems to have had special importance thanks to its place as a minster church, its probable royal foundation (which ensured its prosperity), and the presence of relics that received veneration (hence the ring-crypt). It is unclear whether the monastery survived the Danish invasions but the church certainly experienced major alterations immediately before or about the time of the Norman Conquest that may be associated with a change in use.

The interior of All Saints' showing arches of Roman bricks which once led into side chapels or porticus

The most recent and intensive programme of investigation has been conducted by the Brixworth Archaeological Research Committee, which was set up in 1972 as a multi-disciplinary group. Excavations in 1981–82 suggest that the nave, *porticus* and narthex were planned together and that they were probably constructed in the first half of the 8C. Probably the choir is of the same scheme. What is not clear, however, is what function the *porticus* served. They certainly were connected to the nave through four big arches on either side but whether they were all connected to one another in an aisle fashion is not known. What is particularly intriguing is from where the first builders got their stone. The lowest parts of the nave and tower, up to c 10–12ft, have various materials which are definitely not local but which were used in some quantity. They include igneous rocks such as pink granite and dark grey slate which have come, ultimately, from the Charnwood area of Leicestershire. There is an estimated 350 cubic yds of these. Then there are limestones (some 180 cubic yds), probably from Towcester to the S. Another crucial imported material is Roman brick. It seems that the igneous rocks and the lowest occurrences of the brick were salvaged from Roman buildings in Leicester—assuming that they had not already been brought to an earlier building in the vicinity. In either case it is an extraordinary thing to move large quantities of heavy materials so far (Leicester is c 25 miles away, Towcester 15) and it seems that the local quarrying industry was very rudimentary. It is very likely that the stone supply, at least for the earliest phases, could have been given by local rulers.

The main features of the exterior can readily be seen from the S. The nave has four bays with three clerestory windows above, set over the spandrels of the arches. These arches once led into *porticus* but are now blocked. The present blocking is 19C, a product of Watkins's restoration. The treatment of the arch-heads is one of the most distinctive features at Brixworth. They have two flat orders defined by semicircular bands of Roman brick within which further bricks are set, not in a true radial pattern but usually parallel to one another. The effect is often very awkward. Where large areas of stone have replaced brick, these are 1860s infillings of later medieval window embrasures. The clerestory is set back a little from the wall below and the later medieval parapet comes down some way below the tops of the windows. At present (1987) the dating evidence for the clerestory seems to point towards the second phase of work though it is hard to believe it was not part of the primary design (though some rebuilding may have taken place). Over the nave and choir is a continuous high-pitched roof. This represents a heightening during the 1860s restoration to something like its pre-Conquest pitch. Before the 1860s the Verdun chapel had a further W bay. In the W bay of the nave there is a late Norman doorway with a roll-moulded head. At the base of the S face of the tower is a small doorway which linked two compartments of the narthex. There is also the trace of a N–S wall from the narthex. This seems to have had five ground-floor compartments in total but was largely removed when the tower was built and the stair turret added, probably in the 11C. As with so much of the fabric at Brixworth, secondhand materials have been used— see the scatter of pink, fire-damaged stones, for example. Inside, the stairway is covered by a helical barrel-vault. N of the tower a blocked doorway and a stub of wall from the narthex mirror those on the S, while the N elevation of the nave is similar to the S. Note, however, a band of fire-damaged stones some 2ft high above the offset of the clerestory, no doubt caused by a fire of the roof above the *porticus*. Further E is a small doorway, also blocked, connecting a *porticus* to the choir. The E part of the choir is of regular masonry from a rebuild of c 1842.

Moving to the sanctuary, one can immediately see the ring-crypt and steps that led down to it from a doorway in the choir (there is a similar one on the S side). It was tunnel-vaulted and the springing began above the stringcourse three bricks thick that runs round the crypt. The buttresses in the crypt itself date from 1865. The only part of the pre-Conquest sanctuary that survives comprises the two NW bays which are demarcated by buttresses and where one window survives. Note that there are large quantities of tufa—a local rock full of holes and which is concentrated in the 'late' parts. Though the sanctuary is polygonal outside, it is not clear what shape it took inside, though the very limited evidence seems to suggest it was semicircular. A bigger puzzle is how the crypt functioned. It must have been intended for people to view relics but, tragically, the wall below the E bay of the sanctuary has been rebuilt and the evidence is thus obscured. The 19C records are tantalisingly insufficient but it seems there was some sort of access or, at least, means of viewing into the area under the sanctuary.

The scale of the interior is most impressive. The nave is no less than 30ft wide and the whole length of the church (excluding the tower) is 110ft. Beyond the nave is a very wide chancel arch. This is 14C but previously there was a triple-arched arrangement, as at Bradwell (Essex) and Reculver (Kent). Traces of high outer arches can be seen although they are cut into by the present chancel arch. Mr D. Parsons suggests that the desire to make the arch as wide as possible may be linked to the building of the later medieval 'sanctuary' (removed in the 1860s). Perhaps this served as the chancel, and the combined pre-Conquest nave and choir served as an enlarged nave. Roman bricks occur again in the head of the fine arch to the sanctuary. Either side of this are two small windows in the E wall of the choir. At floor level are the remains of the doorways to the ring-crypt. In the W wall of the nave is a doorway into the tower (or former narthex) and above it is a doorway that would have led from the narthex to a gallery. Now this has been cut into by a beautiful triple opening. This has bulbous mid-wall balusters. The Verdun chapel has destroyed much of the S side of the chancel but above its E arch are the remains of an early window. In the chapel is a wall recess containing a cross-legged knight, presumed to be Sir John de Verdun.

Near the pulpit in an iron cage is a very rare object, a medieval reliquary made of stone and dating from c 1300. It is in two pieces and is decorated with a crocketed, gabled design. When it was discovered built into a wall of the Verdun chapel it was found to contain a human throat bone. The suggestion has been made that this belonged to St. Boniface, an Englishman who became the Apostle of Germany and who was murdered in 754. He is a rare saint in England but it is significant that his feast day, June 5th, and the two days either side are those granted to Brixworth in 1253 for a fair. There was also a guild of St. Boniface attached to the church. Mr. D. Parsons suggests that this veneration could be explained by the fact that he is known to have influenced decisions of the synod of Clofesho (see above) in 747 and that the veneration of his relic may have been the motive for building the ring-crypt. Also near the pulpit is part of a late pre-Conquest cross. A further and very fine sculptured fragment with an eagle is near the S doorway (seen from the inner porch). A 15C screen with one-light divisions stands (not *in situ*) between the choir and the Verdun chapel.

I am most grateful to Mr. D. Parsons for much advice on this entry.

Cottesbrooke, *All Saints*. All Saints' is a large, long church and has the rare distinction of being all of one period, probably just before 1300. There are extensive 18C furnishings and a good array of monuments. There are no aisles, but it was cruciform, though the N transept has been demolished. During the 18C there was still a slab in the chancel marking the tomb of William de Botevylan, Rector from 1285 to 1325; and on each face of the W tower parapet the arms of his family still appear. It seems likely that William or his father were the main benefactors of the building of the church.

The tower has fine pairs of two-light belfry windows with Y-tracery and circular mullions. The twinning motif is an early example in this area, which was to recur. The W window is Geometrical and, unlike the large ones elsewhere, does retain its cusping. The scar from the removal of the N transept can clearly be seen. The church is entered through an 18C porch.

The interior retains its 18C three-decker pulpit and high box-pews. There are stairs to a private pew in the S transept, which is complete with a fireplace. The nave is ceiled and its coving has mock plasterwork. The chancel and transept ceilings were removed in 1959–60 at Lord Mottistone's restoration to reveal Perpendicular tiebeam roofs. The reredos and communion table are also Mottistone's and are set part-way down the chancel to form a vestry behind. There is a squint from the transept to the chancel and a Rood loft opening set extremely high up. The 18C movable wooden font and cover have out-survived a stone font of 1853 by G.E. Street, which has been transferred to Uppingham in Rutland.

In the S transept is the monument of John Rede (died 1604), of alabaster and marble. He lies between two columns with ten children kneeling on the ground. The inscription is under a shallow arch. Then comes Sir John Langham (died 1671) and his wife. He was a London merchant and the monument was made in 1676 by Thomas Cartwright senior for £290. In the chancel is the monument to Mrs. Mary Langham (died 1773), by J.F. Moore. Sir James Langham (died 1795) is commemorated by a lengthy inscription and by a lady standing beside an urn. In the nave is a free-standing monument of unusual design to Sir William Langham (died 1812), erected in 1815.

Daventry, *Holy Cross.* Since the 1960s Daventry has expanded considerably as an overspill town for Birmingham, but the church and many of the elegant buildings tell of late 18C prosperity. Standing at the SE corner of the market place, Holy Cross Church was rebuilt in 1752–58 by David Hiorne (died 1758) and is one of relatively few town churches dating from that time. It has a distinguished façade and an internal elegance worthy of a London church.

The exterior is built of Northampton Sand and has two storeys, which reflect the internal galleries. The spacious central bay of the principal façade has a pedimented porch put up in 1951 but which is entirely in keeping with the character of the building. Above is a lunette window and a pedimented gable. Then the tower and spire begin, first a rusticated stage and then the belfry with large round-arched windows and flat pilasters. The obelisk spire grows out of an octagonal clock stage. An openwork parapet runs all around the church. The nave has six bays. On the S the bays are divided by broad flat pilasters. The ground floor is rusticated. The N side is very much plainer.

Internally, the nave has tall Tuscan columns which carry on up without any reference to the galleries. They are capped by an awkward arrangement of an entablature and a big projection below the springing of the plaster groin-vault. The chancel continues beyond with two tunnel-vaulted bays and terminates with a Venetian window (glass by William Wailes), set high up. The reredos is a fine piece with prominent Doric pilasters but with inappropriate modern paintings. The pulpit is original and has lovely marquetry stars. The interior was restored to its original splendour by S.E. Dykes Bower in 1961.

Earls Barton, *All Saints.* The W tower at Earls Barton is justly famous as the most highly decorated pre-Conquest tower in the country. It stands on a rise above the town and immediately S of a motte belonging to a Norman castle. The extreme proximity of the two have suggested that the earthworks may be associated with the pre-Conquest church, but this is unproven. Though overshadowed by the earlier work, the Norman contributions are important too.

The tower dates from the later 10C and seems to have served as a turriform nave. Clearly there was no provision for a nave to the W, and the fact that the long-and-short work is fully developed at all four corners indicates that a structure to the E would have been narrower. The tower is 60ft high and has a 15C parapet. It is of four stages, each set back a little from, and rather lower than, the one below. Between the raised decoration the walls are stuccoed, no doubt as in pre-Conquest times. The detail of each stage varies but the common element is the use of vertical pilaster strips in decorative schemes that may owe something to the appearance of walls of timbered buildings. There is no regularity to the fenestration except in the top stage, where each face has five tall, narrow openings divided by bulbous balusters. In the ground stage there is a W doorway, characterised by massive masonry.

The head of the doorway is made of only two stones. Surrounding it are two raised, concentric bands. Above are the remains of a two-light window. Another two-light window survives on the S; its heads

10th CENTURY TOWER ♦ ALL SAINTS'
EARLS BARTON ♦ Northamptonshire.

are cut from single stones carved with small crosses and the outer face is divided by turned balusters. In each opening there is a mid-wall slab pierced by a cross. To the left is a raised circle bearing another cross. Above this window, in the second stage of the S face, is a completely preserved doorway which would have been approached by a ladder from outside. A similar doorway on the W has been blocked. In the third stage of each face there is a triangular-headed window.

The Norman remodelling is represented outside by the reset S doorway of c 1180. Its head has beakhead in the inner order and zigzag in the outer. The Norman church seems to have been aisleless as the straight joints at all the corners of the nave, except the NW, reveal. The E end of the chancel with its three lancet windows is 13C. The aisles have Reticulated windows. The 15C provided some chancel windows and the clerestory.

There is a significant amount of Norman work internally. The earliest is the chancel arch responds, with their blocky capitals. The arch above is a 14C remodelling. The Normans were also responsible for cutting a larger arch in the tower and, as at the chancel entrance, the arch above was rebuilt with a pointed form, though reusing a profusion of billet ornament. The most lavish work was in the chancel where the N and S walls were supplied with blank arches covered with zigzag. (Similar wall arcading occurs at King's Sutton.) The graduated sedilia are in the same design but they have been relocated in the 13C extension. Aisles were added in the late 13C or in c 1300, the N arcade being slightly the earlier. In 1868–70, at the restoration by E.F. Law of Northampton, the arcades were rebuilt, as was the porch.

The much restored 15C Rood screen is vaulted; it was painted in 1935 by Henry Bird. The hexagonal Jacobean pulpit has very rich panels. Beside the tower arch is a brass to John Muscote (died 1512) and his wife Alice.

East Carlton, *St. Peter.* Commanding a fine view over the Welland Valley, St. Peter's is a notable case of faithful Gothic in the late 18C. It was completed in 1788 to the designs of John Wing the Younger, who had built the even more ambitious King's Norton Church in Leicestershire (q.v.). The W tower is gracefully proportioned and has a general similarity to several late medieval ones in E Leicestershire. Unlike King's Norton, there are 'transepts' at the E end, the S one a mortuary chapel for Wing's patrons, the Palmer family (note the skull-head stops on the E window), the N one a vestry. The windows have accurately detailed medieval tracery ranging from Geometrical to flowing. Note how the size of the masonry blocks diminishes with height. The interior retains its high box-pews either side of a wide alley which was no doubt filled with open benches for the poor. The two-decker pulpit has attractive marquetry in the IHS symbol. An unusual feature for an 18C church is the mock tower arch. In the chapel is an odd monument to Sir Geoffrey Palmer (died 1673) and his wife, attributed to Joshua Marshall. Their alabaster figures are dressed in shrouds and the couple stand expectantly looking upwards. On either side are tablets with long inscriptions and made to look like doors opened to reveal the figures. Another good monument is to Jeffrey Palmer (died 1661), 'the ornament of ye society and hopes of the age'. The stained glass in the four-light E window is by Clayton & Bell. The transepts have 17C heraldic stained glass.

Finedon, St. Mary. This is a tall, large church, complete with aisles and transepts, and strikingly built of dark Northampton Sand with contrasting limestone dressings. With the Vicarage of 1688 and the Hall it forms part of an important group of buildings. The church is the result of one campaign, starting in the early 14C. The most distinguished feature within is the strainer arch between the E pair of piers.

The big W tower, evidently, was started before the nave was finished as the very clear straight joints between them show. The whole building is embattled and has mainly tall, narrow Reticulated windows under ogee heads; unusually, the tracery has no cusping. The clerestory is also 14C and the hoods on the windows carry crockets. The five-light E window continues with the Reticulated motif, but has an awkward plain circle at the apex. The porch has two storeys, the upper housing a library of some 1000 theological books which was given by Sir John English Dolben in 1788 and dating from the late 15C. Access is by an external staircase of 1794. Under the E end and visible from outside is the vault of c 1710 of the Dolben family (see below), with the busts of Mary (died 1710) and Elizabeth (died 1736).

Inside, the beautiful strainer arch is formed by two curves which meet in the middle. (There are parallels at Easton Maudit and Rushden.) It takes the thrust of the E walls of the transepts. The arcades have three wide bays plus the transepts. On the N are conventional quatrefoil piers; the two on the S were rebuilt in 1957. At the entrance to the chancel is an open stone screen. It was rebuilt in 1858 and a small, worn fragment survives at the N end. In the chancel the windows are shafted and it is clear that vaulting was originally intended. A further change of mind in the early campaign is shown by the interference with the priest's door by the window above. The once fine sedilia have also been interfered with. Apart from the chancel, the church retains its simple, old cambered tiebeam roofs. There was a major restoration in 1858 by William Slater. The Ten Commandments painted prominently over the chancel arch probably date from this time.

Of the furnishings, the most conspicuous and important is the organ in the W gallery. It was built in 1717 by Christopher Shrider and was presented by Sir John Dolben, Vicar and later Lord of the Manor. The first organist was James Kent, who later became organist at Winchester Cathedral. The font seems to be Norman but was recut with scenes in later medieval times: the Baptism of Christ (W) and the Annunciation (E) are still discernible.

In the N aisle is a copy of 1803 of a painting by Peter Lely, showing John Fell (Bishop of Oxford), Richard Allestry and John Dolben (Archbishop of York), who, during the Commonwealth, maintained the sacraments at Oxford.

Fotheringhay, St. Mary and All Saints. Fotheringhay is famous for two things—the castle (of which only the earthworks remain) where Mary, Queen of Scots was beheaded in 1587, and the grand 15C church. This is the parochial part of a once much vaster structure which housed an important college of priests. Formerly in the castle, the college was transferred to the church by Edward, Duke of York, under letters patent of 1411. He died at Agincourt in 1415 and was buried in the church that was then under construction. The college was dissolved in 1548 and passed to John Dudley, Duke of Northumberland, who immediately started to dismantle the choir. The parochial part was built under a contract between the agents of Richard, Duke of York and William Horwode, freemason of Fotheringhay, dated 1434. Horwode was to be paid £300 if the work was satisfactory. Had it proved otherwise he was to go to prison (!).

Apart from minor details the church is as specified in the contract, which stipulated that it was to resemble the choir. At the W end is a tower embraced by the aisles and topped by an octagonal lantern (cf. Lowick and Irthlingborough). The church has large windows and flying buttresses. The height and scale of the exterior are mirrored by the spacious, light interior. There are five bays with piers of complicated section. The E bay is filled by walling that separated the altars in the aisles from those on either side of the middle door of the pulpitum. The church was complete by c 1441 except for the vaulting of the tower: the date obscurely carved on the NW springer is probably 1529. The Perpendicular pulpit has a 17C tester. At the E end of the nave are two identical chaste, non-figurative monuments erected in 1573 by Queen Elizabeth I to commemorate Edward and Richard, Dukes of York, whose previous monuments had been destroyed when the choir was lost.

Great Brington, St. Mary. The importance of Great Brington is in the N chapel and its monuments of the Spencer family, whose members have resided at nearby Althorp since 1508. The chapel, completed in 1514, is a good example of late Perpendicular church building. The rest of the church is of various dates, stretching back to the 13C. A later connection of interest is that an ancestor of George Washington, first President of the U.S.A., is buried here.

Sir Robert Spencer (1570–1627) was ennobled as Baron Spencer of Wormleighton in 1603. The third Baron was created first Earl of Sunderland in 1643. The sixth Earl became the third Duke of Marlborough in 1733 under a special remainder and moved to Blenheim. Althorp passed to his younger brother, John, whose son, also called John (1734–83), was created first Earl Spencer in 1765. The present Earl Spencer is his direct descendant. All these generations of Spencers have left a spectacular array of monuments in the Spencer chapel at Great Brington. The monuments are set behind the original iron railings and many retain their original colour. The five earliest were restored in 1951–52. The three largest are tomb-chests with canopies and lie under the arcade between the chancel and chapel. The E one is to the first Spencer, Sir John (died 1522), and his wife Isabella. They lie beneath a panelled four-centred arch at the apex of which is a lively angel holding the Spencer arms. In the central bay is Sir John (died 1586) and his wife Katherine; she lies beneath an extraordinarily large hood. She was the first cousin of Laurence Washington of Sulgrave, who was in turn the grandfather of Laurence and Robert Washington, who are buried in this church. The monument is by Jasper Hollemans of Burton-on-Trent. The W bay has the tomb of Robert, first Baron Spencer, whose monument, and that of his father (in the NE corner), were made in 1599, 28 years before his own death. His wife Margaret (died 1597) has an amazing heraldic coverlet over the lower part of her body. This monument, and that of Sir John (died 1599) and his wife Mary, are by Hollemans. The latter is very tall and the canopy is carried on four thin, square pillars. Like Katherine, Mary has a strange hood. William (died 1636) and his wife Penelope lie under a stately canopy supported on eight black Corinthian columns in the NW part of the chapel. It was built for Penelope in 1638 (29 years before her death) by Nicholas Stone, who received £600. In the SE corner is a strange symbolic monument by Stone's son, John. It is to Sir Edward (died 1655) and was put up in 1656. He rises out of a funerary urn in the act of resurrection. His right arm once held the sword of the Spirit and rests on the square pillar of the Word of God. His left hand holds a Bible on the column of Truth. Sir John (died 1783) has a large wall monument by Joseph Nollekens. His head is in profile on a medallion held by a female figure. The extension of 1846 contains the coffin plates from the vault below. The roof of this area follows the spirit of King Henry VII's chapel in Westminster Abbey. Stained glass paid for from the will of Sir John Spencer (1532) survives in the chancel SW window.

The Washington connection stems from c 1600 when Laurence Washington, the great-great-great-grandfather of the first President of the United States of America, settled with his younger brother, Robert, in Brington from Sulgrave. Robert, who farmed about 60 acres, became a churchwarden in 1601, died in 1622 and is buried with his wife Elizabeth in the central alley of the nave towards the E end. His tombstone bears two brasses, one with his arms, the other with an inscription. (For security, there are locked covers over the brasses.) Laurence (died 1616) lies on the N side of the chancel under a stone bearing the Washington arms impaled with those of his wife Margaret.

Higham Ferrers, St. Mary the Virgin. Higham Ferrers is perhaps the finest of many fine churches in the Nene valley. It has a splendid setting, not only because it lies in one of the more pleasant small towns in Northamptonshire, but also because it shares its spacious churchyard with two attractive 15C buildings—Archbishop Chichele's school and his Bede House (founded in 1428). The church itself has a singularly notable tower and spire, and an interior distinguished by what is effectively a double nave. There is a very fine collection of brasses. The grandeur of the church is more readily understood when one realises that Higham Ferrers was an important town in the Middle Ages.

This building had reached its present length by the middle of the 13C. The E window jambs remain from that time and the steeple was begun then, but the spire was not completed until 100 years later. It soars to 170ft and the spire, particularly, is a most ambitious design and one which may have served as an inspiration at Rushden. The W portal achieves a grandeur rare in parish churches. It has a diapered tunnel-vault and, on the inner face, a pair of segment-headed doorways divided by a trumeau. Round these doorways in the jambs and arches are half-figures. In the head of the main arch, separated by a trefoiled panel containing an image of the Virgin and Child, are two sets of roundels with carvings. On the N they are the Visitation, the Annunciation, the Adoration of the Magi, Christ among the doctors and Christ's baptism; on the S are the Crucifixion, the Vision of Zacharias, the three Maries at the Sepulchre and the Harrowing of Hell. The belfry windows have transoms, an unusual device in the 13C, but these may be additions of 1631–32. At that time the spire and much of the tower were rebuilt following collapse in 1631. The details may have been altered but the whole is faithful to the medieval spirit. The spire, ribbed and crocketed, rises behind a pierced parapet and is linked to the tower pinnacles by pierced flying buttresses. The elevations illustrate the next and very important phase—a remodelling in the second quarter of the 14C. This may have been the work of Henry, second Earl of Lancaster (died 1345) and/or Laurence St. Maur, Rector, 1298–1337. Into the S wall of the chancel were inserted tall windows with ogee heads and elongated Reticulated tracery. It seems likely that before the addition of the Perpendicular clerestory, the walls of the chancel rose above the level of those of the nave. Now the Perpendicular parapet runs without a break over both chancel and chapel. The W end shows how the two N aisles seem to have been part of the same scheme.

The internal appearance from the W end is dramatic, thanks to the scale of the early 14C additions. It would be even more so but for the organ loft of 1920, sited between the aisle and the Lady chapel, and the screenwork between the nave and chancel. There is no chancel arch and the 13C church probably had no such structural division. What survives of the 13C is the four-bay S arcade, fragments of stringcourse in the chancel (e.g. between the two arches on the N) and the shafted tower arch and wall above. The aisle is narrow and, presumably, would have been mirrored by one on the N. At that time the church would have appeared very long and relatively narrow. When expansion took place on the N, the inner arcade was built with a somewhat different rhythm to the one on the S—does it fossilise the earlier arrangements in which the wider W bay might represent the linking up of a pre-tower arcade to the W end of the tower? Curiously, the axis of the tower is displaced slightly S from that of the nave, seemingly to accommodate the small 13C archway on the N side. Was this to be a doorway to a stair? If so, it is rather a puzzle since the original 13C stair was in the SW angle. The E end of the Lady chapel was designed with a portioned-off vestry (cf. Rushden), against which the high altar was placed.

In the chancel is a double piscina and some 20 collegiate stalls all with misericords, including an angel holding the arms of Archbishop Chichele. The arms of the See of Canterbury are found on one of the supporters. There are a number of old screens including the tall Rood screen, of which the wings retain their original colouring. It now carries a Rood loft of 1920 by Sir Ninian Comper. In the W porch is a 12C pillar piscina (?) with fluted shaft and scenes from the four seasons. But the most outstanding feature is the number and quality of the brasses. Under the 14C arch between the chancel and N chapel is a table-tomb, which, on the evidence of the heraldry, was built in the time of the House of Lancaster (possibly Henry, second Earl). In medieval times it no doubt doubled as an Easter sepulchre. The brass of Laurence St. Maur (died 1337) was placed on the top. He is shown in a 5ft 4ins. figure of a priest in vestments, below a canopy populated by angels who hold his soul in a napkin below Christ in glory, and by St. Andrew, St. Peter, St. Paul and St. Thomas. Another superb brass is to Archbishop Chichele's brother (died 1425) and his wife (N chapel). Their figures are 4ft 3ins. long. Chichele's father, Thomas (died 1400) and his mother, Agnes, are marked by a floriated cross. N of the high altar is Richard Wylleys (died 1523?), Warden of the college at Higham Ferrers.

Archbishop Chichele was born here in 1362 and was ordained in 1392. He became Bishop of St. David's in 1408 and Archbishop of Canterbury in 1414. He founded All Souls College at Oxford in 1438. He did not neglect his native town and founded a college here, and refounded a school and a hospital. He died in 1443 and has a tomb in Canterbury Cathedral.

Irthlingborough, *St. Peter.* An extraordinary tower, some 100ft high, presides over an interesting and confused assembly of buildings.

There was a college here, established by John Pyel, the Lord of the Manor, under a licence of 1375. He died c 1380 but the work was continued by his widow Joan. The tower is capped by two octagonal stages, the upper having large, three-light, square-headed windows. Due to its dangerous condition the old tower was taken down in 1887 and was rebuilt fairly faithfully in 1888–93 by Talbot Brown & Fisher of Wellingborough. N of the tower are the remains of two rib-vaulted undercrofts. A room to the E of the tower leads to a porch on the W end of the church. This has aisles, transepts and chancel chapels. Although Norman pier bases can be detected at the foot of the S arcade piers, most of the building is the result of a continuous campaign from the mid-13C. The E window of five grouped lancets is typical of the late 13C. At this time or very slightly later is the peculiar, vast recess in the internal E wall of the N transept, never apparently intended to be cut through; it must have served as a canopy for an altar. Decorated windows were inserted in the W wall and the S transept. In the 15C the clerestory was added in both the nave and the chancel and traces of the old roofline can be seen in the masonry inside. The N chapel is probably early 16C and the work of Sir Thomas Cheyney, whose arms occur in the parapet. Below the S transept is a crypt, approached by steps in the thickness of the W wall. Eight stalls, one with a misericord, survive from the days of the college. In the S chapel the effigies of John and Joan Pyel lie on a table-tomb. At the E end of the chapel is a splendidly ornate, late Perpendicular, Purbeck marble tomb with a canopy over.

Kelmarsh, St. Denys. The importance of Kelmarsh is two-fold and in neither case is it medieval. First comes the unusual N chapel, remodelled in 1638–39. Its parapet has thick, swirling decoration in low relief and an obelisk pinnacle at the corner. Its E window is a very unusual 17C design of circles and lozenges.

The interior has some of the most lavish High Victorian decoration in the Midlands. The architect was J.K. Colling. R.C. Naylor, who had bought the manor in 1865, called him in in 1874 (cf. the work by Colling for Naylor at Hooton, Cheshire, 1858–62). The E window and those on the S of the nave are Colling's 14C designs. In the nave a new arcade with polished Aberdeen granite piers was built, and a fine hammerbeam roof was placed over it. But the richest treatment was reserved for the chancel, which glitters with colour. Naylor had brought back marbles from Rome and these are used on the floor and to face the walls. The upper parts of the walls have marble and mosaic and also figures of St. Denys, the Evangelists, and, on the E wall, St. Peter and St. Paul, all executed in Powell's glass mosaic. The decorative scheme is completed by a rich altar frontal by Morris & Co. and stained glass in the E window by Lavers, Barraud & Westlake, and the chancel S windows by W.M. Pepper.

There are a number of monuments of interest, the earliest being a headless brass to Morrys Osberne (1534) in the N chapel. Here there is the most ambitious recoloured monument to Sir John Hanbury (1639) and his wife Maria.

King's Sutton, St. Peter and St. Paul. This church has a wonderful spire, as fine as any in England. It rises from an already tall, Decorated tower to 198ft. The tower pinnacles are linked by flying buttresses to further, more substantial pinnacles at the base of the spire. The spire itself is ribbed and crocketed at the angles and has a lower tier of lucarnes with the most delicate tracery. The whole thing is beautifully proportioned and probably dates from the close of the 14C. Unusually, there is a large W porch. This is Perpendicular and is tierceron-vaulted. Much of the rest is Decorated, though a Norman corbel course on the chancel tells of earlier times. The Decorated E window of the S aisle is most spectacular: large and with most ingenious tracery. The S arcade is a curious piece and seems to be a remodelling in the early 14C: see the ballflower on one pier, but using essentially late 12C materials. The Norman origins of the chancel are confirmed by the blind arcading—though with new arch-heads—along the walls. The church was restored by Sir Gilbert Scott in 1866. Over the priest's door is an extraordinary monument to Thomas Langton Freke (died 1769), in which the risen Christ stands symbolically over a grisly skeleton.

Lowick, *St. Peter.* This is Perpendicular work at its best though much of it represents a remodelling of the earlier fabric. The outstanding sight is the tower with its octagonal lantern, completed in the late 15C or early 16C. The rest was carried out over a period of 100 years from c 1370, starting with the nave and aisles. Those responsible were the successive members of the Greene family of nearby Drayton and also John Heton, the Rector from 1406 to 1415. One of the Greenes is commemorated in a particularly notable monument.

Fragments of reused 14C masonry can be seen in the right-hand jambs of the chancel S windows, on either side of the N chapel E window. The S aisle has small Perpendicular windows but the N one has a fine display of wide, four-light ones with embattled transoms. The S transept contained a chapel and was built or remodelled as the result of the foundation of a chantry by Henry Greene in 1467. The tower seems to have been in progress in 1479 and bequests in 1512–13 suggest it may not have been completed until the 16C. The buttresses rise up to large pinnacles linked to the octagon by flying buttresses. The octagon itself has large triple-light openings and numerous pinnacles, each with its own weather vane—a most impressive sight. The four-bay arcades seem to have been rebuilt together and their octagonal piers are quite tall and slender. The remodelling in the chancel is shown by the way the SE window and the sedilia fit together awkwardly. It seems that a third and perhaps even a fourth sedile was transferred to the N chapel. These have similar detail to those in the chancel though cusping occurs only on the chapel ones now. If the E 'sedile' in the chapel is ever that, the evidence is largely destroyed by a monument (date of death 1625). Another curious feature is the blocked doorway in the chancel N wall. This must either predate the building of the chapel or have been blocked by the moving of the 'sedilia'. Within one of the chancel sedilia is a squint from outside though the external blocking is not easy to detect. 19C restoration at this church took place in 1869. The S transept is now enclosed by a 19C stone screen.

In the N aisle windows are 16 large stained glass figures which were originally part of a Jesse tree of c 1320. The smaller ones in the tracery are placed awkwardly. The most easterly figure is no doubt the donor, probably either Sir Simon de Drayton or Sir Walter de Vere, who holds a model of the church. The huge painted Hano-verian arms over the chancel arch were discovered in 1937 and probably date from 1718. The monument to Sir Ralph Greene (died 1417) and his wife, between the chapel and the N chapel, is of great beauty. The contract for it, of which a copy is in the church, records that his widow, Katherine, commissioned it from Thomas Prentys and

Robert Sutton of Chellaston, Derbyshire, which was the source of the alabaster. It was to be completed by Easter in the following year at a cost of £40, including gilding and painting. On the tomb-chest are angels; the couple lie on top, holding hands into eternity. Henry Greene (died 1467) and his second wife Margaret (died 1470) have a brass on a tomb-chest in the S transept. Also here is a very fine monument to Edward Stafford, second Earl of Wiltshire (died 1499). He lies on a tomb-chest, his hands clasped in prayer, and he wears an 'SS' collar, indicative of his Lancastrian sympathies. There is a good but sentimental monument in white marble to Charles Sackville Germain, fifth and last Duke of Dorset (died 1843 and the last of his line) by Richard Westmacott, Jr. Two other monuments of some distinction are in the N chapel—Lady Mary Mordaunt, Duchess of Norfolk (died 1705) and Sir John Germain (died 1718).

Middleton Cheney, *All Saints.* The importance of this church lies in its stained glass by Morris & Co. The spire, however, is interesting in that it seems to be a copy, and a simplified one at that, of the magnificent late 14C one at King's Sutton.

The wealth of Morris & Co. glass arises from the fact that the Reverend W.C. Buckley, the Rector, was a close friend of Sir Edward Burne-Jones, a member of the Morris circle. The earliest window is the E one, designed in 1864 and installed the following year. It is a masterly piece with delicate and unusual colouring; in the tracery are the Agnus Dei and censing angels, below the Twelve Tribes of Israel and then tiers of Biblical figures. The chancel SE window (1866–70) is next: Philip Webb was responsible for the tracery glass and Ford Madox Brown the rest. His Cain and Abel are particularly fine. Finally, in the chancel there are two windows on the N side with various New Testament scenes by Burne-Jones in collaboration with Buckley, to whom they are a memorial (he died in 1892). The style, however, is curiously old-fashioned, with small square panels and patterned glass surrounding them. In the N aisle are two windows with impressive, large standing figures dating from 1880. The E window has the Virgin, St. Anne and St. Elizabeth and an Annunciation. In the NE window, Samuel is by Burne-Jones and Elijah by William Morris (or Dante Gabriel Rossetti). The finest window of all is the W one of 1870. The three main lights are by Burne-Jones and depict Shadrach, Meschach and Abednego in the fiery furnace (Daniel 3.19).

Northampton

All Saints. All Saints' lies at the very heart of Northampton. It was almost totally rebuilt between 1676 and 1680 after a disastrous fire. The previous church seems to have been very large. Parts of the present W tower represent the former crossing, and beneath the W area of the chancel and the extreme E of the nave are the traces of an early 14C crypt. The architect for the rebuilding may have been Henry Bell of King's Lynn, who is known to have been a 'manager' of the work at the church. The proud W portico was added in 1701. From the reign of Queen Elizabeth I until the Restoration of 1660, All Saints' was a noted Puritan stronghold. The Cromwellian incumbent Thomas Ball (died 1659) had notably resisted Archbishop Laud's

High Churchmanship. But after the Restoration of 1660, the tide turned; this building seems to say so.

From the E nave the scale and scope of the work of the 1670s can be appreciated, though the effect is marred by the routine Perpendicular War Memorial S chapel of 1920 (by Sir Arthur Blomfield & Sons and A.J. Driver) and the N organ chamber of 1883. The latter reuses 17C materials but destroys the symmetry of the building. In 1680 the church had a nave and aisles (which practically formed a square), a chancel, and vestibules N and S of the tower, which projected slightly beyond the aisles. To the W no rebuilding was undertaken. Over the nave is a lead-covered dome (with cupola of 1704 over) which makes such a distinguished effect inside. The lighting is mostly through three-light round-headed windows with a plain circle in the head and plain pointed lights at the sides. Each has a scrolly keystone. Over the E window is a triangular pediment and, above the slightly projecting centre bays of the aisles, curved ones over oval lights. Though the core of the tower may be 12C, most of the structure is probably 14C. The proud W portico of 1701 is a piece of civic ambition—eight bays wide and two bays deep. The columns are tall, plain and have Ionic capitals. In the centre is a rather small standing statue of King Charles II in Roman costume (of 1712). According to the inscription running along as a frieze, the King 'gave a thousand tuns of timber towards the rebuilding of this church'. The inscription is signed by (John) Hunt of Northampton. Wings sweep up from the vestibules to the tower, which contains a clock prominently dated 1829.

Inside, the cross-in-square plan is clearly apparent and derives from Wren. The cross is marked by four tremendous Ionic columns with elaborate capitals. They stand on high bases and carry a superstructure entirely of plaster and wood (no doubt that given by King Charles II). The interior is treated with great richness. The arms of the cross have tunnel-vaults with panelling and the corners have flat plaster ceilings with enrichment. The lantern rests on decorated pendentives. The effect of all this is somewhat marred by the galleries. The N gallery was erected in 1714 but the S one did not appear until 1815. At the restoration of 1865–66 they were set back from the columns. The seating in the nave uses old woodwork, but was reduced in height and re-arranged in 1865–66. The chancel has an elaborate ceiling from the 1670s with a large, slightly quatrefoiled centrepiece. The walls, however, were plain until 1888 when E.F. Law undertook considerable embellishment, altered the chancel arch and provided the fine twinned, fluted columns below it. The old reredos and the panels of Moses and Aaron (now in the W and N galleries respectively) were removed and a new altarpiece put in, filling the E window.

The church contains some very fine 17C furnishings. The throne at the E end of the N aisle was used for the Consistory Court that met in the S vestibule. The mayor's chair is another sumptuous piece and is dated 1680. The pulpit is of similar date but its base is of 1888. The marble font was given in 1680. Finally, on leaving the church the splendid doorcases from the tower (especially) and vestibules should be noted.

Holy Sepulchre, Sheep Street. The importance of Holy Sepulchre Church lies in its rare round 12C nave. This is the best preserved of the four English survivors. It is impressive internally though the exterior has been visually confused by additions. The round nave (hereafter 'rotunda') owes its inspiration to the church of the Holy Sepulchre in Jerusalem. This made a great impact upon the first Crusaders in the 11C, one of whom was Simon de Senlis, first Earl of Northampton, who seems to have been the founder here. He returned in 1099 and building probably began soon afterwards.

The rotunda is sandwiched between the 14C W tower and the much-expanded E parts. These were lengthened in 1860–64 by Sir Gilbert Scott in 13C style and the effect from the E is one of unfortunate chaos. In fact, there are four elements, the apsidal chancel, flanked by a S aisle, and two N aisles. The tower has massive, ungainly buttresses necessitated by the slope of the ground, renewed Reticulated tracery in the belfry lights and a graceful parapet spire. But something can be seen of the rotunda both N and S. It had flat buttresses (the big ones on the N are no doubt 14C strengthening) and the outer wall had two tiers of windows. Of the lower tier, only one on the S remains intact. Two of the upper windows survive on the N and would have provided light above the internal vaulting to a triforium. All this was much altered in the 14C and the inner clerestory is of that time. The rotunda is capped by an attractive lead-covered roof of 1868.

The rotunda, when entered, has great impact. In the centre are eight massive circular piers. There are traces of former groining over the original windows, which must have met the walling above the piers in an awkward fashion. A puzzle is the tall Norman shaft N of the entrance to the chancel, which is higher than the springing to the vaulting. The capitals and abaci to the piers are varied and include early circular abaci at the W. The pointed arches above the piers are replacements. A bench formerly ran round the ambulatory but only a small part N of the W entrance to the church survives. In the SE part of the rotunda is an extraordinarily tall (nearly 11ft high) banner-stave locker. The rotunda now serves as a baptistery and in the centre is a font by Sir Gilbert Scott, completed in 1867: it is a memorial to the Reverend Thomas James, who was important in Northamptonshire Ecclesiological circles.

To the E lie the remains of the 12C chancel, which for some strange reason was built displaced to the N of the E–W axis of the rotunda. On the N side can be seen the traces of three windows that used to light it (the W one is the best preserved). From the aisles can be seen the remains, partly reset, of the 12C stringcourses. Enlargement began in c 1180 with a two-bay N aisle. The arcade has triple-shafted responds and leaf capitals. The pier, however, is a much more advanced design, having its circular core surrounded by groups of triple shafts. It has been suggested as a mid-13C replacement. The outer N aisle was a late 13C addition and has three bays instead of two (more space at the W due to the curvature of the rotunda). At the E end is an extraordinary pillar piscina. The bowl and Purbeck marble shaft are 19C but are supposed to have been copied from original 13C fragments found at the restoration. The S aisle did not come until the 14C. The medieval chancel stopped after two bays. E is Scott's work and is more florid than anything else—polychrome in the arches, much foliage and some polished granite shafts. The restoration has left the church sadly gloomy and very dark on all but the brightest of days.

Above the wall shaft in the rotunda is an early 12C tympanum with the bust of a man set between a dragon and a small figure. The 15C wooden corbels to the roof in the present nave are delightfully carved with musicians. The screens in the chancel are by J. Oldrid Scott,

1880. There is one monument of note—the brass to George Coles (died 1640), with his two wives (rotunda, N side). In the outer N aisle is a stained glass window of King Richard I, 'Coeur de Lion', at the Battle of Jaffa, by Messrs. Mayer & Co.

St. Matthew, Kettering Road. Dominating a large area of the E of the town, St. Matthew's has two claims to importance. It contains two of the masterpieces of 20C art and is also a splendid building in its own right, built in 1891–93. The architect was Matthew Holding, who had been a pupil of J.L. Pearson. Walter Hussey, Vicar from 1937 to 1955, was a great patron of the arts. He commissioned the Madonna and Child in the N transept from Henry Moore and, when unveiled in 1944, it was one of the sculptor's key works up to that time. It is utterly timeless and full of deep emotion. In a totally different way Graham Sutherland's Crucifixion in the S transept, unveiled in 1946, is another work of enormous power. Against a violent mauve background the agony of the Crucifixion is portrayed. Here the supreme suffering of the sacrifice is brought home to all who stand before it. Patronage of contemporary artists has continued and in 1987 14 sculptured Stations of the Cross by Daniel Thomas were installed.

St. Peter, Marefair. There is no finer example of Norman work in Northamptonshire. The church is largely of c 1150 but with some significant post-medieval rebuilding. It is very long, aisled, and has a continuous roof over the nave and chancel, with no obvious structural division between the two. Its unusual plan suggests it may have been served by a college of priests. The site is at the centre from which medieval Northampton grew, as has been shown by recent extensive excavations. In the 14C *Nova Legenda Angliae*, St. Peter's is credited with housing the shrine of St. Ragener, martyr and nephew of St. Edmund of East Anglia.

In late Norman times it was larger than now, for the tower has been rebuilt further E thus taking up half the W bay of the nave (see how it cuts into a clerestory window). This took place probably in the early 17C at the same time as the rebuilding of the E end. The latter, however, was rebuilt again by Sir Gilbert Scott in 1850–51 and followed as faithfully as possible the original Norman design. This included extending the E wall 12ft E to the late 12C position. The unusual semicircular buttress recurs on the W angles of the tower. In the W face a reused Norman arch gives some idea of the sculptural riches inside and contains a variety of saltires, interlace and stylised foliage. Above is a tier of blind arches of obviously reused masonry and two such tiers on both N and S faces. All this shows that the rebuilders took the Norman work very seriously. The upper stages of the tower probably contain 13C and 14C masonry. St. Peter's is unusual among Norman parish churches in having a clerestory. This comprises blind arcades with a small window set between each five or six blank arches. The aisles may be on the site of their Norman predecessors, though almost everything seems to date from later reworking. The windows are mainly 17C work.

The interior is yet more distinguished—long, with a stately progression of arches to the E, each with a capital of great richness. There can never have been a chancel arch though a close look at the capitals of the main piers on the aisle sides shows that once there were transverse arches (but no signs of vaulting). The nave, as originally built, had three major bays, each divided into two, though the eastward movement of the tower has caused the loss of a minor bay. The major piers are of quatrefoil section and on the nave side rise sheer to the roof where, no doubt in the late 12C, they would have supported the tiebeams. The alternating piers are much smaller and each has a shaft-ring. In the chancel the pattern changes slightly. There are three bays with circular piers (the E pair with shaft-rings). Turning to the capitals, none are identical. Mostly they are of abstract designs but all are carved with great delicacy. The capitals between the nave and chancel, and the E responds in the chancel have addorsed beasts or birds. The tower arch is also very notable and, again, is a fairly careful 17C reuse of late 12C material.

After these architectural splendours the furnishings and fittings are relatively modest, except for a fine grave slab of c 1140 at the E end of the N aisle. It is thought that the slab may have been the lid of a sarcophagus. Its sculptor also carved some of the capitals in St. Peter's. In the S aisle there are two fragments of pre-Conquest interlace. The reredos is of 1879 (completed 1914), by J. Oldrid Scott. A few monuments should be noted, more for the people concerned than their artistic value. At the W end is a bust to William Smith (1769–1839), a key figure in establishing the scientific study of geology in Britain. Nearby is George Baker (1781–1851), the noted historian of Northamptonshire. At the W end of the N aisle is John Smith of London (died 1742), 'The most eminent engraver of Mezzo-Tinto in his time'. Finally, on the N wall of the sanctuary is a brass to the Reverend R.M. Serjeantson (died 1916), who was Rector here and who did much to promote the study of Northamptonshire's churches.

Oundle, _St. Peter._ St. Peter's is a large church with a fairly interesting structural history and a full range of building dates from Norman to Perpendicular. Its stately spire, over 200ft high, is a landmark over a very wide area and dominates this fine limestone town, famous for its school founded in 1556.

The tower and spire are the great features of the exterior. The tower is late 14C and contains both Decorated and Perpendicular elements—the former represented by the ogee on the W doorway and by the Reticulated belfry lights, the latter by the overall emphasis on the vertical. This verticality gives a sense of lightness despite the imposing size of the structure and there is a freshness often lacking in Perpendicular work. There is a shallow, panelled and tunnel-vaulted W portal of the type popular in this district (e.g. Raunds and Higham Ferrers). The upper half of the tower is taken up by the tall belfry stage. At each corner is an octagonal turret and the merlons are pierced by ornamental loopholes. The spire is superbly handled. It is enlivened with ribs and crockets at the angles and three tiers of lucarnes. '1634' carved prominently on the S records a rebuilding. The E window of the N transept has intriguing tracery combining Geometrical and Decorated elements. The two-storeyed vestry is 16C. The E window has somewhat spidery five-light Perpendicular window tracery inserted into earlier walling. The chancel was probably lengthened about 1250–60 when the slender two-light windows with Geometrical tracery were provided in the side walls. The S chapel E window has particularly fine late Decorated tracery. Beneath the S transept is a crypt (entrance in the SW corner). Two lovely rainwater heads dated 1637 can be seen on the Decorated clerestory. The 'goodly sowthe porch' (Leland) is said to have been built in c 1485 by Robert and Joan Wyatt.

The structural development can best be followed from inside. From the N chapel the remains of a Norman window can be seen. It is often said that there was a Norman crossing tower. The small squarish blocks of ashlar masonry in this area no doubt belong to that time and the stub of walling at the NE corner of the S aisle seems to represent the start of a transept (there is an external buttress in the angle between the transept and the Norman nave). Below the crossing responds the plinths may be Norman but there is no structural evidence to support the idea of a crossing tower. The present arches to the transepts are late Decorated. Major 13C changes took place when the chancel was lengthened, side chapels added and aisles thrown out. All this seems to have been done by c 1260. The S aisle is the earlier of the two. The transepts were probably lengthened late in the 13C. The tower was not started until late in the 14C and it was built free-standing initially (see the complete E buttresses) and later joined up to the nave. Thereafter the main change to the interior was Sir Gilbert Scott's restoration of 1864.

The pulpit is a 15C wooden one of the wine-glass type: it was restored by Pauline Plummer in 1966. The lectern, too, is medieval— a 15C brass eagle. The base of the Rood screen survives. Of very unusual design is the 18C font (base of tower). The E window is by Clayton & Bell, 1864, and that on the S of the chancel is by Sir Ninian Comper, 1918. The building is unusually lacking in monuments, though two of some distinction are to Martha Kirkham (died 1616, chancel NE) and Mary Kirkham (died 1607, S chapel).

Polebrook, *All Saints.* This interesting church has an unusually large amount of late 12C and 13C work and very little later. The base of the tower still has round-arched windows and the hoods over the belfry lights are round, too. On the N porch is a riot of 13C decoration. It is inside that the intriguing development can be seen. Although, as at Oundle, claims are made for a Norman crossing tower, there is no obvious evidence to support this idea. An arch to the N transept can be identified as very late 12C on the strength of its waterleaf capitals, and the chancel arch has very similar detail, but none of this is suggestive of a tower. The two W bays of the N arcade must have been added immediately after the arch to the transept and the abacus of their E respond was returned to that of the W respond of the transept arch, proving that by c 1200 there could not have been a tower. Apart from the waterleaf in the capital of the W respond, the other capitals have prominent volutes. Then, early in the 13C, came the building of the SW tower (no room W of the nave) and the S aisle, which has two impressively tall bays, still with round arches. Its capitals have a variety of foliage. The 13C activity was completed about the middle of the century by the lengthening of the chancel (note the richly moulded and shafted triple-lancet E window), N porch and extension of the N transept. This has fine blind arcading with slender shafts lining its N and W walls. The S chapel was extended beyond the S aisle and no attempt was made to balance it with the N transept. There are two double piscinas, one in the chancel (ornate 13C decoration) and one in the S chapel. Also there is a 15C screen, a 17C pulpit and simple 17C benches (graffito of 1663!).

Raunds, *St. Mary.* The church stands on a hill above this large, drab village and has as its most obvious distinction an extraordinarily ornate 13C W tower, but otherwise it has much interest in terms of its evolution, its contents and its E window.

The tower was started perhaps in c 1225. Its surfaces are broken up by a wild variety of ornamentation. The W face is most inventively treated. It all gives the impression of the master mason trying to achieve as exotic an effect as possible within the grammar of architectural ornament available to him. The broach spire was rebuilt after a lightning strike in 1826.

The story is now best taken up inside. From the nave it can be seen how the present church developed from a Norman, cruciform core. On the S wall are the remains of a former arch and, further E, the last pier but one seems to mark the angle into a former S transept (see the little piece of walling between the responds and the angle of masonry above). No evidence survives of a N transept, however. The traces of rubble foundations beneath the arcade piers may be survivals from the 12C building. Next came the tower, which started detached and only later, after settlement, was joined and this by wider arches than in the rest of the arcades. There was work in the 13C in the chancel: at the NE there is a blocked window (probably a lancet) and a similar feature in the S wall. The latter was shortly cut into by a two-bay arcade to the S chapel (dedicated to St. Peter). An odd feature is the half-bay adjoining the chancel arch as though the intention was to carry on further W—but this did not happen. The 13C date of the S chapel is confirmed by the stiff-leaf capitals on the S doorway. Other 13C work exists in the aisle doorways and, finally, in the magnificent Geometrical E window of two pairs of triple lights and a large octofoiled circle in the head. Next, work began on the arcades, starting on the S in c 1300. This and the joining of the S chapel and the S aisle removed the traces of the S transept. Another half-arch was built, this time from the nave to the chancel arch. At the W end, the wide arch was linked to the semicircular respond which presumably had been put in in anticipation of this event. The same happened on the N, though rather later, and the arcade and the aisle are fully Decorated work. The chancel arch was rebuilt with two orders of ballflower in the hollow moulding. The final contribution was Perpendicular, with the addition of the clerestory (the nave roof still contains much medieval work), windows in the chancel (N), S aisle and the E wall of the S chapel. The church was restored by Sir Gilbert Scott in 1873–74.

The most remarkable fitting is a 15C 24-hour clock-face in stone in the tower arch. Beneath is an inscription saying that it was the gift of John Elen and Sara his wife, who appear with angels in the spandrels. Raunds has an important collection of medieval wall paintings discovered at the restoration. On the nave's N wall (from W to E) are the Seven Deadly Sins, St. Christopher, and the Three Living and the Three Dead. St. George over the N doorway, and the stories of St. Catherine on the W wall of the N aisle, are now only marked by traces. On the soffit of the chancel arch are traces of mortice holes for a tympanum. In front of this and the wall above stood the Rood and outline of the cross, and the figures of St. John and the Virgin Mary can be seen. There are many medieval wooden fragments, especially parts of screenwork made up into a screen to the S chapel, and also in the reredos of the N aisle. The wainscot of the Rood screen survives. In the arch to the S chapel is a fragment of plain blank arches which appears to be 13C, with very flat cusping, which would make it a very rare survival. The font, with an extraordinary, lifelike ram's head protruding on the W face, may be 12C. The E window is a rather crowded composition by C.E. Kempe, 1907.

Rothwell, *Holy Trinity.* Rothwell has a church of considerable scale and one with an interesting and complex architectural development. Its length (173ft) and its E window are the largest in the county. There is clear evidence of a substantial Norman building, of further major expansion in the 13C and of various later medieval alterations. The church was larger than now and has lost its S chapels (at an unknown date), the spire (1660) and those parts of the transepts which projected beyond the aisles (1673). The reason for the medieval magnificence was that Rothwell was the second town of Northamptonshire and its Lords of the Manor, the de Clares, were extremely wealthy.

From the S side, various features of the development can be detected. The three Norman clerestory windows and the corbel course above give some idea of the scale of the 12C church. Below, blocked arches led to a two-bay chapel. The E extent of the chancel was probably reached in the 13C—the evidence is inside—though the external detail dates from a later, Perpendicular remodelling. This includes the vast five-light E window. In the two E bays of the S aisle are the arches that led into the once larger transepts. The windows within them are late 13C and have spherical triangles at the top, one with cusps, the other without. In the other S windows are tall, triple-grouped lancets, further evidence of the 13C. Both porches are 13C too. Above the nave is a late 15C Perpendicular clerestory and on its E gable is a sanctus bell turret. This helps make the rather massive, low tower look clumsy, though before 1660 it would have benefited considerably from the existence of the spire. The tower, completed c 1300, was started very early in the 13C, as revealed by the W doorway, so it is clear that in that century the church had already reached its great length. The doorway is interesting in that it contains both Norman and early 13C devices. The zigzag and battlemented ornament of the late 12C seems to have been reworked into the present pointed doorway, which acquired five orders of shafts with shaft-rings and stiff-leaf foliage on either side. On the N is a big 13C stair turret topped by a most impressive spirelet. The strange blind relieving arches on the tower are modern.

The Norman work reappears inside, including the three chancel clerestory windows plus two others adjacent to them. All 12C evidence on the N of the chancel has been lost but a little remains in the nave. This is a bay and a half of stringcourses on both the inside and outside of the 12C church. These are significant as they show there is no evidence for 12C transepts and, though the church was substantial, it may well have been a long, unaisled, non-transeptal one of the type found at St. Mary de Castro, Leicester. However, by the early 13C transepts and aisles were definitely in existence. There are four bays up to the crossing and a further bay to the former transepts. The arcades are undoubtedly the dominant feature of the interior. The piers have sections alternating between square and round cores, each with four shafts. The capitals have early, small-scale, stiff-leaf foliage and the arches are pointed and double-stepped, which creates a sense of severity. It seems that later in the 13C there was a major scheme to widen the aisles which also involved the heightening of the arcades. See how the lower parts of the arcades lack fillets whereas the upper ones have them. This may have taken place no later than 1280–90, which is also the date of the fine tower arch. There is yet more 13C activity in the chancel. Chapels were thrown out on both sides and in effect created double transepts. On the S side this is particularly clear and a pier in the S wall is a clear sign of how the structure went further S. On the N all four bays remain but when and why two of the S ones vanished is not clear. The chapel and transept arrangements were fully in place by the late 13C. The shafts to the otherwise 15C window are a survival from the great building period at Rothwell. The Perpendicular period is also represented by other windows (N side blocked) at the E end of the chancel, some clerestory windows in the chancel and the vault in the tower (angels at the springing).

The most famous feature at Rothwell is the crypt, built in the early 13C S of the then S aisle. There are two rib-vaulted bays. Its original function is uncertain but it came to be used as a charnel house and now contains the bones of some 1500 people. Research by Dr. Trevor and Mr. B. Doughty suggests two main groups of bones. The earlier, characterised by short skulls and an O blood grouping, dates from the 14C. The later group has longer skulls and blood characteristics typical of the 15C onwards. Many may have been removed here after disturbance from the founding of the Jesus Hospital SE of the church in 1591. The crypt was lost to memory until, we are told, it was rediscovered in c 1700 by an unsuspecting grave digger who was precipitated into it. Hythe in Kent has the only other crypt in England to contain bones.

The extensive collection of old photographs and drawings of the church in the S aisle includes views of the unrestored interior complete with box-pews, gallery of 1836 and twin pulpits. These arrangements survived until surprisingly late. The chancel had been partitioned off in 1760 and was not brought back into use until 1848: meantime, it housed the town fire engine bought in 1750. Restoration of the remainder got under way with Sir Arthur Blomfield and a faculty of 1893. In 1921 four clerestory windows were opened and in 1927 the oak reredos was added. The sedilia and piscina in the chancel are late 13C and are considerable rarities. The piscina has three drains but some alterations may have been made later and the four seats of the sedilia are unusual; only some twenty churches in the country have four or more seats. Another oddity is the font. It has a small, shafted bowl and a kind of shelf below the top from which shafts descend to the base. The Perpendicular choirstalls have some misericords.

For such a major church there is no great wealth of monuments. In the chancel (but normally locked) is the brass to William de Rowell (died 1361), who was in charge of provisioning King Edward III's armies in the early phases of the Hundred Years' War (the brass is covered but is exposed once a year). He is depicted in his vestments as Archdeacon of Essex. Owen Ragsdale, who, at his death in 1591, left money for the founding of the Jesus Hospital, is commemorated in the S chapel by a tomb-chest with a brass on it. In the S transept is a brass to Edward Saunders (died 1514) and his wife Joan: he founded a chantry here.

Rushden, St. Mary. This church has a beautiful exterior and many items of interest inside. It has aisles, transepts, N and S chapels and, best of all, a superb Perpendicular steeple. The transeptal plan was laid out by the late 13C as the Geometrical windows show. In the N window of the N transept is an odd design with trefoils in each intersection in the head.

In a county of fine towers and spires, Rushden's stand comparison with any. The tower is of four stages though the definitions are blurred by the strong polychrome of the stonework. In the ground stage is a small stone porch (as at Higham Ferrers), linked to the adjacent buttresses by charming little flying ones. The spire has its base behind an open quatrefoil parapet and its linking by flying buttresses to corner pinnacles on the tower make a textbook example of how the various elements should be handled.

One enters under the Perpendicular vaulted porch to an interior dominated by the Perpendicular reworking. The W arch to the S chapel records that it was made by 'Hue bochar and Julian hise wyf'. But the feature for which the interior is to be remembered is the strainer arch across the nave (cf. Finedon). A similar arch under the tower dates from the restoration of 1870.

There are considerable amounts of Perpendicular screenwork, a pulpit of similar date and much royal original timber in the roofs. In the chancel are particularly graceful sedilia and a piscina of the 13C. There is extensive 15C stained glass. The N or Pemberton chapel has good monuments to Robert Pemberton (died 1609) and Mary his wife, and to Sir Goddard Pemberton (died 1616).

Stanford-on-Avon, *St. Nicholas.* St. Nicholas's is a largish, unrestored church which was almost wholly rebuilt in the early 14C. It is notable for its remarkably fine array of monuments and for its medieval stained glass.

Externally, almost everything appears to be of c 1300–50. Originally, the tower had a spire. The rebuilding seems to have started in the chancel, for none of the windows there have ogee tracery forms. Red Warwickshire sandstone is used in various places: one of the most easterly uses of such stone. Against the E wall of the chancel, up to sill level, is an earth mound covering the burial vault of the Cave family. A large-scale renovation is (in 1987) under way.

The most striking feature of the interior is that it was not restored until 1908–09. Seating is minimal, largely confined to a few benches facing N and S. There are faint but unmistakable traces of work before the 14C, starting with the NE respond. The base and lower parts remain from what has been suggested as a late 11C arcade. A low 13C SE respond survives too, as does the base of the NW one. In the nave is a detached Norman capital with traces of paintwork. Otherwise everything is early 14C. The five-bay arcade is typical of several in this area in that it has no capitals. All the roofs contain ancient main timbers including, perhaps, the original 14C structure in the chancel.

The font dates from the great rebuilding. Under the tower arch is a Perpendicular screen and under the chancel arch is a large screen brought from Lutterworth in 1837. Parts of the original screen are worked up into the pulpit. The stalls are 15C too and there is one simple misericord. Most spectacular of all, with its delicate scrollwork, is the three-tower organ case of c 1625 in the W gallery. It was originally in the Chapel Royal in Whitehall Palace and thus belonged to King Charles I. After his execution it was bought by Magdalen College, Oxford, but was resold to Sir Thomas Cave in 1649 or 1650 and brought here.

Stanford has by far the best collection of medieval stained glass in the county. (The glass is removed for repair as at mid-1987 and this account follows published sources.) The evidence of the royal heraldry in the chancel suggests the earliest work is of 1306–07 or c 1312–27. This includes much of the glass in the chancel such as the Apostles and saints in the side windows, and in the E window the Crucifixion, a small Virgin and donors, the seated Christ, and figures of a saint and abbots. A later group is from c 1330–40. Most of the N aisle E window belongs to this period, including St. Anne teaching the Virgin to read, a bishop with hand raised in blessing, the Resurrection, and the Crucifixion. In the main lights two female martyrs are depicted. The figures in the tracery of the SE window, a kneeling figure in the NW window and an Agnus Dei in the window E of this also belong to this period. The glass of c 1500 is much paler. It includes, in the first window from the E in the S aisle, a Virgin and Child, donor panels, the Assumption and St. John the Evangelist. In the next window are St. Margaret, St. George and the Visitation. The heraldry and donor groups connected with the Cave family are datable to c 1558 and came from Stanford Hall this century.

Apart from the glass the great interest is in the monuments. They are listed here topographically. Most are to the Cave family of Stanford Hall. **Chancel.** Sir Thomas Cave (died 1613) and his wife Eleanor lie on a tomb-chest linked by a small scroll to that of their son Richard (died 1606, aged 19). Dorothy Egeocke (died 1630) has a black marble slab with fine Roman lettering on top of a table-tomb. The front of this has shields linked by Classical swags in a way that is advanced for its time. Sir Thomas Cave (died 1719) and Sir Verney Cave (died 1734) each have a wall monument of some distinction. Thomas Otway Cave (died 1830) is commemorated by a finely carved sentimental death-bed scene. **Nave.** Sir Thomas Cave (died 1558) and his wife. **South Aisle.** The earliest monument is an effigy of a priest (probably early 14C) under a later canopy. Further W is James Callen (died 1734), set up by his son in 1751. At the W end is Sarah, third Baroness Braye (died 1862), probably by Mary Thornycroft. She lies before a large Gothic arch attended by three cherubs (by John Gibson) and a kneeling woman. The delicacy of this marble monument is matched by that in the N aisle (W end) to Robert Otway Cave (died 1844) by Richard Westmacott, Jr. Sir Ambrose Cave (died 1568) has Corinthian columns flanking an achievement of arms and an inscription. Mary Cave, wife of Henry Knollys (c 1600), lies in an awkward attitude on her side. He lies higher up on his back. Finally, Edmund Verney (died 1896) has a medallion portrait on a Baroque-style monument strange for its time. On the left a superb figure in the uniform of the 17th Lancers solemnly lays a wreath.

Wellingborough, St. Mary. The later years of the Gothic Revival are marked by several great churches but few approach the grandeur of St. Mary's and the splendour of its furnishings. The church was begun in the early 20C through a gift of £5000 by the Misses Sharman of Wellingborough. The design was by Sir Ninian Comper and the church had a special place for him in his work: his wife was buried in the N chapel and it was his wish to rest there too (in fact he was buried in Westminster Abbey). The first part (the chapel of the Holy Name of Jesus) was consecrated in 1908, the chancel and one bay of the nave followed in 1915, and the rest was completed in 1930. The final consecration did not take place until October, 1968.

The guiding spirit is Comper's beloved late Perpendicular and the overall feel is that of the larger late medieval churches, especially in East Anglia. There is no division between the nave and the chancel, which are of nine well-lit bays. Aisles stop short before the E end of the chancel but the side chapels lie N and S of these aisles and extend a little beyond them. On the S the sloping site allows parish rooms to be accommodated beneath the chapel of St. John. The details of the N and S sides differ somewhat. The building materials

The interior of St. Mary's, the masterpiece of Sir Ninian Comper, 1908–30 (with later fittings)

are dark Finedon ironstone with Weldon stone dressings. It is the former which helps make the tower a disappointment. Apart from the very routine design the large blank areas of sharply cut masonry are reminiscent of some of the more drastic mid-Victorian restoration schemes in Northamptonshire using dark ironstone. The tower looks as though it needs rather more enrichment to do justice to the rest of the building. The huge vaulted NE porch is almost of tower proportions in itself.

The exterior impresses by its scale, proportions and simplicity of line. Lavishness is reserved for the interior. The open architectural setting is an ideal vehicle for giving free rein to Comper's sumptuous furnishings and every detail (apart from his son's font cover) is by him. The concave-sided piers are tall and carry capitals with lilies. From inside, the clerestory appears quite shallow and is scarcely noticed as one contemplates the glorious lierne-vault, with countless bosses, cusped ribs and enormous pendants which conceal lights. A major feature is the lack of extensive seating and one is reminded of medieval churches where the W ends would have been kept free for parish purposes. Furthermore, the general lack of stained glass contributes to the sense of openness and lightness.

The focal point is Comper's Rood screen in the sixth bay of the church, where he demonstrates his masterly ability to combine historically incompatible motifs. The loft has a close-set Gothic parapet and is brought forward to rest upon three broad Renaissance arches on Tuscan columns. At the back are more round arches, through which one glimpses the high altar and its baldacchino. In the spandrels of the forward arches of the screen are the figures of St. George, St. Anne (with the young Mary), Joachim and St. Thomas Becket. The heads of the rear arches contain busts of Old Testament Prophets and kings in medallions held by putti. Above the loft stands the Rood group flanked by seraphim and presiding over all is Christ in Majesty. It is the colouring of the furnishings that breathes extra life into the church. It glitters with gold and blue, great favourites of Comper's. He aimed to place the choir on two raised lofts on either side of the chancel and provided access by a bridge (as at Chailey, Sussex) from the N chapel. The screen to the N chapel and the organ also glisten with colour. Gold is the overwhelming colour of the baldacchino, a square structure supported on Corinthian columns inhabited by praying angels. On its W edge the risen Christ is surrounded by seven putti. The font is rather plain but is surrounded by a low screen with gilded foliage. The pulpit is a memorial to the Misses Sharman and is unpainted. In this church one is left with an abiding impression of a last, glorious evocation of the churches of the late Middle Ages, unsurpassed this century and unlikely ever to be attempted again.

NORTHUMBERLAND

Northumberland has always been 'border country'. In Roman times Hadrian's Wall ran across the S part of the county, and for long periods the Romans occupied or at least controlled the territory to the N. Throughout the medieval period the area was fought over, and though mostly in English hands, there was scarcely a generation from the mid-13C to the 16C which did not experience Scottish incursions and English counter-attacks. The River Tweed by then formed the boundary between the two kingdoms; but the important town of Berwick, on the N bank, changed hands many times. Even after Berwick finally became English, in the 16C, it was for long regarded as a special place, mentioned separately in Acts of Parliament, treaties and declarations of war. The county is large, with the bleak moorlands of the Pennines and Cheviots to the W, penetrated ' y the long valleys of the N Tyne, Rede, Coquet and Till, with flatter ountry to the E, and a long and magnificent coastline. Not sur-)risingly, given Northumberland's stormy past, defensive structures ibound, from mighty fortresses such as the castles of Newcastle, Alnwick, Warkworth, Bamburgh and Norham, to small free-standing peel-towers, defensible houses not only for lords but also for parsons. Churches, too, were sometimes strengthened with defence in mind, with huge, sturdy W towers and fireproof stone vaults. Northumberland's chief architectural characteristics are several pre-Conquest towers and many churches of the Norman and Early English periods. Long, narrow chancels lit by tall lancet windows are an especial feature. By contrast, late medieval work is scarce, except in the large, prosperous and defended centres of Newcastle and Alnwick. Elsewhere, the unsettled conditions which prevailed until the 16C prevented much rebuilding. It is, however, probably because of these conditions that so much early work survived unaltered.

The earliest church remains are at Hexham, founded as a monastery by St. Wilfrid in c 671–73, soon after Lindisfarne. His crypt survives, a complex of tunnel-vaulted chambers and passages. In the chancel stands a bishop's throne, a stone seat of the 7C or 8C. Roman stones were used in the crypt, and also in the lower part of the tower of Corbridge, c 700, where the tower arch is a reused Roman arch. Lindisfarne was sacked in 793, and the 9C and first half of the 10C saw Danish raids and domination. In 954 King Edred of Wessex reconquered Northumberland. Most of the surviving pre-Conquest features date from the late 10C and 11C. In the Tyne Valley is a group of towers which include Warden, the upper part of Corbridge, Ovingham and St. Andrew's, Bywell. Other towers are at Bolam and at Whittingham (but the top stage removed and rebuilt by John Green in 1840). Part of an important early cross-shaft, of c 800, forms the base of a 17C font at Rothbury. The depiction of the Ascension is the earliest surviving depiction of this scene in England. For the Norman period the most important remains are the monastic ruins of Holy Island and Tynemouth. Holy Island is contemporary with, and under the influence of, Durham Cathedral. Also influenced by Durham, but of the later period of Bishop Le Puiset, is Norham, with S arcade, chancel arch and S chancel windows. Warkworth is almost completely Norman, and has a rare 12C vaulted chancel. Another is at Heddon-on-the-Wall. Several Norman chancel arches remain, of which Old Berwick is amongst the most sumptuous. It also has the arch of a former apse, an arrangement which survives at Seaton

Delaval. Chollerton's Norman S arcade is remarkable in having Roman columns, salvaged from the nearby camp of Chesters. St. Andrew's, Newcastle, has Norman arcades and a chancel arch. In the keep of the castle at Newcastle, built by King Henry II, 1172–77, is a rib-vaulted Norman chapel.

Many Northumberland churches were built or rebuilt in the Early English period. Foremost is Hexham Abbey, built in c 1100–1250. The nave was destroyed by the Scots and rebuilt only in 1907–09 (by Temple Moore), and the E end is an invention of 1858 by John Dobson, based on Whitby Abbey; but the rest is Early English of the highest quality. Less exuberant is Brinkburn Priory, rescued from ruin in 1858 by Thomas Austin. These were, of course, monastic churches, but there are many parochial examples. A chief characteristic is a long, high, narrow chancel with tall lancet windows which are grouped and stepped at the E end. Examples are at Bamburgh, Corbridge, Rothbury and Simonburn (much renewed in the 19C). Haltwhistle is a remarkably complete Early English work, as is Hartburn, and, substantially, St. Peter's, Bywell (sharing a churchyard with St. Andrew's). Several Early English churches have transepts, some, such as Corbridge, Elsdon, Ovingham and Rothbury, with the additional refinement of a W transept aisle. A peculiarity, rather than an example, are the stone vaults at Kirknewton, which spring from the floor like tunnels. At Ancroft is a huge W tower built like a fortress, which indeed it was: the Vicar used it as a peel-tower until the 19C. A similar tower is at Eglingham. Warkworth's Early English tower carries a spire of c 1400, a feature rare in Northumberland. Bellcotes over the W gable are more frequent, supported either by a single or by a double arched buttress. There are examples at Bothal, Felton, Ford, Holy Island and elsewhere. Few 14C and 15C churches were built in the county. The best are Alnwick, St. John's, Newcastle, and St. Nicholas's, Newcastle. The latter, now the cathedral, was parochial until 1882, and may on that account be discussed here. It has interesting arcades without capitals, the arches dying into the piers, a feature of the arcade at Ponteland. St. Nicholas's has the most glorious tower in the county, with its remarkable open, arched crown (its present detailing by Sir Gilbert Scott, 1861). It dates from the mid-15C, earlier than similar crowns at Edinburgh and Aberdeen. The ruins of Tynemouth Priory include the Percy chantry (restored by John Dobson), which is a Perpendicular-style chapel of the 15C, with intricate and elaborate rib-vaults.

After the Reformation there was little notable architectural development until the 19C. The Perpendicular style persisted into the 17C, as seen in the chancel at Eglingham. So did the tradition of providing sturdy stone vaults: Bellingham has a remarkable tunnel-vault, added after 1609. The most accomplished 17C church was Holy Trinity, Berwick. It was built in 1650–52, in the troubled period of the Civil War and Commonwealth. The mason was John Young of London. The style embraced late Perpendicular and early Classical forms. It now seems more decidedly Classical, since several Gothic windows were replaced by plain Venetian windows in the 19C—the reverse of the usual procedure in that century. The earliest surviving purely Classical church in the county, St. Ann's, City Road, Newcastle, dates from 1764–68. The architect was William Newton of Newcastle. It is rectangular and sober, with a small W portico and a steeple and spire in the Gibbs manner. More exuberant and original was David Stephenson's All Saints', Newcastle, 1786–96, with its oval body and many-tiered tower. Also Classical were Christ Church, Tynemouth (North Shields), 1786–92 (chancel 1869), and St. Nicholas's, Gosforth, 1799 by John Dodds (aisles 1818 by John Dobson, chancel 1913). There was little 18C Gothick in Northumberland churches. The rich plasterwork at Alnwick, heavy with pendants, was removed by Anthony Salvin in the 1860s. Long Horsley, rebuilt in 1783 with a pretty trefoiled chancel arch, was abandoned in 1966 in favour of a building in the village. Two early Catholic churches have good Gothick features: Thropton has a chancel arch of 1811 of tripartite form, separated by pendants. More elaborate was Robert Giles's St. Cuthbert's, North Shields (demolished), the chancel foreshortened like a theatrical stage and preceded by a tripartite arch flanked by doors, the whole decorated with flimsy crockets, pinnacles and gables. A group of simple, early Gothic Revival churches, at Greystead, Humshaugh, Thorneyburn and Wark in the North Tyne valley, was provided in 1818–20 by the Governors of Greenwich Hospital for chaplains redundant after the Napoleonic Wars. The architect was H.H. Seward, Sir John Soane's pupil. Many 19C churches in Northumberland were designed in Norman or Early English style, as if in compliment to the medieval church architecture in the county. Local architects predominated, at first John Dobson and John and Benjamin Green of Newcastle. One of Dobson's first works, St. Thomas's, Newcastle, 1825–30, is Early English, correct in detail but rather uncontrolled in feeling, with an outburst of pinnacles and an extraordinarily heightened openwork tower. Inside are galleries and slender quatrefoil piers unconvincingly supporting a stone vault. No more correct (ecclesiologically speaking) are the Greens' churches. Typical is Earsdon, 1836–37, a straightforward 'lancet' body and a sturdy W tower of several stages, each attractive, but the whole effect badly related and unbalanced. The neo-Norman style attracted several architects. Norham, of course, had real Norman work of great energy and distinction, and Bonomi & Cory's additions of 1836–52, sensibly, do not try to outdo it. The Greens' Horsley, 1844, is quiet and restrained, with low apse and pyramid-roofed W tower. Anthony Salvin provided North Sunderland, 1834. Benjamin Ferrey's St. James's, Morpeth, 1843–46, is big and ambitious, with a central tower. Even the screen separating the churchyard from the street is neo-Norman. At Howick the Classical chapel of 1742 was given a convincing neo-Norman disguise in 1849 by F.J. Francis. 'National' architects did little outstanding work in Northumberland, with the notable exception of J.L. Pearson's Cullercoats, 1884. It is big, serious, Early English in style, and somewhat austere. The broach spire and the high stone vault are especially impressive. Less austere but attractively Early English is Holy Trinity, Whitfield, 1859–60, by A.B. Higham. It is cruciform with a central tower and spire. William Butterfield designed the modest church at Etal, 1858; and S.S. Teulon provided Hunstanworth, 1863. Amongst local architects, Dobson was active until 1862. His Jesmond Parish Church, 1858–61, is Geometrical, with a huge E window and a rose window at the W, but the series of aisle gables, each bay containing upper and lower windows lighting N and S galleries, is unconventional. Dobson's pupil, Robert J. Johnson, went into partnership with Thomas Austin and later with William S. Hicks. Johnson's distinctive style was 15C Perpendicular: Stannington, 1871, All Saints', Gosforth, 1887 (tower 1897) and St. Matthew's, Summerhill Street, Newcastle, 1877 are notable examples. Hicks added the tower of St. Matthew's in 1888, continuing Johnson's Perpendicular style. More sturdy and squat are Hicks's towers at St. Cuthbert's, Blyth, 1885, and Shilbottle, 1885. In 1888 Hicks formed a partnership with Henry C. Charlewood, which was continued by their sons into the early 1960s. Outstanding amongst works of restoration and completion was Temple Moore's nave of Hexham Abbey, 1907–09, in an early Decorated style, as if continuing the development of the church after the destruction of the original nave in 1297. Several new churches were provided for the suburbs of Newcastle in the 1920s and 1930s, including Holy Cross, Fenham, 1935–36 by H.L. Hicks (son of W.S. Hicks), a simplified Italian basilican building in brick; and The Venerable Bede, Benwell Grove, by W.B. Edwards, 1936–37, similar in mood but less streamlined in design.

Northumberland is poor in pre-Reformation church furnishings. The best woodwork is at Hexham Abbey, and is of the 15C and early 16C. There the Rood screen and loft survive, supporting a modern organ. The screen has Flamboyant tracery and original paintings of Bishops of Hexham and Lindisfarne on the dado. There are also choirstalls with misericords, 15C wooden sedilia with vaulted canopies, a 15C pulpit or lectern and the remains of a former reredos, both painted, and the chantries of Robert Ogle (died 1410) and Rowland Leschman (died 1491). In St. Nicholas's, Newcastle (the cathedral) is a remarkable font cover of c 1500, two-tiered, with many gables, pinnacles and a spire. The rib-vaulted interior culminates in a charming boss of the Coronation of the Virgin. There is also a big brass eagle lectern of c 1500. St. Andrew's, Newcastle has a 15C font cover similar to St. Nicholas's. The cover at St. John's, said to be 17C, is in the same tradition. Very little early medieval work survives, except for some sculpted fragments, the best being a Norman relief of the Adoration of the Magi, set in the chancel N wall at Kirknewton. Amongst monuments the tomb-chest of Sir Ralph Grey (died 1443) at Chillingham is outstanding. The chest is encrusted with canopies and carving, and 16 figures of saints. The recumbent figures are of alabaster. At Bothal, the tomb-chest of Lord Ogle (died 1516) has similar figures of mourners and angels. The effigy of Prior Leschman at Hexham is remarkably stiff and unstylised, and his cowl covers his eyes. The brass of Roger Thornton (died 1430), formerly at All Saints', Newcastle, has been removed into the cathedral. For stained glass the visitor should go to Bothal, which has fragmentary work of the 14C and 15C, including the Annunciation and the Coronation of the Virgin in tracery heads; and Morpeth, where an interesting 14C Tree of Jesse window, much renewed by William Wailes, survives at the E end. At Earsdon, in a church of 1836–37 by John and Benjamin Green, is an unexpected treasure: some of the Flemish artist Galyon Hone's glass made in the early 16C for King Henry VIII at Hampton Court Palace. It found its way to Lord Hastings, who presented it to Earsdon in 1874.

The best 17C fittings are in Trinity House chapel, Newcastle, and include a pulpit, desks and a W screen. St. John's, Newcastle has a 17C pulpit of bulky proportions, decorated with Corinthian columns and Jacobean arches. A few pieces of Bishop Cosin woodwork have found their way into Northumberland. It is, perhaps, curious, given that the county was part of the Diocese of Durham, that Bishop Cosin's efforts did not extend there. Norham has a pulpit and stall; but the best work is in the chapel of the island of Inner Farne, of all the unlikely places. Archdeacon Thorp of Durham restored the chapel in 1844–48, and carried there parts of the 17C screen and stalls from Durham Cathedral. Berwick has a W gallery and pulpit of c 1650, still in the Jacobean style. At St. Nicholas's (Cathedral), Newcastle there is a Classical organ case of 1676 built for a Renatus Harris instrument. There are no outstanding furnishings of the 18C until the galleries and pews of All Saints', Newcastle. The next work that must be mentioned dates from 1890–1900, the mosaic decoration in the chancel of St. George's, Jesmond, Newcastle. The founder, Charles W. Mitchell, may have supplied the design which James Brown executed. The figures derive from Ravenna and the decoration is almost Art Nouveau. At Berwick is a Classical-style reredos by Sir Edwin Lutyens, an early work of his. Hicks & Charlewood provided a good Classical reredos in 1911 for St. Ann's, Newcastle. Sir Charles Nicholson's Rood and richly coloured and gilt reredos survive at St. John's, Newcastle; and the delicate screen and communion rail around the new crossing altar are by Stephen Dykes Bower. Berwick has roundels of 16C or 17C Flemish stained glass in the W window.

Many of the major 19C designers are represented in the county. William Wailes of Newcastle is everywhere. James Powell & Sons' glass can be seen at Holy Trinity, Whitfield; there is Clayton & Bell glass at Newton Hall and St. Michael's, Alnwick—a church which has glass by many Victorian firms; at St Paul's, Alnwick is glass by Max Ainmuller of Munich, 1856, to designs by William Dyce; and there is glass of 1872 by Morris & Co. at Haltwhistle. The churches of St. Peter and St. Luke, Wallsend have glass of the 1920s by the Dublin artist, Wilhelmina Geddes. The best range of 17C to 20C monuments is to be found in St. Nicholas's (Cathedral), Newcastle, including works by John Flaxman.

Bishop Nicholas Ridley, martyred in Queen Mary I's reign, was (possibly) baptised at Bellingham. Kirkharle was the birthplace of 'Capability' Brown, the 18C landscape gardener. Thomas Bewick, the wood engraver famous for his 'History of British Birds' and 'General History of Quadrupeds', was born at Ovingham and is buried in the church. John Hodgson, author of the first history of Northumberland (1823–34), still a standard work, lived at Kirk-whelpington. The tomb of the second Earl Grey, Prime Minister at the passage of the great Reform Bill of 1832, is at Howick. Grace Darling, Victorian heroine of a daring sea-rescue, is buried at Bamburgh. The site of the Battle of Flodden Field, 1513, is just S of the church at Branxton and is marked with a memorial cross.

Alnwick, _St. Michael._ St. Michael's is a big, impressive Perpendicular church, standing near the River Alne, with the castle park to its N. Its present exterior form resulted from a royal charter of 1464 which granted Alnwick a port and tolls to raise revenue for its building and repair. The chancel was made Gothick in 1781 by Vincent Shepherd, with an elaborate plaster fan-vault with pendants, a new E window and oak screens and canopies, but this was swept away in Anthony Salvin's restoration of 1863.

Both nave and chancel have wide aisles. The pitched roof of the chancel rises above the rest. The windows are Perpendicular, except for those in the N aisle. Here are remains of the earlier church. At the W end is a small lancet with trefoil head. When the aisle was widened in the 14C new three-light windows were inserted. The tracery has ogee heads, like windows in Newcastle Cathedral. The other windows have quite complicated Perpendicular tracery. The E window is Salvin's. He also replaced the W window, which had been a genuine Decorated one. The S aisle has battlements and buttresses rising to pinnacles. At the SE corner is a turret rising high above the parapet, with a newel staircase. The SW tower is stocky and low, and seems over-supported by its corner buttresses. It is capped by diminutive battlements and pinnacles.

Reused Norman zigzag can be seen over the chancel arch. The nave arcades are early 14C, the S with octagonal piers, the N with hexagonal. At the W end a buttress of the tower thrusts itself assertively into the nave. The chancel arcades have quite elaborate decoration. The piers have clustered shafts in a tracery framework, trefoil-headed. The capitals are lush with foliage; at the springing of the arches are angels with shields. One capital has emblems of crescent and fetterlock, a motif of the fourth Earl of Northumberland (died 1489). In the S nave aisle are carved corbel heads, in the spandrels of the arches, formerly supporting a roof.

Under the tower is a lectern, with scrolled metal of c 1700, and two medieval statues (the heads renewed) of King Henry VI and St. Edmund. The chancel woodwork is all of 1863. The reredos in the N chancel aisle (St. Catherine's chapel) is by H.L. Hicks, 1924, and shows the visit of the Magi, the Crucifixion, and the Empty Tomb, with the four archangels. Most windows have Victorian stained glass by the leading designers. Only the N aisle W window preserves any medieval glass, a small 15C roundel of a pelican. The 19C glass includes the W window and St. Paul's chapel windows, of 1865–70, and the W window of the baptistery, of 1871, all by Clayton & Bell; and the chancel E window by Ward & Hughes, 1866. Under the tower there are many medieval slabs with foliated crosses. In the S chancel aisle there are two recumbent effigies under trefoiled canopies, of an early 14C woman with a wimple and a coronet, and of a knight, later 14C. A 14C ecclesiastic is in the porch into the N chancel chapel. St. Paul's chapel, in the SE corner and formerly the Lady chapel, has fittings brought here in 1981 from St. Paul's Church, Alnwick.

Bamburgh, _St. Aidan._ Bamburgh, one of the largest medieval churches in the county, is mostly 13C. It is cruciform, with a W tower. Its churchyard provides views of the coast to N and E. According to Bede, St. Aidan had a church and chamber here, and he died at Bamburgh in 651. Pope Honorius III settled a dispute in 1221 about the ownership of the church, and it was confirmed to the Augustinian canons of Nostell in Yorkshire, who arrived in 1228. The very wide S aisle may have been the parochial part of the church, with a separate entrance: this may account for the two doors on the S side, the W one being for the canons.

The nave, S aisle and S transept have flat roofs, but the other parts of the church have (restored) pitched roofs. The chancel is aisleless and very long. The windows are all lancets, paired on the N and S sides, and in a triplet at the E end, separated by buttresses. There are low-side windows at the W end of both N and S sides. On the S side is a priest's door which had, formerly, a porch or gable over it. Further E is the entrance to a crypt. The windows of the transepts and aisles, nearly all renewed, now have mostly Y-tracery, but the N aisle windows may have been Perpendicular. There are clerestory windows on the S side only, small and square-headed. The aisles engage the tower, which is of four stages, big and unbuttressed, with a renewed top stage, with battlements.

The N transept preserves an E window, round-headed internally, from the pre-13C church. This suggests that the church was cruciform in the Norman period. In c 1200 the N arcade was built and the N aisle added. The arcade, with circular piers and pointed arches, has capitals progressively more richly decorated from W to E. The E bay is much narrower. At the same date the arches of the crossing were rebuilt. The chancel was rebuilt next, presumably after 1228. Later in the 13C the S arcade was built, with circular piers and plain moulded capitals. The tower, with arches into the church on three sides, has a rare square newel staircase. The S aisle was widened in the 14C. From it can be seen the original clerestory windows, above the arcade. The arch into the transept is wide and has, on the S side, a reused corbel with foliage. There are aumbries in the N and S transepts, and a piscina in the S transept, indicating former altars. Two chantries were founded in the church, one in 1316 and the other in 1333. From the S transept a large squint gives a view of the chancel. It has a stone screen with ogee and inverse-ogee tracery. In the S wall of the chancel are a piscina and sedilia with pointed trefoil heads, and an aumbry in similar style is opposite. Under the S part of the chancel is the crypt, which has two chambers, the N one a slim barrel-vaulted passage with a lancet at the E end and stairs, now blocked, at the W, which led into the chancel. The main chamber has very unusual vaulting, a combination of quadripartite and sexpartite forms. At the E end are two small lancets, and another lancet on the S side has a piscina under it.

In a recess W of the sedilia there is a monument of a cross-legged knight, c 1320. Also in the chancel, near the memorial to his children, is the armour of Ferdinando Forster (died 1701), a member of the major local landowning family. The reredos is an elaborate piece of 1895, with saints in canopied niches. At the W end of the N aisle is the Sharp monument by Sir Francis Chantrey, erected in 1839. There is some 20C stained glass. In the S aisle, a window by James Ballantine, 1936, shows a figure of Spring, flanked by St. Frideswide and St. Cuthbert, with Lindisfarne and Bamburgh Castles in the upper lights. It is a memorial to his grandchildren, set up by A.L. Smith, a Master of Balliol College. In the N transept is a window by G.E.R. Smith, illustrating Proverbs 31 with six scenes from the life of a virtuous woman.

The churchyard has a memorial to Grace Darling, the heroine of the audacious rescue of passengers from the 'Forfarshire', which ran aground in a storm in 1838. She and her father, the lighthouse keeper, rowed through stormy seas to reach them. Her monument is Gothic, arched and flat-topped, with metal columns and an open-work metal parapet. The original effigy, by C.R. Smith, 1846, was brought into the church (to the N nave aisle) in 1885 after damage in a storm; the canopy is by W.S. Hicks. The monument is placed some distance from Grace Darling's grave, so that it may be seen by passing ships.

Berwick-upon-Tweed, *Holy Trinity.* This church is remarkable both for its period and its style. Colonel George Fenwicke, Governor of Berwick, caused it to be built in 1650–52. That was the period of the end of the Civil War and the establishment of the Commonwealth, and Cromwell's campaign in Scotland. It was not a period of church building, and it is extraordinary to find one being built in a border garrison town at such a time of uncertainty. The mason was a London man, John Young, and the design seems to derive from St. Katharine Cree in the City of London of 1628–31. The style is a combination of late Gothic and early Classical.

The exterior maintains the Gothic form of a clerestoried nave with aisles and N chapel. A tower is said to have been planned but omitted at Oliver Cromwell's request. The chancel was added in 1855, with other Classical embellishments. It is remarkable that the 19C architect did not Gothicise the church but instead increased its Classical character. The aisle has Venetian windows, Gothic battlements, and a sundial set symmetrically in the centre of the S side. The corners are quoined. At the W corners rise 19C domed turrets, quite whimsical and charming. The W end was Classicised in the 19C, with a pedimented porch and a Venetian window, which replaced a Gothic traceried window. There was a Gothic window at the E end before the chancel was added. The nave parapet is flat, and some of the windows are 19C Venetian. Others, however, are of an odd square-headed Gothic form, a sort of 'Perpendicular Venetian'.

Inside, there is a five-bay arcade with round arches and Tuscan columns. A W gallery survives, but there were formerly N, S, and E galleries also. The gallery is mostly Jacobean in style, but the blank arcading on the front intersects. Bishop Cosin sometimes used this motif in County Durham and derived it from Norman examples. He could not, of course, have influenced Berwick, since he was in exile until 1660. The pulpit is of c 1650, still in the Jacobean style, and with a tester. Sir Edwin Lutyens provided the Tuscan-style reredos in the early 20C. The W window has been filled with 16C or 17C Flemish roundels of stained glass. There is a small tablet of black marble commemorating Colonel Fenwicke, who died in 1656.

Brinkburn Priory, _St. Peter and St. Paul._ Brinkburn is a 19C restoration of the church of a house of Augustinian Canons founded in c 1135 by William Bertram of Mitford. It was used for services until 1683 but was then abandoned and became ruinous. Thomas Austin of Newcastle restored it in 1857–58 for the Cadogan family. It was mostly a reroofing, but he had to recreate the SW corner of the nave, and he made some structural changes in the chancel. The church is now in the guardianship of the State. It stands in the deep and wooded valley of the Coquet. It is contemporary with Hexham Abbey but of a much more chaste Early English style.

The church is cruciform, with a central tower hardly begun. Like Hexham, there is a N aisle only. The transepts have E aisles. The windows throughout are lancets; at the E end they are in three tiers. The topmost tier is round-headed. At the W end is a blank arcade at the bottom, then a triplet of lancets and another stepped triplet in the gable. There is a stair turret at the NW corner. On the N side of the nave is a late Norman doorway with rich detail. Around and above it are Gothic motifs: bands of dogtooth and an arcade of trefoil-headed arches. Two doors on the S side led to the cloister.

The nave arcade is carried on sturdy octagonal columns, moulded capitals and deeply chamfered arches. Above is a triforium (unlike Hexham, which has a gallery) with double, round-headed openings under a double-arched hoodmould. The clerestory windows are round-headed. The transept aisles have stone vaulting. The chancel formerly had an upper chamber (as did Tynemouth Priory) but Austin removed this in 1858. It would have been later than the Early English style of the rest of the church. There is blank arcading in the chancel. The furnishings are all 19C.

Corbridge, _St. Andrew._ Substantial parts are pre-Conquest, and the tower arch is even older. It is Roman, removed no doubt from the nearby camp of _Corstopitum._ Corbridge was possibly founded in the

670s; it was badly damaged by the Danes in the 9C and was much rebuilt and enlarged in the 13C.

Of the pre-Conquest church the tower and masonry of the nave survive. The tower was at first a porch; it was heightened in the 11C, making it tall and very slender. The earliest work can be seen below. On the W side is a blocked arch, showing that there was an outer porch. Above it is an original window. The topmost stage of the tower has been rebuilt; the belfry windows are 18C. To the pre-Conquest nave were added aisles, transepts and a chancel, making the church cruciform. Later, a N chancel aisle and a W aisle to the N transept were added. The S door is Norman, shafted, with two bands of zigzag in the arches, and a hoodmould. The chancel has 13C lancets, and at the E end a triplet of 1857, widely spaced. On the S side the buttresses have gabled set-offs. There is a priest's door with pointed trefoil head, and a low-side window, square-headed, with mullions and transoms. The lancets at the N and S ends of the transepts are also 19C introductions. The chancel aisle and the N transept W aisle had been ruinous for many years before they were restored in 1867.

The Roman tower arch is round-headed. Above it is a small opening, perhaps to a gallery. The proportions of the nave, narrow and high, are typically pre-Conquest. High up, on the N side, one original window head remains. The nave arcades are 13C, of three bays, with octagonal piers and octagonal moulded capitals. The chancel arch is very high and has evidently been widened. It starts from plain corbels, which support short paired shafts below the arch. The chancel is longer and wider than the nave. The arcade to the N chapel, and the transept arches, are similar to the nave arcades. At the W end of the N aisle is a 13C chamber, which may have been a continuation of the aisle, but was converted into a residence for a priest or anchorite. There is a monument in a large recess in the N transept, a slab inscribed to a burgess of Corbridge, 1296 ('here lies in the earth Hugh, son of Aslin').

Hexham, _St. Andrew._ Hexham is one of the great Early English churches of England, monastic until the Reformation and thereafter parochial. Its architecture—especially the interior—is of high quality; and in addition it preserves the richest collection of pre-Reformation woodwork in the county. But its history extends back to the 7C, and it has remains of the first church on the site. The foundation of Hexham by St. Wilfrid in c 671–73 is recorded in much detail by the saint's biographer, Eddius. The church was said to be the most magnificent NW of the Alps, of remarkable length and height, with many chambers, arcades, turrets and precious embellishments. Of this church, Wilfrid's crypt (discovered in 1725) and a stone chair (known as Wilfrid's throne) survive, and the line of the apse has been traced. Hexham was the seat of a bishop from 678 to 821 (but in 1882, when Northumberland became a diocese separate from Durham, Newcastle and not Hexham was chosen as the cathedral city). The church was sacked by the Danes in 875 and was refounded as a monastery of Augustinian Canons in 1113. The present buildings (chancel, transepts and tower) date from c 1180–1250. The Scots destroyed the nave in 1296, and it was not rebuilt until 1907–09, by Temple Moore. The E end later received a large E window which may have been Perpendicular, with a small E transept below it, on the model of the chapel of the Nine Altars at Durham. John Dobson removed this later work in 1858, replacing it with an E end based on Whitby Abbey.

Dobson's work gave the E part of the church a uniform, Early

English appearance. The windows of chancel and transept aisles, and the clerestory, are single lancets, those of the clerestory being set in blind arcading. The low central tower also has sequences of lancets and blind arcading in its belfry stage. Monastic buildings adjoined the S transept to the S and W. On the S side there is only a stepped triplet of lancets high in the gable. Below is a blocked doorway which led from the dormitory to the night stairs. At the base are remains of the vestibule to the chapter house. On the W side, under the clerestory stage of blind and open lancets, is a stage of single lancets. At the base of this wall are remains of the arcade of the cloister, and two doors, one (blocked) leading into the church, the other leading to the slype or passage between transept and chapter house. It is unusual to find the slype as an integral part of the transept. The nave has a N aisle only: the cloister ran along the S

The crypt of Hexham Abbey, a 7C survival from the church built by St. Wilfrid

side. It is in early Decorated style as if Temple Moore were continuing the architectural development of the church after the Scots' destruction of 1296. It incorporates at the W end some remains of 12C walling. The N transept has tall and stately lancets on the W and N sides, and on the N side an upper tier of lancets, stepped, rising into the gable and almost as tall as the lower tier.

The crypt is entered from the nave by a steep descent of 12 steps. It was built of Roman stones from Corbridge, many of them carved or inscribed. At the foot of the stairs is an ante-chamber leading to the main relic chamber. Both are tunnel-vaulted. To the left (or N) of the ante-chamber is a triangle-vaulted space, with a passage leading from it to an original staircase up into the church. To the right (or S) of the relic chamber is a space leading to a corridor and staircase. The three entrances may not be of the same date. The 7C apse was located in the chancel immediately to the E of Wilfrid's throne. The E end and first bay are Dobson's—quite a creditable job. There are five bays of Early English work. The piers are substantial and clustered, the capitals mostly plain, the arches well-moulded. Over the arcade is a large gallery with pairs of pointed arches under one large round arch. The spandrels are decorated with quatrefoils. Above this is the clerestory, three arches to a bay, with clustered shafts in two tiers. Vaulting shafts rise from small stiff-leaf corbels between the gallery bays; but the roof, as in the N and S transepts, is of wood, and dates from the 15C. The aisles of chancel and transepts have rib-vaults, those in the chancel with stiff-leaf bosses. The S transept is dominated by the magnificent night stairs which rise to a balcony over the slype passage, and doors led to the dormitory and treasury. The piers of the arcade are more complicated than those of the chancel, but the gallery copies the chancel's. The clerestory has tall, accentuated arches. Over the balcony are two groups of blocked triple-shafted lancets, with three lancets higher still. On the W side are groups of three stepped lancets with a wall passage, and a clerestory as before. The N transept is the most stately part of the building. Aisle and arcade are much as before. At ground level runs a blank arcade of trefoil-headed arches, with quatrefoils in the spandrels. Above rise the tall lancets, on the N and W sides. They are divided in their lower part, where a passage runs, by clustered shafts, but higher up by double-chamfering. On the N wall tall shafts rise between the lancets but stop abruptly at the upper tier of lancets. The upper tier is stilted like the lower. The W clerestory is shafted to full height. In the SE corner of the nave is some original 7C flooring.

At the crossing is the Rood screen and loft, the most complete in any monastic church in England. It was erected in Prior Smithson's time (1491–1523) and is of wood. It is of verandah type, that is, it has central passages to left and right which led to stairs to the loft. These were removed in 1908. The W front, of five bays, has side arches filled with Flamboyant blank tracery of intricate pattern. Below, on the dado, are original paintings of Bishops of Lindisfarne and Hexham. The coving supports the loft, with 21 niches. On the beam, paterae with interwoven letters contain an inscription to Thomas Smithson 'who made this work'. (The inscription is in Latin.) Over the entrances to the central passages are paintings of the Annunciation and the Visitation. The E front has a projecting pulpitum with paintings of St. John the Evangelist, St. Oswald, St. Etheldreda and St. Andrew. The 15C choirstalls survive. They have carvings on the elbows and ends, and misericords. A few of the return stalls are new. The canopies perished before 1740, when galleries were erected in the chancel. In the centre of the chancel stands Wilfrid's throne, 7C or 8C, a hollowed-out cube of stone, with plaiting on the top of the arms. To the S of the altar are five canopied sedilia, 15C. Opposite is a 15C pulpit or lectern, probably from the monastic refectory. It is painted with figures of Christ, the Virgin and the Apostles. Over it are paintings of the Passion and the Dance of Death, and higher still is a 'choir screen', most probably the reredos of an altar, with paintings of seven of the 12 Bishops of Hexham. E of the pulpit is the Leschman chantry. It suffered much damage and removal in the 19C but was returned to its original position in 1908. The stone base is covered with uncouth carvings, including a lady curling her hair, a Northumberland piper and a fox preaching to geese. The upper part of the chapel is of wood, with complex tracery. Inside is the original altar and reredos with paintings of St. Peter, St. Andrew and St. Paul, and the Instruments of the Passion. Inside, too, is the stiff stone effigy of Prior Leschman, his cowl covering his eyes. Opposite is an earlier chantry, of Robert Ogle, Prior (died 1410). The wooden screens were sold as lumber in 1858, but much was regained, and the remainder has been recreated. At the E end is a painting of Christ, the Virgin and St. John, also sold in 1858, but bequeathed back to the Abbey in the 20C. The painting over the high altar is a copy after Andrea del Sarto. The organ, on the Rood screen, was installed in 1974. In the chancel aisles are many effigies and sculpted fragments. At the W end of the N aisle is an altar-tomb carved with a Tree of Life. It contained the body of a priest, probably a Prior. More sculpted fragments, dating from Roman to Norman times, are in the walls of the nave. The font is at the W end. The bowl is thought to have been part of a Roman pillar, hollowed out in pre-Conquest times. The stem is Early English: four shafts and bands of dogtooth. The simple cover is 17C, but above it hangs an ornate canopy, made by a Belgian refugee in the First World War. It incorporates 15C fragments. In the S transept, under the night stairs, is the tombstone of the Roman standard-bearer Flavinus, with a spirited relief showing the soldier on horseback riding over a crouching Briton, who raises his sword against the horse. Flavinus died at the age of 25, having served seven years. In the E aisle of this transept are remains of a 15C screen. Also in the S transept is a replica of the cross which is thought to have stood at the head of the grave of Acca, St. Wilfrid's successor as Bishop of Hexham (from 709 to 732), who died in 740. (The original is at Durham.) Some poppyhead bench-ends survive in the N transept. At the SE corner is a stone screen with an attractive four-centred arch over a monument. Most of the stained glass is 19C or 20C but the NE aisle window of the nave contains three pieces of Roman glass excavated at Corbridge. They are in the left-hand light. One piece is a white buckle on King Egfrid's shoulder; a yellow piece is near his forearm; and a small piece is a brooch on Queen Etheldreda's breast. In the S choir aisle a glass case in the wall contains a reputed pre-Conquest chalice, but it is more likely to be of the 11C than of St. Wilfrid's time.

Some of the remains of monastic buildings have been converted into a chapel and parish rooms.

(D.P. Kirby (Ed.) 'Saint Wilfrid at Hexham' (1974).)

Holy Island, St. Mary the Virgin. The flattish island of Holy Island or Lindisfarne is reached by a tidal causeway over the sands. It is a most important place in the early Christian history of England. Here St. Aidan arrived in 635 from Iona, invited by King Oswald of

Northumbria to build a monastery and found a bishopric. A little later, the young St. Wilfrid was a pupil in Aidan's school. A further famous figure, St. Cuthbert, was Prior of Lindisfarne in 664 and Bishop in 685. Just over a decade after St. Cuthbert's death, in c 898, the famous Lindisfarne Gospels were written here. This Latin manuscript of the four Gospels is now a major treasure of the British Library. Lindisfarne was sacked by the Danes in 793 and the monks fled with Cuthbert's body, finally settling at Durham where the See was re-established. It was William of St. Calais, Bishop of Durham, who restored monastic life to Lindisfarne after the Norman Conquest. The church stands to the W of the remains of the priory. It is now mostly 13C.

It is a long, low building, with a narrow chancel. The chancel windows are all lancets—at the E end triple, stepped, and with buttresses between. The nave has aisles but no clerestory. The aisle windows are mostly two-light, with Y-tracery, much restored. At the W end is an 18C bellcote with pyramidal cap, supported by two sturdy buttresses which come together in an arch. In the arch is a lancet window.

The N arcade survives from the 12C: three round arches with circular piers and capitals. The voussoirs of the arches are alternately red and white. At the W there was an extension c 1300. About this time, too, the S arcade was built, with pointed arches and octagonal piers. The chancel arch, also pointed, has no capitals. The high altar carpet, 1970, is a copy of a page of the Lindisfarne Gospels, made by local ladies.

Newcastle-upon-Tyne

All Saints. This splendid Classical building of 1786–96 by David Stephenson, known as the 'Oval Church', stands high on the banks of the river near the Tyne Bridge and its tall tower is a conspicuous landmark.

The tower stands on the S side, projecting from the oval body. It is a complicated, many-tiered and graceful composition. Steps lead up to its tetrastyle pedimented Doric portico. The tower has, first, tripartite windows, segment-headed, then engaged pediments and a tall belfry stage with lunette openings. Above this it becomes octagonal and narrows, with Tuscan columns paired at the corners; higher still are balustrading, another small octagon with Tuscan columns, and finally an octagonal obelisk spire. To left and right of the tower are rooms with tripartite windows. Then the oval body of the church follows in two storeys, the lower with more segment-headed tripartite windows, the upper with tall round-headed windows. At the E and W ends are shallow apsidal projections.

The entrance under the tower is circular and domed. Entering the church proper, the main axis is at right angles to the S entrance. Galleries run round the church on three sides, carried on fluted Roman Doric columns. All the woodwork is of mahogany. The ceiling is brightly and recently painted; but the walls, which formerly had painted decoration, are now plain white. The organ stands in the gallery at the W end. A small 18C table stands primly in the E apse, the windows of which have been re-opened. The church used to house—a survival from the medieval church—the largest brass in the country, to Roger Thornton (died 1430) and his wife (died 1411), now transferred to St. Nicholas's Cathedral. It is an incised rectangular plate. The two figures are surrounded by small figures of saints in niches with elaborate canopies; below are the couple's seven sons and seven daughters. There is a marginal inscription. In the tower vestibule is a tablet commemorating the architect of the church, David Stephenson (1757–1819).

The church was closed for worship in 1961. It was bought by Newcastle City Council in 1970 and repaired. The building is now an urban studies centre.

St. John the Baptist, Grainger Street. St John's is a building of the 14C and 15C, cruciform with a W tower. It is a low building, nestling amongst taller buildings in the city centre. The masonry, especially that of the tower, is rough-hewn, and creates a rugged, primitive effect, which is not altogether pleasing. The church possesses a font cover as ambitious as those in the cathedral and St. Andrew's, which is said to be 17C but looks earlier. There are 20C fittings by Sir Charles Nicholson and Stephen Dykes Bower.

The windows are mostly of three or five lights, with low arches. The parapets of the aisles and chancel are adorned with pinnacles but that of the nave clerestory is flat. The tower has octagonal corner buttresses which rise to slight turrets and are crowned with little pinnacles.

The interior is broad and spacious. A boss in the vault of the tower refers to Robert Rhodes (died 1474), who gave money for the tower, and also for the S transept, on the outside of which his arms and an inscription appear. The nave arcades and the arches of the crossing are 14C and are of the same type as those of St. Nicholas's (the cathedral), that is, chamfered arches dying into octagonal piers without capitals. The N transept, also 14C, has a W aisle. The pier there has a capital. In the N wall of the chancel, over the vestry door, is a Norman window-head from an earlier church. Close to it a cross-slit probably indicates the position of an anchorage formerly attached to the church.

The font with its tall cover, decorated with gables and pinnacles, stands under the W tower. Stephen Dykes Bower created a new altar area at the crossing in c 1970. He moved forward by one bay the massive, heavy, 17C pulpit, which has Corinthian columns and blank arches. The base and stair were designed by Dykes Bower. He also designed the attractive chancel screen, two tiers of slim, turned balusters, the lower tier with delicate wrought-iron work in the heads. Above the heavy entablature are finials in the form of candlesticks. The effect is 17C. In the same style are the communion rails which surround the altar on three sides. Beside the altar is a former communion table with an inscribed stone altar slab dated 1712. Of Sir Charles Nicholson's early 20C reordering, there remain the Rood over the chancel arch, the organ case, the S transept or Blessed Sacrament chapel and the high altar reredos, bright with colour and gilding (it was redecorated by Campbell, Smith & Co. of Liverpool under Dykes Bower's supervision, 1969). There are fragments of medieval stained glass, including the earliest representation of the arms of Newcastle (three towers), in a N window of the chancel. The rest of the stained glass is 19C or early 20C, mostly figures of saints. The windows in the S transept are by Atkinson (E), William Wailes (S) and H.M. Barnett (N). 18C and 19C monumental tablets adorn the walls: in the chancel (now the Lady chapel) are David Dunbar's bust, 1835, of J. Taylor, and a neo-Classical tablet to

Nathaniel Clayton (died 1786), with an attractive use of three different marbles.

Norham, *St. Cuthbert.* Norham, on the banks of the Tweed, has many pre-Conquest associations but scant remains. St. Aidan crossed the river here in 635 on his way to found the monastery at Lindisfarne. His first church, a wooden structure, is said to have been re-erected here. A stone church was built c 830. St. Cuthbert's coffin rested here in 875 on its journey round Northumbria when the Danes sacked Lindisfarne. In the pre-Conquest church were buried St. Ceolwulf, King of Northumbria and later a monk, and Gospatric, first Earl of Northumberland. In medieval times Norham was a stronghold of the Bishops of Durham against the Scots. The present church, begun in 1165 at the same time as the castle, retains some impressive Norman features, including the S arcade, with remarkably wide arches.

It is a long, low building with a continuous roofline. The aisles and tower are 19C. The curious rectangular W tower, added in 1836 by Ignatius Bonomi of Durham, struggles to lift the composition. The nearness of the churchyard boundary at this point probably dictated the shape; the central tower of Jarrow perhaps supplied the model. But it is an unhappy design: Norman belfry openings too large, details somewhat coarse, and a tiled parapet giving it an unfinished look. The nave has no clerestory. It is said to have been roofless from 1513 to 1619, when the parishioners restored it. They demolished the old aisles and walled up the arcades. A Norman S transept is shown in a drawing of c 1840 and must have been demolished soon after. Bonomi & Cory rebuilt the S aisle in 1846 and the N aisle in 1852, more acceptably Norman than the tower. The N transept, containing the organ, was added in 1883–84. The chancel is mostly Norman. On the S side, the five bays of windows have ornate decoration of zigzag and beakhead in the arches. Above them runs a corbel table. On the N side, the windows are plain-headed. The E end was damaged when Robert Bruce fortified the church in 1320 while besieging the castle, and replaced c 1340 by the square end with a large five-light E window with Geometrical tracery (now a not-too-close copy of 1875, renewed 1953). To N and S are two-light windows. There are flat buttresses.

Inside, the nave is rather dark but the chancel is long and light. The S arcade, with its massive arches, is now five bays long, with round piers, but octagonal abaci. The capitals of the piers have waterleaf. Over the arches is a frieze of zigzag. The N arcade is of octagonal piers and double-chamfered round arches. The chancel arch has crocket capitals and alternating red and white stones (as has the vestry arch). On the pillar above the lectern is a mason's mark known elsewhere only at Trondheim Cathedral, Norway. There is a 14C piscina in the sanctuary. In the SW corner of the chancel, above the stalls, is a niche, the purpose of which is unknown. It seems not to have been a window.

The furnishings include several pieces of 17C woodwork brought from Durham Cathedral in the 19C by Dr William Gilly, Vicar in 1831–55 and a Canon of Durham. At the W end are the arms of King Charles II, never coloured. The elaborate pulpit and desk are also from Durham and were part of Bishop Cosin's refurnishing after the Restoration. The font, decorated with interlaced Norman arches, was made c 1842, perhaps to Bonomi's design. The clergy stalls in the chancel are made from parts of a 17C family pew. The 17C flower-stands and brass candlesticks on the altar (with iron rings on the feet for chaining) were recently acquired. The cross, in similar style, is modern; and the lectern, of brass, is a copy of the medieval one in Southwell Minister. The wrought-iron communion rails, of the 1950s, incorporate emblems of St. Peter (keys), St. Cuthbert (eider duck) and St. Ceolwulf (crown), recalling the dedication of the pre-Conquest church. The E window has stained glass of 1873 to illustrate the injunction, 'Feed My Lambs'.

In the chancel on the S side is a 14C monument of a knight, placed in a canopied recess with early Decorated tracery in the gable. It was found in the nave in 1883 when 20ins of dirt were removed from the floor. Opposite is J.G. Lough's monument to Dr Gilly (died 1855), a recumbent effigy on a tomb-chest, in a Norman arched recess. In the tower are pre-Conquest carved stones, parts of a cross-shaft and cross-head, found in the churchyard, and now embedded into a square pillar. Near the font in the NW corner are ancient stones removed from the inside wall of the sanctuary in 1953.

In Norham Church in 1292, John Balliol did homage to King Edward I of England for the Kingdom of Scotland. William Gilly, the most famous Vicar, was the historian of the Waldensians, the ancient Protestant Church of the valleys between Italy and France.

Warkworth, *St. Lawrence*. Warkworth is substantially Norman, a rarity in Northumberland. Only the W tower and S aisle are later. The church was probably founded in the 7C by St. Aidan and King Oswald and may have housed the relics of St. Lawrence sent by Pope Vitalian to King Oswin, Oswald's successor.

The N side of the church shows Norman work of c 1120: five small round-headed lancets separated by wide flat buttresses, with two stringcourses, one of which surmounts the windows as hoodmoulds. There is a blocked doorway with shafts flanked by buttresses and with evidence of a former porch. The chancel has more small Norman windows and a narrow S door. The E end was rebuilt by Ewan Christian c 1860. The sturdy W tower was added c 1200, and has paired-lancet belfry openings. It is topped by a broach spire of c 1400. Also of c 1200 is a N vestry with lancets and a W window of three small lights made from a single stone. The S aisle has late 15C windows, tall and with panel tracery (some inserted in 1860), of three lights, and five lights at the E end. The S porch has a chamber over it, approached from outside by a stair in the NE corner. The church formerly had a clerestory and a flat roof like the aisle, but this was destroyed in John Dobson's restoration of 1860.

The W end of the nave shows Norman work. The windows of the N wall are shafted. The Norman chancel arch has three shafts on each side and a much-moulded and enriched head. The chancel, most unusually for the 12C, is stone-vaulted. The vaulting is of two bays, with small shafts and scalloped capitals. These are supported by the sill-level stringcourse. The windows here also have shafts. The S arcade, early 14C, is of five bays with clustered shafts, moulded capitals and arches. The S porch has a stone rib-vault.

The wrought-iron communion rail is of 1710. Also in the chancel are pre-Conquest cross fragments. There is a monument at the W end of the S aisle of a cross-legged 14C knight with shield, finely preserved. The E window of the S aisle has fragments of medieval stained glass. A new reading desk and pulpit, designed by Alfred Southwick and carved by Ralph Hedley, were installed in 1926. The pulpit has five panels depicting St. Benedict Biscop, St. Hilda and Caedmon, Ceolwulf resigning the kingship, the voyage of St. Cuthbert to Coquet Island, and St. Lawrence distributing riches to the poor.

During the Jacobite Rebellion of 1715 the church was seized by supporters of the Old Pretender, who was proclaimed King James VIII and III at the Market Cross, following prayers in the church for his success.

NOTTINGHAMSHIRE

Nottinghamshire is celebrated more for Robin Hood, D.H. Lawrence and its lace than church architecture. However, it does contain some of the great churches of England—Newark, Blyth, Hawton, St. Mary's at Nottingham and Worksop—even though the ordinary village churches are not a match for Norfolk or Northamptonshire. Nottinghamshire is provided with building materials of only ordinary quality. Most of the medieval churches are constructed of New Red Sandstone, usually of buff or greyish hue. Often these sandstones, though excellent for internal carving, wear poorly outside, hence even more Victorian renewal than might normally be expected. Another widely used stone was Magnesian Limestone. In the SE, Jurassic Blue Lias is used as a building material: it is usually in smallish, rather platy blocks. Where there was money, as at Newark in the Middle Ages or Clumber more recently, imported materials can be found; in these cases, Ancaster stone from Lincolnshire and Runcorn stone respectively.

There is only one significant upstanding pre-Conquest work—the 11C tower and rather earlier nave at Carlton-in-Lindrick. At Stapleford there is the most important pre-Conquest carving, a late cross which still retains its original shaft decorated mainly with interlace. At Shelford is a panel with a fine Virgin and Child on one side and on the other an angel with a book. Fragments can be found at East Bridgford (a cross-shaft with interlace in the S aisle and on the aisle SE buttress). Nottinghamshire is a good county for Norman work. Apart from Southwell Minster, the great churches are Blyth and Worksop, which are both partial survivals of monastic churches, the first Benedictine, the second Augustinian. The earlier is Blyth, where the nave is one of the finest examples of early Norman work at its most severe. To stand in the nave at Worksop is a wholly different experience. This is 50 to 100 years later and the brutal strength of Blyth has been mellowed. Worksop and Southwell are the only complete surviving cases of the popular Norman W façade with two towers. Other Norman work of significance includes the crypt at Newark, the arches at South Collingham and South Scarle, and the W tower at South Leverton. Balderton has a fine doorway which includes an inner order of beakhead and Teversal's S doorway is also richly treated. East Bridgford had a long Norman chancel as the wavy stringcourse on the S side shows. There are many Norman fonts but the key one is at Lenton. There the rectangular font from the former Cluniac priory is of the mid-12C and appears to be without stylistic parallels in England. One side has a foliated cross, but the others tell the story of Christ's Baptism, Crucifixion and Resurrection. The other 12C font with figures is at West Markham. Among the most interesting carvings are Calverton, where there is a series of panels of the Labours of the Months. They may have surrounded a doorway. The chancel arch respond contains a tiny figure of St. Wilfrid, to whom the church is dedicated.

There are excellent examples of 13C work but the two finest, Southwell Minster and the W façade of the ruined Newstead Abbey, are outside the scope of this book. The chapter house at Newstead, however, became the chapel of the house.

At Worksop the Lady chapel is a precious survival. It was attached to the S transept and after long lying roofless, was restored in 1922. Among true parish churches the 13C work in the Newark tower is probably the most interesting. It achieves a rather wilful result by the use of elaborate decoration. At Sibthorpe there is a good, tall chancel arch and at Gedling a spacious 13C chancel. W towers start to become more frequent in the 13C and the steeple at Bingham is an impressive example. There are two two-light belfry windows, which was to become a normal feature, and above these, a corbel course and a spire behind a parapet done in the early 14C. The county is not generally one of spires which, no doubt, reflects the fact that it does not have top quality, durable building stone. An early example, in the 13C, is at Gotham. Nottinghamshire has a few cases of round arches surviving into the early 13C as at Ratcliffe-on-Soar and Teversal.

Nottinghamshire excels in early 14C work. Churches are endowed with work of the greatest beauty and of the ornateness that has led to the term 'Decorated' being applied to church architecture of the early 14C. The pre-eminent example is the chancel at Hawton with its overwhelming Easter sepulchre, sedilia and piscina. At Sibthorpe there is an Easter sepulchre that tries to rival Hawton, but it is much more limited in scope and less refined in detail. The Easter sepulchre was certainly popular in S and W Nottinghamshire at this time and other examples are found at Arnold, Fledborough and Laxton. The chancels in which the Easter sepulchres are located were generally rebuilt at the same time and Car Colston, Hawton, Sibthorpe, Strelley and Woodborough are all worth visiting for their chancels. The one at Sibthorpe is known to have been built for the foundation of a college in 1325. At Woodborough the chancel is as large and as high as the rest of the church. At Woodborough and Strelley can be seen another Nottinghamshire speciality, which carries on into the 15C, a keeled vault to the porch. Here there are no transverse ribs of the type found at Bunny, St. Mary's at Nottingham or Scrooby. West Retford and Gedling also have stone-vaulted porches. Gedling is notable for its steeple built onto the NW corner of the church. It is extremely tall and probably dates from the early 14C.

Nottinghamshire is also a good place to find Perpendicular work at its grandest. Even in the 13C Newark was as long as it is now and is one of the largest parish churches in the country. It is largely a Perpendicular remodelling. Into the same category comes St. Mary's, Nottingham, the second largest church in the county. At both Newark and Nottingham the emphasis, as was typical in the 15C, was on wide uninterrupted spaces and large windows and clerestories to achieve as light an interior as possible. The most ambitious churches had two clerestory windows for every bay below as at East Markham, Newark, Nottingham and Laxton. A rare example of a church entirely (apart from the W tower) of one period is at Lambley, which Ralph Cromwell built in the 1460s. Another case where the benefactor is known is Holme-by-Newark, which was rebuilt by the wealth John Barton (died 1491) had amassed in the wool trade. The most unusual piece of Perpendicular architecture must be the steeple at West Retford with its strange transition from tower to spire. In the absence of spires, a speciality that the Perpendicular builders employed in E Nottinghamshire was to crown their towers not with just the usual four pinnacles at the corners but a further four along each side. Travelling through E Nottinghamshire, it seems that almost every parish church is so treated.

Medieval furnishings are not very well represented. The best items are the Perpendicular screens at Strelley and Newark. The Newark screen of 1508 is by a famous medieval craftsman, Thomas

Drawswerd of York. The Laxton screen is a very late example, dated 1532. At Balderton there are 45 bench-ends of the poppyhead type and they have animals placed on the finials. Misericords can be found at Newark (26), St. Stephen's at Nottingham (8), North Collingham (7), Thurgarton and Wysall (4 each) and Screveton (1). Medieval stained glass at East Retford, Newark, Halam, Fledborough and Egmanton is worth seeing. East Leake and South Scarle have two of the country's half-dozen vamping horns.

In the three centuries after the Reformation there is nothing of national importance. St. Nicholas's, Nottingham was rebuilt in brick in 1671–82 and Holme Pierrepont has a most interesting S aisle with Gothic Survival tracery and a Classical S porch of 1666. In the 18C some churches were Classical, notably West Stockwith of 1722, Ossington of 1782–83 by John Carr and Calverton of the 1760s; but Papplewick of 1795 is a delightful piece of Gothick. The churches of East Stoke and Blidworth were much rebuilt in 1738 and 1739 respectively and acquired unusual arcades with Tuscan columns. The strangest pre-Victorian church was built at Milton in 1831–32 as a combined church and mausoleum erected by the fourth Duke of Newcastle in memory of his wife. The architect was Sir Robert Smirke and his building was meant to replace the parish church, which it failed to do. The county is fortunate in retaining many pre-Victorian interiors. Teversal is of the late 17C. Papplewick dates from 100 years later. Also notable are Barnby, Maplebeck, Oxton, Winkburn and Tythby. Two important and rare examples of pre-Victorian stained glass occur at Papplewick and in the Resurrection window of 1830 by Francis Eginton at Babworth. Perhaps the finest 17C or 18C fitting is the reredos at Wollaton of c 1660.

As for Victorian church building, the great masterpiece is Clumber Chapel, built in 1886–89 by Bodley & Garner for the young and ardently High Church seventh Duke of Newcastle. It represents a magnificent late essay in Ecclesiological Gothic. Church architecture was beginning to find freer expression and Mansfield has a particularly good example of such late 19C architecture in Temple Moore's St. Mark's of 1897. Bodley's St. Alban's, Sneinton, Nottingham, is exactly contemporary with Clumber but shows a very different facet of his output—a brick exterior and a tall, spacious aisled nave and chancel which emphasise refinement and dignity rather than overwhelming grandeur. Bodley is also represented at Coddington which he partly rebuilt and decorated and which is notable for its Morris & Co. glass. A further late 19C church of some distinction is W.D. Caroë's St. Stephen's, Bobber's Mill Road, Nottingham, of 1897. Early in the Victorian era town churches were bigger, more portentous, as H.I. Stevens' St. John the Evangelist's, Mansfield of 1854–56 and William Knight's St. Andrew's, Nottingham of 1869–71 amply demonstrate. Other facets of High Victorian architecture are illustrated by the 'roguish' designs of T.C. Hine at Farnsfield of 1869, and the lavish decoration in the chapel of Newstead Abbey, dating from the 1860s. Returning to the end of the century, Egmanton is important for Ninian Comper's work, notably his Rood screen. Comper also designed the reredos at Newark in the 1930s.

The county has two very notable monuments of 20C church building. The earlier is Henry Wilson's treatment of the chapel at Welbeck Abbey. The other is the former chapel at Kelham by C.C. Thompson of Derby for the Society of the Sacred Mission (or Kelham Fathers), which established a famous Anglican theological college here in 1903 in the extraordinary High Victorian house of 1859–62 by

Sir Gilbert Scott. The chapel was never finished but what we see was put up in 1927–28. It is a mighty brick structure which would have been magnificent had its Byzantine conception of a dome over a cross-in-square plan been carried out. Kelham ceased to be a theological college in 1969 and the chapel is now used for entertainments. *Sic transit gloria.*

There are a number of churches with individual monuments or groups of monuments worth visiting. The two best brasses are at Newark and East Markham. At East Markham a beautiful brass commemorates Millicent Meyring (died 1419), attired in the costume of the early 15C. A good monument of similar date is to Sir Sampson de Strelley (died c 1390) and his wife (died 1405), in the chancel which he rebuilt at Strelley. Another important medieval benefactor whose monument survives was John Barton (died 1491), who rebuilt most of the church at Holme. The best collection of monuments is to the Clifton family of Clifton, now a part of Nottingham. It starts in the late 14C. Another splendid collection that goes back to the 14C is of the Willoughby monuments at Willoughby-on-the-Wolds: it is almost like a fossilised medieval dormitory! The most fantastic medieval monument is part of the chantry erected by Anthony Babington in c 1540. The table-tomb has gone, but the four columns that support the canopy are encrusted with small hexagons filled with tracery, heads, figures, etc. The rebus of babes and tuns figures prominently and in the E wall there is a miniaturised Doom. Artistically, Tudor and Elizabethan monuments are more satisfactory than most of the medieval ones and there is a good collection from 1539 to 1625 to the Sacheverells at Ratcliffe-on-Soar. The monuments of the early Byrons of the 16C and 17C have been brought to Newstead Abbey from Colwick, though the sixth Lord Byron, the poet, lies buried at Hucknall. There are few 17C or 18C monuments of great note though the best are probably the two by Joseph Nollekens to William Denison (died 1782) and Robert Denison (died 1785) at Ossington. But undoubtedly the most curious monument of this time is to Sir Thomas Parkyns, 'the Wrestling Baronet' (died 1741), at Bunny. His monument, designed by himself, records his prolific interests—his designs for buildings on his estates, his interests in medicine, mathematics, hydraulics, etc. On the left side, his huge figure is poised to take on his next wrestling opponent. But right, the figure of Time lays him low.

Architecturally, the Free Church places of worship are not noteworthy. One of the more distinguished is the old Meeting House in Mill Walk on the N of Stockwell Gate in Mansfield. It dates back to 1702 and has been much altered and added to. It has been Unitarian since the late 18C. Inside, three arches down the middle create a 'double nave' effect. Historically the most important place is Scrooby, where a group of Independents gathered in the early 17C under the patronage of William Brewster, the Pilgrim Father. They eventually set sail for the New World in 1620. Mansfield was an important centre of Nonconformity in the 17C and Nottingham also long had a strong tradition of Dissent.

The earliest major historical association concerns Harby where Queen Eleanor, the wife of King Edward I, died in 1290. The grief-stricken king erected the beautiful series of Eleanor crosses at the places where her cortège rested on its journey to London. The chantry chapel he built at Harby has long gone. Car Colston is the resting place of Robert Thoroton (1623–78), the Nottinghamshire antiquarian. At Langar there is the tomb of the first Earl Howe (1726–99), who won the naval battle of the Glorious First of June in 1794. Elston has monuments to the Darwin family, ancestors of the famous Charles, author of 'The Origin of Species'.

Blyth, St. Mary and St. Martin. The nave and N aisle are a supreme example of stern early Norman architecture. This awesome building seems fractionally earlier than Southwell and owes its large scale to having been a Benedictine priory, founded in 1088 by Roger de Builli, and to the fact that Blyth was once one of the more important places in Nottinghamshire, deriving its prosperity from its markets, fairs and its site on a major route. This church was once even larger, for the choir and transepts were removed after the Dissolution. The arrangements of the E end were the same as those at Worksop, with an apsidal chancel flanked by two square-ended chapels, plus two more apsidal ones off the transepts. In c 1300 a very large S aisle was added which was as wide as the length of the S transept. Then came a very tall Perpendicular tower as a piece of parochial display. Very interestingly, before the Reformation a wall was thrown up between the monastic and parochial parts, between the E piers of the nave, the two parts being connected by an extant doorway. The church was restored by C. Hodgson Fowler in 1885.

From the SE the church presents an odd appearance, shorn of its E parts and with the gaping space of what was once the W crossing arch. The E face is filled with undignified modern buff bricks. Above the wide S aisle rises the Norman clerestory, the simplicity and directness of which gives a foretaste of what is inside. The S aisle has windows with heavy, renewed intersected tracery with four bays E of the porch and two to the W. This porch goes with the S aisle, though the battlements are later. At ground level the lack of the offset in the walling just S of the tower indicates the width of the aisle in Norman times. N of the tower the early aisle stands undisturbed. The tower is not especially beautiful overall, but has a number of attractive individual features.

The great nave and aisle were probably complete in c 1100 and their severity has only been modified by the addition of quadripartite rib-vaults in the early 13C. Five bays remain undisturbed; the E one was divided off in the late Middle Ages and the W one was swallowed up by the tower (see the start of the vault springing). The S elevation is undisturbed but for the vaulting, though on the N side the gallery level has been filled in by plain Perpendicular windows. The late 11C elevation therefore had three elements, the arcade, a gallery and a clerestory. The arches of the arcade and the gallery have no ornamentation at all. The piers are square, with a flat projection and shafts that would originally have risen right up to a flat roof. They now stop at the springing of the gallery where the vaulting begins. In the E–W direction there are larger semicircular sections with powerful capitals decorated with the most rudimentary volutes. A stringcourse runs below the gallery. In the N aisle there is absolutely nothing after the late 11C for even the roof has plain, groined bays divided by unadorned transverse arches. The E bay of the aisle was divided off as a sacristy (at the time of the blocking of the nave arch?). That the E bay was blocked off in medieval times is evidenced by the fact that the wall has traces of contemporary paintings.

There are three Perpendicular screens. The one in the S aisle is vaulted on both sides; both it and the nave screen have traces of saints in their dados, but they are not of high quality. The font is 17C and has a ring of cherubs' heads round the bowl. The W window in the S aisle has stained glass by C.E. Kempe, 1903. There are a mutilated knight of the mid-13C in the S aisle and a moderately good monument by John Hancock to Edward Mellish (died 1703) in the N aisle.

On the E wall is the largest surviving Doom painting in the N of England, though, artistically, it is not particularly good. It was found in 1985 and uncovered from 1987. Below are other scenes from a Passion series. The E pier in the S chapel has early ashlar painting and also primitive foliage on the capital; a 12C or even 11C date has been claimed. There is also much painting in the nave, but it is obscure; a few stylised flowers and other motifs are just visible.

Car Colston, *St. Mary.* The glorious thing here is the mid-14C chancel, one of several in the district. It has three bays separated by big buttresses and three-light Reticulated windows. The E window is of five lights, with lovely flowing tracery. So grand is the chancel that it is higher and wider than the nave. The lowest part of the tower is 13C, though the base course and buttresses seem to be later additions. The top of the tower was added in the 15C and is capped by an unusual, dumpy stone spire. Inside, the lightness of the chancel contrasts with the gloominess of the rest. Its sedilia are most notable and may be the work of the same craftsman as at Hawton. They are triple, have ogee heads and lavish finials, pinnacles and crockets. Further E is the piscina with a bowed ogee canopy. Also noteworthy in the chancel is the altar rail, given in 1732, which has an attractive and rare semicircular middle section. The nave has tall, four-bay arcades with standard details probably of the 14C. The choir fittings extend one bay into the nave. There is stained glass of 1875 by C.E. Kempe in one three-light window on the S side of the chancel; it depicts St. Raphael, St. Michael and St. Gabriel.

Robert Thoroton (1623–78), the author of 'The Antiquities of Nottinghamshire', published in 1677, lived in this village. His great coped coffin of red Mansfield stone, dug up from in front of the priest's door in 1863, now lies at the W end of the S aisle. His remains were reburied.

Carlton-in-Lindrick, *St. John the Evangelist.* The only pre-Conquest work of any substance in Nottinghamshire is to be found here in the impressively tall 11C W tower. The nave, or at least its W parts, are even older. There are also small windows in the nave and chancel N walls which may be either pre- or post-Conquest. The N arcade and chancel arch jambs are Transitional. The N chapel was added in c 1200 and nothing more was done until the tower top and buttresses were added (perhaps between 1417 and 1443 when a bell was given) and the clerestory was put on. In 1831 the S aisle was built in a remarkably faithful Perpendicular style and the Norman S doorway was moved to the W wall of the tower.

The early phase of the tower is quite plain, its only embellishments being a stringcourse halfway up and the belfry windows. These have two tall openings with mid-wall shafts. The early nature of the tower was revealed only in 1869 when plaster was removed. The E and W windows were unblocked in 1936. As well as the embattled top stage and the big angle buttresses a SW stair turret was added in the 15C. The upper part of the pre-Conquest tower has extensive pitched stonework. The nave is rather earlier than the tower as the latter is not bonded into it and, in fact, the tower's E face is built on top of the nave W wall. The NW quoining is massive and is of the side-alternate pattern.

The early nave and chancel windows can be seen to better advantage inside. There is one over the E pier of the N arcade and another two complete with deep splays in the chancel. On the N side of the nave the three-bay arcade is of Transitional character with circular piers, roll-moulded arches and capitals with volutes or variations on them. The chancel arch has jambs of similar date—note the late use of interlace on the S impost—but a pointed 15C arch. The tower arch is most interesting. On the nave side it is far more elaborate than the tower side and it seems that the former is a later insertion (e.g. see the lack of bond around the imposts). The E face is of two orders supported on shafts which carry capitals with upright leaves, and it could date from the middle, or even the end of the 11C. Over the tower arch is a gallery approached by a pre-Conquest doorway. Over the priest's door (seen from the vestibule) is an early carved stone depicting what appear to be the sun, the moon and two stars. Remarkably, the church has three stone altars, one each in the aisles, and part of the high altar against the E wall. At the E end of the N aisle is a damaged Nottingham alabaster panel depicting the Trinity. Over the E part of the nave is an old (repositioned?) pulley wheel, for raising a veil or font cover.

Clumber, *Chapel of St. Mary the Virgin.* The late 18C seat of the Dukes of Newcastle was pulled down in 1938 but the cathedralesque chapel remains, standing proudly in the centre of extensive parkland. It is one of the very grandest late 19C churches and was erected in 1886–89 at enormous cost (said to be over £40,000) by Henry, seventh Duke of Newcastle, an ardent High Churchman, who began building at the age of 22. His father had begun a chapel in 1865, but work on this ceased in 1868. The seventh Duke's architect was G.F. Bodley, whose inspiration here is his beloved late Decorated and in particular he draws his cruciform plan and the idea of a corona set around a spire from Patrington in Yorkshire.

The chapel is symmetrical about its E–W axis. S of the chancel is the Lady chapel and N of it are vestries. The chancel is just as long as the nave, though its roof ridge is fractionally higher. The stylistic mood is late Decorated, just as Perpendicular was beginning to make its early, tentative appearances (the S transept window, however, is fully Perpendicular). The emphasis is on height. Prominent buttresses mark off each bay and the windows are set high up. The colour contrasts of the walls are very strong: local buff Steetley stone is set against red Runcorn stone. The visual focus is the steeple. Because of the way the set-offs of the buttresses are organised, a tapering effect really begins above the level of the nave and chancel roofs. In the belfry stage there are two twin-light openings and above this an embattled parapet with thin flying buttresses. These link to an octagonal open corona which surrounds the spire. The S side is a magnificent example of the refinement which Bodley was seeking in his work. It is obviously the side to be seen and Bodley concentrates all the 'disruptive' features like stair turrets and vestries on the N. The main entrance is at the W.

The themes of height and grandeur are continued inside. The arrangements are a nave of four bays, plus the crossing and a long four-bay chancel. In the angle between the nave and the N transept is the baptistery. The chapel is vaulted throughout. Although the plan is a cruciform one, Bodley has solved the problem of a crossing being a barrier between nave and chancel. The width of the nave is continued through to the chancel with the crossing arches dying into the walls. There is no triforium stage, but the clerestory windows are given considerable height and are linked together by a wall passage above the arcades. Such architectural ornament as is employed is small-scale and the building is an ideal clothing for the numerous furnishings and fittings. Taken together these tell clearly of the Anglo-Catholic worship favoured by the seventh Duke.

The furnishings are not all Bodley's. His patron quarrelled with him and later work was done by Ninian Comper and the Reverend Ernest Geldart, until 1922. The most prominent of the furnishings is, however, Bodley's, that is the lovely tall vaulted screen set in the E crossing arch. Over it he planned a Rood beam and a Rood group but the present group is Geldart's. The chancel is a model of Anglo-Catholic furnishing. The stalls are Geldart's and date from 1890. On the walls behind the altar and on some of the furnishings are textiles by Watts & Co. Most of the stained glass is by C.E. Kempe, whose restrained and pure style blends so well with Bodley's architecture. His is the E window, representing Biblical scenes, major saints and the Latin Doctors. The other furnishings in the chancel are the altar by Farmer & Brindley (who were responsible for all the stone carving in the chapel); Geldart's iron and copper lamps; and, on the N side, the organ, whose case has a painted front which was restored by S.E. Dykes Bower. S of the chancel is the Lady chapel, with its Bodley altar and reredos. Its windows are by Kempe and commemorate the marriage of the seventh Duke in 1889. Moving into the crossing and nave, the pulpit is by Farmer & Brindley; there are more lamps by Geldart; there are Stations of the Cross in the blind arcades; and there are large wooden figures of the Virgin and Child and St. Joseph, designed by Geldart. All these fittings date from 1912–22. The W window is again by Kempe, as is that in the S transept. On the N wall of the baptistery is a statue of St. John the Baptist by Comper, who also designed the George and the Dragon in the passage leading to the Lady chapel. A very beautiful item which stood here until recently (but now removed to Milton, though out of character with the rest of the building, was the monument in the N transept to Georgiana (died 1822), the wife of the fourth Duke of Newcastle. It was by Sir Richard Westmacott and has the Duchess reclining with her baby children. Behind in a square panel was a magically aetherial figure clad in gossamer bidding the Duchess towards Heaven.

The chapel is in the care of the National Trust but it is still used for services. It has a resident incumbent and regular parishioners.

Coddington, *All Saints.* The delight here is the interior, which has an early decorative scheme by G.F. Bodley and Morris & Co. glass. Everything is restrained in a way that was most unusual when it was done in 1864–65. The ceiling is in effect three-sided, panelled and has stencilled decoration. The chancel walls were originally decorated too. The chancel windows have gentle glass with designs by William Morris and Sir Edward Burne-Jones. The glass in the S aisle is also by Morris & Co., with designs by Ford Madox Brown, Burne-Jones and Morris himself. Bodley, much later, designed the screen (1890–91). The panelling and reredos are of 1869. He was also responsible for much rebuilding. The three-bay arcades, however, are medieval, and the piers have stone seats round them. There are several 15C carved benches in the N aisle.

East Markham, *St. John the Baptist.* This dignified and amply-proportioned church is mainly the work of the early 15C, though the chancel is early 14C. The most distinctive features outside are the twinning of the three-light clerestory windows over each bay to form a continuous row, and the tall tower. This is built in the grand manner and has the eight pinnacles which are usual in this area. On the S side is a medieval statue in a niche. The early 15C windows of the aisles have three panelled lights under nearly triangular heads. At the SE corner of the nave is a prominent Rood loft stair (cf. the big NE one at nearby Gamston). The 14C chancel is of three bays and, as at Hawton, the middle window is sliced into by the priest's doorway. The S porch is rather small but its original roof is worth a glance. The church was restored by John Oldrid Scott in 1883–87 at a cost of £2600.

The interior is splendidly spacious in a way associated more with East Anglia than Nottinghamshire. The Perpendicular love of panelling and crenellating is to be seen in the treatment of the four-bay nave. There are a number of fittings and furnishings of interest. Of these the most conspicuous is the strange font, with probably a 14C bowl but with eight flying buttresses to its lower part. Its pyramidal cover, and also the pulpit and altar rails, are all of the early 17C. A 15C screen stands in the E bay of the S arcade, and contemporary glass has been collected in the tracery lights of the S aisle windows (including two female saints in the E one). The E window in the chancel is by Ninian Comper in 1896, but also incorporates medieval fragments. On the N side of the chancel is the alabaster tomb-chest to Sir John Markham (died 1409), a judge and Lord of the Manor here who was responsible for drafting the document which deposed King Richard II. The effigy no longer exists. In the S aisle is the very fine brass to Lady Millicent Meryng (died 1419) in her elaborate headdress.

Egmanton, *St. Mary.* It is the Anglo-Catholic revival of the late 19C that gives Egmanton a special place among the churches of Nottinghamshire. The prime mover here was the seventh Duke of Newcastle, who spent over £2000 in 1896–98, during which time a statue of Our Lady was set up in the chancel and which, like its medieval predecessor, has made the church a place of pilgrimage. The Duke's architect was the young Ninian Comper, who designed a set of furnishings remarkably rich for an ordinary village church.

The main item is the coloured screen complete with a loft, Rood group (quite advanced for an English church at the time) and a curved celure over the latter. The far side bays have painted panels of Prophets and St. John the Evangelist. The loft has crocketed canopies over the repeated names of Mary and Jesus. The other big item by Comper is the organ case above the S door. Even more overtly High Church than the Rood group is a hanging pyx (six-sided with angels bearing Instruments of the Passion) and the image of the Virgin on the N wall. Also by Comper are the hangings and riddel posts around the altar and the stained glass in the E window, depicting the Virgin crowned and holding the infant Christ and flanked by St. Anne (on her right), St. Mary Magdalene (left) and Salome and Mary Cleopas.

The old parts of the church are undistinguished. There are 14C windows, a routine 15C tower and nave roof, but the oldest work is the four-bay N arcade of the late 12C with round piers and pointed arches.

St. Mary's, refitted by Sir Ninian Comper in 1896–98 for the seventh Duke of Newcastle

The devotion to Mary at Egmanton began when a local woman was supposed to have seen a vision of the Virgin. The image set up in 1897 became the basis of a latter-day shrine and by 1912 a Guild of Our Lady of Egmanton had been created to honour the Virgin. The first pilgrimage took place in 1929 and has been continued each summer to the present day.

Hawton, *All Saints.* The chancel contains some of the richest Decorated work in England and can be compared with the Southwell pulpitum or the Lady chapel at Ely. It was work of the second Sir Robert de Compton, who died in 1330 and who was buried here. Of the rest of the church little need be said. It was heavily and unsympathetically restored in 1880–87 by C. Hodgson Fowler. The N aisle and three-bay arcade are late 13C. The W tower is known to have been erected by Sir Thomas Molyneux in 1482. It has a W door whose intersected ogee tracery may well indicate a 14C date.

The chancel is not large and has three fairly small bays divided by big buttresses. Its S windows are of three lights with two circles and a reticulation over them—that is, Geometrical with the addition of a Decorated feature. The vast E window, which almost fills its wall, also has a Geometrical skeleton but this is dissolved by mouchettes and other ogee forms into a free design. The S doorway is squeezed into the middle bay and slices away part of the adjacent window. All this is appealing enough but the great glory at Hawton is inside the chancel. On the N is a group (from W to E) of a doorway to a former chapel, the founder's tomb-recess and an Easter sepulchre. This is answered on the S by triple sedilia and a double piscina. The three parts of the N group are divided from one another by tall pinnacles which reach up to a horizontal course. The doorway has a surround of many thin mouldings, an ogee head and large cusps. On top of the ogee feature there stands the figure of a bishop. In the tomb-recess is the effigy of Sir Robert, much defaced. Over him is an ogee arch bearing ogee cusps which, in turn, are sub-cusped. Within the largest cusps are carvings of wimpled women with books. On top of the arch there stands another, larger figure of a bishop, his head now lacking. The large plain spandrel areas over the door and the recess are the only ones so treated and must originally have been painted. The Easter sepulchre has four sleeping soldiers at the base and has two upper, unequal tiers which are divided vertically into three. In the main compartment there are two columns at the front and in the wall at the back a figure of the Risen Christ emerges as from the tomb. On the right are the three exquisitely carved Maries, caught in a state of utter amazement. Sadly, all these figures are mutilated. On the left is a niche which would have held the symbolic body of Christ, the Host. Below the top part is the most astonishing wealth of adornment: knobbly leaves on every gable and arch, two diagonal bands with a trail, flat writhing foliage, crockets, finials—indeed, every possible device from the early 14C vocabulary. Above, the Apostles gather at the Ascension as angels hover over them. Christ disappears, except for his feet, into a cloud. Opposite, the triple sedilia are almost equally profuse in decoration. In the cornice angels crown saints. The two central saints are St. Peter (with keys) and St. Nicholas (with anchor). Beneath are three more, including St. Edmund (with arrow). The capitals at the springing of the canopies have interesting carvings including a pelican and grape-pickers.

The chancel of All Saints', showing exceptional 14C Decorated work: a doorway, a benefactor's tomb and an Easter sepulchre

Other items to note are the plain 15C screen and some plain benches. At the NE corner of the nave is a very interesting fragment of a Rood loft. Obviously it was sawn off flush to the wall and exposed again when the plaster was stripped off the walls.

Holme, *St. Giles.* Holme Church is notable for two main reasons—

much of it was rebuilt by a prosperous wool merchant in the late 15C, and what now stands was largely untouched by Victorian restorers. The church is long and low, with a nave, chancel, S aisle and chapel and W steeple. There are Perpendicular windows on the S side made as large as possible. The chapel, the chancel and the other late 15C work were due to John Barton (died 1491), a Lancashire man who came to live in Holme and made his money out of wool. It is claimed there was a verse in a window of his house which ran 'I thanke God, and ever shall,/It is the sheepe hath payed for all'. Barton's church was restored from 1932 in a very careful fashion by R. Harley Smith for Nevil Truman of Nottingham.

The low steeple with its broach spire is from c 1300, but with a huge Perpendicular W window. The N wall is even older and has a plain 13C doorway. It leans out badly and has been given large brick buttresses in post-Reformation times. The chancel is given a lantern effect through its big windows. The late 15C S porch is a rather ungainly affair, but it has seven very interesting later panels. They were probably added by Robert Barton in the mid-16C. In the centre is the crest of the Staple of Calais (with two sheep at the bottom), to which John Barton belonged. To the right of this is 'J.B.' and below, two bales of the precious wool.

The interior is delightfully light and inviting. The greatest interest is at the E end. A chevron stringcourse in the E wall is earlier than anything seen outside. Between the chancel and chapel is the monument to John Barton and his wife Isabella. It is in two tiers, the couple on the top and below them a cadaver as a *momento mori*. In the S chapel is a short, thick stone altar-slab reinstated to its present position in the 1930s. Either side, in the E wall, are two very elaborate niches for statues; the N one contains a mutilated 14C figure. 15C screens survive, and throughout the church there is 15C woodwork. The bench-ends in the chapel are particularly interesting with animals and birds on their shoulders. The altar rails are 17C. The two E windows contain interesting collections of glass, including many fragments with John Barton's merchant's mark, his initials and his rebus—a bar and a tun.

Lambley, *Holy Trinity.* This church is unusual in being largely of one build—in this case the late 1460s under the will of Ralph Cromwell (died 1454), Lord High Treasurer of England. His badge of a purse appears in two panels which flank the E window. The church is aisleless, has a five-light E window and three windows on each side of the nave. The tracery is of the customary panel type but with a pair of mouchettes at the top. The tower is an older feature, started in the very late 12C and heightened in the 14C with a fourth stage. The interior is a finely proportioned tall space, brightly lit by the big windows. At the W end the tower arch—round-arched with waterleaf capitals—is from the late 12C phase. Clearly, there was once a two-storeyed structure to the N of the chancel as the squint into the chancel shows. There are two Rood loft entrances, each with external expression (the S one has a corbelled-out stairway). The screen seems to be late 14C. There is some Jacobean panelling in the stalls and there are 17C communion rails. Some medieval glass survives in the E window, including a Virgin and Child and a Crucifixion. At the back of the church is a bassoon used in the old choir band.

Mansfield, *St. Mark, Nottingham Road.* This was designed in 1894 by Temple Moore and built in 1897. The five-bay S façade does not seem special with its simple Perpendicular tracery, and diminutive SE tower. But inside there is that spatial lucidity and ingenuity which characterises the very best late 19C churches. The nave and chancel form a simple, undivided space, plus a Lady chapel on the N and a vestry beyond the sanctuary, with three E–W orientated bays. Along the sides are passage aisles which have no external expression at all. They are divided from the nave by square piers and the aisle bays are linked by low round arches. Moore reworked this device at St. Cuthbert's, Middlesbrough in 1900–02. These are returned behind the sanctuary to form a further passage. The Calvary is from Oberammergau, 1930. A pity about the modern lurid rainbow treatment in the roof.

Newark, *St. Mary Magdalene.* Rising in the very centre of the town, near the Market Place, this is, by any standards, a noble church, grand in scale and beautiful in execution. At over 220ft long, including a chancel of nearly 90ft, it is one of the largest English parish churches. The building history is from the late 12C to the 16C, but it seems always to have been exceptionally large and had certainly attained its present length by the early 13C. The tower is an extraordinarily florid example of 13C work, a lavishness which was carried forward into the early 14C S aisle, the top stage of the tower and the spire, which stands some 250ft above the ground and which dwarfs all other buildings in the town. There was then a major pause before work began again in the mid-15C; the nave was being roofed in 1460. Then came the remodelling of the chancel and its aisles (completed 1498) and, fractionally later, the building of the transepts. During this Perpendicular phase there was a clear attempt to reduce the wall masonry to a minimum, especially in the transepts. The church was restored by Sir Gilbert Scott in 1855 at a cost of £5000.

The eye is first drawn to the spectacular tower and its tall spire. The work was begun early in the 13C, to which time the W portal with its rich mouldings and dogtooth ornament belongs. Above, a large Perpendicular W window has been cut through the original walling. The 13C activity involves blank arches and niches in a disorderly rhythm. In the third stage are blank arcades, in the spandrels of which is a strident trellis pattern. Then comes the Decorated belfry stage. It has two twinned windows in each face and over each pair an ungainly crocketed gable. In the lower corners of this stage there are niches with statues remaining. Finally comes a quatrefoil frieze, angle pinnacles and then the spire with four tiers of lucarnes under crocketed gables. The tower was embraced by later extensions of the aisles. Moving to the N, we meet entirely Perpendicular aisle windows, whose design is repeated in the chancel aisle and with scarcely any variation in the N transept. The parapets on the transept and chancel have battlements. Further enrichment on the chancel aisle is the use of detached pinnacles rising out of the buttresses. Between the nave and chancel there is a sanctus bell turret. The three-light clerestory windows form a continuous wall of glass, though their height is diminished over the crossing. The chancel aisles were clearly planned together; their E windows are identical and extremely wide. They flank an earlier, rather squashed E bay of the chancel. It is refreshing to return to the fluidity of the Decorated style in the S aisle, which was being built in 1312. It has flowing windows and richly treated buttresses with gabled heads; each had a statue in a niche. The S porch is two-storeyed and cuts awkwardly in half one of the adjacent windows. Its upper storey contains a library which was founded in 1698 by Bishop White of Peterborough, a former Vicar of Newark.

On entering, one cannot fail to be impressed by the cathedral-like vastness of the building and its lightness. The tower stands on massive piers with arches to the N, S and E. One is in full view of the piers of the nave which are reduced to a tall, slender minimum to maximise space. The crossing piers are quite different and would have been inadequate to carry the tower that presumably had existed before. They probably date from the early part of the 13C but incorporate some late 12C components. The piers between the chancel and its aisles are of the same pattern as in the nave, but are shorter due to the higher floor level. At the E end the chancel has an ambulatory containing three chapels. From the middle of one of them, which is the Lady chapel, steps lead down to the two-bay crypt beneath the sanctuary. It dates from the very late 12C and has rectangular, rib-vaulted bays with keeled ribs and two bosses. It was converted in 1981 into a treasury of church plate from the Diocese of Southwell. Between the sanctuary and its aisles are a pair of chantry chapels. That on the S was founded in 1506 by Robert Markham. On the S, facing the aisle, are two painted panels in which a grinning corpse and a finely dressed courtier symbolise the Dance of Death. On the N the chapel was founded in 1500 by Thomas Meyring, who left a flock of sheep for its support.

The fixtures and fittings are of considerable interest. The following summary starts in the N chancel aisle. Here pride of place must be given to the huge and famous brass to Alan Fleming (died 1363), who in 1349 founded a chantry chapel of Corpus Christi in this church. It was made in Flanders and consists of incised brass plates. Fleming is surrounded by many figures in niches. In the SW corner is an attractive monument to John Johnson (died 1659), with his (rather naive) bust in an oval surround framed by a curtain. At the E end is the chapel of St. George fitted out by W.D. Caroë. The E window is by John Hardman & Co. The Lady chapel has a black marble tomb-chest without an effigy. The chapel of the Holy Spirit, to the S, has a six-light E window with 14C and 15C stained glass, restored in 1957. Moving into the chancel the E end is crowned by a Comper reredos designed in 1936. The stalls are very rich and include 26 misericords in the back row. They must date from shortly after 1500. The rood screen dates from 1508 and is work from the famous workshop of Thomas Drawswerd of York. It is vaulted and has one-light openings. At the W corners of the chancel are monuments similar to the one to Johnson but for the lack of curtains: N to Robert Ramsey (died 1639) and S to Thomas Atkinson (died 1661). The S chapel window contains a notable collection of stained glass. The two centre lights have Biblical scenes of c 1300 and the others various illustrations in 15C glass. The E window is a memorial to Prince Albert. The S aisle contains some fine Victorian stained glass. In the SE window there is glass by William Wailes in memory of T.S. Godfrey (died 1859). The next window W is particularly rich in colour and resembles 13C work. It is by Alfred Gérènte of Paris and commemorates Elizabeth Gilstrap (died 1869), but an inscription indicates that the design was by Sir Gilbert Scott. The two full windows W of the porch are by C.E. Kempe (1901). The W window is by Burlison & Grylls, 1887. In the N aisle is a vast painting of the Raising of Lazarus (presented in 1821 and formerly over the high altar), by William Hilton, R.A., a local artist. Near the font is a particularly well-executed monument to

Anne Markham (died 1601). She kneels surrounded by her children amid fine Classical detail. The font has a Perpendicular base with many carved figures and a bowl which is explained by a plaque on the nave SW pier: 'This Font was Demolished by the Rebels May 9th 1646 Rebuilt by the Charity of Nicholas Ridley 1660'.

Newstead Abbey, *Chapel.* The house is set immediately S of the beautiful W front of the priory church. Its important association is with Lord Byron, whose ancestors were granted the priory in 1539 for £810. Sir John Byron promptly pulled down the church but retained the cloisters, around which the house is formed. In the E range is the chapter house which was turned into a chapel. It dates from the 13C and is entered through a fine doorway with detached shafts, flanked by a pair of two-light windows. The rectangular space inside is divided up into six rib-vaulted bays by two very delicate piers. In 1817 Byron sold Newstead to an old school friend, Colonel Wildman, who added the gallery on the N side by building this out over the upper part of the slype. Mr. Webb, who followed Wildman, set about the decoration of the chapel in the 1860s, probably under C.A. Buckler. The chapel now glows with coloured decoration—patterns on the walls, stained glass by John Hardman & Co. and vibrant Minton tiles.

In the undercroft are monuments to three of the first four Byrons of Newstead. The body of the sixth Lord Byron, the poet who died in 1824 in the Greek War of Independence, was brought to Hucknall Church and now rests in the family vault beneath its chancel, where there is a wall tablet to his memory.

Nottingham

Nottingham is something of a one-church city because by far the best and largest is St. Mary's. In fact medieval Nottingham had only three parish churches, surprisingly few for an important town. What is even more dramatic is that originally St. Mary's included all the land belonging to Nottingham and that the other two parishes were carved out of it. Nottingham was a royal borough and the custodian of the castle had extensive rights, putting a brake on the proliferation of churches. The two 'new' churches of St. Peter and St. Nicholas were in existence by c 1109. The present St. Peter's was built in 1671–82 and still has some 17C and 18C furnishings and a plaster ceiling in the chancel. Medieval churches of villages now within the city include Clifton, an impressive, cruciform building with a notable series of monuments, and Lenton, famous for its 12C font.

Despite being a larger place, Nottingham's collection of 19C churches is not as impressive as neighbouring Leicester's. The best is probably G.F. Bodley's St. Alban's, Bond Street, Sneinton of 1886–87. It has a brick exterior, aisles extending to the E end and a typical Bodley blend of Decorated and Perpendicular. The interior has a great sense of refinement, with tall quatrefoil piers and a fine screen. The most ambitious High Victorian church is St. Andrew's, Mansfield Road of 1869–71 by the local architect William Knight. It is a big-boned cruciform structure which calls up French motifs. For the gentler and, really, more innovative architecture of the late 19C there is St. Stephen's, Bubbers Mill Road of 1897, by W.D. Caroë. Of the Free Church buildings, the former Unitarian Church on High Pavement

(1876 by S. Colman of Bristol) is a big but not very successful Gothic essay. The former Baptist Chapel of 1893–94 on Woodborough Road by Watson Fothergill is an extraordinarily idiosyncratic piece of pseudo-High Victorian Gothic stranded at the end of the century.

St. Mary, High Pavement. This is the main church of Nottingham and, after Newark, the largest parish church in the county. It is exclusively Perpendicular but, unfortunately, its grandeur cannot be appreciated from afar because of the tall 19C buildings of Nottingham's Lace Market that surround it. The accent, especially inside, is as much on length as on height. The history of the building probably goes back to a pre-Conquest minster. This was followed by a Norman church, a two-light window of which is built into a warehouse wall in nearby Broadway.

The present church is cruciform, with a six-bay aisled nave, four-bay chancel and a S chapel added by Temple Moore in 1912–13 (but reusing medieval windows from the chancel). The rebuilding of the church probably began in c 1400. The chapter house N of the chancel was added by G.F. Bodley in 1890. There was substantial work in c 1820 by William Stretton and many details may date from that time.

Seen from the SW there is a contrast between the nave, aisles and transepts on the one hand and the tower on the other. The rich detailing of the former creates almost a degree of fussiness, but the latter is surprisingly plain. The lower of its two main storeys has a four-light window in each face and the top stage has two twin-light windows with blank arches either side. There is quite a lot of plain masonry, whereas the aisles and nave are filled with windows and the spaces outside are taken up with buttresses and panelling. Note especially how the N and S windows of the transepts fill the whole of the tops of their walls: they have no fewer than 12 lights and three transoms. The heads of the clerestory windows even infringe slightly the cornice of the parapet above. This line of clerestory windows is continued round the transepts. The clerestory windows are from W.B. Moffatt's work of 1845–53. He also rebuilt the W façade, which generally follows the medieval scheme, known from a 17C drawing, except that there are now two windows at the W end of each aisle instead of one. The treatment of the frames round the windows in the aisles, for example, is interesting and is echoed inside: rolls start near ground level and reach right round each window, of which there are two per bay. The earliest part of the church is the S porch with its extravagantly cusped doorway (shades of Decorated). This motif is repeated inside in the tomb in the S wall of the S transept, which indicates that it was on the S side that the work was started. The porch has that not uncommon Nottinghamshire feature, a heavy stone tunnel-vaulted roof. On the N is a 15C vestry.

The expanses of windows make for a light interior, in which little space is wasted by large piers. In the nave there are lozenge shapes with the long axis N–S. Everywhere mouldings are kept small, except for the large rolls that surround the windows (cf. outside). These rise from low down and where they meet, similar rolls running horizontally create unusual though very plain rectangles and squares. The clerestory windows sit right on top of the arcades. Above the crossing is a vault but this is actually a very convincing wood and plaster replacement by William Stretton, c 1820, for a stone vault that had collapsed in 1558. Over the spacious chancel is a tiebeam roof by Sir Gilbert Scott, 1872; it was coloured by Lawrence Bond in 1965.

The finest fittings are the S doors. They are by Henry Wilson, 1904, and are made of bronze. Above is a very fine Pietà. The woodwork includes a chancel screen and reredos by Bodley & Garner, 1885, a Jacobean communion table in the N transept, and Scott's stalls of 1872. At the SE corner of these is the bishop's throne (Nottingham had a suffragan bishop from 1870), by Bodley, 1890. At the W end the Lion and the Unicorn date from c 1708. On the SE crossing pier is a late 15C painting of the Virgin and Child, given to the church in 1839. In the chapter house is an extensive series of drawings and paintings of the church at various stages of its history. There is extensive 19C glass including work by most of the major makers—Clayton & Bell, Burlison & Grylls, John Hardman & Co., C.E. Kempe and Ward & Hughes. At the E end of the N aisle is a late 18C or early 19C vestry clock, which runs for a month without winding. St. Mary's is poor in monuments. Under the canopy in the S transept lies John Samon (died 1413), three times Mayor of Nottingham. The canopy opposite in the N transept may have been built for John Thurland (died 1473). The slab below is much earlier, perhaps from the tomb of William Amyas (died c 1348–69). The tomb-chest below this is of alabaster and may have belonged to the tomb of John de Tannesly (died 1414). A curiosity near the N doorway is the tablet to Thomas Berdmore (died 1785), who was a highly prosperous dentist (to King George III among others) and is said to have been the inventor of false teeth. In the S chapel is part of a 15C Nottingham alabaster panel, probably depicting St. Thomas Becket's resignation of his see before Pope Alexander III at Sens in 1164.

Papplewick, *St. James.* This is as good an example of late 18C Gothick as can be found. It was rebuilt in 1795 by the squire, Frederick Montagu, and is a long rectangle with a tall S porch and W tower. The latter partly reused materials from the old church, including the attractive belfry windows with flowing tracery. But the strangest feature is inside. The gallery runs the length of the church but on the N side only, plus a short return at the W end. It spans over a third of the width of the church. On entering one can see the stairs up to it. The staircase splits and its right fork enters the gallery but its left one goes upwards to nowhere. The original seats remain in the gallery. At the N end is the squire's pew, which originally had a fireplace. There is a flat plaster ceiling over the whole interior, including two quatrefoil ventilation holes. The E window is an important survival. It is by Francis Eginton and is based upon Joshua Reynolds's window in New College chapel, Oxford. In yellowy and purply brown hues it depicts Faith and Hope looking upwards towards the IHS symbol. In the SW window are some 15C fragments, including figures of St. Peter and St. Stephen. Their survival and the fragments of incised slabs to Sherwood Forest officials (note the arrow and sling on one) are testimony to Montagu's antiquarian interests. Above the S doorway are two sculptured 12C figures.

Retford

East Retford, *St. Swithun*. Delightfully situated near the Market Place, St. Swithun's is an impressive cruciform structure with aisles, a tall tower and a wealth of 19C stained glass. The fancy Perpendicular exterior with lots of panelling on the buttresses and pinnacles are due to a remodelling by G.G. Place of Nottingham in 1854–55. He had already rebuilt the S porch in 1852 and now he rebuilt the N porch, N chancel aisle, rebuilt and enlarged the N aisle and, most significantly, extended the chancel 17ft and provided it with a clerestory. That the old chancel was short was due to a rebuilding in 1658 after the tower had collapsed in 1651. The N transept seems least affected by post-medieval changes and was built largely of reused stone. At its NW corner it has a simple round-arched doorway from the 13C. The chantry chapel, E of this transept, was rebuilt by G.F. Bodley in 1873.

The most distinctive feature inside is the crossing. The 17C builders remodelled it and added odd capitals with an ogee curve. A trace of the old crossing may be seen in the tall shafts visible on the nave side. The church is a textbook of 19C stained glass: E, Clayton & Bell, 1874, with a centre light by Michael O'Connor, 1855; N and S chancel windows by William Wailes, 1858; S transept S, a Boer War memorial by C.E. Kempe, 1903; S transept, SE by Wailes, 1847; NE, by John Hardman & Co., 1866; SW, 15C and 17C fragments; S aisle, second from E by O'Connor (date of death 1866); third from E, Clayton & Bell (date of death 1880); next by Wailes; W of the porch by O'Connor, 1855; N transept E and N windows by Kempe & Co. as a First World War memorial; N aisle, first from W by O'Connor; second and third by Clayton & Bell (dates of death 1885 and 1873) respectively); nave W by Clayton & Bell; N aisle W by O'Connor; S aisle W by Kempe, 1877. Finally, note the splendid Victorian radiators (also at West Retford).

West Retford, *St. Michael*. West Retford lies on the opposite side of the little River Idle and its church is within easy walking distance from St. Swithun's. Its notable feature is the 15C W steeple, which displays an extraordinary transition from square tower to octagonal spire. The N aisle is of 1863; the chancel was also remodelled then and was extended in 1890. The S porch and aisle are Perpendicular. As at St. Swithun's there is an extensive display of 19C stained glass.

Teversal, *St. Catherine*. The interest here is an almost untouched late 17C furnishing scheme and an ornate S doorway. The latter was reset in the S aisle when this was built very early in the 13C (its arcade still has round arches). Curiously, it was not put back together properly, and hence the odd assortment of fragments in the outer order. Inside, the box-pews, W gallery, pulpit, altar rails, communion table and, above all, the manorial pew form a complete late 17C scheme. Mostly the woodwork is quite plain but the manorial pew for the Molyneux family is enriched with barley sugar corner posts. It has regular, window-like openings to the nave and a lovely panelled ceiling. The Molyneux family is commemorated in good wall monuments in the chancel—NW: Francis (died 1674), whose bust emerges in a ridiculous fashion out of wavy drapery; NE: John (died 1691) and his wife Lucy, the most elaborate of them all; SE: Francis (died 1741) and his wife Diana; SW: Francis (died 1812), 'Gentleman Usher of the

Black Rod during the long period of forty-seven years', commemorated by a fine medallion with his profile, and signed by Josephus Kendrick. In the S aisle there are two incised slabs to Roger Greenhalgh (died 1563) and his wife (died 1538). Structurally, most of the church is 13C though the E part of the S aisle was widened in the early 14C. The original aisles are extremely narrow (scarcely over 3ft wide). The tower is Perpendicular.

Welbeck Abbey, *Chapel.* The private chapel here is a magnificent example of turn-of-the-century church furnishing and shows a complete contrast in ideas to the Gothic chapel at Clumber of only a few years before. It was created in the early 1890s by the sixth Duke of Portland using John Dando Sedding (designs of 1889), and his pupil and successor on his death in 1891, Henry Wilson. They transformed a long riding school of 1623 into a library at the E end and a chapel at the W—hence one would not know from the plain exterior that there is indeed a chapel here. The chapel was formally opened in 1892, though many of the refined finishing touches are rather later.

The main entrance under a W gallery at the end of the library leads into a sumptuous rectangular aisled room, four and a half bays long. The dominant feature is the series of tall columns with high rectangular bases and Ionic capitals, supporting a deep cornice and entablature. All this is in pinkish marble and alabaster. The four columns in the sanctuary of one and a half bays are of Bologne (sic) marble, those in the nave of Derbyshire marble. Over the nave and chancel is a continuous plaster tunnel-vault with broad ribs marking off each bay: those in the nave are filled with figures of Prophets; those over the sanctuary have angels with musical instruments. Everywhere there is polished stone gleaming and glistening.

The woodwork too is of the highest quality. In the aisles two rows of benches are arranged college-wise and in the nave the seats face 'E'. The carvings on the choirstalls represent the six days of Creation and those in the aisles the Benedicite or 148th Psalm. On the walls hang old Flemish tapestries. The altar frontal, said to have been bought by Wilson at an Arts and Crafts exhibition, is a relief of silver on copper depicting the Christ child surrounded by his parents, angels and animals. He lies at the foot of the Tree of Life and the whole composition is said to represent the message of Christ to the World. The altarpiece is by the 17C Dutch painter, Gerard van Honthorst. The font is contained within a distinct baptistery and is a glorious piece given by the Duke and his wife to celebrate the baptism of their eldest son in 1893. The bowl is shallow and is made of alabaster, with mother of pearl set in the rim. Bronze gates separate the baptistery from the nave and were given in 1896. At the entrance to the chapel are Wilson's massive bronze doors. Above them is a bronze tympanum with two angels attending a dead figure, presumably Lord William Cavendish-Bentinck, the half-brother of the sixth Duke, who died suddenly in 1903 on his way to India.

Welbeck Abbey remains in the hands of the Cavendish-Bentinck family, but part of it is used as a military college. Everything, including the chapel, is kept immaculately.

Written permission from the Bursar, Welbeck College, Worksop, S80 3LN, is essential for entry.

Worksop, *St. Mary and St. Cuthbert.* This major 12C church is the survival from an Augustinian priory founded by William de Lovetot in c 1120. Its distinction comes from the nave, 135ft long and consisting of ten bays with a most interesting elevation. The Lady chapel, restored in the 20C, is a most beautiful piece of 13C building. The Norman plan, as at Blyth, had a central apse, square-ended chancel chapels and apsidal chapels leading off the transepts. The 20C contributions at Worksop are particularly important and are both extremely good and extremely bad. The problem was to rebuild an E end after the mid-1960s: the luminous simplicity inside works superbly, the external appearance of a functional building block certainly does not.

The W façade is scarcely altered from the 12C. It has two tall flanking towers of the width of the aisles, a central portal, and a smaller N one. The tops of the towers are Perpendicular. The façade is one of great simplicity; only the Transitional doorways introduce any lively features, such as the three shafts with waterleaf capitals and strips of nailhead in between. The buttresses to the towers are very shallow and reach nearly to the top. The belfry windows are twinned two-light ones with small pointed openings under round, shafted superarches. Simplicity again is the keynote of the side elevations. The clerestory has plain 12C windows under hoods and large areas of plain masonry in between. The S aisle has larger quasi-Norman windows by R. Nicholson of Lincoln, who carried out a major restoration in 1845–49. The bays of the S aisle are demarcated by small buttresses, those on the N are not. Now the 20C story begins. The Lady chapel has three lancets in its E wall and three twinned lancets on the S. It had been roofless and detached from the nave since the 16C; in 1922 it was restored to its former beauty by Sir Harold Brakspear. In 1929 he joined it up again to the nave by a S transept which is a convincing piece of 13C design. He went on in 1932 to provide a crossing and a N transept. In 1965 a large legacy prompted the controversial work by Laurence King between 1970 and 1974. All that is visible from the S is the crossing tower with its needle-like flèche. It is very simple—each face composed of three blocks of masonry divided by vertical narrow windows. This is surprisingly effective but when viewed from the NE the great mass of such architecture seems juxtaposed most awkwardly with the 13C Gothic of half a century before. The functional aluminium doors and windows do nothing to help either.

The nave is remarkable for its length and its unity. It has nine bays, with alternating circular and octagonal piers, plus a tenth bay to the ground stages of the W towers. The E bay is the earliest: 1130–50 rather than c 1170 for the W parts. The elevation comprises arcade, gallery and clerestory. The gallery, with plenty of dogtooth and nailhead in addition, has a most interesting design. It does not just consist of large openings as at Blyth but also smaller ones which are placed over the piers below. The big arches are higher and reach up into the clerestory between the windows. All this is an enterprising rhythm which would not be expected in early or mid-Norman work. The wheel window above the W crossing arch was put in by R. Nicholson during the 1840s. From the nave the internal success of the E end may be judged. There is nothing to see of its starkness except the plain strips of the E window but these are not excessive. Rather, what is dominant is the light that envelops the area from high up in the crossing tower.

The late 12C S door has notable ironwork with graceful curves. From a very different era Sir Gilbert Scott's reredos in the N transept is a lavish High Victorian piece. Three medieval effigies survive in the S transept—Sir Thomas Neville (died 1406), Lord High Treasurer of England, his wife Joan and Thomas, Lord Furnival (died 1366).

THE SOKE OF PETERBOROUGH

The Soke is a small area, not ten miles N–S and only some 15 miles E–W, but it does contain a number of ecclesiastical treasures of the first rank. There are 20 village churches of medieval foundation, plus the City of Peterborough with its cathedral, its medieval parish church, five 19C churches and several 20C ones in its recent development. The Soke was a distinct unit of administration for many centuries, and was ruled successively by medieval Abbots of Peterborough, post-Reformation Bishops of Peterborough, and by the Earls and Marquesses of Exeter (of Burghley House, q.v.). The Soke became an independent county under the Local Government Act of 1888. In 1965 it was joined to Huntingdonshire. Finally, since 1974 it has been part of Cambridgeshire. The Soke is fortunate in its building material: the dense, grey limestone from Barnack, which was one of the great stones of medieval England. Also, from just across the border in Northamptonshire there come Collyweston slates which provide one of the most attractive of all roof coverings (e.g. at Wittering).

The important work in the Soke is early and, in particular, there is a remarkable amount of pre-Conquest work: the lavishly ornate tower at Barnack and the remains of the nave there too; the very complete church at Wittering (including a monumental chancel arch); long-and-short quoining at Peakirk; and sculptured fragments at Castor. Castor is to be visited too for its important Norman work, which seems to have been erected before 1124, if its dedication stone is to be relied upon. Castor's great display is its ornamented crossing tower. Maxey and Marholm also have Norman W towers, the former with decoration. Sutton Church has a fine Norman chancel arch. The 13C is represented by several aisle additions (e.g. at Peakirk), the rebuilding of the fine chancel at Castor and by some sedilia and piscinas (e.g. at Bainton). 13C work also appears at Longthorpe, Maxey and Northborough. Several churches retain round arches into the early 13C, which is also a characteristic of adjacent counties. At Etton there is a complete late 13C church showing the transition from the Early English to the Decorated styles. The early Decorated style of c 1300 appears in the chancel at Ufford, with its pair of E windows, and in the tower and spire at Paston. Excellent later Decorated work is displayed in the chancel at Barnack and in the transept at Northborough, which was the start of a major rebuilding which was not completed. Decorated too is the octagonal top to the tower at Helpston. The Perpendicular style is represented in Peterborough's large parish church of St. John the Baptist, which was built on a new site in 1402–07 and has a spacious, airy interior. In some village churches the Perpendicular style is shown in stately additions to earlier fabric, for instance the side chapels at Maxey and Barnack and the chancel at Marholm, whose rebuilding by Sir William Fitzwilliam, who died in 1534, shows that work was continuing right up to the Reformation.

Good stone medieval spires crown eight of the towers. At Helpston and Barnack the upper stages of the towers are octagonal. The most remarkable spire is at Glinton: this is much taller than the tower itself and has an unforgettable outline, with a more pronounced taper in its upper section. A visit to Glinton is also worthwhile for the entertainment provided by its gargoyles. Maxey, Ufford, Marholm and St. John's, Peterborough have interesting square towers. There are medieval bellcotes at Werrington, Peakirk, Northborough and Sutton.

Of post-Reformation work, there are curious and interesting windows at Helpston, dated 1609. Eye Church was rebuilt in 1846 by George Basevi in Early English style. The tower which was added by F.T. Dollman has now lost its spire. Of the 19C churches in Peterborough, the most interesting and distinctive are All Saints' (1894) by Temple Moore and St. Paul's (1868) by James Teale, which has a massive central lantern tower. A remarkable church of our own times is St. Jude's, Westwood—an imaginative and devotional building designed by Jo Robotham and consecrated in 1984.

Two churches—Peakirk and Castor—have 14C wall paintings of considerable interest. Both churches are notable for having unusual dedications to local saints. St. Pega was the sister of St. Guthlac of Crowland. St. Kyneburgha was a 7C princess of the Mercian royal house. Other features of interest are an Easter sepulchre at Maxey, Commandment boards and royal arms of 1790 at Ufford, and a 17C pulpit and rails at Upton. Fine monuments occur at Paston, Barnack, Ufford, Marholm and Upton.

Barnack, *St. John the Baptist.* This large church is especially interesting for its pre-Conquest work. It has a W tower with a profusion of decoration on the pattern of Earl's Barton (Northamptonshire) and Barton-on-Humber (Lincolnshire) and a great many hallmarks of late pre-Conquest work. Of the later work there is something of every medieval period from Transitional to late Perpendicular (plus a couple of Norman fragments). The size and shape of the pre-Conquest church is not clear but aisles were thrown out in the late 12C (N) and mid-13C (S), the chancel and part of the S aisle were enlarged in the early 14C and there were Perpendicular additions (vestry and S chapel). The church serves an attractive stone-built village in the valley of the River Welland. Barnack was one of the great medieval quarrying centres and the local stone, used in the structure of St. John's, was exported down the Welland to many great churches and cathedrals such as Ely.

Dominating the exterior is Barnack's famous tower, erected in c 1000–20 and heightened in c 1200 by the addition of an octagonal belfry, a spire and tall octagonal pinnacles, rising from the four corners. This tower is striking and is worth detailed examination. The most obvious fact is that the pre-Conquest part comprises the two lower stages and that these are divided up by pilaster strips of long-and-short work. Each face has four vertical panels and the lowest pilaster strips rise from simple corbels set at ground level. There is a wide division between the two stages, comprising two stringcourses with a recess between. A similar device occurs above the upper stage, though how the tower was continued in pre-Conquest times we do not know. There is no W doorway but rather one on the S: this has great strength and simplicity. Note the use of large stones and the unadorned imposts. Above this to the E is a large window with animals in the spandrels. Over this is a sundial. In the second stage is a highly decorated tall stone with a bird perching above rows of whorls and foliage. At the top of this stage is a triangular-headed window with a transenna (openwork mid-wall screen) with interlace. The W face has a triangular-headed window in the first stage and another panel with a bird on top of whorls and foliage in the second. N of this is a small aperture and to the S a large doorway for access from outside. Above the W window is an animal-head corbel of a type met with at Deerhurst, Gloucestershire. The N face has another carved panel with a bird, though the details differ from the other two. What was the meaning of this repeated theme? N and S of the tower are the quoins of the pre-Conquest nave. These suggest that the tower had a conventional nave rather than acting as a turriform nave. The tower now has a 13C top, of octagonal shape, with two-light belfry windows and massive pinnacles at the corners. The octagon has a fairly short spire, unusual for lacking lucarnes.

Moving round the church clockwise, the N aisle has a Transitional doorway, including waterleaf decoration. Otherwise the detail of the N aisle is of c 1300. Inside, evidence will show that there was a late 12C N chapel but outside all the detail is later. At the NE is a Perpendicular two-storey vestry. In the E wall of the chancel one is confronted with what is, for a parish church, a spectacular window. It

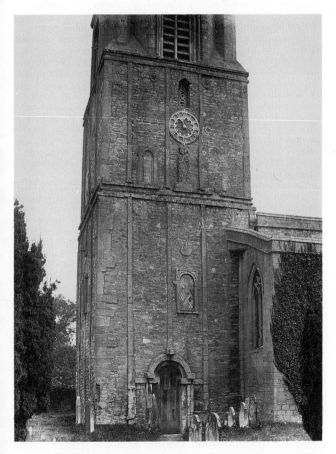

The pre-Conquest lower stages of the tower at St. John the Baptist's, showing long-and-short work, pilaster strips, a doorway and early windows

has five grouped lancets which are dramatised by the inclusion of crocketed straight-headed gables with finials in the heads, a device which is used in the lower parts of the E window of Merton College's chapel at Oxford (dating from the 1290s). The chancel is a rebuilding of the first third of the 14C and is very different from the late Perpendicular S or Lady chapel, which was built by Robert Browne of Walcot (died 1506) and has typical, rather plain windows and patterned parapets and basecourse. Early 14C work reappears in the S aisle and in particular, it has very attractive segmental-arched windows with ogee intersected tracery. The 13C porch is stone-roofed and has an enormously high vault inside. Each inner side wall has four blind arches, and stiff-leaf foliage abounds.

The mighty tower arch, 20ft high, is outlined by stripwork made up of large stones and has imposts of most remarkable appearance. They are wide and, though cut from single blocks, are made to look like a number of platy slabs piled one on top of another. They have been compared to huge stone sandwiches! The central part is set back from the rest. The arch itself and its jambs consist of stones running through the thickness of the wall. In the W wall of the tower is a triangular-headed seat. Whoever occupied it had special status and suggestions have been made that he was presiding over legal or ecclesiastical assemblies. Another feature which may have been part of the early church is the trace of an arch at the E end of the nave and visible from the N aisle. There is no clear evidence as to its date and it could be Norman: certainly it has been cut into by the Transitional N arcade. If it was pre-Conquest, it implies a nave of considerable length. Opposite this arch fragment is a major piece of sculpture, variously dated as early 11C or Norman under earlier influences. It depicts Christ in Majesty, His right hand raised in blessing, His left upon a book.

The three-bay N arcade is a fine piece of late 12C building with its tall, circular piers and enriched arches. The two E bays have zigzag and the W one moulding. The S arcade comes later, very early in the 13C. The piers are quatrefoil with smaller shafts in the angles and shaft-rings. The arches are early enough to still be round-headed, as is so common at this time in Rutland and E Leicestershire. From the chancel one can see the late 12C arch to the N chapel. It has strange decoration on the capital which seems to have evolved out of the waterleaf design. The chancel itself is particularly spacious and has notable sedilia and a piscina. The former is unusually playful with interesting heads on the hood. The piscina is very different and has a bowed ogee canopy and an encrustation of Decorated ornament. On the E wall is a bright mosaic by Salviati put in during the 1852–54 restoration. On the S is the Walcot chapel, reached through a wide, typically late arch. In its E wall are two remarkably ornate niches. The N one is important for a scene depicting what is thought to be the Immaculate Conception, with rays emanating from the Trinity to the figure of the kneeling Virgin.

The font is a remarkable 13C piece. Its bowl is circular with various floral decorations and below, a plain octagonal stem. But flush with the face of the bowl is a series of openwork, trefoiled arches. The Rood screen was designed by Leslie Temple Moore, but incorporates a little 15C work in its base. The reredos and several of the stained glass windows were inserted during the incumbency (1851–92) of the Very Reverend Marsham Argles, who was also Dean of Peterborough and is commemorated by the 19C brass near the vestry door. The earliest monuments of note are the cross-legged knight and a lady of c 1400 under the two arches in the N chapel N wall. In the S or Lady chapel and the S aisle there are two late Perpendicular table-tombs under canopies, without figures. As the chapel was built by Robert Browne, who died in 1506, the table-tomb in the chapel may well be his. The tomb in the S aisle is possibly that of John Browne, Lord Mayor of London (died 1480). On the N wall of the chancel there is a wall monument to Francis Whitstones (died 1598) and his wife. It has lots of small-scale strapwork and various funerary devices. It is signed, unusually and prominently, 'Tomas Greenway of Darby 1612'.

Burghley House, *Chapel.* The chapel is in the E range of the splendid house built in the second half of the 16C by William Cecil (1520–98), first Lord Burghley and Lord High Treasurer under Queen Elizabeth I. The approach to the antechapel is up a stairway dated 1560 from the old kitchen. Burghley is justly famous for its paintings and both the antechapel and the chapel itself have, together, nearly 30, all identified in the official guide book. Particularly notable is Francesco Bassano's dramatic chiaroscuro, 'Agony in the Garden', on the N wall of the antechapel. The chapel proper is a large, square space beyond three round-arched openings with wooden, coffered linings. The flat, plaster-ribbed ceiling is Gothic in conception and possibly dates from 1828. The chapel is comfortably appointed, with an exotic scagliola fireplace on the N wall (it was brought here from Portugal in the 19C), panelling round the walls (attributed to Grinling Gibbons), and a series of swags and flowers between the pictures. The painting behind the altar is of 'Zebedee's Wife Petitioning Our Lord', by Paolo Veronese. A small chamber organ stands in the SW corner. The Gothick seating with open backs, partly of mahogany, is early 19C. Round the sides stand ten Wise Virgins in Coade stone and holding their (unfortunately modern-looking) lamps.

Castor, *St. Kyneburgha.* This church is in the first rank of Norman parish churches in England. Apart from a few reused Roman tiles, it is built entirely of fine grey limestone to a cruciform plan. It occupies a resplendent position, sedately set in its sloping churchyard well back from the A47. It is the only known church which is dedicated to the 7C Mercian princess, St. Kyneburgha. Some way above the priests's door is a tympanum recording the dedication of the church. This gives a date of 1124 but it can be seen that XXIIII has been scratched in later. Presumably the Norman builders erected the stone as building proceeded, not knowing when the dedication would eventually occur. What is Norman is the N transept, part of the W wall of the S transept, the shell of the nave, the tympanum over the S porch and, of course, the wonderfully ornate crossing tower. There was major work in the 13C with the enlargement of the chancel and the addition of a S aisle (early 13C) and the remodelling of the S transept (c 1270–80). The old S transept was smaller, no doubt the same size as the existing N one. The N aisle was added in the 14C (in c 1330) and the tower was vaulted and provided with a spire at that time too. The only Perpendicular activity of importance was the E window and the addition of the clerestory.

The tower has two highly decorated stages above the level of the S transept roof. The lower has two lights under a superarch and zigzag in the heads. The superarch and the tall blind arches to the sides are encrusted with billet and have angle shafts. Over these arches and below the corbel table marking the next stage is scaly lozenge patterning. The upper stage is even more closely decorated with three pairs of openings and flanked by twin blind arches. Again there is a profusion of billet ornament and over the arches there is fish-scale patterning. A corbel course lies beneath the early 14C parapet and behind this there rises the short spire with two tiers of lucarnes. Working anti-clockwise round the church, the S transept and its aisle has Geometrical tracery without cusps (on the S) and the chancel has all the hallmarks of the early 13C—a priest's door (note the dedication stone above) with mouldings but still with a round head, tall lancet windows and flattish buttresses. The E wall has traces of a steeper roof pitch: it would have come lower down than the present one and would have made more sense in relation to the tops of the lancets. In the N transept, the remains of the Norman stringcourse and N window can be seen. The square-headed windows of the N aisle date from its construction in the 14C. In the apex of the nave W wall there is a window from the Norman church. The porch is from the 13C scheme but the S doorway into the aisle is a fine Norman one and was obviously reset—it has a moulded head, billet in the outer order and two orders of angle shafts with sculpted capitals. The timbers of the porch roof are medieval (see the small figures), as is the S door inscribed *Ricardus Beby Rector Ecclecie de Castre fecit* (a Richard of Leicester appears in the list of incumbents in the 14C).

The interior is long and spacious and rises markedly to the E. The nave has three bays and the arches on the S are still round whereas the later ones on the N are pointed. On both sides the piers are round. In the capitals of the crossing piers there is a great variety of 12C carving including men fighting (SW), foliate masks (NW) and hunting (NE). The piers have half-round responds and shafts in the jambs. In the 14C a vault was inserted and has a circular opening for the passage of the bells. Traces of a Norman window in the W wall of the S transept can be seen, though cut into by an early 13C arch. Norman doorways over the crossing arches formerly gave access to roof spaces. The chancel is gloriously spacious and must be a considerable enlargement on its 12C predecessor. It has double sedilia and a double piscina, the latter richly adorned with dogtooth. There is also a 14C piscina in the N wall. There is unusual work between the N aisle and transept—an openwork band of reticulations with five niches over. The roofs in the nave and aisles have medieval work, including figures of angels with musical instruments and Instruments of the Passion (recently coloured). The E end of the N aisle became the chapel of St. Kyneswitha in 1962.

In the SE corner of the chancel there is a pre-Conquest carving under an arch, perhaps of an Apostle or of St. Mark, and clearly one of a series. It probably dates from the early 9C. Inside the N doorway is the fragment of a pre-Conquest cross which may have originally been a Roman altar. In the NW corner of the N aisle is a 14C wall painting with three scenes from the life of St. Catherine—her martyrdom at the wheel, the execution of the philosophers converted by her, and perhaps the entry of Maximin into Alexandria. The Norman font was pieced together from fragments in 1929. In the SE corner of the S aisle is a bread shelf and an inscription. An unusual variant on the *memento mori* is to be discovered on a small gravestone in the extreme NW corner of the S transept. It records: 'Here lyeth the body of William Newman whose days on earth was but a span. Upon the XV day of May his body was laid in clay. In the year of our Lord 1695. This you may read that are alive'.

St. Kyneburgha was the third daughter of Penda, pagan King of Mercia and the sister of Peada, who possibly founded Peterborough Abbey. Perhaps in the 650s she founded, with her sister Kyneswitha, a nunnery at Castor to the N of the present church. They were buried there but in the 11C they were translated to Peterborough and a shrine was built over their relics.

Helpston, *St. Botolph.* Helpston has an attractive church with an unusual early 14C octagonal top to its tower. Below, it is Norman, though rebuilt in 1865. The other most unusual feature is the style of the chancel side windows—pretty work with two tall lights divided by a mullion and with a cusped square at the top of each. One of them (SE) is dated 1609. But it is not for its architecture that Helpston is a place of pilgrimage. It is because it is the birthplace and resting place of John Clare, the great early 19C rural poet. He was born in 1793, the son of a poor farm worker, but by the age of 12 he was writing verse and his first poems were published in 1820. So much of his writing reflects with tenderness and often sadness the area of his home on the edge of the Fens. His life, however, was far from happy as he was trapped in limbo between the life of an agricultural worker and that of a poet. Though known to literary people of his time, he remained desperately poor and, worn out by mental and physical labour, was declared insane in 1837. He continued to write poetry while in Northampton Asylum. This strange, sad life ended in 1864. John Clare is buried beneath a coped grave-cover S of the chancel.

Peakirk, *St. Pega.* The 14C wall paintings are the main reason for visiting this attractive little church. The main scheme depicts the Passion cycle in a series of cartoon-strip-like panels over the Norman N arcade. There are 12 scenes in two tiers. The sequence is interrupted by a sturdy, contemporary St. Christopher. What is unusual about the Passion sequence is the inclusion of certain unusual scenes such as the washing of the disciples' feet and the mocking of Christ, but the exclusion of carrying the Cross and the descent into Hell. The excellent notes in the church prepared by E. Clive Rouse, who restored the paintings, point to a Passion play as the model. In the N aisle is a depiction of the Three Living and the Three Dead with the three horror-struck kings confronted by three dead figures who appear to them against a background of worms, beetles, and other horrid symbols of decay. Also, further W is a warning to gossips, with the Devil pressing together the heads of two gossiping women.

St. Pega was the sister of St. Guthlac of Crowland and after his death in 714 she led a solitary life, it is traditionally said, in Peakirk (which means Pega's church), before dying in Rome on a pilgrimage. The dedication is unique. She is depicted in the E window of 1914 by Kempe & Co. Her anchorage is said to be represented by the late medieval chapel which survives E of the church.

Peterborough, *St. John the Baptist.* St. John's, Peterborough's medieval parish church, lies right in the heart of the city, behind the Market Square and immediately W of the old Guildhall of 1671. St. John's was moved to its present site from a position in Bongate E of the cathedral in 1402–07. Materials from the old church and also from the nave of St. Thomas's Chapel, W of the cathedral, were reused. St.

John's is a large Perpendicular town church, with a long nave and chancel, and aisles which embrace the tower and stretch almost to the E end of the chancel. The clerestory stretches through to the chancel from the nave. There are 11 bays in total. The aisles are lit by four-light Perpendicular windows, with the exception of some towards the W, which have been given intersecting tracery. The graceful W tower has large, four-light belfry windows with transoms and, from the belfry stage, octagonal buttresses which terminate in crocketed spirelets. The tower houses a ring of eight bells. The two-storeyed S porch is unusually long and has a fine tierceron-vault, with the Holy Trinity, the Annunciation and the Crucifixion depicted on carved bosses.

The interior confirms the spaciousness of the building, which has the feel of a town and civic church. Its piers in the seven-bay nave arcades are slender, with typical sections of four shafts and four hollows. The earliest work is the 14C base of the tower, reused from the earlier church. The roofs throughout are of the arch-braced cambered tiebeam variety and these have been tastefully restored. The main restoration took place in 1881–83, under J.L. Pearson.

There is much craftsmanship here of the 19C and 20C. The 20C work includes the screens to the Lady chapel and the organ chamber (1915), the Rood screen (1917), the Rood above it (1938) and the handsome triptych reredos which is sumptuously decorated with gilding and canopies and which has paintings on the wings and statues in the central part. Also of interest is the Ruddle memorial window of 1968, showing famous people associated with Peterborough, including four bishops and portraits of James and Edith Ruddle. This window was designed by A.W. Ruddle and Brian Thomas and was made at Whitefriars Studios. The organ is a fine three-manual instrument by Harrison & Harrison, incorporating pipework from its predecessor by Forster & Andrews. There are two fragments of medieval embroidery in the S aisle, which may have come from an altar frontal.

The Lady chapel contains a large monument to William Wyldbore (died 1781), by Richard Hayward. The memorial to John Image (died 1786) in the S aisle and the John Flaxman memorial to the Squire family in the N aisle are also noteworthy. Robert Scarlett, the sexton at St. John's, buried Queen Katherine of Aragon in 1536 and Mary, Queen of Scots in 1587 in the cathedral. He was himself buried in the cathedral in 1594, at the age of 98.

Wittering, *All Saints*. All Saints' is a remarkably complete, small, late pre-Conquest building which contains a monumental chancel arch, unparalleled in its massiveness. The church has a quiet setting at the S end of the village. Its W tower and stumpy ribbed spire (lit by two tiers of lucarnes) date from c 1320, but the nave and chancel are pre-Conquest and experts have dated them to c 950–81. Although the present windows are later, the pre-Conquest long-and-short work may be seen in the corners and the original walls are of coursed rubble.

The S doorway (of c 1200) admits us to a bright and homely interior, with craftsmanship which spans a thousand years. The pre-Conquest nave and chancel are tall and dignified and the interior is dominated by the massive and very striking chancel arch, which is about 14ft high and 7ft wide. The semicircular arch, embellished with three rolls, rests upon mighty and primitive-looking imposts.

The Normans constructed the two-bay arcade which divides off the N aisle. The arches have zigzag and lozenge moulding and rest upon scalloped capitals. In the chancel there are an aumbry, 17C woodwork incorporated into the later Communion rails, and glass in the E window by C.E. Kempe. The arch to the N chapel has four intriguing corbel faces, including a veiled lady and a man with protruding tongue and big ears! This is the Royal Air Force chapel, which was tastefully refurnished in 1968 to the designs of L. Bond, with most of its furnishings made by members of the R.A.F. The glass in the E window was designed by H.W. Harvey of York.

RUTLAND

The tiny county of Rutland disappeared administratively in 1974 when it was incorporated in Leicestershire. However, it lives on strongly in local consciousness and certainly its churches are of a quality in which Rutlanders can take justifiable pride. There are 50 parish churches, and almost every one is worth a visit. At their best, they stand comparison with the finest in Lincolnshire and Northamptonshire, between which Rutland is sandwiched. The area is particularly fortunate in its building materials. The Jurassic ridge which sweeps down through its neighbours has superb limestones. These are durable, easily carved and weather well to an attractive grey. Ironically, the quarrying industry in Rutland itself seems to have been relatively underdeveloped in the Middle Ages and the great age of the

NORMAN DOORWAY ◇ ◇ ◇
ST MARY'S ◇ ESSENDINE ◇ Rutland.

Clipsham, Ketton, Great Casterton and other quarries only began in about the 16C. Ketton Church, therefore, was built of Barnack stone from Northamptonshire. Ironstone in the W is the other local material and weathers to a delightful series of browns and buffs, though it is less durable than the limestone. Collyweston slates from Northamptonshire form the lovely coverings on some church roofs.

There are perhaps three main characteristics of the Rutland churches: the importance of Transitional architecture, a clutch of several very fine late medieval remodellings, and the frequency of bellcotes. These occur at six churches (plus the hospital chapel at Oakham) and two others have gone in the past 200 years. Mostly they are quite simple (e.g. Little Casterton, Whitwell) but the extraordinarily massive affair at Manton could almost be classed as a tower.

Of pre-Conquest work there is nothing to note apart from the tower arch at Market Overton which has characteristically massive stones. However, what may be a very rare late pre-Conquest font survives at Whitwell. There is a good deal more Norman work and some of it is of considerable interest. A very early feature and a thrilling one is the S doorway at Egleton which has been suggested as Saxo-Norman. It has a tympanum with a wheel-like device flanked by a wyvern and a ?lion. Essendine, the most easterly church in Rutland, has two Norman doorways. The S one is particularly interesting and is of the mid-12C. The tympanum has a dynamic scene of Christ blessing and flanked by angels. The chancel arch is Norman too, though its pointed head seems due to a later reworking. The rich carving on the jambs at Essendine is a similar idea to the treatment on the chancel arch shafts at Stoke Dry, probably of c 1120. Also early 12C is the sturdy W tower at Tixover, a blunt structure speaking of the sternness of post-Conquest England. But pride of place must go to the spectacular late Norman work at Tickencote with its overpowering chancel arch and remarkable sexpartite vaulting in the chancel. Later comes a substantial amount of Transitional work. It can be found at 23 churches plus a secular work of the very greatest importance—the hall of Oakham Castle. This half-world between Norman and Gothic is exemplified by several examples of waterleaf capitals, the introduction of roll-moulding on arches, the development of the double-chamfered arch and, above all in Rutland, the survival of the round arch into the early 13C. Examples of this concentration in Rutland and the adjoining localities are to be found at Great Casterton, Manton and Tixover. In the W front of Ketton there is an elaborate case of Norman and Early English features used side by side.

The arrival of fully-developed Gothic can be seen in the nave of Ketton which seems to be datable to the 1230s. The tower there is also 13C and shows the purity and elegance of Early English work at its best. Great Casterton also has much good 13C work including stiff-leaf ornament and one of the earliest cases of a clerestory. It was in the 13C that the spire was developed into such a work of art in the limestone belt. In Rutland spires take many forms from the stubby 13C example at Glaston to the tremendously florid early 14C one at Ketton. Both these are of the broach type. More idiosyncratic are Cottesmore (ludicrously tall broaches) and Seaton (chamfered-off corners rather than broaches). Later medieval spires were often of the parapet type as at Oakham and South Luffenham, the latter being a case where the angles are enriched (excessively so) with crockets. But the treatment of the spire at Clipsham is the most eccentric of all, as though the 14C builders could not decide what they wanted as the structure stumbled upwards. At Exton, however, they were very clear and the octagon crowned by a short spire makes aesthetic sense of the parapet and octagonal pinnacles that look so bulky at Oakham. Exton was remodelled in the late 13C or 14C and is one of a series of large and beautiful churches for which the county is justly famous and which is a continuation of what may be found in Northamptonshire and Lincolnshire. Another good example from this period is the spacious chancel at North Luffenham with its varied window tracery in which high Decorated starts to make its appearance. Langham (especially on the S side) is a church where work of the mid-14C is lavishly displayed and then come the remodellings at Oakham and Whissendine. There is one rare case of Elizabethan church building in Rutland—Brooke, much rebuilt c 1579. The next interesting work is the Gothick remodelling of Teigh in 1782 and the Norman one at Tickencote ten years afterwards. The latter emulated the work in the chancel and is perhaps the first serious piece of such self-conscious Normanising. There was no need for a crop of new Victorian churches and the only building of note is the chapel at Uppingham School by G.E. Street, 1863–65. Ashwell, however, is an excellent example of a restoration by William Butterfield (1851).

For contents, Lyddington and Stoke Dry are particularly rewarding. Stoke Dry is described in the gazetteer. At Lyddington one can see 15C wall paintings, a screen, and, most interesting of all, the communion rails of 1635 which surround the table on four sides. The reason seems to have been that Bishop Williams of Lincoln, who had a palace at Lyddington (now the Bede House and open to the public), was opposed to the reforms of Archbishop Laud, who required communion tables to be against the E walls of churches. So here the table was moved near the E wall but not up to it. Rutland is quite fortunate in its surviving wall paintings, because apart from Lyddington and Stoke Dry, there are large late 13C figures representing the opposed forces of Synagogue and Church at Little Casterton, and extensive fragments at Great Casterton, North Luffenham and Ketton. Medieval stained glass is best represented in a chancel N window at North Luffenham with three early 14C figures with canopies and shields (it must, however, be said that there were Victorian additions of the missing parts in 1870–71). 15C glass can be seen at Ayston. Medieval screens can be found at Lyddington, Stoke Dry and Whissendine. For monuments the real place of pilgrimage must be to the array of fine monuments in Exton Church.

Brooke, *St. Peter.* Brooke Church has many things of interest. The chief of these is seen in the standard approach from the W, for one is confronted by the immensely steep-pitched roof and by the mullioned window of the N aisle. These are the works of a major remodelling of c 1579, a very rare date in church building. The reason for the activity at this time is, sadly, not known.

The church consists of a nave and chancel which are paralleled by a N aisle and chapel of almost identical size. In addition there is a 13C W tower. Apart from the S wall of the nave and the three-light, square-headed window it contains, nothing else outside is medieval. The Elizabethan work is characterised by plain, square-headed windows with each light under a plain round arch. Both chapel and chancel are under their own steeply pitched roofs. One enters through the S porch of c 1579 which is the only part of the church built then that is not ashlar-faced. The earliest external evidence—

the S doorway—prepares one for the story inside. It probably dates from the third quarter of the 12C, though it was made pointed later on. It has one order of shafts without capitals.

The interior is splendidly light and refreshing and has no overtly Victorian work. It is almost as though the pointed arch had not been invented, for there are the late Norman round arches of the N arcade and then the Renaissance ones of the late 16C work. (The 13C tower arch is pointed, of course.) The N nave arcade is of three bays. At the angles of the capitals there are weighty volutes, with knobbly precursors of stiff-leaf in between. The arches are single-chamfered. The quasi-Classical detailing of the arches from four centuries later is much more refined.

The furnishings and fittings tell a similar late Norman and late 16C (or early 17C) story. On the inside of the N door is the remarkable survival of two late 12C Norman hinges: each is bluntly decorated with seven barbaric Cs. The font is also Norman: its four, square faces are enriched with blind arches. A massive dug-out chest is the only other medieval item. The real importance of the furnishings is that they form a complete scheme of the late 16C or early 17C. There has probably been some reordering, perhaps at the restoration by Ewan Christian (chancel) and by James Tait, 1879, but there is nothing to distract from the pleasure of this complete ensemble— box-pews with plain panelling (bands of hoop-like decoration on the higher backs), a chancel screen (with similar decoration), two family pews, communion table and rail, pulpit (with tester) and so on. In the chapel there is the fine monument to Charles Noel (died 1619 aged 28).

Exton, _St. Peter and St. Paul._ The church lies in a superb setting amid the parkland of Exton Hall. It is a particularly grand building and one which possesses an exceptional series of monuments. The dominant impression is one of height rather than length, due to the towering mass of the steeple, and the high-pitched roofs. It has aisles, small transepts and a clerestory. Much of the late 13C and 14C fabric was renewed in the 1840s and 1850s, hence a superficially Victorian appearance.

The steeple is the most spectacular for many miles around. It is, however, largely a rebuild after a disastrous lightning strike on 25th April, 1843. The architect was probably R.C. Carpenter and it may have taken until 1846 to complete it. The tower is of three stages with set-back buttresses. The real visual interest starts with the twinned two-light Reticulated windows of the belfry stage. Above comes a castellated parapet between four octagonal corner turrets. In the middle of that ensemble there grows an octagonal stage with transomed lights. Finally comes the spire with two tiers of lucarnes. The rest is much more straightforward. Only the S aisle W window (Reticulated) and (blocked) N aisle W window (Y) are original. The rest were the work of J.L. Pearson who restored the church in 1852– 54. Whatever was the reason for the quirky, pastry-cutter designs in the chancel—they certainly were not included in Pearson's original plans? He also replaced an embattled parapet on the nave by a plain one. The interior has a certain drabness arising from the natural-coloured wall rendering from Pearson's restoration. Much was rebuilt here too and one cannot be sure that all the detail is accurate. The brooding hammerbeam roof, however, is very fine. The nave is of four bays (including the openings to the transepts) and on the N has circular piers to the arcade, on the S piers with eight attached shafts.

The responds and E pier on the N have stiff-leaf foliage capitals (note the heads below the leaves on the pier). The chancel arch is 13C and has two moulded orders: the capitals also have stiff-leaf. In the nave there is an array of funeral banners and armour of the Harington and Noel families. The five-light E window (date of death 1866) is by Alexander Gibbs.

The church of St. Peter and St. Paul, which houses fine monuments, 14C to 18C

The exceptional collection of monuments at Exton ranges from the late 14C to the late 18C. The earliest, on the N side of the chancel, is to Nicholas Grene (died c 1379). It is a tomb-chest with panelled sides, the slab having a floriated calvary cross in slight relief. John Harington (died 1524) and his wife Alice lie on a tomb-chest at the W end of the S aisle. It is of alabaster and on the sides are panels with the arms of Harington and Culpeper. At John's feet are a lion and the figure of a bedesman; near Alice's feet are two dogs. In the S part of the S transept is the lawyer Robert Kelway (died 1580), his daughter, her husband (a Harington) and grandchildren. It is an elaborate wall monument and was erected by Kelway's daughter Ann and her husband John, Lord Harington, who kneel in front of the recumbent lawyer. Behind Ann is her daughter. Sir James Harington (died 1591) and his wife Lucy have a monument against the N wall of the chancel. It is of marble and alabaster and the kneeling figures face one another over a prayer desk. In a very different style is the monument at the W end of the N aisle to Anne, wife of Lord Bruce of Kinlosse and granddaughter of the first Lady Harington (died 1627). She died in childbirth in 1627 in her 22nd year. The figure is of great sensitivity and is covered with a lightly folded shroud. The style marks a distinct departure from the formal attitudes in the earlier monuments. It is of black and white marble. Next comes the monument on the W wall of the N transept to James Noel, second Viscount Campden (died 1681 aged 18). He stands somewhat self-consciously with his right elbow on a pedestal on which are his two baby brothers. Also in this transept is the massive monument to Baptist Noel, third Viscount Campden (died 1683) and his fourth wife Elizabeth, who provided funds in her lifetime and instructions for the construction of the monument. It was finished in 1686 at a cost of £1000 and was the work of Grinling Gibbons. It consists of several white marble panels of great artistry depicting the whole family of the Viscount. In all he and his four wives were the parents of no fewer than 19 children. The fecund Lord Campden stands in Roman dress beside a pedestal with Elizabeth on the other side. They are flanked by big obelisks bearing wreaths and topped by black vases. Over the whole is a pediment broken at the top. On the N aisle W wall is Lieut.-General Bennett Noel (died 1766). It is the work of Joseph Nollekens and was erected under a bequest of Noel's widow, Elizabeth (died 1784), who is buried with her husband. A draped female figure leans on an urn which bears the portrait of the deceased. Symbolically she puts out a torch. Another Nollekens monument was erected in 1790 to Elizabeth, Countess of Gains-borough (died 1771) and her two husbands, Baptist, fourth Earl (died 1751), and Thomas Noel of Wilcot Hall, Northamptonshire (died 1788). She reclines on a sarcophagus with her right arm resting on a cornucopia and her left hand pointing to the three persons com-memorated. Below their medallions is a weeping cherub with an extinguished torch.

Great Casterton, *St. Peter and St. Paul.* This is one of the least restored Rutland churches. It also has an unusual amount of 13C work and a structural history, between the 12C and the 14C, that can be read very clearly.

The story starts in the chancel. A straight joint halfway along indicates the extent of the chancel in the 12C. On the S side are the possible remains of a Norman window. The E part of the chancel represents a 13C extension and includes the moderately unusual feature of two lancet windows in the E wall. Above is a niche containing a later figure, probably St. Paul. In the early 13C aisles were built out and the straight joints at their E ends are clear evidence of the unaisled church. There are three-light aisle windows with intersecting tracery. The nave was extended W, and a clerestory with the foiled circular windows, typical of the time, was added. By this time the W end lay near the limit of consecrated ground. So when a tower was determined upon, probably in the late 14C, a drastic expedient was adopted. Rather than building it onto the N or S of the nave, it was placed within the W bay of the nave. This tower is crowned by battlements and vast pinnacles, the SW one of which is dated 1792 (the date of them all?). The rest of the church was given battlements and low-pitched roofs in Perpendicular times. W of the porch is a new room put up in 1982. The S porch is of the 13C; its leaf capitals to the responds give a foretaste of what can be seen inside.

Dominating the interior are the two-bay arcades with their tall circular piers and elegant stiff-leaf capitals. The arches form a good example of the common Rutland round arches still being built in the 13C. Of the two the S arcade is fractionally later than the N; its foliage is slightly more naturalistic and the water-holding hollow found on the base on the N is omitted. The tower arch is impressively tall. At the E end of the N aisle is some simple medieval wall decoration, of a type often used when funds did not run to figure painting. Even though the W gallery was removed in 1894 and the box-pews in 1927, there is much that remains of pre-Victorian arrangements. The communion rail is 18C and so too is the pulpit with tester. Over the tower arch is a plaster tympanum bearing the arms of King George II and on either side, painted on the plaster, is the dictum 'Fear God—Honour Ye King'. Stained glass is almost totally lacking, though the chancel E windows were glazed in 1905 (depicting St. Peter and St. James the Greater). The square font is decorated with concentric lozenges and probably dates from c 1200. In the S aisle there are two 13C tomb-recesses, one inside and one out. The one inside has the effigy of a priest in eucharistic vestments (probably 13C). Outside, the recess has a coffin-lid of the type which shows only the head and feet of the deceased.

Ketton, St. Mary. This is a finely proportioned, largely 13C church, developed from a Norman cruciform building. Its crowning feature is the crossing tower and lavish 150ft high spire which were not completed until the early 14C. We are fortunate in having a date for the 13C work, a grant by Bishop Hugh de Wells of a release of 20 days' penance to those contributing to the work in 1232—though exactly when it began and finished we cannot be sure.

However, that the work in the 1230s was but a modification of the existing fabric can be clearly seen outside. At the W end is an impressive work of c 1190, a portal flanked by pointed, blank arches. The arches have shafts and, flanking them, dogtooth strips. The capitals contain waterleaf decoration and there is a wealth of zigzag. All this is an interesting combination of Norman and Early English motifs but is still a world apart from the serene purity of fully developed Gothic found at Ketton 40 years later. From that time there is little left externally at ground level, only the small W lancets and the evidence of very steeply pitched rooflines on the aisles. But at this time the tower was heightened by a lovely belfry stage. The E angles of the tower are enriched by a roll on what is really a purely ornamental flat buttress. The belfry windows themselves are therefore slightly recessed. They are very tall and each face has two-light openings with Y-tracery. Each opening is divided from its neighbours by rich shafting and dogtooth bands. Below the spire comes a corbel table. The spire itself is reminiscent of nearby St. Mary's, Stamford, with which it shares the unusual feature, confined to this area, of having a moulded cornice at the springing—hence the spire projects out some way from the tower. The broaches and angles of the spire have ribs and at the tops of the broaches are crocketed canopies with figures—SE and SW, the Virgin Mary and Gabriel at the Annunciation, NE and NW, St. Peter and St. Paul. The richness is continued by three tiers of lucarnes under elaborate canopies. The W window is a fine though not wholly appropriate Geometrical design of 1861–62 by Sir Gilbert Scott to replace one that 'has been transformed in a vile manner and has frightful tracery' (Sir Stephen Glynne in 1861). Also by Scott is the Rood loft stair turret on the S side: he built this after the original medieval foundations were discovered. Many windows were renewed by Scott and he also replaced the embattled parapet on the S aisle with a plain one. The chancel was extensively restored by the young T.G. Jackson in 1863, including the provision of a new E window to replace one 'of a sort of Jacobean character and square headed' (Glynne again). A somewhat earlier and very important modification took place under a faculty of 1774. It had generally been assumed that the Norman transepts had been shortened in the 14C but it is now clear that this was done c 1774. The medieval transepts were quite long. It is even possible that the Norman transepts were quite short and were actually lengthened c 1300, which is the date of the reset N and the S windows. The entrance is through the S porch, an early 14C addition to a porchless aisle: see the way the stringcourse passes behind the porch.

The dominant theme of the interior is the work of the early 13C, notably the tall, wide, three-bay arcades. These were erected together and have tall cylindrical piers, moulded capitals with nailhead and double-chamfered arches. Of similar character are the arches into the crossing, which are but the remodelling of a 12C fabric, since above the arch to the nave is a round-headed doorway that would have given access to the Norman roof space. Over the arch from the S aisle to the transept are a couple of large, richly ornamented late Norman fragments (perhaps from a tower arch). The former rooflines at the E end of the nave can be related to the phases before the addition of the Perpendicular clerestory. The chancel has a noticeable lean to the N: its roof is from an attractive scheme by Sir Charles Nicholson in 1950. The 14C font has an octagonal bowl with window tracery panels and flat leaf decoration. Parts of the screen from the S aisle to the transept are original Perpendicular work. Medieval scrollwork survives on the chancel arch. Sir Ninian Comper designed the E window of 1907 commemorating a dedication at the church by Bishop Grosseteste of Lincoln in 1240, the 'English altar' of 1925, and the war memorial in the churchyard.

A notable priest here between 1861 and 1875 was F.H. Sutton. He was a gifted artist and known in Ecclesiological circles. He must have been responsible for the choice of Scott for the 1860s restoration. He designed glass for Brant Broughton (Lincolnshire) and Lincoln Cathedral and at Ketton designed and painted glass in the E window (replaced by Comper), the S transept window and the W windows of the aisles. He was also responsible for designing the pavement under the crossing (includes David playing the Harp).

Normanton, *St. Matthew*. St. Matthew's stands with its lower third ignominiously submerged on the S shores of the vast Rutland Water, a 3500 acre reservoir created in the early 1970s. It was saved by a group of volunteers and is now reached by a short causeway. The medieval church was largely rebuilt in 1764. Then, in 1826, the present W portico and tower were added, the latter being a Baroque piece modelled on St. John's, Smith Square, London. The portico is semicircular with Ionic columns. The architect was probably Thomas Cundy the younger, though his father who died in 1825 might have also been involved in the design. The nave and chancel of 1764 were swept away in 1911, being replaced by a design of 1905 by J.B. Gridley to harmonise with the W end. The three bays with segment-headed windows are divided by Ionic pilasters and at the E end is an apse. Above is a parapet with balusters. Inside, the ceiling is of coved plasterwork. The monuments of the Heathcote family have been moved to Edith Weston Church; the most notable is to Sir Gilbert (died 1733) by J.M. Rysbrack.

Oakham, *All Saints*. All Saints' appears as a large Perpendicular town church with an earlier tower and spire which, at c 162ft in height, dominate this former county town. The Perpendicular remodelling provided large windows, a big clerestory and an abundance of bristling pinnacles and parapets. The story of the growth of the church extends over four centuries and, though complicated, can be traced in the existing fabric.

Unusually, the earliest work can be seen outside. This is the large S doorway which dates from the very early 13C. Its jambs are shafted and on the capitals on the W side are stiff leaves on long upright stalks. The inside of the porch is later 13C and displays four bays of arcading on each wall. Otherwise the only outside work that seems to reach back to that time is the rubble fabric at the E end of the chancel. That this is 13C work is suggested by the contrast with the grey ashlar facing of the rest, and the fact that the arcade to the N chapel is not after the late 13C. This means the church had reached its present E extent by the end of the 13C. The early 14C gave the W limit with the building of the massive steeple. On the W face this has a doorway and small flowing tracery window above, both of these being contained within one superarch. In the next stage are three graduated niches containing original figures, Christ and, probably, St. Peter and St. Paul. The belfry stage exhibits a peculiar and most ungainly feature in the W and S faces: to accommodate the stair, the windows are displaced off-centre. The windows themselves are twinned, tall and have varied tracery and transoms. The parapet arrangements with small piercings and big corner pinnacles are clumpy. Otherwise it is by the Perpendicular contributions that the outside is to be remembered. The windows are of varied forms, those on the N mostly having short transoms in the heads. In the aisles and transepts the Perpendicular appearance is a refacing and heightening of the earlier fabric. The N or Holy Trinity chapel was rebuilt and the S or Lady chapel added. Still later, a vestry was added onto the S chapel (see the awkward tacking on the W side). The final change on the outside was at Sir Gilbert Scott's restoration in 1857–58. Previously the N chapel and chancel shared a common roof. Scott separated the roofs and, much to the disapproval of many of his contemporaries, provided a new E window, replacing the Perpendicular design by his beloved 'Early Middle Pointed'. In itself this is very fine but it simply does not harmonise with the rest of the church.

The interior is light and open: the piers and arches are generally tall and the large windows and clerestory flood the building with light. Visually the N–S axis seems as important as the E–W one: this is due to the scale of the transepts and the fact that the width across the nave and aisles is 5ft more than the length of the nave. There is sufficient evidence to show that the present plan was largely in existence in the 13C. This is a keeled stringcourse under the S aisle and transept windows, part of one in the N aisle, and piscinas in the transepts. Then there is the late 13C work in the arcade between the chancel and the N chapel. It has upright leaves but the piers have been altered when the chapel was rebuilt in the late 15C. The five-bay nave arcades date from a rebuilding in the 14C. The piers themselves are quatrefoil with fillets on the lobes and in the angles. They have an interesting series of carvings. The N ones illustrate demons, monsters and themes of darkness; those on the S (apart from the Reynard capital) have themes of Christianity and Redemption. They are, from the W, **N**: Respond: expulsion of Adam and Eve from the Garden of Eden; Pier 1: grotesques; Pier 2: grotesques and a dragon; Pier 3: leaves and a Green Man; Respond: a beast with a human head playing an instrument; **S**: Respond: pelican feeding her young (symbol of Christ); Pier 1: characters and scenes from the Reynard the Fox stories; Pier 2: four angels; Pier 3: the symbols of the Evangelists; Respond: Adam and Eve before the expulsion; the

Annunciation; the Coronation of the Virgin. At the time of the nave rebuilding the transepts seem to have been heightened. There then followed the Perpendicular phase with the addition of the clerestory, the rebuilding of the N chapel, and the addition of the S one. All this probably took place in the second half of the century with the S chapel being the last scheme, probably c 1480.

For such a grand church the furnishings are surprisingly unexciting. Scott's woodwork of 1857–58 is, as usual, dignified and well-executed and the screens to the chapels are particularly pleasing. The oldest item is the font, very late 12C, standing on a reused piece of the 14C. The big alabaster reredos was installed in 1898: it depicts the Resurrection, angels and the Evangelists, and was made by James Forsyth. There is a remarkable absence of monuments but a late Perpendicular table-tomb in the N chapel, and the kneeling figure of Anne Burton (died 1642) on the W wall of the S aisle, could be noted. She died aged 15 'Whose sweeter sowle, a flower of matchless price/Transplanted is from hence to Paradise'.

S of the church stands the chapel of Oakham School, built in 1924–25 as a war memorial and designed by Granville Streatfeild. It is an ambitious, apsidal structure with flying buttresses on the nave. It is an early 20C recreation of late 14C architecture. The hospital chapel of St. John and St. Anne beside the railway in the W part of the town could also be visited. It is a small rectangular building dating back to the early 14C. It served a hospital founded by John Dolby in 1399 and is now the chapel for the old people's flats that surround it. But no visitor must leave Oakham without visiting the splendid late 12C hall of Oakham Castle just E of the parish church. Its capitals are almost certainly the work of the masons who worked on William of Sens's choir at Canterbury, begun in 1175.

Stoke Dry, *St. Andrew.* St. Andrew's is one of the most delightful Rutland churches, placed on a hillside above the Eye Brook Reservoir. Not only is it largely unrestored, it also has an interesting architectural development and a host of items of interest, including monuments to the Digby family, one of whom was involved in the Gunpowder Plot.

The exterior tells far less of the architectural history than the interior. The most obvious feature is the thin W tower dating from c 1300. Its top may have been rebuilt in 1694. There seems to have been a good deal of work done in the 17C as the alterations to windows in the S aisle show (e.g. W of the porch where the tracery of the three-light window has been replaced by mullions running directly up to the head). The S porch is probably 17C too. The S chapel was added in c 1300 and is rather later than the adjoining aisle. Its S window has bar tracery but the E one is a most unusual design of three lights and in the head there is a spherical triangle containing three strange lobes. The main entrance is through the early 16C two-storeyed N porch, which has a distinctly domestic feel. The upper chamber is lit by a small oriel window.

Inside, the building history can be better traced, starting with Norman work in the chancel. On its N wall is a long piece of stringcourse with indented ornament. On the outside of the Norman chancel (now seen from the S chapel) is a further piece of stringcourse. The responds and one capital of the chancel arch contain some remarkable work of perhaps c 1120. The surfaces are covered with foliage and human and animal figures. On the S side a man tolling a bell can be clearly seen. Otherwise a demon (S), a dragon, a lion, a seated figure and an eagle (N) appear. It seems likely that the Norman church was aisleless. In the early 13C a S aisle was added. The arcade is of three bays, and has circular piers and clustered responds. It will be noticed that the nave is not axial with the chancel, a feature which requires a little explanation. As the chancel seems to be 12C then the displacement must have occurred on the nave side. This probably took place when the N aisle was created in c 1300. There being little land available on the N only a narrow aisle was possible and it seems to have been built at the expense of a little of the nave. The W tower is often taken to be 13C on the evidence of the W lancet, but this could equally be a survival of c 1300 and, if so, the tower was then built axial with the realigned nave. About that time the S chapel was built. All these changes may not have been complete until the end of the second quarter of the century.

The 15C Rood screen is particularly interesting in that it has lateral projections, no doubt for the figures of the Virgin and St. John. Unusually for this area it retains its vaulting. There are a few medieval bench-ends with poppyheads and some 15C glass in the E window. The 17C communion rails remain. In 1898 there was a careful restoration by J. Arthur Reeve and this exposed one of Stoke Dry's greatest treasures, the wall paintings (identified for me by E. Clive Rouse). In the chancel N of the E window is the crucifixion of St. Andrew, with the donor below. To the S is the Virgin and Child enthroned below a trefoiled canopy, with the Annunciation below. On the splays of the E window is scrollwork. All this is late 13C or early 14C. There are 14C paintings in the S chapel too, notably the martyrdom of St. Edmund (note the strange head-dresses of the archers and on St. Christopher). In the splays of the SE window is the crowned figure of St. Margaret (E) and her torture (W). In the nave, above the arcades, are shields with the emblems of the 12 tribes of Israel (probably 16C) but they are only partially conserved. On the N is the ass of Issachar, an unidentified shield and the Lion of Judah. On the S is the barry wavy water for Ruben and another unidentified shield. There are three impressive monuments to the Digby family. The earliest is a table-tomb at the E end of the S aisle with an alabaster slab to Jaqueta Digby (died 1496). From her girdle hangs a pomander box. The headless figure of Sir Everard Digby (died 1540) lies, in plate armour, on a table-tomb in the chapel. Artistically the interest lies in the introduction of Renaissance features at this time. On the wall behind is a canopy with a four-centred arch. In the SE part of the chancel Kenelm Digby (died 1590: his initials and the date 1574 appear on a timber in the chapel roof) and his wife Anne (died 1602) lie upon a table-tomb.

A later Sir Everard Digby was one of the Gunpowder Plot conspirators and was born in this village. He was hanged in 1606. Sadly there is no truth in the attractive but unnecessary tale that the plot was hatched in the room over the porch. Another story concerns a Rector who locked up a witch in the room and starved her to death. But on the veracity of whether her ghost still frequents the church I cannot comment!

Teigh, _Holy Trinity._ In 1782 this church was virtually entirely rebuilt in a delightful Gothick style. The architect was George Richardson and his patron was Robert Sherard, fourth Earl of Harborough, who was also Rector of Teigh. The lower three stages of the 13C and 14C tower were retained but above that the upper part was rebuilt. (There is some doubt over the third stage; it was possibly rebuilt.)

The windows of 1782 were plain pointed ones but were filled with Gothic tracery around the end of the last century. Below the battlements is a delightful frieze loosely modelled on Perpendicular lozenge-patterned examples. The interior is a complete surprise. The tiered seats (three rows each side) are arranged to face N–S and the whole space is covered by a slightly pointed plaster ceiling with Gothic ribbing. The greatest delight of all is the W end where the pulpit floats in mid-air above the W entrance. On either side at a lower level are the sentry-box-like clerk's and reading desks. Above all these a mock window is painted: one gazes past the mock glazing bars at mock leafy trees. Either side of the window are the Lord's Prayer and Creed. To counterbalance these the Ten Commandments flank the window at the E end. The 18C movable wooden font is preserved; the other font is a strange rustic piece carved by another former Rector, A.S. Atcheson, in 1856. A painting of the Flemish School representing the Last Supper after Otto van Veen (1558–1629) serves as a reredos.

The W end of the early Gothic Revival church, Holy Trinity by George Richardson, 1782, showing a pulpit and a false window over the W door, flanked by desks

Tickencote, _St. Peter and St. Paul._ The importance of Tickencote lies in the lavishness of the original Norman work and in an extraordinary Norman remodelling in 1792, arguably the first major case of the Norman revival in England.

What we see externally is largely the work of 1792 when Miss Eliza Wingfield, as the inscription over the S door notes, 'with that true sense of religion and reverence for her maker, which ever distinguished her life, rebuilt this church'. Her architect was S.P. Cockerell, who used fine closely jointed ashlar throughout. The chancel is astonishingly elaborate. The upper part seems to have been completely rebuilt but the N and E façades follow the general original scheme but with changes in detail. The S one is essentially of 1792. Particularly notable are the semicircular buttresses which are rare in England but are paralleled, for example, at St. Peter's,

Northampton. The E wall has five tiers like those of a wedding cake.
The vestry on the N was added in 1792. The windows and decoration
of the nave follow, in a simplified way, the work in the chancel. The
entrance is through the tower of 1792 on the S side.

The interior, when looking E, is stunning. The chancel arch is on
an heroic scale and was not altered in the late 18C. It has become
depressed through settlement and the jambs lean outward. The arch
itself is of six orders, each different. Working inwards from the billet
hoodmould they are: 1. a kind of stepped leaf (reused outside in
1792); 2. zigzag; 3. a wealth of heads and foliage of different designs;
4. battlemented ornament with chevron at the edge; 5. beakheads; 6.
a round soffit roll and an edge roll. The two-bay chancel itself is low
and of immense power, deriving from the most unusual feature of a
Norman sexpartite rib-vault. The ribs, encrusted with zigzag, sweep
upwards to another rare feature, a Norman boss. This shows a
monk's head and two muzzled bears. On the S side is a 14C shaft
below the springing, put in when a chantry chapel was added on the
S. The date of the Norman work has been the subject of much
speculation. Sexpartite vaults do not otherwise appear in England
until after 1175, when they were introduced from France to Canterbury Cathedral. However, the stylistic evidence would suggest an
earlier date for Tickencote, perhaps of c 1160. The lighting is by
small semicircular windows which, on the sides, do not correspond
with the external organisation of the arches. Before 1792 there was a
staircase at the NE corner leading to a priest's chamber above the
chancel, of which slight traces in the stonework are visible.

Remaining in the chancel, a damaged wooden effigy of a knight
can be seen in the recess on the S side. He is said to be Sir Roland le
Daneys (died 1363). The communion table dates from 1627 and
stands on bulbous legs. The font is square and dates from the early
13C. It has intersected arches, and strips of dogtooth at the corners of
the bowl. The E window is by A.K. Nicholson, 1929, and represents
the Beatitudes.

Whissendine, *St. Andrew.* St. Andrew's appears as a fine, spacious
Perpendicular church with a particularly notable 14C tower. The
plan is slightly unusual in that the transepts take off from the chancel
and the S aisle is distinguished by the fact that it is fractionally wider
than the nave.

The crowning feature of the exterior both physically and aesthet-
ically is the 100ft high W tower. It was erected in the first half of the
14C. There are certain common characteristics with Oakham such as
the W doorway and window being framed by one large arch, the idea
of three niches above, the use of small ogee arches in the parapet,
and, most regrettably, the effect of the stair turret on the belfry stage.
This top stage is on a noble scale. The belfry openings are tall, have
two lights and odd little ogees halfway up when one would expect a
transom. But, as at Oakham, the openings on the W and S faces are
displaced to accommodate the stairway in the SW corner. However,
this does not detract from the beautiful height to width proportions,
the sleek handling of the angle buttress details, a fairly well-
developed base course, and the use of shafts and deep mouldings to
enrich the openings. After this the rest of the exterior is more
conventional, and is the product of a Perpendicular remodelling. An
oddity is the big S window in the S transept. The opening is early 14C
but was later given Perpendicular tracery (hence the transom with
strawberry-leaf), and later still the top was destroyed by the

flattening of the roof (possibly in 1640). The E window was put in in 1865 at the start of a protracted restoration (1864–70) by H. Goddard & Son of Leicester. The porch is 14C and it shelters what is the earliest feature that can be seen outside—the 13C S doorway.

There is a good deal more of the 13C inside, notably in the five-bay arcades and the arch from the chancel to the N transept. The N arcade is slightly earlier than the S one but its appearance has been confused in the aisle by the addition in the 17C or even later of three transverse arches to prevent it leaning outwards. The W bay is a later addition to connect it up to the tower. The pier shapes are quite varied, ranging from circular to quatrefoil, and with various enrichments. The chancel arch is modern. The width of the S aisle has already been mentioned. Almost certainly it was a widening in the 14C when the S doorway must have been reset. Whether there was a S transept before the 14C is not known but the fabric of the present one was erected then. It does contain a 13C piscina but this is reset. The addition of the clerestory radically altered the internal atmosphere. At this upper level the seated wooden figures under bowed ogee canopies are an unusual and charming feature and are situated in the wall posts for the roof. The present roof is dated 1728, but contains much medieval work.

The coved screen between the S aisle and the transept is the most notable of the fittings. It was brought here after it had become redundant in 1869 at the rebuilding of St. John's College in Cambridge. It is of 16C date and its doors have Renaissance work. The reredos is of 1912 by Kempe & Co., who had been responsible for the E window in 1892.

SHROPSHIRE

Shropshire, the largest inland county in England, is divided by the Severn; to the N, there is a plain, broken by sandstone ridges which lead to the coalfield and industrial complex around Ironbridge; to the S, there are diagonal valleys separated by steep uplands like Wenlock Edge and the Long Mynd. Although it was the first of the Mercian shires to be named (in 1006), it was not until 1536 that it assumed its present form. Until then it lay in the limbo that was the March of Wales.

So settlement required the protection of castles, and these the Normans quickly provided. In their shadow rose the churches: Acton Burnell, Stokesay, Moreton Corbet, and from these secure centres spread daughter churches and chapels. Such buildings often lay in circular churchyards and were sturdily designed with strong towers and few steeples. Only in the new Norman plantations like Shrewsbury, Ludlow, Bridgnorth, Clun and Bishop's Castle were the larger churches built; and of these, Shrewsbury, which became a staple town for wool and leather in 1326, and Ludlow, which became the headquarters of the Council of the Marches in 1536, were wealthy enough to become grand.

Evidence of pre-Conquest building is slight: the nave at St. Peter's, Diddlebury, and walling at St. Peter's, Stanton Lacy. Unaltered Norman churches are equally rare, with Heath Chapel almost unique. The 12C school of Herefordshire masons left examples of their work on the fonts at Stottesdon and Holdgate and on the tympanum at Aston Eyre. Early English architecture is at its best at Longnor, Acton Burnell, Kinlet and St. Mary's, Shrewsbury. Hodnet has a fine octagonal Decorated tower, while Battlefield (1406–09) has Decorated and Perpendicular tracery side by side. But the Perpendicular style comes into its own at Tong, as it does at Ludlow, where the tower dominates the countryside. Curiously, in such a well-wooded county, there are only two timber-framed churches, Melverley (early 16C) and Halston (late 17C).

Post-Reformation reconstruction can be seen at Church Stretton (1625) and Astley Abbots (1633), while rebuilding after the Civil War occurred at High Ercall (1622), Stokesay (1654 and 1664), Condover (1662), Benthall (1667) and Minsterley (1689). The two chapels of Langley and Halston retain their almost complete 17C furnishing, and at Myddle in 1700, Richard Gough produced the first complete account of a 17C church, its pews, their occupants, and the life of the parish.

The 18C saw the building of six of the county's more memorable churches; two by George Steuart in 1790: Wellington, subsequently wrecked internally by the 1898 restoration, and St. Chad's, Shrewsbury; two by Thomas Telford, at Bridgnorth (1792) and Madeley (1796); and two dedicated to St. Alkmund: one in Shrewsbury by J.H. Haycock and one at Whitchurch by William Smith. During the same century brick became popular and at least 15 churches were built or rebuilt in this way. Perhaps the most pleasing are Leighton (1714) and Quatt, tower only (1763). Many Victorian and Edwardian architects worked in the county: Sir Gilbert Scott at Ellesmere (1849), G.E. Street at St. George's, Oakengates (1861) and Oswestry (1872), Sir Arthur Blomfield at Jackfield (1863) and Bridgnorth (1876), Norman Shaw at Batchcott, Richard's Castle (1891), Sir Aston Webb at

Burford (1899), Sir Ninian Comper at Moreton Corbet (1905), and, perhaps most satisfactorily of all, Detmar Blow at Onibury in 1902.

There are few unusual dedications: St. Eata (a 7C Bishop of Hexham) at Atcham, St. Lucy at Upton Magna, St. Ruthin at Longden, and St. Calixtus (a 3C Pope) at Astley Abbots. Shropshire churches are dominated rather by the tombs of the county families than by the saints to which they are dedicated: Vernons at Tong, Bromleys and Newports at Wroxeter, Corbets at Moreton Corbet, Lees at Acton Burnell, Blounts at Kinlet, Wolryches at Quatt and Cottons at Norton-in-Hales. Nearly all of them are table-tombs with recumbent effigies. Perhaps the most beautiful later memorial is Sir Henry Cheere's Rococo monument to Henrietta Vernon (died 1752) at Hodnet.

Wall painting is rare, though the Battle of Virtues and Vices at Claverley (c 1200) is unique. There is also an exuberantly rustic ceiling (1672) at Bromfield, and some Norman work waiting to be uncovered at Heath Chapel. At Burford there is a very large triptych to the Cornwall family (1568). There are good hatchments in St. Chad's at Shrewsbury, Atcham and Halston. Royal arms are mainly Georgian, the best at Tong, Shifnal, Cheswardine and St. Mary's, Shrewsbury, while Onibury has a rarity in King Edward VII's. There are good roofs at Rushbury and Astley Abbots, screens at Ludlow and Hughley, misericords at Tong and Ludlow, a fine chandelier of 1715 at Whitchurch, and the best of many Jacobean pulpits at Quatt and Petton. Glass by C.E. Kempe and David Evans occurs almost everywhere, and Meole Brace and Calverhall have good examples of work by William Morris. Cast-iron window tracery from Ironbridge can be seen at Longnor, Adderley and Tilstock, iron churchyard monuments at Madeley, Bridgnorth, Leighton and Pontesbury; and Wem acquired a cast-iron pulpit in 1887. There is a fine organ case of 1715 at Whitchurch and good examples of Commandment boards at Ludlow, Lydbury North and Stokesay.

Not many national figures came from Shropshire; it was too pleasant to leave. Warriors had to, and their tombs fill the churches, probably the most famous being John Talbot, Earl of Shrewsbury, whose heart and bones lie at Whitchurch guarded by Talbot dogs. Shakespeare's 'scourge of France', he was killed in battle at the age of 80 in 1453. Elizabeth Fry was moved to become a Quaker at Ironbridge, and there the country's industrialists, Darbys and Wilkinsons, began to change the face of Britain. Richard Baxter preached to 'a dead-hearted unprofitable people' in Bridgnorth. Charles Darwin came from Shrewsbury, Edward German from Whitchurch, Bishop Percy of the Percy Reliques from Bridgnorth, as did Francis Moore of Old Moore's Almanac. A.E. Housman, whose ashes lie at Ludlow, gave the county publicity in his 'Shropshire Lad' and Wilfred Owen's name is on the War Memorial in the Abbey Church in Shrewsbury. From the topographical point of view, not only did Shropshire have in Richard Gough's 'History of Myddle' the first complete village history; but between 1894 and 1912, Dean Cranage gave it in his 'Architectural Account of the Churches of Shropshire' a more detailed and comprehensive history of its ecclesiology than has been given to any other English county.

Acton Burnell, *St. Mary.* Sheltering under the castle walls, but built earlier, this is a church of nave, chancel, N and S transepts, and late Victorian tower. Founded in the mid-13C by Robert Burnell, private chaplain to the future King Edward I, it introduced into rural Shropshire the latest architectural details.

Outwardly, the impression is rather dull, the W front providing the best aspect, with matching buttresses, stepped where they meet the wall, a door with steep, filleted moulding, and a large three-light lancet window above with similar moulding. A corbel table runs below the eaves of both nave and chancel, with weathered heads and grotesque carvings. The Norman N porch has a double-chamfered outer arch, and a recess above contains a free-standing trefoil. The S door has been blocked. The windows in nave and chancel are cusped lancets.

Inside, the church is dark in spite of the impressive windows, especially that at the E end, with four lights separated into pairs by shafts of Purbeck marble, the whole topped by three trefoils and a large cinquefoil. The N and S windows of the chancel are also grouped lancets with trefoil heads. The roof consists of collar-beams on arched braces, and dates from 1571 in the chancel and 1598 in the nave. Short Purbeck marble shafts, standing on stiff-leaf corbels and heads, support the arches of both chancel and transepts. All have similar complex mouldings. The N transept has a floor of medieval tiles, relaid in 1887, while the S transept has traces of wall painting. The large piscina in the chancel has a trefoil arch resting on stiff-leaf capitals and two basins which rest on two projecting small heads. The font is octagonal with shafts and trefoil arches and is possibly contemporary with the original church. The pulpit is Jacobean and there is a 17C collection shovel. More important are the memorials in the N transept. The earliest is the large brass of Sir Nicholas Burnell (died 1382) resting on a table-tomb, in plate armour, jupon and roundel spurs. Alongside is the fine alabaster tomb of Sir Richard Lee (died 1591), lying with his wife on a rolled straw mattress, hands raised in prayer, and a small dog crawling from the gauntlet abandoned at his side. He is in beautifully chased armour and his wife elaborately dressed. Their nine daughters kneel behind them, their eldest son stands at their heads and two more sons at their feet. Below Sir Richard the tomb-chest is banded with straps ending in claws; over him his achievement is supported by caryatids and topped by a skull. There was once his funeral helm with his crest of a squirrel cracking a nut, but it is now in a Shrewsbury museum. On the opposite wall, Sir Humphrey Lee (died 1632) and his wife kneel facing across a prayer-desk on a large hanging monument. Their children are ranged below. The designer was Nicholas Stone. In the same transept there is a wall tablet to Lady Mary Smythe (died 1764), carved with a small cross and two flaring lamps. The cross disappeared from Anglican monuments in the 16C, and this is one of the earliest instances of its cautious reappearance.

Bridgnorth, *St. Mary Magdalene*. A Classical building of 1792 by Thomas Telford, consisting of aisled nave, chancel, apse and N-facing tower, which replaced a collegiate church on the site of the castle chapel. The collapse of Old St. Chad's in Shrewsbury seems to have inspired the people of Bridgnorth to demolish their dilapidated building and employ Telford on the new one. He aligned it with East Castle Street; and the Tuscan columns, pediment, square tower, belfry, polygonal clock turret and leaded dome, make a fine end-piece. It has much in common with St. Chad's, including a round entrance hall. Inside, Ionic columns support a flat ceiling and large round-headed windows lighten the gallery which is arched like a viaduct. Sir Arthur Blomfield raised the chancel in 1876, floored it with local tiles, and added an apse and good iron railings. The church is an example of the way in which Telford was able to enhance the environment by matching his church with the street of fine houses leading to it.

Claverley, *All Saints.* This building is made more remarkable by the wall painting discovered in 1902 and running the length of the nave on the upper part of the N wall. It measures about 50ft in length and the figures are about 4ft in height. It represents the *Psychomachia* or Battle of the Virtues and Vices, but is in effect a battle scene between mounted knights. There are symbolic trees and foliage between the figures and a frieze of running scrollwork above and below. Although it dates from c 1200, the shields, horses and knights have a strong resemblance to the Bayeux Tapestry. The church also contains a good incised slab to Richard Spicer (died 1448) and a fine alabaster tomb to Sir Robert Broke (died 1558), 'the compleatest lawyer of his time', Speaker of the House of Commons and Recorder of London. He lies with his two wives, guarded by their 17 children.

Condover, *St. Mary and St. Andrew.* A church of very mixed descent: a late Norman N transept; W tower, nave and S transept from the Restoration; and a chancel of 1868; but all unified by the same pink sandstone. It contains notable monuments, dominated by G.F. Watts's portrayal of Sir Thomas Cholmondeley (died 1864). He kneels in belted coat and long cloak, hands on the hilt of his sword, his curled beard pointed to heaven. He died on his honeymoon, and close at hand lies his sister-in-law who died in childbirth, her baby at her side and an empty cradle. It was carved by her husband, Reginald Cholmondeley, who had assisted Watts with Sir Thomas's monument. Near them is Roger Owen (died 1746) by L.F. Roubiliac. He is reclining nonchalantly, his wife at his feet watching with concern. Over the vestry door, Martha Owen (died 1641), also with her baby, is commemorated. Back in the S transept against the wall, there is a large memorial to Jane Norton (died 1640) and her husband. They kneel facing one another under arches, with achievement over. Below them, under similar arches, are her father and brother in the same attitude. In the chancel stands a table-tomb with much strapwork to Thomas Scriven (died 1587) and his wife. They lie together in alabaster, their children ranged around the sides.

Halston Chapel, see Melverley, *St. Peter.*

Heath Chapel. Reached along winding lanes, this simplest of Norman churches stands alone in a field. Its barn-like nave and lower chancel has no tower or bellcote. The W end has four distinctive single-light windows, three stepped in the apex and a larger one below in the flat central buttress. Similar flat buttresses continue round the building and the single light at the E end is also set in one of them. There are four matching windows to nave and chancel. The S door with two orders of shafts and weathered capitals has zigzag decoration in the outer arch and in the hoodmould. The tympanum is blank and the door cuts through the stringcourse which runs round the building.

Inside, notable features are a simple Norman font with a double arcade roughly incised at the top and extensive wall painting awaiting restoration. The chancel arch has scalloped capitals and is double-stepped. The furniture is almost all of the 17C, though the box-pew in the chancel is composed of earlier parts. Pulpit, squire's pew, box-pews, many with rosettes carved within diamonds on their doors, and three-sided communion rail, are all in keeping, though the sturdy children's benches (cf. Skenfrith, Monmouthshire) are earlier, as is the ironwork on the W door.

A two-cell Norman church, with flat buttresses, stringcourses and S doorway with shafts and mouldings

Hughley, *St. John the Baptist.* This church possesses a fine screen, similar to the one at Aymestrey (Herefordshire). It features very delicate tracery over the dado, then broad divisions separated by clustered shafts, rising in tiers to lierne-vaulting which intersects in wide crosses enclosing quatrefoils. Elaborate cresting over.

Ludlow, *St. Laurence.* Ludlow Parish Church is one of the finest buildings of the Welsh Marches. Its pinnacled roof and great tower (135ft tall) present a formidable silhouette, especially when seen from the railway (looking up) or from Whitcliff (looking down). In the town itself, however, the church is frequently out of sight behind the tall houses in the narrow streets. It has no churchyard as such, but a garden of rest runs the whole length of its N side, with a simple memorial cross.

One must start with the 15C crossing tower: at its lower stage it has large windows with Y-tracery; this pattern is repeated at the upper stage, whose small bell openings are flanked by figures in niches; these and the elaborate battlements and pinnacles are 19C. The whole building is of red sandstone, much weathered and in places much restored. There were two major Victorian restorations: by Sir Gilbert Scott (1859–60) and by Sir Arthur Blomfield (1889–91).

The transept windows N and S are Decorated. The E window of nine lights is Perpendicular, but has a curious narrow ogee opening below it, and the N aisle of the nave is notable for its six windows of two lights with Geometrical tracery (star within circle). At nearby Leominster these windows would have been encrusted with ball-flower; here, however, it appears only on the aisle window at the W end. The nave W window of seven lights has fine Reticulated tracery with a surprisingly modest W door beneath. The chief feature of the S elevation is the hexagonal porch (early 14C) which has a vaulted ceiling and chamber over. The embattled stair turret is surmounted by a carving of the Pelican in her Piety. The doorway inside the porch has an Early English arch of a single order with bell capitals.

The nave is of six high bays with clerestory. The fine timber roof has tiebeams and 24 gilded bosses. The piers of the arcades each have four shafts, and there are copious masons' marks etched on the stones. N and S aisles terminate in sweeping half-arches where they meet the transepts; evidence of former chantries can be seen in the piscinas in the S aisle wall. There is a recent nave altar in front of the crossing arch. Its imposition was controversial, but the church is long enough and the chancel screen deep enough to justify it. The choirstalls positioned in the crossing appear cramped, however. The view up into the tower from the crossing is dramatic.

The N transept, which formerly housed the Fletchers' chapel, now contains the great organ of 1784 given by the Earl of Powys (whose family still owns Ludlow Castle). The N chapel is entered through a richly carved screen. In the SW corner is the doorway to the tower stairs. The walls have linenfold panelling, and the altar (with a gilded canopy over the E window) is surrounded by 18C communion rails. The great feature of this chapel is its glass: 15C with rather large ungainly figures in the N windows, but a splendid E window of 1460 depicting King Edward the Confessor with the Palmers.

The chancel is entered through a veranda Rood screen. The choirstalls (1447) have a nearly intact set of 30 misericords depicting a cheerful variety of subjects (heraldry, proverbs, local life, etc.). The poppyhead bench-ends are also distinguished. The windows N and S of the sanctuary have double transoms; the E window has three transoms. The roof is richly embossed and painted; the sanctuary has an interesting mosaic floor. There are coloured and gilded monuments to Marcher lords on the walls and at the sides: Ludlow, with its castle and cathedral-like church, was clearly no mean centre of power. Behind the high altar, the stone reredos contains 24 figures and has five panels depicting scenes from the life of Christ.

The S chapel (Lady chapel) is entered through a 15C screen with noble carving. Behind the modern stone mensa set on four posts is a Jesse tree (originally 14C but restored by Hardman & Co. in 1891). In the S wall are a piscina and alcove, with a larger opening that was originally a doorway through which the parish fire engine passed when it was kept in this chapel.

The chapel in the S transept has a modern carved altar and communion rails. The S window has good Reticulated tracery. Beneath it is the alabaster recumbent figure of Dame Mary Eure (1612).

Furnishings of note elsewhere in the church are the W window by Thomas Willement (signed in the bottom right-hand corner) and two good windows by Hardman & Co. (chiefly in yellow, grey and white) in the N aisle; pews in the Lady chapel, probably 17C and much carved upon; and, on the S wall, a late 19C banner depicting St. Laurence: very fine embroidery and laidwork by Watts & Co.

Ludlow Castle, *Chapel.* Of the chapel of Ludlow Castle only the nave remains, and it is circular, located near the centre of the Inner Bailey. The outline of what must have been a very narrow chancel with apse can be traced. The W doorway and chancel arch suggest the mid-12C. This chapel was clearly too small for the growing establishment of the castle, and a larger one was built by the early 14C in the S corner of the Outer Bailey.

Lydbury North, *St. Michael.* An uncompromising Norman church consisting of W tower, nave, N and S transepts and chancel. It stands in a raised churchyard, dominating the village, its history greatly influenced by two powerful local families, the Clives of Walcot in the S transept, and the Plowdens of Plowden in the Catholic N transept.

The heavily buttressed tower is of c 1200 up to the corbel table, and has later battlements and an unobtrusive spirelet. The bell openings are paired lancets and there is a good single-handed clock. The roof is stone-tiled and there are five small Norman windows, two in the nave and three in the chancel which has a strangely large priest's door with single shafts, worn capitals and a zigzag lintel. The nave S door is protected by a handsome timber porch with castellated rafters and waved barge boards. '1901' is carved on the lintel, the date of J.T. Micklethwaite's extensive restoration of the whole building. The windows of the N transept are early 14C, those of the S transept 19C. This transept has an upper room with a door below from the churchyard to its stairs. It was used as the village school from 1662 to 1843.

Inside, the church is light, with plastered walls, few monuments and little stained glass. There is a good roof with collar-beams and wind-braces. The tower arch is a fine one with scallops and a single chamfer. Another Norman arch leads from the nave to the N transept. This, the Plowden chapel, has the distinction of being Catholic, and is separated from the nave by a screen of the early 16C. Inside, the chapel is whitewashed, and the altar is a simple stone ledge below a single-light window. The arch opposite, leading to the Walcot S chapel, is by Micklethwaite (1900) and has Queen Victoria, very placid, as the E capital, and King Edward VII snarling with disapproval at the congregation from the W.

The furnishings include a well-restored screen with Creed, Commandments and Lord's Prayer forming a tympanum over. The lettering is in black-letter and runs the whole length of the screen, the Lord's Prayer being signed by Charles Bright, Churchwarden 1615. The box-pews are carved with dragons and foliage, and the pulpit, similarly carved, dates from 1624. On either side of the communion table are two wooden candlesticks of c 1640. The font is square on a scalloped base and has a sturdy cover. In the Walcot chapel are hatchments of the Clive family with elephants and dragons as supporters. The Walcot chapel takes its name from the house outside the village which was bought by Robert Clive on his return from India. He committed suicide in 1774 and was buried in the parish where he was born, Moreton Say. No stone marks his grave, but there is a brass inside the door to his memory, *'Primus in Indis'*.

Melverley, *St. Peter,* **and Halston Chapel.** These are the only timber-framed churches in Shropshire. St. Peter's is poised like a galleon over the Vyrnwy, one of the Severn's most beautiful tributaries. It dates from the early 16C and consists of nave and chancel in one, with a timber-framed bell tower at the W end. It is almost entirely post and pannel with a few diagonal struts. The robust porch has benches inside. There was considerable restoration in 1878.

The interior is a maze of tiebeams, collar-beams and wind-braces, similar to but sturdier than the timbering at Vowchurch (Herefordshire). The only division is by means of the screen, a simple panelled dado with a door and posts linking it to a tiebeam. According to Dean Cranage, the screen once bore an inscription stating that church and steeple were rebuilt in 1718. The W gallery of 1588 is traditionally associated with the Armada and certainly has the feel of a galleon.

Halston Chapel, of 1690, is smaller and has a brick tower. The timbering of the rest of the building is post and pannel. It stands in the park surrounded by a ditch and sheltering yews. The W door enters into the tower and another door opens into the nave, the pew of squire and servants on either side, then the villagers facing one another on long benches with doors. It is a church with a single liturgical centre, the communion table with its reredos of Decalogue, Creed and Lord's Prayer guarded by Moses and Aaron painted on panels. On the right of the sanctuary, there is an enclosed christening pew with a baluster font; to the left is a double-decker pulpit with '1725' painted on the front. The communion rail, chandelier and royal arms on the front of the gallery are all early 18C. There are several hatchments, a shirt with armorial bearings over the christening pew, and foxes, bears and horses carved on the spandrels of the roof timbers, all very appropriate to a building once owned by 'Mad Jack Mitton'.

Moreton Corbet, *St. Bartholomew*. In the shadow of the ruined castle, this is a compact church of many periods: Norman chancel, mid-14C nave and aisle, and W tower begun in c 1540 but not finished until 1769. The S chapel, which served as the squire's pew, was added in the 1780s. There is a remarkable trefoiled triangular W window and, beautifully set in the door from the tower to the nave, many fragments of 15C glass. The E window and reredos are by Sir Ninian Comper and were well renovated in 1984. The reredos has the figures at the Annunciation, freestanding against the glass and under a canopy resting on pillars supported on elephants' backs and with capitals of castles and squirrels. These Corbet motifs, along with ravens, are repeated on two fine monuments in the S aisle: Sir Robert Corbet (died 1513) and his wife, recumbent on a high table-tomb with small, well-cut figures under ogee arches around the sides. Near them, Sir Richard Corbet (died 1567) and his wife lie on a high tomb-chest with panels around the side containing rather haphazardly, a swaddled baby with a rose and a lily, a squirrel with a nut, shields carried by the Corbet elephant and castle, and ravens. Both tombs are highly coloured. In the squire's pew there is a wall memorial to Richard Corbet, *'vir simplex'* (died 1691). His bust is under a pediment with shield over. In the churchyard, a bronze naked youth by I.H.M. Furse is placed over the grave of Vincent Corbet who died at Eton in 1904, aged 13. He is also commemorated by Comper's reredos.

Shifnal, *St. Andrew*. A large red sandstone church, consisting of aisled nave, chancel with Lady chapel, transepts and central tower, standing in a municipalised and meaningless churchyard. Like many Shropshire churches it was collegiate and was given in 1409 by King Henry IV as an endowment to Battlefield, to help pay for that memorial to those who died at the Battle of Shrewsbury in 1403.

The tower is castellated, as is the nave, and there are traces of early 13C work in the S transept door. The S porch is of two storeys, with a trefoil outer arch and rib-vaults meeting in the central boss. The upper storey protrudes into the nave which has octagonal piers with double-chamfered arches and was built in the early 13C. The crossing tower, which was rebuilt in c 1300, rests on high three-chamfered arches. The hammerbeam roof seems to have been added after the great fire of 1591 when 'the Parish Church together with the chancel and steeple with six bells (was) utterly consumed and molten'. The building was heavily restored in 1876 by Sir Gilbert Scott.

There is a 17C pedestal pulpit, much altered, and very few monuments. The Lady chapel has an effigy of Olive Brigges (died 1596) lying on a table-tomb; Humphry Brigges (died 1626) and his wife also lie there, while in the sanctuary there is the effigy of a former Vicar, Thomas Forster (died 1526). He was also Prior of Wormbridge and lies in alb and chasuble under a four-centred arch. More surprising are the tablets under the crossing: one to William Wakley who died in 1714 at the age of 120, and the other to Mary Yates who died in 1776 at the age of 127, having married her third husband when she was 92.

Shrewsbury

St. Mary. St. Mary's stands in the centre of Shrewsbury surrounded by half-timbered and Georgian buildings. Founded in the later 10C, the present church is notable for its spire and spectacular stained glass. It is cruciform in shape, but with a W tower and additions E of the transepts. The characteristic local sandstone, appealingly varied in colour within the church, is much blackened on the outside. The churchyard affords a rare glimpse of green in a busy townscape.

The earliest visible exterior work is Norman: the lower stages of the tower, parts of the transepts and (most notably) the doorway of the S porch. There are windows and doorways of all periods, especially in the NE corner with an unusually wide triple-lancet group in the N sanctuary wall. The two E windows look Perpendicular but are essentially Victorian. A head of Queen Victoria forms a stop to the moulding over the Trinity chapel door, E of the S transept. The spire, rebuilt after it had collapsed in a storm (1894), is markedly tall. The total height is 222ft.

The church is entered through the N porch. Seen from beneath the tower arch, the nave arcades of four wide bays with a late 15C clerestory give a sense of space and light. The greatest impact, however, comes from the eight-light E window, framed in the chancel arch. The N transept chapels can be glimpsed, but the Trinity chapel, S of the chancel, is not seen at first.

The tower arch is pointed, but rests on responds with Norman carving. There is a traceried wooden screen dividing the tower from the nave. This survived the destruction caused by the collapsing spire; the present nave roof is, of course, post-1894 but is a detailed reconstruction with good bosses. The piers of the arcades are made up of four clusters of triple shafts. The waterleaf and stiff-leaf capitals are all different and excellent. Some have faces protruding from the foliage.

Above the chancel arch is a pair of two-light openings of the early 13C. The choir is actually in the crossing area, and the chancel proper is marked by a step and low wall. The sanctuary's width is emphasised by its spaciousness. Behind the bishop's throne on the S side are traces of Norman arcading, perhaps from a sedilia. The high altar is curtained in the English altar style.

In the N transept there are two altars: St. Nicholas (recessed under a tunnel-vault) and St. Catherine. The Trinity chapel stretches from the S transept eastwards and was established as a Drapers' chapel in 1460; more recently it was used by the pupils of Shrewsbury School. It has an imposing E window and S windows with late Decorated or early Perpendicular tracery.

The oldest surviving furnishing is the font—interesting 14C work with a hollow stem and tracery panels. The stained glass is remarkable, not least because little of it was designed for St. Mary's. The great Jesse window (mid-14C) above the high altar was previously in Old St. Chad's, Shrewsbury. Much of the remaining glass comes from the Low Countries and Germany: Trier, Cologne and Liège. It was collected and inserted by a Victorian Vicar, W.G. Rowland. The N windows show scenes from the life of St. Bernard of Clairvaux. In the St. Nicholas chapel are monochrome roundels depicting events from the Book of Tobit. The organ case dates from the early 18C, when James Burney, younger brother of Dr Charles Burney, was organist for 54 years. The tiles are worth noting: many are by Godwin of Lugwardine (nave and chancel) but there is a particularly interesting pavement in the St. Catherine chapel, and art nouveau tiles in muted red and green in the arcading behind the Trinity chapel altar.

There are several monuments of note: a 14C knight recumbent on a chest in the Trinity chapel, an incised marble slab depicting Nicholas Stafford and his wife (died 1471 and 1463) in the St. Catherine chapel's N wall, and beside it a memorial to Admiral Benbow, described as 'the Nelson of his times'. On the W wall of the nave there is a good Victorian brass memorial to the second Afghan War (1879–80). Most poignant of all is a memorial on the outside tower W wall to Robert Cadman who in 1739 launched himself from the spire, hoping to fly across the Severn. His failure is recorded in a melancholy epitaph. This church has recently been declared redundant.

St. Chad. St. Chad's occupies a prominent position on the Town Walls overlooking the Quarry, the gardens that attractively slope down to the Severn. It was built in 1790–92 in Grecian Revival style by George Steuart following the collapse of Old St. Chad's. It has a circular nave, and is today the most impressive and prospering Anglican church in Shrewsbury.

Built of white Grinshill stone, St. Chad's most prominent feature is its tower: the first stage is square, flanked by side wings and a portico so that it hardly looks like a tower at all. Then there is an octagonal belfry, above which is a slender colonnade supporting a cupola with gilded cross on top. A circular section links the tower with the rotunda (100ft in diameter) that houses the nave. This has square windows below and tall round-headed windows at gallery level.

The interior is more remarkable still. One enters under the tower into a circular vestibule and passes into the larger antechamber, also circular and with a delicate staircase coiling around each side up to the gallery entrance. The third and largest circular chamber is the nave itself, a splendid auditorium, strikingly white except for the dark oak of the curved pews and the gilt work on the pillars (Ionic below, supporting the gallery; fluted Corinthian above). The gallery runs nearly all around; the only break is for the recessed sanctuary, whose arch is supported by pairs of huge Corinthian columns. The reredos by Cecil Hare (1923) is a fine design in Renaissance style; above it is the sanctuary window by David Evans. Its chief subject is the Descent from the Cross (a poor and strident copy of Rubens), but there are unexpected and charming details in the margins of the window, for example a peacock in a walled garden. The other glass, in the nave, is also by Evans in his characteristic manner. There is a notable set of hatchments around the wall. The font is of Silurian marble and the pulpit, of copper and brass, owes something to art nouveau but is not out of place. The organ (Norman & Beard 1908) is in the gallery.

The chapel of St. Aidan (ritual S of the vestibule) is easily overlooked but is, in its different way, as original as the church. Dedicated in 1951 as a memorial chapel of the King's Shropshire Light Infantry and the Herefordshire Regiment, it has oak panelled walls and an apsidal sanctuary with black and white tiles in a 'Festival of Britain style' pattern. There is a miniature Rood beam and carved Rood, and the handmade chairs all have appealingly-adzed seats. The chapel is an example of postwar Anglican style at its best.

St. Chad's, by George Steuart, 1790–92, with the circular nave in the background

St. Alkmund. Of the medieval church, only the Perpendicular tower and spire survive; the present church was dedicated in 1795. Interesting pre-archaeological Gothic by Carline & Tilley, originally with cast-iron tracery made in Coalbrookdale in the windows (still retained in the E window and the W windows of the aisles, but elsewhere replaced with stone). The rectangular plan (no chancel, minimal sanctuary) is still essentially Classical. The walls have a wooden dado all round. Notable painted E window: a bizarre version of 'The Assumption' by Guido Reni, signed Francis Eginton, 1795, with the Virgin transmuted into Faith, aptly for the Evangelical temper of this church. The wife of one Victorian incumbent, C.E.L. Wightman, was the moving spirit behind the Church of England Temperance Society.

Unitarian Chapel. Founded in 1662, with an 18C frontage flush with the building line of the High Street. The interior is a rectangular room (rather narrow) with neat pews and a gallery containing the organ and a clock dated 1724. At the other end, above the pulpit, there are fine royal arms of King George I. There is a flat ceiling with plaster decoration and a frieze of swags. On the walls are simple memorials, including one to Charles Darwin, born in Shrewsbury in 1809 and a worshipper here.

Stottesdon, St. Mary. A large church with W tower, aisled nave and chancel. It is remarkable for the tympanum of a much earlier church and a splendid font of c 1160. The tympanum is now inside the tower: almost triangular, there is a bearded face at the apex; below are saltire crosses arranged in disconnected groups, while on the lintel are primitive beasts, two of them upside down. Nothing like as crude is the font carved by one of the craftsmen working in Herefordshire in the mid-12C. Many of the features common to that school are here: elaborate interlace, birds with long claws, dragons eating their tails, the Agnus Dei, all held together in circles of medallions whose bands issue from the mouths of beasts with pricked ears and ribbed cheeks. It dates from c 1160 and is in excellent condition.

Tong, St. Mary and St. Bartholomew. A collegiate church, of nave, S porch, central tower with transepts and chancel, on the site of an earlier building. It was built between 1411 and 1430 by Lady Isabella de Pembruge so that Masses could be said for her three husbands. Her daughter, Benedicta, married Sir Richard Vernon, and the church then became the mausoleum of that family. Although collegiate, it survived the Reformation relatively unscathed as one of the inspecting commissioners was a Vernon. It was restored in 1892 by Ewan Christian.

Once guarded by Tong Castle, it is now encompassed by the M54 and its approach roads. Built of reddish sandstone on a raised churchyard, almost the whole church is castellated, the buttresses rising above the battlements in pinnacles. The central tower has a square first stage, then an octagonal second section with a parapet of pinnacled merlons, and finally a small spire.

The interior is overwhelmed by the tombs. The piers of the arcades are octagonal and the nave roof has moulded beams and bosses. The Vernon S chapel is fan-vaulted with elegant pendants. The chancel has 16 stalls with misericords and there is a pulpit of 1629. The royal arms are well-carved and commemorate the Peace of Paris, 1814.

The E window contains some medieval glass, and the W window has glass by C.E. Kempe.

The abundant tombs lie everywhere, many of them of alabaster. They include Sir Fulke de Pembruge (died 1409) and his wife Isabella, the builder of the church who died in 1446. He lies on a table-tomb in chain armour, his head on his helmet which in turn rests on a female head; his wife, in widow's weeds, rests her feet on a fawn. The tomb lies to the N of the nave; to the S is the table-tomb of Sir Richard Vernon (died 1451), Speaker of the House of Commons, in plate armour, his feet on a lion, laurel leaves around his head; his wife, Benedicta, with beringed fingers and a mitred head-dress.

Effigies of Sir Richard Vernon (died 1451) and his wife Benedicta

Their son, Sir William Vernon, Knight Constable of England, lies to the W, on a tomb of Purbeck marble inlaid with brasses. He is in armour, the boar's head crest at his head; his wife with hood and wimple has her feet on an elephant; their 12 children are around the base. Across the nave to the N is the alabaster tomb of Richard Vernon (died 1517). He lies in plate armour beside his wife Margaret. To the S of Sir Richard Vernon is Sir Thomas Stanley (died 1576) and his wife Margaret. He was Governor of the Isle of Man and lies with his wife on a two-tiered tomb with allegorical figures and obelisks. On the lower tier is their son, Sir Edward, who died in 1632, having sold Tong. The tomb has a long inscription and two verses attributed by Sir William Dugdale to Shakespeare, one beginning, 'Aske who lyes heare but do not weep', the other, 'Not monumental tombe preserve our Fame'. To the S at the entrance to the Golden chapel is the tomb of Sir Henry Vernon (died 1515). There is an elegant canopy over the effigies of Sir Henry in plate armour and of his wife in a long dress overlapping two small hounds. There are bedesmen at the base of the tomb. The Golden chapel is entered through an ogee arch and traces of the gilding which gave it the name can be seen on the vaulted ceiling. It contains brasses and an impressive half-figure of Arthur Vernon resting on a bracket under a canopy. He is holding a book. On the floor below there is a fine brass to the same man, a Cambridge graduate who died in 1517. There are many other monuments, including one to George Durant (died 1780), a mourning figure at an urn. His son inherited Tong and increased the population by 54, 12 children by his first wife, ten by his second and 32 by the village.

Tong is not only rich in tombs. It has a great bell of 1518 and nicely painted ringing rules of 1694. There is a pulpit fall of c 1600 and good medieval tiles in the Golden chapel. The plate includes the famous Tong ciborium described as 'a cup of goulde and christall' and made c 1545. The church also possesses Napoleon's travelling cup and Little Nell's fictional grave. Charles Dickens in 'The Old Curiosity Shop' buried her at Tong, and so an enterprising verger erected a small inscribed stone, inserted her name in the register, and then benefited from the many visitors to whom he acted as guide. Robert Eyton, in his 'Antiquities of Shropshire' wrote: 'If there be a place in Shropshire calculated alike to impress the moralist, to instruct the antiquary, and interest the historian, that place is Tong'. This is still true.

Wroxeter, *St. Andrew*. The church comprises W tower, nave and chancel, erected by the Normans using some Roman and pre-Conquest material. The pillars to the churchyard are Roman and the porch is Victorian. Inside, the base of the huge font is probably Roman, and in the S wall of the nave is a 9C cross-shaft with dragons, foliage and interlace. Wroxeter is especially notable for four monuments in the chancel. Chronologically, they commemorate Lord Chief Justice Bromley (died 1555) and his wife 'on whose Sowles God have mercy', lying side by side in alabaster on a tomb-chest which is divided into panels with candelabra and a girl. Alongside are their daughter and her husband, Sir Richard Newport (died 1570). The mourners around the sides hold out shields like matadors with their capes. Although he was one of King Henry VIII's executors, he was reckoned to be 'a Papist at heart'. There is a similar tomb to John Barber and his wife (died 1618); but the fourth to Francis Newport, Earl of Bradford, has no recumbent effigy but mourning angels on either side of an urn with a reredos background. He died in 1708.

Richard Baxter went to school in the church and for a short time taught there.

STAFFORDSHIRE

Staffordshire is a county of great contrasts both in terms of scenery and of man's impact on the landscape. Between the great industrial areas of the Potteries in the NW, the sprawl of the West Midlands conurbation in the SW, and to a lesser degree, Burton-on-Trent, there is a rural landscape ranging from some of the finest moorland scenery in England to the lush countryside which runs in a broad band across the middle of the county. The county is one of sandstone for building, closely followed by brick. The Potteries supplied tiles, bricks, etc not just to Staffordshire but to the rest of England. In addition, Staffordshire has been the source of much alabaster. Industrialisation led of course to the creation of great wealth and Staffordshire is blessed with many Victorian churches, a few of which are masterpieces.

The pre-Conquest period is poorly represented. The excavated remains of St. Bertelin's, in front of St. Mary's at Stafford, reveal a simple two-cell church. There are in addition a blocked S doorway at Ilam and merely the hint of an early cruciform church at Tamworth. But the pre-Conquest period in Staffordshire is best exemplified by the group of crosses, most important of which are those at Wolverhampton (9C), Ilam and Leek. Finally, it might be recalled that St. Chad (died 672) was the founder of the See of Lichfield, where his shrine once stood, and that a successor in the late 8C became for a few years the third archbishop in England, a mirror of the power of Offa, King of the Mercians, whose capital was Tamworth. The Norman period is represented by the major part of the church at Tutbury with its elaborate W doorway, the small but largely restored cruciform church of St. Chad at Stafford, the remains of cruciform churches at Gnosall and Tamworth, by Longdon Church and by a group of fonts (St. Mary's at Stafford, Ilam and Armitage being the best).

The Early English style appears in the chancel and arcades of the church at Eccleshall and in the chancel of Brewood. Early English too is work at St. Chad's, Lichfield and St. Mary's, Stafford. There is also a fine 13C S doorway at Checkley. The Decorated style is much more comprehensively represented, with pride of place going to the large church at Clifton Campville, which was so beloved by John Betjeman. The large church at Tamworth was substantially rebuilt in the 14C. Decorated too are Checkley (chancel), Hamstall Ridware, Norbury, Uttoxeter (spire) and Wolverhampton St. Peter (crossing and S transept).

The Perpendicular style has five outstanding examples in Barton-under-Needwood (whole church c 1533), Penkridge, Stafford St. Mary (the crossing tower, clerestory and windows), Wolverhampton St. Peter (the crossing tower and N transept) and finally, from as late as 1633, Broughton. Broughton is 'Gothic Survival' or simplified Perpendicular. 17C Gothic is also found at Checkley (e.g. N windows). The full Classical style is separated by just 43 years from Broughton—at Ingestre, which is believed to be the work of Sir Christopher Wren. It is a well-preserved and important 17C church. Most of the Classical churches are 18C. Among the more important are St. Modwen's, Burton-on-Trent (1726 by William and Francis Smith), Patshull (1743 by James Gibbs), Wolverhampton St. John (1758–76 by William Baker) and on into the early 19C with two

Catholic churches by Joseph Ireland at Wolverhampton (St. Peter and St. Paul, 1825–27), and at Walsall (St. Mary, also 1825–27). Forton is a medieval church which was Classicised in 1723. Stone (1753–58 by William Robinson) is Gothick.

With the 1818 Church Building Act came a spate of Commissioners' churches which were felt necessary in the burgeoning industrial areas. In the Potteries, St. Peter ad Vincula at Stoke was rebuilt in the Commissioners' style by Trubshaw & Johnson in 1826–29, and at Hanley, St. Mark's was built in 1831–33 by J. Oates.

Staffordshire comes into its own later in the 19C with contributions from many of the great names of Victorian architecture. A.W.N. Pugin designed the interior of the chapel at Alton Towers (c 1839) and St. Giles's at Cheadle, his masterpiece (1841–46). Gilbert Scott is represented by Holy Trinity, Stoke (1842) and by restorations at St. Mary's, Stafford (1840–44) and St. Giles's, Newcastle (1873–76). William Butterfield designed the church, schoolhouse and rectory at Sheen, 1850–52. G.E. Street is well-represented at Denstone (1860–62), an important early work of his. G.F. Bodley has two of his greatest works in the county, one in mid-career and the other late, Hoar Cross (1872–1876) and St. Chad's, Burton-on-Trent (1903–1910). Norman Shaw's idiosyncratic All Saints', Leek dates from 1887. Gerald Horsley, a pupil of Shaw, is represented at Longsdon (1903–05). Further architects represented are Basil Champneys (Glascote, 1880), John Douglas at Hopwas, 1881, and J.O. Scott at Newborough (where the extraordinary tower and spire may be later by another architect).

In the 20C, Lavender & Twentyman's St. Martin's, Ettingshall, Wolverhampton (1938–39), is a notable example of interwar architecture. Postwar, the rebuilding of St. Michael's, Tettenhall, Wolverhampton, by Bernard Miller in 1950 stands out as exceptional.

Among medieval fittings of fine workmanship and importance are the 14C and 15C wooden screens at Clifton Campville, which also possesses a good collection of misericords dating from the same centuries. There are further misericords at Eccleshall and Penkridge. The 15C stalls at Wolverhampton St. Peter came from Lilleshall Abbey. A Perpendicular stone pulpit complete with stairs survives in the same church. Carved bench-ends of the 16C can be seen at Checkley. Alstonefield has a 17C pulpit, pews, screen, etc.; Ingestre retains its Wren-style fittings from the late 17C. 18C and later interiors follow contemporary buildings (see above). Denstone and Hoar Cross are important 19C examples.

The county is thin on brasses (Norbury, Clifton Campville and Ashley, all 14C, and Kinver, 16C) but exceptionally rich in alabaster tombs and incised slabs. These can best be seen at Hanbury (the oldest in alabaster), Elford, Tamworth, Checkley, Patshull, Penkridge, Wolverhampton St. Peter, Stafford St. Mary, Brewood and, arguably the finest of them all, at Clifton Campville. Most monuments are 15C–17C. Alabaster continued in use to the end of the 17C, most notably by the sculptors from Burton-on-Trent. From later periods, notable monuments exist at Ingestre (of Chetwynds and Talbots, 17C–19C), Tamworth (including one by Arnold Quellin), Stone (of the Jervis family, mainly early 19C), Stoke-on-Trent (of Wedgwoods, Spodes and other potters, 18C and 19C), Ilam (Sir Francis Chantrey's memorial of 1831 to David Pike Watts in its own octagonal chapel), Ashley (including works by Joseph Nollekens and Chantrey), and Hoar Cross (exceptional monuments by Bodley & Garner). Mention should finally be made of Eccleshall, which has the tombs of six Bishops of Lichfield, and of Ilam, which has the remains of a 13C shrine to St. Bertelin.

There is some good medieval stained glass, predominantly 14C and 15C, with Checkley possessing the best collection and a further good group surviving at Broughton. However, it is only in the 19C that stained glass becomes plentiful. Morris & Co. glass can be found at Leek (both St. Edward the Confessor's and All Saints'), Tamworth, Cheddleton, Madeley and Ingestre. William Wailes made the glass for Pugin's church at Cheadle; Clayton & Bell made the complete sequence of windows at Denstone. At the end of the 19C Burlison & Grylls provided the glass at Hoar Cross, to Thomas Garner's design. Good ranges of Victorian glass from various firms can be seen at Stafford St. Mary, Tamworth, Wolverhampton St. Peter, Newcastle St. Giles, Leek St. Edward the Confessor, Leek All Saints, Cheddleton and Eccleshall. Comper windows are found at Checkley, which also has a number of his fittings, and at Longsdon. Of more recent 20C glass, John Piper's E window in St. John's Hospital chapel, Lichfield (1984), is outstanding.

The Catholic presence in Staffordshire has been strong due to the great families such as the Talbots. The county also possesses at Mow Cop the birthplace of Primitive Methodism, which was strong in industrial areas.

Broughton, *St. Peter.* St. Peter's, built in 1630–34, was consecrated on 1st September 1633. It is built in the local red sandstone in a loose Perpendicular style. Its chief features are its Georgian box-pews and its windows. The E window, reused from an earlier building, contains a jumble of medieval, mostly 15C glass. It includes figures of a king, St. George, St. Roche (the French patron saint of plague victims) and St. Andrew. There is also a fragment which bears the date 1543.

The S chancel window is a memorial to Sir John Delves who died in the Battle of Tewkesbury in 1471. Both he and his wife appear beneath the figures of the Virgin Mary and St. Francis. The N chancel window dates from the early 17C and is purely heraldic, depicting the arms of local families.

The S aisle window is by C.E. Kempe (1894), and depicts the Easter story. The S aisle E window depicts St. Peter and the Good Centurion (1888). The W window contains modern armorial designs.

Burton-on-Trent, *St. Chad, Hunter Street.* This is one of the last major undertakings by G.F. Bodley, being started in 1903 and finished by his partner Cecil Hare after his death. It was built at a cost of £38,000 by Lord Burton in Bodley's favourite Decorated style.

The church, built of sandstone, is in appearance long and low, being dominated by the tall NW tower which is joined to the body of the church by a single-storey, stone-vaulted corridor. The entrance is in the N face of the tower. The walls of the tower and the church are mostly plain, only occasionally being relieved by decorative or architectural features. On the W side of the tower there is a battlemented polygonal stair turret. Above the doorway on the N side there is a niche containing a statue of St. Chad. In the upper stage each face has a pair of tall two-light belfry openings, and the tower is topped by battlements and a recessed spire. The nave is lit by triple-light windows and the chancel by double-light windows. The appearance of the E end is unusual, for the chancel is longer than the S aisle but in turn the N aisle with its taller Lady chapel extends beyond the chancel. On the S side, attached to the S aisle, is Cecil Hare's octagonal vestry which looks like a chapter house.

Internally the church consists of a five-bay nave, with quatrefoil piers with additional strips in the recesses. The piers support moulded capitals and Decorated arches. The nave roof is a wooden barrel-vault, the aisles having simple lean-to roofs. In the last bay of the nave on the S side, in front of the chancel screen, there stands the magnificent five-sided stone pulpit. Each face has a carved figure. The decoration continues in the stone screen which runs from the pulpit to the S wall of the S aisle. There are carvings of four angels making music. Above this is the organ case. The wooden chancel screen is typical of Bodley. It has vaulting and three intricately traceried arches on each side of the entrance. The marble-floored chancel, raised on one step, has a wooden barrel-vaulted roof. The sanctuary is raised on a further step, the high altar on three more. Behind this stands the reredos depicting the Last Supper. There are wooden canopied sedilia on the N side and a priest's chair on the S side. A wooden screen separates the chancel and sanctuary from the Lady chapel on the N side, whose outstanding feature is the very large stone reredos. It has carved scenes of the Crucifixion and (below) the Nativity. The reredos is the work of Bridgeman's.

The church has a small number of stained glass windows. The large W window was installed in memory of the first Lord Burton (died 1909) and depicts the Apostles. In the sanctuary the E window, of five lights, depicts Christ on the Cross surrounded by saints and angels. The sanctuary S window, of two lights, shows St. Peter and St. Paul.

Cheadle, St. Giles. St. Giles's was designed by A.W.N. Pugin and built at the expense of the 16th Earl of Shrewsbury in 1841–46. The combination of the Earl's wealth and Pugin's vision led to what is one of the seminal buildings of the Gothic Revival. The result is a red sandstone building with a tower and spire soaring to 200ft and dominating the surrounding countryside. Internally, the absence of financial restraint allowed a riot of colour and decoration.

The style is Decorated. The relative plainness of the exterior is relieved by the large buttresses along the S side, by roof cresting and an E gable cross, and by a bellcote at the junction of nave and chancel. At the E end there are statues of St. John the Baptist and St. John the Evangelist, and a niche above containing three angels carrying the emblems of the Eucharist. The S porch is more elaborate than its N counterpart, in keeping with the richer detailing of the S side. Perhaps the most arresting detail is the pair of tower or W doors. They are virtually covered with hinges which have been enlarged into the form of two gilt rampant lions, which are part of the Shrewsbury family crest, and which stand against a background painted red within gilt engrailed borders.

Within, the impact is one of rich decoration everywhere, dimly lit through the stained glass windows. The nave is of five bays with octagonal pillars and richly decorated foliate capitals. Each pillar has a different painted pattern applied. Indeed, every inch of the church is covered in decoration. Above each arch in the nave are pairs of circular copper plates with painted Prophets upon them. Above the chancel arch is the Doom or Last Judgement painting by Hauser. The N aisle with the chapel of Our Lady at its E end has a decorative scheme which is predominantly blue, the colour associated with the Virgin Mary. The S aisle has a red scheme, this being associated with

Our Lord. All round the church to a height of approximately 4ft, the walls are lined with tiles of yellow and blue glaze. To the walls of the N and S aisles are fixed the Stations of the Cross put up in 1864. The roofs of the nave and aisles are all constructed of oak and highly decorated. The wall posts are supported on stone corbels which are carved as angels playing musical instruments.

Throughout the church the floors are tiled with the products of Minton and Wedgwood. The chapel of Our Lady is separated from the rest of the aisle and from the nave by a low screen. Its altar is of alabaster, intricately carved and decorated. Above this is a 15C Flemish oak triptych, which has been dubiously covered in gilt paint since Pugin bought it. The pulpit was carved from one block by Thomas Roddis. The seven panels represent St. Francis of Assisi, St. Anthony of Padua, St. Bernadino of Siena and the remaining four panels are devoted to St. John the Baptist preaching in the wilderness. Interestingly, the pulpit is reached via the sacristy. The chancel is separated from the nave by a superb Rood screen, with figures of Christ on the Cross, St. John and Our Lady. The chancel is raised on two steps and the sanctuary on a further four, each step bearing an inscription in Latin. The inscription on the chancel steps reads, 'All nations will come unto it and will say: Come and let us go up to the mountain of the Lord and the house of the God of Jacob'. The sanctuary steps have the words of the antiphon and psalm said at the beginning of Mass. The walls of the chancel and sanctuary have

The W door of St. Giles's by A.W.N. Pugin; the church was built in 1841–46 for the 16th Earl of Shrewsbury

painted angels holding texts from the Te Deum, Benedictus and Psalms of Praise. This work was undertaken by J.D. Crace. At the roofline around the chancel and sanctuary are carved angels holding crowns. The high altar with its ornate carving, and the reredos behind, are the work of Thomas Roddis. High above the altar and the E window there is a canopy of honour. In the S wall of the sanctuary there are markedly ornate sedilia. Opposite is the Easter sepulchre under a cusped ogee arch. The recess has a painting depicting the Dead Christ supported by angels. The corona hanging in the chancel is reputed to have been bought by Pugin in Flanders and restored by him. The S wall of the chancel is pierced by an arch to the Blessed Sacrament chapel which is filled by an elaborate metal screen. The chapel is really a sixth bay of the S aisle and is the most lavishly decorated part of the church. The symbol of the Eucharist, the Lamb and Flag, appears repeatedly in this chapel. At the other end of the S aisle, the last bay is the baptistery, partitioned off by oak and brass screens. The alabaster font is octagonal and its base has four monsters being symbolically crushed. There is an elaborate pin-nacled canopy.

All the stained glass was manufactured by William Wailes. Starting with the N aisle, the first N wall window from the W has six roundels of pre-Conquest saints: Edmund, Edward the Martyr, Edward the Confessor, Etheldreda, Ethelburga and Mildred. The following window shows St. Peter and his crucifixion, and St. Paul with his Letter to the Romans. The next window depicts the seven corporal works of mercy, plus the Holy Spirit represented by a dove. The three-light window in the chapel of Our Lady depicts the Virgin and Child in the centre light and the Annunciation in the outer two lights. The E window depicts the Tree of Jesse. The Blessed Sacrament chapel's E window depicts Christ with angels, with inscriptions from St. John's Gospel. The S aisle's second window is the patron's window and its three lights have images of St. John, St. Giles and St. Chad. The baptistery's three-light window depicts St. John the Baptist holding a lamb with a flag, with a dove overhead. He is surrounded by depictions of virtues triumphing over vices.

Checkley, *St. Mary and All Saints*. An impressive and large church, of red sandstone, set in a churchyard on a bank and surrounded by trees, in a village which has been very quiet since the opening of the bypass. John Betjeman referred to it as 'the best medieval church in North Staffordshire'. There is evidence of a church on the site since c 800, with the remains in the churchyard of three pre-Conquest crosses. The church reveals a confusing architectural picture from the Norman period to the 20C.

The large W tower has lower stages of Norman workmanship. The top stage is Perpendicular. The battlemented nave and aisles seem Perpendicular, but much of the church was rebuilt in the 17C, reusing old materials. The N aisle windows, in which the mullions rise to the heads without tracery, are clearly 17C. The S doorway dates from c 1300; the vaulted porch is probably a later rebuilding. It is believed that some of its materials and carving came from nearby Croxden Abbey. At the E end of the S aisle the windowsill has been worn by medieval archers sharpening their arrowheads. The chancel of four bays has windows with intersecting tracery, all c 1300. In the churchyard near the S porch are the remains of three pre-Conquest crosses bearing geometric patterns. On the largest of the three is a panel with three figures, identified with three bishops supposedly killed locally at the Battle of Deadmans Green.

Internally, the four-bay nave has 12C and 13C details, some perhaps remodelled. The pillars on the S side have late Norman capitals of c 1150, whilst the N side and N aisle represent the transition to Early English, c 1200. There are 17C Perpendicular clerestory windows. The tower arch is Decorated and compares with the chancel arch. The nave's kingpost roof with fine carved heads dates from the 17C, contemporary with the clerestory. In front of the tower arch is a late pre-Conquest or early Norman drum-shaped font, with vigorous carving of a donkey on it. In front of the early 20C wooden vestry screen, at the W end of the S aisle, is a large chest inscribed AMH 1694. The E bay of the S aisle is a memorial chapel, enclosed by wooden parclose screens designed by Sir Ninian Comper in 1922.

The oak stalls in the chancel date from c 1535. Those on the S side are the Beamhurst family stalls. Another belonged to Anthony Draycott MP. The ends have linenfold panelling and very stylised poppyheads. There are also carvings of the heads of two 'Red Indians' along with the Tudor rose and initials. The N stalls have carvings of fish. Against the S wall of the chancel is the alabaster tomb-chest and recumbent effigies of Godfrey Foljambe (died 1560) and his wife Margaret. Set in the floor nearby is a much worn alabaster slab. This is the tomb of Thomas Chawner (died 1544), the last Abbot of Croxden. Against the N wall is a weathered cross-legged 14C knight. The wooden chancel roof apparently came from Croxden Abbey some years after its Dissolution, for 10s 6d. The high altar was designed by Comper, complete with riddel posts surmounted by gilded candle-carrying angels. An altar under the chancel arch was dedicated in 1986.

There is 14C glass in the E window and in the chancel NE and SE windows. The E window has two rows of figures. In the top row are St. Chad, an evangelist, St. Thomas Becket, a prophet and St. Nicholas. The lower row depicts the stoning of St. Stephen, the sacrifice of Isaac, the Crucifixion, St. Margaret and the dragon, and the martyrdom of St. Thomas Becket. The NE chancel window depicts Moses, St. John, St. Peter and the arms of the Draycots, Bassets, Meverells and Talbots. The SW chancel window contains seven remaining 17C Dutch roundels of the months of the year. The S aisle E window (1919) is by Comper. It represents Christ on the Cross surrounded by mounted soldiers, complete with the banners of the allied nations of the First World War. In the foreground are the correct Biblical figures with the addition (right) of a kneeling army officer in contemporary battle dress. An almost identical window can be seen in Stockcross Church in Berkshire. In the N aisle a window with a large roundel of St. George slaying the dragon is also the work of Comper. The roundel is surrounded with heraldic devices and dated 1912, with Comper's wild strawberry at bottom right.

In the tower space a board lists the Vicars since 1238. Between 1791 and 1908 there were just three: 1791–1839 Samuel Langley, 1839–78 William Hutchinson and 1878–1909 Edward Philips.

Clifton Campville, *St. Andrew.* St. Andrew's has justifiably been called one of the great parish churches of England. It was one of the great medieval livings, held by a number of men destined for high office in Church and State. It is basically a Decorated rebuild of an

Early English church, and is justly famous for its soaring spire, its wealth of medieval woodwork and its monuments.

Set at the top of the hill above the village, the dominant feature is the Decorated tower and tapering spire, rising to 189ft. The spire made the national news twice in 1984. On January 2nd it was struck by lightning and in November it partly collapsed. It has now been fully restored. The spire is supported at its base by four flying buttresses.

The exterior reveals the extent of the 14C rebuilding. The alterations were started in 1361 and took c 15 years to complete. E of the N door is the Chantry chapel which was the N transept of the earlier church. Above the chapel is the priest's room, reached by a spiral staircase, built in the angle between chapel and chancel. The chapel is Early English in detail. The chancel also reveals some Early English detailing in the buttresses and the lancet window of the N wall.

The plan reveals how the tower, nave, S aisle, S porch and Lady chapel have been added to a smaller, cruciform church. The first impression internally is one of light and spaciousness, due in part to the three large windows in the first stage of the tower. Three Decorated arches separate the nave and S aisle. A continuation E of the S aisle acts as the Lady chapel, which is separated from the chancel by three more Decorated arches. The Chantry chapel has an Early English entrance arch and a groined roof and lancet window. It was thoroughly restored in 1975.

The chancel and Lady chapel are enclosed by a series of wooden screens. The Rood screen is 16C, with the addition of two doors, inscribed 'Master Gilbert Parson of Clifton in the year of Our Lord 1634'. The Lady chapel is enclosed by four parclose screens, three of which are contemporary with the building of the chapel, c 1350. The fourth screen, separating the Lady chapel from the S aisle, is signed 'H.G.1634'. There are seven misericords in the chancel, dating from the early 14C, the carving alternating between heads and naturalistic foliage. A well-designed oak screen (1975), filled with clear glass, separates the Chantry chapel from the nave. The chancel, Lady chapel, nave and S aisle retain medieval roofs, although the nave roof was restored and raised in 1906.

In the Lady chapel is the imposing alabaster tomb-chest of Sir John Vernon (died 1545) and his wife Ellen. Their recumbent effigies are surrounded by exceptionally well-carved figures of children and bedesmen, and shields. On the floor of the Lady chapel is part of a palimpsest brass of c 1360, possibly to Maud, the second wife of Sir Richard Stafford. The reverse shows part of the effigy of a cross-legged knight of c 1300. In the chancel are two purely architectural marble monuments of 1736 by J.M. Rysbrack, to Sir Charles Pye (died 1721), Sir Richard Pye (died 1724) and Sir Robert Pye (died 1734). In the nave N wall, under a low arch, is a tomb, believed to be that of Isabella (died 1356), first wife of Sir Richard Stafford. He died in 1381 and is buried opposite, beneath a large arch in the S aisle wall. The panel within the arch contains the remains of a 14C wall painting of the Coronation of the Virgin, uncovered in 1933 by Professor E.W. Tristram. Also in the S aisle are monuments by Sir Richard Westmacott to Charles S. Watkins (died 1813), depicting a kneeling woman, and by William Behnes to John Watkins (died 1833), of a seated young man in mourning.

The medieval manor was held by a number of illustrious figures. Sir Richard Stafford, responsible for rebuilding the church, was succeeded by his eldest son Edmund, who became Rector (1393–95), Dean of York, and in 1395 Bishop of Exeter. He was later to rise to be Lord Chancellor of England. Subsequent Rectors in the 15C secured similar preferment in Church and State.

Denstone, *All Saints.* All Saints' was built in 1860–62 to the designs of G.E. Street. It is a building of national importance, due in part to the majesty of its simplicity and the completeness of its fittings. The church has remained virtually unaltered since its completion and is a perfect example of the ideals of the Oxford Movement. Stylistically, it belongs to the 13C and early 14C, that is to say the Decorated style. The church was paid for by Sir Percival Thomas Heywood as a memorial to three generations of his family.

The church, churchyard cross, lychgate, school and vicarage, all designed by Street, form a linear development on a rising slope between the road and a disused railway line. The strong simple vertical lines of the nave, the apsidal E end with its higher pitched roof and the circular N tower, are offset by the horizontal bands of polychromatic decoration. The windows are good examples of Street's plate tracery.

Entry is gained by the S porch, which has a high pitched roof starting very low, a typical feature by Street. The plan is of an aisleless nave and a chancel with an apse. The interior is faced in rough stone with sandstone dressings. The subdued use of polychromy in both horizontal bands and the voussoirs echo the exterior treatment. The aisleless nave rises to a simply treated raftered roof. The plainness of the nave highlights the simplicity of the lancets and plate tracery. This acts as a foil to the richness of the Clayton & Bell stained glass. The chancel, raised on two steps, is separated from the nave by a low marble screen. As with the nave, the walls of the chancel and apse rise to a wooden barrel-vaulted roof. The shafts of the chancel and apse windows and the sedilia are of black Purbeck marble, introducing a further touch of opulence.

Directly opposite the S entrance, in the NW corner, is the font, designed by Street and carved by Thomas Earp. The corners of the bowl are angels holding jars representing the four rivers of paradise. The carving of the chancel arch capitals, pulpit and reredos is also by Earp. The low chancel screen is surmounted by a brass rail, emphasising the division between chancel and nave. The chancel contains plain wooden choirstalls and is separated from the organ chamber on the N by an iron screen designed by Street. The altar is raised on two steps and has a low marble reredos. Around the church on the various windowsills is a series of two-armed candlesticks in brass. Coronae for electric 'candles' hang in the nave.

The outstanding feature is the complete set of windows by Clayton & Bell. The richness and brilliance of the colour and design exemplify Clayton & Bell at their best. The apse windows depict the Annunciation and the Nativity (N); Passion scenes (centre); and Resurrection scenes (S). The chancel S window shows Christ appearing to the Disciples and the Virgin Mary. The two quatrefoils high up in the chancel depict St. George and St. Michael. The S side of the nave has three triple-light windows. They mainly depict stories of the Apostles. The N side of the nave has four lancet windows which depict (from the E) St. Paul, St. Stephen, St. Chad and St. John.

Eccleshall, *Holy Trinity.* One of the most impressive churches in Staffordshire, Holy Trinity stands at the W end of the High Street, set in a churchyard sloping down to the N to the lush water meadows which lay between it and the castle. The present church is largely an Early English rebuild in local red sandstone of a substantial Norman church, with extensive Perpendicular additions. The large scale of the church and its regional importance stem from its being close to Eccleshall Castle, which was the principal residence of the Bishops of Lichfield from 1066 until 1868. Five of them are buried in the church and one in the churchyard.

The exterior shows well the three distinct Gothic styles. The 13C chancel is the oldest part, comprising five bays, with tall thin lancet windows. In one of the bays are the remains of arrow whets, where medieval archers sharpened their arrow heads on the chancel wall to bring them luck. The E window of five lancets was inserted by G.E. Street, 1866. The nave, S aisle and porch reveal extensive 15C rebuilding. Under the S aisle window are the remains of a 'mass clock', a seven-inch circle inscribed with marks. The tower reveals evidence of all three Gothic styles. The lower stage is Early English, the middle Decorated and the upper Perpendicular. The vestries N and S of the tower were added by G.E. Street in 1866-69. The porch and tower have some particularly good gargoyles.

The nave of five bays has round pillars and Transitional arches. Each pillar has differently carved capitals of foliate decoration. Above are Perpendicular clerestory windows. Built into the W wall of the nave are a number of reused carved pre-Conquest stones. The markedly large chancel was much restored by Street.

The reredos behind the high altar, carved from local alabaster, was designed by Basil Champneys and installed in 1893. It depicts the Crucifixion, the Last Supper and groups of Old (left) and New (right) Testament figures under wonderfully intricate tabernacles. The chancel contains a fine wooden Bishop's Throne, from which Bishop Lonsdale ordained 567 deacons and 646 priests. The large organ case (N side of the chancel), and the Lady Chapel altar, reredos, canopy and screens were all carved out of limed oak: magnificent early 20C Gothic woodwork. They were designed by W.D. Caroë in 1930-31. The pulpit is of stone and dates from Street's restoration. At the W end, under the tower arch, is the 13C font and on the sill of the tower W window are fixed three medieval misericords. At the W end of the S aisle is a large royal arms dated 1687. In the N aisle there is a highly imaginative and fanciful 17C painting of the castle.

In the N wall of the sanctuary a recess shelters the alabaster effigy of Bishop James Bowstead (died 1843), who was the first Bishop of Coventry after it had been separated from Lichfield. Also against the N wall of the chancel is the large and impressive alabaster tomb of Bishop Overton (died 1609). The tomb was made six years before his death. There is an elaborate tomb-chest with figures and shields, a recumbent effigy and, against the wall, two Corinthian columns supporting a frieze with shields above. Inset in arches are the figures of his two wives both kneeling and looking E. Bishop Overton was responsible for bringing glassmaking to the Eccleshall area. In the S tower vestry is the incised alabaster tomb-chest of Bishop Thomas Bentham (died 1578), who was responsible for contributing Ezekiel and Daniel to the 'Bishops' Bible' in 1568. Against the tower arch is a badly defaced and worn effigy in an upright position, believed to be the remains of the tomb of Bishop Robert Wright. He died in 1643, besieged in Eccleshall Castle by the Parliamentary forces. Finally, in the NE corner of the churchyard, is a 6ft tall marble cross which marks the grave of Bishop Lonsdale (died 1867).

The church contains a fine collection of Victorian stained glass. The E window depicts the Easter story and is the work of Clayton & Bell, who also made the S aisle E window, depicting the Nativity (1874). The S aisle W window depicts the raising of Lazarus and dates from 1862. The first S aisle window E of the S porch is by H.W. Bryans (1898). It depicts the women at the empty tomb.

Hoar Cross, *Holy Angels.* This is one of the most important Victorian churches in England, the masterpiece of G.F. Bodley and his partner Thomas Garner. It is built entirely in the Decorated style, in the local red sandstone. It was started in 1872, dedicated in 1876, and extended at a unknown later date. The Lady chapel was added in 1891, All Souls' chapel in 1900 and finally the narthex in 1906, which was designed by Bodley but carried out by his successor, Cecil Hare. The church was paid for by Emily Charlotte Meynell Ingram as a memorial to her husband, Hugo Francis, who had died in 1871.

The church sits astride a hilltop some 400ft above sea level in the Needwood forest, dominating the surrounding countryside. The church consists of a three-bay nave and narthex, a tall central tower, short transepts and a three-bay clerestoried chancel, higher than the nave, with adjoining side chapels. The battlemented central tower of two stages has three vertical divisions recessed between buttresses. Each division has two-light tracery, all blank except for the upper stage of the central division. The nave is low and relatively plain when compared to the chancel. The windows are larger and more numerous in the chancel, where they rise above the Lady chapel and St. Hugh's chapel on the N side, and the Chantry chapel and the chapel of All Souls on the S. The short transepts are the same height as the nave but have pointed windows, in contrast to the square-headed N and S windows of the nave and chancel. The main E window of six lights has complex 14C tracery.

The immediate impact of the nave upon entering is one of darkness, owing to the relative smallness of the nave windows and to the fact that all the windows are filled with stained glass. The result is that the eye is drawn through the ornate Rood screen to the light-filled chancel, with its soaring stone tierceron-vault. The chancel has the only stone vault, the nave and transepts having wooden wagon roofs.

The chequered black and white marble flooring was a device much favoured by Bodley. Around the walls of the aisles are the Stations of the Cross, carved in Antwerp by De Wint and Boeck, and coloured by Powell's. All the other furnishings were designed by Bodley & Garner, to whom a memorial is placed in the narthex. Garner's contribution centred on the chancel and on the carving. S of the chancel the Chantry chapel contains the tombs of Hugo Francis Meynell Ingram (died 1871) and his wife Emily (died 1904). Both comprise recumbent effigies of white marble on alabaster tomb-chests. Over his tomb is a lavish ogee arch and over hers a wooden canopy. The tombs were executed by Farmer & Brindley. The Chantry chapel also has the memorial to F.G. Lindley Meynell (died 1910), designed by Cecil Hare and executed by Bridgeman & Sons; the memorial tablet to Lady Mary Meynell (died 1937) by H.S. Goodhart-Rendel; and a tablet to F.H. Lindley Meynell (died 1941), by Sir Charles Nicholson. The fine organ case was designed by Canon Frederick Sutton, who often collaborated with Bodley. All the stained glass was designed by Garner and made by Burlison & Grylls. Saints are depicted in almost every window. The N chancel window represents the Latin Doctors, and its counterpart on the S the Greek Doctors. Otherwise, early martyrs and English saints predominate (see the church's booklet).

The church possesses a large collection of vestments, the most important being a chasuble, which apparently belonged to Pope Gregory XI, c 1378.

Ilam, *Holy Cross.* Holy Cross, set in outstanding scenery, is a medieval church, to which was added the very large octagonal Watts Russell memorial chapel in 1831. The church was drastically restored in 1855–56 by Gilbert Scott. Internally much is by Scott including the reredos, the sanctuary tiling and the iron screens, made by Francis Skidmore. The Norman font has six highly individualistic carved panels. There are three outstanding tombs. Firstly, the medieval shrine of St. Bertelin, which consists of a base with open quatrefoil decoration. Secondly, the large alabaster tomb to Robert Meverell (died 1626) and his wife. However, the chief glory of the church is what is undoubtedly one of Sir Francis Chantrey's greatest works, the memorial to David Pike Watts, carved in marble in 1831. He is reclining on a couch with his daughter and her three children kneeling at his side. All this is life-size and carefully lit in an otherwise bare chapel. In the churchyard are the remains of three pre-Conquest crosses.

Ingestre, *St. Mary the Virgin.* St. Mary's is set in an isolated position at the end of a long unmade dead-end track, with just the very large mansion and stable blocks for company. It is almost certainly the work of Sir Christopher Wren in 1673–76 and has remained virtually unaltered since that date. The present church replaces an older church whose site is unknown. It was in 1671 that Walter Chetwynd petitioned for permission to demolish the old building and erect a new church on a new site.

The church, built in ashlar, consists of a W tower, a four-bay aisled nave and a chancel. The tower has three distinct stages. The lowest stage has a prominent pedimented W doorway, supported by Tuscan columns, and alternating quoins on the W face. The middle stage bears the Chetwynd arms (W) and has circular windows to N and S. These continue into the clerestory of the nave and visually link it with the tower. The top stage has a louvred round-headed window in each face. The tower is surmounted by a balustrade with an urn at each corner. The aisles and chancel have the same large round-headed windows. Entrance through the W door gives an immediate impact of richness, well-lit by the large windows. The walls, pillars and ceilings are white, adding to the quality of lightness. The nave is divided from the aisles by pillars which are each made up of four three-quarter Tuscan columns. These support block entablatures and rounded arches with cherubs as keystones. The chancel arch and tower arch have heads which are supposed to represent Sir Christopher Wren and, at the W end, Walter Chetwynd. The box-pews, although cut down in the Victorian period, are contemporary with the church and are plainly decorated with inset panels. The flat nave ceiling is a sumptuous example of the plasterer's art. During its restoration in the late 1960s, two names were discovered, Gilbert and S. Hand. Hand was the name of the family in charge of quarrying the stone for St. Paul's Cathedral. The chancel ceiling is barrel-vaulted, with plaster panels containing various armorial and heraldic devices.

The church has fine monuments, fittings and stained glass. At the

W end is a painting depicting Doubting Thomas, executed in 1871 by the Belgian artist Forasyn the Elder. It was presented by the 19th Earl of Shrewsbury. In the N aisle at the W end is the white marble font, the bowl being fluted and supported on an enlarged baluster. The ornate wrought-iron light fittings, each supporting two glass lamp shades, were made in 1886 by Thomas Taylor-Smith and installed by the Domestic Electric Light Company of London. Ingestre was one of the first electrically-lit churches outside London. The chancel screen is of three arches divided by Corinthian pilasters. Within the spandrels are cherubs' heads and further rich decoration includes festoons and garlands. All this is surmounted by the superbly carved royal arms. The double-decker pulpit and its tester are also richly decorated with carving. Similar decoration is used in the panelling of the chancel. The wooden altar rails have Ionic capitals on the balusters. The two carved figures of the Virgin Mary and the Archangel Gabriel above the wooden reredos were bought in Belgium by the 19th Earl in 1871.

In the chancel there are many monuments to the Chetwynd family. Against the N wall is the large marble tomb-chest, with recumbent effigy in robes of state, of the 18th Earl of Shrewsbury (died 1868). The monument is by Sir John Steell and was executed in 1873. On the S side of the chancel are wall monuments to Catherine Talbot (died 1785) and John Chetwynd (died 1741). Against the S wall at the E end is the marble sarcophagus, surmounted by the busts of a woman and child, to Francesca Tomasine, Countess Talbot (died 1819), by Thomas Kirk. Next to this against the S wall is the marble tomb-chest with recumbent effigy of the second Earl Talbot (died 1848), by the younger Richard Westmacott. On the E wall of the N aisle are two marble monuments by Sir Francis Chantrey. The lower one to Viscount Ingestre (died 1826) is a marble tablet with a panel depicting the Viscount's fatal accident. Above this is the memorial to John Chetwynd-Talbot (died 1825). It is in the form of a pedimented slab with a frontal carving of a priest. On the E wall is the marble relief carving, by Ernesto Cali of Naples (1857), to Lady Victoria Susan Talbot (died 1856). She is depicted asleep on a day bed. In front of the E wall stands the large tomb, with a recumbent effigy in ceremonial uniform, of Viscount Ingestre (died 1915). The tomb-chest is in black marble and the effigy and swags on the sides are in bronze. It was executed by Lady Feodora Gleichen in 1918.

In the N aisle there is a particularly fine window with brilliant colours by Sir Edward Burne-Jones, 1897–98. It depicts two angels with a pelican feeding its young. The window next to this and its opposite number in the S aisle have some heraldic roundels which apparently came from the previous church. The chancel N window is by Thomas Willement, 1852. In the S aisle there is a memorial window to Georgina Rose McDonald, made in 1907 by Baroness Gleichen in the Morris & Co. workshops.

Leek

All Saints. All Saints' is a masterful and powerful display of the architectural talents of Richard Norman Shaw. It was built in 1885–87 and contains fittings by a number of key artistic figures of the late 19C and early 20C. There is much stained glass designed by Sir Edward Burne-Jones and made by Morris & Co., and glass and wall paintings by J. Edgar Platt, head of the Leek School of Art at the beginning of the century. The wall paintings in the chancel as well as the bishop's chair and roof of the porch are the work of one of Shaw's pupils, Gerald Horsley. Another pupil, William Lethaby, was responsible for the pulpit and the scheme for the reredos. The set of altar frontals is the work of the Leek School of Embroidery.

St. Edward the Confessor. St. Edward's is the mother church of Leek. It is chiefly of the 14C and 17C, with a major restoration by G.E. Street in 1865–67. There are four items worthy of note. The W end is taken up by an enormous gallery which rises steeply to the roof. The stained glass ranges from two small medieval panels in the tower to work by Morris & Co. (N transept E, 1902, and S transept S, 1907), two large rose windows by G.F. Bodley (1903), chancel windows by Clayton & Bell (1867) and the N transept N window by J.H. Dearle (1907). The church also has a series of frontals and other embroidery by the Leek School of Embroidery from the 1870s onwards. Finally, there are the remains of two pre-Conquest crosses, both inside and in the churchyard.

Lichfield

St. Chad. St. Chad's is built of the local red sandstone, with a late 17C redbrick clerestory, and is set in rural surroundings, with a magnificent view across the wide expanse of Stowe Pool to the cathedral. The church has a fine Decorated W tower with a stair turret at the SE angle. The battlemented Early English S aisle retains a splendid original doorway, sheltered by the S porch.

Internally, the nave of five bays has octagonal piers, those on the S side being Early English. The N arcade is Perpendicular. The W tower arch, W window and chancel E window date from the Decorated period, but the chancel preserves two 13C lancets as well. At the W end there is a wooden tower screen, surmounted by a statue of St. Chad, which was erected as a memorial to Joseph Deacon (died 1942). There is a chest dated 1669 in the nave. The high altar is wooden and its front is divided by four pairs of Ionic columns. Within the arches are painted panels of St. Aidan, St. Chad and St. Oswald. The wooden pulpit is unusual in that its base is set in a sunken square in the floor. In the S aisle the altar is a plain wooden table dated 1658. The church has a number of Victorian stained glass windows. The five-light E window depicts Christ as the Good Shepherd. There are a number of good 18C and 19C memorial tablets.

St. Mary. A large church with a fine W tower and spire which stands up well against the triple spires of the nearby cathedral. The spire is the work of G.E. Street, 1852–54. The rest was rebuilt in 1868–70 by

James Fowler. The church has been converted into the St. Mary's Heritage Centre (opened 1981), comprising a shop, offices, a large café and an historical exhibition, but the former chancel and Dyott chapel have been kept for worship. In the former chancel there is an ornate reredos with mosaic inlay panels. The E window of seven lights depicts the Crucifixion (by Clayton & Bell). On the N side of the chancel is the Dyott chapel which contains monuments to the Dyott family. The small wooden altar has painted panels of Noah in the Ark. The E window has scenes from the New Testament. The two-light side window depicts St. Richard of Chichester and St. George.

St. Michael. Set on a hill surrounded by its nine-acre graveyard, this sandstone church has a spectacular view across Lichfield to the cathedral. The chief monument of the church is the floor slab to Samuel Johnson's parents and brother.

The main external feature is the W tower and recessed spire. The tower shows evidence of Early English work; but it is chiefly Perpendicular. The church was subsequently added to and restored on a number of occasions, repairs being recorded in the 1570s, 1590s and in 1677–80. In 1842–43 Thomas Johnson largely rebuilt the church in the Early English style. This accounts for the comparative unity of appearance of the exterior. Finally, J. Oldrid Scott undertook essential repairs in 1890–93.

The nave is of four bays with octagonal piers and moulded capitals. The chancel is 13C in origin; the present Perpendicular E window dates from J. Oldrid Scott's restoration of 1890–93. The oak reredos dates from 1926 and the wooden panelling in the sanctuary was installed in 1944. The brass eagle lectern was given in 1905. Above the chancel arch is a painted panel bearing the arms of Queen Anne, 1711. The octagonal font dates from 1669. In an arched recess in the chancel is the well-preserved tomb of William Walton (died c 1350). His recumbent effigy has its feet resting on his pet dog. William Walton was the first recorded benefactor of St. Michael's. In his will he left 'Three acres of land for one waxen light, of a good size, to burn in the said chapel on all feast days'.

In the floor of the centre aisle of the nave is the incised marble slab to Samuel Johnson's father, mother and brother. The inscription in Latin records the life and character of Michael Johnson (died 1731), Sarah (died 1759) and Nathaniel (died 1737). Dr Johnson wrote 'Rasselas or the Prince of Abyssinia' to raise money for his mother in her final illness, but in the event it paid for her funeral and memorial. The stained glass is all late 19C and early 20C. The N aisle has a three-light window depicting Jesus appearing to the women in the garden by T.F. Curtis of Ward & Hughes (1915). The E window was filled with stained glass in 1893–97, depicting the triumphant re-entry of Christ into Heaven.

In the churchyard, which is one of the largest and oldest continually used in England (it may be of Roman origin), there is the grave of Trooper John Brown, who sounded the charge for the Light Brigade at the Battle of Balaclava (1854) in the Crimean War.

Sheen, *St. Luke.* St. Luke's presents the appearance of being just another small Victorian church set in remote moorland scenery and built out of the local gritstone. A church dating from 1554 was replaced in 1828–32 by Isaac Billinge. In 1850 the church underwent a further rebuilding, to the designs of C.W. Burleigh of Leeds. Within a short time the architect was replaced by William Butterfield. Butterfield was introduced by the patron, A.J.B. Beresford Hope, who also persuaded Benjamin Webb, co-founder of the Cambridge Camden Society, to accept the living in 1853 and to stay until 1862. Beresford Hope had visions of making Sheen 'a centre for Anglo-Catholicism' and an 'Athens in the Moorlands'.

The church has a three-stage W tower with a recessed pyramidal roof, an aisleless nave, a S porch and a two-bay chancel and N vestry. Surrounded by its graveyard, the church adjoins Butterfield's school and parsonage, both of which are now private houses. Externally, just what is the work of Butterfield is unclear. Certainly his is the pyramidal roof on the tower and the gable crosses. It is inside that his hand can be seen clearly.

The aisleless nave is lit by three windows in 13C style on each side. At the W end the large pointed arch leads into the tower space. The chancel has a stone tunnel-vault with five transverse ribs. This is the work of Butterfield and this roofing is used too in the adjacent vestry. The chancel is divided from the nave by a wooden screen, erected in 1903 by Professor Sheldon as a memorial to the Prince family. Above this, suspended from the chancel arch, is a large cross. It is floriated and has an image of Our Lord based on the work of Murillo. There is a similar chancel cross in Butterfield's great London church of All Saints, Margaret Street. Many of the fittings in the chancel came from the Margaret Street Chapel which Butterfield replaced by All Saints'. The inlaid marble altar was installed in 1869; it was sent from London at the expense of Beresford Hope. The reredos of alabaster and local marble was designed by Butterfield, as were the altar candlesticks. The orange altar hangings are unfortunate. The pulpit, by Butterfield, was brought from the Margaret Street Chapel, where it had been used by Edward Pusey and John Henry Newman. The large font with its massive wooden cover and its iron swivelling gantry stands under the tower arch. In the tower space on the S wall is a board listing the benefactors of the poor in 1674–1780, which was restored in 1896. All the stained glass is the work of Michael O'Connor except for one N nave window (1924), which shows Christ as the Good Shepherd and was inserted as a memorial to Professor Sheldon and his wife Margaret. The chancel E window (1854) depicts St. Bede, St. Luke and St. Etheldreda. In the tracery is Our Lord in Majesty displaying the Stigmata and seated on a rainbow. The brass eagle lectern was given by the parish as a memorial to T.E. Heygate, a priest who served the parish for 40 years until his death in 1903. In the chancel on the S wall is a brass tablet commemorating A.J.B. Beresford Hope: 'To the glory of God and in memory of the rebuilder of this church, vicarage and schools, A.J.B. Beresford Hope of Beresford Hall—MP, member of Her Majesty's Privy Council, born January 25 1820, died October 20 1887, buried at Christ Church, Kilndown, Kent. This brass is given by his children and friends.' Opposite this on the N wall is a memorial with a portrait medallion to Beresford Hope's wife, Lady Mildred (died 1881).

Stafford

St. Chad. St. Chad's is a much-restored cruciform Norman church. It is set back from the main street and was originally fronted by shops. The church was stated as being ruinous by 1650. Restoration started in 1854 under Henry Ward and was completed by Sir Gilbert Scott between 1873 and 1886. By the 19C the S transept and the aisles had gone, and the nave arcades had been blocked in. The W front, hemmed in on each side by commercial premises, was designed and built by Scott in 1873–74. Above the elaborate central doorway is a row of round-headed arches, the middle three being glazed. In the gable there is a niche containing a statue of St. Chad presented by Scott. From the NE side the only view of the building as a whole can be gained. The aisles with their small windows are restorations, whereas the clerestory windows of the nave are original. The central tower is Perpendicular. The N transept, again a restoration, has as its chief feature a rose window. The chancel is much restored and Norman in inspiration, but with an Early English E window.

The nave retains the original massive drum piers, with simple capitals and with incised decoration on the single-step arches. Original too is the W crossing arch which has two rows of zigzag and beakhead decoration. On the abacus of the NE tower pier is a carved inscription and some guilloche and fleur-de-lis decoration. The inscription reads *Orm Vocatur Qui Me Condidit*, and literally translates 'He who founded me is called Orm'. It is a rare example of a dedicatory inscription giving the name of the benefactor or founder. The style moves to Early English in the arches to the N transept and chancel. The chancel, although heavily restored, possesses some marvellous intersecting blind arcading on both sides. The overall impact is one of a dark and sombre interior, lit mainly by small, clear windows.

The font has an extremely convincing Norman bowl, but dates from 1856. Surmounting this is an ornate and tall Gothic cover designed by Sir Charles Nicholson. The splendid reredos (c 1910) is by Sir Walter Tapper. The Rood was given in 1922. The church is singularly devoid of monuments and stained glass. In the N aisle there is a memorial window to George Arthur Wroe, Vicar 1942–68.

St. Mary. St. Mary's is a very large church, formerly collegiate, with a complex building history represented by the Early English, Decorated and Perpendicular styles. The church was extensively restored and rebuilt by Gilbert Scott in 1840–44. There are a number of important monuments and fittings. Chief among these are the Norman font and the alabaster tomb to Sir Edward Aston (died 1568) and his wife Joan Boules.

The church is surrounded by a churchyard which has been cleared and lawned. This forms an oasis of peace, reached through narrow alleyways from the main shopping centre to the E. The building is dominated by the octagonal Perpendicular central tower, rising above the impressively large church. Just W of the church lie the remains of a simple two-cell pre-Conquest church, dedicated to St. Bertelin, a local saint. It had survived much altered as a school until 1801, when it was demolished. It was excavated in 1954 and its foundations laid bare.

The immediate impact of the interior is one of great spaciousness and size. The nave is Early English of c 1200, five bays in length, with

Perpendicular clerestory windows higher than the original roofline. Above the chancel arch is an impressive display of Early English arcading, behind which is the bell chamber. The S transept collapsed in 1845 and was rebuilt by Scott in 13C style, as was the S aisle of the chancel, now used as the Lady chapel, which had collapsed in 1843. The chancel is impressively long, almost as long as the nave. The N transept is the jewel of the church. It is much larger than the S transept and was built between 1320 and 1340 in the Decorated style. There is blind arcading between the clerestory windows, and its N wall is supported by some elaborate detached buttresses and pinnacles.

The most important fitting is the font, which is Norman and seemingly much influenced by the Eastern Mediterranean. The bowl is a quatrefoil shape, supported by squat crouching figures and by lions beneath them. There are inscriptions which translate 'You bring from Jerusalem life-giving water, making me both beautiful and special' and 'You are unwise if you do not flee; see the lions'. The font has been given a conjectured date of c 1148. The church possesses two organs; the larger, in a fine case but blocking most of the W window, was first built by John Geib of London in 1789–90. In the N transept is the alabaster tomb with recumbent effigies of Sir Edward Aston (died 1568) and his wife, Joan Boules. In the N aisle there is a 19C memorial bust to Izaak Walton, who was baptised here in 1593. There is a good range of stained glass, including some medieval fragments in a N aisle window. The W window of that aisle was designed in 1846 by A.W.N. Pugin and was executed by John Hardman. The main W window, now almost totally obscured by the organ, was designed by Alfred Gérente (1855). The N transept E window is by C.E. Kempe and the S aisle and Lady chapel contain windows by Mayer & Co.

Stoke on Trent, *St. Peter ad Vincula.* Set in a large churchyard, opposite the Classical town hall, it is the mother church of the Potteries. The present church was built N of the site of the medieval church in 1826–29 at a cost of c £14,000 by Trubshaw & Johnson in the style of Commissioners' churches. It was consecrated in 1830. The most important aspect of the church is its monuments to local pottery families such as Wedgwood and Spode. In the churchyard there are the remains of a pre-Conquest cross with interlace decoration. Set up S of the present church are two much-restored Decorated arches on the site of the earlier church. Nearby is the simple tomb-slab marking the grave of Josiah Wedgwood (died 1795).

The church has a three-stage W tower with octagonal corner turrets. The nave of five bays has buttresses carrying pinnacles. Both the nave and chancel are battlemented. The chancel of two bays has octagonal turrets at its E end. Internally there is a gallery running from the W end round the N and S sides. This forms aisles, and an internal porch at the W end. Both above and below the gallery, the N and S elevations have five three-light windows. The roof of the nave is coffered. The chancel has a five-light E window and a plaster vault.

In the chancel there is a fine alabaster reredos (1888) depicting the Crucifixion, Christ washing the Disciples' feet and Christ as the Good Shepherd. The E window has glass depicting the Apostles by David Evans. The N wall of the chancel has a marble tablet to Sarah Wedgwood (died 1815), widow of Josiah, and a marble portrait medallion by John Flaxman to Josiah himself (died 1795). The month of the date of birth is wrong. There is a large marble angel in memory of John Bourne (died 1833), by William Behnes. Nearby is a marble tablet to Sir Lovelace Tomlinson Stamer, Bt (died 1908), who was Rector and later Bishop Suffragan of Shrewsbury. Also on the N wall is a tablet with a marble bust by Behnes to John Tomlinson (died 1838). Along the S wall is a memorial to William Adams, an important potter, with a black stone portrait medallion. There is also a large marble memorial depicting a woman weeping at the sarcophagus, by Behnes, in memory of Josiah Spode (died 1829). Next to this is a tablet to Josiah Spode (died 1827), by Humphrey Hopper and another to the founder of the firm (1797). Nearby is a marble tablet to William Taylor Copeland (died 1868), master potter, MP for Stoke, Lord Mayor of London in 1836 and a founder of the local hospital. The two windows in the S wall of the chancel are by Mayer & Co. In the N aisle against the gallery screen is an altar with a tapestry dated 1911, depicting the angel breaking St. Peter's chains. A nearby window is in memory of George Augustus Selwyn, Bishop of Lichfield, and is dated 1879. Beneath another N window is a pre-Conquest font. N of the chancel arch is the stone pulpit which has above it a 17C crucifix, believed to be Spanish. The Minton family vault is under the S vestry; there is a brass plaque to the family on the vestry wall.

The churchyard contains an interesting grave slab to Sibil Clark (died 1684 aged 112) and her husband, Henry, who also died aged 112.

Stone, _St. Michael._ St. Michael's is a Georgian Gothick foundation. A petition for a new church in 1735 led to its construction in 1753–58. The 1885 restoration produced a Perpendicular chancel and a complete set of stained glass windows. There are a number of features of note. Firstly, the church has retained its Georgian box-pews and galleries and is considered by English Heritage as one of the four best remaining examples in the country. Secondly, it has a remarkably large number of windows by C.E. Kempe (20), dating from 1894–1901. Thirdly, there are monuments from Stone Priory, a pair of probable 13C effigies, and a 16C brass to one Thomas Crompton, and monuments to the Parker Jervis family. Most important of these are those at the W end, to the first Earl St. Vincent (died 1823) and to the fourth Earl St. Vincent (died 1885). The tablet to the first Earl is by William Whitelaw, with the naval trophies and bust above reputedly by Chantrey. There are life-size busts to the two Earls by Chantrey at the W end. Outside the church at the E end is the free-standing Parker Jervis mausoleum, designed by William Robinson in the form of a Greek Doric temple.

Tamworth, _St. Editha._ A large and complex church over 190ft long, it sits on a slight rise in a turfed churchyard. Once the church and castle dominated the town and surrounding countryside but the '60s' planners have dominated them with an appallingly sited group of tower blocks. The church, built of local sandstone, houses a wealth of stained glass and monuments. The present church is largely of the Decorated period, the result of rebuilding after a fire in 1345.

The most impressive and dominant feature is the largely Perpendicular W tower. There are pairs of small two-light belfry windows with far larger windows below. The belfry windows look 13C. On the N side there is a partly renewed lancet. The W doorway is by Basil

Champneys. The top stage is surmounted by four large corner pinnacles. In the SW corner of the tower there is the rare feature of a double spiral staircase.

The four-bay nave has quatrefoil piers with smaller shafts in the recesses. These support large Decorated arches which carry the Perpendicular clerestory. At the W end the tower arch is filled with a screen and above this is stone tracery in the Perpendicular style, echoing the W window. There is no chancel arch; there was once a Norman crossing tower, and its E and W arches have gone. The N and S arches with zigzag decoration remain, opening into the transepts. The clerestory continues at the same level in the chancel as in the nave. The lack of a chancel arch and the continuous clerestory gives the church a feeling of great length. In the N wall of the chancel there are three 14C tomb recesses which pierce the wall into St. George's chapel. Above are three two-light openings, once external. At the W end of the S aisle a rather incongruous low concrete wall surrounds steps to the crypt, which is now used as a coffee bar and meeting room.

Under the tower against the N wall is the very large monument to John Ferrers (died 1680) and his son Humphrey (died 1678). They are depicted life-size, kneeling towards each other but turned outwards and with a large inscription between them. Above are family crests, putti, garlands, an urn and a sarcophagus. The tomb has been ascribed to Grinling Gibbons but it was probably executed by Arnold Quellin. Opposite this on the S wall there is a marble monument to John Clarke (died 1818), depicting a kneeling, mourning woman against a sarcophagus. In the centre aisle of the nave at the W end is the octagonal font which dates from 1854 and was designed by Sir Gilbert Scott. The chancel screen is 18C wrought-iron, an agreeably light work. The S aisle has at its E end the remains of some Perpendicular stonework which has been identified as the base of a font. The aisle now serves as the Lady chapel. Also in the S aisle is a Classical tablet depicting a mourning woman, kneeling beneath a weeping willow; it commemorates Elizabeth Blood (died 1899) but looks early 19C. In the N aisle a monument to John Horner (died 1769) shows a putto crying over a portrait medallion with another putto above. In the N transept, in front of the screens separating St. George's chapel, there are the remains of a stone coffin and fragments of a stone effigy of a 15C knight.

The chancel is mainly 14C fabric and 19C fittings. The proud reredos was designed by Scott in 1852; the statues were carved by J. Birnie Philip. The mosaic panels, made by Salviati in 1887, are placed between the Purbeck marble shafts. In the N wall of the sanctuary the recesses shelter three tombs. To the E there is an alabaster tomb-chest with the recumbent effigies of Sir John Ferrers (died 1512) and his wife. The chest bears a series of small female figures under canopies, most of whose heads have been hacked off. The second monument is 14C, in freestone, and perhaps commemorates Lady Joan de Freville (died 1339). The third tomb consists of the badly damaged figures of a knight, possibly Sir Baldwin Freville (died 1400) and his wife. In the N wall of St. George's chapel, under a large arched recess, there is a 14C effigy, possibly that of the man responsible for rebuilding the church after the fire in 1345, Baldwin de Witney (died 1369).

The chief feature of the church is its collection of mainly 19C stained glass. The E window is filled with glass by William Wailes (1870) and depicts the Apostles. In the S wall of the chancel there are three clerestory windows which were designed by Ford Madox Brown and made by Morris & Co. in 1873. In St. George's chapel the E window has glass by Sir Edward Burne-Jones, 1874. In the N wall are four windows filled with later Morris & Co. glass. In the S transept is a large three-light window depicting scenes from the life of Christ. The S aisle has three windows which depict scenes and figures from the Old Testament, by Powell's, 1881–86. In the N aisle a memorial to the dead of the First World War (Christ surrounded by the Heavenly Host) and a window in memory of Maurice Berkeley Peel (killed in 1917) are the work of Henry Holiday. In the W window, under the tower, is stained glass of 1975 by Alan Younger. It is abstract in form, relying on colour, and is based on a passage from Revelation about the New Jerusalem.

Tutbury, *St. Mary the Virgin.* St. Mary's is all that remains of a Benedictine priory built on the S flank of the hill below Tutbury

St. Mary's: a grand 12C Norman W front, with later window tracery

Castle. It was founded in 1089 by Henry de Ferrers. At the Dissolution most of the nave was left for the use of the town and the rest was demolished or allowed to fall into decay. The result is an impressive Norman fragment, with the additions of the tower, chancel and apse by G.E. Street in 1866–68.

The exterior reveals four periods of building. The most impressive feature is the magnificent W end of c 1150–70. The exceptional W door has seven orders of decoration. The order of beakheads is notable for being of alabaster, the earliest use of the material in England. The door itself is Street's, as is the gable above. The SW corner has a squat tower, a 16C addition, which appears totally out of scale and sympathy with the W front. The S door has a very worn carving in the tympanum representing a boar hunt. The N aisle was added in 1820–22 by Joseph B.H. Bennett in very loose Gothic.

Internally, it is the nave which holds one's attention. It is six bays in length (originally eight) and reveals the change in Norman style over the 50-odd years of its construction. The easternmost two piers of each arcade are circular, the rest are a peculiar quatrefoil shape. The decoration of the capitals is very simple. There are two roll-mouldings to each arch. The W end has been dated as late as 1150 because of the sumptuousness of its detail. The massive W door has zigzag decoration and above there is some particularly fine interlaced arcading. The tracery of the large Decorated W window was designed by G.F. Bodley in 1890. The clerestory of the nave has 16C windows. At the Dissolution the original roof and clerestory were taken down and replaced by a flat ceiling, with the triforium becoming the clerestory. The flat ceiling was in turn replaced by Street's wooden barrel-vaulted roof. The S aisle reveals some 14C rebuilding. The very large pointed chancel arch, by Street, replaced a large blank 16C wall. The chancel and apse complement the Norman nave. All the fittings in the chancel are the designs of Street, who awarded the makers, Ward & Critchlow of Uttoxeter, a first-class certificate. The reredos in the S aisle was designed by Cecil Hare in 1919 and was made from a single block of alabaster by Bridgeman's. The S aisle also possesses no less than 39 Glastonbury chairs of different designs. In the N aisle there are two monuments of interest. The first is a marble tablet, depicting a weeping man against a pillar, in memory of George Robinson (died 1837), by Joseph Hall of Derby. The second is an alabaster coffin which was uncovered in 1972. It contained the remains of a woman. The use of alabaster for this and for the W door is hardly surprising when you consider that Tutbury is built on alabaster. All the stained glass is the work of Burlison & Grylls and dates from 1890 to 1939.

Walsall, *St. Mary*. This is the main Catholic church of Walsall, by Joseph Ireland, 1825–27. It is set on what is locally known as the Mount, with a view of central Walsall. It presents a whitewashed, rectangular, pedimented box with four giant Doric pilasters at the W and E ends. The church has five tapering oblong windows on each side, filled with glass by Hardman's. Internally, there is a coffered tunnel-vaulted roof. The sanctuary has four fluted Ionic pilasters and painted panels depicting the Evangelists and the Crucifixion.

Wolverhampton

St. Peter. This large and imposing church was collegiate in the medieval period and between 1479 and 1846 it was a Royal Peculiar united with the Deanery of Windsor. A church has existed on the site since 994, when one dedicated to St. Mary was founded by Lady Wulfrun. Evidence from this early date is the famous pre-Conquest cross in the churchyard. The present building has work of all periods from the 13C to the 20C. It is rich in fittings and stained glass.

The church is situated at the highest point of the town, set now in a relatively peaceful part of the civic complex. It is built of locally quarried sandstone and is dominated by the four-storey Perpendicular central tower. The four-bay chancel and polygonal apse are in the Decorated style and were built by Ewan Christian during the 1860s, replacing a chancel of 1682–84. The nave, aisles, transepts, S porch and vestries on the N side are all Perpendicular, so giving the exterior a sense of architectural unity. Near the S porch is the 14ft shaft of a 9C cross. Although it is much worn, it reveals bands of decoration of acanthus and triangles. The W end of the churchyard falls away steeply in a series of steps and terraces. Here is the war memorial designed by C.T. Armstrong in 1922. From the civic complex to the W, the church presents an impressive view.

Internally, the atmosphere is light and spacious. The five-bay nave is lit by unusual Perpendicular clerestory windows, which are repeated in the S transept, now used as a Lady chapel. The nave dates from c 1450–80. The four tower arches are the oldest fabric, c 1205. The N transept (the war memorial chapel) dates from the 15C and has blind arcading along the N wall. Two massive windows with a singular lack of tracery and unusual leading flood the transept with light. The chancel, four bays long and with a polygonal apse, was designed in the Decorated style by Ewan Christian in the 1860s. The S porch, vestries and W front are also by Christian.

The inner S porch is an outstanding example of modern woodcarving (1929), in highly decorative Gothic. The octagonal font with its bowl supported by statues is dated 1660. At the W end of the nave is the Jacobean gallery built at the expense of the Merchant Taylors Company for the use of Wolverhampton Grammar School. The nave roof has a wealth of carving, much of it gilded. The main cross beams are supported by angels. The Perpendicular stone pulpit forms part of one of the nave pillars. Its stone staircase is guarded by a large seated lion. Twelve Perpendicular stalls came from Lilleshall Abbey in 1546 and the lectern is supposed to have come from Halesowen Abbey. Above the nave tower arch is the organ built by Henry Willis in the 1860s and rebuilt on a number of occasions since. The S transept which contains the Lady chapel is enclosed by two wooden screens. The altar, with Ionic columns as riddel posts and altar rails, is Jacobean; it was possibly consecrated by Archbishop Laud. Next to this against the S wall is an alabaster tomb-chest, with recumbent effigies of John Leveson (died 1575) and his wife Joyce. It is a late example of the work of the Royleys of Burton-on-Trent. Against the tower pier is the life-size bronze statue of Admiral Sir Richard Leveson (died 1605) and two putti. It was made in 1634 by the French court sculptor to King Charles I, Hubert Le Sueur. The N transept, enclosed by two parclose screens, contains the alabaster tomb-chest with recumbent effigies of Thomas Lane (died 1588) and his wife Katherine. Around the sides are gathered their children and shields.

It is the work of the Royleys of Burton. The alabaster and marble monument to Col. John Lane (died 1667) is by Jasper Latham. Col. Lane was the person responsible for hiding King Charles II and then helping him escape after the Battle of Worcester. His family received the special honour of bearing the royal lions of England on their crest.

The church possesses a fine range of stained glass. The seven windows of the apse are filled with rich Victorian glass of New Testament scenes. The chancel windows contain fragments of medieval glass, German and Flemish, presented in 1959 by Theodosia Hinckes. The Lady chapel E window represents the Tree of Jesse. The N transept contains three Victorian roundels depicting Christ with the sick and children. The N aisle has a window to the memory of Archibald Fisher Smith, who fell at Ypres in the First World War. It was made by A.J. Davies and represents a soldier praying before an altar. The W window (1852) was a memorial to the Duke of Wellington and depicts Moses, Joshua, Gideon and David, each with a scene from their stories underneath. The three windows of the S aisle are by C.E. Kempe.

There are many monuments, especially along the S aisle wall. Amongst these are a memorial brass to Troop Sergeant Major John Stratford, who was the oldest soldier in the British Empire. He died in 1932 aged 102, having served in the British Army for 68 years (1846–1914). Next to this is a brass to John Marston (died 1918), twice Mayor of Wolverhampton and the key figure in the development of the motor-cycle and car industry in the area. The church also contains a number of monuments to the Mander family, another important local family of industrialists.

St. Martin, Ettingshall. Arguably one of the finest 1930s churches in the Midlands, it was designed by Messrs. Lavender & Twentyman in 1939. It is of brick construction with a W tower almost devoid of architectural features. Above the W door is a life-size statue of St. Martin by Donald Potter. The windows are tall, arched lancets. The low, flat-roofed aisles have simple rectangular openings. The vicarage is joined to the church by a triple-arched covered way, forming a counterbalance to the mass of the tower.

The six-bay nave has plain arches, from above each of which a wooden beam extends carrying the light fittings. The flat roof of the nave is relieved by the 31 white-painted roof beams alternating with the red background. The sanctuary has a tall red drape behind the altar, rising to a tester on an otherwise blank E wall. The altar is of Australian Walnut, with rails of a simplified Greek key pattern. The pulpit has a carving of the Lamb of God by Donald Potter. On the S side of the sanctuary the piscina and sedilia are merely rectangular openings of different sizes. At the W end the tower arch is filled with a metal grille which was originally open but which now has black insulation board behind it. It looks most effective. Below this is the circular granite font with carving of five figures holding outstretched hands, between which are plants. The cover has a central handle in the form of a baby in a cupped hand. The font and its cover are by Donald Potter.

St. Michael and All Angels, Tettenhall. The church is set on a hillside surrounded by its crowded graveyard. Until a disastrous fire in 1950 a major medieval church stood on the site. Of this, only the Perpendicular W tower and Victorian S porch, designed by A.E.

Street in 1882–83, remain. The present idiosyncratic building is the work of Bernard Miller in 1952–55. Three gabled projections from each aisle are filled with very original tracery. Internally, simple woodwork abounds, with the nave pillars reaching their capitals barely 4ft off the ground. The lighting is suspended from curious bell-shaped copper covers. The E window of the Lady chapel is by George Cooper-Abbs and depicts the Triumphant Christ, Archangels and the Last Supper.

WARWICKSHIRE

Warwickshire is roughly an oval with its long axis running due N–S but with its W side nibbled away by Worcestershire. Most counties seem to have to be described as ones of contrast but this well-worn description is most certainly true of Warwickshire. The contrast in this case is between industrial and suburban development and unspoiled rural beauty. The former is dominated by Birmingham and Coventry and their surroundings; the latter is at its best as the county drives the wedge of the Vale of the Red Horse between Gloucestershire and Oxfordshire in the extreme S. As for churches, Warwickshire is neither one of the foremost counties nor is it without much of considerable beauty and interest. Undoubtedly the most-visited church is Stratford, where Shakespeare draws pilgrims as the most holy relics of saints would have done centuries ago. Yet Stratford and its church have less to offer the architecturally-minded visitor than the lovely county town a few miles away. There, both the castle and St. Mary's Church are worth travelling a very long way to see. Leamington is a delightful Georgian place where the best church is one of the few by G.G. Scott, Jr—St. Mark's of 1879. Rugby is about the school and William Butterfield, whose school chapel is the quintessence of Victorian Christian expression in architecture. Birmingham, for its size (and excepting its two cathedrals), is slightly disappointing for its churches. Coventry is most visited for its new cathedral, still built to a traditional Gothic plan but given modern dress. Besides this there are two important ancient churches.

The most common building material is Triassic sandstone, either of a red or a buff colour. It does not weather particularly well: fine carving quickly turns to a blur and restoration work has often had to be heavy. In the Coventry area the stone from the Keuper Sandstone beds is particularly red in hue and gives an unusual and, to my mind, unattractive appearance to churches. In the SE, Warwickshire borders on to the Cotswolds which are part of the great Jurassic ridge. Here limestone comes into use.

Late pre-Conquest architecture can be seen at Wootton Wawen and Tredington. At Wootton Wawen the central tower survives and the church has grown around it. At Tredington there are the traces of a sizeable aisleless nave which had eight windows and two door-ways. The latter were in fact elevated and must have provided access from outside to a gallery over the W part of the nave. A problematic piece of pre-Conquest work is the octagonal W part of the crypt at Berkswell and though the visual evidence is 12C it has been suggested that this is a reworking of a pre-Conquest shrine.

Berkswell is a key site for 12C work because, apart from its most interesting and extensive crypt, it has an impressive, almost perfectly preserved chancel. There is much worthwhile Norman activity at Stoneleigh. Particularly notable is the high decorated chancel arch with its strong detail and the font with named Apostles. The chancel was once vaulted. The E and S walls have much-restored blind arches with pointed heads, reminiscent of the decoration in the churches of Devizes in Wiltshire. Perhaps the best example of Norman might and power is the large crypt beneath the chancel at St. Mary's, Warwick. There are substantial remains of Norman work at five other churches, Beaudesert, Polesworth, Corley, Wyken and Ryton-on-Dunsmore. Beaudesert has an entire Norman chancel (plus vaulting by Thomas Garner in 1865), chancel arch and N and S doorways. Polesworth survives from a Benedictine nunnery which had been founded by St. Modwen in c 827 and whose first abbess was St. Edith of Polesworth, the daughter of King Egbert. The present church has an impressive Norman N arcade of eight bays with round piers and scalloped capitals. The N aisle has been widened later to give a two-nave effect, a plan common in neighbouring W Leicestershire in the 14C. Corley also has a late 12C N arcade, which cuts into an early 12C nave. There is also a Norman doorway and plainish tympanum. Wyken, now a suburb of Coventry, is a fairly complete example of a small Norman village church, and much of the fabric at Ryton-on-Dunsmore is early Norman. At Halford there is an interesting tympanum which contains the best piece of 12C figure sculpture in the county. An angel sits with a scroll draped between his outstretched hands. The whole composition, completely symmetrical, has a serene, majestic quality.

There is some notable 13C church architecture though the quantity is limited. The most impressive is at Temple Balsall, followed by the nave at Merevale. These, along with the ambitious early to mid-13C chancel at King's Norton in Birmingham, are described in the gazetteer. There is also a worthwhile chancel at Pillerton Hersey which probably dates from the middle of the century. From the late 13C, Solihull has pretty chancel windows and a most interesting and lovely chapel raised above a low crypt on the N side. In the big town churches there is little from the 13C though the meagre evidence at Holy Trinity, Coventry and also at the old cathedral shows that these were very substantial buildings at this time.

There was extensive work throughout the county in c 1300 which was evidently a time of relative prosperity (cf. neighbouring Leicestershire). Much of the work is fairly routine with such oft-repeated motifs as Y- or intersected tracery. Many aisles were added at this time. As for Decorated work, one of the best pieces is what now forms the nave of Astley: originally this was the vast chancel of a collegiate church of 1343.

In contrast to work of the 13C and 14C there is Perpendicular activity of the highest order in Warwickshire. St. Michael's, Coventry, later the cathedral, and Holy Trinity in the same city were remodelled and were among the largest late medieval parish churches. At St. Michael's work on the tower began in 1371 and at Holy Trinity on the chancel in 1395. They both illustrate very well the trend towards building side chapels in the 15C and 16C, and in these cases they were built by the prosperous and influential guilds of Coventry. Warwick possesses at St. Mary's Church a chantry chapel which is unsurpassed in England: the Beauchamp chapel, started in 1443 under the will of Richard Beauchamp. The prolific statuary round the E window is among the masterpieces of late medieval English art. Half a century earlier the vaulting in the chancel at St. Mary's is remarkable for having flying ribs to enhance its lightness and beauty. Brailes has a splendid tower with twinned belfry windows. Other late 15C towers, and in these cases surmounted by tall spires, are at Coleshill, King's Norton and Yardley, the latter two in suburbs of Birmingham. A church that appears to be almost wholly Perpendicular, but which was founded in 1342 and was remodelled in the 15C, is St. John the Baptist's, Coventry, established as a chantry by Queen Isabella. It is a classic example of a local red sandstone building and is interesting in that it has a cruciform plan, unusual at this late date. Other Perpendicular work of interest includes the chapel of the Guild of the Holy Cross in Stratford, the chancel of the parish church in Stratford, the remodelling of Lapworth with its N tower detached from the main body of the church and a (? relic) chamber at the W end, and Knowle, which was all built in c 1400. The date of some of the very latest medieval work in the county is known. This is at Solihull, where the W front and S aisle are from 1535.

There was much church building and remodelling in the 17C and 18C. Undoubtedly the most important is the late 18C church of Great Packington, an extraordinary neo-Classical edifice like nothing else in the kingdom. The largest work was the rebuilding of the W parts of St. Mary's, Warwick after the Great Fire of Warwick of 1694. Sir William Wilson of Sutton Coldfield provided a new nave and aisles on the lines of a Continental hall church and lit by enormous sub-Gothic windows. There are 17C and 18C chapels in major houses in Warwickshire that are worth seeing: Arbury Hall, which also has some of the most ornate Strawberry Hill Gothick in England in the domestic rooms; Compton Verney, designed by Lancelot 'Capability' Brown, who probably designed the splendid setting; Stoneleigh, which retains its original 18C furnishings; and Compton Wynyates, where the mid-17C chapel, still in Perpendicular Gothic, is detached from the superb Tudor house. The S chapel at Stoneleigh Parish Church was built in 1665 and it, too, is Gothic and convincing Perpendicular at that. Other churches from the 17C and 18C of note are Honiley, Over Whitacre and the small and delightful building at Binley on the outskirts of Coventry. This has a gem of an interior. These three are all Classical.

The major churches of the 19C are all Gothic, though not necessarily Victorian. Two from the 1820s, in particular, are noteworthy— Holy Trinity, Camp Hill, Bordesley, in Birmingham, and Hampton Lucy. At the latter (by Rickman & Hutchinson) the style is Decorated in an exciting, lavish way that was unknown in early 14C Warwickshire. The first major Victorian parish church (which excludes Pugin's Birmingham Catholic Cathedral in 1839–41) was St. Andrew's, Bordesley, Birmingham. Tragically, this was demolished in 1986. It was an important example of an early, Ecclesiologically correct church and was erected in 1844–46. Gilbert Scott, of course, always aspired to Ecclesiological correctness and this certainly applies to his best work in Warwickshire, Sherbourne, rebuilt in 1862–64 in his beloved style of c 1300. It is a lavish estate church which cost some £20,000. Scott also added a 'proper' chancel at Hampton Lucy in 1856, which seems to try to outdo Rickman & Hutchinson at their own game. The 1860s brought Rogue Gothicism to Warwickshire in the form of Lower Shuckburgh, by J. Croft (1864). It is not the most exotic of Croft's Gothic fantasy churches but nonetheless it does assail one's senses about ecclesiastical propriety, especially the SW tower and the contrived transition from tower to spire. J.P. Seddon usually strove for the unusual but in a more restrained way and his Ullenhall (1875) is an interesting essay in the reworking of 13C motifs; his ceiling is most attractively decorated. J.L. Pearson built three churches: Newbold Pacey (1881–82), St. Patrick's, Bordesley, in Birmingham (1896) and a masterpiece at St. Alban's, Birmingham (1879–81). Another great architect at work in Warwickshire was William Butterfield, whose local masterpiece is the chapel at Rugby School of 1872. Leamington Spa is fortunate in having one of the rare major churches by G.G. Scott, Jr, his St. Mark's, Rugby Road of 1879. It is a stately building which reworks a combination of Decorated and Perpendicular in a most enterprising fashion. A local architect of considerable distinction at the turn of the century was W.H. Bidlake of Birmingham. His two great works are St. Agatha's, Sparkbrook, of 1899–1901, and the vaulted cemetery chapel at Handsworth. This is insufficiently known and must rank as good an example of this building type as any in the country.

One of England's masterpieces of mid-20C church building is in Birmingham: St. Matthew's, Perry Beeches by Robert Maguire and Keith Murray, where close inspection reveals that the apparently uncompromising exterior conceals an ingenious spatial arrangement and a perfect interior for modern Anglican worship. How many future parish churches will even approach its distinction?

For church furnishings and fittings, perhaps the most interesting item of woodwork is the set of stalls at Astley, in what was the collegiate chancel. They are not particularly lavish but are notable for the paintings of Prophets and Apostles on their backs. They date from c 1400 and have misericords. Good Perpendicular screens are to be found at Wormleighton and Alcester. The former came from Southam and is tall, elegantly traceried and has a Rood loft parapet above the vaulting. A late 17C screen (1677) survives at Bagington in front of the Bromley vault. Indeed, Bagington is an excellent example of typical pre-Victorian furnishing as it also has 18C box-pews, W gallery, pulpit, panelling and an altar rail. For pre-19C furnishings in a private chapel, the collection at Compton Wynyates is particularly complete. Among stone fittings there are at Withybrook the remains of an Easter sepulchre: above a tomb-chest which used to depict sleeping soldiers, are other soldiers and an angel. The most impressive wall painting is the Doom at the Guild Chapel in Stratford. Medieval stained glass is not generally of a high order but the remains of an early 14C Jesse window at Merevale are notable. For its time—1837—the E window at Hampton Lucy by Thomas Willement is of the greatest importance nationally, both in terms of its scale and quality of execution.

By far the most important place for medieval monuments is St. Mary's, Warwick. Specifically, this is because of those to Thomas Beauchamp I (died 1369) and Richard Beauchamp (erected 1449–53) and also for the brass to Thomas II (died 1401). Thomas I's effigy is of alabaster but that of Richard, under a hooped, gilded canopy is probably the supreme example of large-scale late medieval metalwork in England. At Merevale there is a fine brass of 1412 to Robert, Earl Ferrers and also an excellent though unfortunately mutilated figure of a knight from the late 13C. However, the brass that is most worth seeking out is at Wixford, of Thomas de Cruwe and Julian his wife (died 1411). Their carefully poised figures, he in armour, she in a flowing dress, stand with their hands clasped in prayer beneath two canopies.

St. Mary's, Warwick is also a key church for post-Reformation monuments, including a number from the Elizabethan and Jacobean years. But the monument that probably draws most visitors is that to William Shakespeare (died 1616) at Stratford, though in itself it is not very distinguished. Stratford has other monuments including the only Rysbrack in Warwickshire, to James Kendall (died 1756). Charlecote has three monuments from the first half of the 17C to the Lucy family, including one to Sir Thomas Lucy (died 1640) in black and white marble which is probably the work (except for the effigies) of the great early 17C English sculptor, Nicholas Stone. He was also responsible for the tomb-chest at Charlecote to Richard Verney (died 1630) and the stately Classical, but unfigured monument to Sir

Thomas Puckering (1639) at Warwick. More ostentatious is the vast monument at Stoneleigh to Alice, Duchess of Dudley (died 1668): this is a vast marble affair showing the duchess and her daughter in shrouds. Finally, for pre-19C monuments, there is Preston-on-Stour, where the dates range from Sir Nicholas Kemp's monument (died 1624) to the late 18C, including one by Sir Richard Westmacott in Grecian mode to James West (died 1797). Into the 19C, Richard Westmacott, Jr is represented at Preston-on-Stour, in the monument to J.R. West (died 1838), again with Greek figures. His father's work in the one to Mrs. Eardley-Wilmot (died 1818) at Berkswell is remarkable for its ethereal embracing angels. Notable monuments tend to be to landowners or officials rather than industrialists but that to James Watt (died 1819) at Handsworth, Birmingham is a masterly exception. Handsworth has other monuments to Watts's associates and great industrial pioneers.

Among non-Anglican churches and chapels the most important is the chapel at Oscott, which was finished by A.W.N.Pugin and which was his first major work. The Oratory Church on the Hagley Road, Birmingham, is an expensive Roman-style building erected in 1903–09 as a memorial to Cardinal Newman. The Catholic church at Wootton Wawen of 1813 is an imposing building too. Free Church buildings, of course, tend to be much plainer. The Gothic Baptist Chapel at Umberslade near Nuthurst, however, is the most lavish Free Church building in the county. The Umberslade Chapel was built by George Ingall of Birmingham in 1877 for the wealthy industrialist, G.F. Muntz. Warwickshire has a number of early Friends' meeting houses with that at Ettington, from the 1680s, being a particularly good and complete example. Other examples are Shipston-on-Stour (of c 1690 and now a library), Warwick (High Street, 1695) and Tredington, Armscote (1725). The earliest Baptist chapel is at Alcester (c 1736) and is attached to a later chapel. The only Presbyterian, later Congregational, church from the early 18C is at Bedworth (1727).

Several Warwickshire churches and chapels have links with famous people. The most obvious is Stratford and Shakespeare, followed closely by St. Mary's, Warwick and the Beauchamp Earls. Another famous figure associated with Warwick is the legendary Guy, a pre-Conquest Earl of Warwick who undertook heroic deeds against dragons and fearsome animals. Eventually he went to the Holy Land, slew an evil giant and on his return lived secretly in a cave unbeknown to his wife. At Guy's Cliffe, the chantry chapel of St. Mary Magdalen, now owned by the Freemasons, contains a larger than life-size statue of Guy carved from the solid rock and dating from the early 15C. The chapel was founded in 1422. Literary associations may be traced at the chapels of Arbury Hall and Stoneleigh Abbey. The former is associated with George Eliot and the latter with Jane Austen; they used the chapels as models for their writings. At the school chapel at Rugby there are monuments to many important figures, notably to Thomas Arnold, who was a key figure in shaping public school education in the last century. At Binton the W window is dedicated to Scott of the Antarctic, who in 1908 married the daughter of the Rector. Warwickshire has important connections with modern Catholic history through Oscott College, where Newman was confirmed as a Catholic, and the Oratory Church, where he lived from 1852. Nonconformity in 19C Birmingham was highly important and two key figures were Joseph Chamberlain, whose family worshipped at the church of the Messiah in Broad Street (now demolished), and Robert William Dale, the Congregational minister from 1859 at Carr's Lane Chapel, who played an influential part in the development of Birmingham.

Arbury Hall, *Chapel.* The late 17C chapel is notable for its superb plaster ceiling. The Hall itself was a mansion of c 1580 which has been the home of the Newdigate family since 1586. Apart from the chapel, its other and greater claim to fame is the astonishingly ornate work which makes it one of, if not the, best Gothick building of the late 18C. This work was carried out by Sir Roger Newdigate from c 1750 until just before his death in 1806.

Externally there is nothing to distinguish the chapel, which was created by Sir Richard Newdigate and completed in c 1678. The walls were refaced during Sir Roger's campaigns. The interior is a white, bright rectangle with a black and white marble chequered floor. The great achievement is the plasterwork executed by Edward Martin for £48 plus his expenses. On the ceiling there is an astonishing display of fruit, leaves and flowers, arranged in friezes and swags around a central oval, all in extraordinarily high relief. Either side of the E window are panels containing the Ten Commandments, painted on boards and dated 1631. The triptych reredos is 16C Flemish work and was one of many pieces brought to the Hall by Sir Roger in the late 18C (he did the Grand Tour twice!). The W end does not form part of the same scheme as the main portion of the chapel and was probably altered by Sir Roger. In its W wall there is an open panel with mock organ pipes. The lovely lock on the door dates from c 1680 and was made by John Wilkes of Birmingham.

George Eliot the novelist (Mary Anne Evans), the daughter of the land agent, was born on the estate in 1819. She was well aware of Sir Roger Newdigate's transforming zeal and it appears only thinly disguised in 'Mr. Gilfil's Love Story'.

Astley, *St. Mary the Virgin.* St. Mary's has a most unusual history and an interesting array of features inside. In medieval times it must have been a vast building, for the present nave is only the chancel of the collegiate church founded by Sir Thomas Astley in 1343. This languished from its dissolution in 1545 until 1607–08, when Richard Chamberlayne re-established the building as a parish church and built the present nave and tower, no doubt reusing old materials.

From a casual glance one would not suspect all this, because the tower is a fairly convincing Perpendicular structure. More closely examined, its details are not totally authentic, and the two-bay chancel with mixed Gothic windows is too small for a normal medieval piece. The W windows are rather Gothick in spirit and the broad openwork of the parapets is post-medieval. It is dated prominently '1608' on the S and is dwarfed by the mighty 'nave'. This has three bays, each with a window of fine flowing tracery. In its E gable is a rose window and, below, the remains of a vast Perpendicular E window. Traces of the doorways to the vanished collegiate buildings can be seen.

The interior is an impressive unaisled space. One is immediately struck by the remnants of the former seven-light E window over the chancel arch, flanked by two niches. The chancel, covered by a panelled Gothick plaster vault which one would normally expect to be later than 1608, is intimate in comparison. But the greatest interest lies in the stalls which date from c 1400. There are 18 under a broad frieze, each one with a fringe of cusping above and divided from its neighbour by a thin shaft. The backs have a remarkable collection of paintings: on the N, Apostles and on the S, Prophets. Each bears a scroll on which the medieval inscription was overwritten by a goodly text in 1624. On the walls is a further collection of Biblical texts, the Lord's Prayer, Creed and, in the chancel, the Ten Commandments. The pulpit and lectern have good detail and seem to be of the late 17C. The rest of the seating seems 17C too, though plainer and somewhat reorganised later. On the N are fragments of medieval glass. The reredos is a Flemish triptych of c 1600 depicting the Descent from the Cross. Three good medieval alabaster figures lie in the tower space: they are probably Sir Edward Grey, Lord Ferrers (died 1457); Elizabeth Talbot, the wife of Edward Grey, Lord Lisle (died c 1483); and Cecily Bonneville, wife of Sir Thomas Grey, Marquess of Dorset (died c 1530). On the N wall of the nave is a monument to Robert Freeman (died 1855), chaplain to the army before Sebastopol.

N of the church are the remains of the moated Astley Castle, owned by the Grey family of Leicestershire, to which Lady Jane Grey belonged.

Berkswell, *St. John the Baptist.* There are many items of interest here but pride of place must go to the *two* crypts. They are Norman and like the chancel, which is long by 12C standards, they imply an importance about Berkswell at which we can now only guess. Nearby is the well of Berkswell, a 'large spring which boileth up on the south side of the churchyard' (Dugdale) and which was restored in 1851.

The Norman chancel, like much of the church, is built of red sandstone in squarish blocks. At each corner are two half-round buttresses and halfway down the sides is a similar one. The windows are set above a stringcourse and in the E wall there are three of them, with two more small ones in the gable. The main windows are shafted and the central one in the E wall has waterleaf capitals. Assuming these are faithful to the original ornament, they indicate a date of c 1170–80. On each side there are flat 'buttresses' below the stringcourse which widen below and embrace further windows at ground level. These are related to the crypt and suggest that the chancel and crypt were planned together. The other exciting feature outside is the 16C S porch, a two-storey structure, the jettied upper part of which has closely-set studding, side windows and a gable just like that in many a cottage. It is entered by an external stair. The S aisle is 14C (with renewed windows), the plain, unbuttressed W tower is late 15C and the N aisle was rebuilt in the same century. The clerestory seems post-medieval (?17C). The church is entered through a reset Norman S doorway, again with a waterleaf capital.

The internal floor rises towards the E, reflecting the height of the crypts beneath. Access to the E crypt was by doorways low down on either side of the chancel arch, as was common for the circulation of pilgrims. There is, however, no record of Berkswell as a place of pilgrimage and, furthermore, there is no appreciable wear on the steps. The real surprise is the W crypt, octagonal in shape and lying beneath the E bay of the nave. It is wider than the E crypt, reflecting the slightly greater width of the nave compared with that of the chancel. The two-bay E crypt is the earlier as can plainly be seen at the junction between the two. The end of the W crypt has been butted up to existing walling and moulding. The latter turns N–S and, from what can be seen through the aperture cut in the SE face of the W crypt, there is a stretch of masonry predating the octagon. What does all this mean? The idea of an octagonal crypt is paralleled in pre-Conquest work as at St. Augustine's, Canterbury. But the Berkswell example is emphatically not pre-Conquest. Both crypts have rib-vaults, with chamfered ribs on short wall shafts. In the W one there appears waterleaf detailing, again reasserting a late 12C date. The octagon is usually suggested as perhaps a reworking of a pre-Conquest plan and there is a reference in Leland in the mid-16C that Berkswell was the burial place of St. Milred, Bishop of Worcester, who died in 772. More recently it was suggested that there may have been a relic of St. Mildred, Abbess of Minster-in-Thanet, Kent (died 725), obtained by the Mercian King Aethelbald, who (Leland says) had a palace nearby and who was a kinsman of St. Mildred. Excavations in the 19C showed what could have been the base of a shrine in the middle of the octagon. Perhaps there was a plan to turn a pre-Conquest octagon into a square space that was abandoned, and then it was totally remodelled instead. Low stone seats run round the walls of the crypts and painting at the E end of the E crypt suggests its use as a chapel in late medieval times. The W crypt does have an effect above ground in the planning of the nave. The two Norman bays on the N stop short just before the octagon, as it was obviously intended to light it from outside. Expansion took place in the 14C when a chapel was thrown out and linked to the N aisle. Of similar date is the S aisle and three-bay arcade. Note the somewhat unusual capitals with demi-octagonal lobes set on plain, octagonal piers. The chancel was restored in 1909 by W.D. Caroë.

Some 18C box-pews and open seats remain. Over the S aisle is a gallery, converted in c 1983 into a room which can be curtained off. The N and W galleries have gone. Perpendicular one-light parclose screenwork survives. Parts of the barrel-vaulted timber roof in the chancel are medieval. There are two monuments of some distinction in the chancel: Lady Eardley, signed by John Bacon, 1795, and Mrs. Elizabeth Eardley-Wilmot (died 1818) by Sir Richard Westmacott. This has two lovely angels embracing and clothed in drapery of ethereal lightness.

Binley, *St. Bartholomew.* This is a gem of a church, built in 1771–73 by Lord Craven. Unfortunately his architect is not known. The plan is a rectangular nave and chancel, with a semicircular apse for the sanctuary, plus a N chapel and vestibule for the Craven family. The W entrance is through a portico flanked by Tuscan columns *in antis* and over this is an octagonal bell turret and a cupola. On the N the Cravens had their own columned portico. The real delight is inside and this must be what led the irascible Lord Torrington to say the church was 'built in the Venetian ballroom taste'. The most striking thing is the segmental tunnel-vault, decorated with floral garlands and medallions of figures. These details are picked out in white against a recent blue background, just like a piece of blue Wedgwood (previously, light green and pink were the main colours). Flanking the entrance to the sanctuary are pairs of marble columns (cf. between the Craven chapel and nave), with details reminiscent of Robert Adam. The altar is interesting in that it is curved, following the apse, and is made of a thin slab of marble. In the E window is enamelled glass of 1776 by William Peckitt of York. He had done much to revive coloured glass and he did work for York Minster, and for Lincoln and Exeter Cathedrals. It is brightly coloured and depicts the Virgin and Child in late 18C garb. The W gallery is routine but has a very early use of cast-iron columns.

Birmingham

The medieval parish of Birmingham was fairly insignificant and had for its mother church St. Martin's in the Bull Ring. In the early 18C, the estates on the NW had been developed sufficiently for the building of Thomas Archer's ambitious Baroque church of St. Philip (1711–25), which became the cathedral in 1905. Later came Roger Eykyns' new chapel of St. Paul, a little further out, a rectangular Classical building with a tower and spire over the W entrance and galleries round three sides. Further Anglican churches were added in the 18C and early 19C and a great many more in Victorian times. A particularly good example of a Commissioners' church is Holy Trinity in Camp Hill, Bordesley, built in 1820–22 by Francis Goodwin, and now a shelter for the homeless. It is an ambitious Perpendicular rectangle and, in line with a brief fashion, has cast-iron tracery throughout. J.L. Pearson's St. Alban's, Bordesley and W.H. Bidlake's St. Agatha's, Sparkbrook are Victorian masterpieces.

Birmingham has a strong Nonconformist tradition and many chapels of all denominations were added. The two key figures during the latter part of the 19C were Joseph Chamberlain and R. W. Dale. Dr. Dale became minister at Carr's Lane Chapel in 1853 and was a friend and supporter of Chamberlain, the Radical politician, who was a Unitarian. Chamberlain played a key role in Birmingham's politics in the 1860s and 1870s, served as Mayor in 1873–76, became an MP in 1876 and went on to a distinguished national political career. Dale's church has now been replaced by a functional structure of c 1970 and Chamberlain's Church of the Messiah in Broad Street has also been demolished and a nondescript modern edifice has been put up nearby instead.

There are two Catholic centres of national importance, Oscott College on the N and the Oratory on the Hagley Road to the W.

St. Martin. Now surrounded by the bleak modernity that characterises so much of Birmingham, St. Martin's is the mother church of the city. Today the rock-faced sandstone church appears as an ambitious Victorian evocation of the 14C, with lots of external crocketing, gabling, friezes and Decorated windows. There was a large church here in the 13C which occupied the present plan of the nave, aisles, NW tower and had two crypts (under the nave and under the W end of the S aisle). In 1690 it was cased in brick apart from the spire. Work to restore the church to a more acceptable appearance started in 1853–55, when P.C. Hardwick restored the steeple, note his outdoor pulpit on the N. This is not a happy composition: the angle buttresses are over-large and there is lots of frivolously applied ornament. The rest was rebuilt by J.A. Chatwin in 1873–75. He added the transepts. The interior is lofty and has an impressive hammerbeam roof modelled on that of Westminster Hall. The detailing of the interior is all 14C but the overall effect is dark, serious and dull, as so often in the 1870s and 1880s. In the N chancel aisle there are three effigies believed to be members of the de Bermingham family. The oldest (SW), Sir William (c 1325), is a cross-legged knight; Sir Fulk (c 1370) is badly worn; and on the N is Sir John (c 1390), on an alabaster tomb-chest.

Bordesley, St. Alban. St. Alban's, built in 1879–81, is one of several major town churches designed by J.L. Pearson and has many similarities to St. Michael and All Angels', Croydon, designed a little time before. In a poor area, it grew out of a mission church founded in 1865, which was served by J.S. Pollack and his brother Thomas. They were keen ritualists and their church was the centre of disturbances against their activities.

The main features of the exterior are tall lancet and two-light windows, an apsidal E end, a fine W façade, which projects slightly from the nave, a S transept flush with the S chapel and a rather unfortunate, sparely designed tower erected in 1938 by E.F. Reynolds in place of Pearson's steeple, which was never built.

The interior is majestically conceived. It is not very large but the vaulting, the stateliness of the high clerestory windows and the chasteness of the design give it a cathedralesque quality. An ambulatory, divided from the chancel by steeply pointed arches, enhances the air of mystery at the E end. The elevations are divided into three fairly low arches, then a triforium reduced to an openwork parapet with walkway behind, which binds the church together horizontally, and lastly the tall clerestory. On the S is St. Patrick's chapel, where Reservation of the Sacrament was introduced in 1911.

Edgbaston, Oratory Church of the Immaculate Conception. The church lies off the busy Hagley Road, scarcely visible outside but for its copper-covered dome and something of the Renaissance E end. It was built in 1903–09 to the designs of E. Doran Webb as a memorial to Cardinal Newman. The original Oratory was founded in Rome by St. Philip Neri c 1552. Oratories—groups of secular priests—were founded in other countries in the 17C and 18C but their history in England dates from Newman's decision to set up a house at Old Oscott in 1848. This Oratory moved to Edgbaston in 1852. Newman lived here until his death in 1890.

The church is approached through a corridor past a cloister built in the 1860s by Henry Clutton. The interior is big, with shallow transepts, aisles and a dome over the crossing. Very appropriately the atmosphere is Roman, including the use of lintels, not arches, on the tall black and white marble columns. The piers on the nave side are set in slightly and the space between them determines the width of the rest of the church further E. At the E end is a tall, blind apse with mosaic decoration. Mosaics also fill the squinches of the crossing and the walls of the dome. At the W end is a gallery and in the wall of the aisles there is a complex series of openings to altars, confessionals and offices.

Handsworth, St. Mary. The interest at Handsworth is not in the architecture, which is largely the result of 19C remodellings, but that it is the resting place for three of the great pioneers of the Industrial Revolution. Pride of place must go to the beautiful monument to James Watt (1736–1819), set in a purpose-built chapel of 1826 by Thomas Rickman S of the chancel. The son of a Scottish hardware manufacturer, he was a great engineer whose mechanical genius was linked in 1774 to the entrepreneurial skills of Matthew Boulton (1728–1809). At Boulton's Soho Manufactory they developed Watt's application of steam to motive power. Watt's seated figure is by Sir

Francis Chantrey and is a superb composition in white marble, which reveals a great mind in thoughtful contemplation. In the E window contemporary glass includes the Scotch thistle. On the N wall of the chancel is John Flaxman's monument to Boulton who 'improved, embellished, and extended the arts and manufactures of his country'. Below, one of the putti holds a low relief of the Soho Manufactory. The other great pioneer was William Murdock (1754–1839). He was assistant to Watt and the engineer who first applied gas lighting with success in 1782 and was the constructor of the first locomotive. His bust by Chantrey faces that of Boulton. He bears a rather gaunt, anxious expression. An attractive medallion wall monument at the E end of the S aisle is to Sergius Swellengrebel (died 1770), an agent for Boulton's silver goods in the East Indies.

Handsworth Cemetery Chapel. In 1909–10 W.H. Bidlake built this inspired chapel for Handsworth's cemetery: a tall building of immense grace and lightness, built of red brick with stone dressings. The side windows are set high up and are separated by tall buttresses. The E end has a polygonal apse but the W end, with two turrets, is sadly fussy. The interior is a surprise with a ring of high, clustered columns of variegated sandstone set near the walls and carrying tierceron-vaulting. The actual space is quite small but Bidlake creates out of it a cathedralesque quality. At the W end is a glassed-in, traceried screen forming a mortuary area. The infilling of the vaulting is simply red roof tiles laid face outwards—an odd piece of economy in an otherwise sumptuous building.

King's Norton, St. Nicholas. This is a large church in a delightful setting. From the S are two features of real interest, a 15C steeple, rising to 180ft, and the treatment of the S aisle. The tower has four stages, including an especially elaborate belfry stage. The S aisle, a 14C structure, has been crowned by unusual 17C cross-gables with three-light mullioned windows. The chancel was lengthened in the 13C. On the N is a reset Norman window (another is visible below it inside). Are the small square blocks also Norman masonry? The interior, despite a gloomy restoration by W.J. Hopkins in 1872, is impressive for its length and for the large number of arcade arches—seven, with different pier shapes. Hopkins's hammerbeam roof over the nave is impressive in a massive way—and altogether too much for the church! There is good 19C stained glass here. The E window is by C.E. Kempe (1899). The windows in the N aisle are by a local firm, Swaine & Bourne, and the rest, apart from the E window of the S aisle, were by John Hardman in the 1870s. By far the best monument is to Sir Richard Grevis (died 1632) and his wife Ann under the tower.

Northfield, St. Laurence. This red sandstone church has been much restored but is noteworthy for its work of the 13C. This is the date of the lower part of the tower and the most imposing chancel. It is of three bays and has a triple-lancet E window. Inside, the bays are all divided by slender shafts which begin at floor level, and the windows are all shafted and make an elegant display. In the NW corner is a low-side window. There is no chancel arch and what seem to be the boards of a tympanic filling remain in place. The S arcade is 14C and was copied by G. F. Bodley when he added the unassuming N aisle in 1898–1900. Some bits of a 15C screen are reused in the pulpit.

Oscott, St. Mary's College, Chapel. Oscott occupies a special place in the history of English Catholicism and it was the place where

A.W.N. Pugin undertook his first major commission. A Catholic mission had been founded at Old Oscott (now called Maryvale) in the late 17C and there, in 1794, the first students were received. It was the first Catholic school to combine religious and secular education. The present college, now the seminary for the Archdiocese of Birmingham, was founded under Bishop Thomas Walsh with the assistance of the Earl of Shrewsbury. The site was bought in 1835 and building commenced under the Lichfield architect, Joseph Potter. Pugin came on the scene in 1837, having been introduced by Lord Shrewsbury, who had employed him at Alton Towers in Staffordshire. Pugin swept all before him, including Potter, whom he replaced as architect. Most of the structure was complete, so Pugin's contribution was chiefly the internal decoration and the addition of the polygonal apse to the chapel. This is of six bays, built of red brick with four-light Perpendicular sandstone windows, buttressed between the bays and with an embattled parapet. On the S is the Weedall chantry begun in 1861 by E.W. Pugin and eventually completed in 1909.

It is the interior that counts. It was here that Pugin was able to put into practice what he preached in his 'Contrasts' of 1836 and as Professor of Ecclesiastical Antiquities here at Oscott. The chief glory is the decoration. On the panelled nave roof is a blue ground powdered with gold stars and oft-repeated sacred emblems in the centre of each panel. The vault of the sanctuary is also blue with gold stars. Its walls are blue with fleur-de-lis above, while below there are bold red and gold floral designs. On the N wall are paintings of St. Athanasius and St. Leo and on the S St. Gregory and St. Thomas Aquinas. The pulpit is Pugin's and is approached via a stair in the wall. The stalls at the E end of the nave are by Pugin and so is the design of William Warrington's glass in the sanctuary. The complex reredos is also Pugin's design and incorporates Flemish 15C work. The magnificent communion rail (dated 1680 on the right-hand door) came from Louvain and its rich, swirling decoration depicts the Abundance of Life. The florid confessional with its caryatid figures framing the three openings is also a 17C imported piece. What a pity about the incongruous modern stainless-steel-framed altar, chairs and lectern.

In the 1840s Oscott attracted many famous converts to Catholicism and it was here in 1845 that John Henry Newman was confirmed as a Catholic.

(Written applications for admission to the Rector, Oscott College, Chester Road, Sutton Coldfield, B73 5AA.)

Perry Beeches, St. Matthew. When the history of church building in the mid-20C comes to be written, St. Matthew's will occupy an important place in it. It dates from 1962–64 and was designed by Robert Maguire and Keith Murray. The initial impression is of a strange, angular jumble of inclined, lead-covered roofs and wedge-shaped windows round a tall hexagonal core. The walls are of buff brick with thick horizontal concrete bands. Inside, the ingenious simplicity is revealed. The plan is an irregular hexagon and there are no visually divisive elements like piers or screens. An impressively large space is built up stage by stage until, over the altar, there is a towering open void, 47ft up to the eaves. All this is achieved by slicing away the side walls of the hexagon to an ever-increasing height to create a semi-hexagonal space on each face—that is, in the area of the entrance a sixth of the total height is cut away, then two-sixths, then three-sixths and so on, so that, finally, one ends up with the underside of a vast staircase. The brick and concrete bands are reiterated and mark off the ascending stages. All the light falls into the building through the wedge-shaped windows and the narrow bands connecting them. Instead of dispersing the liturgical centres the architects have unified them. Symbolically, the font, built of blue engineering bricks, is placed near the doorway and between it and the altar is what can only be described as the 20C equivalent of a three-decker pulpit. The seating consists of chunky open benches carved from English ash. At St. Matthew's the medieval plan, which endured down to the new Coventry Cathedral, has finally been exorcised. The wonder here is that simplicity of line and materials does not lead to a sterile space, but a very living one, in which grandeur and intimacy are brilliantly fused.

Sparkbrook, St. Agatha. St. Agatha's is one of the finest churches from around the turn of the century. It is also one of the relatively few to show a strong Arts and Crafts influence, and that comes out most strongly in the highly inventive tower. The church is the masterwork of W.H. Bidlake and was built in 1899–1901. Like nearby St. Alban's, it has long been a centre of High Church worship in Birmingham. It consists of a 'W' tower (actually at the E), nave, aisles (which expand into side chapels), chancel, S chapel and vestries on the N. It was severely damaged by bombing at the E end in 1940 and all the woodwork was destroyed in 1959 in a fire started by a 13-year-old arsonist.

The exterior, faced with bluish brick, is scarcely seen apart from the 'W' façade, tower and clerestory. The tympana over the portals depict scenes from the life of St. Agatha: being comforted in prison by St. Peter and being burnt. Then comes a window and next a low-relief sculpture of Christ in Majesty, with adoring angels at a slightly lower level. Then come two twinned Reticulated windows in a short stage and the tall belfry lights with enormous louvres. The tower is capped by a delicate openwork parapet and four open pinnacles. It is Gothic architecture surely enough but a Gothic that is not rooted in any specific period, a melting down of many ideas and recasting them into something new.

The interior is long, light and serene. It is faced with light buff brick with arches and dressings of rather darker buff sandstone. The impression, especially from the 'E', is of a modern version of one of the grander East Anglian Perpendicular churches. The piers are lozenges, much more elongated on the sides to the nave than on those to the aisles. At the E end can be seen slight changes in the colour of the brickwork which marks the difference between the original structure and the rebuilt one after 1959. The altar, one of the finer pieces among modern church fittings, is made of Westmorland slate and rests on a tapering single block.

Coventry

For a city that was perhaps the fifth in medieval England, Coventry has very few medieval parish churches. It seems its prosperous citizens preferred to establish chapels within the two great churches of St. Michael and Holy Trinity, which they remodelled. There were, however, several hospitals and other religious houses, remains of some of which survived the Second World War. They are now surrounded by the dismal buildings that make modern Coventry so depressing. Ecclesiastically, the key event was the founding of the Benedictine priory (just N of Holy Trinity) in 1043 by Leofric, Earl of Chester, and his wife Godiva. The priory was very rich and Coventry was divided into the Prior's Half and the Earl's Half. Holy Trinity was founded before 1113 and served the tenants of the former, whereas St. Michael's served the latter. Both churches are within a few yards of each other. St. Michael's became the main civic church and eventually a cathedral in 1918. St. John's, Bablake became a parish church only in 1734. It had been founded as a collegiate church in 1342 by Queen Isabella. The first church to be built since the Reformation came only in 1830–32 (Christ Church), followed by others in the 1840s.

Holy Trinity. Holy Trinity is a mighty late medieval town church, largely built between the mid-14C and the eve of the Reformation. Of the Norman church which was destroyed by fire in 1257, nothing survives, though its 13C successor is represented by the inner N porch (normally closed, but blocked lancet windows to the N aisle can be seen) and water-holding bases to three of the four arches W of the crossing. The church has a spreading plan with a long chancel (two aisles N), transepts, aisles and a complicated arrangement N of the N aisle where chapels have filled in the angles created by the porch and N transept. The dominant feature is the late medieval tower and spire of 237ft which rival but do not equal the adjacent St. Michael's. The spire and upper part of the tower were rebuilt after falling in a storm on 24th January, 1665: the work seems to have been done in 1666–68. The tower was cased in 1826 by Thomas Rickman and both tower and spire were refaced in 1915–18 by Sir T.G. Jackson in red Woolton sandstone (which is starting to decay again). Much of the rest of the exterior was refaced between 1843 and 1849 by R.C. Hussey in Bath stone, which is rather out of place in sandstone Coventry. Outside, Holy Trinity shows Perpendicular work of various types (but the E window is of 1854), including a clerestory which continues with nine closely-set bays in the chancel. The latest pre-Reformation addition was the Marler chapel as an outer chancel aisle, c 1530. A curious feature is the flight of steps between the S aisle and transept. This gave access to the S transept because until 1834 a public passageway passed under it. The reason seems to be the building of Jesus Hall against the S transept in c 1500 and the need to maintain a thoroughfare.

The impressive scale of the church can best be appreciated inside. The nave has four bays; the chancel, 16ft longer than the nave, has four arched bays plus the sanctuary. Rebuilding of the nave seems to have occurred in the late 14C. The chancel was intended to be rebuilt with an extension 24ft E in 1391, but all the present work is later. At the W end of the chancel two 13C arches have been left in place (with rebuilt jambs), presumably to avoid disturbance of the tower. The crossing is a most impressive space: above the arches are three panelled stages, two of which flood the area with light. The vaulting is of wood and was put in by Sir Gilbert Scott in 1854–55; its painting is now sadly deteriorated. On the E wall of the nave is a blackened Doom, discovered in 1831. The late Perpendicular pulpit is an interesting piece, of stone, attached to the SE crossing pier at an unusually high level. The stalls from the Whitefriars have a variety of misericords. The brass eagle lectern is medieval too. It survived the Commonwealth by being turned into a collecting box (coins in the beak, emptied through the tail). The W window has impressive but very brightly coloured glass by Hugh Easton, dedicated in 1955. Sir Ninian Comper's E window, also completed in 1955, depicts the Crucifixion but is lifeless and conventional (although with well-drawn figures) in comparison.

George Eliot, the novelist, attended this church from 1840 to 1849, where her father was a sidesman.

St. John the Baptist. St. John's is a tall, compressed building of red sandstone that presents an almost entirely Perpendicular appearance. It started with a grant of land in 1344 by Queen Isabella, widow of King Edward II, to the Guild of St. John the Baptist for building a chantry chapel for the soul of her husband, other members of the royal family and the Guild members. It was dedicated in 1350 and at that time there were two chaplains. In 1357 provision was made for a S aisle and, when this was built, the chapel perhaps covered the area of the present chancel and S chapel. Building work continued to the end of the century and beyond. What we see today is essentially the work of the 15C and early 16C, during which time the number of priests increased considerably so that by 1461 there were a warden, 11 priests and two clerks to serve five altars. The piecemeal nature of the work is clear on close inspection. After sporadic use following the suppression of the college in 1548, it eventually became a parish church in 1734.

The church has a late example of a central tower. At the corners it has the rare feature of bartizans. Also unusual are the tall clerestory windows in the chancel and on the S of the nave. The N side has 14C Reticulated ones, reused. The windows are mostly Perpendicular of various designs though the E one is Gilbert Scott's (restorations of 1858–61 and 1875–77). Apart from tracery renewal, Scott replaced the embattled parapets on the chancel, S chapel, S transept and tower. He added the flying buttress on the S of the nave, allegedly in accordance with archaeological evidence. To start to appreciate the fragmented nature of the medieval building campaigns one should look at the S transept. Its big eight-light S window has no relation to what happens below, though this is not the case to the N, and it seems that the idea of the tall transepts occurred after the aisles were already in existence. There is more of such evidence inside.

First, it is clear that the nave and chancel are not on the same axis, because presumably when the nave was planned it had to be turned a little N to stop it encroaching on the street. Also the S aisle windows are not in line with the arcade arches, the E and W crossing piers differ in detail (the E ones provide for vaulting), and the E and W windows high up in the transepts have to accommodate the slope of the aisle roofs. Unfortunately, the bare sandstone gives a drab, unkempt appearance to what is otherwise a fine interior. It is likely that the only 14C parts to survive are the S wall of the S aisle, the masonry low down in the S chapel, the lowest course of the W wall of the church and part of the N wall of the Lady chapel. It seems that the remodelling began at the W end and proceeded E. The screen is of 1886 by John Oldrid Scott and the Rood group was added in 1908.

Hospital of St. John the Baptist, Hales Street. A short walk E of St. John's is all that remains of the Hospital of St. John the Baptist. This 14C red sandstone chapel served a hospital founded in the 12C. After the dissolution of the hospital in 1544, it housed the Free Grammar School until 1885. At some stage after the dissolution the two-bay S aisle was demolished. The W end was shortened in the late 18C and the big W window with its clumsy flowing tracery dates from that time. There is no internal division between the nave and chancel and a plaster tunnel-vault, no doubt from the 18C, runs along both.

Great Packington, *St. James.* In the 700-acre park surrounding Packington Hall there stands one of the most remarkable churches in England—remarkable for the originality of its architecture and for the circumstances under which it was built. The work of replacing the medieval church was begun in 1789 by the fourth Earl of Aylesford to commemorate King George III's return to health. It was completed in 1790. The plan is a cross-in-square, rare in the late 18C but known within the work of Wren. 18C church exteriors could be quite simple but here the design is carried to the point of uncompromising bluntness and yet the interior is a masterpiece of serene beauty. Use is made of Greek architectural elements in a way that is unprecedented, yet the overall style cannot be conventionally categorised. Marcus Binney ('Country Life', Vol. 150 (1972), pp 110–15) described it as one of the very first truly international buildings of the neo-Classical movement. He shows that the inspirational force

St. James's by Joseph Bonomi, 1789–90, built for the fourth Earl of Aylesford

behind it was almost certainly Lord Aylesford himself, who had a deep interest in architecture, was a talented artist and had known Classical buildings at first hand in Italy. Binney suggests that Lord Aylesford incorporated the architectural elements that most fascinated him. The task of welding them together was probably undertaken by the architect, Joseph Bonomi, who was perhaps responsible for the plan. But to Lord Aylesford we must almost certainly attribute the Greek Revival elements, notably the massive Doric columns inside which carry arches for the first time in English architecture. This idea, like several others, was probably modelled after the Baths of Diocletian in Rome.

The outside walls are red brick. There is not a great deal of difference in the treatment of each face. The E end has a vestry projecting at the NE corner and only a blind arch in place of the big lunette windows on the other faces. These windows are sliced into three by plain brick mullions, another idea taken from the Baths of Diocletian. The cross-in-square plan is marked out by the small square towers over each corner space; each tower carries a low lead dome. In the centre of each face is a large sandstone pediment, broken at the bottom by the windows. Underneath the church is a crypt, apparently designed for storage.

If the outside is worldly and functional, the interior conveys spiritual calm and strength. Despite the massive constructions at the corners of the central space and the vaulting throughout, it is anything but heavy. Off the nave open the sanctuary, the 'transepts' (for seating) and the vestibule, through which one enters from the W. All the arches are round. How the corner spaces were originally used is not clear and they seem to have been the functionless consequences of the plan. The font was originally central and why the vestry was not placed in one of the corners instead of detracting from the external symmetry is strange. The most conspicuous features are the enormous fluted Doric sandstone columns at the corners of the central space (cf. the columns before the sanctuary in the Catholic chapel at Wootton Wawen). These powerful columns have exaggerated entasis and were an astonishing idea in 1789. Above them is a bulky triglyph frieze. Originally there was a W gallery.

The costliness of this interior is reflected in the fittings, notably the altarpiece. This has marble Corinthian columns and pediment and, in the centre, a painting of the Ascension by J.F. Rigaud, who also worked at the Hall, died there in 1810 and was buried in the churchyard. Before it stands the marble communion rail with balusters. The pulpit is extraordinary for its time: it is also of marble and its three sides carry the IHS symbol, the cross and XPI. It could pass more easily as a piece from the 1850s rather than from 1790. The organ is a beautifully toned instrument and came to the church from Gopsall Hall, Leicestershire, via Packington Hall, where it arrived in 1773. It was originally built in c 1750 by Thomas Parker for Charles Jennens of Gopsall to a specification by Handel.

Hampton Lucy, *St. Peter ad Vincula.* Built in 1822–26 by Thomas Rickman and Henry Hutchinson for John Lucy, this is one of the grandest essays in Gothic church building early in the 19C. They took their Gothic seriously but not in a heavy-handed way. The church has a tall tower, nave and aisles, all in a Decorated style and with lots of openwork parapets and friezes. Sir Gilbert Scott added a polygonal apse in 1858, each face under a gable, and all following in a sensitive fashion what had been built before. The interior, plaster-vaulted in its 1820s part, impresses by its gracious verticality and by the ring of large windows at the E end. The E window glass was adapted from the 1837 schemes by Thomas Willement, showing the life of St. Peter (a very early date for so major a scheme).

Knowle, *St. John the Baptist, St. Lawrence and St. Anne.* In a large attractive churchyard in the centre of Knowle stands this large, stately and entirely Perpendicular church. In 1396 Walter Cook, a native of Knowle, founded a chapel here, which was consecrated in 1402 and additions to which were made in c 1412. In 1416 it became collegiate and further additions were probably made then. It is faced with red and grey sandstone, though at the E end is some rubbly marly stone (once stuccoed), which may be from the earliest phase. There are big windows throughout, those in the chancel being particularly tall. Interestingly, the E bay of the chancel is canted in. Below it there was a passageway presumably used for processions in medieval times. Why it was needed is something of a mystery, since there seems to be plenty of land to the E. It was blocked in the 1740s.

The substantial early 15C Perpendicular St. John the Baptist's. Both S aisle and S clerestory have buttresses, pinnacles and three-light windows

Inside, the lack of a chancel arch emphasises the length. The nave has five narrow arches on either side. In the chancel the elevated position of the sedilia and piscina reflects the subway beneath. Oddly there are traces of other sedilia and a piscina near the W end of the chancel (what phase did they belong to?). There are a number of simple misericords and an elaborate, vaulted screen. On the pulpit is a most attractive hourglass from the late 17C. The church also possesses two dug-out chests.

Lapworth, *St. Mary the Virgin.* Here there is a most curious plan and many intriguing details. The most obvious feature is that the 14C tower was detached on the N, there being insufficient room between the Norman nave and the road. It is linked to the church by a renewed corridor. The other rare feature is the W 'porch' of two storeys, with a processional way beneath, but which probably served as a relic chamber. Then there are the highly odd low windows along the S wall of the S aisle. Outwardly the greatest display is the Perpendicular work with its large, four-bay clerestory and battlements.

At this church it is best to start inside. It has grown from a compact Norman nave, one window of which probably survives at the NE end. Then in the 13C came the N chapel (still with a round arch) and the arcades starting with the N. The bays are very narrow, caused by the squeezing in of four rather than three. On the N the arches are acutely pointed; all the capitals and bases have slight variations of detail. It does not seem to have been built all at the same time and the W arch particularly seems to have been awkwardly rebuilt. The S arcade is more harmonious and all of one build. The chancel arch, widened in medieval times, perhaps has reused 12C responds. The chancel contains basically 13C fabric, though the S wall was probably rebuilt in the early 14C, when the two short, wide, three-light windows were put in. The S wall of the S aisle is puzzling. Towards the W are two short broad lancets set low down and further E are two more 13C blocked windows. Above these, low spreading Perpendicular windows with foliated hoodmoulds have been put in. Presumably the lowness of the windows arises from the fact that the 13C roof came very low down. The 14C tower is not attractive in its details. At the NW corner is an ungainly octagonal stair turret. At the W end is the most interesting feature of all. Its function can only be guessed at, but on the ground stage there are two doorways which lead to spiral staircases. One would have been for going up, the other down. There was no access to the church and it seems highly likely on the evidence of the staircases that a relic or relics were displayed and the arrangements were to allow the free passage of pilgrims. There is now a stairway down into the church through one of two tall lancets in the W wall of the nave.

It is a modern monument that is of interest among the furnishings and fittings: a wall tablet by Eric Gill, 1928, to Florence Bradshaw (died 1922) of the 'mater amabilis', a tender but unsentimental low relief of the Virgin and Child.

Merevale, St. Mary the Virgin. The interest about this church is its relationship to the monastic site, its strange plan, glass and pulpitum. The Cistercian Abbey of Merevale was founded in 1148 by Robert, Earl Ferrers and lay to the E. The present church is likely to have been a chapel near the entrance to the abbey with a substantial chancel for the monks and a small nave for the lay brethren and parishioners. The architectural history can be traced back to the mid-13C when the chancel and nave seem to have been as long as they are now. The suggestion that they were erected while the abbey church was being rebuilt is plausible enough but they clearly remained of much importance since there was large and expensive remodelling in the early 14C and c 1500.

The visitor approaches through a gatehouse of c 1840 by Henry Clutton and Edward Blore and is faced by a towerless structure, a short two-bay nave that has lost its aisles—probably in the 18C—and a long chancel with a four-bay N aisle and with small-scale late Perpendicular details. Over the junction between nave and chancel is a modern bell turret and clock. Working anti-clockwise, the W end of the mid-13C nave is clearly revealed in the doorway and grouped triple-lancet above. It is clear that the old S aisle roof came low down and the Reticulated W window of the chancel S aisle stood above it. On the S of the aisle are three richly detailed flowing windows of c 1340. The ugly SE buttress is 18C. At the E end can be seen traces of the original chancel. The big modern buttresses incorporate the lower parts of the old thin ones. The N aisle is from the remodelling of c 1500 and has prominent, tall pinnacles.

The arcades of the mid-13C are clearly seen inside. The piers are octagonal and low. Above the capitals is a short vertical piece into which the double-chamfered arches die. The chancel arch also is mid-13C and over it there is a circular window that has lost any tracery or glazing. It is hard to see that it was ever an outside window. Beyond the chancel arch the church opens out and is dominated by the remodelling of c 1500. The piers have a slender lozenge-section with thin mouldings and diminutive capitals. From the valleys vertical pieces rise up to a corbel course that runs level with the tops of the arches. In the N aisle, wall shafts rise the full height of the walls through the springing of the roof.

One of the great treasures is the 14C Jesse window set in the later E window. During the Civil War it was taken out; it was discovered in the grounds of the Hall in the 19C and much of it is glass of that time. There are 15 figures. The second row has David (with harp), Solomon (with sword), and Hezekiah (with sceptre). Malachi and Moses are on either side. Christ is in the centre of the top row, flanked by a king and, in the other lights, a prophet. The figures of Jesse himself and the Virgin are missing. The tracery lights above contain 15C glass. Further medieval glass is to be found in the N aisle. In the tracery lights are various figures of c 1500 including the risen Christ appearing to St. Mary Magdalene, St. Peter, St. Stephen, St. Margaret, and St. Anne teaching the Virgin to read. In the SW window is further ancient glass (14C). The other great survival is the 15C pulpitum, now at the W end. There is no particular reason to believe that it came from the abbey church because it could have stood quite satisfactorily in front of the chancel arch: the returned parts of the loft are carved and could have been visible in the E arches of the nave. Over the entrance is a projecting part, perhaps for an organ. It was presumably transferred to the W end after the Reformation to act as a gallery. In the chancel is a brass with a pair of figures of c 1400. They may be Robert, Earl Ferrers (died 1412) and Margaret his wife. On the N of the nave is a very fine though headless and feetless effigy of a cross-legged knight from the mid-13C in chain armour and a long surcoat. On the S is a tomb-chest with an alabaster knight and lady of c 1440. It may be the tomb of William, Earl Ferrers and his wife Elizabeth.

Rugby School, *Chapel.* Rugby School has a stunning chapel, built in 1867–72 by William Butterfield and replacing a chapel of 1818–21 by Henry Hakewill. The top of the tower (1883) and two bays of the nave were added later. The chapel shows the powerful and inventive force of mid-Victorian architecture and is a marked contrast to the timid First World War chapel of 1920–23 by Sir Charles Nicholson to the S.

To appreciate the chapel best one should stand on the playing fields. The building is full of complexity and angular detail. There is tension between the horizontal dimension, represented by the polychrome striping in the red and buff bricks and stone, and the vertical, represented by the tall windows and tower. It is not immediately obvious how the building hangs together and to understand it one needs to go inside. The tower squats over the chancel and to the

E is a projecting sanctuary (the plan Butterfield had used 20 years before at St. Matthias', Stoke Newington). Around the sanctuary the buttresses are pierced below, not for processional use but for the drain gulley. The tower has big buttresses, above which are broaches which turn the square tower into an octagon. These tops of the buttresses are covered with a scaly motif, popular with Butterfield. The belfry windows are tall and span both the tower and octagonal top. This has a ring of three-light, square-headed windows covered by a short, scaly spire from which gargoyles thrust outward. Further W on the chapel is a short projection and then two transept bays under gables. W from these is a short nave and it is clear on close examination that the detailing is a little less strident than the remainder. The reason is that it was built much later, being completed in 1898. The architect was T.G. Jackson, working under the approval of the then aged Butterfield.

The interior, which is tall and a striking comment on the confidence of Victorian religion in public schools, continues some of the themes from the exterior—its large scale, original detailing and the use of polychromy. However, there is practically no trace of the tower, only two arches, which explains the need for the large buttresses outside. Between these two arches are further diaphragm arches, a relatively early use of this motif in 19C architecture. The chapel is long but there is also a major accent on the central area in the region of the transepts, which forms a focus for the seating. The three arches to the transepts are carried on very tall polychrome piers, somewhat set back from the line of the nave walls. Over the apse is a mosaic of 1883 by Salviati of Venice. The roof over the nave and central area is a bold and complex one with both hammerbeams and tiebeams luridly painted in black and white.

The windows are all glazed. The following list proceeds from the nave and round the N side. N side: Crimean window, by John Hardman, commemorating 33 Rugbeians who died. Opposite is the Indian mutiny window, again by Hardman, and commemorates 27 dead. Christ before Pilate is 16C Continental glass. On the N is Christ after the Resurrection, which was brought from Aerschott near Louvain by Thomas Arnold to the old chapel in 1836. W wall of the N transept: left light by Hardman, central one (Christ blessing) by William Wailes, right by Wailes and Hardman. The Thomas window is by Thomas Willement and was originally installed in 1842. The four small windows in the apse are of 1872, designed by Butterfield and executed by Alexander Gibbs. The E window was the first that Arnold brought from abroad and came from Aerschott in 1834. On the S is the South African memorial window, 1904, by H. Dearle and executed by Morris & Co. The Presentation in the Temple is said to have come from Rouen in 1839. Two further windows on the S are by Gibbs, designed by Butterfield. The E.M. Goulburn window is by C.E. Kempe. In the S aisle are four windows by Morris & Co. The great W window of 1902 was designed by H. Dearle and was made by Morris & Co. It depicts the reunion in Paradise of kindred and friends.

There are innumerable memorials to former Rugbeians. Dr. Thomas James (Headmaster, 1778–94) is by Sir Francis Chantrey (1824), showing him seated and with the busts of Virgil and Homer. Opposite is Dr. Wooll (Headmaster 1806–29), by Richard Westmacott, Jr, again seated. Dr. Thomas Arnold (died 1842) reclines beneath a late Gothic canopy.

Thomas Arnold came as Headmaster in 1828 and his example did much to regenerate public school education. He embodied and inculcated so many of what we regard as typical Victorian values—strong religious belief, a belief in morality and duty, the stress on Classical education in moulding the youthful mind to the proper pattern. The stone beneath the lectern marks his vault. His eldest son was Matthew Arnold, the poet (memorial on N side). Another memorial on the N is to Matthew Holbeche Bloxam (died 1888), who was an important writer on church architecture.

Solihull, *St. Alphege.* Solihull is a big, prosperous town on the SE edge of Birmingham and has a large and distinguished red sandstone church. It has a crossing tower, nave, aisles, transepts and chancel with a N chapel attached at the E end. Most of the structure dates from the last quarter of the 13C and the very early years of the 14C.

The plan may have a Norman origin but the bulk of the tower now dates from the 13C and early 14C, except for the belfry stage and its spire. The spire, rising to 168ft, was rebuilt after being blown down in 1757. The great attraction of the exterior is the chancel and its N chapel which were put up in the late 13C. They have most attractive windows due to the ingenious cusps. The chancel is high, the reason for which is apparent inside. The N aisle is 14C, but the W end and the S aisle were remodelled or built in the 16C, and a precise date, 1535, is known.

The nave is 16C and has five tall bays with octagonal piers. Just W of the tower the walling of the nave is from a much earlier phase, hence the Norman window traces on the S. There have been problems with the stability of the arcades and flying buttresses have been inserted within the aisles to stabilise them. The chancel is very spacious and has an attractive stringcourse which runs round the windows and which is formed into blind trefoils between them. On the N it is evident that the N chapel is in two storeys. Below is a two-bay crypt with a simple rib-vault and steps down to it. The chapel has the attractive feature of windows between it and the chancel and containing the same tracery as the other chancel windows.

The church still has two medieval stone altar slabs, one in the N chapel and the other at the E end of the S aisle. The sedilia in the chancel are curious, consisting simply of three stepped stone seats and it is hard to imagine how canopies could have existed without major interference with the window above. At the E end of the S aisle is a Perpendicular stone reredos with a row of panelling. Another reredos, of wood, is in the N aisle and probably dates from c 1700. The communion rails are exceedingly elaborate, late 17C in date with twisted balusters and lots of rich foliage. Further old woodwork exists in the 15C screen to the N transept and in the pulpit of 1610. There is a good window of c 1901 by C.E. Kempe, showing the Resurrection and post-Resurrection appearances.

Stoneleigh Abbey, *Chapel.* This is the finest example of a private chapel within a stately home in Warwickshire (Compton Wynyates and Capability Brown's chapel at Compton Verney are detached). It lies within the S part of the magnificent W range built in 1714–26 by Francis Smith of Warwick for the third Lord Leigh of the first creation. The house itself takes its name from the Cistercian abbey founded in 1154.

Externally the 18C chapel has no distinguishing features. It occupies the two lower storeys of the new wing and is much larger than the rather earlier chapel at Arbury. Its most notable feature is the decorative plasterwork, probably completed in the 1770s by Francis Smith's nephew, William, and a local craftsman, John Wright. The wall treatment is quite restrained with light surrounds to the four windows and panels of sharply wrought decoration. The *tour-de-force* is the ceiling, the centrepiece of which is a huge rayed IHS symbol with cherubs surrounding it. At the 'E' (= S) end, amid much trumpet-blowing, is a Resurrection scene with extraordinarily crude perspective. Note the all-seeing eye of God in a triangle. At the 'W' end is a strangely inept Hope and Anchor. The ceiling depends for its effect on its total impression, even though the details often do not bear scrutiny. The pew in the 'SE' corner is the Leigh family pew.

The Leigh family has occupied Stoneleigh Abbey since it was bought in 1561 by Sir Thomas Leigh, a wealthy London merchant. The chapel was used by Jane Austen as a model for Southerton chapel in 'Mansfield Park'. She visited Stoneleigh in 1806 with her mother, who had been born into a branch of the Leigh family.

Stratford-upon-Avon

Holy Trinity. It is the grave of William Shakespeare that brings so many people to this church, delightfully situated on the banks of the Avon. It is also a building of some architectural distinction and dates from the early 13C to the late 18C. Exaggerated claims on behalf of its beauty and content in popular guides, however, should be treated with a little circumspection! In the later Middle Ages it was collegiate, following the foundation of a chantry in the chapel of St. Thomas the Martyr in 1331 in the S aisle by John de Stratford, later Bishop of Winchester.

The approach is either along the river bank or down a fine avenue of lime trees from the road. All the periods of its development can be seen outside. The earliest work is in the transepts whose lancet windows indicate a large cruciform structure of the early 13C. The lower stage of the crossing tower is also 13C, and has twinned lights with a shaft between. Above comes 14C work with unusual (renewed) circular windows. The spire is much later, having been built in 1763 by William Hiorn of Warwick to replace a wooden one. It was rebuilt again in 1867 by Joseph Latimer. The 14C work was even more extensive in the body of the church. The work in the aisles seems to date from the second quarter of the century on the basis of the window evidence. It is the chancel that is the most striking part of all, and it is part of the Perpendicular works, being rebuilt by Dean Thomas Balshall (died 1491). The side walls have five large graceful windows of four transomed lights, divided by buttresses with ornate tops. In the E window are seven lights with restrained but by no means severe tracery. On the NE wall are the faint traces of a structure demolished in 1799. This is shown in an old picture as a two-storeyed building and it served in its lower part as a charnel house. Elsewhere the 15C added the clerestory of 12 large windows (two per bay), the W window and two-storeyed N porch.

As one stands in the W part of the nave four things are striking: the brightly-lit spaciousness of the nave, the fact that its axis is markedly different from that of the chancel, that none of the work one can see is prior to the 14C, and that one is in perhaps the most-visited (and most-commercialised) parish church in the land. Everything W of the crossing was rebuilt in the 14C, a scheme which involved the remodelling of the base of the tower too, though there is clear external evidence that the tower dates from the 13C. Unusually the piers are hexagonal. There was much remodelling when the clerestory was put in late in the 15C—hence the panelling over the arches and the triple shafts rising from the valleys of the arches. There is a little evidence of the 13C but one has to stand inside the N transept (now a vestry). In both E and W walls are the N responds of the 13C arches which must be contemporaneous with the lancets seen outside. They suggest very narrow aisles to the nave and chancel. The chancel is lit by the big windows and contains a rich display of ornamentation to the window heads, panelling between the windows and a fine four-centred doorway in the second bay from the E on the N. This led to the charnel house. Its hoodstops are huge: the W one with a St. Christopher, the E one, symbolically, with Christ rising from the tomb.

The most interesting furnishings are the stalls. They have 26 misericords with a wide variety of carvings including a domestic quarrel, a merman and mermaid, the unicorn and virgin, etc. The screen into the N transept is original 15C work. In the chancel stands the mutilated Perpendicular font, returned to the church in 1823, in which it is reasonably presumed that Shakespeare was baptised. The fine organ case stands (over?) prominently at the E end of the nave and is by Bodley & Garner, who restored the church in 1888–92. In the S window of the S transept is the 'American window', unveiled in 1896 by the American Ambassador as a gift from his nation; it includes figures from England and the New World.

On 23rd April, 1616 William Shakespeare died at the age of 52 and was buried in the chancel just beyond the altar rails, towards the N. Above his grave is a short verse, said to have been penned by Shakespeare himself:

Good friend for Jesus sake forbeare
To digg the dust encloased heare
Bleste be the man that spares thes stones
And curst be he that moves my bones.

On the wall to the N is Shakespeare's monument by Gerard Johnson. Below is a long Latin inscription and above, two cherubs sit beside an achievement of arms. Between two marble Corinthian columns is a half-figure of Shakespeare in restored colours. He holds a quill pen but the likeness is unflattering as the poet bears a bemused expression as if in doubt as to where the next word will come from. N of Shakespeare's grave is that of his wife Anne (died 1623, aged 67). The church has a number of other interesting monuments. In the chancel is Dean Thomas Balshall (died 1491), builder of the chancel (N wall). It was evidently intended to double as an Easter sepulchre: the sides of the table-tomb have scenes from the Passion and Resurrection. Against the E wall (N) is John Combe (died 1614) a friend of Shakespeare's, who lies beneath a round-arched recess between columns. Against the N wall is Judith Combe (died 1649), whose bust appears hand-in-hand with her betrothed Richard (by Thomas Stanton). The monument to James Kendall (died 1756) is by J.M. Rysbrack. The E end of the N aisle is the Clopton chapel. Hugh Clopton (died 1496) lies in an extensively restored tomb between aisle and nave. William Clopton (died 1592) and his wife Anne lie on a table-tomb in the NE corner; their seven children are depicted in a frieze above. Against the E wall is the splendid monument by Edward Marshall, later master mason to King Charles II, to Joyce

Clopton (died 1635), who married George Carew, Earl of Totnes (died 1629). The powder kegs, guns, etc. in the base record the fact that he was Master in Ordnance to King James I.

Guild Chapel of the Holy Cross. The guild was founded in 1269 and by the Dissolution was the most important body in Stratford. During the 15C it included the Duke of Clarence and the Earl of Warwick. The E and S walls of the chancel may date from the 13C but the rest of this part was remodelled, and the N wall was rebuilt, in 1450. The aisleless nave was rebuilt by Hugh Clopton and the building was mentioned in his will of 1496, when work may have been under way. The chancel is quite humble, but the nave has four big four-light Perpendicular windows to the street. Inside, the space is clear and light, something enhanced by the plain plaster ceilings, which are probably of 1804. The most noteworthy feature comprises the remains of late medieval wall paintings. Over the chancel arch is a Doom which can perhaps be best appreciated from a drawing in the church, based on one of 1804. The ground is dark green. On the dexter side is an architecturally splendid New Jerusalem and on the sinister, jolly-looking demons round up miscreants who, according to the inscriptions, have been guilty of the Seven Deadly Sins. The font is a typically 18C piece of black marble.

Temple Balsall, *St. Mary.* This is a remarkable church in a remarkable setting. Balsall was given by Roger de Mowbray to the Knights Templar (whence *Temple* Balsall). After their suppression in 1307, it passed to their successors, the Knights of St. John (or 'Hospitallers'). At the Reformation the estate passed via Catherine Parr and the Earl of Leicester to Lady Anne Holbourne and her sister, Lady Katherine Leveson (died 1674), who founded the hospital and school under her will. The hospital was rebuilt in 1725–27 by Francis Smith of Warwick, from which time the present lovely buildings date.

The church, made parochial in 1863, was built some time around 1300, though whether in the last days of the Templars or the early ones of the Hospitallers is not known. It is one vast rectangle with four bays each side and a high gabled roof behind plain parapets. There are two particularly remarkable windows on the S, one with a rose with radiating panels in the head and another with a mullion rising straight to the apex (an extraordinary thing at that time). The building was very extensively restored in 1845–49 by Gilbert Scott, though it seems faithfully in line with documentary evidence of 1541. The windows are mostly shafted inside and the floor levels rise appreciably to the E.

Warwick, *St. Mary.* This, the main church of Warwick, is a fitting place of worship for this historic county town. It is on the top of the hill and its tower is a landmark for many miles around. Apart from its considerable architectural significance, it has important associations with the Earls of Warwick, several of whom are buried here. There was a large-scale Norman church as can be imagined from the extensive crypt. In 1123 Roger de Newburgh, second Norman Earl of Warwick, made the church collegiate. There is then nothing until the 14C, the time of the Beauchamp Earls, who played a major part in national and, indeed, international affairs. Thomas Beauchamp I began the rebuilding, using money obtained from the ransom of a French archbishop and, after his death in 1369, the work was continued by his son, Thomas II. Their campaign provided the chancel, completed in 1392. In the next century the most magnificent part was added—the Beauchamp chantry chapel, built under the will of Richard, the greatest of the Beauchamp Earls, who died in 1439. His executors determined upon a worthy building. It took 20 years to build, starting in 1443, cost £2481 4s 7½d and was provided with the magnificent ostentation that so fascinated the later Middle Ages. In 1694 an event took place that has radically affected the appearance of the church. In a great fire—or *conflagratione stupenda* as it says on the tower—the centre of Warwick was destroyed and with it, the church W of the chancel. Rebuilding started in 1698, was complete in 1704 and the new parts are a most interesting essay in contemporary Gothic. Drawings by Wren in 1696 were rejected and the executed work was designed by Sir William Wilson of Sutton Coldfield.

The main feature of the exterior is the 174ft high tower which projects into the road and has open arches on three sides as a *porte-cochère*. It is a most imposing shape but its repetitive details do not stand close scrutiny. It is in three stages, each of which has two large niches up the sides like the footholds for a giant. There are also large, dull Gothic blind windows on the two lower stages and an odd composition for the two-light belfry openings. Moving to the N, the nave has three bays and huge windows with very free Gothic tracery, which is also repeated on the N face of the N transept. Above the nave is a parapet with balusters and urns. The N side of the chancel is a graceless assemblage of vestries and a projecting chapter house but behind these can be seen flying buttresses to the chancel. The roofline of the chancel arcs upwards at the E to allow a larger E façade. This is filled with a six-light window surrounded by panelling. On the S comes the famous Beauchamp chapel where every surface is filled either with windows or with more panelling. It has three bays, each with six-light windows and beyond its main E wall a low vestry. Returning to the W end, the work of c 1700 on the S side mirrors that on the N.

The interior is large and has an enormous amount to see. It is described here starting with the W parts of c 1700, proceeding via the vestries N of the chancel and ending with the Beauchamp chapel. A remarkable aspect of the work of c 1700 is its un-English atmosphere. The aisles rise to the same height as the nave in the fashion of a Continental hall church and the nave and aisles have plaster tierceron-vaulting which springs from little winged heads above the capitals. The sense of height is emphasised by the extreme tallness of the piers. Their capitals are right below the vaulting. Acanthus leaves reappear and the abaci have the egg-and-dart motif. The piers themselves are of conventional Perpendicular plan with four rolls and four hollow chamfers. There are four bays to the nave and, while it is clear that there is no special treatment of the piers marking off the transept bays, the W pair of piers is of enormous and incongruous size. The reason is simply that it was intended to build the tower over the W bay of the nave, but structural problems were encountered and the tower was built W of the nave instead. Mounted on the two would-be tower piers are a fine clock and a matching arms of Queen Anne which were donated in 1706 when building work was finished. At the W end of the S aisle are a pair of dole shelves for bread for the poor and a record of who left how much for this worthy cause. Near this in the nave are two lovely mace-rests by the civic seats. Looking back, the W bay of the nave contains the organ which partly dates from 1730, when the maker was Thomas Schwarbrick. The N transept is the regimental chapel of the Royal Warwickshire Regiment, completed in 1952. Nearby, at the entrance to the vestry, is the brass to Thomas Oken (died 1573) and his wife. He was a major benefactor of the town and established several charities.

N of the chancel lies the long, low tierceron-vaulted vestries of the late 14C. Off them lies the chapter house with nine seats round the apse. It is now virtually filled with the monument to Fulke Greville (died 1628), who was granted Warwick Castle by King James I in 1604. The Greville family were wool merchants from Chipping Campden and, eventually, in 1759, obtained the Earldom of Warwick which, unlike the castle, they retain to this day. The monument here is by Thomas Ashby and is a huge rather austere six-poster. The sarcophagus and columns are of black marble. On the W wall of the vestry is an excellent monument to Sir Thomas Puckering (died 1636) in a very refined Classical style by Nicholas Stone. From the W vestry one can descend into the Norman crypt. This has two rows of mighty piers, and vaulting with strong ribs. The crypt is all that remains of the 12C building but seems to somewhat post-date the collegiate foundation of 1123. It was extended E by one bay as part of the Beauchamps' building activities in the 14C. The NE part is divided off and since 1770 has served as the mausoleum of the Grevilles. A rarity in the crypt is the trolley from a ducking stool for medieval miscreants.

In the chancel the walls are panelled all over and the space is covered by a spectacular tierceron-vault. The windows are all set up high above the flanking buildings. The most striking effect of the building efforts of the 14C Beauchamps are the flying ribs. There are three for each cluster of springing and the space between each member and its corresponding main rib is filled with a pair of mouchettes placed back to back. The panelling on the ground stage is employed to surround an Easter sepulchre with three openings on the N and a quadruple sedilia and a piscina on the S. In the centre of the chancel is the Beauchamp who started rebuilding the church, Thomas I (died 1369). He was a commander at the battle of Crecy in 1346 (when he was only 17), at Poitiers in 1356 and was a guardian of the Black Prince. It was he who began the rebuilding of Warwick Castle, but he died prematurely of plague during the siege of Calais. His alabaster effigy lies on his table-tomb, holding the hand of his wife Catherine in a slightly stylised gesture of affection. The reredos is by Butterfield, who was at work here in 1883–86.

Steps lead down into a most interesting space between the chancel and the Beauchamp chapel. What has happened is that the space between the two has large buttresses, and openings have been cut through these. In the W part a lobby with a longitudinally panelled roof has been formed and it gives access to a staircase to the roof. To the E is an extraordinary room, a tiny chapel known as the Dean's chapel, incorporating decoration of the greatest delicacy. The roof has mini fan-vaulting with pendants and at the E end are two frilly niches and a little frieze between. On the N, stairs lead up to an even tinier space which is just large enough for a prayer desk in the thickness of the chancel S wall. At the E end there is a squint to the high altar. On the S open panelling gives a view of the Beauchamp chapel. Moving to the S transept one can see from the masonry of the E wall how the work of c 1700 slightly extended the wall S. The iron screen formerly surrounded the tomb of Robert Dudley in the Beauchamp chapel and was made by Nicholas Parris of Warwick in

1716. On the E wall are the large brasses of Thomas Beauchamp II (died 1401) and his wife Margaret. This is all that survives from their monument that was destroyed in the fire of 1694. The entrance to the chapel is through a porch of 1704 by Samuel Dunckley of Warwick. It passes as extremely convincing 15C Gothic except for certain details such as the cornices.

What now remains is the Beauchamp chapel itself, dedicated to Our Lady, decorated with all the apparatus of mid-15C architecture and containing one of the most famous monuments in the country. It is a three-bay hall with windows made as large as they could be and, in the centre, in accordance with his will, the tomb of Richard Beauchamp. There is an abundance of stone panelling and the chapel is, of course, vaulted. In the centre of each bay is a complex figure of eight round-nosed triangles containing heraldic and religious figures. The finest work of all is the E window. It has two enlarged mullions rising to the head and round the frame are two orders. These mullions and window frame are filled with superb figures. Most are angels, representing all nine orders, but at each side are two female saints, St. Barbara and St. Catherine to the N, and St. Mary Magdalene and St. Margaret to the S. Below the E window at the sides is delicate canopy-work of the type found in the Dean's chapel. In the middle is the stone reredos of c 1760, not really appropriate but an extraordinarily ornate piece of Gothic for its time. The surround was designed and made by a local man, Timothy Lightholer. The figure sculpture depicts the Annunciation and is by William Collins. On the W wall is a Doom. This strange piece is a repainting of 1678 by Richard Bird of London of an earlier representation but 'in the manner of Mr. Michaelangelo'. Despite much Puritan zeal, a lot of 15C stained glass made by John Prudde survives, and in the side tracery lights many angels remain together with the music for their song. This has been identified as the *Gaudeamus* (which is the introit at the Mass of the Assumption), the *Gloria* (for the greater double feasts), and the Marian antiphon, *Ave regina caelorum*. A contract was made in 1449 for the two tiers of stalls at the W end but the existing woodwork is later.

Richard Beauchamp was the confidant of King Henry V, Captain of Calais and was involved in the trial and death of Joan of Arc. He lies on a tomb-chest delicately carved out of Purbeck marble. The contracts for the work specify the names of the craftsmen, for example John Bourde of Corfe, Dorset, who supplied the stone, William Austen of London who cast the effigy, Bartholomew Lamberspring who did the gilding, and others too. The magnificent figure of Richard, like the hooped canopy over it, is of gilded latten. It was apparently cast in a number of pieces and then fastened together. As specified in the contract, he is represented by 'an image of a man armed' (the details are of c 1460) but there is no reason to suppose that the exceedingly realistic face is actually that of Richard himself. He lies with his hands slightly apart in adoration and contemplation of the celestial vision of the E window. At his feet are a griffin and a miserable looking bear. Around the monument are weepers of gilded latten, who can be identified by their armorial bearings. The man at the E on the S is Richard Neville or 'Warwick the Kingmaker'. The Dudleys, who succeeded to the Earldom in the 16C, are represented in the other monuments. Robert Dudley (died 1588) was also Earl of Leicester and a favourite of Queen Elizabeth I. He and his wife Lettice (died 1634) are the recumbent effigies on the large monument on the N of the chancel. This is by far the most lavish monument in the church. To the S is Ambrose Dudley (died 1590) on a tomb-chest which bears very fine shields. His coronet is 18C and made of iron. In the SE corner is Robert Dudley, who died as a child in 1584 and is called on his inscription 'the noble Impe'. On the N wall is a wooden tablet imitating a brass in praise of Lettice Dudley, who lived on after her husband's death to the age of 95.

(I am most grateful to Miss Stella Fletcher for assistance on this entry).

Other Buildings. Both the E and W gates support chapels. That on the E gate is a pretty building of 1788, dedicated to St. Peter, by Francis Hiorn. It has a charming small W tower on the top of which is a recessed wooden stage with traceried sides. At the other end of the ancient town the W gate is a particularly impressive affair. The entrance to the town was through a long tunnel, the E part of which has transverse vaulting ribs and the W part tierceron-vaulting. Above it is the chapel of St. James, now part of the Lord Leycester Hospital. The tower stands above the tierceron-vaulted section. The N side is heavily buttressed with the buttresses flying over a passage.

The chapel at Warwick Castle faces the courtyard and was built by Fulke Greville, who acquired the castle from King James in 1604. The interior is mostly from 1759, a date recorded in the E window which was given at that time by the Earl of Exeter and which includes medieval glass. The ceiling has panelling and tiny pendants. Between the antechapel and chapel is a 19C stone screen. Among the contents are a spectacularly large Italian alabaster vase of 1830, an even more virtuoso piece of Flemish woodcarving of c 1740 depicting a battle between Greeks and Amazons, the chapel plate of 1753, a Polish brass chandelier of c 1700 and a Brussels tapestry from the mid-16C.

Wootton Wawen

St. Peter. Apart from its picturesque site, the interest here is the pre-Conquest work and the subsequent development of the church. A pre-Conquest tower, which can be only loosely dated to the 10C or early 11C, stands stranded in the middle of a church which has grown around it. That it was central before the Conquest is shown clearly by arches on all four sides in the ground stage, each with upright and flat stonework. To N and S there were openings to *porticus* and, indeed, on the N two substantial stubs of walling survive. Recent work suggests that the present nave was laid out later in pre-Conquest or early Norman times. A small Norman window on the N is from a slightly later Norman phase but still not necessarily 12C. Even the chancel, it seems, may be 12C but with secondary, 13C features. In the 13C the S *porticus* was replaced by a transept with an E chapel, and a S aisle was added. The Lady chapel was modified in the 14C and is now as big as the nave or chancel. The pulpit is Perpendicular and there are a number of worthwhile monuments.

Chapel, next to Wootton Hall. This is a remarkable building for its date. It was erected in 1813, only 22 years after the toleration of Catholic worship. Attached to the rear of the Hall, it is of red brick and is tall, spacious and severe. The sides have, low down, round-arched windows and the apse has three lunette lights set very high.

The only internal division is by two enormous Doric columns at the entrance to the altar space. There is a segmental vaulted ceiling divided into panels. The building has had an unusual use since 1905 when a new church was erected in the village. It was turned into a ballroom for the Hall and, even now, it is cleared occasionally for this purpose. Otherwise its survival is secured as a store for the caravan site company.

WESTMORLAND

Westmorland occupies the SE corner of the Lake District, thence extending E across the valley of the River Eden to the Pennine foothills, and S across the N shores of Morecambe Bay. Appleby was the county town until 1974, but Kendal is the only major town and most churches are found in rural or semi-rural situations. Approximately half the Anglican churches were built in the 19C at a time of religious revival and economic development and, apart from St. Mary's, Ambleside, designed by Sir Gilbert Scott, St. Peter's at Askham, by Robert Smirke, and Anthony Salvin's St. Patrick's at Patterdale, most of them were designed by local or North Country architects. Among the churches built in the 17C and 18C, Witherslack in the S of the county, erected c 1669, and Hugill, otherwise known as Ings, near Kendal, of 1743, are worthy of note. The remainder, considerable in number, are generally Norman foundations, much altered and restored over the centuries, and preserving a legacy of Norman, Early English, Decorated and Perpendicular styles, original and modern. An outstanding Norman survival is the Durham-style W end of the N arcade at Kirkby Lonsdale. The only pre-Conquest tower W of the N Pennines is to be found at Morland. For building material generally, sandstone, attractive for its widely-varying hues, limestone and flagstone have been available. By unusual contrast, the church at Tebay, once a railway village on the main line between Lancaster and Carlisle, is of rock-faced granite from the nearby Shap Quarry.

Notable monuments are the tombs at St. Lawrence's, Appleby, of Lady Anne Clifford and her mother, the Countess of Cumberland, the many Lowther memorials at St. Michael's Lowther, and a tablet at Holy Trinity, Kendal, by John Flaxman.

Stained glass of the 14C and 15C may be seen in a fine window at Bowness-on-Windermere, some of which is said to have come from Cartmel Priory after the Dissolution. Otherwise, early glass survives only as fragments re-erected in later times. There is, however, a wealth of 19C and 20C glass throughout the county, to which the studio of Shrigley & Hunt, of Lancaster, has contributed in large measure. By Morris & Co. (the figures and panels being by Sir Edward Burne-Jones and Ford Madox Brown), is the fine E window at Jesus Chapel, Troutbeck and by Henry Holiday the series of windows, including an interesting pair illustrating the words of the Benedicite, to be found at Holy Trinity, Casterton, near Kirkby Lonsdale.

Visitors to William Wordsworth's 'Dove Cottage' may like to be reminded that the poet is buried in nearby Grasmere churchyard. Near him lies the young Hartley Coleridge.

Appleby, St. Lawrence. Of the Norman church founded c 1130 nothing now remains except the lower stage of the tower, the building having suffered from damage by fire at the hands of the Scots in 1174, and again in 1388. From a gradual rebuilding of the fabric between these events the church has retained its early 14C stonework, while restoration and extension in more settled times after 1388 have added the prominent Perpendicular features. In 1654–55 Lady Anne Clifford, who lived in Appleby Castle and who was closely associated with the church, undertook extensive repairs and rebuilding, but did not depart from the existing styles of architecture.

Externally, the upper part of the W tower, the three-light clerestory windows above the nave, the battlements of the nave and the now-weathered pinnacles and gargoyles represent the prominent Perpendicular style of the structure. In contrast, the aisle windows, many of them Victorian replacements of 1861–62, are of the Decorated period. They are square-headed windows, each of two ogee lights. A fragment of the original tracery is preserved as the lintel to a side gate to the churchyard, W of the tower. The aisles have plain parapets. The S entrance porch, surmounted by a sandstone sundial, is 17C and has a reused 13C piece as the doorway. A barbican of 1811 by Robert Smirke stands at the main entrance to the churchyard.

In the interior the nave is separated from the aisles by early 14C sandstone arcades of five bays, with quatrefoil piers and double-chamfered arches. The chancel and side chapels at the E end are set apart by two-bay arcades, of which the N arcade is of Lady Anne Clifford's time in Perpendicular style. At the W end, the Norman stage of the tower is open to both nave and W bay of the S aisle by 14C arches. A Norman window pierces the 5ft-thick N wall of the tower. The carved heads that adorn the nave arcades are 19C. The narrow arch on the S side of the main altar is 14C and overlooked the churchyard before a 15C chantry chapel and the S aisle became one in the 17C. The panelled plaster ceiling in the nave is early 19C.

Dominating the W end of the church is the organ, arranged in three turrets, said to be the second oldest instrument in service in the country, the date of the case being c 1542–47. Originally in Carlisle Cathedral, it was given in 1683 by the Dean and Chapter to the Mayor and Corporation of Appleby for use in the church. Some 40 years elapsed before it was erected at the W end in 1722. In 1836 it was moved to the N chapel. Restored to its former magnificence in 1976, the organ returned to the W end of the nave. The escutcheon of King Henry II, who granted a charter to Appleby in the 12C, adorns the wall adjacent to the porch and may have been intended to crown the instrument at its inauguration in 1722.

Below the pulpit on the N side of the nave are pews, decorated with carved panels from the organ case, for the Mayor and Corporation, and on an adjacent pillar there is an early 18C wrought-iron rest for the sword and mace. Affixed to the wall above the chancel arch is a Restoration coat of arms, at the foot of which is painted, possibly by direction of Lady Anne Clifford, a passage from Isaiah, chapter 33, verses 15 and 17. Lining the arcades behind the choirstalls are carved wooden screens of the 15C. In the S chapel, cut in a roof beam, are the words 'Ann Conntesse of Pembroke in Ano 1655 repaired all this building'. In the baptistery, in the SW corner of the church, are three chained volumes of Foxe's 'Acts and Monuments of the Martyrs', printed in 1631 and given by their publisher, Richard More, an Appleby tradesman's son. The octagonal font and plinth are of 1886, of polished fossilised limestone. Some medieval glass has been reset in the Victorian N chapel window tracery: a shield with the azure lion rampant of the Northumberland Percies, from whom Lady Anne claimed descent, and one with the arms of Beaumont, both said to be 15C. An escutcheon with the arms of France and England is believed to be 14C. The stained glass in the chancel E window is of 1872 by Wailes & Strang and depicts, in the upper part, Jesus turning the water into wine at the marriage at Cana, and in the lower, the Adoration of the Magi. In the S aisle are three windows of c 1902 by Heaton, Butler &

Bayne, which are pictorial representations of Faith, Hope and Charity.

The two most important monuments, both erected by Lady Anne Clifford, are in the N chapel. Dating from 1617, the recumbent effigy in alabaster of her mother, Margaret, Countess of Cumberland, wearing a coronet of gilded metal, her widow's mantle covering her bodice and gown, lies on a black marble tomb-chest decorated with funerary trophies. It is placed to the left of the high altar. The excellent workmanship of the monument and the resemblance of the effigy to that of Queen Elizabeth I in Westminster Abbey has led to the conjecture that the same sculptor, Maximilian Colt, may have executed the work. Nearby is the tomb of Lady Anne herself, erected during her lifetime, possessing a reredos, made of alabaster and black marble, of Classical columns and broken segmental pediment, embellished with 24 shields, all emblazoned, which trace the descent of the Clifford family. Lady Anne died in 1676.

William Paley, the eminent theologian, Professor of Divinity at Cambridge, was Vicar from 1777 to 1789. John Robinson, MP for Westmorland from 1764 to 1774, who became a household word as the butt of Sheridan's famous retort in Parliament, 'I could name him as soon as I could say Jack Robinson', was baptised in this church in 1727.

Bowness-on-Windermere, _St. Martin._ St. Martin's was consecrated in 1483 when it replaced an earlier chapel destroyed by fire. It is noteworthy for the glass of 1480 in the E window, some of which is believed on good grounds to have come from Cartmel Priory and some to have been made specifically for the church. In the tracery are some 20 coats of arms of the important families of the time, among them one of the Washington family, forebears of George Washington, first President of the United States of America. Also in the tracery is what is considered to be the oldest piece, an early 14C Virgin and Child, and a 15C coat of arms of King Edward V, whose short reign began and ended in the year the church was consecrated. Of the 15C are the main lights, the centrepiece of which is the Crucifixion, and the monks and lay people of Cartmel Priory, all kneeling, in the predellae. The window suffered some restoration in c 1870. The church possesses a rare equestrian statue in polished wood of St. Martin and the Beggar.

Crosby Ravensworth, _St. Lawrence._ The main body of the church is a rebuilding and enlargement in the Early English style in 1867–86 by J.S. Crowther for Canon George Frederick Weston, Vicar from 1848 to 1887. The tower is 15C with a Victorian upper stage. The windows of the N chapel are Decorated, its low Perpendicular arch into the chancel being 16C. The S doorway to the nave, the nave arcades and the tripartite piers of the crossing are the remains of a 13C rebuilding after the destruction of the Norman church of c 1100 by the Scots.

In appearance the church is like a miniature cathedral in a rural setting, its transepts (removed in the 15C) restored, the roof raised, a clerestory of quatrefoil windows added, and the imposing upper stage of the tower built with its battlements and stair turret, gargoyles and carved heads. The Gothicised S porches were built in 1811 by Robert Smirke, fresh from his monumental success with the building of Lowther Castle; notice his symbols of bread and wine, the carved texts, and the words _'Ecce Sponsus Venit'_. Of the many carved heads decorating the exterior there is one at roof level between the tower and the adjacent S porch of a man swallowing a mouse. In the churchyard stands the shaft of a cross, perhaps 10C.

The inner S doorway with two orders of colonnettes and dogtooth decoration is of c 1240. The 15C tower is open to a nave divided from the aisles by early 13C double-chamfered three-bay arcades, the S arcade, with nailhead decoration and leaf paterae, being later in date than the N arcade. At the crossing the tripartite piers are of c 1200. The inclusion in the NW pier of a low shaft and respond indicates the raising of the nave floor before the erection of the N arcade. Note the triple-arched opening in the W wall of the crossing and the four dormer windows above, both designed to bring light to a dark nave. The rebuilt chancel arch leads into a chancel raised in two stages, the 19C vestry occupying the NE corner.

The outstanding memorial is the chapel of the Dent family of Flass in the S transept. Victorian Early English in style, it has busts on the walls, memorial plaques under pointed arcading and a fresco of Our Lord blessing children on the S wall. Stained glass fills the rose window and lancets, with angels in the foils of the rose, and scenes from the life of Our Lord in the lancets. The seating provided was for family and staff. In the N chancel chapel stands the tomb-chest of Sir Lancelot Threlkeld, died c 1512, a massive marble slab on a fluted and gadrooned softstone chest. In the tower, statuettes of Faith, Hope and Charity in an architectural setting of c 1835 by David Dunbar of Newcastle form a memorial to George Gibson, a benefactor of the church. The musical still-life at the foot is appropriate to the man who built the first organ in the church for his own use. The stained glass is 19C. The chancel E window is by Clayton & Bell and depicts in its four lights Christ's Passion, Crucifixion, Deposition from the Cross and Resurrection. Also by Clayton & Bell are the windows in the N aisle, those in the Dent chapel, and the geometrical and floral designs in the clerestory and N transept. The S chancel window of c 1889 to Canon Weston, whose kneeling figure is seen in the predella and an angel choir of nine in the three lights, is by Shrigley & Hunt. The carved wood reredos is of 1897, its central panel, the Last Supper, being by a local craftsman, and the side panels by the village carving class. Interesting pew-ends are to be found in the S aisle; the pews are said to have come from a local 18C dale chapel.

A father who enjoyed royal patronage and had a famous son was born in the parish. Launcelot Addison, Chaplain to King Charles II, who became Dean of Lichfield, was the father; the son was Joseph Addison, essayist, playwright, and Secretary of State.

Kendal, *Holy Trinity, Kirkland.* This is the Perpendicular, double-aisled parish church of the largest town in Westmorland, which from medieval times has been a centre for the wool trade and weaving manufacture. As the town prospered and the population increased, the earlier 13C church grew in size. The S aisle is said to have been built to accommodate the Flemish weavers who came to the town in 1331, while with the increase in the number of affluent families chantry chapels were founded. Of these chapels only four now remain with their tombs and memorials and some early 16C Flamboyant screenwork. In the late 16C the N aisle was added and the church rebuilt in the Perpendicular style. By the mid-19C this structure was showing signs of serious decay and a drastic restoration was undertaken in c 1850–70. The present century has seen some re-arrangement and reordering of the interior. The stained glass in the church is an important feature.

The church is situated to the S of the town, the W end overlooking a busy thoroughfare appropriately named Kirkland, while the E end rises above the grassed churchyard beyond which flows the River Kent. Externally it is a late Perpendicular building of red sandstone and yellow freestone, the walls and clerestory decorated with battlements, crocketed pinnacles and gargoyles, the length being divided by stepped buttresses into nine bays. Viewed from the W the buttressed, 80ft-high, square tower significantly dwarfs the inner and outer aisles on either side, while from the E the view is truly majestic, the inspired fitting of the rose window during the 19C in place of three clerestory windows being a contributory factor.

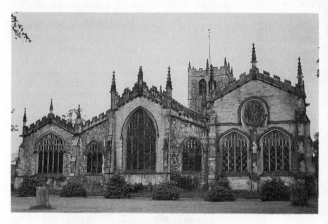

Holy Trinity Church, an exceptionally wide late Perpendicular church, much restored in the 19C

The S porch by which one enters accords in style with the external stonework of the E window, and is Victorian. It replaced the more modest structure which may be seen pictured in a stained glass window in the W end. The first impression of the perfectly rectangular interior is the width, its 103ft almost rivalling that of a cathedral. Above, the roof is embellished with angels. Four arcades run the length of the interior and divide it into nave, aisles and outer aisles. In the inner arcades there are four bays to the nave and four to the chancel, but the outer arcades run from E to W without a break. At the W end stand the colossal octagonal E piers of the tower which have no capitals. The octagonal piers and capitals of the outer N arcade are Perpendicular, while those of the 14C outer S aisle are, surprisingly, of an elementary 13C style. The nave arcades have piers and capitals of both types arranged alternately, two in the W bay, and two at a point where a chancel arch may have stood in the 13C, having no capitals. The E bays of the nave arcades are Victorian replacements, several of them bearing a nailhead decoration. The altar has been brought forward from the E end. Its removal has revealed the fine carved reredos of Caen stone with pillars of Orton marble of 1867. Suspended above the altar is a modern, stainless steel Crown of Thorns, given by the Gilpin Trust in memory of Bernard Gilpin, 'The Apostle of the North' (1517–83).

During the Victorian restoration the NE Bellingham chapel was re-roofed and refurbished, the present colourful, ribbed ceiling incorporating the original bosses. A tomb-chest has good brass effigies of Sir Roger Bellingham (died 1533) and his wife. In the N wall will be seen a brass of Sir Alan Bellingham (died 1577). The inner chapel on the N side, dedicated to St. Thomas Becket, has desks with carved mitre heads, and on the wall hangs a framed painting of the arms of a Howard Earl. In the Strickland chapel stands an old tomb-chest with coats of arms, and a table-tomb on Tuscan columns covering the effigy (disfigured) of the boy Walter Strickland, son of Sir Thomas, who died in 1656. The Parr chapel, which now extends into the S aisle, has a slab tomb believed to be that of Sir William Parr, grandfather of Katharine Parr, who married King Henry VIII in his last years, and survived him. The fine carved screen enclosing the chapel is modern, designed and executed by local craftsmen.

The octagonal font is of black marble, with concave sides bearing blank shields, and is 15C. The wooden, 8ft-high cover is of 1898, and is said to have been carved from a single block. In the nave are choirstalls with carved poppyheads, and in the outer N aisle, bench-ends with similar decoration. In the outer S aisle the benches with poppyheads are modern. A fine set of carved stalls stands against the W wall in the baptistery. On a windowsill in the Parr chapel will be found a fragment of a 9C cross-shaft with a scrollwork design of grapes and leaves. Of the many 18C and 19C monuments decorating the walls an outstanding one is by John Flaxman in white marble in memory of Zachary Hubbersty (died 1787). In the tympanum an angel hovers over the prostrate widow, whose six children are gathered at her feet. A modern sculpture by Josephina de Vasconcellos of Mary, Jesus and two children of different ethnic origin, typifying the refugee problem, stands at the entrance to the Parr chapel.

Apart from a small coat of arms in the Bellingham chapel and some ancient glass said to have been set in the clerestory windows, all surviving stained glass is 19C or 20C. Four windows in the SW corner, one of which is now hidden by the organ, are by William Warrington. Two of these incorporate heraldic work. Ward & Hughes made the NW window and the heavily sentimental Sinkinson window in the S aisle. Shrigley & Hunt erected the glass of the rose window. The Valley of the Shadow of Death window in the S aisle was made to the design of M. Alice Gordon. The E window, the earliest in date, is of 1854 by Michael O'Connor. It depicts the Crucifixion, the Resurrection and the Evangelists. In the Parr chapel, the fine five-light E window, with the Virgin and Child flanked by four archangels, and with 14 women saints in the tracery, is attributed to J.C.N. Bewsey, a pupil of C.E. Kempe. The clerestory glass dates from the 19C restoration period; some was by Warrington, some by Pilkington.

The celebrated portrait painter George Romney died in 1802 at Kendal, where, half a century earlier, he had been apprenticed to an artist. A memorial to him, a Grecian urn in relief in black marble, erected by his son, is on the W wall adjacent to the porch. Celebrated by his association with Lady Anne Clifford is George Sedgwick, died 1685, who is buried beneath the floor of the church. A framed inscription on the W wall records that he was secretary to Lady Anne for 18 years, during which time she dictated to him her famous diaries.

Kirkby Lonsdale, *St. Mary the Virgin.* St. Mary the Virgin is the parish church of a small country town of narrow, winding streets and quiet byways, situated on the high W bank of the River Lune. The building had its beginnings in the early 12C. Its major feature is a magnificent display of Norman architecture at the W end: one that is unique in the county. A break in construction occurred and, when work was restarted, it was on the basis of changed plans and on a reduced scale. In the 13C the church thus completed was extended E, and in the following century the hitherto narrow nave aisles were widened. In the later 15C or early 16C the Perpendicular N arcade was erected, its outer aisle being extended, after the Reformation, into the area of the Middleton chantry which had been built c 1486 in the NE corner. The church underwent an extensive restoration in 1866.

The church stands in a spacious churchyard from the NE corner of which the view to the River Lune and the Barbon Fells beyond was admired by Ruskin and painted by Turner. The exterior of the building is of sandstone rubble and ashlar, its walls embattled in the

The early 12C N arcade of St. Mary's

19C. Embraced by the aisles, the four-stage tower, with its battlements and pinnacles, is the result of heightening and reconstruction on several occasions, the latest in 1705. The lowest stage is 12C, while above, the openings are 15C or 16C in style. At the foot is the Norman W door with several orders of shafts and capitals, and inner mouldings, the weather-worn remains of carved decoration still visible in the arches. The exterior reveals a wide range of architectural styles: Perpendicular in the N and S aisles, in the modern N roof lights and in the chantry E window; early 13C lancets in the chancel E window, and 14C Reticulated tracery in the adjacent nave aisle windows. The N aisle W door and the clergy door on the S side are Norman pieces reused. There are Norman windows at the W ends of the aisles. The roof of the nave continues over the aisles, but to the N there is an outer aisle, separately roofed. The aisles are buttressed.

One enters the church by an elegant Norman-style porch of 1866, part of the inner doorway being a reused 12C piece. Seven-bay arcades course the interior from W to E without any intervening chancel arch. At the W end of the N arcade of the nave stands the massive fragment of 12C architecture: a respond of triple shafts, and three piers on high bases, the centre one compound, all bridged by round arches, each arch consisting of a different moulding, and each abacus and capital of different design. The two cylindrical shafts have a diamond pattern overall, one deeply cut, the other marked by triple parallel scoring, both almost certainly inspired by similar designs at Durham Cathedral. The S arcade, started later in the 12C, has three round arches at the W end, but the scale is much reduced, and both nave arcades were continued, with pointed double-chamfered arches and round or octagonal piers, to the E window, where the three lancets have internal arches supported by slim detached shafts. The E bay of the outer N arcade will be seen to die into an impost in the E wall in the form of a 15C carved human head.

Examples of fine woodcarving are the pulpit, part of the original three-decker, dated 1619, a sanctuary chair of 1629, a cupboard made from a former pew for the Vicar bearing the words 'Sedes Vicar', and another, with crowded intricate design, of the Jacobean period. A stone coffin in the chantry is believed to be 13C. Among the stained glass windows is one in the S aisle of c 1878 designed by Henry Holiday and executed by Powell's of Whitefriars. Figures of Faith, Hope and Charity adorn the three lights. Victorian iron screens surround the chancel. The reredos is also 19C.

Kirkby Stephen, St. Stephen. St. Stephen's is the large and impressive church of a small market town. Although the building was extensively restored and rebuilt in 1847–74, it retains stonework of five successive centuries, the earliest, in the NW corner, being a fragment of walling of c 1170. In the early 13C, a mere 50 years later, possibly due to unsure foundations or structural failure, a new church on a cruciform plan with central tower arose. The S aisle of this building was widened in the 15C, and following the collapse of its central tower, the W tower of c 1506 was erected.

To appreciate the detail, proportions and style of the exterior it must be viewed from the S. There is the lofty, three-stage tower with its twin two-light bell openings under ogee gables, battlements and pinnacles; the clerestory, raised in height and rebuilt in the 19C, and the wall of the S aisle below it, both with plain parapets; the shallow gable-end of the transept; and the side chapel and the chancel with its markedly steep roof. The chancel lancets are 13C in style, the side chapel window has Decorated tracery and the rest is Perpendicular. Brockram was used for the external stonework during the building of the E end in the 19C, with the unfortunate result that the red and red-brown colour of the sandstone structure contrasts strongly with the pale, purplish colour of the clastic Brockram. The churchyard is entered from the market place by an attractive Classical porch of 1810 by George Gibson.

The church is entered by a 19C porch with an ogee outer gable and an inner 15C doorway, to reveal the nave, aisles, transepts, chancel and chancel chapels. The ground plan is asymmetrical, for whereas the wall of the widened S aisle lines up with the gable-end of the transept and the wall of the chapel on the S side, on the N side the elements of cruciform structure are maintained. Seven-bay arcades of the 13C divide the aisles from the nave. There are cylindrical piers with wide bases, octagonal moulded capitals and double-chamfered arches. Above the arcades and over the crossing, between the strikingly high tower arch and the modern chancel arch, is the 16C roof with painted and emblazoned bosses. E of the nave the interior was mostly rebuilt in a 13C style in 1847–51 (by R.C. Carpenter), the exceptions being the N transept, which has a Decorated N window and a Perpendicular reredos niche, and the late 13C sedilia and piscina of the chancel, which Carpenter reused.

The Musgrave (or Hartley) chapel on the S side of the chancel is enclosed by wooden and glass screens. Above the entrance there is an engraved glass panel depicting the martyred St. Stephen by John Hutton. Inside the chapel, whose painted roof bosses are said to be medieval, there is set at the foot of the altar a red sandstone tomb-slab decorated with a worn floriated cross, sword and shield, believed to be that of Sir Thomas Musgrave of Hartley Castle, who died in 1376. Freestanding nearby, to the N, is a tomb-chest carved with niches with crocketed ogee canopies alternating with pilasters crowned by pinnacles, which bears the recumbent sandstone effigy of Sir Richard Musgrave of c 1409. In the S wall, in an alcove with a gable of coarsely carved leaves surmounted by his coat of arms, stands the plain tomb-chest of another Sir Richard Musgrave and his wife, of c 1464.

In the N chapel restored in 1849 stands the Wharton monument, unfortunately damaged and disfigured. On the tomb-slab, supported by corner balusters, are the recumbent effigies of Thomas, first Lord Wharton (died 1568) and of Eleanor Stapleton, his first wife, on his left, and Anne Talbot, his second wife, on his right. Lord Wharton, his head on a tilting helmet, is in armour, the ladies in caps, bodices and full skirts, the Lady Eleanor wearing a ruff. On the sides of the chest, in relief, are the figures of sons and daughters, numerous achievements, and a dedication, while on the chamfered edge of the tomb-slab is Lord Wharton's epitaph in Latin, in lettering worthy of study.

On view in the nave are a number of pre-Conquest and Norman relics, among them part of a cross-shaft of c 870 carved with the bound figure of a horned Loki, a symbol in the early Christian Church of the Evil One; part of a 10C Viking hogback tombstone; a delicately carved capital from the first of the Norman churches; and a stone coffin of c 1150–1200. The ornate marble and granite pulpit on its Caen stone base was a gift to the church in 1871.

Among the stained glass windows are two by Clayton & Bell: in the S transept one of 1874 depicting the Ascension, with Moses and Elijah on either hand, and, in the S aisle, inserted c 1903, another depicting St. Luke the physician in the centre light, and the visitation of the sick and those in prison in the side lights. At the W end there is a window of 1903 designed by James Clarke of Casterton and executed by Arthur J. Dix. It depicts the aged Samuel, Mary of Bethany, Eunice and the young Timothy, and St. Peter with a staff and a lamb in its four lights.

Lowther, *St. Michael.* St. Michael's has internal stonework of the 12C and 13C, external walls of 1686 pierced by rectangular windows, and an upper stage of the tower of 1856. It is well-known for its many monuments to members of the Lowther family from Elizabethan times to the present century. In the porch are pre-Conquest hogback tombstones and fragments of stone with cablework and interlace. The E window, designed by Herbert Hendrie and executed by Charles Blakeman of London, features St. Cuthbert and St. George, and commemorates the home nurse, the shepherd, ploughman and woodman of the Lowther Estates during the Second World War.

Morland, *St. Laurence.* The church can claim to have the only pre-Conquest tower W of the N Pennines, the long ridge of which, dominated by Cross Fell, can be seen from the vicinity of the church. Sturdy, with 5ft-thick walls built of sandstone rubble blocks pierced by small narrow window openings, the round-headed twin bell openings with a deeply-recessed rounded mid-shaft supporting the lintel, distinguish it for what it is. The present top stage is a late 16C addition, the original capping stones being reused. The low parapet spire was an afterthought. Inside the tower the massive two-stage ladder was cut from a single oak tree over 300 years ago and is still in use.

WORCESTERSHIRE

John Betjeman, in 1958, likened Worcestershire to a fruit tart: a central plain of orchards, surrounded by a crust of hills, burnt where they merge into the Black Country. Since he wrote, that damaged section has spread S. At the same time key towns, like Worcester and Kidderminster, have been abandoned to the motorist and suburban development has begun to overwhelm the villages. Only on the fringes of the S half and in the Teme valley is the countryside still dominant.

This has not made it easier for those who have to maintain their churches. Many seem to be permanently locked, and in this respect Worcester itself sets a deplorable example. Apart from the cathedral, the town is a frustrating and dispiriting experience for the church visitor. Several of the city centre churches are redundant or threatened with redundancy; those that are not often remain tightly locked against vandals. Some buildings have been given worthwhile new roles: St. Helen's is now the County Record Office; the Countess of Huntingdon's Chapel, a most interesting early 19C building, is being converted into a concert hall. Others have been less fortunate: St. Mary Magdalene's (by Frederick Preedy 1876–77) is empty and derelict. One fears for St. Paul's, with its important set of C.E. Kempe windows. Of the redundant churches only St. Swithun's remains intact and unchanged from its 18C heyday. This church alone makes Worcester worth visiting.

In the countryside there is much to be seen, though the predominance of the New Red Sandstone as a building material has added to the diocese's problems as it does not weather well. Only around Broadway is the limestone of the Cotswolds available as a more permanent foundation. Curiously, half-timbering, which is so common in domestic building, is rare in churches. Besford is probably the best example, though the towers of Warndon and Pirton, with crucked side aisles, are memorable. Timber roofs of the trussed rafter type abound, and Ribbesford has an arcade of wooden piers and arches. Worcestershire is a county of brick houses but brick churches are uncommon, though Hanley Castle (1674) and Wolverley (1722) are exceptions, while Pirton has chancel windows with brick tracery.

Pre-Conquest remains are few. Only the Cropthorne cross-head and the mysterious Lechmere Stone have survived. After the Norman Conquest the county came under the domination of its four great Benedictine abbeys: Worcester, Pershore, Evesham and Malvern, all founded before the Domesday Survey. In 1218 the Premonstratensian house at Halesowen was added. Only the crypt of the cathedral has survived from the late 11C, but there was a great deal of building in the 12C, St. Peter's, Rock and St. Martin's, Holt being good examples, both large and both containing good Norman sculpture. Size is also a characteristic of such cruciform churches as Bredon, Ripple and Broadway, while Ribbesford and Powick are also considerable buildings. The county is not distinguished by its Early English and Decorated architecture, though Pershore has both, and Chaddesley Corbett a beautiful Decorated chancel. The Perpendicular style is at its best in the side chapel of All Saints', Evesham and in the nave of Malvern Priory.

Although many churches are rich in 16C and 17C funerary monuments, few churches were built then, and it is not until the 18C that local architecture begins to flower again: at St. Swithun's, Worcester (1734–36) and St. Anne's, Bewdley (1745–48), both by Thomas Woodward; at St. Thomas's, Stourbridge (1728–36) and Great Witley (1735); at St. Mary Magdalene's, Croome d'Abitot (1763) by Lancelot Brown and Robert Adam; and at St. Bartholomew's, Tardebigge (1777) by Francis Hiorn. Many of these churches were monuments to the wealth of the local nobility, but by the 19C this was no longer the case. Even so there was much restoration and some new building. This was especially true of Malvern which acquired the church of Our Lady and St. Alphonsus by Charles Hansom in 1846 and St. Gabriel's by Sir Gilbert Scott in 1872, both at Hanley Swan; then the chapel of the Convent of the Holy Name by Sir Ninian Comper in 1893 and the church of the Ascension by Sir Walter Tapper in 1903, both at Malvern Link. Tenbury Wells was taken over by Henry Woodyer when he built the church of St. Michael for Sir Frederick Gore Ouseley in 1856, and joined it by cloister to St. Michael's College, founded to promote the services of the Church of England, and to give a liberal and classical education to the sons of the clergy and others. Sir Frederick, a fine musician and composer of many anthems, hymns and cantatas, was the largest benefactor and guiding influence. Two curiosities are the Perpendicular reconstruction of Pensax by Thomas Jones in 1832, and the red and black brick tower at Wythall by W.H. Bidlake in 1903. Perhaps the most satisfactory 20C work is the restoration of St. John the Baptist at Wickhamford by G.C. Lees Milne in 1949.

Examples of Norman sculpture can be found on the corbel tables at Holt, Astley and Rock, while of the many fonts, the most spectacular is that at Chaddesley Corbett, and the most unusual at Halesowen, with primitive dragons and thick early interlace. More important are the two rare stone lecterns: at Crowle a tense figure, clutching tendrils, knees bent and feet braced against the front of the lectern; at Norton, a more relaxed cleric, leaning from the foliage, his hand raised in blessing. From the 12C, too, come the small Pirton stone of the Crucifixion and the majestic figure of the seated Christ above the S door at Rous Lench. Wall painting has survived in fragments at Pinvin, Martley and Wickhamford.

Early glass is rare outside Malvern, but pieces have survived from the 14C at Bredon, Birtsmorton and Fladbury, where one showing the Virgin and Child has been imaginatively set as the centrepiece of a cross in the Lady chapel and lit from behind. Matching fragments can be seen at Warndon, and at Eaton Bishop in Herefordshire. St. Michael's College at Tenbury Wells has good stained glass by John Hardman & Co., as has Hanley Castle by Clayton & Bell. Rochford has a very early (1863) E window by William Morris, while Wilden has much later Morris & Co. glass in all its windows. The latter were commissioned by Alfred Baldwin, a relative of Sir Edward Burne-Jones, and the donor of another Morris & Co. window at Ribbesford.

Pre-Reformation memorials include a fine 14C slab at Bredon and good brasses at Strensham, Fladbury and Kidderminster. Perhaps the most unusual Elizabethan memorial is the alabaster effigy of Richard Harewell (died 1576) at Besford and the accompanying triptych to another member of the family who died at the same time. It has hinged sides, painted back and front, and is similar to the Cornwall triptych (1568) at Burford (Shropshire). The 17C saw the local gentry embellish their churches with many notable effigies, the most splendid being those of the Sandys family at Wickhamford (1626), the Savage family at Elmley Castle (1631) and the vast memorial to

Giles Reed at Bredon (1611). Of a more restrained nature is Nicholas Stone's monument to the first Lord Coventry at Croome d'Abitot (1639) and Thomas Scheemakers's extremely beautiful memorial to Mary Russell at Powick (1786), with a roundel showing her teaching her child music. Even larger than the Reed monument at Bredon is J.M. Rysbrack's homage to the first Lord Foley at Great Witley. Good 19C memorials are not common, though Sir Francis Chantrey's to the sixth Earl of Plymouth at Tardebigge (1835) has sentimental grace.

Malvern has a large collection of 15C wall tiles, and there are other groups at Bredon and Broadway. Ripple has a set of 15C misericords illustrating the labours of the farming year. Croome has a superb wooden font, and pulpit with tester, both by Robert Adam. The chapel at Madresfield Court has good Arts and Crafts decoration, dated between 1902 and 1923, and described by Evelyn Waugh in 'Brideshead Revisited'. Newland Church has extensive mural decoration by Clayton & Bell. Rochford has a fine late 18C organ case with double-headed eagle over. Royal arms are fairly numerous, amongst the best being those of Charles I at Broadway, Charles II at Wickhamford, early Georgian at Rochford, Martley, Powick and Ripple, George III at Bredon and Strensham, George IV at Grimley, and Elizabeth II in mahogany at Hanbury. Curious dedications include St. Cassian at Chaddesley Corbett, St. Ecgwin at Church Honeybourne and St. Denys at Severn Stoke.

In spite of King John and Prince Arthur in the cathedral, Worcestershire has not produced many great men. Samuel Butler is commemorated at Strensham, Edward Elgar was born at Broadheath, and Rowland Hill has a statue at Kidderminster. More representative are the two engine drivers, Thomas Scaife and Joseph Rutherford, whose fine headstones, complete with engines, adorn Bromsgrove churchyard. More influential have been the women: Hannah Snell, the woman soldier, Mrs Henry Wood, and Mrs Sherwood of the Fairchild Family, all born at Worcester; Frances Ridley Havergal, born and buried at Astley; and most influential of all, Hannah Macdonald, a Methodist minister's wife, commemorated in a window by Sir Edward Burne-Jones at Ribbesford. She had four daughters: one married Burne-Jones, another Sir William Poynter, the third became the mother of Rudyard Kipling and the fourth the mother of Stanley Baldwin.

Beckford, *St. John the Baptist.* Comprising a nave, central tower and chancel, this church is notable for the tympana over the N and S doors. The latter has two orders of columns and an arch with zigzag decoration. The tympanum rests on corbels, each with two heads, and contains a central cross, with an eye to the left and a bird on the right. Facing each other below the cross are two prancing animals with long ears and horns. The N door has been sealed and has weathered beast-heads and a tympanum of the Harrowing of Hell. It shows Christ choking a dragon with his cross while dragging a man on a rope from the pit. The W arch of the central tower is Norman with zigzag decoration and has at the base of the N shaft a primitively carved centaur and two beak-like heads.

Besford, *St. Peter.* This is the only timber-framed church left in Worcestershire, with nave, oak-shingled bellcote and stone chancel (1881). It is similar to Melverley (Shropshire) though here the timbering is in large squares with occasional diagonal braces rather than closely spaced uprights. The nave dates from the 14C and the timber porch from the 15C. The W window has tracery and mullions in wood and the Rood loft contains quatrefoils, each surrounding a rose. It has red, blue and gold colouring. On the S wall of the nave is a triptych, painted on both sides as at Burford (Shropshire). It commemorates a member of the Harewell family who died young in the late 16C. The outsides have shields and angels, the central panel has the deceased kneeling amongst children while, overhead, badly damaged, was Christ with a rainbow. Below is a verse which includes the words: 'An impe entombed heere dothe lie,/In tender years bereft of breath...' He was not alone. Richard Harewell died in 1576 at the age of 15 and his effigy in alabaster lies on a table-tomb with a small boy on a panel below. Similarly, the tomb of Sir Edward Sebright (died 1679) by William Stanton, has his small daughters, chins on hands and hoods over their plaits, gazing at an inscription stating that Anne died in 1673, aged two, and Elizabeth in 1674, aged five.

Bredon, St. Giles. This outstanding church, with central tower and spire, long chancel, and wide-aisled nave, was built between 1190 and 1350. It is surrounded by a large churchyard and several resplendent buildings, mansion house, manor house, tithe barn and rectory, which a Victorian rector extended to 18 rooms. There was a pre-Conquest monastery here but there are no remains.

The embattled tower, narrower than either nave or chancel, has a slender hexagonal recessed 14C spire with a fine weathercock by Sir Ninian Comper. The chancel has grotesque heads pressed between the buttresses and the stone-tiled roof. The W front has square pinnacles at the angles and a Perpendicular window over a Norman door with beast-head label-stops. There are two small Norman windows on either side of the W end of the nave, but the S aisle or Mitton chapel has double-lancet windows with trefoil heads, while the chancel windows have tracery of c 1300. The vaulted Norman porch faces N and has a room over. Both outer and inner doors have zigzag decoration with good ironwork on hinges and handle. The corbel table has weathered badly, but there are four well-preserved scratch dials near the SW angle of the nave.

The whitewashed walls and abundance of clear glass make the church marvellously light. The W tower arch is pointed with two orders of chevrons, separated by a roll-moulding, resting on scalloped capitals. The Mitton chapel is separated from the nave by two bays on quatrefoil piers, and has lancet windows with detached shafts of Purbeck marble standing on wide sills. The sanctuary has three steps, the risers lined with medieval tiles, probably from Repton, while the nave has a chequered pattern of red, yellow and black tiles, polished by long use. The sanctuary contains sedilia, piscina and Easter sepulchre with crockets and finials. The window in the N wall of the chancel has two fine panels of 14C glass showing St. Mary of Egypt and St. Mary Magdalene.

In the Mitton chapel heraldic glass from Hadzor has been inserted into a plain background to commemorate the Silver Jubilee of Queen Elizabeth II. Small windows in the walls of the tower have glass by Sir Ninian Comper, who was also responsible for the altar, raised behind Jacobean communion rails which have long pendants between the balusters. The seating in the chancel is open-backed, while the nave pews have decorated ends. There are 86 medieval tiles with 39 different coats of arms, including Bohun, Mortimer, Berkeley, Clare, England, Castile and Leon. Amongst the monuments in the chancel is a slab carved with Christ on a tree cross and the heads of a man and a woman over the arms and under trefoil canopies (14C). To the W is a recessed tomb of similar date with the diminutive figures of William Reed, his wife and child. On a very different scale is the enormous śarcophagus of Giles Reed and his wife, a daughter of Fulke Greville. They died in 1611 and lie beneath a canopy rich in obelisks and putti, two of whom are extinguishing their torches in skulls. The children kneel on either side under square pavilions. Sir Giles's helmet hangs on the wall beside. In the N aisle is a large canvas arms of King George III.

Amongst the notables buried here is Bishop Prideaux. Born in 1578, he became Regius Professor of Divinity and Vice-Chancellor of Oxford University, and chaplain to Prince Henry, King James VI and I and King Charles I. He was driven from the See of Worcester during the Civil War and died in poverty at Bredon in 1650. Greatly loved, he is commemorated here in glass, stone, bronze and brass, 'a man of learning, munificence and ability, a servant of God and his King.'

Broadway, St. Eadburgha. Eluding the tourist chaos of England's most publicised village, St. Eadburgha's lies tranquilly below the escarpment down the Snowshill road. Beautifully maintained and built of mellowed Cotswold stone, it consists of chancel, crossing tower, transepts and aisled nave. Externally, it is all Perpendicular, but the foundations are of the early 13C. It stands in a well-kept churchyard with clipped yews and lichen-covered tombstones, many with good calligraphy by F.R. Kempson. The central tower is of three stages with embattled parapet and pinnacles at the corners. The S aisle has a flat roof and similar parapet. The nave doors have metal grilles with shutters behind.

The interior benefits from the lack of pews, the simple tiled floor, and the absence of coloured glass. So the honey-coloured stone of the scalloped and moulded capitals of the arcade is, for once, adequately lit. The central tower is vaulted, with radiating ribs, and seems to have been superimposed on what was once the Norman nave. It rests on 14C arches with double chamfers to the E and W, but the early 13C chancel arch is also used. The nave roof rests on a pleasantly flowered wall plate. Most of the windows are Perpendicular and in keeping; so are the fittings. The font, a plain stone vase, is surrounded by medieval tiles. The pulpit, barrel-shaped, seems to have come from St. Michael's, the present parish church of 1839. In exchange, St. Eadburgha's lost her splendid Elizabethan pulpit with its writhing dragons and large tester. In the nave is a simple pillared collecting box, and over the crossing arch large arms of King George I. The chancel has Jacobean communion rails and table, and on the N wall a seemingly Flemish panel, carved with eight saints. The S transept is occupied by a monumental parish bier of 1888 with solid chariot wheels and rope-like tyres. There are few memorials, the most pleasing being a tablet with shield, columns and putti to Walter Savage (died 1640), and a large monument to William Taylor (1741) by Samuel Chandler.

Unobtrusive, at the W end, is a small slate tablet to David Davies who died in 1819 after serving as curate here for 42 years. And in the chancel a marble memorial commemorates one of the country's greatest bibliophiles, the 'Vello-maniac', Sir Thomas Phillips (1792–1872), who kept his great collection of books and documents across the road at Middle Hill.

Chaddesley Corbett, *St. Cassian.* A church consisting of an 18C W tower, 12C nave, 14C chancel, N and S aisles, 13C St. Nicholas's chapel, and 16C vestry. It stands in a large churchyard at the end of a pleasant village street. The chancel is notable, especially the Decorated tracery of the E window.

The W tower was rebuilt by James Rose, a local architect, in 1779. It has a battlemented parapet, recessed spire with bands of quatrefoils, and seems to have been built a little W of the original so that there appear to be two tower arches. The E window is such a fine example of 14C tracery, containing such a dreadful example of Victorian glass, that it is best viewed from the outside.

Inside, the three NE single-stepped arches of the nave date from c 1150 and rest on rounded piers with scalloped capitals and square abaci. To this arcade was added a later W bay, contemporary with the S arcade. The aisles were enlarged in the 14C and the chancel rebuilt in lavish style. Extensive but restrained restoration by William Butterfield took place in 1863–64. It included the removal of the galleries and box-pews, a new pulpit, re-tiling of the floors and a rebuilding of the N wall of the nave. He also removed the flat nave ceiling and opened up the fine timbers of the roof. Inevitably, the plaster was stripped. The furnishings include a Norman font, cup-shaped, and carved with dragons, interlace and plaiting. A section of a mid-12C tympanum, showing Christ holding a book, has also been retained. In the chancel is an aumbry with ogee canopy, crocketed, and resting on heads. Of the same 14C date are the sedilia and piscina, this time resting on long-haired heads.

The monuments include a brass of 1511 of the parker of Duncient Park with his wife and 11 children and the limestone effigy (c 1290) of one of the Corbets, in chain-mail, with shield, sword and crossed legs. The 17C memorials have been recently vividly restored. Humfrey Pakington (died 1631) is commemorated by a long eulogy beginning, 'In memory of you who did despise/Vain pomp...'. It is enclosed by Classical pillars, in black and white marble, with an achievement in a broken pediment over. Inside the S door are good benefaction boards, dated 1759. The glass is poor except for a window in the N aisle by A.J. Davies of the Bromsgrove Guild.

The dedication to St. Cassian is unique in England. There were three of them: a 4C Greek Bishop of Autun, a French abbot, and a Roman schoolmaster stabbed to death by his pupils with their styli. It is probably the first of these to whom this dedication relates.

Croome d'Abitot, *St. Mary Magdalene.* Positioned to overlook the park, a convincingly Gothic Revival church with a W tower, nave and chancel within an embattled parapet, built in mellow cream Cotswold ashlar. The sixth Earl of Coventry received permission to demolish the old church of St. James to rebuild Croome Court in 1758. He undertook to build a new church and employed Capability Brown and Sanderson Miller to build the Court, drain and landscape the park, and place the church on a hill in front of the house. It was Brown's first major commission after leaving Stowe, and with Robert Adam's help, the church of St. Mary Magdalene was completed and consecrated in 1763.

The W tower is of three stages, has slender buttresses at the angles, rising to pinnacles above the pierced parapet. The W door opens into a vaulted porch with radiating ribs; the second stage has encircled quatrefoils, while the belfry has elaborately traceried openings. The battlements of the nave and chancel are pierced, and interspersed with pinnacles as on the tower. The windows have Y- or intersecting tracery, all cusped. The churchyard retains the old dedication to St. James the Apostle.

The porch, which is under the tower, is plastered like the rest of the building and the impression on entering the nave is of light, and a delicate mixture of Classical and Gothic detail. The roof is coved and rests on slender clustered piers separating the nave from the aisles which have flat ceilings. All are decorated with stucco borders and roundels. An ogee arch leads to the chancel which is long and has an E window of intersecting tracery. The glass is clear throughout and the benches are panelled and carved. Although Brown seems to have had overall control, Robert Adam worked on the interior and the furnishings. If that had been the end of the matter, all would have been well. Unfortunately, Lord Coventry then moved his ancestor's monuments into the narrow chancel, a space too constricted for them. Nor are they all good, the best being that of the first Baron (died 1639), attributed to Nicholas Stone. In black and white marble he is shown reclining above the emblems of his office. He was Keeper of the Great Seal and a figure of Justice is holding it. The monument is of better quality than the large memorial to the fourth Baron by Grinling Gibbons which faces it. He died in 1686 and is propped above his ridiculously small coronet (once balanced on his head), gazing at close range into the bosom of Hope who is pointing upwards to higher things. In quite another class are the font and pulpit by Robert Adam. The latter has an elegant tester and the wooden font is carved round the bowl with angels and leaf bands. It rests on a narrow stem, decorated with swags and twisted fluting, and stands on a spreading, fluted base. The cover is carved with leafage and has a fluted dome. Not all members of the family clutter the chancel. The founder's wife, the beautiful Maria Gunning, who died from consumption and lead poisoning from the over-use of cosmetics, is not here, nor is the first Earl (died 1699) who married one of his servants, which so shocked his heir that he refused to have the monument she had commissioned from William Stanton in the church. She then married Thomas Savage of Elmley Castle and her first husband's handsome memorial was placed in that church. Croome became redundant in 1973 and is now under the care of the Redundant Churches Fund. Until recently the Court harboured a Buddhist community, and on the edge of the churchyard stood a notice, 'No meditating beyond this point'. It is now permissible, and there are few Worcestershire churchyards more congenial for this exercise.

Elmley Castle, *St. Mary.* A Norman church with an embattled 13C tower, nave, chancel and transept, standing at the end of the main street. Apart from the herringbone masonry in the chancel, the church is notable for two of the finest memorials in the county. On the W side of the S transept are three members of the Savage family (1631). They lie side by side in translucent alabaster, William praying, Giles with his hand on his sword, and the latter's wife in an elegant cape holding her child, described by Mrs Esdaile as 'the most delightful long-clothes baby in England'. At the feet of their parents are four kneeling children, three with their hands clasped in prayer, the fourth, a boy, with one hand on his heart and the other on the hilt of his sword. In front of the children is a line of animal heads, including a stag with an arrow through its neck. Opposite is the large monument of the first Earl of Coventry (died 1699) intended for

Croome d'Abitot (q.v.) but placed in front of the Jesse window here instead. He lies, peacefully leaning against a column, heavily bewigged, with puffed sleeves and fine cravat. His eyes look heaven-ward but his left hand gropes lovingly towards the coronet lying by his side. He is guarded by two tall and elegant angels. It is by William Stanton.

Evesham, All Saints and St. Lawrence. Two churches and a detached bell tower stand in the precincts of a great Benedictine abbey. The complex is approached from the town through a Norman gateway which has been rebuilt with Tudor timber-framing. St. Lawrence's, redundant and firmly shut, is a Perpendicular building, restored in 1836, and consisting of a tower with squat spire, chancel, nave, side aisles and S chapel. It is this last addition, probably built by Abbot Lichfield in 1520, with battlements, a five-light window, and fan-vaulting with a central pediment, which is the best feature.

All Saints', a Norman building of W tower with recessed spire, chancel, aisled nave and S chapel, is approached from the gatehouse to the N. The porch into the tower is an exuberant addition to the battlements and pinnacles over the aisles. Once again, Abbot Lichfield provided a beautiful S chapel in 1513, intending it as his own resting place. It is of two bays and has a flowered frieze, battlements and pinnacles. The interior is dark with few monuments except for a small, lively, 13C twisted figure of Moses (?) in the porch. There are good Arts and Crafts chancel gates and several bosses from the abbey.

The chief glory of Evesham, however, again the work of Abbot Lichfield, is the free-standing bell tower. It is panelled to the N and S, with four-light windows and two-light bell openings crowned by ogee gables. The top has pierced battlements, while the archway under the tower opens onto well-kept municipal parkland. Consider-ing that so much of what Abbot Lichfield built was undertaken within barely 25 years of the closure of his abbey, his splendid buildings are a tribute, not only to his taste, but to the surety of his faith. The tower he erected in 1513 is today a confirmation of both.

Great Witley, St. Michael. Witley Court is an awesome ruin; mirac-ulously, when the house was destroyed by fire in 1937, the adjoining church was spared. Completed in 1735, it was built (perhaps by James Gibbs) for the widow of Lord Foley. The church is rectangular, ashlared and with a dignified balustrade for a parapet. The W tower sits on the roof and has two stages: the first houses the clock, and above is an octagonal lantern surmounted by orb and cross. The porch consists of a portico supported on Tuscan columns.

The excitement is all reserved for the interior. The first impression is of white and gold everywhere. There are vivid early 18C stained glass windows and three large ceiling paintings mounted in a spectacular decoration of papier-mâché. The paintings and stained glass came from the former chapel of the Duke of Chandos at Canons, Edgware. The papier-mâché work was modelled on the stucco ceilings at Canons by Bagutti; the paintings are by Antonio Bellucci and the stained glass is signed and dated by Joshua Price, who worked to the designs of Francesco Sleter (or Slater). The glazing is all in squares and the windows are purely paintings. In 'The Adoration of the Kings', the Virgin sits in front of a Classical ruin and a squadron of flying cherubs hovers in attendance. The organ case, although from Canons, seems almost a part of the W wall: the console is enclosed by a semicircular balcony. The delicate font, by James Forsyth, is a marble bowl supported by four angels; the pulpit is much more robust and Baroque, but it is actually by S.W. Dawkes, the builder of mid-Victorian Witley Court. Dawkes was also responsible for the pews; but, like the pulpit, these harmonise well with the original Foley conception of the church. There is a huge monument to the first Lord Foley, by J.M. Rysbrack.

The interior facing W of St. Michael's, an Italianate extravaganza of 1735, perhaps by James Gibbs

Hanley Swan, *Our Lady and St. Alphonsus.* A commanding church consisting of nave, chancel and bellcote at the E end. There is a small convent and presbytery attached. It stands on the edge of Blackmore Park, the home in the 19C of Thomas Hornyold, the most influential Catholic in the county. It was the second Redemptorist foundation in England, and became a secular parish in 1851. It cost £30,000 in 1846 and was built by Charles Hansom, a brother of the inventor of the Hansom cab. The money came chiefly from the Hornyold and Gandolfi families. The church is in the Early English style and was consecrated in 1846. It is most lavishly decorated, with a finely carved reredos, painted light hangings, a Rood screen, and angels with musical instruments in the springing of the rib-vaulting. The furniture has been attributed to A.W.N. Pugin.

Holt, St. Martin. Consisting of tower, chancel, nave and S arcade, it stands close to the castle, overlooking vast gravel pits. Only Rock has more Norman decoration than Holt, which starts with the reset door in the lychgate. The S and N doors have elaborately carved capitals on two orders of columns. They include foliate heads, a monster biting its tail, and a fox and a bird drinking from a barrel. The chancel arch and S arcade are rounded, and there is a fine Norman window in the N side of the nave. The font is round, on a thick stem cut with diagonal grooves, and the sides are ringed by monstrous faces, linked mouth to mouth, by trailing foliage. Over the chancel arch is a Victorian mosaic, copied from Ravenna, and in the S arcade some 15C glass. The E window is by C.E. Kempe (1892). Amongst all this exclusively masculine decoration it is gratifying to find that the screen and lectern were carved by the wife of a 19C Vicar.

Kidderminster, St. Mary and All Saints. A noble SW tower, aisled nave with clerestory, choir with aisles and side chapels, in a municipalised churchyard, looking down on a jungle of roads, shopping precincts and car parks. Church Street, one of the better streets left, is severed from its church by a ring road which can only be crossed through a graffiti-covered underpass. A major restoration of St. Mary's took place in 1895 but the older parts date from the early 1500s.

Once the ring road has been conquered, well-restored gates lead to the tower which rises in three stages to an embattled and panelled parapet with pinnacles at the angles. The bottom stage has a five-light W window, the second has stepped niches, and the third has two-light bell openings with blank replicas on either side. The clerestory has a matching panelled parapet with battlements and is lit by straight-headed two-light windows. Beyond the sanctuary, the Lady chapel, which was once free-standing, has now been joined to the church by a vestry. On the N side, the Whittal chapel was designed by Sir Giles Gilbert Scott and dedicated in 1922.

The interior is made more complicated by the sepulchral darkness caused by the Victorian glass. Even the huge eight-light W window admits little light. The nave has arcades of four bays standing on octagonal piers and the roof is said to be a replica of that of the Guesten Hall of Worcester Cathedral. Most of the memorials from the 15C have been damaged. The fine tomb of Lady Joyce Beauchamp has her effigy protected by slender buttresses supporting a canopy which has lost its pinnacles and on which the four guardian angels have lost their heads. More impressive is the huge brass to Sir John Phelip (died 1415) and Walter Cookesey (died 1407). They stand on lions under a triple canopy, in full armour, their hands in prayer, on either side of Matilda, the demure wife they shared. Below them a Latin inscription states that Sir John fought at Harfleur and that King Henry V loved him as a friend. He died three weeks before Agincourt.

Richard Baxter was appointed as curate in 1641 and remained

there until 1660. The pillar on the N side of the nave shows the marks of the fastenings which held the pulpit from which he preached. On the back of the pillar are some words from Tyndale's Bible: 'We preach not ourselves but Jesus Christe our Lorde. We are not as the moste parte are which choppe and change with the word of God'. It is a pity that the planners who have done so much to ruin this town, did not heed these words and chop and change a little less brutally.

Malvern

Malvern Priory, *St. Mary and St. Michael.* Malvern Priory is a richly rewarding church. The refinement of its Perpendicular exterior, the dignity of its Norman nave, the warmth of its multi-coloured stone, the exhilaration of its stained glass, the harmoniousness of its setting—all these make Malvern memorable. But it only just survived the Dissolution: in 1541 a group of parishoners, led by one John Pope, had to pay £20 to preserve the remaining parts of the building: the Lady chapel and S transept had already been demolished.

Externally, only the E and N elevations are closely accessible. Below the great E window is a depressed arch and doorway while, almost at ground level, traces of the Norman crypt under the now-vanished Lady chapel can be seen. The finest features of the N side are the clerestory windows, all transomed. The six-light N transept window also has good Perpendicular tracery. The unity of this whole elevation is enhanced by the buttresses, parapets and pinnacles and (above all, of course) by the crossing tower. By contrast with its near contemporary, Ludlow, Malvern's is not a tall tower, but any suggestion of squatness is offset by the slender buttressing, by the tall ogee gables over the bell openings and by the pierced battlements and corner turrets. The S elevation, with amputated transept, quite lacks the impact of the N, but once boasted the cloisters.

Given the area of glass in the windows, the interior is not surprisingly light. The pale pink-grey stone of the nave and the plastered aisle walls reflect this light generously: thus walls and furnishings glow, including the panelled flat wooden roof with good recent painting and gilding. One can take in the length and height of the building without difficulty, since there is no chancel screen and only a level floor almost as far as the sanctuary. Remarkably, however, this sense of space and light is achieved in an uncompromisingly Norman nave of six bays, whose uncarved drum pillars sustain the round two-step arches and the dauntingly strong walls above them. The N aisle is twice the width of the S. The N transept, formerly known as the Jesus chapel, is dominated by its spectacular Coronation of Mary window. The crossing has a rather heavy lierne-vault beneath the tower. The present choirstalls are situated in the crossing, as is the organ (N side). The N chancel aisle and the curved ambulatory behind the high altar terminate abruptly with the parclose screen of the St. Anne chapel that completely absorbs what would have been the S chancel aisle.

Malvern boasts the finest collection of medieval wall tiles in Britain. More than 1000 tiles with nearly 100 different patterns can be seen on the curved wall behind the high altar, in the N chancel aisle and beside the reredos (glass mosaic, by Sir Arthur Blomfield, 1884). Mid-15C Malvern tiles like these can be found in churches throughout the S and W Midlands. The nave has rush-seated chairs instead of pews; the present choirstalls are Victorian, but are overshadowed by the monks' stalls beyond with their misericords. The earliest of these are mid-14C. There is a calendar set (15C) and a number of easily detected replacements, but the general standard of design is high and the range of subjects unusually varied. In the ambulatory is a strange pair of weighty Gothick chairs, an interesting provincial attempt, perhaps, at emulating a new fashion. The most notable modern woodwork is the organ case (by W.D. Caroë) in confident Jacobean style.

N of the high altar is a mutilated tomb of a 13C knight holding a battle axe. On the other side is the Knottesford tomb—alabaster, and depicting John Knottesford with his wife; it was commissioned by their daughter Anne, who is seen kneeling piously at their feet— Elizabethan costume and design of a high order. The war memorial in the S aisle, again by Caroë, is an effective marble monument; less flamboyant than the organ case, but still in Jacobean style. Also in the S aisle is a fine banner designed by Ninian Comper and made in 1910 at St. Mary's Convent, Wantage.

No brief paragraph can do justice to the 15C glass of Malvern Priory. In importance it ranks with that of York Minster. The Coronation of Mary window in the N transept is one of the finest works of art of its date (c 1501) anywhere in Britain. The joys of Mary are represented and the Virgin herself appears in a halo of golden light with a blue nimbus, while King Henry VII and Prince Arthur, his heir, kneel in the bottom panels. The E window depicts first benefactors of the priory, then the Passion with the Crucifixion in the centre. The chancel clerestory windows chiefly show saints, martyrs and doctors of the Church, each figure in his own canopy-worked niche. It was these windows that inspired C.E. Kempe at the start of his career; his own work is seen in the E window of the St. Anne chapel. In this chapel the S windows present a delightful gallery of Old Testament stories. In the N aisle the 1887 Jubilee window by T.W. Camm is notable, its three lights presenting the accession of Queen Victoria, her coronation, and the Jubilee service in Westminster Abbey.

Malvern Link, *The Ascension.* The Ascension (dedicated 1903) is an important church by Sir Walter Tapper, and one of the most interesting buildings in Malvern. Its exterior is austere, though it dominates the surrounding streets and houses; its interior and furnishings are restrained but uplifting. Here if anywhere is evidence that the legacy of G.F. Bodley was not merely 'good taste' (Tapper had been chief draughtsman to Bodley & Garner).

The church has a cross-gabled W tower, slightly recessed into the nave. Below the W gable a carved figure of the Ascended Christ (by Harry Hems) stands in stone relief. The N and S bell openings are of Y-tracery with shafts instead of mullions. There are no louvres. A triple-lancet window dominates the W face and there is no tower door. The nave's four bays are defined by flat buttresses with pairs of lancets between them all set high beneath the steeply overhanging eaves of the slate roof. A bellcote marks the division between nave and chancel, but the chancel is also narrower and has three tall, single lancets each side. The S door is approached down an impressive avenue of yews. The walls are stucco, but all stone dressings are Cotswold stone.

The interior is aisleless: there are chairs instead of pews and the emphasis is all on height. The four nave bays are divided by responds supporting rib arches, and there is a plaster wagon-vault ceiling. The high windows have running in front of them an arcaded wall passage. The chancel arch is narrow and rises to the apex of the roof. Through it can be seen the lierne-vault of the chancel and the E end; this has a powerfully unified triple focus of three-lancet window, reredos and raised altar. The chancel floor is tiled black and white (as is the baptistery, recessed under the tower arch). The font itself is a beautifully scalloped octagonal bowl of black stone, supported by free-standing clusters of piers, and with a black and gilt cover suspended from the ceiling. The wooden pulpit by contrast sits modestly in the NE corner of the nave, quite overshadowed by the Rood (from Oberammergau) and the fine wrought-iron screen (black and gilded again) whose Art Nouveau frieze by William Bainbridge Reynolds features angels holding shields depicting the Instruments

The interior facing E of the chapel of the Convent of the Holy Name by Sir Ninian Comper, 1903

of the Passion. There is a single range of stalls each side of the chancel (and the organ is in a tower gallery) so nothing obscures the view of the high altar and the reredos. The frontals are by Watts & Co.; the reredos is a triptych with dominant colours of red and gold, depicting saints.

Malvern Link, *Convent of the Holy Name.* Sir Ninian Comper designed the Convent chapel in 1903, and continued designing furnishings for it up to 1950. Externally it is of red brick with a stone parapet running the whole length of the building and with tall, two-light windows. The porch is placed half-way along the cloister on the S side of the chapel.

The chapel is of seven bays, the windows so deeply set that the wall shafts are, in effect, internal buttresses. The interior is notable both for its height and light: walls, wagon roof, even the W screen are all white. By contrast the panelling and stalls are dark oak, and Comper's glass is predominantly blue and purple. At the W end is a gallery, originally for the girls of the convent's reformatory.

Comper's most characteristic work is at the E end. There is an English altar with two pairs of cast metal angels topping the riddel posts. Behind is a stone screen running the entire width of the sanctuary and with ogee-headed doors either side of the altar. Much delightfully idiosyncratic colour and decoration is on this screen: pelicans, dolphins etc. The alabaster reredos has as its central figure a beardless Christ. One expects the sacristy to be behind the screen, but it isn't. Indeed the screen was a later addition to the chapel when the introduction of a hanging pyx (another Comper hallmark) required that the altar should stand forward of the E window. The pyx itself is exquisite: hexagonal, with perfect miniature Gothic details and an angel on the door. Also of great beauty are a ciborium and chalice made to Comper's designs by W.F. Knight. The Convent is now empty and the future of its buildings and furnishings is uncertain.

Little Malvern Priory, *St. Giles.* The Priory, together with Little Malvern Court alongside, forms a picturesque group at the foot of the Malvern Hills.

Originally a small Benedictine monastery founded in 1125, the church was dedicated to St. Mary, St. Giles and St. John. Of the original buildings only fragments remain. What survive are the tower and the former chancel. The 14C screen has the intricately carved Rood beam resting upon it, and there are 15C Malvern tiles still *in situ* in the sanctuary floor. The figures in the E window are portraits of the Yorkist royal family during the Wars of the Roses.

Newland, *St. Leonard.* In 1855 'The Ecclesiologist' praised the little wooden roadside chapel of Newland, recommending it as 'an excellent model for a church of the simplest type in many colonial situations, or for a temporary church at home'. Within ten years, however, it had been replaced by a stone building that was to be not only the parish church of Newland, but the chapel of the adjoining almshouses, all erected by Earl Beauchamp. P.C. Hardwick's church is of stone, his almshouses are redbrick; the former is externally modest, the latter are grandiose. The church has a long roof, a N porch and a small crocketed spire at the SE corner. A passage connects the tower with a tiny mortuary chapel, half-timbered with wooden tracery windows. Evidently, this was built from the remains of the original church.

Nothing about the outside prepares one for the extraordinary richness of the interior. Not an inch of roof or wall is left undecorated. The decoration was by Clayton & Bell. The chancel, almost as long as the nave, is entered through a low wall and elaborate wrought-iron gates (by Francis Skidmore to Hardwick's design). The E window (of three lights, with Geometrical tracery) stands above a richly gilded reredos, but this is entirely outshone by the triple sedilia placed in the first bay of the chancel arcade: the extravagant canopy work is supported by free-standing black marble shafts, and the seats are also panelled with marble. Chancel and sanctuary floors are tiled throughout in a style more Levantine than Gothic. The chancel arcade, of three bays, is supported by pairs of polished marble pillars with straps and exaggerated carved capitals. What is in effect the S chancel aisle houses the organ, the vestry and additional choirstalls. There are rose windows with unusual tracery at both ends and a small dormer above the doorway leading to the mortuary chapel. As in the chancel itself, every surface is covered with designs both formal and figurative, chiefly in terracotta, blue and green.

The nave is muted only in comparison with the chancel. Here the chief colours are terracotta and white, but the marble pulpit, the inlay of the low chancel wall, and the decoration of the chancel arch, window reveals and roof timbers give a remarkable unity to the whole building. Set in the W wall is perhaps the most bizarre feature of all: a Venetian-style oriel window with dark green leaded glass. This was built to allow occupants of the Infirmary to watch the services, and is placed off-centre to avoid obstructing the W rose window above or the font below.

The font, presumably 12C and shaped like a large cheese with a band of dogtooth decoration just below the rim, is the only pre-1864 furnishing in the church. The stained glass in the E window is by John Hardman & Co., in the W rose window by Lavers & Barraud, and the rest is by Clayton & Bell, especially good in the other rose windows (N.B. the baptismal themes above the font) and in the dormer. On the W wall of the chancel aisle is an impressive brass and enamel memorial to the third Earl Beauchamp, the church's founder.

Pershore, *Holy Cross and St. Edburgha.* The crossing tower, S transept and a small section of the nave are left from the great Benedictine abbey demolished in 1540. What remained was bought by the townsfolk for £400 and became the parish church. It stands upright and a little forlorn in a large churchyard, overlooking posts which mark a nave, once as long as that at Tewkesbury. It bears many marks of destruction and restoration: buttresses erected after the collapse of the N transept in 1686; a totally inadequate apse built on the site of the Lady chapel in 1846; and reconstruction work by Sir Gilbert Scott in 1862–63 and Sir Harold Brakspear in 1920.

The height of the crowning tower, now at the W end of the chancel, accentuates the constriction below. It is of three stages, with much ballflower decoration, and is capped by finials shaped like candle snuffers. The second stage has delicate 14C two-light windows, while the bell openings of the third stage are flanked by blank recesses of the same design. The belfry contains a famous ring of Rudhall bells from Gloucester (1715). The early 13C chancel has a parapet, flying buttresses and Early English Decorated windows. There is Norman arcading near the gable of the 12C S transept and the marks of the roofline of the monks' dormitory.

Inside, the church is of great beauty. The best approach is from the

W end, looking towards the chancel with its four bays and multiple-shafted piers. It was consecrated in 1239. The superb vaulting rises from between the clerestory windows and the triforium passage on double shafts springing from the spandrels. The ribs then meet like stars around the 41 splendid bosses containing beasts, foliar heads and exotic leaf patterns. All this is from the 13C; earlier is the S transept, with blank Norman arcading and columns with zigzag decoration.

The furnishings include a badly worn Norman font with Christ and the Apostles under an arcade. The S chapel has an E window by C.E. Kempe and medieval tiles in the floor. Two 15C windows in the S aisle have glass by John Hardman & Co. illustrating the history of the abbey. The tombs include a 13C knight and 16C and 17C monuments to the Haselwood family. There are several hatchments, the remains of a wall painting, and part of a screen in the N transept which has the heads of an abbot and of King Henry VI, inscribed Ao XII (1434). Near the N door is a large benefaction board recording the gift of £50 to the poor by Henry Smith in 1626. The long inscription consists chiefly of those who should not benefit.

Ripple, *St. Mary.* A cruciform building with chancel, tower and transepts, and nave with clerestory and aisles, one of the few, almost complete, Early English churches in the county. Most features date from the 12C, the chancel from the 13C. The Perpendicular tower has an 18C balustrade. The N porch was given an upper storey in 1797 and, according to John Noake, was used by the parson to hang his game. The church is famous for its 16 misericords, dating from the 15C, illustrating the monthly labours of the farming year. The E window, until it was destroyed in the Civil War, contained the arms of King Henry V and his family. The remains have been found and placed in the S window of the chancel. The E window now has glass by H.W. Bryans, a pupil of C.E. Kempe, who was responsible for the W window. In the chancel is a brass to John Woodward (died 1596) 'sometime yeoman of the Gard with King Phillipe and allso to Queen Elizabeth'. His grandson 'was laid down to sleep with his grandfather in the dust of the same grave' in 1668. The arms are of King George I.

Strensham, *St. Philip and St. James.* An unassuming W tower, nave, chancel and S porch, isolated above the Avon and cut off from its village. It contains royal arms (Hanoverian) and hatchments over the chancel arch; 16C benches with linenfold ends and matching wall panelling with hat pegs; family pew and two-decker pulpit; medieval tiles in the nave floor; and a painted W gallery of c 1500. Once part of the screen, the gallery consists of 23 vertical boards each painted with the figure of a saint and stands on elaborately carved posts and spandrels, probably from the same source. There are also memorials of the Russell family: four fine brasses, two (1390 and 1405) under the chancel carpet, and the others (1502 and 1562) in the chancel wall. Less restrained are the Russell tombs. Sir Thomas (died 1632) lies with his wife on a tomb-chest open to show a coffin and skulls. Columns support an open pediment, all skilfully enriched. It lies opposite the monument to Sir Francis (died 1705) by Edward Stanton. He lies, body twisted towards his wife, one hand with broken fingers gesturing towards his coronet which is being carried into the clouds by putti. His wife, hand raised in admonishment, seems to be advising him to think of other things. There is also a small memorial to Samuel Butler, the author of 'Hudibras', who was born here.

Tardebigge, *St. Bartholomew.* Francis Hiorn's slender spire of 1777 dominates an auditory church to which Henry Rowe of Worcester added an apsidal chancel in 1879. The tower is memorable, with a pillared portico to the W and a Baroque concave bellcote with paired pillars supporting elegant urns. The whole is surmounted by the fine spire. The nave is lit by tall round-headed windows of clear glass. The interior has benefited from the work of members of the Bromsgrove Guild, especially the bronze lectern of 1907, the chancel seating of the same date, and the oak doors of the portico. There are also two fine monuments. In the chancel a white marble memorial to Other Archer by Sir Francis Chantrey (1835) shows a woman in long Grecian clothes weeping over an urn. Facing the nave, there is a large tablet to Lady Mary Cookes and her husband (died 1693). Twisted columns support an oval in which half-length reliefs of husband and wife gaze at the congregation. It has been attributed to William Stanton, but has more in common with Edward Stanton's memorial to Richard Acton at Acton Round (Shropshire). Apart from its superb position, St. Bartholomew's is rare in this part of the county for its beautifully kept churchyard, its church school and its sturdy defence of the Book of Common Prayer.

Wickhamford, *St. John the Baptist.* The church consists of a 17C W tower, a rebuilt 17C nave and a 13C chancel. It was unobtrusively restored in 1949 by G.C. Lees Milne and has retained most of its main features, plastered walls, a huge tympanum over the chancel arch with the arms of King Charles II, and Jacobean panelling. The chancel is separated from the nave by gates and all the liturgical furniture is in the nave, including the lower part of a three-decker pulpit, box-pews and a beautiful W gallery. This leaves the chancel empty except for three-sided communion rails, a 13C wall painting of the Virgin, and the superb alabaster tombs (repainted in 1956) of Sir Samuel and Sir Edwyn Sandys, father and heir, who died within three weeks of each other in 1626. They lie under canopies supported on black pillars, with their wives and kneeling children. The ledger stone in the sanctuary to Penelope Washington (died 1697) has the arms (two bars, three molets) which foreshadowed the stars and stripes of America. A very well-kept church.

Worcester

St. Swithun (in the care of the Redundant Churches Fund). A perfect 18C city church on the corner of the High Street, still surrounded by street traders and pedestrians. Apart from its Perpendicular tower, the building is all of the 1730s, and its façade is at the E end with Venetian window, broad pediment and a clock mounted above the gable. There are doorways at either corner. The N and S sides have six bays, with fluted Doric pilasters and round-arched windows. The stonework of the parapet is in places badly decayed.

   The interior is at first sight conventional, but has some intriguing details. One enters under the tower and passes through the vestibule into the aisleless church proper. There are box-pews everywhere, and facing in all directions. There are no choirstalls, of course, and the communion table is contained between two screens on top of which are hefty Doric pillars rising to the ceiling. The ceiling is fascinating: apparently coved and plastered, it actually exhibits a very rudimentary attempt at Gothic vaulting supported by cheerfully repainted Gothic cherubs on high corbels. The effect is utterly unselfconscious. On the W wall is an organ gallery with fluted square pillars underneath. The three-decker pulpit dominates the building: the staircase twists elegantly behind, and the tester has an elaborate cresting including the Pelican in her Piety and a large anchor dangling beneath her. In front of the pulpit is the Mayor's pew, containing a high-backed chair from the top of which sprouts an elaborate sword rest including the Corporation badge and the royal monogram, G.R., on top.

There are no outstanding memorials on the walls, but several are of interest, among them Edward Milton's (1629), a model of Jacobean formal simplicity, and Elizabeth Barker's (1692) with an elaborate cartouche, and a skull and hourglass motif below. The only jarring note in the whole church is struck by the hideous plastic lampshades, but one must be grateful that the church has been otherwise so well-preserved.

St. Nicholas. Externally, this is the grandest of the 18C churches in Worcester; internally, it is the most disappointing. It was built in 1730 by Humphrey Hollins. The W tower has side bays, the church itself has four bays and the usual round-arched windows. At the E end there is a miniature apse for the sanctuary. The complete church cost £3345 and most of that money must have been spent on the W façade and tower. A massive portal is flanked by Tuscan pillars supporting a broken-back pediment. Above the pediment is a finely carved royal arms. Pilasters define the side bays which also have balustraded parapets. The tower is based on a pattern from James Gibbs's 'Book of Architecture' and is an undoubted landmark. The first stage is square, the second square with rounded edges; the bell stage is octagonal surmounted by a cupola with an imposing weather vane on top.

The interior shows all too clearly the damage done by the restoration of 1867. The galleries, pulpit and communion rails, of wood and iron, are dismal when contrasted with the fittings of St. Swithun's. The windows of the aisles have very early crown glass in their surrounds. The font has a conventional baluster shape, and cherub decorations, with a ceramic lining to the stone bowl. Underneath the S staircase in the vestibule is a bookcase that looks like a converted 17C breadshelf. Fluted Doric pilasters support a segmental pediment. Just legible are the words 'He that giveth to the Poor Lendeth to the Lord'.

Old St. Martin's (St. Martin in Cornmarket). This is a brick building with rusticated stone dressings. A simple balustrade tops the tower, while the E façade is unadorned. The entrance porch stands in a small courtyard on the S side.

The interior is bizarre: here is an 18C church (1768 by Anthony Keck) entirely formal and conventional in design given an evangelical face-lift in the 1850s with a poor Gothic E window and 'Worship The Lord In The Beauty of Holiness' inscribed above; then more recently adopting all the trappings of full-blooded ritualism. Pugin would have despaired. The 18C panelling and communion rails have survived, as has the balustraded W gallery. The capitals and entablatures of the pillars have been well picked out in a recent redecoration, but the painted stonework of the Victorian font is a fearful lapse. The stained glass belongs firmly to St. Martin's evangelical phase. A confessional box of quaint design sits in the NW corner.

St. Martin, London Road. This is an impressive example of an Edwardian town church, built by the prolific G.H. Fellowes Prynne (foundation stone 9 October 1909) but with every sign of care and originality. Red rockfaced stone is used throughout except for windows. There is no tower but an intricate wood and copper bell turret marks the division between nave and chancel. The E window seems very high up because there is an undercroft beneath the chancel. The W window has emphatic curvilinear tracery and a modern baptistery. The S elevation fronting the road is enhanced by the addition of a well-detailed porch and transept, terminating in an apsidal E corner.

The interior is spacious and uncluttered: chairs, not pews, a low wall instead of a chancel screen, narrow passage aisles, tall red and white piers, a wagon roof. The baptistery (1961) is more effective when seen from inside the church. Mass and proportion, not decoration, create the impact throughout. There is an interesting contrast, however, in the little chapel enclosed within the apse of the S transept. There are modern Stations of the Cross in appliqué and embroidery.

CITY OF YORK

York is so dominated ecclesiastically and architecturally by the Minster that the churches and chapels of the city can be easily overlooked. This is not altogether surprising, because many surviving medieval churches are small and rather insignificant. Some, it is true, are redeemed by individual features of interest: a fine spire or lantern tower, or fittings, or (above all) by stained glass. More medieval glass survives in the Minster and the parish churches than in any other city in England. Traditionally, its preservation during the Civil War and Commonwealth is ascribed to the firm control of Lord Fairfax, who became Governor of York after it fell to Parliament in 1644. Before the Reformation there were more than 40 parish churches within the city walls. Now there are fewer than 20, and some of these are no longer in religious use. The churches are mostly built of white magnesian limestone from Tadcaster, but there was much infilling and rebuilding with brick.

Most of the churches are built in 15C Perpendicular style. A few earlier features can be singled out for mention. The major pre-Conquest survival is the W tower of St. Mary Bishophill Junior. Its lower part reuses Roman stone. Above is rough masonry in herringbone pattern; and the belfry stage has twin bell openings with a central shaft (the W opening has 13C Y-tracery). There is 11C walling round the chancel arch of St. Mary, Castlegate and the E wall of St. Cuthbert's, Peaseholme Green is 11C, using Roman bricks and stones. From the Norman period two doors survive, both reset. At St. Denys's, Walmgate the nave was demolished in 1797 and the door was reset in the (former) S chancel aisle. The S doorway at St. Margaret's, Walmgate does not belong to the church at all, but was brought from St. Nicholas's Hospital outside the city, which had been ruined in the siege of 1644. On the arches are Zodiac signs and Labours of the Months. At St. Michael's, Spurriergate the Transitional piers, capitals and arches were reused in the 15C rebuilding, and the 15C tower arches have piers and capitals which—astonishingly—reproduce the 12C form, a most unusual example of 'revival'. Little 13C work survives. For the Decorated style, the Reticulated S windows of Holy Trinity, Goodramgate, and the flowing tracery of the SE window of St. Denys's, Walmgate can be studied. In the 15C most churches assumed their surviving form. Some fine towers were built, from the plain but well-proportioned St. Saviour's, St. Saviourgate (largely rebuilt 1844–45) to St. Martin-le-Grand, Coney Street. This tower, and the surviving S aisle (the rest was bombed in the 1940s and restored by George Pace, 1961) represent the most ornate Perpendicular exterior, with detached, crocketed pinnacles and openwork battlements. Two churches have prominent spires on octagonal belfry stages: St. Mary's, Castlegate and All Saints', North Street. All Saints', Pavement has the finest tower of any York church, the magnificent openwork lantern of 1475–1501, and this seems to have inspired the diminutive lanterns on the W gables of St. Helen's, St. Helen's Square and St. Michael-le-Belfry. Both lanterns surmount giant arches framing the W window. All three lanterns, and the W fronts of St. Helen's and St. Michael's, are 19C reconstructions, but they reproduce more or less what was there before.

The post-Reformation period is mostly a history of patching-up, partial demolition and 19C reconstruction. St. John's, Micklegate has a short timber and brick tower of 1646, with a pyramidal roof, quaint rather than attractive. St. Margaret's, Walmgate has a brick tower of 1684; and the brick tower of St. Martin-cum-Gregory, Micklegate is as late as 1844. Holy Trinity, Micklegate is the much-reduced remnant of a priory founded in 1089. The W front of 1902–04 is a fine work by C. Hodgson Fowler, inspired by the Minster's S transept. Of post-Reformation churches and chapels, the earliest surviving is the Unitarian Chapel, St. Saviourgate, built in 1692 of brick. The Greek cross plan, with a central, blank tower topped by a pyramidal roof, is unusual. The round-headed windows are of 1839. The finest 18C chapel is the Bar Convent's chapel built in 1767–70 by Thomas Atkinson for the Institute of the Blessed Virgin Mary. Of 19C chapels the Centenary Methodist Church, St. Saviourgate, of 1839–40, is the best. It is by James Simpson and has a grand Ionic pedimented portico. George Goldie's Catholic church of St. Wilfred, Duncombe Place, is the proudest Gothic Revival church in York, bold and assertive in 13C style with a big SW tower. It needed to be bold, with the huge mass of the Minster looming behind it, and with its different alignment it deliberately snubs its ponderous neighbour. In the 20C some sensitive restoration was done by George Pace (St. Martin-le-Grand, Coney Street and St. Michael's, Spurriergate), and when St. Mary Bishophill Senior was demolished in 1963 Pace incorporated parts of that church in his new church of the Holy Redeemer, Boroughbridge Road, 1965.

Holy Trinity, Goodramgate, unaltered by the Victorians, has fittings of 17C and 18C date, box-pews, a double-decker pulpit, and altar furnishings of 1715. This arrangement, of a big wooden reredos in the Classical style, and a communion rail with a central semicircular projection, can be found also at St. Michael-le-Belfry (1712), St. Michael's, Spurriergate (early 18C) and St. Martin-cum-Gregory, Micklegate (1749–53). Several 17C pulpits survive, in St. Denys's, Walmgate (early 17C), All Saints', Pavement (1634), St. Martin-cum-Gregory (1636) and All Saints', North Street (1675). Some churches have late 17C font covers with scrolled and openwork tops: St. Martin-cum-Gregory and St. Mary Bishophill Junior. Slightly later are those at Holy Trinity, Micklegate (1717, from demolished St. Saviour's) and St. Martin-le-Grand, Coney Street (1717). A few medieval fittings survive. The oldest are the 13C closing-ring at All Saints', Pavement, and a late 12C font with Norman blank arcading on the bowl, at St. Helen's. 15C doors, with Perpendicular panel tracery, are at St. Cuthbert's, Peaseholme Green, St. Crux Hall, Pavement (from the demolished church), St. Sampson's, Church Street, and Holy Trinity, Micklegate. All Saints', Pavement has a 15C lectern from St. Crux. There are late 15C stalls at All Saints', North Street, and early 16C benches in St. Michael-le-Belfry. Good 19C fittings, a three-sided gallery, mahogany pulpit and organ case, survive in the Centenary Methodist Church. St. Mary Bishophill Junior has an early 20C reredos by Temple Moore.

Most York churches have fragments of medieval stained glass, and some have impressive surviving schemes. The windows of All Saints', Pavement, All Saints', North Street, Holy Trinity, Goodramgate and St. Michael-le-Belfry are described in the gazetteer. St. Denys's, Walmgate has the oldest glass, 13C, small roundels in grisaille, illustrating scenes from the life of St. Theophilus. This is in the N aisle. In the same aisle is 14C glass with figures of saints. The E window, mid-15C, has the Crucifixion and the Virgin and St. John, a central feature also of the E window of Holy Trinity, Goodramgate.

The N aisle E window was once a Tree of Jesse window, but is now a jumble of fragments. The Tree of Jesse features also in the stained glass of St. Michael's, Spurriergate. The Jesse window has some similarities with John Thornton's work in the Minster. It was restored from confusion in 1948, but is somewhat faded. Amongst the other windows is one showing the Nine Orders of Angels, a subject also at All Saints', North Street and St. Martin-le-Grand, Coney Street. The former W window was reset in the N wall of the smaller church. The angels are in the tracery lights; the main window depicts the story of St. Martin. The 18C stained glass artist William Peckitt is represented at St. Martin-cum-Gregory, Micklegate, in memorial windows to members of his family, in the N aisle.

The York churches do not yield many outstanding monuments. St. Crux Hall has several good memorials saved from the demolished church. The only early 17C monument with recumbent effigies and an architectural canopy, to Sir Robert Walter, is here. A tablet to Roger Belwood (died 1694) calls him 'a learned man' and is set against a bookcase, as if to emphasise the point. The Fisher family of late 18C sculptors provided the monument to Henry Waite (died 1780), with his profile portrait in a medallion. St. Michael's, Spurriergate has a charming neo-Classical wall monument by the Fishers to William Hutchinson (died 1772). The best 18C monument is to Robert Squire and his wife in St. Michael-le-Belfry. Another at St. Olave's, Marygate to William Thornton (died 1721) is a ponderous oval tablet with cherubs, festoons and a flaming urn. Thornton was the celebrated engineer of the great wooden frame which restored the leaning N front of Beverley Minster to the perpendicular in c 1716. In the churchyard is a monument to William Etty the painter (died 1849). At Holy Trinity, Micklegate is an early Gothic Revival monument to Dr. John Burton (died 1771). He was the author of 'Monasticon Eboracense' and the two volumes are placed on top of a plaque and parchment. In the churchyard opposite St. George's, George Street, the highwayman Dick Turpin is buried. There is no monument.

All Saints, North Street. All Saints' has two remarkably fine 15C stained glass windows, illustrating the 'Corporal Acts of Mercy' and the 'Pricke of Conscience'. It has much other medieval glass besides. Remarkable too, though less admirable perhaps, is the collection of ecclesiastical bric-a-brac, statuettes, dark paintings and the like, displayed in the spacious interior. The church was extensively restored by the York Civic Trust in 1977.

The 15C W tower, with an octagonal upper stage and spire, 120ft high, adds dignity to the exterior. At the E end are windows with Decorated tracery; most of the aisle windows are 15C square-headed, three-light Perpendicular. At the SW corner E. Ridsdale Tate added an 'anchorage' in the early 20C, its concrete sub-structure mostly concealed by applied half-timbering.

The interior is light. There is no structural division between nave and chancel. The aisles, as wide as the nave, are separated from the latter by arcades of six bays, the piers variously late 12C to 15C. Over the chancel and its aisles are fine hammerbeam roofs with bosses and angel corbels. The chancel and sanctuary are separated by wooden screens by E. Ridsdale Tate, of different styles and dates (but all early 20C). They were originally stained but were stripped in the Civic Trust's 1977 restoration, perhaps to imitate a medieval effect. Inside are late 15C stalls, with one original misericord. The pulpit, which stands in the N aisle, is of 1675, six-sided, with painted figures on each face.

The 'Pricke of Conscience' window is the NE window. It is very early 15C, and may be the work of John Thornton, glazier of the E window of the Minster, or by his workshop. It depicts the various disasters which will befall the world in the last 15 days, as told in a medieval poem. The cycle starts at bottom left. The sea rises/falls back/to its original level/sea monsters emerge onto land/the sea burns/trees burn and drop their fruit/a great earthquake/rocks burn/ men hide in holes in the earth (restored)/only earth and sky are seen/ men and women emerge and pray/bones begin to rise in their coffins/the stars fall/all shall die/the world burns and everything ends. Each scene has a couplet, as in the last: 'The XV day this sall betyde/The world sall bryn (burn) on every side'. In the tracery above are scenes from the Last Judgement: St. Peter receiving (?) the Virgin in Heaven, and demons casting souls into Hell. Below are three donors (restored). Also in the N aisle (second window from the E) is the Corporal Acts of Mercy window, 15C. Many details of contemporary life are depicted in this setting of Christ's words in St. Matthew's Gospel, 'I was thirsty, and ye gave me drink', and the like. The hungry are fed, the stranger is received, the naked clothed, the sick are visited, the prisoners comforted. Below, from other windows, are a kneeling priest, and a man and a woman, and the sun encircled by seven stars. In the E window of this aisle is early 14C glass, with intense colours, depicting the Epiphany, Crucifixion and Coronation of the Virgin in the upper lights, the Annunciation, Nativity and Resurrection below. The E window of the chancel, c 1412–28, shows St. John the Baptist, St. Anne teaching the Virgin to read, and St. Christopher, under elaborate canopies. In the lower lights are members of the Blackburn family and a representation of the Trinity. The three windows at the E end were restored in the 19C by William Wailes of Newcastle. In the S aisle, the third window from the E is early 15C and depicts the Nine Orders of Angels. The other windows have mostly saints, archbishops and shields.

There are no outstanding monuments in the church, but a tablet to Rebecca and Susannah Thorpe, undated, erected by a modest relation 'who valued them when living, & laments them now dead'.

All Saints, Pavement. The tall and stately 15C lantern on the W tower of All Saints' is a prominent feature of the city centre. It still houses a light, and in former centuries it was a beacon to guide travellers to York at night. The chancel was demolished in 1782 to make way for a market; much of the church, including the tower, was reconstructed in 1835–37; a new E end was built in 1887 to the design of Fisher & Hepper. The church contains interesting panels of 14C glass from the church of St. Saviour.

The nave has a 15C clerestory with square-headed windows and a battlemented parapet. The aisles, embracing the tower, have pointed windows with Reticulated tracery. Similar tracery was used in the 19C E window. The tower is large and bulky, and is pierced by a huge W window of five lights, with Perpendicular panel tracery. Over the tower soars the octagonal openwork lantern, built in 1475–1501, tall, slender and elegant, crowned with a lacy parapet of crocketed gables and pinnacles.

The nave is of four bays, the tower forming a fifth. The piers are octagonal, the capitals rather plainly moulded. The big W window allows much light into the church; the E window is set in the former

All Saints' seen from the E; the 15C lantern was copied in other churches

chancel arch. The roof, restored in 1987, shows on the bosses the merchants' marks of those who contributed to the building. On the N door, outside, is a small 13C closing-ring with the head of a lion or dragon swallowing a man. At the E end is a 15C lectern from the demolished St. Crux Church. The base, carved with figures of the Evangelists, is 19C. Nearby is a small, graceful pulpit with tester of 1634, made by Nicholas Hall. It stands on a slim goblet stem, and is ornamented with blank arches and carved bands and restrained colouring of red and gold. Cherubs' heads emerge from the scroll-work above the tester. It has inscriptions which read 'Preach the Word be instant in season and out of season. Timo(thy)' and 'Where there is no vision the people perish. Proverbs 29.18'. The organ, originally built by Snetzler, 1812, has been rebuilt twice and in 1963 was installed in its present split position at the E end of the aisles, in cases built by Robert Thompson of Kilburn. His also is the panelling flanking the reredos, carved with symbols of the Passion. In the reredos, the figures are St. Peter, the Evangelists and St. Paul, with Christ in the centre. The aisles are lined with panelling from old box-pews removed in the mid-19C. In the S aisle are shields of the city's guilds, and a board listing Lord Mayors from the parish. Royal arms of 1688 in this aisle are from St. Crux Church; another set, of the 18C, is at the W end. Raised pews under the W windows are seats for the churchwardens. Attached to the W piers are benefaction boards. The W window has stained glass of c 1370 by Richard Caldbeck, removed from St. Saviour's and painstakingly reassembled from a state of great confusion by the Minster glaziers. The top row, left to right, shows: Christ nailed to the Cross; the Crucifixion; and the Deposition. Below: the Entombment; the Harrowing of Hell (Adam and Eve the first to emerge); and the Resurrection. Third row: The Woman and Angel at the Tomb; Christ appearing to St. Mary Magdalene; the Meal at Emmaus. Bottom: Christ appearing to St. Thomas; fragments; the Ascension (Christ's feet and hem of garment; footmarks left behind). There are several 19C windows by C.E. Kempe. The E window (1887), rather fussy and cluttered, has a host of saints. The N aisle E window (1893) shows the Virgin and Child with angels around. The S aisle E window of 1903 has three holy mothers with their sons—Hannah and Samuel, the Virgin and Child, and St. Elizabeth with St. John the Baptist. The S aisle window (1897) has three northern saint-bishops—Aidan, Paulinus and Cuthbert. In the N aisle is a brass to Sir Robert Askwith, Lord Mayor 1609 and 1617, brought from St. Crux in 1887, and also a monument to Tate Wilkinson, a successful 18C manager of York's Theatre Royal.

Bar Convent, Chapel. This small community of Catholic sisters of the Institute of the Blessed Virgin Mary was founded next to Micklegate Bar in 1686 by Mother Frances Bedingfield. Ann Aspinal became Superior in 1760, and during her rule the present buildings were erected to the designs of Thomas Atkinson. The splendid neo-Classical chapel was built in 1766–70, and the new building was

The Bar Convent Chapel, just outside Micklegate, by Thomas Atkinson, 1765–69

completed with the street front in 1787. The chapel was licensed as a place of worship in 1791, and was in public use until 1828. In 1985, following a reorganisation of Catholic education in York, the Georgian buildings became a Museum of Catholic History.

The chapel is a circular, domed room, with shallow transepts and a nave with round-headed recesses in the side walls. The dome is shallow and top-lit by a small glazed cupola. It is painted white, and the decoration of wreaths and festoons is picked out in gold. Eight white fluted columns with gilded Ionic capitals support the dome. These are free-standing on the nave side and are set against the green panelled walls of the chancel. Against the E wall is a reredos, white and gilt, surmounted by figures of the Latin Doctors. There is a free-standing altar table in modern Catholic fashion, and beneath it is placed a gilt sculpture of a Pelican in her Piety, designed by Thomas Atkinson.

Joseph Aloysius Hansom, the 19C architect and originator of the Hansom cab, was baptised here in 1803.

Holy Trinity, Goodramgate. Hidden from view in a secluded churchyard behind Goodramgate, and unnoticed by 19C restorers, Holy Trinity has irregular box-pews and other 17C and 18C fittings, and some attractive medieval stained glass. It is now vested in the Redundant Churches Fund. It is a simple, unpretentious building, mostly 15C, with nave and chancel in one, aisles embracing the W tower, and a projecting S chapel. The tower has belfry windows of two lights, with panel tracery. The windows of the S side are Decorated, being square-headed with Reticulated tracery.

The interior is low and undulating, the arcades askew and the floor uneven. The arcades are of four bays, with octagonal piers. One of the capitals has foliage, and may be 13C, reused. There is no clerestory. The chancel arch was removed in 1633. A broad, four-centred arch opens into the S chapel (a chantry chapel of St. James). The walls are unplastered or (more likely) have been stripped at some time. The church is furnished with a variety of box-pews, some Jacobean, more 18C. Rising amidst them is a plain double-decker pulpit of 1695, remodelled in 1785. At the E end is an early 18C communion rail, three-sided, with turned balusters, and semicircular gates projecting in the middle. Against the E wall is a low, panelled reredos of 1691. At the W end is the usual stand for the mace of the Lord Mayor. The list of names of Lord Mayors of York includes George Hudson, 'the railway king'. The five-light E window contains glass given by the Rector, John Walker, in 1471. He was an official of the two most important York guilds, of Corpus Christi and of St. Christopher and St. George. The lights show, from left to right, St. George slaying the Dragon; St. John the Baptist (with camel skin hanging between his legs); Corpus Christi (with the donor kneeling); St. John the Evangelist; St. Christopher. Below are St. Mary Cleopas, her husband Alphaeus and four children; St. Anne and St. Joachim with the young Virgin (and child!); the Trinity, crowned (Christ's crown incorporating the Crown of Thorns) about to crown the Virgin; Salome and Zebedee with St. John the Evangelist (a tiny eagle perched on his Gospel); St. Ursula embracing a pope, a king and some of the virgins who were martyred with her. The window once had two lower rows, one row with five representations of the Virgin, each in a rayed mandorla. Some lights were moved to the N aisle E window in the 18C or 19C. This window has a light of the Virgin at

top left; at top right is an archbishop in another mandorla symbolising, perhaps, the Church as ruler of the world. There are 15C
fragments also in the S aisle E window: St. Paulinus at top left, and
perhaps St. Olave at top right.

St. Mary, Castlegate. This church, mostly 15C, with an imposing
spire rising from an octagonal stage of the W tower, now houses an
exhibition on the history of York. It contains some fragments of
medieval stained glass and an important pre-Conquest dedication
stone, discovered during William Butterfield's restoration of 1868–70.
The stone is damaged, and the date is missing, but it records the
building of the church by Efrard, Grim and Aese, in a mixture of Latin
and Old English, and has been dated to c 1020. The three benefactors, who have Viking names, built the church 'in the name of the
holy Lord Christ and of St. Mary and St. Martin and St. (?) Cuthbert
and All Saints'. The stone is placed at the top of the stairs in the N
aisle.

St. Michael-le-Belfry. The church shelters under the Minster's huge
mass, on its S side. It was entirely rebuilt in 1525–37, at the time of
the Reformation, to the design of John Forman, master mason of the
Minster. Until the 1850s the W front was hidden behind a cluster of
houses. G.T. Andrews rebuilt the turret over the W gable in 1855, and
G. Fowler Jones refitted the interior in 1853 and completed the
external restoration in 1867.

St. Michael-le-Belfry is broad and squat, and its lowness is exaggerated by the Minster's height. It has nave and chancel in one, and
N and S aisles. The W end, though almost completely 19C, is a close
reproduction of the original. From a slightly projecting W porch with
gabled door, a giant arch rises to enclose the W window. The arch
has a flat parapet and is crowned with pinnacles at the ends and a
central openwork lantern, a miniature version of the one at All
Saints', Pavement. Over the aisles are stepped parapets; at the SW
corner is an octagonal turret with blank panel tracery in its upper
stages. The buttresses of the aisles were formerly crowned with
pinnacles. Under the windows of the S side is a frieze of shields in
quatrefoils, bearing the arms of St. William, Archbishop Zouche, St.
Peter, the See of York and the See of London. The four-light windows
of the aisles have Perpendicular tracery rather squashed into the
heads of the lights.

The interior is surprisingly spacious and well lit by the square-
headed clerestory windows. The arcades of six bays have four-
centred arches on tall, slim piers. The spandrels are decorated with
carving: quatrefoils flanked by pointed trefoils, with angels bearing
shields below. In the quatrefoils are sculpted heads and other
decorations. The ceilings are flat and panelled. At the E end is a
sumptuous reredos of 1712, dark-stained and gilded, by William Etty.
Four fluted Corinthian columns support an entablature and frame the
usual Commandment boards and, in the centre, a painting of the
Adoration of the Shepherds. Etty also designed the altar rails, with a
semicircular projection. There are some 16C benches with poppyheads and traceried ends. Most of the seats are 19C, cut-down box-
pews. The W gallery of 1785, which stretches across nave and aisles,
has the arms of Queen Victoria. The organ, with its unstained case,
stands in the N aisle. The walls of this aisle are lined with massive
benefaction boards. Much medieval stained glass survives. In the
five-light E window 14C glass has been reset, presumably from

the earlier church. In the main tier, from left to right, are St. Peter and St. Paul; the Annunciation, the Nativity, the Resurrection; and the Coronation of the Virgin. Below, a donor gives the window; two figures kneel; the Crucifixion; two more figures kneel; and St. James the Great. The aisle windows have striking 16C glass installed at the rebuilding. In the N aisle, from E to W, are: four scenes from the life of St. Thomas Becket (the series is continued from windows in the Minster); then St. Michael and St. Christopher; the Annunciation; and St. Ursula. In the lower panels are donors. On the S side, the E window is 19C; then follow St. John the Baptist, St. Peter, a damaged figure, St. Wilfrid, with donors and a large family below. Then St. Hugh; St. Paul; St. Peter; St. William; St. George; St. Martin; a bishop, crowned; St. Christopher; a knight; St. James the Great; a bishop; St. James the Less, his heart pierced; roundels of shields and kneeling donors below. The inscriptions, though modern, reproduce the 16C texts, which are recorded in a Bodleian manuscript. At the E end of the S aisle is the imposing 18C monument to Robert Squire (died 1709) and his wife, Priscilla. The couple stand, looking very self-assured, resting their elbows on urns. Above them hover cherubs raising aloft a celestial crown, in the arch of an elaborate canopy. An original iron railing protects the monument. There are many 18C and 19C wall tablets, obelisks, etc., including a lively Baroque cartouche to Mary Woodyeare (died 1728), with swags, cherubs' heads, and a death's head at the base.

Guy Fawkes was baptised in this church in 1570.

THE EAST RIDING OF YORKSHIRE

The East Riding has an unusual number of exceptionally large and important churches. They are Holy Trinity, Hull; Howden Minster; St. Mary's, Hemingbrough; Beverley Minster; St. Mary's at Beverley; St. Patrick's, Patrington; St. Augustine's, Hedon; and Bridlington Priory. The last of these was monastic; the minsters at Howden and Beverley were collegiate; but the others were parochial. All of them are of exceptional size or have exceptional features. If it is recalled that transepts in English churches very rarely have aisles, the exceptional size of these East Riding churches is shown by the fact that seven of the eight have, or have had, aisled transepts. Five of the eight have, or have had, an ambulatory around the choir. Beverley Minster, which claims to descend from St. John of Beverley's 7C foundation—the best-known site of the early Church in the East Riding—is appropriately the grandest of all. Its present fabric derives from a rebuilding of considerable grandeur between the 13C and the 15C. However, Holy Trinity Church at Hull—the only one of the eight to lack transept aisles—is actually larger than Beverley Minster overall, and it is reputed to be the largest parish church in England by area.

The East Riding is the smallest of the three Ridings and the least spectacular in its landscapes. The undulating Wolds form its main physical feature and they contrast markedly with the Moors and the Dales of the West and North Ridings. The Riding is overwhelmingly an agricultural one, in marked contrast to the West Riding. Churches have been built throughout the centuries from agricultural wealth, except along the Humber, where merchant wealth from the ports was available. Of the ports, Hull has been the most important since the 14C. It is the only town in the East Riding of really significant size. Amongst the building materials mention must be made of the early use of brick, especially in Hull and Beverley. Holy Trinity Church at Hull is a major example of the use of brick as early as the 14C. Howden Minster and Beverley Minster both have brick infilling in their vaults. The same two churches, plus St. Mary's at Beverley, are also examples of the use of magnesian limestone from near Tadcaster in the West Riding.

The East Riding has few pre-Conquest survivals of any note. The churches of Skipwith and Wharram-le-Street have plain 11C W towers. At Aldbrough there is an inscription of similar date which records that Ulf built a church there. Beverley Minster has a *frithstool* or seat, which would have been placed at the E end of a pre-Conquest church. St. James's, Nunburnholme possesses the remains of an early cross; its carvings depict the Virgin and Child and a number of monsters and mythical beasts. Finally, Stillingfleet has famous ironwork on its S door, whose 'Viking' character seems to belie an original association with its 12C setting. The ironwork may have been reused, or else it was a markedly late use of a bygone style. Norman work is relatively frequent. Two churches of the mid-12C stand out for their completeness: St. Nicholas's, North Newbald and St. Mary's, Kirkburn. The former is aisleless and cruciform, with a central battlemented tower and an elaborate S doorway, above which a vesica niche houses a carving of Christ in Majesty. Kirkburn has a W tower, an aisleless nave and a chancel. Its fittings include a Norman carved font. St. Michael's at Garton-on-the-Wolds has the typical features of a Norman village church: flat buttresses, a corbel table, small windows which are splayed within, plain arched doorways and a plan of chancel, aisleless nave and W tower. Etton has similar features, but there as much is neo-Norman as is original. Weaverthorpe is an impressive, simple Norman church, which seems to have been built in the early 12C. Other Norman survivals of note are Kirby Underdale, Millington, Riccall (S doorway), Thwing (a carving of the Agnus Dei in the tympanum), Stillingfleet (the S doorway, later than mid-12C, and the simpler N doorway), Bridlington Priory (a fragment of the 12C cloister), Goodmanham (S doorway and chancel arch), and fonts at Everingham (in the Catholic church), Beverley Minster, Langtoft and Cowlam.

An instructive example of the lancet phase of the Early English style is St. Oswald's, Filey. The lancets there are particularly tall. Work of similar date may be seen at Hedon (trefoil-headed doorways, lancet windows) and Hemingbrough (parts of the arcades and transepts). St. Andrew's at Middleton-on-the-Wolds has a long 13C chancel with stepped lancets at the E end. The N side of Bridlington Priory and the E parts of Beverley Minster are also 13C in date. Beverley Minster shows a lavish use of Purbeck marble shafting and a copying of ideas from Lincoln. From late in the 13C there are Geometrical windows at Howden Minster and the very attractive square-headed windows in the chancel at Skipwith. The change from Early English to Decorated may be studied in the Riding's major churches. In Beverley Minster the nave is 14C, but begins by copying the 13C fabric to the E. Beverley Minster also has the most elaborate Decorated feature in the East Riding, the Percy tomb, which dates from after 1339. At Hedon the lancet style of the chancel and transepts is succeeded by intersected tracery in the nave aisles and finally by 'flowing' or fully Decorated tracery at the W end. The church possesses, too, a Decorated font, octagonal and with cusped and crocketed gables rising from the underside of the bowl. A font of similar date and style exists in Holy Trinity Church, Hull. St. Patrick's at Patrington, 'the Queen of Holderness', is the most complete Decorated church in the East Riding and a markedly splendid one. It shows some variety of forms, from the late 13C Geometrical in the transepts to the Reticulated and 'flowing' of the nave and chancel. Within the church, the Easter sepulchre, piscina and sedilia are famous examples of fittings in the ogee style. In St. Mary's at Beverley, the vaulted NE chapel is an attractive Decorated addition of the second quarter of the 14C. St. Andrew's, Bainton was rebuilt by its Rector, William de Brocklesby, just before the mid-14C; the church had been attacked by the Scots in 1322. The chancel of St. Mary's, Lockington has 14C Reticulated windows. Holy Trinity Church, Hull was substantially built in the 14C, but the tall, thin piers of the 14C chancel differ little from the later Perpendicular piers of the nave. The Decorated style is shown clearly only in the windows at the E end and in the transepts. The nave of the church is a standard Perpendicular work, with immense windows and an emphasis on height. The central tower of the church was the last major part of the fabric to be completed, by the end of the 15C. This pattern of a new Perpendicular tower was repeated elsewhere, notably at Hedon and Howden. Both have central towers with two tiers of tall three-light belfry windows. Hedon's tower is capped by eight pinnacles, which is a characteristic 15C feature in the East Riding. The most ornate 'typical' tower is that of All Saints', Great Driffield, with set-back buttresses, transomed three-light belfry windows, panelled battlements, eight pinnacles, and niches in both buttresses and pinnacles. At St. Mary's, Hemingbrough, the earlier fabric was capped by a substantial mid-15C recessed spire, which is twice as high as the tower. Patrington Church also has a spire, which emerges from a Perpendicular open octagonal screen or corona. The W end of Beverley Minster, comprising the two towers, a central doorway, a S tower doorway, a W window of nine lights and endless panelling, is an immensely impressive 15C composition. A final Perpendicular work which must be mentioned is the church of St. Augustine at Skirlaugh, which was rebuilt in the very early 15C by Bishop Skirlaugh of Durham, a native of the village. It is small and chapel-like, but well-detailed and of the one style throughout.

Between the 15C and the 19C there is little of note. The prosperity of Hull and Beverley in the 18C produced no great town churches of that time. In the East Riding as a whole, only two 18C church buildings deserve a reference: St. Andrew's at Boynton of 1768–70 by John Carr, which is more of interest for its internal plan and for its fittings than for its Gothick architecture; and the chapel of the Charterhouse in Hull (serving almshouses) of 1778–80. Mercantile prosperity in Hull certainly prompted some important buildings in the first half of the 19C, but almost all of them have been demolished. There remains the chapel of Trinity House, built in 1839–43 by H.F. Lockwood, to represent Hull's Classical places of worship. The Catholic church of St. Charles Borromeo in Jarratt Street also survives, but it was substantially altered in the later 19C from its original appearance in 1829. Another Catholic church, dedicated to St. Mary and St. Everilda, was built in Classical style and to a basilican plan by Agostino Giorgioli in 1836–39 next to Everingham Hall. With these exceptions—and they are not particularly striking ones—the 19C in the East Riding is very much a matter of the Gothic Revival. Indeed, it is a surprisingly rich area for works by two of the leading Victorian architects, J.L. Pearson and G.E. Street. The Sykes family of Sledmere stands out as the most significant source of patronage by far. The fourth and fifth Baronets, both called Sir Tatton, commissioned new churches and major restorations of old ones from the 1850s until the early 1900s. The fourth Baronet began by restoring churches to J.L. Pearson's designs at Garton-on-the-Wolds, Kirkburn and Bishop Wilton and by building a new one at Hilston. In 1865, the fifth Baronet, who had succeeded his father two years before, turned to G.E. Street instead. Over the next dozen years a substantial programme of building and restoring was undertaken. The grandest of the new churches was St. Andrew's, East Heslerton (1873–77), but even that is not large by Victorian standards. The younger Sir Tatton had turned to Street on the strength of his churches at Whitwell-on-the-Hill (1858–60), built just across the border in the North Riding for the Lechmeres, and at Howsham (1859–60), built for the Cholmleys. The fifth Baronet's commissions more or less stopped in the late 1870s. He returned to church building in the late 1890s and early 1900s. He commissioned Temple Moore and Charles Hodgson Fowler for various works, of which Temple Moore's rebuilding of the church at Sledmere itself is the most attractive. Temple Moore also worked independently of Sir Tatton at Great Driffield, where he designed screens in the early 20C, and at St. Mary's, Sculcoates, Hull, where he replaced an 18C church in 1916. G.E. Street had designed another Hull church, All Saints' at Sculcoates (1866–69), but otherwise 19C prosperity brought no notable Victorian rivals to the city's medieval churches. Street also undertook much restoration at Hedon from the late 1860s.

Two churches by J.L. Pearson, which were not parts of his work for the Sykes family, are arguably the grandest 19C works in the East Riding: St. Leonard's at Scorborough (1857–59) and St. Mary's at South Dalton (1858–61). Both churches are unusually lavish, with elaborate carvings and good contemporary fittings. Finally, no comments on 19C work can omit a mention of Sir Gilbert Scott's restorations of many of the major churches, especially of Bridlington Priory and of Beverley Minster where he designed the present organ screen. The screen was made by James Elwell of Beverley, who also worked with Sir Gilbert's son, G.G. Scott Jr, at Great Driffield in 1878–80.

Fittings of significance are chiefly to be found in the eight major churches. Beverley Minster has a famous group of 68 16C misericords, 14C wooden sedilia, a rare medieval wooden treadwheel windlass (above the crossing), a major font cover of 1726, two 18C statues of King Athelstan and St. John of Beverley, and Sir Gilbert Scott's organ screen. Medieval carvings in the Minster provide a major source for early musical instruments. The church also has 15C glass in its E window, re-arranged from fragmentary survivals throughout the building, and a wealth of 19C glass, especially by John Hardman & Co.. St. Mary's at Beverley is also notable for 19C glass, including some by Hardman to Pugin's designs, and by Clayton & Bell. The chancel ceiling at St. Mary's bears the famous 15C painted panels of medieval kings. On a N arcade pier there are the equally famous 16C painted carvings of minstrels. Howden Minster has preserved its 15C pulpitum, albeit in detached sections; St. Oswald's at Flamborough retains a substantial 15C Rood screen; and Hemingbrough Church possesses one very early misericord (of c 1200). Lissett possesses the oldest-dated church bell in the country. Holy Trinity, Hull has some notable carved stall-ends, a fine 14C font, an altar table of 1770 and a huge eagle lectern of 1847. Medieval stained glass may be seen at Nunburnholme (14C, in a chancel window), Skipwith and Skirlaugh (mostly fragments in both). 18C glass by William Peckitt exists at Boynton, Harpham and in the chapel of the mansion at Burton Constable. Peckitt was the first stained glass artist to emerge at York after the medieval tradition had lapsed. The 19C produced immense quantities of stained glass. Clayton & Bell is well-represented in the churches designed or restored by Street and Pearson, especially at Scorborough, South Dalton, Howsham and Weaverthorpe. Bridlington Priory has work by William Wailes. Holy Trinity, Hull has two windows of the turn of this century by Walter Crane. The Belgian artist, Jean Baptiste Capronnier, is widely represented, at Howden, Etton, Foxholes and Cottingham.

Monuments might be said to begin with the 12C Tournai marble slab at Bridlington Priory, which could be part of a memorial to the founder. The next significant monuments date from the 14C. In Holy Trinity Church, Hull there are some memorials to members of the de la Pole family, who were leading 14C merchants. At Bainton a monument of c 1331 to Sir Edmund de Mauley shows affinities to the famous Percy tomb in Beverley Minster, which was made after 1339 to an unidentified member of the great Percy family. Howden Minster has a pair of early 14C effigies, possibly of Sir John Metham (died 1311) and his wife. In Cottingham Church there is a notable brass to Nicholas of Louth (died 1384), who built the chancel; he is shown as a friar under an ogee canopy. Another significant 14C memorial, at Lowthorpe, depicts Sir Thomas Heslerton and his wife.

The effigies are overlaid by a stylised tree. 14C and 15C memorials remain at Harpham, including a brass to Sir Thomas de St. Quintin (died 1418) and his wife. Swine Church has monuments of the same period to members of the Hilton family. At Bainton there is a brass in the chancel to Roger Godeale, Rector (died 1429), which shows him in his vestments and with a chalice. Another Rector, Thomas Tonge (died 1472), is shown in a brass at Beeford. The church at Burton Agnes has notable monuments from the 15C to the 18C, beginning with a pair of 15C alabaster effigies on a decorated tomb-chest, and later including a memorial to Sir Henry Griffith (died 1645), which makes much play of skulls and bones. A late 17C monument at South Dalton, commemorating Sir John Hotham and possibly designed by John Bushnell, has a full-scale *memento mori* on a slab beneath the main effigy. Beverley Minster has a second Percy tomb in the NE corner, commemorating Henry, fourth Earl of Northumberland (died 1489)—a very plain tomb-chest in contrast to its 14C Percy neighbour. Later monuments in the Minster include those at the E end to 17C and 18C members of the Warton family. Peter Scheemakers designed the one to Sir Michael Warton (died 1725). John Bacon, Jr designed the memorials to William Hutchinson in St. Mary's, Beverley, 1808, and to Joseph Sykes at Kirk Ella, 1809. His contemporary, the Danish sculptor Bertel Thorwaldsen, designed Lady Lawley's monument at Escrick in 1828.

The historical associations must begin with St. John of Beverley, a revered figure in the early English Church. He was born at Harpham, where the church is named after him. The first church on the site of Beverley Minster is traditionally said to have been founded by him in the late 7C, and he died there in 721. His fame derived largely from his miracles of healing. Another local St. John—of Bridlington—was canonised in 1401. He was John de Thwing, Prior of Bridlington in the 14C. A third local figure, John de Howden, who died in 1275, was culted as a saint at Howden Minster but never achieved formal canonisation. Rare dedications include St. Magnus at Bessingby, St. German (a 5C Bishop of Auxerre in France) at Winestead, St. Edith at Bishop Wilton, St. Elgin at North Frodingham (apparently the same as St. Elphin of Warrington, Lancashire), St. Everilda (a 7C nun) at Everingham, St. Augustine of Hippo at Hedon and St. Margaret of Scotland (died 1093) at Hilston. The Riding has more dedications to both St. Oswald and St. Helen than is usual. From before even John of Beverley's time, there descends the story (via Bede) of Coifi's destruction of the idols at Goodmanham. Coifi was the pagan high priest who converted to Christianity along with King Edwin, King of Northumbria, in c 627.

William Wilberforce was associated with St. Mary's, Lowgate, Hull. His grandfather served there as churchwarden. His second son, Robert, was Rector of Burton Agnes from 1840 to 1854 and was also Archdeacon of the East Riding. St. Mary's in Hull had three generations of Scotts as 19C incumbents. They were the cousins of the leading Victorian architect, Sir Gilbert Scott. Holy Trinity, Hull is associated with another distinguished Victorian architect, G.F. Bodley. His sister married the son of the Reverend J.H. Bromby, who was Vicar of Holy Trinity from 1797 to 1866. A 20C association is the burial of Winifred Holtby, the novelist, at Rudston in 1936.

Beverley Minster, *St. John the Evangelist*. This famous church, which dates from between the 13C and the 15C, was collegiate throughout the Middle Ages. Upon the Dissolution of colleges under

King Edward VI, it became parochial. It is of cathedral size, and yet it has never been a bishop's seat. Its origins are closely tied to St. John of Beverley (died 721), whose life is described in the pages of Bede's 'Ecclesiastical History'. St. John was in fact the bishop who ordained Bede. He was a native of Harpham in the East Riding, who served as Bishop of Hexham from 687 to 705 and as Bishop of York from 705 to 717. At Beverley he founded a monastery, to which he retired and where he was buried in 721. He was canonised in 1037. By then the early monastery had gone, but King Athelstan had revived the religious importance of the site by establishing a college of secular canons. Building and rebuilding occurred in numerous phases both before and after the Norman Conquest. Then a fire in the late 12C and the collapse of a tower in c 1213 occasioned the building, with some grandeur, of the church which stands today. The choir and transepts were completed in the 13C, the nave followed in the 14C, and the W front was added by c 1420.

Beverley Minster stands at the S end of the town, within sight of the railway station. Until recently, open land lay to its S. To its N, an agreeable street of old buildings (Highgate) leads into the town centre. The church comprises a nave with N and S aisles and two W towers, N and S transepts, each with E and W aisles, a choir with N and S aisles, smaller transepts at the E with an E aisle, and a small NE or Percy chapel. All the fabric E of and including the transepts dates from c 1220 to c 1260, except that the small Percy chapel was added at the end of the 15C, the nine-light E window replaced an earlier window or windows in the same century, and the S choir aisle also has 15C windows. The remainder of the windows to the E are therefore lancets, all of them shafted and the upper ones flanked by narrower blank arcading. The ends of the E transepts have paired lancets in three tiers. The main transepts have two tiers of three lancets, then a rose and finally a single, narrow opening in the gable. The main transepts also have doorways in their end walls. They are round-headed, shafted (with stiff-leaf capitals) and flanked by blank pointed arches. Shafted choir aisle buttresses rise to very plain gables, from which spring flying supports to the upper walls of the choir and the transepts. A very low tower covers the crossing. W of the main transepts comes the 14C nave. Here the windows have Decorated tracery—four-light in the aisles, with mouchettes and ogee designs, three-light and basically intersecting in the clerestory. There are N and S nave porches, the N one (the Highgate porch) being markedly elaborate. The W front is Beverley Minster's familiar face, comprising two symmetrical flanking towers, which are set quite close together, and the great nine-light W window between them. This window is very similar to the main E window. The W front is successful partly because the wall between the towers is built up well above the nave's roofline. The towers do not therefore seem disproportionately tall. Also, the front is pulled together by its uniform enrichment of panelling and blank arcading. The towers have substantial gabled buttresses, which recede in stages. The belfry windows are of three tall transomed lights, with crocketed ogee gables above. Fourteen pinnacles surmount each tower, the corner ones being higher than the rest.

Entering by the Highgate porch on the S, the nave is seen to be of ten bays (counting the tower bays). The piers have four major shafts and four more in the diagonals. The triforium follows that of the earlier choir in comprising trefoil-headed arches, enriched with dogtooth, set in front of lower and simpler arches. The clerestory above has Purbeck shafting—the only uniform use of Purbeck in the nave. In the E bay, however, Purbeck is used at all levels, a feature which copies the choir. Both the nave and its aisles are vaulted, with painting in the angles of the nave's main ribs, and with painted bosses. The W end has an elaborate doorway and surround. The door itself was carved in the 18C by William Thornton with figures of the four Evangelists and their symbols. Arcading flanks the doorway at ground level, and above are rows of niches with modern figures up to the W window. The stained glass of the window is by John Hardman & Co., 1865. The nave aisles have blank arcading, with carved label stops of great interest. In the S nave aisle, raised on three steps, stands the 12C font of Frosterley marble and its huge, ornate suspended cover of 1726. To its N, two 18C figures of King Athelstan and St. John of Beverley stand in the S doorway. One bay further to the N, under the S arcade, lies a tomb-chest under a considerable canopy with cusping, pinnacles and finials.

The crossing brings the visitor to the 13C parts. Purbeck marble will now be seen everywhere. There are rib-vaults, a tall clerestory and a diminutive triforium which consists of two layers, the outer trefoil-headed with Purbeck shafting and dogtooth, the inner much simpler. Under the crossing there stands a circular nave altar of 1970, placed on two receding circular platforms and flanked by tripod candlesticks. Above it will be seen the boss in the roof of the crossing. The boss is movable and allows items to be taken to and from the tower. The crane used to do so is perhaps Beverley Minster's single most interesting possession, a wooden treadwheel windlass. Of the main transepts, the N was saved from collapse in the early 18C by Nicholas Hawksmoor and William Thornton, who devised an ingenious machine to do so. Today its E aisle is used as a shop, but it also contains a fine 15C effigy of a priest on a tomb-chest.

The choir is separated from the crossing by a fine wooden organ screen, which was designed by Sir Gilbert Scott and made by James Elwell. The organ above (of which the rest is in the S choir aisle) was last rebuilt by Hill, Norman & Beard in 1962. The choir itself has particularly splendid woodwork, of 16C and later date. The stalls have traceried ends with the usual carved finials. The canopies are very detailed. There are no fewer than 68 misericords. They include the outer return stall on the S (the Archbishop of York's stall), which shows a Pelican in her Piety; on the N side, the second stall from the W at the back depicts a fox in a friar's gown and holding a rosary in the act of preaching to seven geese, with a monkey and another fox behind him; and on the S side, the first front stall from the E has an elephant with a howdah, driven by an ape. The lighting of the choirstalls, by elegant brass lamps with triplets of globes, was installed in 1985. Further E, the sanctuary is flanked by the famous Percy tomb on the N and by the sedilia on the S. The tomb is the most elaborate of 14C monuments, comprising a huge and finely detailed nodding ogee canopy over a tomb-chest. Curiously, it is not known whom it commemorates, other than a member of the Percy family in the mid-14C. At the bottom of the monument, the tomb-chest is entirely plain and it carries no effigy. All the detail is reserved for the canopy. The ogee arch, cusped and sub-cusped, is set within a gable. Flanking pinnacles rise from the corners. Carving is liberally supplied to the spandrels, ends of cusps, crockets and above all to the upper parts of the main gable. A statue of Christ is placed on each side above the apex of the ogee arch. Angels flank the main gable on both choir and aisle sides; those facing the choir hold Instruments of the Passion. Opposite this tomb, on the S side of the sanctuary, are the sedilia. They comprise four canopied wooden seats of the 14C. Each canopy consists of a nodding ogee arch under a gable, all supported on panelled posts which rise to crocketed pinnacles. The sanctuary also possesses a frithstool, a pre-Conquest stone seat whose arms and back are of equal height. It is unadorned. Originally, it was a seat of authority which would have stood at the E end of a pre-Conquest church.

The reredos, which separates the sanctuary and choir from the retrochoir, is of 14C origin but underwent much restoration in 1826. Beyond the reredos, the retrochoir is now the Lady chapel. In the Middle Ages, it housed the rich shrine of St. John of Beverley. The E side of the reredos is a three-bay vaulted canopy. The back and sides of it have blank Reticulated tracery. There are in the retrochoir some grandiose 17C and 18C monuments to members of the Warton family, including one by Peter Scheemakers to Sir Michael Warton (died 1725). Above is the great E window, whose stained glass dates from the 15C. Note the four Latin Doctors at the sides of the upper tier.

The N choir aisle has a stairway under trefoiled arches which once led into the chapter house between the main and subsidiary N transepts. To the S, a fine 15C open wooden screen leads into the choir. To the E of the stairs, there are fine 18C wrought-iron gates. Further E comes the Percy or Northumberland chapel, which was built in c 1490 to house the tomb of Henry Percy, fourth Earl of Northumberland (died 1489).

Beverley, *St. Mary.* St. Mary's was founded in the 12C as a daughter church of the minster. It was soon adopted by the townspeople as their favoured parish church, for the minster was understandably under the sway of high ecclesiastics and of royalty. Some traces of the original building survive, but the church's appearance today is the result of some centuries of enlargement and rebuilding. The late Middle Ages contributed much to the fabric, making the Perpendicular style predominant in the building.

St. Mary's stands at a street corner, stretching E along a narrow side street where it can hardly be appreciated from a distance. Only the central tower may be seen from Beverley's principal market place, over the rooftops. The tower was finished by 1524 to replace one which had collapsed in 1520. It possesses four-light, transomed belfry windows, a battlemented parapet and no fewer than 16 pinnacles. The other prominent part of the exterior is the splendid W front, which comprises a massive Perpendicular window of seven lights and flanking octagonal turrets which rise above the parapet, adorned with open tracery. The nave and aisles are surmounted by decorated parapets and battlements, with added pinnacles on the nave. The S porch has an ogee gable, four narrow two-light windows, battlements, niches on either side of the entrance and vaulting within. It is of the 15C, with 16C additions. The inner doorway is Norman.

The plan of the church consists of a nave of six bays, with wide N and S aisles, the crossing tower, N and S transepts, E aisles in the transepts (the N one extended E as Holy Trinity chapel, with a crypt below), a spacious chancel of five bays (which is divided into a choir, sanctuary and retrochoir), chancel aisles, a vestry leading from the N chancel aisle which was originally a chapel, and a sacristy which is also N of the chancel. The nave was largely rebuilt after 1520. There are piers with four shafts and intervening hollows; blank tracery in the spandrels; a tall clerestory of three-light Perpendicular windows, all with clear glass and with panelling below them; hoodmould stops; and nave and aisle ceilings which are painted with gold stars on a blue background. The capital of the easternmost pier of the nave's N arcade bears five stone figures of musicians to mark the benefaction of a guild of minstrels in the 1520s. The chancel is of the late 13C and early 14C, the S side being earlier than the N. The three easternmost bays of the N chancel aisle form St. Michael's chapel, built in the second quarter of the 14C. It is of Decorated work of the first quality and magnificence, including flowing and Reticulated tracery and tierceron vaulting. A priest's quarters exist over the chapel; and to the N of the chapel, extending just one bay outwards, is a sacristy. On account of an inscription found in the priest's quarters, Mr W.C.B. Smith, historian of St. Mary's, has attributed St. Michael's chapel to Ivo de Raughton. The S chancel aisle forms St. Katharine's chapel. There are two remnants of the 12C church: some zigzag between the N transept and the N chancel aisle; and part of the original exterior wall in the S chancel aisle.

In the nave, to the left of the tower arch, stands an alabaster pulpit by Sir Gilbert Scott, who worked on the church in the 1860s. A screen of 1893, which incorporates some 15C work, stands just W of the arch leading from the crossing into the choir. The designer was John Bilson. The 28 choirstalls, with misericords, are of 1445, the work of the Ripon school of carvers. Of the same date are the painted panels of the ceiling, which depict English monarchs from the 7C until King Henry VI. The panels were repainted in the 1860s and again in 1939, when the figure of King George VI was added. The reredos is of 1875–76 by John Oldrid Scott; it includes a depiction of the Last Supper. The font of Derbyshire marble, which stands in the NW corner, dates from 1530.

St. Mary's possesses much 19C stained glass. The E window has two tiers of figures in its five lights, by Clayton & Bell. The great W window has two rows of seven figures each, designed by A.W.N. Pugin and made by John Hardman & Co. The E window of St. Michael's chapel, of four lights, is by Clayton & Bell. The corresponding window in the S chancel aisle is by Hardman.

Robert Fisher, the father of John Fisher—Bishop of Rochester and 16C martyr, whom Pope Pius XI canonised in 1935—was buried here in 1477.

Boynton, St. Andrew. St. Andrew's comprises a brick Gothick aisleless nave and lower chancel of 1768–70, designed by John Carr, and a stone-built 15C W tower. Within, the nave and chancel are divided by a double screen formed by pairs of rather eccentric Gothic columns and capitals on each side. The double screen marks out a separate space which has been the sanctuary since 1987, reviving a plan which had applied until a reordering in 1910. The double screen provides what is in effect the altar's canopy. The setting of the altar is very tasteful. The chancel of 1910–87 (now E of the altar), which is entered through a wrought-iron rail, is raised by one step. There is a N recess for the organ. The N and S windows, which have stone surrounds, have intersecting leadwork but no tracery. The E window, however, has stone tracery of two trefoiled lights, with a trefoil within a circle in the head. It has some coloured heraldic glass by William Peckitt. The W gallery was a private pew of the Strickland family of Boynton Hall. Together with the benches in the nave, it is painted green. There is a cylindrical font with decoration of intersecting arches. The numerous monuments of the 17C and the 18C at the E end are of the Stricklands.

St. Andrew's, a Gothick rebuilding by John Carr, 1768–70

Bridlington Priory, *St. Mary.* St. Mary's comprises the nave, N and S nave aisles, and two W towers of an Augustinian priory church which was founded by Walter de Gant (or Gaunt) in c 1113–24. The medieval priory was distinguished by the canonisation in 1401 of a 14C Prior, John de Thwing, who became St. John of Bridlington. Upon the Dissolution, the transepts, crossing tower, choir and conventual buildings were demolished, reducing the church from c 333ft in length to 185ft. Restoration in the 19C was undertaken by Edmund Sharpe in the 1840s and by Sir Gilbert Scott in the 1870s. Scott rebuilt the upper parts of the two W towers.

The familiar view of the church is of its asymmetrical W front, comprising a flat-topped NW tower, a huge nine-light Perpendicular window, and a much taller and more elaborate SW tower. Scott provided the Perpendicular details of this tower. The main doorway of the W front is very elaborate. The NW tower has a round-headed doorway which dates from the 13C. Of the same date are the lancet windows of the N side and the notable N porch, although the latter was much restored by Scott. The lights are paired E of the porch. The E front is the patched-up and heavily buttressed legacy of the Dissolution, save that the main seven-light E window is Scott's insertion in Geometrical style. The former crossing, transepts and choir were all markedly askew to the nave. A small part of the N transept's W wall still remains. On the S side of the exterior, the scars of the formerly attached conventual buildings may be seen. It will be noticed that the roof of the S aisle is lower than that of the N. The S clerestory windows are therefore larger, with a transom. They are four-light and Geometrical, except for the three clerestory windows to the W, which are Perpendicular replacements.

The interior is markedly spacious. There are ten bays, with very tall piers of four major shafts and a further two minor ones in each angle. The capitals and arches are moulded. On the S side, the three piers at the W end have panelled and traceried sides, dating from the 15C. Above the N arcade there is a triforium, but on the S there is double tracery to the lower part of the clerestory windows. At the W end, the great Perpendicular window has a very wide transom; above it the window is set back by nine inches. All the roofs are wooden, but vaulting was once intended for the aisles. The W end of the nave has hammerbeams, the rest has kingposts. Note the doorway into the N porch. It has well-carved capitals of foliage and of the heads of a king, queen and archbishop.

The Caen stone reredos of 1875 has five crocketed gables, somewhat dwarfed by the huge E window. The pulpit against the N arcade was made in 1850, but the elaborate and agreeable hexagonal canopy, plus the stairs, are additions of 1960. The eagle lectern to the S is of 1873. The two elaborate stalls in the chancel were carved by Robert Thompson of Kilburn. At the W end of the N aisle there are placed reconstructed parts of the 12C cloister, which pre-date any of the standing fabric. In the opposite aisle there are a number of relatively old gravestones, including one to Robert Brystwyk, Prior, who died in 1493. Also to be seen is the so-called breadstone, a slab of Tournai marble on which bread for the poor was once placed. It may be a 12C memorial stone of the founder of the priory.

The church has a notable collection of 19C and 20C stained glass. The E window is a Tree of Jesse. St. John of Bridlington is depicted in a S aisle window, the first beyond the screen. This window is a postwar replacement by G.E.R. Smith for one which was destroyed in the Second World War. The N aisle windows are all of Old Testament subjects. The great W window has figures in each of the principal or upper tier of lights. From the S, they are St. Peter, St. Matthew, St. John the Evangelist, the Virgin Mary, Christ, St. John the Baptist, St. Mark, St. Luke and St. Paul. Each figure is surmounted by an appropriate symbol. Below, in the central panel, is St. Thomas, the only full-length figure in the lower tier.

Filey, _St. Oswald._ St. Oswald's is a cruciform church which was built between c 1180 and c 1230. Its predominant style is Early English, but there are also late Norman elements. A W tower was originally intended, probably with an aisled nave and chancel; the crossing tower and transepts were additions to the plan in the early 13C. Restoration was undertaken in 1885. The fittings are largely of the late 19C and early 20C.

The crossing tower is very wide and not particularly tall. The shadows of former roofs of steeper pitch may be seen on the W, N and E faces. In the upper stage of each face, above a stringcourse, there is a pair of pointed belfry openings under a rounded arch. Battlements form the parapet. The transepts and chancel are of the same height as the nave, but because the nave has lower lean-to aisles, the details of the transepts and chancel are larger and impress more readily. There are tall lancet windows with hoodmoulds. In each face of the transepts there are central, chamfered buttresses, on either side of which, close up, a lancet is placed. A stringcourse runs immediately below the lancets. The transepts have angle buttresses in addition to the central ones. The chancel has an E window of three lancets (which are shafted within). The clerestory above the nave has diminutive Norman windows. At the W end of the nave there is, surprisingly, a single lancet, but the W window of the N aisle is Norman, deeply splayed within. The S door is late Norman.

Within, the fairly narrow five-bay nave has columns which are alternately round and octagonal. There are double-chamfered pointed arches and moulded capitals with varying detail. The benches in the nave are arranged unusually, so that there is no central alley. The deeply splayed Norman clerestory windows are placed directly above the apex of the nave arches. One bay at the W shows the evidence for an intended tower; columns for a tower arch stand against the arcades. There are fine 13C sedilia in the chancel. There is much stained glass by C.E. Kempe, by his successor company and by Bryans & Webb. In the S transept, the S window depicts King Aethelberht of Kent (left) and St. Augustine of Canterbury and St. Gregory (right). St. Gregory is shown saying *'non Angli sed Angeli'*, in the incident in Rome which preceded his sending St. Augustine to England. The four lancets on the S side of the chancel depict more early saints, including the church's patron, St. Oswald, King of Northumbria, and the Celtic missionary whom he supported, St. Aidan. The reredos is of 1911 by C. Hodgson Fowler. There are attractive candelabra of the 19C or early 20C. Over the N door are 18C royal arms.

Canon Arthur Neville Cooper, Vicar of Filey for 55 years from 1880, achieved fame as a long-distance pedestrian. He walked from Filey to Rome and from Filey to Venice on separate occasions! Various books record his experiences as a pedestrian. His pastoral work in Filey itself endeared him to the townsfolk.

Garton-on-the-Wolds, *St. Michael*. St. Michael's is largely a 12C Norman building of W tower, aisleless nave and chancel. There is a S door of three orders with zigzag moulding and a W door with four orders of the same. Two Norman lancets pierce both the N and S walls and there is a fifth, with zigzag, in the W face of the tower. All are deeply splayed within. One three-light S window has Decorated tracery. A corbel table below the roof presents many animal carvings. There are the usual flat buttresses on the nave. The top of the tower is Perpendicular. Otherwise, the dominant influence here is of the 19C. At the expense of Sir Tatton Sykes, J.L. Pearson rebuilt the chancel in 1856 in Norman style. He supplied blind arcading on the E front above three lancets. Then in 1865 G.E. Street refitted the interior and called in Clayton & Bell to paint it. The walls and roofs are completely painted in a 13C style, except for a dado of Staffordshire tiles. The N wall bears the story of the Creation and the S has aspects of life in every month of the year. On either side of the tower arch are the four Greek Doctors; the chancel arch is flanked by the four Latin Doctors. Restoration work on the mural paintings began in October, 1986, under Wolfgang Gärtner. A 19C screen is fitted within the 12C chancel arch, which is very wide and high. The fine 19C font and cover stand in the SW corner of the nave. There are mosaic pavements. The Decorated window in the S wall has 19C stained glass, comprising nine Passion scenes.

Hedon, *St. Augustine*. St. Augustine's is a substantial cruciform church whose fabric dates mainly from the late 12C to the 15C. It is known as 'The King of Holderness'. It comprises a five-bay nave, a proud crossing tower which is 129ft high to the top of the pinnacles, N and S transepts, a chancel and a SE vestry. The transepts and chancel are of the same height as the nave. At one time, there were E aisles to the transepts and a chapel to the S of the chancel. The chancel and transepts date from the late 12C and the first half of the 13C; the nave is substantially of the end of the 13C; the extreme W end was remodelled in the early 14C; and the crossing tower is a Perpendicular work which was built after 1428. The size of St. Augustine's speaks of Hedon's medieval wealth as a port, at least until the rise of Kingston-upon-Hull. G.E. Street restored the church between 1867 and 1875. In recent years, much money has been spent on the fabric, especially on the tower and N transept.

The 15C crossing tower has angle buttresses and a central buttress in each face. There are two tiers of pairs of three-light windows, an openwork parapet and eight pinnacles. The windows of the body of the church present an interesting range of medieval styles. Lancets from the late 12C or early 13C are to be found in the N wall of the chancel, the W wall of the vestry (which was once the E window of the S chancel chapel) and in the transepts (but bearing in mind that G.E. Street renewed the ends of the transepts, especially on the S). The S transept has slightly earlier features than the N transept: look especially at their W faces and at their doorways. Of the four nave aisle windows, the three to the E have Reticulated tracery of c 1300. The westernmost windows of the nave aisles, however, have flowing Decorated tracery. The five-light W window of the nave is also Decorated. At the other end of the church, the main E window of five transomed lights is Perpendicular. Doorways merit some attention. The N doorway of the N transept is a splendid Early English work, with much dogtooth decoration. Its counterpart to the S is earlier, for it has a round arch. The nave has trefoil-headed 13C doorways to N and S. Finally, notice the scars of the S chancel chapel and of the E aisles of the transepts.

The interior reflects the building history recounted above. The S side of the chancel reflects the removal of the S chapel (which was a chantry of St. Mary), except for its E wall, which became the W wall of the 15C vestry. A doorway leads from the chancel into the vestry. Remains of the sedilia survive to its W. On the N side of the chancel there is Geometrical blank tracery. The chancel and the transepts have clerestory wall passages. Stiff-leaf may be seen in the arch leading from the S transept into the S nave aisle. The nave itself has tall piers with four major shafts and four minor ones.

The reredos is Victorian, but upholds the older tradition of including the inscribed panels of the Commandments, the Creed and the Lord's Prayer. Modern choir fittings, all lightly stained, stand W of the crossing. Their 19C equivalents remain in the chancel proper. The font, in the SW corner, is an octagonal Decorated example. It has crocketed gables which rise from the curved underside of the bowl, and also bears quatrefoils and other enrichment. A three-manual organ of 1926 is placed to the N of the crossing. In the N transept itself are placed the arms of King George II, 1741, and a 13C black marble grave-cover, which bears a cross in relief. A 14C stone effigy lies in the chancel. The stained glass is all relatively modern. The glass in the E window was inserted in 1900. The Ascension and the Crucifixion are its main subjects, surrounded by a large number of figures including St. Augustine of Hippo, the church's patron, and his mother, St. Monica.

Hemingbrough, *St. Mary the Virgin*. This substantial, cruciform church was largely built in the 13C, but its most notable feature, the thin, needle-like recessed spire, 190ft in height, was added in the early 15C. In 1426, St. Mary's became a collegiate church under the patronage of the Bishop of Durham and it has sometimes been known as 'Hemingbrough Minster'. A misericord in the church, dated to c 1200, is possibly the earliest in England.

The church comprises a four-bay nave, N and S nave aisles, a crossing tower, N and S transepts, a chancel and a S chancel aisle. The spire seems to be twice as tall as the tower, behind whose battlements it is markedly recessed. The thinness of the spire preserves a sense of harmony. To the 13C belong the Y-traceried N windows of the chancel and the E window of five stepped and cusped lights. 13C lancet windows also appear on the E and W faces of the S transept. The five-light S window of this transept, however, is clearly Perpendicular. To its W, the S aisle windows are Decorated. The W front and the N side of the church W of the chancel have 15C windows, and the clerestory windows are of the same date.

Within, the nave arcades have two rounded E bays and two pointed W ones. The earlier bays have round piers, octagonal abaci and moulded arches. Then comes a notably thick pier on each side (the second pier from the W), marking an earlier W end. The bays to the W are different from their E neighbours only in being pointed, and so they are not much later in date. The N nave aisle is very wide—wider than the nave itself. The N transept has a very narrow W aisle, with a two-bay arcade. The four-bay S chancel arcade is of the 15C.

There are many fittings of interest in the church. In the nave there are bench-ends carved with four-light tracery. In the SW corner stands the font of c 1190, decorated with blank arcading. Various memorial tablets are affixed over the N arcade. The Burton chantry in the SE corner of the church has an attractive modern screen and stalls, by Robert Thompson of Kilburn, with carvings of squirrels, cats and mice. The four-light E window of the chantry has stained glass of c 1900. A late medieval cadaver effigy is placed in the Babthorpe chantry (or N chapel). The church's one misericord, situated to the right of the chancel arch, is a remarkably early one, of c 1200; it has stylised leaves and stalks arranged in curving patterns. An attractive 'English altar' with blue hangings stands in the N transept. Nearby is a medieval stone table, formerly in the Babthorpe chantry. It is carved with tracery of a pair of two ogee lights, with quatrefoils in the heads. There is also carved cresting. It would appear to be of the 14C or 15C. There are 16C parclose screens.

Howden Minster, *St. Peter and St. Paul.* The present church is the surviving portion of a cruciform collegiate building, which was under the patronage of the Prior and Convent of Durham and of the Bishops of Durham in the Middle Ages. Like Bridlington Priory, Howden has lost its choir, but unlike Bridlington, it has retained its transepts and crossing tower. King William I gave Howden to the Bishop of Durham in 1080. The bishop kept the manor but gave the advowson to Durham's Prior and Convent. In 1267 the church was made collegiate and ultimately had six secular canons. Rebuilding subsequently took place and most of the present building is of the 13C and early 14C, though the tower and chapter house date from the following century. After the Dissolution (in this case under King Edward VI), Howden became poor. The choir was abandoned in 1609 and its vault fell in 1696. The remaining fabric was restored between 1843 and 1854. A fire in the tower in 1929 necessitated further restoration.

The church comprises a six-bay nave, N and S nave aisles, a S porch, a former school attached at the SW corner, a crossing tower, N and S transepts, and chapels which are really the extended E aisles of the transepts. To the E is the ruined choir and to the S of that, the ruined chapter house. The tower is the dominant exterior feature. It was built in two phases in the 15C. Money was given for the first phase in the will, dated 1403, of Bishop Skirlaugh of Durham. Skirlaugh's lower stage has pairs of immensely tall three-light windows, each with two transoms, in each face, flanked by gabled buttresses. The upper stage, which was added later in the 15C, has pairs of three-light windows with one transom. The parapet is battlemented. It is a noble tower, a late medieval lantern, and we are lucky that it survived Howden's lean times after the Dissolution. The transepts and nave were built within about 30 years of Howden becoming collegiate. The arms of Bishop Bek of Durham date the W front to between 1306 and 1311. The window tracery of all this late 13C and early 14C work is Geometrical.

The W front—the one complete elevation which can be appreciated clearly—has four hexagonal turrets with openwork tracery, flanking both nave and aisles. There are straight-topped W ends to the lean-to aisles. To the S, what appears to be an outer aisle is a school of c 1500. It is attached to the two W bays of the S aisle and is two-storeyed. Immediately to its E is the S porch, also two-storeyed, which has been a vestry since 1843. It is of the same date as the nave. The ruined choir is said to date from a little later than the nave, but its details are very similar. Undoubtedly later is the octagonal chapter house, Decorated below and Perpendicular above. Its original roof fell in 1750.

The interior is spacious to the W and perhaps a little crowded to the E. The chancel, so to speak, comprises the crossing and one bay of the nave. The E end is occupied by the surviving 15C pulpitum, a very fine work of four large canopied niches and a wide ogee arch in the centre. To its S lies the Lady chapel (in the S transept), to which is attached a SE chapel or Saltmarshe chantry. The organ is divided between the nave's E arches, above the choirstalls. The piers of the nave have four shafts and four hollows, and moulded capitals. The clerestory above has a wall passage. The roof is a replacement of 1854.

The pulpitum has 14C statues in its four niches which were brought from the ruined choir between 1784 and 1799 and which therefore show weathering. They depict St. Peter, St. Paul, a blind-folded woman and St. John the Evangelist. The central archway of the pulpitum is now St. Cuthbert's chapel, where the Blessed Sacrament is reserved. The woodwork of the altar was carved by Robert Thompson of Kilburn after the fire of 1929. In the S transept there is a 14C statue of the Virgin Mary (also brought from the choir). On her shoulder perches a dove to represent the Annunciation. Below the statue there is a brass of c 1480 of an unidentified knight. Both the S transept and the adjoining Saltmarshe chantry have numerous monuments. Among the medieval tombstones in the transept is one of John Cobe (died 1467), a chantry priest. There is also a late 13C effigy of a priest in eucharistic vestments, standing on a tomb-chest to which it does not belong. It is thought to represent St. John of Howden. A 17C drawing shows a recumbent effigy, once thought to be the one now standing on the tomb-chest, in the recess in the SE chapel, with an inscription identifying it as that of John de Metham, Rector of Patrington from 1379 to 1399. The standing statue, however, is too early to be of John de Metham, and *his* effigy must have been destroyed. In the recess today there are two further medieval effigies, which are thought to be of Sir John Metham (died 1311) and his wife. Also in the chapel are a parish coffin of 1664 (used to transport bodies to the graveside before burial in shrouds) and a gravestone which covered the entrails of Walter de Kirkham, Bishop of Durham, who died at Howden in 1260. A fine eagle lectern stands in the nave on the N. Huge royal arms of King George I, 1718, are placed in the N transept. There too is stained glass of 1953, by H. Stammers, to commemorate the present Queen's coronation. It depicts Bishop Skirlaugh, Roger de Hoveden (or Howden, Rector from 1174 to 1197, who was a notable chronicler), and St. Osanna, whom Gerald of Wales (died 1220) alleged to be buried at Howden and identified as the sister of a King Osred, of whom two of the name lived in the 8C. No more is known of her. The W window of the nave has 19C stained glass by Jean Baptiste Capronnier, rather yellow in effect. The same artist also designed the W windows of the aisles.

One of the earliest canons of Howden in the 13C, John de Howden, was regarded as a saint after his death in 1275, but he was never formally canonised. The 16C historian, Leland, recorded his tomb in the choir. Offerings from pilgrims to his tomb helped to pay for building work in the 13C and 14C.

Kingston-upon-Hull

The largest town in the East Riding, usually known simply as Hull, rose to prominence in the 14C as the chief port on the River Humber. It rapidly became a place of merchant wealth as notable as any in England. The size of the principal church, Holy Trinity, built in the 14C and 15C, underlines the wealth of the place. The medieval town grew up in the angle between the Rivers Hull and Humber, and hinged on the High Street which still runs parallel with the River Hull. Georgian expansion took place a little to the N and later development has carried the boundaries far from the old centre.

The two medieval churches of Hull proper, Holy Trinity and St. Mary's in Lowgate, were both long dependent on Hessle and North Ferriby respectively, at least in theory. Other medieval churches now within Hull's boundaries formerly served separate villages. The next group of churches and chapels to survive are Georgian and very early Victorian. Of these, the chapel of Trinity House deserves a special mention. Trinity House is a foremost institutional reminder of Hull's maritime history. The present chapel was built in 1839–43 to the designs of H.F. Lockwood. It is a large Classical work, whose interior comprises a vaulted square with three barrel-vaulted arms and an apse with large columns. There are box-pews and a good pulpit. Earlier and less grand Classical works are the chapel of the Charterhouse, of c 1779–80, in an Adam style and probably by Joseph Hargrave, and the Catholic church of St. Charles Borromeo in Jarratt Street, originally of 1829 by John Earle.

The Victorian age and the 20C have been responsible for the overwhelming majority of Hull's churches. G.E. Street designed All Saints', Margaret Street, Sculcoates, a redbrick church of 1866–69; Samuel Musgrave added the tower in 1883. St. Mary's, at one time the main church of Sculcoates, was largely rebuilt by Temple Moore in 1916. He reused some 18C Tuscan columns from the earlier church. Also by Temple Moore is St. Augustine's of 1890–96. Both churches have Decorated tracery and both lack towers. Of the 20C buildings, a surprising number date from the 1950s. St. Michael's, Orchard Park Road, by F.F. Johnson, 1957–58, has the Norman font from Wharram Percy.

Hull deserves some fame for being the birthplace in 1827 of G.F. Bodley, one of the most distinguished architects of the Gothic Revival. His former master, Sir Gilbert Scott, also had links with Hull. Three successive Vicars of St. Mary's in Lowgate were his cousins.

Holy Trinity. Holy Trinity Church claims the distinction of being the largest English parish church by area. It was built mainly between the late 13C and the early 15C and speaks very clearly of Hull's medieval wealth as a port. The church is a notably early example of the use of brick, which was locally kilned. The building suffered from misuse during the Commonwealth and from other post-medieval alterations. Major restoration was undertaken by H.F. Lockwood in 1841–46 and by Sir Gilbert Scott a little later.

The church stands next to the Market Place, just to the W of the commercial centre of medieval Hull. It is 285ft long and has a tower which is 150ft high. The plan comprises an eight-bay nave with N and S aisles, a crossing tower, a five-bay chancel with N and S aisles, shallow N and S transepts, and a series of rooms added to the S aisle. The transepts, chancel and lower part of the tower are of brick. The transepts were built first, by the early 14C, the chancel followed in the full flower of the Decorated period, and then the nave was built in the late 14C and early 15C. The building was consecrated in 1425. The crossing tower was added later, perhaps by the end of the 15C. The exterior is one of huge windows and pinnacled buttresses. The E window is of seven lights, with two transoms; the E windows of the chancel aisles are of five lights and have splendid Decorated tracery; the chancel windows are of four wide lights, again with full Decorated tracery; the transepts have windows of Geometrical tracery veering towards the Decorated; the nave has Perpendicular windows, five-light to N and S, nine-light at the W and seven-light at the W ends of the aisles. The tower has two tiers of windows with battlemented transoms, the lower windows glazed, the upper louvred. There is a tall openwork parapet with corner pinnacles, and shorter ones are centrally placed.

The interior has tall and slender piers which comprise four shafts with four intervening hollows and which have foliage capitals. There is a nave altar under the W arch of the crossing tower. A screen of 1900 stands under the tower's E arch. Another screen, of four Perpendicular divisions, stands under the S arch and is the surviving centre of the medieval Rood screen. The choir is accorded three bays, the sanctuary one and the last bay is an ambulatory. A stone screen separates sanctuary from ambulatory, and screens also divide the choir and sanctuary from the aisles.

The pulpit of of 1846 by H.F. Lockwood. To its N is the lectern of 1847, which is 7ft high and weighs 7cwt and was made locally by George Parker. The 16-sided font at the W end dates from the 14C and is made of coralloid marble. The choir has some attractive 14C, 15C and 18C bench-ends. Note St. Peter and St. Paul. The stone screen in the chancel dates from 1886. The communion table which now stands on the E side of the screen behind the high altar was bought for the church in 1770. In the N chancel aisle hangs a painting of the Last Supper by James Parmentier, 1711. It once covered the lower part of the E window. It was later reduced in size and now depicts ten Apostles instead of 12. To the N of the S porch is a worn sculpture of the Holy Trinity, placed in an arch which once led into a chantry chapel founded by John Alcock, Bishop of Worcester and later of Ely, in the 15C.

There are a number of monuments in the church. The earliest is an effigy of Eleanor Box, a Mayoress of Hull who died in 1380, which lies against the W wall of the S transept. Just to the E of the S transept is the Broadley chapel, which was renamed after its restorer in 1863. Previously it was known as the de la Pole chapel. A canopied tomb, to a de la Pole but without an effigy, opens into the S chancel aisle. A little to the E of this arch is the tomb of Sir William de la Pole (died 1366) and his wife Katherine de Norwich (died 1381). Sir William was the first Mayor of Hull in 1331. Their effigies are of Chellaston alabaster from Derbyshire and lie under an ogee canopy, cusped and sub-cusped. A tomb-chest in the S chancel aisle bears a brass of Richard and Margaret Byll, who both died in 1451. They are represented by half-length figures and there are the Evangelists' symbols at the four corners. Nearby, against the S wall, is a frontal bust of Thomas Whincop, 1624, Lecturer at Holy Trinity and Master of the Charterhouse in Hull.

Relatively few of the church's innumerable windows have stained glass. In the S nave aisle there are two windows by Walter Crane, which are known as the Earle and Brooks windows. The former is of 1897 and represents the 148th Psalm. The latter is of 1907 and depicts Calvary. Over the S porch is stained glass of 1952 by H.J. Stammers of York, which depicts events in Hull's history. The E window of the chancel is by Clayton & Bell. There are two minor roundels of 14C glass, depicting Noah and the Judgement of Solomon.

John Healey Bromby was Vicar of this parish from 1797 to 1866, no fewer than 69 years. His son, Charles Henry Bromby, married the sister of the architect, George Frederick Bodley. The Bodleys lived in Hull from 1817 to 1839 and the future architect was born there in 1827. Charles Bromby later became the Bishop of Tasmania.

Patrington, *St. Patrick.* St. Patrick's is one of the most important Decorated churches in England, built on an ambitious scale and with notable details. It is widely known as 'The Queen of Holderness'. The present church replaced an earlier one and it is accepted that it was rebuilt in stages, the transepts first, then the nave and lastly the chancel, all between c 1275 and c 1350. There is no agreement, however, whether the present plan reflects an earlier one, and in particular it has been debated whether the crossing tower, which has Early English elements, is a survival of the earlier church or an anomalous part of the rebuilding. The lavishness of the building may be compared with Hawton in Nottinghamshire and Heckington in Lincolnshire in its Decorated details, but in its plan and scale it is much more impressive than them.

St. Patrick's comprises a five-bay nave with N and S aisles, a crossing tower with spire, N and S transepts each with E and W aisles of three bays, an aisleless chancel, a NE sacristy and N and S porches, the S one being two-storeyed. The middle bay of the S transept's E aisle has an apse, which represents the Lady chapel. There is no clerestory. The spire rises to 189ft, the church's internal length is 141ft and its width at the transepts is 86ft. Buttresses rising to crocketed pinnacles surround the building. The buttresses all bear

St. Patrick's, a splendid 14C cruciform church in Holderness

gargoyles and those to the transepts have niches. The N and S nave aisles have windows of three lights which are conventionally Decorated. The N transept N window and its counterpart in the S window are of four lights, transomed, and entirely Decorated. The seven-light E window, however, is Perpendicular. There is an elaborate N doorway to the N transept, with animal supporters and a gable. The crossing tower has lancets in its lowest stage. Above comes the belfry stage, with four arches, of which the outer two are blank and the others are plain, louvred openings. The lancets and the arcading are the details which are cited as evidence in arguing that the tower is earlier. The impression it gives, however, is not divergent but rather one of harmony with the rest of the building. There is a plain parapet and small corner pinnacles, which are connected to the spire by flying buttresses. An octagonal corona of cusped arches, with pinnacles, stands to a height of 25ft around the base of the spire. It was to be the model for G.F. Bodley's spire at Clumber in Nottinghamshire. A 13C sculpture of the Virgin and Child is placed below the E window.

The interior is very light, for there is little stained glass. The piers of the nave have clustered shafts and capitals with very accomplished foliage. One pier, at the W end on the N, has an earlier, wide base. The arcades of the transepts entail that the crossing tower rests only on its four piers. The church therefore seems to have an 'open plan', but the two arcades in each transept bring innumerable piers and arches into many vistas. The E aisle of the S transept has an original rib-vault. The middle bay of this aisle has a lantern-type boss, which is carved on three sides with the Annunciation, St. John the Baptist and St. Catherine; it may have been a reliquary. The nave and transepts have original roofs, but that of the chancel is of c 1880.

There is a chancel screen of 14C character, the divisions being of two lights with ogee tracery. It is much restored. To the N of the sanctuary is a notable Easter sepulchre. Its lowest stage bears carvings of three sleeping Roman soldiers, each under a rich bowed ogee canopy. Above was once an open shelf, which is now used for the Reserved Sacrament. Then comes a Resurrection scene, with two censing angels flanking the figure of Christ. Finally, there is a blank space where one might expect an Ascension, surmounted by a depressed ogee arch. The lateral shafts ascend into crocketed pinnacles. To the S of the sanctuary there are sedilia and a piscina. They have shafts, pinnacles and ogee arches which correspond with those of the Easter sepulchre. The reredos is perhaps the most spectacular fitting in the church. It is of gilded oak and almost stretches across the entire E wall. It was made in 1936 to the designs of J. Harold Gibbons. It has 13 canopied niches, which are filled with statues of the Virgin Mary and 12 Northumbrian saints, flanked by two much larger ones (for St. Patrick, N, and St. George, S), which are surmounted by pinnacles to the N and S of the E window. The E window has stained glass of 1884, a little dark perhaps, but better than a clear window above such a rich reredos. The Lady chapel in the S transept has three empty niches, whose canopies are similar to those of the sedilia. The blank panel below represents the position of the former reredos. At the W end is the font, whose 12 sides have very worn gabled tracery in the Decorated style. In the S transept are some pews of 1684. The pulpit dates from 1612. The organ is by Forster & Andrews, 1891.

Scorborough, *St. Leonard* and South Dalton, *St. Mary*. These two churches stand just a few miles apart. Both were built in 13C style to the designs of J.L. Pearson, the former in 1857–59 and the latter in 1858–61. Pearson's patron at Scorborough was James Hall, whose family had risen to be landowners after serving the Hotham family of Dalton Hall. The rebuilding of St. Leonard's prompted the third Baron Hotham to do the same at South Dalton, but on an even larger and more lavish scale.

St. Leonard's stands at the end of a lane some four miles N of Beverley. It comprises an aisleless nave, a chancel and a W tower with a spire. There are gabled belfry windows in the tower. The spire has corner pinnacles rising from the broaches.

The interior is rich in detail. The windows of paired lancets are set behind arches on detached marble shafts. The W window is set behind two trefoiled arches supported by clustered marble pillars. Over the side windows are quatrefoils, all with double tracery. Nave and chancel are divided by pairs of columns on each side. The stone pulpit bears carved figures of the four Latin Doctors. The font and the reredos have similar elaborate decorative carving. The stained glass, which is by the firm of Clayton & Bell, includes the depiction in the E window of the Annunciation, the Nativity, the Last Supper, the Crucifixion, the Entombment, the Resurrection and, in the rose above, Christ in Glory. On the sanctuary step is an inscription which states that James Hall had rebuilt the church as a thank-offering. In the NE corner of the sanctuary, there is an early 16C effigy of Henry de Middleton, priest, shown in his vestments and with a chalice.

St. Mary's serves the parish of Dalton Holme, which united the previously separate parishes of South Dalton and Holme on the Wolds in 1861. The church stands at the N end of South Dalton. It is a substantial cruciform church, comprising an aisleless nave, N and S transepts, chancel, chancel aisles and W tower and spire. It cost its builder some £25,000. The spire rises to a height of 208ft, which is higher than both Patrington and Hemingbrough. Such a large church inevitably imposes problems of upkeep on its rural parish.

The tower has tall, three-light belfry openings with low gables, recessed between sharp horizontal features above and below. Octagonal buttresses to the belfry are carried up as pinnacles, keeping close to the spire. The latter has gabled lucarnes near its base. The windows of the church have Geometrical tracery. Chancel, nave and transepts all have gable crosses.

Within, there is blind arcading between the windows of the aisleless nave. The sanctuary also has arcading, with attached shafts. The tower arch is remarkably tall. The church is richly appointed, with a tiled floor in the nave as well as in the chancel, carved bench-ends, attractive coronae for the church's lighting, a font cover of elaborate ironwork, and a substantial metal screen to the S chancel chapel by Skidmore's. As at Scorborough, there is stained glass by Clayton & Bell. The Day of Judgement is depicted in the E window of 1861, arranged in ten panels. The W window shows eight pairs of Old Testament figures. The S transept window depicts Melchizedek, St. John the Baptist, St. Stephen and St. Augustine. The S chancel aisle contains a large memorial to Sir John Hotham (died 1689). This monument, which is attributed to John Bushnell, comprises an effigy on a black marble slab, supported by four allegorical figures of Virtues, and a lower black slab with a *memento mori*. In the same aisle there is a tablet to the church's builder, the third Baron Hotham, who died in 1870.

Sledmere House, *Chapel of St. Mark.* Sledmere House is a careful restoration of 1912–17 by Walter Brierley of an 18C building, which had been burnt in 1911. Richard Sykes (1706–61) inherited Sledmere in 1748 and began a new house in 1751. His nephew, Sir Christopher, the second Baronet (1749–1801), extended and remodelled it in the 1780s and 1790s, acting as his own designer, but with the advice of John Carr and Samuel Wyatt. The chapel was an addition after the fire by Walter Brierley. It is a rectangular room, which is divided from a five-sided E end by a screen of two marbled Composite columns and two responds. The three E windows behind the altar have stained glass of 1979, designed by Angela, Countess of Antrim (sister of Sir Richard Sykes, seventh Baronet) and made by Patrick Reyntiens and David Wasley. French and Italian religious paintings hang in the body of the chapel.

Weaverthorpe, St. Andrew. St. Andrew's is a fine Norman building of W tower, nave, S porch and chancel, which was sympathetically restored and refitted by G.E. Street in 1870–72. The 14C S porch is the only addition to the original plan. The church was built in the early 12C by Herbert of Winchester (or Herbert the Chamberlain) whose dedication inscription is placed over the S door. His son, William Fitzherbert, became Archbishop of York in 1143 and was canonised as St. William of York in 1226.

The church stands on rising ground to the N of the village in a very large churchyard. It is built of small, squared stone blocks in the Norman fashion. The tall, unbuttressed W tower has arched belfry openings, which are divided by a central shaft. A semicircular projection from the SE corner carries the staircase up to the belfry. There are N and S Norman doors, both very simple, with blank tympana. Over the S door, however, is the sundial, which bears this inscription: + IN HONORE SCI ANDREÆ/APOSTOLI HEREBERTVS/ WINTONIE/HOC MONASTERI/VM FECIT IN TEMPORE RE (Herbert of Winchester built this minster in honour of St. Andrew the Apostle in the time of...). A minster was usually a parish church of importance beyond its own town or village. The N and S nave walls are both pierced by two Norman windows; the S wall also has one 14C cusped, ogee lancet. The square-headed chancel windows are of the 14C, two-light except for the E window which has three lights. The exterior has no buttresses or stringcourses.

The aisleless nave is bounded at the W end by the very tall, narrow, Norman tower arch, and at the E by the very wide, stepped Norman chancel arch. Above the tower arch is an opening into the ringing chamber. The iron tower and brass chancel screens were designed by G.E. Street and were made by T. Potter & Son as parts of the works of 1870–72. A bust of Sir Tatton Sykes, Bt. (died 1913), who commissioned Street's restoration, stands on the ledge of the 14C S window. The stained glass in that window depicts St. Peter, including his crucifixion upside down. The Norman windows on the S have stained glass of St. James the Less (E) and St. John (W); the two on the N depict the Virgin Mary (E) and St. Mary Magdalene (W). All the stained glass is by Clayton & Bell. The pulpit of iron openwork (made by Leaver of Maidenhead) and the lectern are also by Street. To the right of the chancel arch is a large sculpture of St. Andrew, by James Redfern, 1872. The saint holds his symbol of a saltire cross. The cylindrical font is Norman and is decorated with a diapered pattern of octagons and circles. Street added the present wagon roof, which is painted. In the chancel, the folding altarpiece is by Clayton & Bell. The E window above depicts the Agnus Dei in the central light. Other chancel windows show the Annunciation, St. Mary Magdalene at the Tomb, and the Crucifixion of St. Andrew.

THE NORTH RIDING OF YORKSHIRE

The North Riding emerged from the reorganisation of 1974 as the much-changed North Yorkshire. In its old form the N boundary was the River Tees, and its S tip was the City of York. It comprised the Vale of York in the centre, with South Teesdale, Swaledale and Wensleydale on one side, and Cleveland and the Vale of Pickering on the other, and with the abrupt mass of the North York Moors rising up between. Yet for so large, varied and impressive a county, the churches are surprisingly poor. Certainly it was not, in medieval times, a prosperous part of the country; and perhaps the building materials available—soft sandstones and dull limestones—did not inspire ambitious architectural ideas. The churches are less grand and exciting than many in neighbouring County Durham or the East Riding. Some have fine and interesting features; but only Whitby, with its extraordinary 18C interior, might be regarded as the best church of its kind in the country. This is by no means true, however, of the North Riding's great monastic churches, now ruined, and beyond the scope of this book: Rievaulx, Whitby, Guisborough, Byland and others were the greatest churches of the county, and of national significance.

There are few pre-Conquest buildings (but many sculpted fragments). Kirkdale's tower arch and sundial, and Hovingham's sculpted altar frontal and tower, are described in the gazetteer. Hackness has a chancel arch of probably 11C date; other towers are at Appleton-le-Street and Hornby. Masham has an impressive but worn 9C cross-shaft with figures in tiers of arches, a Mercian motif; at Brompton-in-Allertonshire are several well-preserved hogback tombstones of Anglo-Danish design, the ends carved with bears, some with muzzled snouts. From the Norman period the crypt at Lastingham is outstanding. There are many Norman chancel arches, the best at Felixkirk and at Liverton. Alne has a splendid S doorway, richly carved with Zodiac signs, Labours of the Months and animals and mythical beasts. Barton-le-Street, a neo-Norman concoction of 1871 using many genuine Norman parts, has the former S door inside the N porch, equally richly decorated, with reliefs above of the Magi and the Virgin and Child, in bed, with bearded angels swinging censers. The only Norman tympanum *in situ* is at Danby Wiske. Yarm exhibits a stocky Norman W front, tacked on now to a Classical body of 1730. The best Norman arcade is the N arcade of Hornby, late 12C. A good Norman tower can be seen at Leake. Whitby's tower is late Transitional.

The Cistercians introduced pointed arches at Rievaulx Abbey in the 1130s. A little later is the surviving part of the W front of the former Gilbertine Priory of Old Malton, still with a Transitional appearance. Fully-fledged Early English emerges in the charming little church at Skelton of the mid-13C, derived stylistically from the S transept of York Minster. For the Decorated period, the S arcade and aisle of Patrick Brompton are worth examining, and the E window of Great Langton. Of the Perpendicular style, Thirsk is outstanding (though modest in national terms). Northallerton has a big, stern central tower and Perpendicular windows of transepts and aisles, but the chancel is of 1885. Bedale has a Perpendicular belfry and an E window said to have come out of Jervaulx Abbey. More pleasing, perhaps, are the smaller churches of this period: Coxwold, with its rare octagonal tower; Catterick ('improved' with a clerestory in 1872); Askrigg; and Burneston, with a spire—scarce in the North Riding.

The 17C is almost barren in architectural terms. Amongst 18C Classical churches, Yarm (1730) is competent but not outstanding. The finest 18C building is the Hospital chapel at Kirkleatham of the 1740s, most probably by James Gibbs. Kirkleatham Church, a little later, more modest and much plainer, is the best parochial example of the Classical style, and Gibbs's overpowering Turner Mausoleum of 1739 is the finest such addition in the county. For ingenious planning, Thomas Atkinson's Brandsby, 1767–70, with a centrally planned interior stressed externally by an open cupola, can be mentioned. Sir Thomas Robinson's church at Rokeby of the mid-1760s is a modest essay by this skilled amateur. The Gothic Revival came slowly to the North Riding. H.H. Seward's substantial church at East Witton, 1809, anticipates it. The first real and remarkable product of the Revival is the Catholic chapel at Brough Hall, 1837, in the Early English style, designed by Sir William Lawson and Ignatius Bonomi as a close copy of the medieval Minster Library at York. There is an interesting group of churches of the 1840s, more or less eccentric, by the wayward E.B. Lamb, at Bagby, Sowerby, Healey, Aldwark and Thirkleby. G.E. Street is represented by Whitwell-on-the-Hill, 1858–60, with a fine spire, and Robin Hood's Bay, 1868–70, sober and serious. William Butterfield built Sessay, 1847–48, and Dalton (near Topcliffe), 1868. G.F. Bodley's fine work at St. Martin's, Scarborough, 1861–63, is described in the gazetteer. J.L. Pearson's Appleton-le-Moors, 1863–65, is a powerful work with a tall and assertive spire. Local architects naturally found much work in the 19C. Two examples are John Norton's church of St. John the Evangelist, Middlesbrough, 1864–66, with spire of 1883, showing how brick could be used to create a grand Early English design; and R.J. Johnson's St. Hilda's, Whitby, 1884–86 (the tower by G.E. Charlewood, 1938), grand, Decorated and restrained. Temple Moore was much employed in the North Riding, and his churches show a sensitivity of scale and feeling for location, exemplified by East Moors, 1882. His church of St. Cuthbert, Middlesbrough, 1902, a polygonal redbrick fortress once crammed into a difficult, confined space, looks sadly ridiculous now in the middle of a car park. Finally, Sir Giles Gilbert Scott's Ampleforth Abbey is a grand church of 1922–61: a surprising sight in a sleepy village in the Vale of Pickering.

In furnishings, the North Riding has little that is really outstanding. There are a number of Norman fonts, of which the best is probably at West Rounton. A splendid font cover of 1352 survives at Well, with a crocketed spire and pre-Perpendicular tracery. Somewhat later is the tall cover at Middleham. Several medieval screens remain, including two at Aysgarth (one dated 1536). At Hornby the lower panels have preserved the original painting of foliage and birds. The screen at Wensley was used in the late 17C for the back of the Scrope family pew. The main survivals from the dissolved monasteries are two sets of stalls. One set, now in Richmond Church, is early 16C and came from Easby Abbey. It has delightful misericords. The other set is dispersed, and its provenance is a mystery. It may have come from Jervaulx Abbey. The bench-ends are characterised by detached shafts supporting charming little beasts. The main group is in Wensley, Aysgarth and Hauxwell; others are at Leake and Over Silton. Three churches preserve significant sections of wall painting. At Easby (near Richmond) are mid-13C scenes from the Old and New Testaments, and Labours of the Months; at Wensley is an early representation, mid-14C, of the Three Quick and the Three Dead; the most extensive scheme is at Pickering. Of medieval monuments, the following are outstanding. At Bedale is an early 14C recumbent effigy of alabaster to Sir Brian Fitzalan, one of the earliest surviving uses of that material. Ampleforth has a damaged mid-14C slab showing a bearded man with a woman lurking behind him, peering over his shoulder. Fine brasses survive at Topcliffe, to Thomas de Topcliffe (died 1394) and his wife, and at Wensley, to Simon de Wenslaw (died 1394), priest. Finally, at Guisborough is the Brus Cenotaph, an early 16C tomb-chest with carved figures of knights, originally erected in the priory by Prior Cockerell.

Good sets of 17C benches survive at Wensley, Burneston, Leake and Hutton Rudby. At the last church is a pretty inlaid pulpit of 1594. Kirklington has a pulpit on bulbous legs, said to have been made from a Jacobean four-poster bed. Seamer (near Scarborough) has a fine, arched Jacobean screen. Stonegrave's charming screen of 1637 has had its dado used as panelling around the church. For a late 17C interior with intact fittings, Carlton Husthwaite can be studied. For grandeur and sheer pompousness the raised Milbanke Pew at Croft, 1680, reached by a grand staircase, cannot be bettered in the county. Equally presumptuous is the Cholmley pew at Whitby, late 17C, thrown across the chancel arch by the Lord of the Manor. Whitby's furnishings sum up perfectly the 18C approach to church furnishing. A perfectly preserved pre-Victorian interior, with box-pews, triple-decker pulpit and Commandment boards, survives in the old church of Robin Hood's Bay, 1821; another is at Skelton-in-Cleveland. The most neo-Classical furnishing is probably the font at Rokeby, a tripod in the form of an antique incense burner; the earliest Gothic Revival piece is the Decorated style font at Hornby, remarkably convincing for 1783. Of 19C Gothic Revival furnishings, the best are probably in Bodley's St. Martin's, Scarborough, especially the lovely Morris & Co. pulpit. Butterfield's Dalton has a complete mid-19C interior. Bolton-upon-Swale has interior decorations, tiled dados and wall paintings of c 1877 by Eden Nesfield. In the 20C many churches received woodwork and oak furnishings by Robert Thompson of Kilburn, the 'mouse man' (after the mouse carved on all his work). It is quiet, attractive but undemonstrative, and is easily over-looked.

There are few outstanding 17C monuments: one of the best is at Masham, to Sir Marmaduke Wyvill, 1613. For the 18C, there are fine ensembles at Kirkleatham and Coxwold; a good architectural monument at Nunnington to Lord Widdrington (died 1743) by James Gibbs, sculpted by J.M. Rysbrack; John Flaxman's Sir Thomas Frankland, 1803, husband and wife grieving the loss of their children, at Thirkleby; the same sculptor's Reverend Thomas Brand (died 1814) at Wath; and Sir Francis Chantrey's Mrs. Johnstone (died 1819) at Hackness. Her husband weeps on her lap as she dies after childbirth.

The medieval stained glass is fragmentary. Kirkleatham's Turner Hospital chapel has a good early 18C E window. At Yarm a window of 1768 by William Peckitt survives. It features Moses. John Hardman's glass in George Goldie's Catholic church at Ugthorpe, 1855–57, may be from designs by A.W.N. Pugin. Robin Hood's Bay has fine windows of c 1875 by Henry Holiday. At St. Martin's, Scarborough is glass by D.G. Rossetti, William Morris, Sir Edward Burne-Jones and Ford Madox Brown. William Morris provided fine glass for Butterfield's Dalton.

Brough, *St. Paulinus.* St Paulinus' was the private Catholic chapel of the Hall, and stands proudly in a parkland setting. Completed in 1837, it is a close copy of the Archbishop's Chapel at York, now the Minster Library. Sir William Lawson, the patron, chose the model, William Browne of York supplied the drawings, and Ignatius Bonomi of Durham was the executant architect.

It is a tall, two-storeyed building with a presbytery attached to the N side. Below is a schoolroom and above, reached by an internal stair, is the chapel. The style is Early English, though even the later windows of the ground floor of the Minster Library are reproduced. The lofty interior is lit on the S side by paired and triple lancets under round arches, with slender pointed arches between. There is much carved decoration on the shafts and foliage capitals. At the E and W ends are five stepped lancets, with small trefoil windows in the gables. On the N side, near the altar, is an aisle or tribune, with seats for the Lawson family, with two round arches and a low arcade or railing (the design for which came from a tomb in the N transept of York Minster).

The E window has stained glass by Thomas Willement of Newcastle, 1837, based on the Five Sisters window at York. The windows on the S side are by William Wailes, 1857–62. Under the altar are the remains of St. Innocent Martyr, found in the Roman catacombs and presented to Sir William Lawson by Pope Gregory XVI in 1837.

Castle Howard, *Chapel.* The chapel occupies the N end of the W wing of the house. The visitor reaches it at the end of the tour. After passing through 18C interiors, it is something of a surprise to come upon the chapel, with its sumptuous decoration in a rich Victorian style of 1875–78.

The W wing was designed by Sir Thomas Robinson and built for the fourth Earl of Carlisle in 1753–59. The chapel was probably fitted up at this time. The basic design survives: the tall, fluted columns with Corinthian capitals, screening the sanctuary, and the flat ceiling with imitation coffering, copied from the ceiling of the chapel of St. James's Palace of the 1530s. In 1875–78 Admiral Edward Howard, Lord Lanerton, transformed the chapel. R.J. Johnson of Newcastle was the architect. The floor was lowered—it was originally at the level of the altar—and the pillars and ceiling were redecorated. C.E. Kempe supplied the altar painting (Christ at the Column), and pupils of Kempe painted the frescoes of saints which form a frieze on the S wall. In the windows, hinged panels were inserted, and filled with stained glass designed by Sir Edward Burne-Jones and executed by Morris & Co., scenes from the life of Christ in Classical surrounds. Behind the font is a polychrome plaster bas-relief of the Virgin and Child by Andrea Sansovino (1460–1529). The woodwork—stalls in a Renaissance style, pews in a flowing 19C style—was carved by local craftsmen.

Catterick, *St. Anne.* Rebuilt 1412–15; remarkably, the original contract survives. It was between Katherine Burgh and her son William, and Richard de Cracall (Crakehall), mason. He undertook to 'make the Kirke of Katrick newe als Workmanschippe and mason crafte will' and to finish the work in three years. 'Tusses'—projecting stones—were to be left for the addition of a tower and vestry. The contract reveals many 15C methods.

A tower was added afterwards; the N chapel is of 1491 and the S chapel is of 1505. C.G. Wray rebuilt the clerestory in 1872. A black marble octagonal font bears the initials of William Burgh and arms of other local families. The E window has stained glass of 1862 by William Wailes (Last Supper); in the S aisle the E and SE windows are by C.E. Kempe, 1896 and 1900. There are several brasses to the Burgh family in the N chapel and aisle: John de Burgh (died 1412) and his wife Katherine; William Burgh (died 1442) and his son William (died 1465); William Burgh (died 1492), who founded a chantry with Richard Swaldall, a yeoman. Swaldall's brass is in the nave. In the S aisle is an effigy of a knight in armour, supposed to be Walter de Urswicke, Keeper of Richmond Castle in the reign of King Edward III. In the chancel is a brass inscription to Grace Lowther, 1594, who was 'so mindful of death that, for the last seven years of her pilgrimage, she would never go of a journey without taking her winding sheet about with her'.

Coxwold, *St. Michael.* The village is a single street of neat stone cottages fronted by wide greens. The street rises to the W, and the church stands in a commanding position at the top. It is a 15C building, with tower and nave of that date, and a chancel rebuilt in 1777 by Thomas Atkinson.

The most notable external feature is the octagonal W tower, sturdy rather than stately, with thin buttresses rising to crocketed pinnacles, openwork battlements, and two-light bell openings. The nave is low, with large three-light windows, buttresses with detached shafts and gargoyles, more openwork battlements (cruder than those of the tower), and crocketed pinnacles. The chancel has a large E window with elaborate tracery (of 1912, when the S window was inserted), but no N windows.

Inside, the church is of 18C character. In the nave are box-pews (cut down in 1906). The pulpit, with tester, was formerly a triple-decker. It lost a stage in 1906. On the other side of the chancel arch is an enclosure with an altar against the E wall, formerly the Lord of the Manor's pew. The W gallery survives, and so does the flat ceiling. The bosses are old and have been reset. Coats of arms are arranged around the chancel arch. In the centre are the arms of King George II, flanked by those of Thomas, Earl Fauconberg, and his nephew the third Viscount Fauconberg. The arms are decorated with crossed palm branches. Above, a scroll dates the composition to 1732.

The chancel holds the chief glory of Coxwold. Monuments of the Fauconbergs line the walls. To the left of the altar is the earliest, to Sir William Belassys (died 1603). It is signed at the bottom 'Thomas Browne did carve this tombe him selfe alone of Hessalwood stone'. There are recumbent effigies, three sons kneeling below, and a son and a daughter on either side. Above is an extravagant and elaborately decorated monument—niches, heraldry, obelisks, strapwork and inscriptions. Opposite it is the restrained monument, architectural without exuberance, to Thomas Bellasis, Viscount Fauconberg, and Barbara his wife. It was designed in 1632 by Nicholas Stone (Lord Fauconberg did not die until 1653). The life-size figures kneel in a columned aperture, with triangular and segmental pediments and a coat of arms above. Opposite and W is an early 18C monument to Henry Bellasis (died 1647) and his brother Thomas, Earl of Fauconberg (died 1700). Two standing figures engage in conversation, the Earl in coronation robes, his brother in Roman costume. Above, putti hover in a cloud, bearing crown and palm. Pilasters rise to a flat entablature, and there are large urns on either side. Opposite this is a Gothic altar-tomb to the second Earl of Fauconberg (of the second creation) who died in 1802. Closest to the chancel arch are two very similar Gothic plaques, one (to the N) to Sir George Wombwell, Bt., of nearby Newburgh Priory (died 1855) and the other to Rear Admiral Lord Adolphus Fitzclarence, illegitimate son of King William IV, who died at Newburgh in 1856 and is buried in the Fauconberg vault.

The monuments leave little room for furniture, and much of the central space is filled with a long W projection of the early 18C altar rail. There is 15C stained glass in the heads of most nave windows; and on the S side of the nave, 18C coats of arms by William Peckitt of York.

Near the church stands Shandy Hall, the home of Lawrence Sterne (1713–68), author of 'Tristram Shandy', who was incumbent of Coxwold from 1760 until his death. His memorial stone stands outside the S wall of the nave.

Hovingham, *All Saints.* The church preserves a fine pre-Conquest sculpture at the E end of the S aisle. It is perhaps the frontal of an altar, and is dated to c 800. Formerly it was outside, built into the S face of the tower, and is consequently somewhat decayed. A row of eight figures is arranged under arches, with doves in the spandrels. The first two on the left depict the Annunciation; the right-hand figure is probably an angel; interpretation of the rest is uncertain. The tower is either very late pre-Conquest or very early post-Conquest. The rest of the church was rebuilt in 1860 by Rhode Hawkins.

Kirkdale, *St. Gregory.* The church lies hidden in a secluded wooded setting beside a stream. It is noted for its pre-Conquest remains, including a sundial with a long inscription. Temple Moore restored the church in 1907–09.

The church consists of nave with N aisle, a small W tower of 1827, and a high chancel of 1881, with N chapel. The fabric of the nave is pre-Conquest, and can be dated to c 1060. Over the S door is a sundial with flanking inscriptions. The dial was in the centre, with an inscription: THIS IS DAEGES SOL MERCA AETILCUMTIDE (This is the day's sun mark for every hour) AND HAWARTH ME WROHTE AND BRAND PRS (Hawarth and Brand the priests made me). The inscriptions on either side read: ORM GAMAL/SUNA BOHTE SCS/GREGORIUS MIN/STER THONNE HI/T WES AEL TOBRO/CAN & TOFALAN & HE/HIT LET MACAN NEWAN FROM/GRUNDE XPE & SCS GREGORI/US IN EAD-WARD DAGUM CNG/& N TOSTI DAGUM EORL (Orm, Gamal's son, bought St. Gregory's Minster when it was all ruined and fallen and he had it rebuilt from the ground to Christ and St. Gregory in King Edward's days and in Earl Tosti's days). Tosti was Earl of Northumbria, 1056–65.

Inside, a pre-Conquest arch, high and round-headed and very narrow, opens from the nave to the tower. It was blocked until the late 19C. Also pre-Conquest is the chancel arch. There is a N arcade of pointed arches (the aisle was built c 1200), but the octagonal capitals with volutes, and the E respond with waterleaf, are older in style. The chancel was rebuilt in 1881, reusing parts of the old E windows (triple lancets), and preserving the medieval arch into the N chapel. The stained glass in the E lancets is by Kempe & Co. There are some sculptural fragments, including a large pre-Conquest cross with Crucifixus, a 7C slab with scrolled cross, another with interlace ornament, and (at the E end of the N aisle) a late 14C statue of the Virgin.

Kirkleatham

St. Cuthbert. A modest Classical building of 1761–63 (but the tower
is 1731), dominated externally by the grand mausoleum of the
Turners at its E end. The mausoleum was erected by Cholmley
Turner in 1740 to Marwood Turner, 'the best of sons' (see the
inscription on the outside), who died on the Grand Tour. James
Gibbs was the designer of the mausoleum. The church was rebuilt by
Robert Corney, a local architect, either to his own design or to that of
John Carr.   The most impressive view is from the E. The
mausoleum, a bold Baroque octagon topped by a tall pyramid and
urn, stands on the N side. Its base has blank arches and rusticated
bands, volute-topped buttresses and round windows above. The
chancel has a Venetian E window in a round arch, quoined corners
and a pediment. In the S wall of the chancel, in another round arch, is
a window with pedimented top, formerly a door. The other windows
are round-headed with wooden glazing bars. Heavy plain pedimented parapets conceal the roof.

The interior is plain but dignified: Tuscan columns support flat
ceilings, with pilasters at the chancel opening. The former box-pews
and triple-decker pulpit were cut down into their present shape in
1855; the chancel furnishings, including the altar carved with putti,
were installed between 1919 and 1931. In the chancel is the door to
the mausoleum, under an arch designed by Gibbs 'in the Gothick
manner'. In 1740 it would have harmonised with the medieval
chancel. The mausoleum originally had fine plasterwork, but is now
plain after reconstruction in 1839.

Near the entrance is the 18C font of white and green marble. The
pyramidal oak cover, carved with cherubim foliage and putti, is
perhaps 16C. In the N aisle is a large ironbound chest with monsters
on the posts and blank tracery on the front, made to hold the seal of a
chantry founded in 1348. In the chancel are two 17C brasses, to
Robert Coulthirst (died 1631) and Dorothy Turner (died 1628). On the
N wall of the chancel is a a skull-crowned cartouche of black and
white marble by Joshua Marshall to John Turner (died 1643) and his
wife. Opposite is their son John Turner, Sergeant-at-Law (died
1688): a tall statue by Peter Scheemakers, c 1740, in a Classical
niche. In the mausoleum, Turner statues stand in niches around the
table-tomb of Sir William Turner (this formerly stood where the
organ now is). Marwood Turner (died 1739) is by Scheemakers: a
young man, his elbow resting on books lying on a pillar. Cholmley
Turner (died 1757) is by Sir Henry Cheere. Sir Charles Turner (died
1810), the last of the line, is commemorated by a Grecian female
figure standing by a sarcophagus, by Sir Richard Westmacott.

The E window has stained glass of 1931 by A.K. Nicholson,
showing the Ascension flanked by St. Cuthbert on Lindisfarne and
St. Hilda at Whitby. In the S aisle is a window of 1933 depicting
Moses, Ruth, Naomi and the Israelites.

Sir William Turner's Hospital, Chapel. The Hospital is a dignified
quadrangle of almshouses with a splendid chapel almost certainly
designed by James Gibbs. The founder, Sir William Turner (1615–
92), was a successful City merchant and Lord Mayor of London; his
great-nephew, Cholmley Turner, rebuilt the Hospital in the 1740s.
The chapel is at the centre of the S range. Its stone entrance front
contrasts with the mellow brick of the domestic buildings. It is

dominated by a tall, many-staged clock-tower, octagonal and domed at the top. Its base, open on three sides and arched, forms the porch. Above it is set a stone with the foundation inscription.

The interior, unaltered from 1740, is square, with an apsidal sanctuary. Four fluted Ionic columns—of wood, painted to resemble stone—divide the body of the chapel Greek-cross-wise, and the compartments of the ceiling are groin-vaulted, with ribbonwork decoration on the transverse arches. Two galleries, entered from the adjacent houses, fill the aisles, and are linked over the main entrance by a stepped passage, with excellent wrought-iron railings, rising to a central balcony. From the balcony a door leads to the tower. It has a scrolled pediment top, and above, a bust of Cholmley Turner in a medallion, flanked by eagles in plaster. Below, the arch of the entrance has delicate woodcarving. The pews run lengthways under the galleries. The seats to left and right of the entrance have doors with Rococo carving. The gilt chandelier and altar chairs were bought by Turner in 1747 and came from the Duke of Chandos's chapel at Canons. The E window is filled with Flemish stained glass; in the centre the Adoration of the Magi, and left and right John Turner, Sergeant-at-law, and Sir William Turner, Lord Mayor.

Lastingham, *St. Mary.* St. Cedd founded a monastery at Lastingham at the invitation of King Ethelwald of Northumbria. The site was, according to Bede, 'among mountains, difficult of access and remote, where there appeared to be fitter dwelling places for thieves and wild beasts than for man'. St. Cedd had been a pupil of St. Aidan at Lindisfarne and acted as an interpreter at the Synod of Whitby. He died in 664. A stone church was built, and Cedd's body was buried at the high altar. The monastery was probably destroyed by the Danes in c 870. In 1078 Stephen of Whitby and some other monks refounded it, and began to build a church which forms the nucleus of the present building. In 1086, however, they abandoned the site, leaving the church unfinished, and removed to York. The church became parochial in 1228 when it was converted into its present form. J.L. Pearson restored it extensively in 1879.

The structure of the church differs considerably from Stephen's original project. What we see now as a simple aisled nave and apsidal chancel masks the more ambitious and unfinished plan. The present nave represents Stephen's crossing tower and chancel. The E end was his presbytery and apse. He intended transepts and a nave extending W of the present tower. There is structural evidence for this outside and inside the church. When the church was reoccupied in the early 13C the W side of the crossing was walled up, arcades were opened, and aisles were added.

The churchyard slopes to the E, making the apse very tall. The lower part of the apse has small windows at ground level, lighting the crypt. High up are three round-headed windows. The two on the N and S sides of the presbytery were inserted by Pearson. He renewed the corbel tables. A continuous sill runs under the windows. Between the apse windows flattish buttresses run down to the ground. On the N and S sides are large blank arches at ground level. The lancets of the clerestory were inserted by Pearson. The other windows of the church are in 14C and 15C style, mostly square-headed. The 13C S door was reset when the aisle was widened. It is round-headed, and the rere-arch is made from an ancient tombstone. The S porch is 19C.

The small two-stage tower was added in the 15C. On either side of it is the evidence for Stephen's planned nave. Two Norman responds have early scalloped capitals. The foundations of a nave are reported to have been found in the churchyard, but there is no evidence above ground.

The attractive stone vaults of the church were all constructed by Pearson. In the apse the Norman windows have single shafts. Under the SE window is a trefoil-headed piscina, and W of this are trefoil-headed sedilia, cut into the wall. The 19C arches of the apse and presbytery rest on original shafts and responds, the W set with crude volute capitals. What is now the nave is four bays long. The two E bays were the Norman chancel, the two W bays forming the crossing. At the junction are triple piers with shafted responds and volute capitals W and E (as in the presbytery). There is evidence of aisles flanking the Norman chancel. In the 13C pointed arches were inserted, forming the present four bays. There are central clustered piers with moulded capitals. In the aisles, at the position of the projected crossing, high shafts for the crossing arches can be seen. A pointed arch, springing directly from the walls, opens into the tower. Under the SE window of the S aisle is a small pointed piscina and credence table. The NE corner of the N aisle has been blocked off to form a vestry.

Steps in the centre of the church descend to the low and cavernous crypt. It is lit by three small windows at the E. In form it reproduces the original upper church: an apse, presbytery and aisled chancel. But the piers are so huge, and the groin vaults so heavy and pronounced, that the effect is rather of many small compartments. The four free-standing piers are amazingly squat, as if they have been driven into the ground by the weight of the church above. Some of the capitals of the piers and responds are plain cushion capitals. Others are more elaborate, being carved with interlace, pointed leaves and crude volutes. From the N aisle a passage runs E, the original entrance to the crypt.

In the crypt are several pre-Conquest sculpted fragments. There is the head of an early cross, which probably stood over 20ft high. Pieces of carved wood came possibly from a medieval roof. The fittings are mostly 19C. The pulpit encases part of one of the 13C piers. The font is circular and of the late 12C. A painting of the Mount of Olives is by John Jackson R.A., a native of Lastingham (after Correggio). The stained glass of the apse is by U. de Matteis of Florence, 1880. In a two-light window in the N wall is stained glass of St. Cedd and St. Chad, signed by C.E. Kempe, c 1899.

Pickering, St. Peter and St. Paul. The church is sited away from the main street and is reached by steps. It possesses a remarkable series of medieval wall paintings which were discovered in 1851, covered again, and revealed and over-restored in 1878–80.

The church is cruciform, with a W tower and a S chancel chapel. The tower is early 13C with Decorated belfry windows and a high octagonal spire. Early 13C also is the S aisle. In the 14C the chancel was widened and rebuilt: it has a five-light E window and other windows with intersecting tracery of a late, uncertain date. The N transept, N aisle and S porch are also 14C. In the 15C the S chapel (originally two-storeyed) and a N chapel (demolished) were added and the nave clerestory, with square-headed, two-light windows and battlements, was built. The whole church was extensively restored in 1876–79.

The nave has four-bay Norman arcades, the N being mid-12C with round piers and scalloped capitals, the S a little later, with square piers having semicircular attached shafts and waterleaf capitals. The W bay of the S aisle was crudely remodelled in Perpendicular style. The chancel arch and the transept arches are 14C. In the chancel are 14C sedilia and a piscina: monsters and heads support crocketed gables. In the N wall of the chancel is a plain aumbry.

The font has an early bowl, but is somewhat patched up: the register records that it was damaged in 1644. The screen, now under the tower, has an original door and neo-Jacobean surround. The chancel screen and Rood are of 1927. The circular pulpit is mid-18C and there are 18C chandeliers. The wall paintings, above the nave arcades, are remarkably complete and vivid, and date from the mid-15C. The N series depicts, from W to E: St. George on horseback slaying the dragon—St. Christopher leaning on a sprouting staff, an eel coiled around his right leg, and a hermit bearing a lantern on his left—the story of Herod's Feast (on the right, Salome dancing and St. John the Baptist warning; on the left, St. John executed; in the centre, Salome bearing his head on a charger) with the Coronation of the Virgin above—St. Edmund, King and Martyr, tied naked to a tree and pierced with arrows from two archers; above, the martyrdom of St. Thomas Becket. On the S side, from E to W, 11 stories of St. Catherine: rebuking Maxentius for idol worship—taken to prison—arguing with the king's wise men—massacre of the wise men converted by Catherine—in prison—scourged—again thrown into prison—visited by the Empress Faustina—on the wheel—taken to execution—awaiting execution. Then the seven corporal acts of mercy with the Annunciation (or possibly the Assumption) above; seven scenes from the Passion (Christ healing Malchus's ear—before Pilate—scourging—bearing the Cross—Crucifixion—Descent from the Cross—entombment) with the Burial of the Virgin above (a row of Apostles in front, and the Jewish prince Belzeray sitting astride the coffin) and the Resurrection and the Descent into Hell below (represented by a dragon's mouth). Near the lectern is an effigy of a cross-legged man, c 1350, probably Sir William Bruce, who founded a chantry here in 1337. His hands hold his heart, and there are angels beside his pillow. A truncated knight of c 1400, in alabaster, is near the pulpit; and in the S chapel are two fine alabaster effigies, probably Sir David de Roucliffe and his wife Margery, he in armour and surcoat, wearing a collar of SS. At the chancel entrance is a brass plate with fine lettering, in a stone surround, to Joshua Newton (died 1712).

Scarborough

St. Mary the Virgin. The parish church of Scarborough stands above the old town but below the castle. Its odd appearance, with the tower at the E end, is due to damage dramatically sustained during the siege of Scarborough Castle in 1644–45. The besieging Parliament-arians brought cannon into the church, knocked out the E window and demolished part of the castle keep. In retaliation, the Royalists in the castle demolished the chancel with their guns, and so weakened the tower that it fell in 1659. It was rebuilt but the chancel and N transept were not replaced. The W towers have vanished also; only the bases remain. Ewan Christian made a thorough-going restoration in 1848–50.

The W end, of the late 12C, is the oldest part. It has three stepped and shafted lancets. In the tower bases are single lancets. The W door was added in the 14C. It has sculpted heads said to be King Edward III and Queen Philippa, who were married at York in 1328. The front was heavily restored by Christian, and the wheel window in the gable is his. The church is approached from the S, and presents an irregular gabled appearance. Instead of a S aisle there is a series of projecting chapels, roofed in stone. From the W, they are the two-storey porch, then a chapel equal in height, with a large four-light window with flowing tracery, renewed in the 19C. E of this are three smaller chapels with identical Geometrical tracery, and then the S transept, with crocketed pinnacles and an original five-light window with Reticulated tracery. The four chapels were chantries, and were built between 1380 and 1400. The tower was rebuilt between 1660 and 1669. The arrangement of belfry windows is most elaborate on the S side, with a central two-light opening flanked by lancets: this may be original. The other three faces look like a 17C (or later) rebuilding. On the N side of the church is an outer aisle, St. Nicholas's aisle, which was of 1350, but was rebuilt by Ewan Christian. The windows have Reticulated tracery.

The rather dark interior has solid arcades of c 1200, probably cut through old walls. The N arcade and the two E bays of the S arcade were built first, with circular piers and triple-chamfered arches. The rest of the S arcade continues in a different style, with a clumsy join. There is a shafted pier, then an octagonal one, and the last is quatrefoil with fillets. The clerestory of plain lancets is shafted, and vaulting shafts rise up between. At the W door are two crisply carved 14C heads of ladies wearing wimples; and at the apex of the chancel arch is a humorous carving of a man and woman fighting over a money bag which is firmly grasped by the woman. The arcade to the outer N aisle has vigorously sculpted capitals of monsters, men and animals. The stonework of the E window, comprising mullions only, is by George Pace, 1957. The chapels on the S side of the church are known (from the W) as St. Mary's, St. Stephen's, St. Nicholas's and St. James's. St. Mary's chapel has been the baptistery since 1971. The font of 1869 has a gilded oak cover of 1961 by George Pace.

There are few furnishings of note. In 1978 the reredos, lectern, altar rail, choirstalls and war memorial were brought from Christ Church, Scarborough on its closure and installed in St. Nicholas's aisle. The pews in the nave came from St. John's, Driffield in 1969. The organ was rebuilt in 1985 on a platform above the clergy vestry in the inner N aisle. There is much 19C and 20C stained glass. The E window, designed by H.J. Stammers in 1958, illustrates the Benedicite. The S clerestory windows show northern saints—from E to W Paulinus, Hilda, John of Beverley, Aidan, Wilfrid and Cuthbert. The baptistery window of 1896 portrays the Magnificat, and in the other chapels are figures of saints by William Wailes, c 1850, set in clear glass in 1940. The E window of St. Nicholas's aisle was brought from the demolished All Saints' Church in 1974. The W lancets have medallions of 1850 in a late 13C style. On many walls of the church are about 200 small brass plates, mostly 18C, removed from headstones in the churchyard. On the N wall of St. Nicholas's aisle is a marble medallion to Elizabeth Craven (died 1728) by L.F. Roubiliac; and on the W wall of St. Stephen's chapel is E.V. Physick's monument to William Woodall (died 1830) and his wife, showing a woman kneeling beside a sarcophagus.

In the churchyard is the grave and headstone of the novelist, Anne Brontë (died 1849).

St. Martin-on-the-Hill. St. Martin's was built between 1861 and 1863. It is a notable work by G.F. Bodley and an important example of Bodley's early collaboration with Morris & Co. The church was given largely by Mary Craven in memory of her father, Martin Craven, a surgeon who had been a neighbour of Bodley's father, a physician, in Albion Street, Hull, before 1839. Bodley extended the original church to the W in 1879 and added a Lady chapel in 1902. The fittings were inserted under his supervision over many years.

The church comprises a six-bay nave, N and S aisles, a chancel, a Lady chapel to the N of the chancel and an organ chamber to the S of

Morris & Co.'s pulpit in St. Martin's, a church built by G.F. Bodley, 1861–63

it, an embattled W narthex and a gabled tower, 100ft high, which stands over the N aisle in the second bay from the W. The tower has full-height, flat angle buttresses which are themselves gabled. The use of a gabled tower and the placing of a circular window above two lancets at the W end clearly assign the church to the early years of Bodley's career. The building material is Whitby stone. Bodley declared of the church that its 'chief merit is a certain look of size about the interior'. It is an austere interior, unplastered and lacking the painted decoration which Bodley was sometimes able to lavish on his churches. There are six-bay arcades with either octagonal piers and octagonal moulded capitals or clustered shafts. The clerestory windows are of two unfoliated lights with sexfoiled circles in the heads. The nave is of considerable height, well above that of the lean-to aisles, and has a steeply-pitched roof. Above the statue of St. Martin on the S arcade can be seen the shadow of the original W end. The E window, set high in the wall, is of three lights with one large circle and two smaller ones in the head. The aisle windows are of two or three lights, largely uncusped, with simple tracery in the heads.

The gilded chancel screen, with Rood above, was designed by Bodley after 1889. In front of it, to the S, stands the pulpit, the church's most notable fitting. It is oblong and has ten painted panels in two tiers, eight on the front and two on the N side. The two panels on the side, by Dante Gabriel Rossetti, depict the Annunciation. On the front, the upper panels show the Evangelists (designed by Ford Madox Brown, painted by George Campfield) and the lower show the Latin Doctors (designed by William Morris, painted by George Campfield). There are also little punning emblems of martins. The lectern was made by Watts & Co., of which Bodley was a co-founder. The reredos is a triptych, in which the wings each have three painted figures and the centre is a bas-relief of the Annunciation by Farmer & Brindley. Above the reredos are traceried panels painted onto the wall. The central panel depicts the Adoration of the Magi, flanked by angels, and the side panels contain saints, all painted by Campfield, possibly to designs by Sir Edward Burne-Jones; by 1889, however, the painting had so deteriorated that it was entirely re-done by Farren of Scarborough. The ceiling of the chancel and of the W part of the Lady chapel is by Morris and Philip Webb. Bodley designed the reredos in the Lady chapel and the patterning on the E and W walls. The organ case was also designed by Bodley, but bears in addition four angels which were painted by J.R. Spencer Stanhope of Morris & Co. They are on its W side. The church possesses a red altar frontal, lately repaired, which was designed by William Morris in 1862 and was probably sewn by his wife. The square font, raised on two steps, which stands in the W bay on the N side, is made of York stone and bears Bodley's characteristic Greek cross. Note the nearby cupboards, perhaps by Morris & Co.

The stained glass is very largely by Morris & Co. The E window depicts the Crucifixion (by Ford Madox Brown, 1862) and the Parable of the Vineyard in seven panels (by Dante Gabriel Rossetti, 1861). The rose windows high up in the N and S walls of the chancel show the symbols of the Evangelists. The windows of the N aisle have Old Testament figures and those of the S aisle New Testament figures. The stained glass of the baptistery and narthex was designed by Burlison & Grylls, a firm Bodley much employed in his later years. Note the contrast in St. George's chapel, in the SW corner of the church, between the two-light W window of the story of St. Martin, by Ford Madox Brown and the three-light S window of St.

Augustine, St. Monica and St. George, executed by Burlison & Grylls in 1884. The earlier window is markedly obscure in contrast to the clarity of the three saints. The W windows depict, in the two long lancets, Adam and Eve, to represent the Fall, and above—in the rose—the Annunciation.

S.C.H.

Sheriff Hutton, *St. Helen and the Holy Cross.* A tomb in the N aisle (reassembled in 1950) supposedly represents King Richard III's son, Edward, Prince of Wales (died 1484). Stylistically, however, it is early 15C, and it may actually commemorate Ralph, son of Richard Neville, Earl of Salisbury, who is known to have been buried here. A mutilated alabaster effigy of a boy rests on a tomb-chest with a representation of the Trinity between angels and saints. The child wears a long coat with bag sleeves, and a coronet or cap of maintenance. The tomb was restored in 1985.

The tower and nave are Norman in origin. The chancel was added in the 13C, and the five-light E window is 15C. The aisles are 14C, and were extended E to form chapels in the 15C. The furnishings include a Jacobean communion rail, and box-pews of the 17C to 19C. There is a brass at the E end of the N chapel to Dorothy and John Fenys (or Fiennes) who died in 1491 in infancy and were the children of Lord Dacre: they are shown in swaddling clothes. The E window has stained glass of 1861 by J.W. Knowles.

Skelton, *St. Giles.* A small, remarkably fine Early English church, possibly part of a more ambitious project which was curtailed. Parish tradition states that it was built with stone left over in the building of the S transept of York Minster, and by the same workmen. The S transept was started c 1225; and in 1247 Archbishop de Gray confirmed a donation to Skelton by Robert Haget, Treasurer of York Minster. Many of the present external details of Skelton may be due to Henry Graham, who was entrusted with its restoration in 1814 (when he was only 19!); but Ewan Christian, writing on the church in 1846, suggests that Graham did a sensitive job, employing skilled masons from York Minster.

The exterior, with its large spreading roof springing from low side walls, suggests a single chamber, with only the double bellcote, topped by a floriated cross, to mark the division between nave and chancel. There are similar crosses on the E and W gables. Only the E one survived the restoration of 1814–18. The S doorway has profuse and ornate decoration, with many orders of shafts (originally of Purbeck marble, replaced with limestone in 1814–18), stiff-leaf capitals, and bands of dogtooth in the arches. The side windows are plain lancets, separated by buttresses. A course of roll-mouldings and nailhead runs right round the walls. At the E end is a fine arrangement of triple lancets, shafted, and separated by buttresses from smaller aisle windows, and a vesica window above. The W end has a single shafted nave lancet and a round window above, and smaller aisle lancets.

Inside, the short, two-bay nave is divided from the chancel by massive piers which may have been intended as part of a crossing tower. The ceiling is of 1880. Originally it was flat and boarded; in 1814 Henry Graham inserted a plaster groin-vault of his own invention. Ewan Christian regretted this insertion, but admitted that 'in themselves the parts are correctly designed, in accordance with the style of the building, and ... the enrichments have been carefully modelled upon existing examples of the same date, in York Minster'. E and W windows have shafts and dogtooth. In the chancel the piscina is adorned with foliage and fluting. Most of the stained glass is by Lavers, Barraud & Westlake. In the S chapel floor is a monument to Robert Lovell (died 1421) and his wife. At the N door is a monument to the young Henry Graham, testifying to 'the ardent pursuit of improvement in his profession as an Architect'. He died in 1819, aged 24.

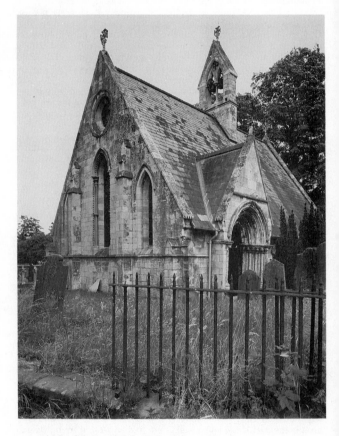

St. Giles's, 13C Early English work

Thirsk, St. Mary. Thirsk, though not Perpendicular at its most magnificent, is the finest example of its style in the North Riding. Rebuilding started in c 1430 and continued into the 16C. Licence was given in 1431 for a chantry founded by Robert Thirsk (died 1419). This seems to have been the signal for rebuilding. The church was restored, quite sensitively, by G.E. Street in 1877.

The buttressed tower is sturdy and of three stages. The nave and aisles are tall and handsome, more windows than wall; the chancel is lower. All parapets have pierced, openwork battlements, bold yet delicate; and on the body of the church they are punctuated by crocketed pinnacles. All windows except the E are of three lights, with tracery: in the aisles and tower they are pointed, and in the clerestory and chancel nearly rounded. The S porch has a chamber over it: it was restored in 1857, preserving the old door. Under the chancel, where the ground falls away sharply, is a tunnel-vaulted crypt. A sculpture of the Virgin and Child, 15C or earlier, is above the W window, in a niche in the W face of the tower.

Inside are six-bay nave arcades; the chancel arch is by Street. The nave has a wagon roof with bosses and other adornment. The chancel roof, formerly flat, was raised in 1844 and the bosses were painted. In the S chapel there are a piscina and a bracket for a statue. The medieval wooden screens to the N and S chapels survive. The font has a wooden Perpendicular spired canopy. The communion table was 'recently placed' in 1849. There are 17C wall paintings of the Apostles: five on the N side, three on the S. Some 15C stained glass is collected in the S aisle E window. The main E window has glass of 1844, of the Saviour and the Evangelists, designed by Lady Walsingham and her daughters, of Thirkleby Park, and executed by William Wailes. Of the SE window of 1875 in the S aisle by Henry Holiday, only the figures in the tracery survive. There is a brass to Robert Thirsk 'clerus nup. Rector eccl ... a ... fundator istius cantariae' (priest, lately Rector of this church and founder of this chantry) at the E end of the S aisle. (The chantry, dedicated to St. Anne, was in the S aisle.) It shows a half-length figure with angels to left and right.

Whitby, *St. Mary.* Whitby Church is unforgettable both in its setting and in its internal arrangement. It is neither beautiful nor of strictly architectural importance; but its quaint charm rarely fails to captivate. It stands exposed to the cold North Sea, high on the East Cliff above the old fishing town and harbour, with the gaunt ruins of the abbey rising behind. It is approached through the winding streets and up the cliff by the 199 steps called Church Stairs, or by car to Abbey Plain.

It was originally a Norman building of c 1110–20, consisting of nave and chancel, to which transepts and a tower (but never aisles) were added. In 1818 the walls of the N side were thrown outwards to form a large square room. The S side (by which one enters) retains 12C features. The tower is Norman, but with Early English bell openings. Two Norman windows survive in the S wall of the nave (the E one lengthened). The original Norman S doorway also remains. The S transept has one Early English window on its S side, with many fine mouldings. In the chancel there are more Norman windows and a corbel table. The hoodmould of another Early English window survives in the E wall of the N transept. In that transept also, there are triple lancet windows remodelled in 1744. On this medieval framework a Georgian overlay has been applied—the pretty S porch of 1821–23 with its Gothick, ogee arch; sash windows of different shapes and sizes, with wooden glazing bars; and external stairs giving access to various parts of the church.

All these Georgian hints do not, however, fully prepare the visitor for the surprise of the interior. It is a perfect pre-Victorian setting, completely (and remarkably) untouched by 19C restorers, all clutter and confusion, with high box-pews, galleries on every side, and sturdy pillars rising to a flattish roof pierced with dormer windows. It has often and aptly been likened to below-deck in a big sailing ship. Ships' carpenters were, in fact, responsible for making the roof and sturdy piers which have Gothic clustered shafts and stiff acanthus capitals. In the centre of the nave the very high, slender, triple-decker pulpit rises somewhat precariously. It is of 1778. It originally stood over the aisle on iron props, but was moved in 1847. The tester, resting on slim supports of clustered shafts (similar to the piers of 1818), has a scrolly openwork top rising to a pineapple finial. Attached to the back of the pulpit are two ear-trumpets, used by the rather deaf Mrs. Andrew, whose husband was minister in the early 19C. In front of the pulpit, the church stove thrusts its inelegant flue up to the roof. The galleries gradually encircled the nave. First in the 17C the Cholmley Pew was set uncompromisingly across the Norman chancel arch. It rests on four vigorously twisted columns with Composite capitals, and is decorated rather heavily with swags of fruit and flowers, cherubs' heads and an acanthus frieze. In front is a clock of c 1770; above, the arms of Queen Victoria, 1840. The other galleries were erected in the following order: W gallery 1700; N transept 1744; S transept 1759; nave S side 1764; N gallery and W balcony 1818. All are painted white, and rest on Tuscan columns. The box-pews range from the 17C to the 19C, the early ones with knobs on the ends. Some pew-ends are inscribed 'free'. Around the walls hang 18C Commandment boards. The church is lit by candles only: the large brass chandelier is of 1769. The chancel, dark and private, approached up several steps, was restored in 1905. It has a communion table and rails of the late 16C. In the sanctuary is a chair carved with nautical emblems, made from wood of the wreck of the 'Royal Charter'. It commemorates the Reverend William Scoresby (1789–1857), mariner-turned-minister and a Whitby man, who devised an improved magnetic compass which was adopted by the Admiralty, and which he tested on an Antarctic voyage on board the 'Royal Charter' in 1856. The chair, presented in 1922, includes a compass in its decorative scheme. The stained glass windows of the chancel are by C.E. Kempe, 1907. In the vestibule of the church is a marble rotunda on a pedestal, commemorating 12 lifeboatmen who were lost in a storm in 1861.

In the churchyard near the steps is a tall cross, erected in 1898, based on the great 7C cross at Ruthwell. It commemorates Caedmon, a cowherd at St. Hilda's monastery, who, though illiterate, was miraculously inspired to compose sacred poetry of great beauty, and who died in 680.

Whitby was the location of the famous Synod of 663 (some scholars say 664), which decided that the Church in Northumbria would follow Roman rather than Celtic traditions. It was also where St. Hilda became abbess of a monastery in 657, and where she remained until her death in 680.

THE WEST RIDING OF YORKSHIRE

The West Riding is the largest of all the historic English counties, and one of the most diverse. It is readily identified with the major industrial cities of Leeds, Sheffield, Bradford, Halifax, Rotherham and so forth, which are grouped in its S and central parts. To the N and NW there are the moors and the dales. To the E there is the unspectacular countryside in the vicinity of York. In the SE corner there are the upper reaches of the Humber, low-lying and marshy. Wakefield was the ancient county town, but long ago it was over-taken by Leeds as the main commercial centre. The re-arrangement of counties in 1974 dismantled the West Riding more drastically than any other county. Two new counties of South Yorkshire and West Yorkshire were created, and districts were transferred to North Yorkshire, Humberside and Cumbria. Ecclesiastically, the Sees of Ripon, Wakefield, Sheffield and Bradford have all been created in the last century and a half to divide the ancient See of York. In the Roman Catholic Church there are Dioceses of Leeds and Hallam, the latter based on Sheffield.

The West Riding is very well-known for its medieval monastic remains and associations: Kirkstall, Fountains, Selby, Roche, Bolton and Nostell. It has representative churches of every period, but inevitably the rise of the industrial cities has left a disproportionately large number of 19C and 20C buildings. None of the industrial cities was anciently subdivided into numerous small parishes on the lines of York or Norwich: they were towns with one major church. Leeds, for example, had just one parish church until 1634. (Leeds also had a bridge chapel, which, in addition to the surviving examples at Wakefield and Rotherham, 14C and 15C respectively, might be said to form a local group.) Leeds, however, does have one link of high antiquity which is exceptional within Yorkshire. There is a possibility that Christianity in the district E of Leeds, anciently known as Elmet, has had a continuous history since Roman times. The name Leeds, which has the older form of *Loidis*, is Celtic and not English. Elmet was the name of a Celtic kingdom which existed from after the collapse of the Roman province until it was incorporated in the 7C by the English Kingdom of Northumbria under King Edwin. Since King Edwin was the first English Christian ruler in the N, it is possible that Christian continuity was maintained from, say, the 4C onwards—a very rare circumstance. *Elmet* remains in such place-names as Sherburn-in-Elmet.

No known Christian building, of course, has survived from ancient Elmet. The earliest fabric in the West Riding is the famous crypt at Ripon Cathedral, which was built for St. Wilfrid in the 670s. The principal pre-Conquest parish churches are Kirk Hammerton and Ledsham. Both are more or less complete pre-Conquest buildings to which later additions have been made. St. John's, Kirk Hammerton comprises a chancel, nave and W tower, with extensions of 1890–91 amounting to a new church to the N. All Saints', Ledsham has a two-storey, pre-Conquest W porch now incorporated in the tower, a S *porticus* and a number of early windows. This fabric could be as early as the 8C. The churches at Bardsey and Monk Fryston both have plain pre-Conquest W towers. St. Peter's, Leeds has a late pre-Conquest standing cross, which combines Christianity with Germanic legends. A cross of rather Viking appearance survives at Marton. St. Michael's, Thornhill has fragmentary crosses with inscriptions which make it clear that the crosses are memorials. Finally, All Saints', Ilkley has three 9C crosses of millstone grit, one over 8ft in height and bearing the Evangelists' symbols, Christ and the usual interlace. Norman remains are fairly numerous and frequently distinguished. The most conspicuous example is Selby Abbey. The most complete Norman parish churches are at Birkin and Adel. Both are two-cell 12C churches, although at Birkin a vaulted, apsidal sanctuary divides from the chancel. Adel has splendid sculptures around its S doorway and its chancel arch, and a late Norman bronze closing-ring. St. John's, Healaugh is substantially a mid-12C church, whose W tower and S doorway are notable features. Notable too is the W tower of St. Mary Magdalene's, Campsall, which is unusually grand. The same church has a small capital of Viking style, yet another instance in Yorkshire of Viking influence, sometimes shown long after the Norman Conquest. Other churches with significant Norman fabric are St. Oswald's, Farnham (the chancel); St. Peter's, Thorpe Salvin (arcades, tower and chancel arches, S doorway, windows and font); St. Cuthbert's, Fishlake (the S doorway); St. Mary's, Kippax (much herringbone masonry); St. Wilfrid's, Brayton; St. Nicholas's, Askham Bryan; St. Mary's Askham Richard (late 12C doorways); and All Saints', Sherburn-in-Elmet (nave arcades).

The various Gothic styles are not evenly represented. Perpendicular fabric is far more frequent than its predecessors. The great Early English work is the W front of Ripon Cathedral, built in the first half of the 13C. The best example described in the text is St. Mary's, Nun Monkton. The lower part of its W front is late Norman, but above there are shafted lancets, with shaft-rings and dogtooth. The interior N and S walls have blind arches between the lancet windows, forming a developed and attractive composition of the Early English style. St. Cuthbert's, Adlingfleet might also be mentioned for its 13C work. The Decorated style is represented by the splendid mid-14C bridge chapel at Wakefield, whose windows have flowing tracery. St. Oswald's, Methley is also Decorated. It has Reticulated windows and a standard 14C S arcade of octagonal piers and double-chamfered arches. St. John's at Wadworth has a Decorated S chapel whose E window has unusual tracery. All four lights include mouchettes which point towards the centre, and the two outer mullions are carried up to the frame where a horizontal connects them to form a square-cut box within the pointed window. Wadsworth's S chapel also has an ogee piscina and sedilia. A S chapel of similar date exists in St. John's, Knaresborough. Other 14C work of note may be seen at St. Peter's, Walton; Selby Abbey (the E end); and St. Cuthbert's, Fishlake (the chancel).

The Perpendicular style has left many examples. The principal churches of the trading towns typically date from that period. The cathedrals of Wakefield, Sheffield and Bradford, which were parochial until 1888, 1914 and 1919 respectively, are 15C parish churches in appearance, despite modern additions. St. John's, Halifax and All Saints', Rotherham, which remain parish churches, are further examples of the type. Both have darkened stone. In the S of the West Riding, by contrast, white magnesian limestone gives an added attraction to some large 15C churches: Ecclesfield, Tickhill and the central tower at Hatfield near Doncaster. Ecclesfield has pinnacled buttresses which are almost detached from the walls. Tickhill is exceptionally large for the present village, but in the Middle Ages it was an important castle town. All Saints' at Harewood is a consistent Perpendicular church, spacious but fairly plain. Its tall piers lack capitals. St. Oswald's, Methley has a S chapel which may be dated to c 1483–84 and whose window tracery includes the arched lights which were to continue until the 17C. The church of All Saints, Bolton Percy may also be closely dated, to c 1411- 24. Holy Trinity, Skipton, long and low with many square-headed windows, is an exemplar of the late medieval churches of Craven in the NW of the Riding.

The West Riding has one 17C church of the first importance: St. John's, Leeds (1632–34). Its exterior is of the simplified late Gothic which is labelled 'Gothic Survival'. Its interior, however, is fitted with sumptuous woodwork of Renaissance inspiration. Fabric and fittings of the 17C also survive in the Red House Chapel at Moor Monkton: again, Renaissance woodwork in a late Gothic building. Classical fabric of the 17C, by contrast, may be seen on the S front of the ruined old church at Wentworth. In 1684 a pedimented projection was added to the nave. Note the contrast with the early 17C chapels to the E. What is also notable in the 17C is the group of early Nonconformist chapels. Two are as early as any in England: Bramhope and Great Houghton. They are frequently referred to as 'Puritan chapels'. Both are of the mid-17C, that is Cromwell's Commonwealth, when they were not in fact out of conformity with the Presbyterian ascendancy of the time. The two chapels are late Gothic in style, rectangular, with arched lights to the windows and with surviving 17C fittings. Similar in style is the chapel which Lady Anne Clifford built for Barden Tower. The type is represented at Midhopestones as late as 1705: a rectangle with mullioned windows. From later in the 17C there are two venerable Friends' meeting houses, at Brigflatts near Sedbergh (1675) and at Farfield (1689). Here, in contrast to the two 'Puritan chapels', we have the typical domestic architecture of early non-Anglican places of worship. Important non-Anglican churches survive too from the 18C. At Stannington, Sheffield, the Unitarian Underbank Chapel of 1742 survives. Its principal elevation has two tall arched windows flanked by square-headed doors with small circular windows above them. A further 18C non-Anglican church of interest is at Fulneck, part of a Moravian village which is an instructive reminder of an important 18C religious movement.

Returning to the mainstream Anglican churches, the 18C produced both Classical and early Gothic buildings. The Classical buildings included a number built to increase the church provision in the major towns. Many of these have unfortunately been demolished. Holy Trinity Church in Boar Lane, Leeds, however, survives. It was built in 1721–27 by William Halfpenny, except that its noticeable steeple is of 1839 by R.D. Chantrell. Chantrell, the architect of the Gothic Leeds Parish Church, produced here a convincing 18C steeple to accord with Halfpenny's essay in the style of Wren and Gibbs. A modest village Classical church of the same period is St. James's, Tong, of 1727. In the rural NE of the Riding St. Martin's, Allerton Mauleverer is an early attempt at neo-Norman. It was built in 1745–46, perhaps by James Paine or John Vardy. The obvious 18C element is mixed with neo-Norman features and with some reused medieval fabric. A stately Classical church from later in the 18C is St. Peter's, Horbury, of 1791–94 by John Carr. This distinguished architect was born there in 1723 and built the church at his own expense. The plan is that of a wide preaching room. Stately too is the Classical St. Peter's, Sowerby (1763–66, with a tower of 1781). Gothick designs appeared at

Ravenfield (1756, by John Carr) and at Aldfield (c 1783, with Y-tracery).

The 19C in the West Riding overshadows all earlier periods in its number of new churches, especially in the industrial towns. The 'Commissioners' churches' of the early decades of the century continued the 18C process of increasing church accommodation in the major towns. Typical churches of that period were Christ Church in Meadow Lane, Leeds (1823–26, by R.D. Chantrell), and St. George's, Sheffield (1821–25, by Hurst & Woodland). After c 1840 new church provision multiplied markedly. In addition, non-Anglican churches were built on a scale and often in a grandeur which had not applied previously. In two major towns, the principal parish church was rebuilt. St. Peter's, Leeds was rebuilt in 1838–41 by R.D. Chantrell for Walter Farquhar Hook, the influential Vicar from 1837 to 1859. The new church was a serious and worthy Gothic building, a thoughtful development from the standard Georgian interior. Just over a decade later Sir Gilbert Scott rebuilt St. George's, Doncaster (1854–58) after a fire. He produced a proud, cruciform church in his usual Geometrical style. Halifax acquired a major church too—All Souls', Haley Hill (1856–59)—which easily achieved prominence by means of a tall spire on an already high point. All Souls' was also by Sir Gilbert Scott, and was the church which he considered to be his best. Typically Victorian was the fact that the church was the gift of a manufacturer, Edward Akroyd, and typical too was its rivalry in spire height with the Square Congregational Church of 1855–57. As the Free Churches built more grandly and more assertively, the Church of England built grandly in reply. At Todmorden the Unitarians built a huge Gothic church in Fielden Square in 1869, with a spire of 196ft, marble enrichment, stained glass by J.B. Capronnier and accomplished woodwork. The architect was John Gibson and the donors were the sons of John Fielden, local mill-owner and MP. The United Reformed Church at Saltaire, built in 1858–59 by Lockwood & Mawson for Sir Titus Salt, is equally lavish, but in this case Classical. The church has a tall semicircular portico, a circular tower and an aisleless interior whose walls are divided by full-height Corinthian columns. Norman Shaw designed Holy Trinity Church at Bingley (1866–68, with a later tower), gaunt externally, more appealing within. St. Saviour's at Leeds (1842–45) was a serious early work of the Gothic Revival by John Macduff Derick. Nearby is the Catholic church of Mount St. Mary, 1852–66, by Joseph Hansom, William Wardell and E.W. Pugin. An earlier Catholic church of interest is St. Edward's, Clifford, a neo-Norman building of the 1840s. William Burges designed two churches near Ripon on the most lavish scale: Christ the Consoler at Skelton-on-Ure (1871–76) and St. Mary's at Studley Royal (1871–78). J.L. Pearson designed the stately church of Holy Trinity at Wentworth (1875–77) and also St. Margaret's at Horsforth (1877–83). The church at Wentworth is entirely stone-vaulted as one would expect of Pearson. G.F. Bodley worked at Cawthorne in the 1870s in remodelling All Saints' Church. His more important work, St. Edward's, Holbeck, Leeds (1903–04), has unfortunately been demolished. A little earlier than St. Edward's is Sir Thomas Jackson's chapel for Giggleswick School (1897–1901), which is a Latin cross with a prominent dome over the crossing. The early 20C also saw the building of St. Wilfrid's at Harrogate (1905–14), by Temple Moore. The church has an air of strength and solidity, and a sense of refinement like that of Bodley. At Mirfield, Sir Walter Tapper and

Michael Tapper designed the church for the College of the Resurrection (1911–37). The E parts are the earlier and the style is more
or less Norman. Nearly contemporary is the church of St. John the
Evangelist and St. Mary Magdalene (1916), built at Goldthorpe for
Lord Halifax by A.Y. Nutt. The style is Italian and the building is
notable for its use of reinforced concrete. The church of the Epiphany, Gipton, Leeds (1938), by N.F. Cachemaille-Day, was built to
a Gothic plan but with elements typically 20C in their bareness. Tall
circular concrete pillars rise to the roof without ornament of any
kind. Equally minimal in its Gothic allusions is St. Wilfrid's, Leeds
(1937–39), by Randall Wells. The church of the First Martyrs, Bradford (1935), by J.H. Langtry-Langton, is notable for its early use of a
central altar, which is set under a cantilevered dome and lantern.
Finally, mention must be made of the widespread work in recent
decades of George Pace (died 1975), mainly in new fittings and
reorderings.

Amongst medieval fittings of note, the most unusual is a wooden
15C canopied chest at Cowthorpe, which is thought to have been an
Easter sepulchre. St. Mary's, Sprotbrough has a stone seat of pre-
Conquest appearance whose decorative details, however, are of the
14C. Medieval screenwork is fairly frequent. A good Rood screen
with ogee arches, restored in 1881, remains in St. Helen's, Burgh-
wallis. Hubberholme retains a Rood loft of 1558, one of only two in
Yorkshire. Other screens of interest are at Kirk Sandal, Rotherham
(All Saints'), Mitton, Batley, Hatfield, Campsall and Ecclesfield.
Virtually all of them are of the 15C. All Saints' at Rotherham
additionally has 15C stalls with attractive carvings and some trace-
ried bench-ends. Misericords survive at Ecclesfield, Sprotbrough and
Loversall. Medieval stained glass is to be seen at Bolton Percy (a 15C
E window), Thornhill (all 15C, including an inscription to the builder
of the Savile chapel in 1447), Dewsbury (13C and 14C), Acaster
Malbis (a 14C E window), Elland (15C scenes of the Virgin Mary),
Almondbury, Emley and Aldborough. St. Oswald's at Methley has a
distinguished lectern of c 1500 of Low Countries design. St. John's,
Halifax has a 15C font cover in the form of a soaring spire. All
Hallows' at Almondbury has a distinguished font cover from the early
16C. A Janus cross, a two-sided cross-head under a gable, remains
from the 15C at Sherburn-in-Elmet. Drax Church possesses mid-16C
bench-ends which show some Renaissance influence. In the 17C
square-topped bench-ends with knobs as finials became common.
They are to be found in St. John's at Halifax, Bolton Percy, Darfield,
Arksey, Barnoldswick and St. John's at Leeds. The last-named
church has the most magnificent collection of 17C fittings, all
carefully restored at the end of the 19C. 17C fittings may also be seen
at Beauchief (Sheffield), Arksey, Slaidburn and in the Red House
Chapel at Moor Monkton. Non-Anglican interiors of the 17C survive
at Bramhope (originally Presbyterian) and Brigflatts (a simple
Friends' meeting house of 1675). Finally from the 17C there must be
mentioned a number of poor boxes: Knaresborough, Sedbergh and
the much-loved figure in St. John's, Halifax known as Old
Tristram.

From the very beginning of the 18C, stained glass by Henry Gyles
remains at Adel and Denton. Tong Church has an intact interior of
1727, including a squire's pew. 18C bread shelves survive at
Aldborough. St. Laurence's, Aldfield retains unaltered fittings of
c 1783. The 19C is represented very widely, especially by stained
glass. Substantial collections exist in St. George's, Doncaster and in

Ecclesfield, both by various firms. Burges's churches at Skelton-on-Ure and Studley Royal have schemes of stained glass by Frederick Weekes, executed by Saunders & Co. Glass designed by A.W.N. Pugin exists in St. Edward's, Clifford and in St. Saviour's, Leeds. Nun Monkton has good Morris & Co. glass of c 1873 at its E end. From the end of the century, C.E. Kempe's windows appear almost everywhere. The W window at Harewood is one of the grandest. 19C interiors have naturally managed to survive more or less intact more often than the arrangements of earlier centuries. Leeds Parish Church represents the earliest Victorian ideas, though some items there are later. The great reredos, for example, is of 1872 by G.E. Street. The best High Victorian interiors are those in the two churches by Burges and in All Souls', Halifax. Amongst individual fittings, Campsall Church has Pugin's altar from the former chapel at Ackworth Grange, and Cawthorne Church has a fine pulpit painted by J.R. Spencer Stanhope. From the end of the 19C, Comper's splendid ensemble of Rood screen, parclose screens, canopied high altar, stained glass and painted decoration at St. Wilfrid's, Cantley is a very early example of his work. He repeated it in the 20C at Frickley, High Melton and at St. Peter's, Huddersfield. Notable mid-20C glass by J.E. Nuttgens exists at Aldwick-le-Street.

Monuments of note begin with an exceptional 12C coped tomb-chest at Conisbrough. Only in the 14C, however, do monuments become numerous. Effigies from that time survive at Birkin (a civilian), Goldsborough (two cross-legged knights), Allerton Mauleverer (two worn oaken effigies of knights), Barnbrough (also of oak) and Ripley (a knight and his wife). From the same century there survives a notable brass of c 1360 of William de Aldeburgh at St. Andrew's, Aldborough. Harewood Church possesses an unrivalled series of alabaster monuments from the 15C and 16C: they are described in the gazetteer. Wentworth Old Church has a number of monuments from the 15C to the 17C, including one of the first Earl of Strafford, who was beheaded in 1641. At Kirk Sandal there is a monument to William Rokeby (died 1521), who was Vicar both there and at Halifax, and also Archbishop of Dublin. All Saints' at Aston has the kneeling figures of Lord Darcy (died 1624) and his three wives. Tickhill Church has two late medieval tomb-chests, of which one shows Renaissance influence. In St. Oswald's at Methley the tomb of Sir Robert Waterton (died 1424) and his wife is an excellent 15C example. The same church has numerous later monuments of the Savile family, including one attributed to Maximilian Colt and one by Peter Scheemakers. Scheemakers was also responsible for the memorial to Lady Betty Hastings at Ledsham. Knaresborough Church has a long series of Slingsby monuments, beginning in 1602. The most notable are of two upright figures in niches, of the 1630s, attributed to Epiphanius Evesham. All Hallows' at Great Mitton has a series of Sherburne family memorials, many of them by William Stanton in the late 17C and early 18C. From the late 18C, Joseph Wilton's statue of Archbishop Tillotson at Sowerby must be mentioned. Good monuments by John Flaxman exist at Campsall (1803), Rotherham (1806) and St. Peter's, Leeds (1811). The Victorians returned to medieval types in monuments as in other matters. Sir Gilbert Scott's monument to Dean Hook (died 1875) in Leeds Parish Church is worthy of any medieval bishop. A fine mural brass to John Sharp, Vicar, exists at Horbury. A group of late 19C and early 20C memorials is to be seen at Hickleton. Finally, at Studley Royal there is the large Edwardian monument of the first Marquess and Marchioness of Ripon.

Perhaps the most famous historical association is that of the Brontës with Haworth, but the present St. Michael's Church very largely dates from after their time. Patrick Brontë was the incumbent there from 1820 to 1861. He had also been Vicar of St. Peter's, Hartshead, in 1810–15 and in 1812 he had married Maria Bramwell at St. Oswald's, Guisely, a church which also has links with Longfellow's forbears. Knaresborough has two notable early associations. The first known royal Maundy ceremony took place there under King John in 1210 and in the same period the town was the home of a hermit who was later known as St. Robert of Knaresborough. The church at Bolton Percy has the tomb of Ferdinando, second Lord Fairfax (died 1648), the Cromwellian commander. John Tillotson, Archbishop of Canterbury in the 1690s, was born near Sowerby and is commemorated in St. Peter's Church there by a late 18C statue. The famous cabinet maker, Thomas Chippendale, was baptised at All Saints', Otley in 1718. Giggleswick is connected with George Birkbeck, the founder of the movement for mechanics' institutes and after whom Birkbeck College in London is named. Lord Grimthorpe (1816–1905), who is well-known as the ruthless restorer of St. Alban's Abbey, came from the Beckett family, bankers of Leeds. He served for many years as Chancellor of the Diocese of York, in which capacity he bullied architects and parishes and generally tried to act as a dictator in the world of Yorkshire's church architecture. A Churchman who wrote an immense number of books, including many novels, Sabine Baring-Gould (1834–1924), served as a curate at St. Peter's, Horbury in 1864–67. Horbury was also the birthplace and burial place of John Carr, the 18C Yorkshire architect. He designed the present St. Peter's. Finally, St. Wilfrid's at Hickleton is closely associated with the two Viscounts Halifax of the later 19C and early 20C, lay leaders of the Anglo-Catholic movement. The architect, G.F. Bodley, also has a memorial there.

Unusual dedications are St. Ricarius at Aberford, a 7C abbot from Celles near Amiens (known in France as St. Riquier); St. Alkelda at Giggleswick, reputed to be a martyr of Viking times; St. Everilda at Nether Poppleton, a 7C nun (cf. Everingham, East Riding); and St. Lucius at Farnley Tyas, a 3C martyr who is also called St. Lucian of Beauvais.

Adel, *St. John the Baptist.* Adel, on the N side of Leeds, is still a distinct village. Its church, which stands in a churchyard of substantial size, is a notable two-cell 12C Norman building, whose S door and chancel arch are of the first importance for their architectural sculpture.

The church comprises an aisleless nave, with a W bellcote of two openings of 1839, a square-ended chancel and a NE vestry. The three E windows in Norman style are of 1879. The two lower W windows are also modern, but genuinely Norman are the upper W window, two lancets on each side of the chancel and the windows set high up in the nave walls, above a stringcourse, one to the S and four to the N. The vestry has a three-light E window which until 1879 was the E window of the chancel. There is a low 14C window in the SW corner of the chancel and two square-headed 16C windows in the S wall of the nave. There is a corbel frieze below the entirely modern roofs. Flat buttresses may be seen at the W end. A simple arched priest's door in the chancel contrasts with the other door which is the

CHURCH of ST JOHN the BAPTIST : ADEL

glory of the exterior, the S nave door of four orders, which projects from the wall and is gabled above. The inner order has beakhead, the second has zigzag, the third two roll-mouldings and the fourth also zigzag. The decoration of the two inner orders is carried below the capitals, whereas the two outer orders have shafts and bases. Above in the gable are sculptures in box frames. Christ in Majesty is placed immediately above the arch and above Him is the Lamb. To the left and right are the symbols of the Evangelists. The entire composition represents the fourth chapter of the Revelation of St. John. On the door is a Norman bronze closing-ring, comprising a grotesque animal which both holds the ring and swallows a man.

Within, the chancel arch of three orders is visually dominant. The inner arch has zigzag moulding, the middle two roll-mouldings joined by bands to form a ladder pattern, and the outer is of beakheads. The 37 heads of this outer order are all different. The capitals bear carvings which represent the Redemption of Man. The N respond has the Baptism of Christ. The River Jordan is shown by concentric arches forming a mound of water. Above Christ is the dove of the Holy Spirit. Just to the right, beyond St. John the Baptist, is King David, for Christ was of his line. The Devil, bottom left, attempts to drink the river, to prevent the Redemption. Above left is an angel, seen sideways, holding Christ's clothes. On the S respond is the Crucifixion. Joseph of Arimathea and Nicodemus take down the body from the Cross, with St. John and the Virgin standing by. The Devil is slinking away in the lower right-hand corner, defeated. The middle capitals show, N, a centaur, and S, a knight with a lance; the one representing raw Nature, the other the Church Triumphant, proclaiming the Redemption.

The three paintings in the nave, of the Crucifixion, Ascension and the Garden of Gethsemane, are by Vanderbank and were given in 1745. The font cover is of 1921 by Eric Gill. Of the stained glass, the vestry E window depicts the arms of King Charles II by Henry Gyles. By him also is the chancel SW window, a memorial to Thomas Kirke (died 1706), who had given the royal arms. The E windows, of Our

CHURCH OF ST JOHN THE BAPTIST : ADEL

Lord (centre), St. John the Baptist and St. Peter, date from 1879. St. Luke and St. Stephen, in the sanctuary N and S windows, are by Harry Harvey, 1969. The window in the S nave wall, towards the chancel arch, depicts Norman landowners and ecclesiastics. It is of 1933 by F.C. Eden.

Allerton Mauleverer, *St. Martin*. St. Martin's was rebuilt in 1745–46 in a vaguely neo-Norman style at the expense of Richard Arundell of Allerton Park, the heir of the Mauleverers who had held the manor from the 12C. (Mauleverer means 'poor harrier'.) The design has most plausibly been attributed to James Paine or John Vardy. The 18C rebuilding preserved no more than a S arcade, three bells and some medieval tombs of the Mauleverers. The inconsistent effect of the new church has led writers to suggest that various features are reused, but this is not the case. The church was declared redundant in 1971 and passed to the Redundant Churches Fund in 1973. Peter Hill of Boston Spa subsequently restored it.

The church comprises a nave with N and S aisles, N and S transepts opening off the E bay of the nave, a central tower to the E of the nave with flanking chambers (the former vestry to the S, the belfry stairs to the N), and, for the 18C, a surprisingly long chancel. The previous church, which is depicted in a drawing of 1734 and which may be the one depicted in the present E window, had a W tower and spire, but no transepts. The W façade is a curious composition. The nave is gabled, with a circular window flanked by two neo-Norman ones above, and a plain, round-headed doorway below. The N and S aisles project very slightly to the W and have broken pediments and wide, flat buttresses on either side of single arched windows, of 18C rather than Norman size. The contrast between the steeply-pitched nave roof and the shallow aisle roofs is somewhat clumsy. It might also be concluded that a Norman architect would have provided a richer W door than his 18C successor. The tower, with two thin, arched windows in each face and a low, pyramidal capping, also tries to be Norman. The E window, however, is in a five-light Perpendicular style, of a type which could be 17C rather than 15C. Above it, the E end has a broken pediment. The transepts have two-light windows with quatrefoils above. The S side of the nave has four slightly pointed windows. All of this was new in the 18C.

Within, the one genuine medieval survival of the fabric is the 14C S arcade of four bays, with octagonal piers but no capitals. The arch from the nave to the tower is relatively low and narrow, and so the vista to the chancel is restricted. The visitor will be surprised to see a hammerbeam roof in the nave—again, new in 1745–46. The nave has both box-pews and open benches with carved ends. There is a two-decker pulpit on the N side. Above the tower arch is a huge 18C painting of Moses and Aaron, who hold panels of the Command-ments. Below, on either side of the arch, are smaller panels of the Lord's Prayer and Creed. There are metal gates below the arch. The chancel is rather bare. The E window has 18C glass by William Peckitt of York. In the S transept is the large tomb of Mary Thornton (died 1800), whose husband bought Allerton Park in 1789. The N transept has two cross-legged wooden knights, probably of 14C Mauleverers, alabaster effigies of Sir John Mauleverer (died 1468) and his wife, Alyson, and brass figures of Sir John Mauleverer (died 1400) and his wife, Eleanor. In the window of this transept is an 18C coat of arms of the Mauleverers. The corresponding window in the S transept has the arms of the Arundells.

Birkin, _St. Mary._ St. Mary's is a two-cell Norman church of much interest and distinction. Its 14C and 15C additions have added to its qualities without detracting from its Norman character. The plan is of a W tower, a nave, a S aisle and an apsidal E end. It is built of small, squared stones in the Norman fashion.

The W tower is tall and unbuttressed. The lower or Norman part is entirely plain, except for two narrow lights in its W face. The top is 15C, with two-light belfry windows, battlements and corner pinna-cles. On the N side of the church and around the E end there are large, shafted Norman windows and a corbel table. The three windows of the apse are decorated with zigzag, beakhead and medallions; the central one has 14C tracery. There are flat buttresses to the apse. To the W, there is a reset Norman S nave door, a showpiece of the church. It has four orders, the inner one plain, then beakhead, then zigzag and finally medallions. There are three shafts each side, with scalloped capitals. It was reset when the S aisle was built as a chantry in 1329 by John and Beatrice de Everingham. Its windows have Decorated tracery, five-light to the E, three-light to S and W (the latter gable-headed). The aisle has a substantial plinth.

Within, the church reveals surprisingly large chancel and tower arches and vaulting within the apse. The S arcade is of two bays, very tall, with double-chamfered arches supported on an octagonal pier with an octagonal moulded capital and on carved-head responds. The chancel arch has a square-cut outer order, a soffit roll and semicircular responds. The capitals are scalloped. The tower arch is similar, but a little lower and a little plainer, and almost entirely obscured by the organ. The Norman windows are shafted inside as well as out. The E window of the apse has zigzag decoration.

The Classical pulpit is of the 18C, with a large tester. The font is of 1663. The arms of King George II are placed on the N wall. Nearby is a memorial to George Dixon Todd (died 1929), a local physician, who is represented on horseback, as he was known in life. A little to the E, there is a recess in the N wall which contains a 14C effigy in civil dress, holding a heart in his hands. The tiles in the chancel and sanctuary (as in 1988) are to be replaced with stone floors. The E window of c 1893 has stained glass of the Nativity, showing the Adoration of the Kings and the Adoration of the Shepherds. A little 14C glass remains in the tracery of the S aisle's E window. An ogee piscina remains below, in the S wall. Nearby is an incised 13C gravestone, brought into the church in 1982.

Bolton Percy, *All Saints.* All Saints' was built in white magnesian limestone in 1411–23 and was consecrated in 1424. It comprises a W tower, a wide four-bay nave with N and S aisles, a spacious chancel and a S porch. The porch is modern. The unbuttressed tower has battlements and corner pinnacles. The nave and chancel have buttresses, the chancel's rising to pinnacles. The windows are Perpendicular.

Within, the nave arcades have octagonal piers, octagonal moulded capitals and double-chamfered arches. The fittings of the church are quite distinguished. 17C box-pews survive, with rounded knobs as finials, and in the chancel, the return stalls are 15C. The pulpit and sounding-board, to the right of the nave, are 18C. An older, 17C, hexagonal pulpit, which stands to the left, is now used as a lectern. In the chancel there are fine sedilia with three ogee canopies and crocketed 'spires'. On the S wall of the chancel there are displayed sections and elevations of the church by Martin Shaw Briggs, 1904. Over the tower arch are placed the arms of King George III. The octagonal font cover is Jacobean, with tracery in each face. The font itself is Norman.

All Saints' has 15C stained glass in its E window: in its lower lights, five early Yorkshire saints (Paulinus, Chad, Wilfrid, John of Beverley and William of York) and, in its upper lights, St. Peter, St. Anne, the Virgin and Child, St. Elizabeth and St. John the Evangelist. The medieval glass was much restored by William Warrington in 1866. The E window of the N aisle is by C.E. Kempe, 1907. To its W, there are depictions of the Baptism of Christ (1880) and of the Annunciation (1876). The E window of the S aisle is earlier—c 1855—and shows scenes of the Passion.

A railed monument in the S aisle commemorates Ferdinando, Lord Fairfax (died 1648), who commanded the parliamentary armies in Yorkshire during the Civil War.

Bramhope, *Puritan Chapel.* The Puritan Chapel at Bramhope is a building of 1649 which preserves a rare interior from the days of Cromwell's Commonwealth. The simple rectangular building has a W bellcote. Its windows are mullioned and square-headed, with arched lights. There is a two-light W window, a five-light E window and four windows in the S elevation. There are two S doors. Inside, darkly stained box-pews are placed in obedience to a three-decker pulpit, which stands against the N wall and which is accorded an additional window on that side. The communion table is screened by metal rails. At the W end is a narrow, hexagonal font of 1673 and a number of monuments.

Brigflatts, *Friends' Meeting House.* Brigflatts is a hamlet a mile and a half S of Sedbergh. Its meeting house of 1675 is the oldest Friends' place of worship in the N of England and one which preserves the atmosphere of its beginnings. George Fox, the founder of the

Friends, during his visit to the district in 1652, stayed at Brigflatts in the farm which lies at the end of the lane past the meeting house.

In common with other late 17C meeting houses, Brigflatts is domestic in scale, a white-painted stone oblong, but distinguished for what it is by an inscribed two-storey E porch and by its irregular windows. There are square-headed windows, each divided by two mullions, at three levels on the E side. The two at the N end, one set above the other, reflect the gallery within and the two placed side by side to the right of the porch, halfway up the wall, reflect the internal dais. The two windows at the S end, balancing those to the N, light the caretaker's quarters. The upper room of the porch has one small arched window.

Within, immediately ahead of the door is the staircase, which leads to the oak gallery. This extends around the S, W and N sides and leads to the room over the porch. The dais is under the windows on the E side. There are wooden forms with simple backs. In the 18C, a pen for sheepdogs was placed at the foot of the stairs.

Campsall, *St. Mary Magdalene.* St. Mary Magdalene's is the greater part of a notable Norman cruciform church which retains an elaborate 12C tower. The church also possesses Early English work of good quality, which may be seen in the chancel and at the W end of the S aisle.

The church comprises a W tower, a nave, low N and S nave aisles, a S porch, N and S transepts, and a chancel. The W tower is the showpiece of the exterior. At its base is a doorway of three orders of shafts with scalloped capitals, and arches decorated with a roll-moulding and zigzag. Above the doorway there is a small arcade of five bays with diminutive cushion capitals. Then comes a single arched window with shafts, a clock-face and, above a stringcourse, a pair of belfry openings, each of them divided by a central shaft and set under a superarch. Surmounting all are 15C battlements and short corner pinnacles. The W ends of the nave aisles, which embrace the tower, are Early English. The windows are cusped lancets; some of them are shouldered. The W bay of the S aisle is two-storeyed. The rest of the S aisle has Perpendicular windows. Above are the nave's 15C battlements and pinnacles, and three-light clerestory windows. The S porch, however, is Decorated and the S transept also has Decorated features. The chancel has 13C lancets and Y-tracery, but the E window with intersecting tracery is a 19C insertion. On the N side of the chancel one shafted Norman window survives, flanked by flat buttresses.

The interior reveals the same story of enlargements and alterations from the 12C to the 15C. The fact that the Norman church was cruciform is shown by the blocked Norman window which is visible in the N transept. Norman aisles are demonstrated by the arch from the N aisle into the N transept, which has zigzag decoration. The arches from the nave to the transepts are a little later. Of the 13C is the rib-vaulted W bay of the S aisle, whose exterior was mentioned above. It forms the baptistery and was restored in 1983. The upper room was a priest's chamber. The nave arcades were rebuilt in the 15C.

The 15C oak chancel screen survives, tall but fairly plain, though with its coving. The screen carries a long inscription, beginning 'Let fal downe thy ne and lift up thy hart...'. The E window has stained glass of 1964: a Te Deum. The pulpit is Jacobean. There are two fonts: a newer one in the S transept and a 14C one in the SW corner.

One notable monument at the E end commemorates the Yarborough family by John Flaxman. A stone altar in the S transept, brought from the chapel of Ackworth Grange in 1959, was designed by A.W.N. Pugin.

Cantley, *St. Wilfrid.* Cantley is an ancient village which is now a suburb of Doncaster. St. Wilfrid's has fabric which dates from as far back as the 12C, but it is chiefly distinguished by the work which Sir Ninian Comper undertook in 1894 under the guidance of William Meaburn Tatham, Vicar from 1893 to 1938. Comper transformed the interior for the Anglo-Catholic tradition of worship, which the parish has maintained, and it forms an important early work in his career.

The church comprises a W tower, nave with N and S aisles, and a chancel. The priest's door is 12C Transitional and the S nave doorway is 13C. The 15C tower has diagonal buttresses, battlements and corner pinnacles. The nave has three-bay arcades, with octagonal piers and octagonal moulded capitals. The S aisle is original 14C, but the N aisle was added in 1894. The aisles are lit by two-light, square-headed windows, except for one four-light window in the N aisle. There is no clerestory. The chancel has a three-light E window (of 13C stepped lancets) and two windows of irregular pattern to both N and S.

Comper was responsible for practically all the fittings, decoration and stained glass of the church. The most notable fittings are the screens, all of 1894. There is a chancel screen, with Rood above, carved by McCulloch of Kennington, and parclose screens to the E ends of the nave aisles, forming a Lady chapel to the S and a Jesus chapel to the N. All are painted red and green and also gilded. Comper painted the window splays in the chancel, which were conserved by Peter Larkworthy in recent years, and designed the 'English altar', with its canopy and hanging pyx. The E window behind it has stained glass of St. Wilfrid, the Virgin and Child, and St. John of Beverley. The S window of the sanctuary, whose ledge served as sedilia, has glass which was copied by Comper from St. Michael Spurriergate in York. On the N side of the chancel there is a statue of St. Wilfrid. Figures of St. Peter and St. Paul flank the E window. The organ of 1905 stands at the W end and the font, with a tall cover, stands in the SW corner.

The Childers family of Cantley Hall long held the advowson. The one memorial of note, under the tower, is to John Walbank Childers (died 1812). Gladstone's Chancellor of the Exchequer in the 1880s, Hugh Childers, and his wife, lent their likenesses to the figures in the chancel SW window (St. Victoria and St. Hugh of Lincoln).

The church presently has 84 sittings, which, it is gratifying to hear, is insufficient for its congregation. After much debate, a plan to extend the building has been approved. The present N wall is to be moved out by 30ft and an extension to the W wall will be made to line up with the existing vestry. The plans have been made by Donald Buttress.

Clifford, *St. Edward.* St. Edward's Catholic Church stands prominently in the middle of this village in Wharfedale, a neo-Norman work of 1845–48. The formal or superintending architect was J.A. Hansom, but in this case he is said to have been given a design by an amateur called Ramsay, from Traquair near Peebles. In addition, much of the work of translating ideas into reality fell onto George Roberts, a local builder. The tall W tower was built later, in 1859–60 and 1866–67, by George Goldie. The church is a product of the Catholic landed families of Yorkshire, particularly the Vavasours of Hazlewood Castle and the Grimstons, of whom Mrs. Ralph Grimston must rank as the effective foundress of St. Edward's.

The church comprises a W tower, nave, lean-to aisles and a lower Lady chapel at the E end. The tower is of four storeys. At its base is an open porch. Above are arched windows in various arrangements, a protruding SW staircase (square below, circular above) and a pyramidal roof. The arched aisle windows have single external shafts. The windows are separated by flat buttresses. The two lights of each clerestory window are divided by a shaft and placed within a larger, blind arch.

The interior has nave arcades of seven bays, two of which form the sanctuary and a third of which, much narrower than the rest, stands between the sanctuary and the E wall of the body of the church. There are cylindrical piers of heavy Norman style, plain capitals, octagonal abaci and moulded arches. A low wall and gates (the latter bearing the device of King Edward the Confessor, the church's patron) divide nave from sanctuary. To the N, E and S of the sanctuary is a stone screen with round arches. Just to the E of this screen is the E wall, which is pierced by one large arch flanked by two lower ones and above by two vesica windows on either side of the Rood and by a wheel window just below the roof.

The pulpit has blind arcading enriched with zigzag mouldings. The Lady chapel has a statue of the Virgin Mary, signed by K. Hoffman, Rome, 1844, which is placed within an elaborate neo-Norman arch inscribed 'Exaltata sum quasi plentatio rosae in Hiericho' (I am raised up like a rose planted in Jericho). The church has some notable stained glass. Four windows of 1848–51 are known to be by A.W.N. Pugin. They include the windows of the Lady chapel, which commemorate George Vavasour and depict events in the life of Our Lady. The figure of St. Augustine of Canterbury in the N aisle is also attributed to Pugin. The window of St. Edward the Confessor, also in the N aisle, is of c 1850 by A. Lusson. The windows of the N and S aisles contain figures of a wide range of saints. St. Hilda appears with St. Clare and St. Teresa of Avila, and amongst the familiar St. George and St. John the Baptist there is the less familiar St. Thomas of Hereford, who was once Rector of nearby Spofforth.

(H. Lane Fox, 'Chronicles of a Wharfedale Parish' (1909).)

Cowthorpe, *St. Michael*. St. Michael's is a rebuilding of 1456–58 at the expense of Brian Roucliff, who was Lord of the Manor and patron of the benefice. The church passed to the Redundant Churches Fund in 1977. It is notable for its W tower, which sits astride the W wall with minimal supports, and for its 15C wooden Easter sepulchre.

The building comprises a nave and chancel and a tower which sits rather awkwardly on the W end, half out and half in. There are two large external buttresses, which are joined by an arch. Deep within this arch is the three-light, transomed W window. The tower has a battlemented parapet which would fit a castle's turret more than a small church. The nave and chancel have square-headed windows. The S porch is 16C.

Within, the tower's apparently limited internal supports—corbels—may be seen. There is a chancel arch, but it is so wide and high that the church is virtually a single-cell building. On the chancel N wall there is a brass memorial to the founder (died 1495) and his wife. The brass is mutilated and has lost the inscription which called Brian

Roucliff 'the founder and builder of this church and of all the work up to its completion', but it retains his figure holding a model of the building. In the NW corner stands the wooden Easter sepulchre, which would once have stood against the chancel N wall. It comprises a canopy, with elaborate cresting, over a chest with six cusped panels. The communion rails are 17C. The fittings are otherwise all 19C. Note particularly the 19C lamps on the choirstalls. In the heads of two E window lights there is some 15C glass.

Doncaster, *St. George*. St. George's is a rebuilding of 1854–58 by Sir Gilbert Scott, after a fire had destroyed the previous building in 1853. Various features of the present building, most notably the crossing tower, more or less reproduce parts of its predecessor. It is nevertheless unmistakably the product of a proud 19C city and equally unmistakably a work by Scott. His pupil, G.F. Bodley, in speaking of his own design of 1858 for St. Michael's, Brighton, stated that he was 'tired of mouldings', after a surfeit of them in Scott's office. St. George's is a major example of what Bodley had in mind, a confident, exuberant crowning of the first accurate wave of the Gothic Revival.

The church has a nave, nave aisles, a two-storey S porch, a crossing tower, transepts, a choir and slightly projecting sanctuary, and choir aisles. The foursquare, 170ft tower is very tall in proportion to the body of the church and is visible from afar. Each face has two tiers of windows, the lower being pairs of two-light windows with cinquefoil heads, the upper being very tall three-light louvred openings, with intersecting tracery and crocketed gable hoods. There are traceried angle buttresses up to the heads of the belfry openings, with no fewer than four crocketed gable heads each. Surmounting the tower is an openwork parapet of 12 arches to each face, divided by 15 pinnacles. The nave towers over the lean-to aisles. The W front comprises a seven-light W window, with Geometrical tracery, flanked by gabled buttresses which rise into crocketed spirelets. The W door is gabled and crocketed. The choir and shallow transepts are of the same height as the nave. The choir aisles are more generous than their counterparts of the nave. The E front is similar to the W front but, in the absence of a door, the window is larger.

The nave arcades are of five bays, comprising clustered shafts, stiff-leaf capitals and much-moulded arches. The spandrels are decorated with quatrefoils which are filled by busts of Old Testament prophets and kings. The choir has arcades of three bays; the E bays have open tracery. The spandrels in the choir bear busts of the Apostles. The S choir aisle, known as the Forman chapel, is elaborately treated. It has three four-light windows to the S and a five-light E window.

The reredos behind the high altar is a characteristic work by Scott: an arcade of five cusped arches surmounted by crocketed gables. The five panels are filled with paintings of Christ and the Evangelists. The arcading of the reredos is continued at a lower level around the sanctuary. The font of black Serpentine marble stands in the middle of the Forman chapel, surrounded by a Minton tiled floor. The small reredos in this chapel is most attractive; it dates from 1913 and includes alabaster figures of the Crucifixion and the Evangelists. The organ by Edmund Schulze, 1862, occupies much of the N choir aisle. The memorials include one in the N nave aisle to Captain Ian North, who died when the 'Atlantic Conveyor' was sunk in the Falklands War in 1982.

St. George's has a superb collection of 19C stained glass, all of it inserted between 1857 and 1872, except for two windows of 1896 which replaced earlier ones. The E window of the choir, of 1862 by John Hardman, depicts the Passion, Resurrection and Ascension. The windows of the Forman chapel were all made by William Wailes and inserted in 1858. The chapel's E window recounts the story of the Passion. The S windows treat the Apostles. The S transept window is by Clayton & Bell. The main W window is by Ward & Hughes and depicts the genealogy of Jesus as given by St. Matthew.

Ecclesfield, *St. Mary the Virgin.* This is a large Perpendicular church which has a nave with N and S aisles, a S porch, a crossing tower, N and S transepts, and a chancel with N and S chapels. The tower is fairly plain. It has two-light, transomed belfry openings, battlements and eight short pinnacles. The parapets throughout the church have battlements and pinnacles which rise from somewhat detached buttresses. All the tall side windows are of three transomed lights. The E, W and transept end windows have five lights.

The interior has five-bay nave arcades of octagonal or cylindrical piers, moulded capitals and double-chamfered arches. The piers have wide, slightly clumsy bases. Above are the three-light clerestory windows and a striking new roof. There is a nave altar, with choirstalls placed beneath the crossing tower, and to the E follows the chancel screen. Two-bay arcades separate the chancel from its chapels.

The church possesses much stained glass. The W window of the N nave aisle wall has jumbled medieval glass, mainly heraldic. The rest is all 19C. Two windows of c 1883 and c 1895 in the S nave aisle are by C.E. Kempe. The S transept S window of 1874 is very attractive. The nave has traceried bench-ends. Elsewhere there are benches and stalls which have small carved figures. The pulpit is richly carved. On the N nave wall there are the colours, swords and bugles of the Ecclesfield Regiment of Volunteers of 1803, raised to face Napoleon's feared invasion. (A further connection from that time is that Nelson's chaplain at Trafalgar, Alexander John Scott, is buried just N of the church.) In the S transept there is a portion of a pre-Conquest cross-shaft. The one notable monument, in the S chancel chapel, is of Sir Richard Scott (died 1640).

Fulneck, *Moravian Church.* The growth of the Moravian Church in England was a notable part of the religious history of the 18C. The settlement at Fulneck began in 1742 and gradually grew into a separate Moravian village. Its church, built in 1746–48, today has 150 communicant members. The rectangular building has a dignified Classical interior. There are galleries on three sides and against the fourth or S side is placed the pulpit, the focus of the church. The gallery over the main or N entrance houses a Snetzler organ of 1748. There are four arched windows in the S wall, with some stained glass of 1933. Benjamin Latrobe, the American architect, was baptised here. His father was the minister from 1757 to 1768.

Halifax

St. John the Baptist. The principal parish church of Halifax is a substantial 15C building, set in the middle of this ancient town of the wool trade, against a background of steep hills. The 15C church incorporates some 12C zigzag mouldings and, more prominently, 13C N aisle windows. Restoration took place in 1878–79 under J. Oldrid Scott.

The exterior is very dark. The tall W tower of 1449–82 has angle buttresses, pairs of tall two-light belfry openings in each face, and an embattled and pinnacled parapet which is noticeably set back. Gargoyles protrude from below the parapet. The body of the church has a nave and chancel with roofs of equal height, N and S aisles which continue as chancel aisles, an outer S aisle, a N chapel in the position of a transept, and N and S porches. All except the nave have pinnacles and either battlements or a poppyhead cresting. The windows are mostly Perpendicular, including the five-light E window of the outer S aisle and the particularly large E window of the chancel, which is of seven transomed lights. In the older N aisle, the windows have Y-tracery. Only the chancel has a clerestory. Beneath the windows of the chancel aisles are small square-headed windows which light an E crypt.

The nave arcades are of five bays. There are octagonal piers, each with four concave sides, octagonal moulded capitals and concave moulded arches. The chancel has four structural bays, but the chancel screen stands two bays E of the chancel arch. In front of it stands a nave altar, installed in 1983. The details of the nave are more accomplished than those of the chancel. The SW corner shows evidence of an intended tower, abandoned in favour of the present one. The roofs of the chancel and nave date from the 17C and bear the coats of arms of Vicars of Halifax and of local families. The organ (partly by Snetzler, 1766) occupies part of the N chancel aisle. The outer S aisle is the Holdsworth chapel, built by Robert Holdsworth, Vicar of Halifax (died 1556). The N or Rokeby chapel recalls another Vicar, William Rokeby (died 1521). The S chancel aisle (or chapel of the Resurrection) has been the regimental chapel of the Duke of Wellington's Regiment since 1951.

The font cover at the W end is a soaring 15C example: two receding stages with elaborate openwork tracery and cresting, and a tall crocketed spire. The seating is of cut-down box-pews, of 1633, with rounded knobs as finials. The pulpit is 19C. The choirstalls are of the 15C, but plain. Three more, used as sedilia, are of better craftsmanship and possibly came from Kirkstall Abbey. The altar rails date from 1698. In the SW corner there stands a full-size figure known as Old Tristram, who holds an almsbox. The box itself dates from 1701, but the figure is probably older. The royal arms are those of Queen Anne, 1705. The E window has stained glass of 1851 by George Hedgeland, showing scenes of Christ's Passion. The Crucifixion is in the central light. Below it is shown the Judgement of Pilate; Pilate looks not at all Roman. At the W end, under the tower, there is a table-tomb with effigy to Charles Musgrave, first Archdeacon of Craven (died 1880). A cusped, ogee wall canopy in the SW corner commemorates Robert Ferrar, the 16C martyr. It was made in 1847.

All Souls, Haley Hill. All Souls' was built in 1856–59 by Sir Gilbert

Scott for Edward Akroyd, a rich Halifax manufacturer. The church was part of Akroyd's model suburb, but it was also intended to outshine the Square Congregational Church, which had been built by his industrial rivals, the Crossleys. All Souls' has a commanding spire of 236ft, one foot higher than that of the Congregational Church. Scott considered that All Souls' was 'on the whole, my best church', but he lamented that the overall design was less grand than it might have been. In 1977 the church became redundant and its future looked bleak. In 1981 an All Souls' Haley Hill Preservation Trust was set up to lease the church from the Diocese of Wakefield. The trust raised much money directly, but chiefly depended on grants from the National Heritage Memorial Fund and the Historic Buildings Council. The roof was repaired in 1982–83 and the tower and spire in 1985. The lease was relinquished in 1988 and the church's future again became uncertain.

The church comprises a nave with N and S aisles, a SW porch, N and S transepts which are attached to the E bay of the nave, a chancel with a chapel to the S and an organ chamber and vestries to the N, and a NW tower and spire. The church is built of millstone grit, with dressings of Steetley magnesian limestone. The tower has gabled angle buttresses in its lower stages. Above, there are clasping octagonal buttresses which rise into crocketed pinnacles. Statues adorn both types of buttress: in gabled niches below and under small canopies above. All the statues were carved by J.B. Philip. There are pairs of recessed, two-light belfry openings in each face. The parapet projects slightly and provides a necessary horizontal foil to the effect of the buttresses, pinnacles and spire. Tall, thin, gabled, two-light lucarnes adorn the foot of the spire and there are two small tiers of lucarnes above. The W face of the nave, which adjoins the tower to the S, has an elaborate W door and a tall five-light window with Geometrical tracery. This was Scott's favourite style, the style of the late 13C. The E window virtually repeats the W. The aisle windows are of three lights, the clerestory windows of two, each light being shafted, except for the W bay on the S, which has three lights. There are gabled buttresses to the aisles, transepts and chancel, all of which have statues in niches. The exterior statues, 27 in total, are all by J.B. Philip. To the S of the nave, there stands a statue of Edward Akroyd.

The interior has Ringley stone ashlar facing. The nave is of five bays, if the taller and wider bay which leads into the transepts is counted. The capitals have splendid carved foliage. In the spandrels there are roundels which house busts of the Latin Doctors on the N and of four early bishops (St. Polycarp, St. Ignatius, St. Cyprian and St. Clement) on the S. The tympanum of the W door has a carving of a Pelican in her Piety. Shafts of Derbyshire marble and Peterhead granite adorn the clerestory. The baptistery occupies the space beneath the tower. The chancel has blank arcading and a tiled floor. The alabaster reredos and the pulpit of Caen stone with inlaid marble decoration are both by J.B. Philip. The low iron screen to the chancel, which stands on an alabaster plinth, and the screen to the S chapel, were made by Francis Skidmore. The stained glass of the E and W windows is by John Hardman. The E window of 1860 shows ten scenes from the life of Christ. The W window of 1859 depicts the Last Judgement. Hardman also provided the chancel's N and S windows, which depict the Baptism of Christ and the Last Supper respectively, and the lights of the S chapel. The 15 clerestory lights show the Apostles and the Evangelists by Clayton & Bell, 1859. By the same firm and in the same year are the transept end windows, concerning St. Peter (S) and St. John the Baptist (N).

Harewood, *All Saints.* The church was built almost entirely in the 15C. It is famous for six pairs of effigies on tomb-chests, all of alabaster, which were made between c 1419 and c 1510. Minor alterations to the exterior were undertaken by John Carr in the late 18C, and in 1862–63 Sir Gilbert Scott considerably reordered the interior. The church passed to the Redundant Churches Fund in 1978. Much repair of the monuments took place in 1979–81.

All Saints' stands in the parkland of Harewood House. Harewood village was rebuilt away from the church in the late 18C for Edwin, first Lord Harewood. All Saints' comprises a nave with N and S aisles, a S porch, a chancel with N and S chancel chapels, a projecting sanctuary and a W tower. The low tower has battlements and two-light belfry windows. There are battlements, too, at the E and W ends of the church, parts of the alterations of 1793 by John Carr. The N and S aisle parapets are plain. The roof of the nave continues down over the aisles and continues to the E over the chancel without a break. The buttressed aisles have three-light Perpendicular windows; the E and W windows have five lights. There are N, S and W doors, the last being the main entrance today.

The interior has four-bay nave arcades of double-chamfered arches and tall, octagonal piers which lack capitals. One arch to the N and S separates the chancel from its chapels, and a smaller arch follows to the E on each side to shelter a monument. The chancel has 19C tiles and there is a good 19C pulpit next to the chancel arch. The font in the S aisle, however, is Norman. The E window has stained glass of 1855 by M. & A. O'Connor, depicting the Crucifixion and the Ascension and other scenes from the life of Christ. The W window of c 1892, by C.E. Kempe, shows St. John the Baptist, St. Peter, Christ, St. John the Evangelist and King David. The W window of the S aisle is by Powell Bros. of Leeds.

Three Gascoigne monuments stand in a line in the S aisle and the S chapel. Their present positions date from the restoration of 1979–81. The monument to the W is of Sir William Gascoigne and his wife Margaret, c 1487. The tomb-chest has niches with crocketed canopies which house weepers and saints. Sir William is in armour; his wife wears a long gown and a veil. The next monument E was formerly placed against the wall in the SE corner of the S chapel. Its tomb-chest is substantially new; what is original is very similar to the preceding monument. Those commemorated are another Sir William Gascoigne (again in armour) and another Margaret, of c 1465. Further E, in the S chapel proper, lie a third Sir William Gascoigne and his wife Elizabeth, whose monument of c 1419 is the earliest of the series. This Sir William, the grandfather of the preceding, was Lord Chief Justice and is thus the odd one out in wearing judge's robes rather than armour. In Shakespeare's 'Henry IV', he takes the future King Henry V to court for youthful misdemeanours. The tomb-chest has angels holding shields. The inscription strip around the edges of the chest's top is 19C. To the N of this monument, under the arch which opens into the chancel, stands the memorial of Sir William Ryther and his wife Sybil, of c 1425. This memorial forms a pair with the contemporary one on the N side to Sir Richard Redman and his wife Elizabeth. The two wives were the daughters and co-heiresses of Sir William Aldburgh of Harewood Castle. They both have detailed flowered head-dresses. The tomb-chests are plainer than those of the later monuments. The final monument lies in the N chapel and commemorates Sir Edward Redman and his wife Elizabeth, of c 1510. The elaborate tomb-chest has weepers, saints, and angels with shields in canopied niches. Under one of Sir Edward's feet is a bedesman, who prays for the deceased.

The communion rails were given in memory of King George V by his only daughter, Princess Mary (Princess Royal), who married the sixth Earl of Harewood. Her own memorial is placed on the S aisle wall. She died in 1965. A fine memorial to be noted is of an 18C judge, Sir Thomas Denison (died 1765), on the E wall of the S or Gascoigne chapel. Sir Thomas's memorial includes a portrait bust.

Harrogate, *St. Wilfrid.* St. Wilfrid's is a distinguished early 20C church which has a number of unusual features. The nave and chancel were built by Temple Moore in 1905–14; the transepts and the Lady chapel were added by Leslie Moore between 1928 and 1935. The style is Early English, but the overall effect is closer to G.F. Bodley in spirit than it is to mid-Victorian essays in 13C style.

The church stands in Duchy Road, in a spaciously laid-out district of this spa town. The exterior shows a substantial cruciform church, with a central tower standing between a nave and a chancel of roughly equal length. The tower is embattled and carries a low capping. The small belfry windows are flanked by blind arches. The E end of the chancel is notably high, with tower-like N and S corners. The W end, unusually, is V-shaped. Also unusual are the N and S transepts, both markedly tall, the S one apsidal, the N one tower-like, foursquare and embattled. The majority of windows are fairly wide lancets, mainly paired. Above the high altar there are three two-light windows and, higher still, five unequal lancets. The S transept has very tall and narrow lancets. The N transept acts as an entrance porch.

St. Wilfrid's, a distinctive masterpiece of 1905–14 by Temple Moore

The interior has three-bay nave arcades, with triple-chamfered arches resting on either cylindrical or octagonal piers with moulded capitals. The crossing has clustered piers. To the E there are three-bay arcades in the chancel, above which runs a triforium. Behind the high altar there are three arches, through which yet further three-bay arcades may be seen in the Lady chapel. This chapel is an extended octagon, with very narrow aisles and with wall seating in medieval fashion. The entire building is rib-vaulted. The chancel is surrounded by an ambulatory, and beyond that there are chapels to the N, S and E. The chancel screen of 1919 has a Rood high above it. The inscription repeats one in Antwerp. The translation is: 'When you pass before this image of Christ, reverence it with humility: but worship not the image, but Him whom it depicts'. The large pulpit has painted panels and a small circular tester. The font at the W end is made of Verona marble. The symbols of the Holy Spirit above it are by Leslie Durbin. The 450 kneelers in the church were made by parishioners in the 12 years after 1965. The reliefs in the nave were designed by Frances Darlington. Most of the stained glass is by Victor Milner. Note in particular the three-light window in St. Wilfrid's chapel which shows nine scenes from the saint's life. The seven lancets of the S transept depict the seven Sacraments, of which Harry Harvey of York designed the Holy Unction window in 1981. A window in the N transept is a memorial to Temple Moore.

Hatfield, *St. Lawrence.* St Lawrence's is a fine cruciform church which is largely Perpendicular but which also possesses significant Norman and 13C features. The church stands quite clear of other buildings and impresses as much by its attractive white magnesian limestone as by its substantial size.

The commanding central tower, 100ft in height, has lower windows of four arched lights and upper pairs of two-light, transomed windows. There are battlements and eight pinnacles. The tower bears the arms of the Savage family: Thomas Savage was Archbishop of York from 1501 to 1507 and his brother became Bailiff of Hatfield in 1485. The work seems to have been carried out in the early 16C. The rest of the church comprises a nave with N and S aisles, and a chancel with N and S chapels. The nave and chancel are of equal height, but only the nave has a clerestory, which comprises tall three-light windows. The nave, the chancel and the chancel chapels are all battlemented, and there are pinnacles on the nave parapets and at the E end. The main E and W windows and the end windows of the transepts are all of five transomed lights, the lights being uncusped and virtually arched; this would appear to be very late Perpendicular work. The main W window, however, is placed above the earliest feature of the exterior, a Norman W doorway of three orders with colonnettes. It looks much restored. Norman, too, is the W window of the N aisle and the S doorway. The doorway has circular or pellet moulding. The door itself has apparently old ironwork of two large Cs, one on each side. The final feature of the exterior to be noticed is the group of Decorated windows in the S nave aisle.

Within, the nave has five-bay arcades of round piers, octagonal capitals and double-chamfered pointed arches. On the N side, there are transverse arches across the aisle from each nave pier, presumably put in when the Perpendicular clerestory was added. The crossing arches are very tall. Light comes from the lower tier of tower windows; Sir Thomas Jackson raised the floor of the ringing chamber in 1872 for this purpose. There are two-bay arcades with octagonal piers between the chancel and its chapels. The transepts are relatively shallow.

The chancel screen has four one-light openings and a central archway. Each opening has a pendant to separate two arches and there is a bigger pendant in the central opening. To the N, there is a simpler screen to the chancel chapel. The high altar has riddel posts and gilded angels, a 20C work by Leslie Moore. The pulpit, which is presumably 19C, has fine detailed tracery. To the S of the S door there is an attractive benefaction board. Two windows in the S aisle have stained glass by C.E. Kempe and his successor company: a three-light window of c 1904 depicting St. Paulinus, St. Edwin and St. Oswald, and a four-light window to its E of c 1925 which shows St. Aidan, St. Cuthbert, St. Bede and St. Hilda. The main E window has stained glass of c 1868, presenting ten scenes from the life of Christ. More recent stained glass was designed by George Pace. Three monuments deserve notice. There is a plain tomb-chest in the N transept. Another tomb-chest, in the NE corner of the S chancel chapel, has shields enclosed by lozenges. In the N chancel chapel there is an attractive carved wall tablet to John and Frances Hatfield (died 1693 and 1698) and to John, Jr and his wife (died 1720 and 1730).

Horbury, St. Peter and St. Leonard. Horbury is a small town SW of Wakefield. Its church is a worthy Classical building of 1791–94 by John Carr, who was born here in 1723 and was eventually buried here. He built the church at his own expense. Over the S door is the inscription: HANC AEDEM SACRAM, PIETATIS IN DEUM ET AMORIS IN SOLUM NATALE MONIMENTUM, PROPRIIS SUMPTIBUS EXTRUXIT IOANNES CARR, ARCHITECTUS (John Carr, architect, built this church at his own expense in honour of God and for love of his birthplace).

The church comprises a W tower and a nave with shallow N and S transepts and polygonal E and W ends. The stone looks very clean and fresh. The W steeple has six receding stages. The lowest stage is plain with blank windows, one arched and the other square-headed, the latter above the former, in the N, S and W faces. Then there is a rusticated stage, with clock-faces, and next a stage with arched louvred openings, flanked by pairs of pilasters. The fourth stage repeats the third, but substitutes recessed pillars for the outer pilasters. This is then surmounted by a rotunda of small columns and finally by a conical spire. The S door is grandly treated with a portico of four attached Ionic columns and a pediment.

The interior presents an interesting plan. To N and S there are two fluted Corinthian columns which support the entablature of the nave and which screen the N and S transepts, but one might term them aisles. The effect is really of a very wide nave. A small SE chapel opens off the S transept. The E end is apsidal, the W end likewise, with a gallery for the organ. There are four fluted and gilded Corinthian pilasters at the E end. The ceiling, a shallow barrel-vault, is painted. To the left of the nave is a fine pulpit with tester. On the N wall there is a splendid brass to John Sharp (1810–1903), Vicar from 1834 to 1899, which presents views of local institutions he had founded.

Sabine Baring-Gould was curate of Horbury from 1864 to 1867. He devoted a chapter of his 'Further Reminiscences' (1925) to his years here under John Sharp. Here he wrote 'Onward, Christian Soldiers' (first sung at a children's Whitsunday procession at Horbury Brig in 1865) and also 'On the Resurrection Morning'. For these he is still famous today, long after his enormous number of books have been largely forgotten.

Kirk Hammerton, St. John the Baptist. St. John's incorporates an entire pre-Conquest building within a much larger 19C church, which was built in 1890–91 to the designs of Charles Hodgson Fowler. The 19C church largely replaced a late 12C lean-to N aisle, but whereas the old N aisle was subsidiary to the pre-Conquest church, the 19C building reversed the relationship and made the ancient church its S aisle.

The church comprises a nave, nave aisles, chancel, SE chapel, SW tower and NE vestry. In effect, there are two churches. On the S side there are the tower, nave and chancel of the pre-Conquest building, and to their N there is a largely 19C church of nave, chancel, N aisle and vestry. The unbuttressed SW tower has an arched W doorway of two orders, with large imposts and jambs; an upper storey divided from the lower by a bold stringcourse and pierced by two arched belfry openings, separated by a small column, in each face; and a low pyramidal capping. The pre-Conquest nave has a S door like that of the tower, but much renewed. The square-headed window in the S wall is a later, probably 14C, insertion. This window cuts into a blocked pre-Conquest doorway, the use of which has long been debated. A chapel or transept has usually been suggested. The pre-Conquest chancel also has an inserted three-light E window, but in its S wall are two windows of Norman date, the W one much taller than the other, and also a blocked pre-Conquest light. The 19C church to the N has a four-light W window, a three-light E window which is genuinely Perpendicular and a lean-to N aisle with windows in the Decorated style.

Entering by the S door, the pre-Conquest building is seen to have a tall but entirely plain arch to the tower and a chancel arch which employs large, plain stones for its imposts and capitals. The arcade, which was cut in the N wall of the pre-Conquest church, is of two bays. There is one cylindrical column, with an octagonal capital. The arches are slightly pointed. This is very early Gothic work. By contrast, the 19C N arcade, of three bays, uses a later medieval style of properly pointed arches, octagonal columns and moulded capitals. The chancel screen, pulpit and lectern are all 19C. The wooden reredos in the chancel has paintings of St. John the Baptist holding Kirk Hammerton Church and St. Peter with York Minster (both to the N), and St. Hilda with Whitby Abbey and St. Wilfrid with Ripon Cathedral (both to the S). The SE chapel has an elaborate reredos, 16C Dutch work but painted by George Ostrehan in the 1890s. George Ostrehan also painted the lower walls of the chancel and its roof. The E window has stained glass of the Crucifixion, with the Virgin Mary and St. John the Baptist, by C.E. Tute, 1893, after C.E. Kempe. Tute also designed the stained glass in the SE chapel. Its E window depicts the Virgin and Child, St. John the Baptist and St. Mary Magdalen. The communion rails of the chapel are Jacobean.

Knaresborough, *St. John the Baptist*. St. John's is a substantial cruciform church which has fabric of various medieval styles. The present crossing and chancel appear to possess the earliest surviving fabric: two blocked 12C windows on either side of the chancel's E window, and the crossing arches which are of the late 12C. The 13C saw the addition of the chancel chapels, the 15C the nave aisles and, as elsewhere, the 15C also altered roofs and windows to give the semblance of a Perpendicular church. The 14C has also left its mark on the E end and in particular on the SE or St. Edmund's chapel. Major restoration took place in 1870–72 and a reordering of the nave and crossing was undertaken in 1977–78.

The church comprises a nave with lean-to N and S aisles, a crossing tower, a chancel, a NE or St. Mary Magdalene's or Slingsby chapel, a SE or St. Edmund's chapel, and a S porch. The tower has small corner pinnacles and a Hertfordshire spike. The shadows of former transept roofs may be seen on its N and S faces. The nave aisles have buttresses which rise to pinnacles. The windows are variously Reticulated, intersecting and Perpendicular. There are diminutive three-light clerestory windows in the nave. The W front, which is entirely Perpendicular, has niches on either side of the central doorway.

Entering through the S porch, there is a four-bay nave with very tall arcades of octagonal piers and octagonal moulded capitals. The dominant impression in the nave is of the 15C. The crossing has 12C piers which have three plain shafts. The original transepts are now incorporated in the aisles. There is a fairly elaborate Early English arch from the former S transept into St. Edmund's chapel. Both this chapel and the E end of the chancel are Decorated in style. The chapel has 14C sedilia and a piscina, a recess with an ogee canopy, a S window with intersecting tracery and a Reticulated E window. The chancel has a five-light Reticulated E window, with stained glass of Christ and the Evangelists. The reredos and the arcading which flanks it are 19C. The nave altar, furnished with a fall drape, dates from 1977. The wooden font cover at the W end is an elaborate work of c 1700. The octagonal font is 15C. Royal arms of King William III, 1700, surmount the S door. The stained glass in the W window commemorates Sir Charles Slingsby, who died in 1869.

The interesting memorials are to members of the Slingsby family, all placed in the NE chapel. A table-tomb with two effigies in the centre commemorates Francis and Mary Slingsby (died 1600 and 1598). He is shown in full armour. The tomb was made in 1601–02 by Thomas Browne. Their son, Sir Henry (died 1634), is represented by an upright figure in white marble, set against the N wall. He is shown in a shroud. His brother, Sir William, who died in 1638, is commemorated by another upright figure, placed against the S wall. The figure, which is larger than Sir Henry's, stands in a round-headed recess. Sir William's memorial was made in 1634, at the same time as his brother's, and both are apparently by Epiphanius Evesham. Sir William rests his rather tired face on his left hand, and in turn his left arm rests on the guard of his sword. He wears a large hat, and boots with spurs. In his right hand he holds a large heraldic cartouche. Sir Henry Slingsby, who was beheaded under Cromwell in 1658, has a black marble slab of 1693 which is inscribed 'a tyranno Cromwellio capite mulctatus' (beheaded by Cromwell the tyrant). Sir Charles Slingsby, the tenth and last Baronet (died 1869), has a table-tomb with an effigy, by J.E. Boehm.

Knaresborough is distinguished for its own medieval saint—St. Robert (1160–1218), a hermit who received gifts from King John, among others. It was in King John's reign, in 1210, that the earliest recorded royal Maundy ceremony took place in the town.

Ledsham, *All Saints*. All Saints' is outwardly a church of various Gothic styles, but incorporates a pre-Conquest building which may be as early as the 8C. The lower part of the W tower and the present S wall provide the principal pre-Conquest evidence. The church was much enlarged and altered in the 14C and 15C and it was restored by Henry Curzon in the 19C.

The church comprises a W tower, nave, N nave aisle, chancel, N

chancel aisle (the Lady chapel) and a NE vestry. The pre-Conquest
building seems to have comprised the present tower and nave, plus a
small chancel, with N and S nave chambers, of which the S one is
now represented by the S porch. The W tower is pre-Conquest in its
lower stage, Norman above, with two louvred openings separated by
a colonnette within a blank round arch. The 15C added the battlements, corner pinnacles and recessed stone spire. The pre-Conquest
portion of the tower was a two-storey W porch, which had a S door
and not a W one. This door survives, albeit after 19C restoration: a
very low opening, decorated with interlace and scrolls. The W
window of the tower is Norman. In the nave S wall, the porch and
three-light windows are 15C. There are blocked pre-Conquest windows, with monolithic heads, in this wall. To the E, the chancel has
13C lancets in its S wall. Its E window in the Decorated style is 19C.

Entering by the S porch, the evidence for the pre-Conquest S
chamber is seen above the present S doorway. A markedly tall and
narrow opening is indicated. Pre-Conquest naves were often very tall
and it seems that the S chamber, being of similar height, had a tall
connecting arch. The chancel arch is pre-Conquest, perhaps with
some restoration. The arch to the tower is Norman, but above it is a
pre-Conquest window, originally serving the upper storey of the W
porch. The three-bay nave arcade has octagonal piers, with moulded
capitals and double-chamfered arches. A similar two-bay arcade
separates the chancel from the Lady chapel. The N aisle and the
Lady chapel are late medieval.

One S window has 15C glass, including an Annunciation, which
was removed from the E window in 1900. The chancel fittings all
appear to be 19C. The altar and communion rails of the Lady chapel
are of 1929. The principal monuments stand in this chapel. The
monument of Lady Elizabeth Hastings is by Peter Scheemakers. Her
reclining effigy is flanked by two statues of her half-sisters, who
represent Piety and Prudence. Nearby, Sir John and Lady Lewis
recline on two levels above a sarcophagus in black and white marble.
The monument was by Thomas Cartwright, 1677. The third monument of note is that to Lady Mary Bolles (died 1662), who was created
a baroness in her own right. Her tomb in the NW corner of the
chapel comprises a recumbent effigy in a shroud, in white marble, on
a black and white tomb-chest, whose Ionic columns separate heraldic panels and a central inscription.

Lady Elizabeth Hastings deserves additional attention. She was
the daughter of the seventh Earl of Huntingdon and his wife,
Elizabeth, who was herself the daughter of Sir John and Lady Lewis
of Ledston Hall. She inherited the estate and devoted herself to good
works. Her tomb records: '...she dispensed Justice, Honour, Truth,
so earnestly and sincerely and candidly that she won for herself a
name more lofty than any inscription can record, more lasting than
any monument'.

Leeds

St. Peter, Kirkgate. Leeds Parish Church was rebuilt in 1838–41 to the designs of R.D. Chantrell for Walter Farquhar Hook, a most influential Vicar of Leeds (1837–59) who later became Dean of Chichester. The present church is primarily of interest as an example of early Victorian design and planning, but as the successor building of the oldest church foundation in Leeds, it also has some ancient possessions and associations, above all the 10C Leeds Cross.

The church stands a little outside the obvious centre of modern Leeds. Within Kirkgate, however, the church stands prominently. Its N elevation fronts the street and in the middle of that elevation is placed a dominating, foursquare tower. At its foot is the main entrance. The tower is all the more dominating because it rises from the low outer N aisle. It has gabled angle buttresses, which recede in stages; tall openwork parapets; eight crocketed pinnacles, the corner ones higher than the rest; pairs of transomed two-light belfry openings, beneath which there are clock-faces; and much traceried panelling in the lower stages. The tower is a serious and detailed work for 1838–41. The same may be said of the body of the church. There are four aisled bays to E and W of the crossing, an apse and further low extensions at the E end, and a S transept to balance the N tower. The aisles are notably tall but there is still a clerestory to nave and chancel. The parapets are plain except on the outer N aisle (the show front), where there are pinnacled buttresses. The same aisle has square-headed Reticulated windows. The other N and S windows have simpler tracery. The E windows are decidedly Perpendicular: a transomed five-light main window flanked by transomed three-light windows.

Entering by the N door, the visitor comes into the crossing. Neither the N tower nor the S transept extend beyond the outer walls, but there is a sufficient N–S axis to call the church cruciform. The crossing arches are significant features of the interior. The E and W arms are of equal length, with the same tall arcade. Blank panelling decorates the surfaces between the arches and the clerestory windows. The most noticeable feature of the interior, however, is the very heavy group of galleries to N, S and W, which are darkly stained and decorated with crocketed ogee panelling. An eagle lectern and Chantrell's elaborate pulpit are placed at the crossing amidst these galleries, prompting thoughts of Georgian 'preaching box' arrangements. The choir is placed E of the crossing. The previous church had a surpliced choir as early as 1818, which was markedly advanced. The E end provides a focus by virtue of its fan-vaulted apse, by its ornate reredos and ornate blank arches which flank it, by its being raised on several steps, and finally by the fact that the galleries stop well short of the E end. There is a spaciousness to the E which contrasts with the rest of the church. The E end was remodelled by G.E. Street in the 1870s, but the present arrangements are substantially those of 1841. Some features were 'advanced' for 1841, but others are clearly contrary to the thinking of the next Victorian generation. Dr Hook was a High Churchman of a 17C sort, who was somewhat detached from the Oxford and Ecclesiological Movements. The architect, R.D. Chantrell, at one point considered that 'The Ecclesiologist', the journal of the most serious Gothic Revivalists, was 'a mischievous tissue of imbecility and fanaticism'. So St. Peter's is neither High Victorian nor entirely pre-Ecclesiological. It is an interesting reflection of earlier High Church ideas, dressed in a serious but independent Gothic Revival style.

The present reredos of 1872 was designed by G.E. Street, replacing an altarpiece of 1841 which looked back to the 18C. The mosaic panels of the reredos are by Clayton & Bell. The panels of the apse, which depict the Apostles, are by Salviati of Venice. C.E. Kempe designed the sedilia of 1891. An even later addition of much significance and beauty was the reredos of the Lady chapel (N of the chancel), which was designed by F.C. Eden as part of a war memorial completed in 1922. No new font was provided in 1841; the 15C font from the old church had been retained. It was replaced in 1883 by an elaborate font designed by William Butterfield. Stained glass is prominent in the church. The E window has Flemish or French glass of the 16C, which was arranged by John Summers for the new church. The flanking windows have stained glass by Thomas Wilmshurst, who clung to a pictorial style as it ceased to be fashionable. William Wailes made the E window of the S aisle in memory of a Leeds industrialist, Benjamin Gott, and his wife. The main W window is of 1856, designed by Chantrell and made by David Evans of Shrewsbury. The heraldry represents the patrons of the new church.

Special mention must be made of the Leeds Cross. It was found in pieces in 1838 and put together by Chantrell. It stands on the S side at the E end, 13ft high. The side which faces the centre of the church is the reverse; the obverse or true front faces the S wall. The present reconstruction has seven stages of shaft and a cross-head. Some parts were new in the 19C. It has been argued that one or two further stages are missing and that the cross-head does not belong to this shaft. The cross is usually concluded to be of the 10C, but an argument has been made, too, for the 11C. The carvings represent at least two Evangelists, and perhaps all four, but in addition a Germanic legendary character, Weland the Smith, has been identified. There is also much vine-scroll and interlace decoration. (See Alec McGuire and Ann Clark, 'The Leeds Crosses' (1987).)

St. Peter's has a number of notable monuments. Walter Hook has a prominent monument to the N of the chancel, designed by Sir Gilbert Scott. A recumbent effigy with hands clasped in prayer lies on a tomb-chest with five open arches on each side. Attractive foliage fills their spandrels. Nearby is a memorial to Ralph Thoresby (died 1725), a famous antiquary who wrote the first history of Leeds. Also in the NE corner is a monument of 1812 by John Flaxman to Captain Samuel Walker and Captain Richard Beckett, two local men who fell in the Peninsular War. A figure of Victory mourns by a palm tree. In the S chancel aisle there is an incomplete early 14C effigy of a knight. Some 15C brasses are also preserved there. A more modern monument of note is by Baron Marochetti to William Beckett (died 1863), a Leeds banker; his portrait is accompanied by a representation of Charity.

In the 19C and early 20C, Leeds Parish Church was well-known as a training school for curates. The tradition began with Walter Hook. The church has also been distinguished for its music. S.S. Wesley was its organist from 1842 to 1849.

St. John the Evangelist, New Briggate. St. John's was founded by John Harrison (1579–1656) and built in 1632–34. Harrison was a rich cloth merchant and magistrate who made many benefactions to Leeds. It was fortunate that St. John's was built in the Laudian period. Its particularly rich set of fittings is immediately reminiscent of the church interiors associated with Bishop Cosin in County Durham. Cosin was a preacher on the day when St. John's was opened, but if there was a connection, it was St. John's which influenced Cosin and not the reverse. The church was rather drastically restored by Richard Norman Shaw in 1866–68. To be fair to him, he had intervened to save the church from demolition, and after support for its retention had been won from Sir Gilbert Scott, the price of retention was a drastic reordering. Most of the regrettable changes were reversed by Temple Moore in the late 19C and early 20C. The population of the parish dwindled in the 20C and St. John's was eventually declared redundant. It is now in the care of the Redundant Churches Fund.

St. John's comprises a nave and S aisle, a S porch, a NW tower and a NW vestry. The tower has battlements and corner pinnacles, and tall three-light, transomed windows with ogee hoodmoulds. Lower down there are gabled diagonal buttresses. The details of the tower look a little fanciful for the 17C and indeed it was rebuilt in 1838 by John Clark. The S porch and the NW vestry are both by Shaw. The body of the church has square-headed windows of arched but cusped lights. There are battlements on the S side, but those on the N were removed in c 1800. Gothic Survival is the label which we must give the style of the 17C exterior, the 19C tower alone showing any conscious attempt at reviving Gothic.

St. John's, a two-naved church whose interior originally focused on the pulpit against the N wall

The interior is not so straightforward as it seems. It is proper today to speak of a nave and a S aisle, but originally a different arrangement existed. The church is a rectangle which is divided by a central arcade of seven bays. A screen which stretches across the full width of the church divides the two E bays from the rest. Before 1787 the communion table was placed in the S chancel; it is possible that its removal to the N chancel was a reversion to the arrangement of 1634.

So we might speak of two naves or perhaps, in the 18C, of a nave and N aisle. But before a reordering in 1807–08, the pulpit stood centrally against the N wall and the pews were arranged to face it. The central arcade thus linked two spans of one nave rather than divided the nave from an aisle. The arcade has octagonal piers, which consist of four main flat sides and four rounded ones in the recessed angles. The capitals look faintly Classical. The two roofs have prominent tiebeams, kingposts and plastered panels. The tiebeam above the chancel screen has a wooden chancel arch attached beneath it, with much strapwork between the two. The screen itself is very elaborately carved and has substantial strapwork cresting. It is attributed to Francis Gunby. Above the opening into the N chancel are the 17C royal arms, which have been restored to that position in recent years. The late 19C carvings which took their place are now fixed to the W wall. The pulpit, and its large tester ornamented with strapwork and obelisks, now stands against the N wall near the screen. Eagles, symbolic of St. John the Evangelist, flank the wall plate. All around are the 17C box-pews, now lacking their doors and 'cut down', but retaining their decorated ends and knobs as finials. In the N chancel there is an ornate 19C reredos by Salviati of Venice, set within a frame by Temple Moore, surprisingly congruous with the 17C fittings. An alpha and an omega appear prominently on two flanking panels. The font is Shaw's.

The stained glass is entirely agreeable. Most of the N and S windows have central picture-panels only, thus keeping the church light. All the glass is late 19C and early 20C, by C.E. Tute, Ward & Hughes, Victor Milner, John Hardman & Co. and Burlison & Grylls. A sequence of subjects begins with the Annunciation towards the E end of the S wall. Not in this sequence is the Harrison memorial window (the E window of the S chancel, or Harrison chapel), by Burlison & Grylls, 1885. Scenes from John Harrison's life, including the building of St. John's, form the lower panels; the upper scenes concern St. John the Evangelist. John Harrison's portrait hangs on the W wall of the nave.

The church has many minor wall tablets and brass plates. One commemorates Robert Todd (died 1661), the first incumbent. He was a Puritan who was deprived in 1660, but he was nevertheless buried in St. John's.

St. Saviour, Ellerby Road. St. Saviour's was built in 1842–45 to the designs of John Macduff Derick and at the instigation of Edward Pusey, one of the leading Tractarians. Walter Hook, the Vicar of Leeds, who was a High Churchman of an older school, had considered the building of more churches in the city from 1839. Pusey offered to pay for one church anonymously. Hook later became uncomfortable about the churchmanship at St. Saviour's, which one commentator saw in 1851 as an 'ante-chamber to the Vatican', for so many of its priests and congregation had seceded to Rome. In fact, St. Saviour's was more unstable than influential; only under John Wylde, Vicar from 1877 to 1929, did it secure stability and acceptance.

The architecture and fittings of St. Saviour's were initially 'serious' and worthy, but were not an uninhibited display of Ecclesiology. Pusey insisted that the Decalogue be placed over the altar. The church has a nave with aisles, transepts, a crossing tower and an aisleless chancel. G.F. Bodley added the Lady chapel (or Pusey chapel) in 1890. The tower was heightened by Leslie Moore in 1937.

It has a pierced parapet and corner pinnacles. The transepts are tall and the E gable is also tall. There is a five-light E window with Geometrical tracery, which is flanked by gabled buttresses. The W window and the principal transept windows are also of five lights. The tracery is of late 13C style throughout. The church stands on high ground not very far to the SE of Leeds Parish Church, but its surroundings are somewhat depressing and its stone is now very darkened and sombre.

The four-bay nave has tall, thin octagonal piers. The impression throughout is one of height. The chancel is of three bays. A substantial reredos stands at the E end, incorporating canopied statues. It is by Temple Moore, 1921. The church has fine chancel and N aisle screens. Of considerable interest is the stained glass. The four five-light windows have glass which was designed by A.W.N. Pugin and was made by Michael O'Connor. Dr Pusey supervised the scheme in collaboration with Benjamin Webb, the leading Ecclesiologist. A N aisle window was added by Morris & Co. in the 1870s.

Methley, *St. Oswald*. St. Oswald's is of considerable interest for its Decorated and Perpendicular work, despite substantial restoration in the 19C and 20C. It is also notable for its monuments. The church stands in a fairly rural setting in an otherwise industrial part of Yorkshire, between Castleford and Leeds.

The church comprises a W tower, nave, chancel, S aisle, SE or Waterton chapel and NE vestry. The N and S windows are 14C. In the N wall are three-light Reticulated windows. The S aisle has one such window and windows with ogee lights in the S wall and at the W end. To the left of the middle window in the N wall, however, there is—inside the church—part of a 13C lancet. The fabric was thus substantially remodelled in the 14C rather than totally rebuilt. Further work was undertaken in the 15C. The W tower, buttressed and battlemented, is Perpendicular. So too is the Waterton chapel, whose E window of four arched lights is of c 1483–84. The chancel was rebuilt in 1926; its E window is Perpendicular in style.

Within, the three-bay S arcade is seen to be 14C: octagonal piers, octagonal moulded capitals and double-chamfered arches. The arcade and the N and S nave windows make the body of the church largely Decorated. To the E, however, the predominant impression is Perpendicular, from both the 15C Waterton chapel and the 20C chancel.

In the N wall of the nave and in the S aisle wall directly opposite, there are ogee recesses with effigies of a priest and a layman. An inscription made them brothers and attributed to them the 14C remodelling of the church. In the S aisle is a tall tomb-chest, with effigies of Sir Henry Savile (died 1632), his wife and his father, Sir John (died 1606). There are attached Ionic columns, painted black. In the Waterton chapel, against the S wall, there is a large, restless monument by J. Wilton, 1780, to John Savile, first Earl of Mexborough (died 1778). Opposite is a memorial to Charles and Aletheia Savile (died 1741 and 1759), also rather restless, by Peter Scheemakers. To the S of the sanctuary of the chapel is a tomb-chest with eight angels bearing shields and two large effigies, of Lord Welles (died 1461 in the Battle of Towton) and his wife. Of alabaster, the tomb is somewhat decayed. Finally, under a cusped canopy or arch between the chapel and the chancel, is the tomb-chest of Sir Robert Waterton (died 1424) and his wife. He founded the chantry which the later SE chapel was to house. The monument is of alabaster and bears angels and traceried sides.

The pulpit is a dignified Classical work of Queen Anne's time. To the right of the chancel arch is a stone sculpture of St. Oswald. The lectern has a Flemish base of c 1500, with a surmounting 19C eagle. The font cover, a steeple, was made under a will of 1584. The Waterton chapel has a 15C screen to the aisle but a 20C one to the chancel. The E window of the chapel has 15C glass: Christ and the Virgin Mary, St. John the Evangelist and St. John the Baptist, and the Latin Doctors, plus many angels. The E window of the chancel has stained glass by A.K. Nicholson, inserted after the chancel's rebuilding in 1926.

Carvings in this church, particularly the head corbels of the chancel arch, inspired Henry Moore at the beginning of his career.

Nun Monkton, *St. Mary.* St. Mary's has a magnificent setting, beyond a wide green with a pond and approached by an avenue. Attractive 17C and 18C buildings flank it. The church is the surviving nave of a Benedictine nunnery church which was founded in c 1153. Its style is a mixture of Transitional and more fully developed Early English.

The W end has a late Norman doorway of five orders and much zigzag decoration, surmounted by a gable and trefoil-headed niche and flanked by two arched niches on each side. In the right-hand niche there is a much-worn, 13C shrouded figure. Above the door are three stepped and fully Early English lancets, which are externally shafted, with two tiers of shaft-rings to the central light and one to each of the flanking lights. Dogtooth moulding adjoins all the shafts. The central portion of the W front rises into a short tower, with plain parapet, low capping and single louvred belfry openings. There are two late Norman S doorways.

The aisleless interior presents a rich Early English impression. There are seven lancet windows in the N and S walls, all deeply splayed and all set back behind a wall passage at sill level which is fronted by arcading. Between the lancets are tall, thin, two-light shafted openings, the shafts bearing shaft-rings, with niches over. At the W end two huge pillars, arched to the W wall, form the internal supports of the tower. The E end was rebuilt in 1873 by J.W. Walton, who inserted three stepped lancets.

The 19C reredos is of five gabled arches, the central one larger, with arcading to left and right. It is a work reminiscent of Sir Gilbert Scott's style. 19C too are the piscina, sedilia, pulpit, lectern and low sanctuary wall and gates. The E window has stained glass by Morris & Co.. In the central light, amidst much foliage, is 'verbum caro factum est alleluia alleluia' (the Word was made flesh...). The stained glass in the W lancets is of St. Etheldreda (S), St. Hilda (centre) and St. Chad (N).

Rotherham

All Saints. All Saints' is a monumental cruciform church which is almost entirely of the 15C and whose spire of c 180ft dominates the centre of this steel town. It includes a notable SE or Jesus chapel, which was founded in 1480 as a chantry by Thomas Rotherham, who was Archbishop of York from 1480 to 1500. A little later, in 1482, he set up a College of Jesus. These benefactions were augmented in 1505 by Henry Carnebull, Archdeacon of York. The church was much altered and restored in the 18C and again by Sir Gilbert Scott in 1873–75.

The church comprises a nave with aisles, a S porch, a crossing tower with spire, transepts, a chancel, chancel chapels, and a NE vestry. It is built of Rotherham red sandstone, looking very dark and sombre. The recessed and crocketed octagonal spire rises from a tower with pairs of four-light and double-transomed windows in each face. Small spirelets rise from the foot of the spire. The tower is battlemented and pinnacled, as are all the other parapets. A surviving record shows that the tower was built from c 1409. The windows of the church are all large and Perpendicular. At the E end, Scott inserted the present seven-light transomed window. The chancel's clerestory, an addition of 1508–12, is notably tall.

The interior is spacious and tall, more richly fitted towards the E. The four-bay nave arcades have capitals which are not more than bands of decoration. Very modern and somewhat unsympathetic light fittings hang in the nave. The crossing tower is fan-vaulted. To its E, there are two-bay arcades between the chancel and the chancel aisles. These arcades look much earlier than those of the nave: 14C rather than 15C. The piers have castellated moulded capitals. But above them, the chancel clerestory is late Perpendicular. The SE or Jesus chapel has a roof which has been redecorated in recent years. The screen which separates it from the S transept is a surviving portion of the medieval chancel screen. It is darkly stained and comprises two large four-light bays with open panels below.

The finely carved and embellished pulpit on the N side of the nave dates from 1604; its canopy is 18C. At the E end of the N aisle there stands an ancient font, brought back into the church after long disuse. Its Victorian replacement stands at the W end of the S aisle. The N transept houses the organ, originally by Snetzler, 1777. Its case in dark woodwork, setting off the gilded pipes, is a fine Classical work of the 18C. The chancel has an interesting collection of 15C bench-ends with carved figures. They depict the Annunciation and the Adoration of the Magi. In the late Middle Ages, the return stall on the S was the Vicar's and that on the N was for the Provost of the College of Jesus. The reredos and the eagle lectern both date from the 1870s. The ogee sedilia seem to match the chancel arcades in date. In the Jesus chapel, the altarpiece was introduced in 1921 by Temple Moore. Of the stained glass, the main E window, a Te Deum, was designed by Scott and made by Clayton & Bell. The S window of the S transept, of 1859 by A. Gibbs, shows the Annunciation, the Adoration of the Kings, the healing of Bartimeus, 'suffer little children', the commissioning of St. Peter, the Entry into Jerusalem, the Last Supper, the Agony in the Garden and St. Peter healing the man at the Beautiful Gate (Acts 3). A window of 1963 by Harry Harvey of York illustrates the life of Thomas Rotherham. The E window of the Jesus chapel, of 1921, depicts St. Anne, St. Gabriel, the Virgin and Child, St. Michael and St. Elizabeth.

At the E end of the N chancel aisle stands the canopied wall monument of Robert Swifte (died 1561) and of his wife Anne (died 1539). The monument is square-topped with cresting and quatrefoil decoration. A large brass plate is fixed to the back wall, declaring: 'Christ is oure lyfe/and deathe is our advantage'. In the S transept there is a memorial to 50 people, most of them children, who died at the launching of a vessel at Masbrough in 1841. What was intended as a treat turned into a tragedy. Their names and ages are inscribed on the memorial.

Rotherham's most famous son, the 15C archbishop, was successively Bishop of Rochester and Bishop of Lincoln before being preferred to York. Among his many gifts to his native town, he bequeathed an elaborate mitre for the use of the 'boy bishop' each December. Archbishop Rotherham died in 1500 and was buried at York.

Chapel of Our Lady on Rotherham Bridge. Rotherham's bridge chapel remains attached to the medieval bridge, which has been superseded by an adjacent modern bridge. The chapel was built in c 1483, probably under Archbishop Rotherham's patronage. It lasted just 60 years as a chapel. From the mid-16C until 1924 it was put to a variety of secular uses. A full restoration of the fabric for worship came in 1924. Six years later, the new Chantry Bridge was opened. The chapel has a tall profile in the centre of the old bridge. There are two three-light windows to N and S and a four-light E window. The latter has stained glass of 1975 by Alan Younger. The traceried bench-ends match those in All Saints' Church. Services are held here at 11.00 on Tuesdays and 10.00 on Saturdays.

Saltaire, *United Reformed Church, Victoria Road.* Saltaire is a 19C mill town, the creation in its entirety of Sir Titus Salt, one of Victorian Bradford's most successful manufacturers. As a part of this new town, Sir Titus built a Congregational church in 1858–59 to the designs of Lockwood & Mawson. It still stands proudly today and it is still in use as a United Reformed church, whereas the *raison d'être* of the town, the mill, was closed completely in 1986. The church is one of the grandest buildings erected for the Free Churches in the 19C.

The church is set back from Victoria Road and stands apart from neighbouring buildings. It has a stately W front which comprises a semicircular portico of six Corinthian columns and, above, a short tower which narrows to an octagonal lantern, surmounted by a small dome and a copper spike. There are six square-headed windows N and S, each framed by giant Corinthian pilasters. A mausoleum is attached to the NE end of the church.

The interior is aisleless and presents a rich effect of 19C Classical details and woodwork. There is a barrel-vault, panelled and decorated, with breaks for the windows. There are dark columns along the side walls, but with gilded capitals. The window surrounds are of yellowish marble. The walls are painted a fairly dark blue. The W end has a vestibule under the tower and a shallow W gallery in the church proper. The E end is recessed and partly houses the organ, in front of which stands the pulpit. The benches have carved scroll ends. Two huge chandeliers hang like inverted umbrellas. In the W vestibule, to the right, is a bust of Sir Titus Salt, dating from 1856.

Sherburn-in-Elmet, *All Saints.* All Saints' is outwardly a Perpendicular building with an Early English chancel. It is in fact a late medieval remodelling of a 12C church, whose nave arcades survive, and the chancel is substantially of 1857 by Anthony Salvin. The impressive size of the late Norman church seems to derive from the presence of a house of the Archbishops of York.

The church stands on a hill to the W of the village, in a markedly large and sloping churchyard. It is built of the very white limestone which is such an attractive feature of churches in the S of Yorkshire. The building comprises a W tower, a nave with aisles which embrace the tower and extend for one bay E of the nave, an aisleless chancel, a S porch and a chamber attached to the E side of that porch. The tower has battlements, corner pinnacles and gargoyles, all 15C. The heavy buttressing points to a 15C heightening of an earlier tower, and indeed the lower part is late Norman. The evidence lies within. The battlemented nave has three-light Perpendicular clerestory windows. The aisles have Perpendicular windows, too, but the narrower N aisle also has a surviving Norman window. Thus the S aisle is a 15C widening of a Norman aisled church. The S porch is Salvin's apart from some reused Norman fabric. The chancel is of 1857 above the footings; it has lancet windows and a vesica window high in the gable.

Within, there are four-bay Norman nave arcades with cylindrical piers, scalloped capitals and two bands of miniature arcading above each arch. The NE respond has volutes, the SW waterleaf. The tower has rounded but triple-chamfered arches to N, S and E. Above the E arch there is a Norman window, arched with shafts. The chancel arch is double-chamfered, with the inner chamfer resting on semicircular shafts. The nave roof is 17C; the chancel's, of 1857, rests on large carved corbels. The S wall has three pointed-arch recesses. Also in that wall is an opening of irregular shape which connects with the outer S chapel, just E of the porch. This outer S chapel was founded as St. Martin's chantry in the early 16C. In recent years it has been refitted to serve as a meeting room as well as a chapel.

The fittings and adornments are mostly 19C and 20C (and especially of 1857). There are two exceptions: the W window contains some medieval heraldic glass; and in the S aisle there are the two halves of a 15C Janus Cross, a two-sided Crucifixion with the figures of the Virgin Mary and St. John, set under a gable and ornamented with tracery and Instruments of the Passion, which were split from one another long ago. Of the 19C stained glass, mention might be made of the New Testament scenes in the E window of the S aisle, 1875.

Studley Royal, *St. Mary* and Skelton-on-Ure, *Christ the Consoler.* These are two of the most important Victorian churches in Yorkshire, standing just six miles apart, and both were designed by William Burges at the instance of members of the Vyner family. The church of Christ the Consoler, Skelton, was built in 1871–76 by Lady Mary Vyner in memory of her son, Frederick Grantham Vyner, who had been murdered by Greek brigands in 1870. St. Mary's, Studley Royal (1871–78) was built by Henrietta, Marchioness of Ripon, who was Lady Mary's daughter.

The church of Christ the Consoler stands near the gates of Newby Park, where Lady Mary Vyner lived. It serves as a normal parish church in a way that St. Mary's, standing in the middle of parkland, could never have done. It comprises a N tower with spire, an aisled four-bay nave with S porch, and an aisleless chancel, all in 13C style. The W end has a large rose window, there is a carving of the Good Shepherd over the S porch, the clerestory comprises groups of three shafted lancets, and the chancel has large Vyner shields on its buttresses, plus gargoyles. The interior is rich and sombre. There are blind arcades along the aisle walls, seven blind arches at the W end beneath the rose, and four statue-filled arches, surmounted by two roundels and a vesica, all forming an Ascension group carved by Thomas Nicholls, above the chancel arch. In the nave, black marble shafts attached to the piers are carried up to the roof corbels. The chancel is vaulted, has double tracery to its windows and features much red and green marble shafting. There are return stalls of walnut with angel carvings, in front of the low white marble chancel screen. A rather heavy organ fills the E bay of the N nave arcade, the corbels of its gallery featuring various fierce animals. The elaborate font cover in the SW corner has four traceried gables in its main stage, and then two smaller stages and a spire. At the W end a tablet remembers the foundress, who died in 1892. The stained glass throughout the church was designed by Fred Weekes and H.W. Lonsdale and made by Saunders & Co., under Burges's control. The E window shows the Crucifixion and its prefigurations. The aisle windows feature Christ's parables and miracles; the clerestory has Prophets.

St. Mary's is a much larger church and stands in 18C parkland at the head of an avenue which frames a view of Ripon Cathedral. Elsewhere in the park there are the spectacular ruins of Fountains Abbey. The church was declared redundant in 1970 and is now run by the National Trust on behalf of English Heritage. The plan is of an aisled nave with S porch, a W tower and spire, an aisleless chancel and a NE ve .try. As at Skelton, the style is 13C. The tower has set-back buttresses which become pinnacles at the base of the spire. The louvred single belfry openings have gables which rise against the spire. It is notable that the belfry stage is octagonal to accord with the spire. The E and W windows have Geometrical tracery, both including a rose. Above the E window there are three large gabled statue niches, with flanking crocketed pinnacles rising above the roof. The N and S windows are all paired, those of the chancel being more elaborate, with crocketed gables.

The interior follows Skelton in many details: in its Purbeck marble shafting, in its scheme of stained glass by Saunders & Co. to the designs of Fred Weekes, in its heavy organ filling a bay of the N aisle, and in the greater richness of its chancel, where double tracery, a painted roof, a mosaic floor, brasswork, gilding and alabaster all make a sumptuous display. A carved lion, typical of Burges, bears a shaft above the sedilia. At the E end of the S aisle there is a table-tomb with an arcaded and crested screen to the first Marquess of Ripon (died 1909) and his wife, the builder of the church (died 1907). The monument is in coloured marbles.

Tickhill, *St. Mary the Virgin.* St. Mary's is a church whose size and quality reflect the medieval importance and wealth of this castle town. It is a late 14C and early 15C remodelling and enlargement of an already substantial building.

The exterior presents that very white magnesian limestone which is so attractive in many churches in S Yorkshire. Tickhill's W tower of 120ft, which was repaired in 1979–80, commands the scene. Its lower part is 13C. There is a splendid W doorway with three orders of shafts

The stately 15C church of St. Mary

and dogtooth decoration. The earlier part of the tower also has large, flat, clasping buttresses. Between them, and over the W door, there is an inserted Perpendicular W window of five transomed lights. The upper part of the tower is wholly Perpendicular. There are pairs of three-light, transomed belfry openings, eight pinnacles and a parapet which is formed by crocketed and cusped open gables being placed over the openings of the battlements. The upper part of the tower has angle buttresses with two tiers of small gables. Below the belfry there are statues in niches. Heraldry on the tower dates from the late 14C, including John of Gaunt's arms of Castile and Leon, which he was entitled to bear between 1373 and 1399. The body of the church comprises a nave with aisles, N and S porches, and a chancel with N and S chapels. There are battlements and pinnacles throughout; those on the N chancel chapel are 19C additions. The nave aisle windows are Perpendicular. So too is the E window of the chancel. The chancel is markedly lower than the nave, so that there is room for a five-light window in the E gable of the nave. The three-light clerestory windows, which are inevitably Perpendicular, are paired to each nave bay below.

The interior repeats and confirms the story of the exterior. The tower has arches to E, N and S, speaking of aisles in the 13C church. The springers of vaulting ribs may be seen beneath the tower. The immense E arch leads into a four-bay nave with very high arches, each of which has an ogee gable whose finial reaches between the clerestory windows. The chancel has a wide W arch, a three-bay S arcade of octagonal piers and double-chamfered arches (but the E bay is narrower and taller), and a single arch into the N chapel. Also on the N side, just E of the arch, is a 13C lancet and the shadow of part of another, which demonstrate that the 13C church was as long as the present one. The interior was thoroughly cleaned in 1982–83.

The late medieval font beneath the tower has a canopy of 1959 by George Pace. A painted panel of the Georgian royal arms is placed over the N door. They are of King George I, c 1724. The pulpit is Jacobean, c 1606. The brass eagle lectern was made in 1908; the design is rather square in shape. The high altar also dates from 1908, standing in front of a reredos of 1881. Windows in the S aisle preserve much late 15C glass. The first window E of the S door depicts six Apostles, each of whom holds a scroll inscribed in Latin with parts of the Creed. The next two windows to the E have glass which seems to concern the Holy Trinity, perhaps in association with the known medieval chantry of that dedication. The remaining stained glass is of the late 19C and early 20C. C.E. Kempe designed the window above the chancel arch (1895, depicting the Transfiguration), and the E and N windows of the N chancel chapel (1906). The chancel's E window shows the Ascension, by Powell Bros. of Leeds, 1883. By the same firm are the main W window (1885, depicting the Creation) and windows to the SW and NE. Heaton, Butler & Bayne made the memorial window of 1887 to the Reverend E.H. Brooksbank in the SE corner.

The church has some notable monuments in the NW corner. There are three table-tombs. One bears the effigies of Sir Thomas Fitz-william (died 1497) and his wife, Lucy Neville. It was enrailed in the 18C. The tomb dates from c 1530 and shows early Renaissance features. The second tomb is of William Estfeld (died 1386) and his wife Margaret. The tomb-chest is decorated with quatrefoils between cusped lancets, but bears no effigies. It was formerly sited in the chancel where a brass inscription which belongs to it is now fixed to the N wall. The third monument commemorates Louisa Blanche Foljambe (died 1871) and her son. The effigies of alabaster, by William Calder Marshall, lie on a stone base.

Tong, *St. James.* The church was rebuilt in 1727 by Sir George Tempest of Tong Hall. It is notable because it preserves to an unusual extent its 18C fittings. Its setting is attractive too, for despite being just outside Bradford, Tong remains a proper village. Considerable restoration was undertaken in 1979–80.

The church comprises a nave, a N aisle, a NE vestry and a W tower, all built in very dark stone (some reused from the earlier building). The W tower has a single arched belfry window in the N, S and E faces and a window of two cusped lights in the W face. The parapet is plain. The S nave wall has large arched lights with enhanced keystones. On the N side there are square-headed windows of two arched lights. The E window is 19C.

Within, the three-bay N arcade has round arches on Tuscan piers. All around are box-pews, including the Tempest family pew—complete with fireplace—against the N wall towards the E. Opposite it is a three-decker pulpit, whose tester is inscribed with the date of the church, 1727. There is a W gallery, whose front bears the arms of King George III and which houses the organ. At the E end, four hatchments hang on the N wall and one on the S. On the N wall of the sanctuary there is a big memorial of 1919 to Sir Robert Tempest (died 1901) and his wife, and to the fourth Baronet (died 1909) and his wife. The usual inscribed boards are placed to the left and right of the E window. In the vestry there is placed the exceptionally well-preserved gravestone of Nathan Kirshaw (died 1677).

Wakefield, *Chantry Chapel of St. Mary on the Bridge.* Five bridge chapels remain in England today, but those at Rotherham, Derby, Bradford-on-Avon and St. Ives must defer to the example at Wakefield in importance. It is placed halfway across a mid-14C bridge. Drastic restoration took place under Sir Gilbert Scott in 1847 and again under Sir Charles Nicholson in 1939. The original W front was replaced entirely by Scott and was re-erected in the grounds of Kettlethorpe Hall, Wakefield, in 1847.

The chapel is a miniature essay in an elaborate Decorated style. The W front in Derbyshire stone is of five bays, each with blank flowing tracery. Each bay is gabled, with panelled uprights in between. The parapet is embellished with carvings of the Annunciation, the Nativity, the Resurrection, the Ascension and Pentecost. Before 1847, the fifth panel represented the Coronation of the Virgin. Crocketed pinnacles flank the W front. On the N and S sides there are three square-headed, three-light windows with flowing tracery. The E window is of five lights. An octagonal NE stair turret, whose top is embattled, gives access to an E crypt. The chapel is still used for worship.

Womersley, *St. Martin.* St. Martin's is a cruciform church with a broach spire, whose predominant character is that of the early 14C but which has fabric of all styles from Norman to Perpendicular. The village lies in the countryside between Doncaster and Selby.

The church comprises a nave with a wide S aisle and a narrower N aisle, a S porch, a crossing tower with spire, N and S transepts, a chancel and a NE vestry. The exterior presents the white magnesian limestone which is an attractive feature of many churches in the S of Yorkshire. The 14C broach spire sits on a plain and fairly low tower. The nave is very tall and has two-light clerestory windows, the E one on the N being longer than the rest. Their tracery is 14C. The low, lean-to N aisle has two-light windows and buttresses. Rood loft stairs rise against the W side of the N transept and are carried over the aisle roof at its E end. The N transept has a N window of two ogee lights. The chancel, wide and fairly tall, has no E window. On the S side, the E window of the transept is Reticulated. One window E of the porch is square-headed Perpendicular. The main W window is also Perpendicular.

The interior has a character which is chiefly determined by fittings of the late 19C. Cassandra, Countess of Rosse was responsible for much of the work. There is a chancel screen by G.F. Bodley with elaborate tracery in the upper parts of the openings. Above the screen is a loft and a Rood group flanked by angels with outstretched wings and holding candles. The medieval fabric of the nave reveals no predominant style. The N arcade of five bays has round piers with moulded capitals and pointed, double-chamfered arches. The chamfering is of the slight early type. The W arch of the arcade is narrower than its neighbour; it dies into the W wall and into the first pier. The E arch is also narrower and was presumably built to link an existing arcade with the new 14C crossing tower. The S arcade is of only two bays; there is no S aisle at the W end. The octagonal pier and moulded capital, and double-chamfered arches make the arcade 14C. It fits in entirely with the 14C tower. The S transept has a screen and an elaborately painted roof.

There is much stained glass by C.E. Kempe: the E window of the S transept of 1895, depicting the Virgin and Child in the central light; a three-light window of 1904 in the S aisle showing St. Sebastian, St. George and St. Maurice; and three windows in the N aisle, of which one (of 1895) depicts St. Hubert and St. Dominic. One S chancel window is by Mayer of Munich. In the S transept there is a round-arched and cusped tomb-recess. Nearby, in the wide S aisle, there is a worn 14C effigy of a cross-legged knight (perhaps Adam de Newmarch, who owned the manor). The representation of the Last Supper in tilework dates from the 17C and was brought from Spain.

Old Counties

SCOTLAND

NORTHUMBER-LAND

CUMBERLAND   DURHAM

WEST-MORLAND   North Riding

Y O R K S H I R E

East Riding

West Riding

LANCASHIRE

Lindsey

CHESHIRE   DERBY   L I N C O L N

NOTTS

ENGLAND   Holland

STAFFORD   Kesteven

SHROPSHIRE   LEICESTER   1   NORFOLK

WALES   2   3

WARWICK   SUFFOLK

NORTHAMPTON   West   East

WORCESTER

HEREFORD   4

GLOUCESTER   OXFORD   BUCKS   HERTFORD   ESSEX

GREATER LONDON

BERKSHIRE

WILTSHIRE   SURREY   KENT

HAMPSHIRE   S U S S E X

SOMERSET   West   East

DEVON   DORSET

CORNWALL

ENGLISH COUNTIES
1. RUTLAND
2. HUNTINGDON AND PETERBOROUGH
3. CAMBRIDGE AND ISLE OF ELY
4. BEDFORDSHIRE

Post 1973-75
Reorganisation of Counties

SCOTLAND

NORTHUMBER
LAND

1

DURHAM

2

CUMBRIA

NORTH YORKSHIRE

HUMBERSIDE

LANCASHIRE

WEST
YORKSHIRE

3

4

5

CHESHIRE

DERBY

NOTTS

LINCOLN

ENGLAND

SHROPSHIRE

STAFFORD

LEICESTER

NORFOLK

6

WALES

HEREFORD
AND
WORCESTER

WARWICK

NORTHAMPTON

CAMBRIDGE

SUFFOLK

7

HERTFORD

ESSEX

GLOUCESTER

OXFORD

BUCKS

GREATER
LONDON

AVON

WILTSHIRE

BERKSHIRE

SURREY

KENT

SOMERSET

HAMPSHIRE

WEST
SUSSEX

EAST
SUSSEX

DEVON

DORSET

8

CORNWALL

ENGLISH COUNTIES

1. TYNE AND WEAR
2. CLEVELAND
3. SOUTH YORKSHIRE
4. MERSEYSIDE
5. GREATER MANCHESTER
6. WEST MIDLANDS
7. BEDFORDSHIRE
8. ISLE OF WIGHT

INDEX OF ARCHITECTS, ARTISTS AND CRAFTSMEN

INDEX TO CHURCHES AND CHAPELS